The Indian Sign Language

THE
INDIAN SIGN LANGUAGE

W. P. Clark

University of Nebraska Press
Lincoln and London

Manufactured in the United States of America

First Bison Book printing: 1982
Most recent printing indicated by the first digit below:
4   5   6   7   8   9   10

Library of Congress Cataloging in Publication Data
Clark, W. P. (William Philo), 1845?–1884.
  The Indian sign language.
  Reprint. Originally published: Philadelphia : L. R. Hamersly, 1885.
  Includes index.
  1. Indians of North America—Sign language. 2. Indians of North
America—Great Plains. I. Title.
E98.S5C59 1982   419   81–16420
ISBN 0–8032–1414–6   AACR2
ISBN 0–8032–6309–0 (pbk.)

*The Indian Sign Language, with Brief Explanatory Notes of the Gestures Taught
Deaf-Mutes in Our Institutions for Their Instruction, and a Description of Some of
the Peculiar Laws, Customs, Myths, Superstitions, Ways of Living, Code of Peace
and War Signals of Our Aborigines*, was first published in 1885 by L. R.
Hamersly & Co.

∞

MAP SHOWING

Indian Reservations
in the United States
West of the 84th Meridian
and the Number of Indians
belonging thereto in 1882

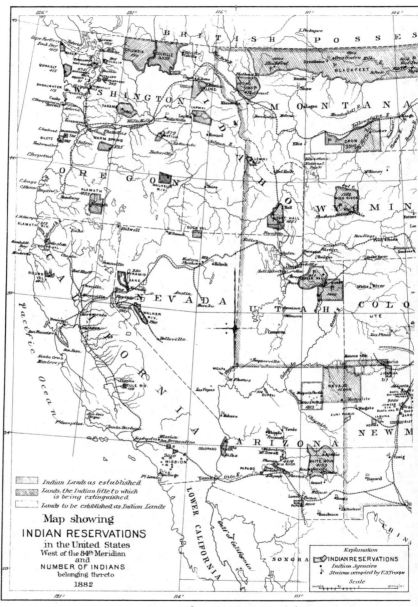

Map showing
INDIAN RESERVATIONS
in the United States
West of the 84th Meridian
and
NUMBER OF INDIANS
belonging thereto
1882

Indian Lands as established
Lands, the Indian title to which
is being extinguished
Lands to be established as Indian Lands

Explanation

INDIAN RESERVATIONS
• Indian Agencies
⚑ Stations occupied by U.S.Troops
Scale

⚑ Agencies visited under special instructions of the Lieut General
〜〜〜 Boundary of the Military Division of the Missouri
Number of Indians in United States (I.C's Report of 1881) 261,851
— do — do — Mil. Div. Mo. — do —— 175,813

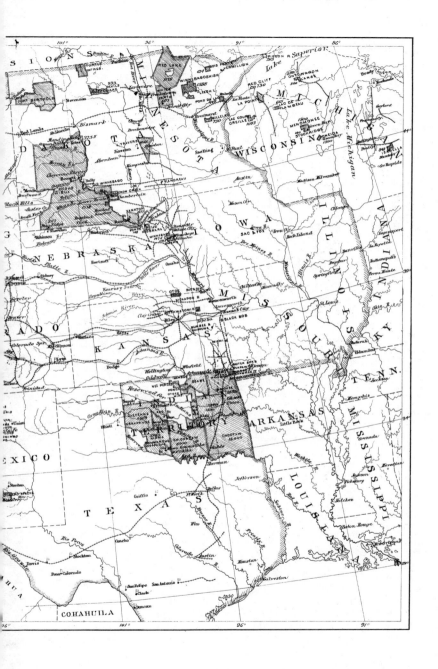

The Indian Sign Language

HEADQUARTERS ARMY OF THE UNITED STATES,

WASHINGTON, D.C., *July 7th,* 1884.

LIEUT.-GENERAL P. H. SHERIDAN.

SIR,—I have the honor to submit herewith, in compliance with your instructions, a work upon the Sign Language of the Indians living within the territory of the United States, with some account of their tribal histories and race peculiarities.

This work is based upon my own observations, made among the Indians themselves during a period of more than six years, supplemented by a careful study of the principal authorities on Indian habits and customs.

Very respectfully,

Your obedient servant,

W. P. CLARK,

Captain Second Cavalry.

INTRODUCTORY.

IT seems proper in submitting this work that a brief account should first be given of the manner in which I acquired a knowledge of the sign language of the Indians, and that I should at least outline some of the opportunities which have been given me for gaining an understanding of race peculiarities, as I think something will thereby be added to the weight of the expressed opinions not only in regard to the language, but to other matters pertaining to our aborigines which I have touched upon.

During the Sioux and Cheyenne war of 1876–7, in November of 1876, I found myself in command of some three hundred friendly enlisted Indian scouts of the Pawnee, Shoshone, Arapahoe, Cheyenne, Crow, and Sioux tribes; six tribes having six different vocal languages. I had, of course, before known of the sign language used by our Indians, but here I was strongly impressed with its value and beauty. On the march, by their camp-fires at night, and in the early gray of morning, just before charging down on a hostile Indian village, I took my first lessons in this language and in Indian tactics. I observed that these Indians, having different vocal languages, had no difficulty in communicating with each other, and held constant intercourse by means of gestures. For the practical benefits which would immediately ensue, I devoted myself to the study of the gesture language and the people. I found that the Indians were wonderfully good and patient instructors, and that the gesture speech was easy to acquire and remember.

The campaign ended. I was ordered to Red Cloud Agency, and remained there and at Spotted Tail Agency for a year, my duties bringing me in close and constant contact and intercourse with the Sioux, Cheyennes, and Arapahoes,—in their camps, at their feasts, festivals, and funerals, and in the field with scouting-parties.

In 1878–9 and 1880, my duties carried me farther to the northwest, and though engaged mostly in field operations during these years, the character of the service was such that I was thrown into intimate relations with the Cheyennes, Sioux, Crows, Bannacks, Assinaboines, Gros Ventres of the Prairie, Mandans, Arickarees, and other tribes in that region, and had almost constant use for my knowledge of gesture speech. I found this of great value, not only in imparting and receiving information, but as a check upon unreliable interpreters.

5

In 1881 I was directed by Lieutenant-General Sheridan to submit to him a work on the Indian sign language, with such remarks upon the habits, manners, and customs of the Indians as might be considered necessary and proper. To complete and perfect my study of the language and people, I, under orders from him, visited several tribes in the Indian Territory, in Minnesota, Manitoba, Northwest Territory, Dakota, Montana, Nebraska, Utah, Wyoming, and Idaho. Upon the accompanying map are indicated the locations of the agencies and tribes where I made this special investigation. I have faithfully endeavored to ascertain the facts, and to complete my study of this language so far as I was able to do so by personal conversation in gesture speech with the Indians of the tribes which I visited, and to learn whatever I could of its existence or non-existence at present, and its status in olden times.

To insure all this I prepared a list of words, phrases, idioms, etc., and on reaching the different agencies or encampments, obtained an interpreter, and secured the services of some of the Indians who were reported as the most accomplished in gesture speech. The interpreter translated the words, etc., the Indians made the signs, and I, taking the sign language as I had learned it as a standard, noted the differences where there were any, provided always, of course, that the differences were not merely personal flourishes or careless abbreviations; *i.e.*, in case the root of the sign was changed or did not appear, I carefully noted it. Although individuals may obscure the meaning of these gestures through carelessness, awkwardness, or efforts to secure a superabundance of graceful execution, yet one skilled in the sign language will instantly recognize them, provided that they possess the radical or essential part.

This careful comparison finished, I then entered into conversation personally by signs with the Indians, and had them relate to me stories, autobiographies, etc. In this way I was of course able to discover if my method of making signs was understood, and detect any gesture that I had not before seen. I then mixed with the Indians generally, visited their camps, and endeavored to ascertain the extent of the understanding of gesture speech in the tribe or band. I also interviewed some of the old Jesuit fathers, interpreters, traders, trappers, half-breeds, and others who had had a long experience with these people. I discovered that to have the Indians first make the gestures was absolutely necessary, because, if one makes a sign to an Indian in a certain way, the chances are ten to one he will return it in the same way, even though he may never have seen it before. For instance, if a person in conversation in gestures with a Crow Indian were to use the Ute sign for pony, the Indian, should he have occasion to make the sign in return to the same person within a few minutes' time, would use the same gesture, and in this way unintentionally deceive the investigator.

I have noted under SIGN LANGUAGE the evidence obtained from the Indians in regard to the use and extent of the language at the present time and in remote periods of their history, and have elsewhere given my reasons for the similarity of gestures among all the tribes; and my personal experience fully sustains Professor Whitney's statement, that "the art of talking by gesture is too natural to man ever to be lost, though put down by, on the whole, greater availability of utterance as proved by experience, and if two men, who have not learned each other's tongue, meet and desire to exchange thoughts at all, they will resort to gesture and arrive at a mutual understanding on many points, whether they have a common origin and certain traces of hereditary (rather traditional) habits, or whether they have merely the accordant endowments of a common humanity."

ORIGIN OF THE AMERICAN INDIANS.

I am not prepared to discuss the origin of man, and I wish in this work to enter as little as possible the fields of speculation and conjecture, but "human science shows that the world has unfolded from small beginnings, and it is reasonable to suppose that so the race has unfolded," and having thought much, and observed closely the Indian as he is found at present, both in his debased condition near our civilization, and in his wild state before coming in contact with it, I feel that I should at least place some of my views on record, and I unhesitatingly pronounce in favor of the Autochthonic theory of the origin of our aborigines.

I think Mr. H. H. Bancroft happily summarizes the views that have been advanced in regard to this subject when he says, "The American Indians, their origin and consanguinity, have from the days of Columbus to the present time proved no less a knotty question. Schoolmen and scientists count their theories by hundreds, each sustaining some pet conjecture with a logical clearness equalled only by the facility with which he demolishes all the rest. One proves their origin by Holy Writ, another by the sage sayings of the fathers. One discovers in them Phœnician merchants, another the ten lost tribes of Israel. They are tracked with equal certainty from Scandinavia, from Ireland, from Iceland, from Greenland, across Behring Strait, across the Northern Pacific, the Southern Pacific, from the Polynesian Islands, from Australia, from Africa. Venturesome Carthaginians were thrown upon the eastern shore, Japanese junks on the western. The breezes that wafted hither America's primogenitors are still blowing, and the ocean currents by which they came cease not yet to flow. The finely-spun webs of logic by which these fancies are maintained would prove amusing did not the profound earnestness of their respective advocates render them ridiculous."

Not only has the origin of the race been settled by these visionary theorists, but the origin and migrations of separate tribes carefully set forth, one writer claiming that those speaking the Sioux and kindred languages landed on this continent near the Gulf of St. Lawrence about the same time, probably at least three thousand years ago. Another insists that in the Mandans he discovered a lost

Welsh colony, and proves his statement by a description of some of their physical peculiarities, such as light hair and blue eyes, and more startling and conclusive still, discovered through a Welshman he had with him that they spoke the Welsh language. It is hardly necessary now to say that the Welshman wantonly imposed upon the searcher after savage lore, and the light hair and blue eyes have since been accounted for.

Believing, then, that the American man "is as indigenous as the *fauna* and *flora*," it does not matter, and at this late day it certainly cannot be determined, whether the tribes found on this continent at the time of its discovery were unfolded from several groups of savages occupying widely separated geographical areas, or were slowly evolved from one. The erosion of time has worn away all records, but it seems proper to briefly outline the reasons for this belief. There was certainly nothing in the languages of the different tribes which justified a belief in this early migration ; no trace of ancient arts and inscriptions, or of monumental data, has been discovered among them, and certainly it is only reasonable to suppose that a people sufficiently advanced to conquer the obstacles of such a migration would have been developed intellectually and physically to a degree beyond that required for preserving some evidence of such a wonderful event in their lives; but from the fretted shores of the Atlantic to the fair waters of the Pacific nothing of this kind has ever been found, and there is no evidence of a foreign origin in their traditions or myths, although these go back in the eternity of the past to the time of their creation,—to the flood,—to the period in their development when they first used the bow and arrow.

The mere fact that they had certain customs, habits, manners, and religious rites common to humanity in some other parts of the world, only shows that man in the same plane, stage, or period of savagery, barbarism, or civilization, possesses many similar traits, mentally, morally, and physically.

I cannot point to a more striking illustration of this than to call attention to the astronomical discoveries, and to the wonderful inventions which have simultaneously sprung into existence; in short, to the results which have been achieved by the scientific minds of different nations of the world, working out their problems at widely separated geographical points, the one entirely ignorant of the existence of the other, and though their minds were subjected to different surroundings and influence, still becoming pregnant with the same ideas at the same time. These things are more strange and peculiar to me than that in the lower stages of human evolution the sun should have been regarded with superstitious awe, or that certain rude social customs of the Indians should have been similar to those of the peoples of some other country.

It would, indeed, be rash to make any positive assertions as to race origin. One must not attempt, as Professor Whitney tersely says, "to carry too definite a light too far back into the obscure past." It is safe to say, however, that all writers agree in giving to the nations of America a remote antiquity. Traditions, ruins, moral and physical peculiarities, all denote that, several thousand years ago, humanity existed on this continent. Of what type history gives no information, science can throw no definite light, and conjecture affords no satisfaction. The data in regard to the Plains Indians are even more unsatisfactory than with other native nations. Their history mostly hangs on the slender threads of oral tradition and picture-writing. The latter is a sort of hieroglyphical chart upon which each figure represents the most important event that happened to the band or tribe during the year,—the death of a noted chief, the scourge of smallpox or measles, the capture of a woolly pony from some adjacent tribe,—and these charts rarely go back more than one hundred years.

Picture-writings which represent the histories of individuals are so common that many writers have wrongly asserted that these were the only ones kept.

The trail of their migration on the vast prairies is like the track left by a vessel on the troubled waters of the ocean. But hopeless as the task at first glance appears, poor as the guides are which lead us into the chaos of the past, yet scientific investigation has even at this late day done much to crystallize the unknown into the known, and the power and force of civilization, guided by the hand of genius, may yet trace the lines which mark much of the growth of primitive man on this continent, through a part of the long dark period of savagery and the gray light which dawned upon him in his early stage of barbarism.

ORIGIN OF INDIAN SIGN LANGUAGE.

In regard to the degree of intelligence necessary for the invention and use of gesture speech there is a great variety of opinion among scientific investigators. Says one, "What gesture language can be more expressive than that employed by the horse with its ears, and the dog with its tail, wherein are manifestations of every shade of joy, sorrow, courage, shame, and anger?" Another claims that " it is not at all probable that a system of gesture language was ever employed by any primitive people prior or in preference to vocal language. To communicate by signs requires no little skill, and implies a degree of artifice and forethought far beyond that required in vocal or emotional language. Long before a child arrives at the point of intelligence necessary for conveying thoughts by signs it is well advanced in a vocal language of its own."

Kant held the opinion that the mind of a deaf-mute was incapable of development; but the wonderful success of our modern institutions has dissipated forever that idea; and I have seen the little three-years-old child of a deaf-mute Indian hold up its tiny hands and carry on a conversation (without any attempt at vocal speech) which would have done credit to any child of that age.

Broadly, the term language may be applied to whatever means

social beings employ to communicate passion or sentiment, or to influence one another ; whatever is made a vehicle of intelligence, idiographic or phonetic, is language, and the object of language is to arrive by skilful combinations of known signs at the expression of something unknown to one of the parties ; *i.e.*, the idea to be conveyed.

At a very early period of the savage state the necessity for communication developed certain signs, visible and vocal, which met the wants of the necessity felt at the time. In all probability vocal signs were not at first as rapidly developed as gestures, but though of slower growth, they finally crowded out, and in a measure took the place of facial expression and bodily movements, so that by the time when the later stage or period of savagery, or perhaps barbarism, was reached, each group in this unfolding process, which might be called a family, band, or tribe, had retained only a few of their original gestures, and had for the communication of conceptions and the operations of thought a rude and imperfect articulate language. Extreme poverty in such language would undoubtedly require gesture to confirm and elucidate the meaning intended to be conveyed, and in the beginning, whatever other uncertainties may thickly cluster about and obscure the subject, no one, I think, will question the poverty of their articulate speech.

The myths of nearly every tribe of Indians seem to evidence the fact that there was a time in their development when they did not have the bow and arrow. This is interesting and important only as showing the growth of their inventive and imitative faculties, essential qualities in language-making.

Whether, as I have before stated, the North American Indians are the result of the growth or unfolding of one or several groups of savages, the great number of distinct vocal languages, about seventy-six, and the great variety of dialects of the same language, need not be to the philological student so much a matter of surprise, for through natural causes, such as internal trouble, wars with other tribes, in short, the segregation which takes place when humanity is in the hunter state, the savages would necessarily have crystallized into separate families or bands, and in these bands, after a long period of time, an articulate speech would have been developed, perfected, and marked by the influence of their surroundings, such as food, climate, occupation, etc. After such development of utterance these bands may, in the course of time, have been broken by causes similar to those which brought about the original segregation, and the fragments may have drifted to widely-separated geographical areas, and the philologist now finding them, discovers that their vocal languages belong to what he terms a "common stock." Laying aside all conjectures as to race origin, and simply taking the savages as they were found in recent times, we find that after each group or tribe had developed a distinct set of vocal signs, forming a marked and peculiar articulate speech which was useful as a means of communicating ideas only to the members of the group, the tribes again met as is illustrated by our Plains Indians. Here again the necessity for intercommunication between tribes having different vocal speech developed gesture speech, the sign language I have described, so that the many-tongued hordes of the vast sea-like prairies can at least be credited with perfecting and beautifying the language, which in all probability, with vocal imitations, formed the vehicle for the expression of the budding thoughts of primitive man on this continent.

Before considering this special growth I will briefly touch on the status of some of the Eastern tribes and their languages in former times, so far as history sheds any light on the subject.

That we find no positive evidence of the existence and use of gesture speech does not necessarily show that there was none, as is shown by the following notable examples. Circumstances forced Lewis and Clarke in their exploration of the then unknown West to spend the winter of 1804–5 with the Mandans, Gros Ventres, and Arickarees in their village on the Missouri, only a short distance below the present site of their camp at Fort Berthold. During the winter the Cheyennes and Sioux visited this village, and there can be no doubt that gesture speech was daily and hourly used by the members of these tribes as it is to-day when they meet, but no mention is made of the fact, and not until these explorers met the Shoshones near the headwaters of the Missouri do we find any note made of signs being used. If these explorers who entered so minutely into the characteristics of the Indians in their writings failed to make a record of this language, I do not think it very surprising that earlier investigators should have, under less favorable auspices, also neglected it.

I have called attention to the lack of any systematic code of gestures among the Algonquins, and given some idea of the great geographical area covered by their language, and I believe this to be the reason for the non-culture and lack of general use of signs.

Mr. Bancroft makes the vocal language even more comprehensive than I have claimed, for he says, "The most widely diffused and the most fertile in dialects of all North American languages, the Algonquin, was the mother-tongue of those who welcomed the Pilgrims to Plymouth. It was heard from the Bay of Gaspé to the valley of the Des Moines, from Cape Fear, and it may be from Savannah, to the land of the Eskimos, from the Cumberland River of Kentucky to the southern bank of the Mississippi. It was spoken, though not exclusively, in a territory that extended through sixty degrees of longitude and more than twenty degrees of latitude."

The six nations forming the Iroquois League, according to Mr. Morgan, were all able to understand each other with readiness in conversation, though he says, "Of the six dialects in which it is now spoken (Iroquois language), the Mohawk and Oneida have a close resemblance to each other, the Cayuga and Seneca the same, while the Onondaga and Tuscarora are not only unlike each other, but are also distinguished from the other four by strong dialectical differences."

The Iroquois League at the time spoken of by Mr. Morgan did not need gestures to communicate with each other, but it must be remembered that prior to the greatness, power, and advanced stage of barbarism which this confederacy achieved, many of them were living in amity with the Algonquins, and at this time, probably, gestures were used. Of this period Mr. Morgan says, "Their remote origin and their history anterior to the discovery are both enshrouded with obscurity. Tradition interposes its feeble light to extricate from the confusion which time has wrought some of the leading events which preceded and marked their political organization. It informs us that prior to their occupation of New York they resided in the vicinity of Montreal, upon the northern bank of the St. Lawrence, where they lived in subjection to the Adirondacks, a branch of the Algonquin race then in possession of the whole country north of that river. At that time the Iroquois were but one nation and few in number. From the Adirondacks they learned the art of husbandry, and while associated with them became inured to the hardships of the war-path and of the chase. After they had multiplied in numbers and improved by experience, they made an attempt to secure the independent possession of the country they occupied, but having been in the struggle overpowered and vanquished by the Adirondacks, they were compelled to retire from the country to escape extermination."

As I have stated, there is scarcely anything in written history to guide one, and I doubt the reliability of any of the traditions which can now be gathered from the wretched remnants of these once powerful tribes. It required long and patient study and investigation to obtain reliable data from the Plains Indians in regard to the growth of the language with them. It was easy and safe, and disposed of the matter at once to say, it was a gift from God, and many of them answered my inquiries as did "Iron Hawk," the Sioux chief, when he said, "The whites have had the power given them by the Great Spirit to read and write, and convey information in this way. He gave us the power to talk with our hands and arms, and send information with the mirror, blanket, and pony far away, and when we meet with Indians who have a different spoken language from ours, we can talk to them in signs."

Schoolcraft gives something, but the little that is noted relates rather more to signals than signs. Wampum seems to have been given rather than tobacco to indicate a friendly feeling.

A sapling cut to within two or three feet of the ground, its bark carefully peeled off, so as to be conspicuous, and a stone placed on the stump, indicated that the Oneidas were in the vicinity, and a signal-fire lighted near the Oneida stone warned them for many miles east, west, north, and south. Existence of war was indicated by a tomahawk painted red, ornamented with red feathers, and with black wampum struck in the war-post in each village of the league.

At their night encampments they cut upon the trees certain devices to indicate their numbers and destination. On their return they did the same, showing also the number of captives and the number slain.

The condition of affairs in the South was, however, much more favorable to the growth or perfection of gesture speech than in the North, for there were many different vocal languages spoken by the various tribes in that section. In regard to this Dr. J. Hammond Trumbull says,—

"The Chahta Muskokis family, comprising the Choctaws and Chickasas, Muskokis or Creeks, Seminoles, Coussattis, Alabamas, and Hitchitis, occupied the territory now constituting the States of Georgia, Alabama, Mississippi, and Florida, with a portion of Louisiana, east of the Mississippi, except the shore of the Gulf of Mobile westward, and the banks of the Mississippi inhabited by various small tribes, and a tract in Northern Alabama, on both sides of the Tennessee River, which belonged to the Cherokees.

"The Choctaws and Chickasas speak nearly related dialects of the same language, to which probably the Hitchiti also belongs. The Creeks, Seminoles, and small tribes of Coussattis and Alabamas, speak dialects of another language of the same stock."

The necessity for intercommunication between tribes existed, the vocal languages were different, and it is only reasonable to suppose that gestures were used.

After so much uncertainty in the East, and such great poverty of reliable data in the extreme West, it is with comfort and satisfaction that we contemplate the present status, and examine the traditional evidence of the growth of the language with our Plains Indians, and in my mind there is no doubt that this language, viewed in the light of rapidly communicating ideas, has been greatly enriched by them within the last two hundred years. I consider it at least unwise to say that any one particular tribe invented it and taught it to the others. All languages have of course needed the healthy stimulus of inventive and imitative faculties, but they, like humanity, *grow*, and very slowly, into beauty and usefulness.

It will readily be seen that the predatory hordes occupying the great plains, and having but recently come into a better means of transporting their possessions over long distances, viz., by the pony in place of the dog, would naturally and necessarily need and use signs much more than mountain tribes, whose habitat did not change from year's end to year's end, unless they were compelled to move by some superior force, and whose surroundings and occupation did not bring them in contact with strange tongues.

Linguistically considered, the tribes which during the last one hundred or one hundred and fifty years have had determined centres, if not of origin, certainly of perfection and propagation of gesture speech, may be divided into five groups, as follows:

First. The *Cheyennes* and *Arapahoes*, who, for mutual protection or other causes, had been together for a long time,—since their meeting in Western Minnesota. They were alike in many of their manners and customs, but each had a vocal language totally different from the other, and both were difficult to acquire; the Arapahoe tongue being almost impossible to master.

These two tribes were at this time a powerful nation, numbering probably not less than four thousand lodges, and perhaps five, the present Northern and Southern bands being united. (See CHEYENNE.) Not only were their vocal languages different from each other, but they were also totally unlike that of any of the tribes which surrounded them; and in their prairie driftings, in their search for game, in their relations both of peace and war with these tribes, there was constantly with them the necessity for gesture speech, and in its growth and perfection I consider that these two tribes exercised a greater influence than any of the rest.

Second. The *Mandans, Gros Ventres,* and *Arickarees,* with whom similar conditions obtained as with the Arapahoes and Cheyennes; the Mandan language ranking in difficulty of acquirement about with the Arapahoe. They were also numerous and powerful, but maintained almost constant warfare with the surrounding tribes, and this, taken in connection with their permanent villages, limited their influence.

Third. The *Crows.* These Indians were literally surrounded by tribes, with whom they came constantly in contact, who spoke (with the exception of their kin, the Gros Ventres) languages different from their own, and their relations with these tribes seemed to vibrate between peace and war. In later years the Nez Perces, Bannacks, Snakes, and Crows confederated in their annual buffalo-hunt to protect themselves from the Blackfeet, Sioux, Cheyennes, and Arapahoes, and not many years ago the Crows formed an alliance with the Blackfeet and Gros Ventres of the prairie, when the Cheyennes, Sioux, and Arapahoes drove them northwest out of their country.

Fourth. The *Blackfeet.* These had been joined by the Gros Ventres of the prairie soon after the Cheyennes and Arapahoes crossed the Missouri River, and they lived in harmony together until within a few years. Their vocal languages were totally different, and they had constant intercourse with other tribes. A few years since the Gros Ventres of the prairie joined the Assinaboines, with whom they are now living.

Fifth. The *Kiowas* and *Apaches.* The time when these tribes first joined their forces is beyond the reach of tradition. When the Cheyennes crossed the Missouri they were living together west of the Black Hills of Dakota, and were forced south by the Cheyennes and Arapahoes on the north, the Utes on the west, and the Pawnees, Omahas, and others to the east, until they found refuge and protection with the powerful Comanche nation.

Here again vocal languages were different, and daily communication with each other and with surrounding tribes was necessary, so that in all probability when they joined the Comanches they were much more proficient in the use of gesture speech than were the members of that tribe, and as a consequence some writers, basing their belief on the evidence of Southern Indians, have stated that the Kiowas "invented the sign language."

The confederation of the Cheyennes, Sioux, Arapahoes, Kiowas, Comanches, Apaches, and some other tribes, against the Utes, which took place about fifty years ago, though of short duration, still must have exercised a marked influence in weeding out undesirable gestures and establishing better ones.

Other centres of influence, growth, or perfection could be cited, but I have instanced the most pronounced.

It should be clearly borne in mind that the stimulus of outside intercourse is necessary to keep alive the interest required for the maintenance and development of the language. Without this intercourse the weaker tribe is absorbed in the stronger, and the vocal language most easily acquired prevails. This is strikingly illustrated in the case of the Bannacks and Shoshones. Nearly every Bannack speaks the Shoshone language fluently and well, but there are very few of the Shoshones who have any knowledge of the Bannack tongue. Some claim that it is even more difficult to master than Arapahoe, while the Shoshone is easily acquired.

Even in my comparatively short experience with the Indians, I have observed the birth, growth, and death of many gestures.

Before the introduction of the coffee-mill among the Indians, coffee was represented as a *grain*, or more elaborately by describing the process of preparing and drinking the beverage. The little coffee-mill killed off these gestures at once, and the motion made as though turning the crank of the mill to grind the parched berry is to-day understood as meaning *coffee* by nearly all the Plains tribes.

The origin of the Indian sign language is, then, I think it safe to say, coincident with his primitive condition, with his first necessity for communication with his fellow-man ; and its development and perfection are also the result of the necessity of intercommunication between tribes, who, long ages after its first use, had developed different vocal languages.

Could this work have been illustrated, it would have added greatly to the facility of understanding and making the gestures, for it is extremely difficult to describe the most simple movements of the hands in space, so that a person who had never seen the movements would, by following the descriptions, make the correct motions. To this part of the work I have given great care, have devoted much time and thought, and if the directions contained in the brief descriptions are carried out, I am confident that the most of the signs will be made in such a manner as to be readily recognized by those conversant with the language. In fact, nearly all of the descriptions have been tested and found to contain these essential elements.

In my description of the different parts of the hands, to determine their positions and movements, I have adopted the terms in common use, rather than the precise anatomical nomenclature. The

joints are numbered from the extremities of the fingers.   The radial
side or edge of the hand is called the *upper* edge, and the ulnar side
or edge the *lower* edge; the palmar surface, *palm* of hand, and
dorsal surface, back of hand.   The thumb and index finger extended
and abducted are termed *spread* thumb and index.   The term *compressed hand* is used to mean the position or arrangement of the
hand in which the fingers are extended, but the tips of index and
little fingers are brought as near each other as possible, under and
pressing against second and third fingers, and the palmar surface of
extended thumb, from tip to first articulation, presses against palmar
surface of second and third fingers behind their second articulation.
The word *outwards* is used as synonymous with *front; i.e.*, neither to
the right nor left of the median line of the body.   In speaking of
horizontal and vertical curves, of course the planes of these curves
are intended to be represented as horizontal or vertical.

   To reduce verbiage, the designation *Southern Indians* is used to
include the southern bands of Cheyennes and Arapahoes, the Kiowas,
Apaches, Caddos, Comanches, Wichitas, and generally the tribes in
the Indian Territory; *Berthold Indians* for the Hidatsas or Gros
Ventres, Mandans, and Arickarees; *Belknap Indians* for the Gros
Ventres of the Prairie and Assinaboines; *Blackfeet Indians* for the
Bloods, Blackfeet, and Piegans; *Missoula Indians* for the Nez Perces,
Flatheads, Pend d'Oreilles, and Koutenays.

   In addition to the practical value of communicating directly with
the Indians,—*i.e.*, without the aid of an interpreter,—gesture speech
discloses much of the sociological status of our aborigines, and discovers the meaning of many words in their different languages which
would otherwise remain obscure if not unknown.   It also leads in
some cases directly to correct information in regard to the segregation of the tribe into bands, and the origin of the causes which produced it, so that a thorough knowledge of signs must necessarily be
of great assistance in anthropological studies.   For instance, the
tribal sign for the Sioux or Dakota Indians reveals the custom, which
they in olden times practised, of cutting off the heads of their slain
enemies ; and the signs for the Ogalalla, Minnecoujon, and Uncapapa bands furnish a clue to the correct interpretation of these
words, and the traditional account of the origin of the bands, which
the etymology of the words does not.   The Pacific slope Indians,
even including the Utes and Nez Perces, have a general sign for the
Prairie tribes, viz., *Dog-Eaters*,—and I believe these tribes mark the
western limit where the dog is considered a luxury as food.   The
tribal signs for the Mandans and Wichitas discover the now discarded
practice of tattooing, the former the cheeks and the latter the breasts
of the women.
   I have heard Indians declare that they had always located the
Great Spirit in the heavens, and yet in gestures they would indicate
that this was the location of the white man's God, and for their

Great Mystery would point to the north, south, or east for its location.

The sign for the Milky-Way led me to make special inquiry in regard to this starry pathway, and I was rewarded with the story of its being the direct and easy trail to the Happy Hunting-Ground, made by those who had been killed in battle.

The mysteries of their myths are illuminated by this language, and traditions, which otherwise would have long since passed into the shades of forgetfulness and oblivion, are kept alive and green in the memories of the present generation.

To comprehend the *conceptions* and attain proficiency in the Indian sign language one should have some knowledge of their race peculiarities (and I have briefly described such as seemed most necessary). So important was this knowledge considered by a recent writer that he claims, "To learn it sufficiently well for ordinary intercourse is no more difficult than to learn any foreign language; to master it, one must have been born in a lodge of Plains Indians, and have been accustomed to its daily and hourly use from his earliest to mature years."

I have conversed in gestures with nearly every tribe of the Plains Indians from the British to the Mexican line, and though I admit that a knowledge of their ways is necessary to secure proficiency, still I consider the above expression too strong. Educated as the Indians are by nature, and drawing many of their metaphors and comparisons from her abundant reservoirs, it is no wonder that one must know something of their lives to talk fluently and understand quickly. To become, in short, accomplished, one must train the mind to *think* like the Indians. It can be readily understood that this language would seem meaningless and contemptible in a land of art and science, but beautiful, graceful, rich, and useful in the realm of nature. Vividness of description is secured by exactness, earnestness, and vigor of gesture; a graceful execution can only result from long practice. Rapid and vehement signs have the same force in this language that such a manner of utterance would give in speech, while a languid and slovenly method of making gestures would exhibit weakness and worthlessness, just as it would in a vocal language. It must be borne in mind that this is in a great measure a pantomimic language, and the air-pictures must at least be fair imitations to be worthy of recognition.

The phrases and proper names given in the Appendix outline the grammar of the language, but the following imaginary speech may give a clearer idea of its construction, its syntax, and it is very important that this should be well understood: "I arrived here to-day to make a treaty,—my one hundred lodges are camped beyond the Black Hills, near the Yellowstone River. You are a great chief,— pity me, I am poor, my five children are sick and have nothing to eat. The snow is deep and the weather intensely cold. Perhaps God sees me. I am going. In one month I shall reach my camp." In signs this literally translated would read, I—arrive here—to-day

—to make—treaty. My—hundred—lodge—camp—beyond—Hills
—Black—near—river—called—Elk—you—chief—great—pity me—
I—poor—My—five—child—sick—food—all gone (or wiped out)—
Snow—deep—cold—brave or strong.   Perhaps—chief great (or
Great Mystery)—above—see—me—I—go.   Moon—die—I—arrive
there— my—camp.

It will be observed that the articles, conjunctions, and preposi-
tions are omitted, and adjectives follow the nouns.   Verbs are used
in the present tense, nouns and verbs are used in the singular number,
the idea of plurality being expressed in some other way.   Abbreviation is constantly practised.   An Indian in closing or terminating
a talk or speech wishing to say, I have finished my speech or conversation, or, I have nothing more to say, simply makes the sign for
Done or Finished.

In addition to the description of peculiar customs which seemed
necessary for an understanding of their gesture speech, I have touched
upon such subjects as have, in many instances, been glaringly distorted and misrepresented, such as the underlying motives of the
Indians in their practice of the Sun-Dance ; the origin of the custom
of, and reasons for, scalping ; their ideas of God, and many other
subjects.

Nearly all the habits, religious beliefs, customs, traditional histories, mythological stories, about which I have written, are such as
have come under my personal observation, or have been secured
directly from the Indians, without having been filtered through and
fancifully colored by an interpreter, thus eliminating some of the
elements of intentional and unintentional deception.

I have in several places attributed good traits of character to Indians, and they possess many, notwithstanding the fact that some
good people of our race seem to think them only worthy of extermination.   Mr. Bancroft presents this matter in a happy light when
he says,—

"It is common for those unaccustomed to look below the surface
of things to regard Indians as scarcely within the category of humanity.   Especially is this the case when we, maddened by some
treacherous outrage, some diabolical act of cruelty, hastily pronounce
them incorrigibly wicked, inhumanly malignant, a nest of vipers,
the extermination of which is a righteous act, all of which may be
true ; but judged by this standard, has not every nation on earth
incurred the death-penalty?"

The Indians were not favored at the first discovery of this country with inquisitive, learned, and disinterested historians, and it is
a difficult task now to correctly represent them, on account of the
great changes that have taken place.   If the Indians form their
ideas of us from the traders, land speculators, and common white
people with whom alone they associate, they will not commit a
greater error than Europeans do when they form their ideas of the
character of the Indians from those who hang about the settlements

and traffic with the frontier inhabitants. Sickly philanthropy is too weak-eyed to see the vices which inherently belong to their stage of the development of man, and the bitter sentiments entertained by those who have suffered cruel outrages at the hands of these barbarians make them blind to any good that they may possess.

I have not, I repeat, tried to draw a veil over evils to soften the cruelties which these people are capable of, or excuse their barbarism and excesses, but it is not a difficult matter, I think, to show how the fires of hell have been kindled in their savage breasts. The frontier sentiment in regard to our Indians is not as well known as the kindly feeling entertained by those who have formed their ideas from the pleasant descriptions of Eastern writers. The following concise statement made by Mr. James W. Steele correctly represents this sentiment: "The most extraordinary of all the efforts of American romance are those which, without any foundation in truth, have created the widely-accepted picture of the American Indian. When confronted with the actual hero, the beautiful characters of Cooper cease to attract, and, indeed, become in a sense ridiculous. Lordly, reticent, content, eloquent, brave, faithful, magnanimous, and truthful he made those sons of the forest seem, whose scattered descendants now linger upon coveted reservations, and, in happy squalor, seem patiently, if not lazily, to await final oblivion. Filthy, brutal, cunning, and very treacherous and thievish are their descendants and relatives who still wander in a condition of marauding independence west of us. Every tradition repeating the story of Indian bravery, generosity, and hospitality fades like mist before the actual man. The quality of moral degradation, inborn and unmitigated, runs through the whole kindred, from King Philip and Red Jacket down to San-tan-te, Sitting Bull, Kicking Bird, and Spotted Tail. The common instincts of savagery, as illustrated in all the tribes and kindreds of the world, are intensified in these. Brave only in superior numbers or in ambush, honest only in being a consummate hypocrite, merry only at the sight of suffering inflicted by his own hand, friendly only through cunning, and hospitable never, and, above all, sublimely mendacious and a liar always, the Indian, as he really is to those who unfortunately know him, seems poor material out of which to manufacture a hero or frame a romance. All missionary and philanthropic efforts made in his behalf have thus far failed to amend his life or change his morals. Always prominent in the history of the country, ever to the fore in philanthropic literature and high-plane oratory, always the impediment to be removed, and afterward the dependant to be supported, mollified by semi-annual gifts, and oiled and pacified by periodical talks about the Great Father and blarney about 'brothers,' through campaigns, councils, treaties, and tribal relations, he has finally come to almost the last years of his career, with only the one redeeming fact upon his record, that he has never been tamed and never been a servant. Neither has the hyena."

This is a terribly severe arraignment, and yet it is true of a class,—those who have been debauched and demoralized by our civilization, and our system of dealing with them, and it also accurately portrays the status of a few others; but it would be no more fair to judge the Indian from this description than it would to rate our civilization as on a level with the crime and border-ruffianism that are seen on the crest of the advance wave of our Western emigration. The characteristics I have described are such as the most of our wild Indians possess, or at least such as they seemed to me to possess.

In the Appendix will be found a description of such signals made with the pony, smoke, mirror, and blanket as are in most common use. Writers have generally given the Indians credit for a much more extensive code, but I believe I have done full justice to their system; though it is possible that the code of smoke signals of the Apaches may be more extensive and perfect than that of other tribes. I have also noted some of the metaphors and idioms which are in constant use, and these metaphoric idioms, if I may so call them, are very important. I might say a knowledge of them is absolutely essential to a correct understanding of the language. I have also given some of the Indian names for a few of the prominent rivers and mountains which have not been preserved on our maps, as well as some of the personal names which are difficult to express by means of gestures.

The description of the gestures made by our instructed deaf-mutes is brief, but it is believed is sufficiently accurate for comparison with the Indian sign language.

I am indebted to Dr. Philip Gillett for assistance in this part of the work, and under great obligation to Mr. Ezra G. Valentine of this city, who for some seven years was an instructor in the Deaf-Mute College at Jacksonville, Illinois, and who with patience, courtesy, and kindness went over my entire vocabulary and made for me the gesture for each word. Mr. Valentine agreed with me in considering many of the Indian gestures superior to those made by instructed deaf-mutes, while of course some of those in our system are better than those made by the Indians. Many are exactly alike. I am indebted to General Robert Williams, U. S. Army, for advice and suggestions, and to Lieutenant-Colonel James F. Gregory, A.D.C., for much healthy criticism and material assistance running through the preparation of the entire work.

THE INDIAN SIGN LANGUAGE.

A.

Abandoned. Conception: Thrown away. Bring both closed hands, backs up, in front of and little to left of body, hands near each other, right in front of and little higher than left; lower the hands, at same time carry them to left and rear, and simultaneously open the hands with a snap to the fingers in extending them. This sign, like many others, can be made with one hand and be understood, but in all these cases, where practicable, it is better to use both. When an Indian becomes sick or tired of his wife, or if in his mind he has good reason for what we would call a divorce, he, as they say, "simply abandons her," "throws her away," and she goes back to her parents or other kinsfolk. If on account of age or other reason the Indians displace the chief of a band or tribe, he is "thrown away," the above sign being used to express the change.

Red Dog, an Uncapapa Sioux at Red Cloud Agency, was at one time an able orator and a man of some considerable influence with the Ogalallas. Age only having brought him boastfulness, his influence became entirely a thing of the past; and as I ignored him he became incensed, and asked for a transfer from the agency, saying, "You have thrown me away;" and, to make it still more emphatic, added, "Yes, you have thrown a blanket over me!"—meaning that I had not only deposed and suppressed him as a chief or headman, but had also placed him out of the sight of his people.

Deaf-mutes, to express the same idea, open the hands similarly, but move them to the front and downward, holding them in front of centre of body, drawing the hands back after the movement.

Aboard. Conception: Sitting down on. Make the sign for conveyance or vehicle, then bring left hand back down in front of body some ten inches, fingers extended, touching and pointing to right and front, left forearm horizontal. Bring the closed right hand so that little finger and lower edge shall rest on palm of left, back of right hand to right and front, right forearm about horizontal.

Deaf-mutes hold right hand on back of left, and usually hands are extended and palm of right resting on back of left.

Abortion. Make sign for FEMALE, for GROS VENTRE (BIG BELLY), for KILL (this latter gesture made towards abdomen), and sign for PARTURITION. A simple miscarriage would be expressed by saying that the young (of creature spoken of) was dead before birth. The Crow Indians are, so far as I know, the only tribe who openly justify abortion. They claim that they were authorized to commit it by the God who created them. (See Crow.) "Whirlwind," of the Southern Cheyennes, in the Indian Territory, said to me "that they did not like to talk of such matters,—it was not a fit subject for chiefs to discuss;" but, after an elaborate explanation on my part, said "he had heard of but one tribe who practised abortion;" and when asked what tribe this was, replied, "the whites." The Arapahoes cannot be said to sanction the action of their women in committing abortion, but they look at the offence with indifference. Indian women sometimes throw themselves violently across a log or stone, or lean suddenly and heavily forward on the high pommels of their saddles. Some of the Southern tribes are said to produce abortion by the most violent measures. A pregnant woman will lie on the ground and permit another woman to strike her with a club several severe blows upon the abdomen, or to lay thereon hot flat stones. It is hardly necessary to add that these violent and extreme means frequently kill the woman as well as the fœtus. Some tribes, it is claimed, make decoctions from roots or plants, which, when taken internally, produce abortion without pain or injury ; but this I have been unable to authenticate. It is safe to say, in conclusion, that the crime of producing abortion in any manner is of very infrequent perpetration.

Deaf-mutes sometimes indicate this by revolving the hands in front of body, which denotes failure ; but a more complete way would be to make signs for *baby, kill,* and *parturition.*

Above. In the sense of one thing above another, bring the left hand, back up, fingers extended and touching in front of and a little to left of body ; left forearm horizontal, fingers pointing to right and front ; bring right hand, back up, some inches over left (according as it is desired to represent a great or small distance), fingers extended and touching, and pointing in a direction perpendicular to the direction of fingers of left hand.

Above, in the sense of above the earth, in the heavens above the clouds, is indicated by simply pointing towards the zenith with index finger of right hand, others and thumb closed.

In the sense of one above another in authority, social position, favor, or esteem, also one above many, or above the people generally, the vertical motion of fingers is used as explained under SUPERIOR.

Deaf-mutes make very nearly the same gesture.

Absent. Make sign for SIT and No. This is used in such expressions as "He is not here," etc.

Deaf-mutes simply wave the right hand outwards from the body.

Abuse. Conception : Throwing lies or mistakes against one. When speaking of abusing, scolding, defaming some other person, bring the right hand back outwards some eight inches in front of body, first and second fingers extended and separated, others and thumb closed, index finger and forearm horizontal, nearly parallel to body; move the hand rather sharply outwards, or towards the person indicated, mostly by wrist action, several inches; return hand and repeat motion several times.

To indicate that others scold or defame, or detract from your merits, bring the right hand, back to right, some eight inches in front of right breast, first and second fingers extended and separated, others and thumb closed, index and forearm horizontal, extended fingers pointing to left and front; move the hand rather sharply, mostly by wrist action, several inches towards left breast; return hand to first position and repeat motion two or three times. The Flatheads and many other tribes make the sign for *bad* after *talk*, while others simply touch the mouth and then make sign for *bad*. Some tribes use the gesture I have described in the sense of joking, fooling, etc.

Deaf-mutes bring the closed left hand, back to left, in front of centre of body, and thrust the right index about horizontally, other fingers and thumb closed; from rear to front over left hand, right index grazing left hand at thumb and index as it passes.

Accident. This requires the metaphoric idiom used by the Indians, as noted under "By Itself." Explain how or in what manner (which would, as a rule, be known from the conversation or the circumstances), and then make sign for "By Itself." I was accidentally shot, would be in sign, I shot "*by itself*," meaning there was no reason or cause for the shooting; no one to blame or responsible for it. This peculiar metaphoric idiom is much more frequently used by the Cheyennes, Arapahoes, and Sioux than by other tribes.

Deaf-mutes bring the hands well in front of body, equidistant from it and opposite each other, some six inches apart, index fingers alone extended and held about horizontally, and pointing about to front; by wrist action suddenly turn the hands, backs towards each other.

Accompany. See With.

Accost. See Question. Deaf-mutes strike the horizontal left forearm near wrist, with palmar surface of finger of right hand; point right index at person, and then crook same, drawing hand slightly to rear.

Ache. Conception: From the throbbing pulsation of the blood, or the darting sensations of pain. In the former case, see Sick. In the latter, bring the extended index finger of right hand, others and thumb closed, over and parallel to the surface of the afflicted part; move the hand sharply a few inches, so as to thrust index finger in several different directions, keeping it so far as practicable parallel to the surface. For a headache, frequently the sign for *sick* is first made near head, and then the above sign. Indians not fully conversant with the sign language make signs for lying down, and then breathe in a distressed manner.

Deaf-mutes hold the extended index finger, others and thumb

closed, over and parallel to surface, and then make thrusting motion to indicate the darting pain, sometimes first making the sign for *sick*.

Across. The left hand is usually used to denote the object crossed, the sign for which would be made, and then holding extended left hand in front of body, back up, fingers pointing to right; pass the partially compressed and slightly curved right hand, back to right, over left on a curve upwards to front and then downwards. Across, in the sense of, on the other side, the right hand, after passing beyond left, is held with back nearly to front, fingers pointing about to left (this position taken by wrist action just as right hand passes left), as though something was laid on the other side; and in case of some one waiting on the other side, the right hand would be closed as it is moved over left, and after passing beyond, the sign for SIT made; literally, sitting on the other side.

The deaf-mute gesture is the same.

Add. This is expressed by the sign for WITH. In the sense of putting one thing on another, indicate the piling up by natural gesture.

Deaf-mutes bring the tips of fingers and thumb together, then holding left hand, back down, in front of body, bring the tips of right against left, right hand back up and held over left.

Adultery. Make proper sign for *person*, then the sign for AN-OTHER; sign for COPULATE, and sign for PRIVATE. The sign is rarely used, except to relate to the woman. Some tribes make sign for cutting off the nose. In former times many tribes punished the woman by cutting off the cartilaginous portion of the nose, and the Blackfeet included the lower part of the ears; the man was sometimes whipped, and usually had to pay roundly for the crime in ponies or whatever other property he might possess. If the wife of a chief dishonored him, she as well as her paramour would sometimes be killed by the enraged husband. I heard the story of an old Comanche chief whose young wife had run away with a robust warrior of the tribe. The husband pursuing them for three months from camp to camp and over desolate prairies, finally overtook them, killed the young man, and, taking away the wife's moccasins, with his knife cut long gashes in the soles of her feet and left her dismounted on the prairie, hundreds of miles away from any camp. The Bannocks claim that formerly they did not punish the woman, but took property from the man, and sometimes killed him.

Deaf-mutes make the sign for *ashamed* and *copulate*,—a shameful connection.

Advance. Bring the right hand, back up, fingers extended, touching, pointing to front and slightly upwards, in front of body, and about ten inches distant; bring the left hand in a similar position, but between right and body; move the hands simultaneously to the front by gentle jerks. To indicate that a village was moving, extend the index fingers of each hand, others and thumbs closed; bring the hands near each other, crossing the index fingers at first joints, right above the left, palms of hands towards each other; move the hands in this position to front, to the right, left, or rear, to indicate the direction of movement or advancement, keeping backs of hands towards the direction indicated. This is frequently used to indicate any advance or movement of men or animals, though, strictly, it relates to a village, and the crossed index fingers represent the tepee-poles. As a rule, however, it would be necessary to explain what was moving, and hold the hands correspondingly ; if a column of white troops, the hands nearly closed, backs up, are held in front of body, left several inches in front of right and a trifle higher, and then the hands moved simultaneously to front by gentle jerks. Many of the Southern tribes—Comanches, Kiowas, and others—hold slightly compressed and nearly extended hands in front of body, wrists crossed, left in front of right, backs of hands outwards, hands few inches apart, fingers of left pointing to right and upwards, of the right to left and upwards ; move the hands in this position by gentle jerks. They claim the conception of the sign is from carrying something in the arms, or something laid in hollow of left arm or elbow.

Deaf-mutes simply move the extended right hand, either back up or back to right, to front, from near body about opposite, though a little lower, than right shoulder.

Advance Guard. Bring the left hand, back up, fingers extended and touching, some ten inches in front of centre of body, fingers pointing to front and slightly upwards; bring right hand, index finger extended, others and thumb closed, in front of left hand a few inches, index finger pointing to front and upwards, it being in front of centre of left hand (this indicates the person in front or in advance of the rest); then, still holding hands in same position, extend second finger of right hand, keeping first and second well separated, and by wrist action move this hand horizontally several times from right to left (indicates looking about). If desiring to express the idea of the advance-guard looking for trail, etc., of course the fingers would in the movement point towards the ground. Their advance-guard and flankers are called SCOUTS.

Afraid. Conception : Cannot stand up before ; shrinks back from. Bring both hands well out in front of body, or to either side (well out), backs of hands up, hands about height of breast, index fingers extended, pointing upwards and to front, others and thumbs closed, hands about eight inches apart at same height and advanced equally ; bring the hands back a few inches with a downward movement, a partial jerk, and simultaneously curve the index fingers. The hands should be put out towards and drawn back from the person or thing which causes fear. Usually only one hand is used in making this gesture. Indians consider bravery the highest, most perfect virtue ; physical cowardice the meanest, most abject vice. Their education and training from infancy create in their minds and hearts a condition of affairs which elicits spontaneous reverence for the one, contempt and scorn, beyond words, for the other.

The sign for HEART is made by some, and then the right hand, still held in this position over the heart, is lifted up a few inches quickly two or three times, to indicate the throbbing action of the heart under the influence of fear ; others hold the hand as in HEART, and then raise the hand as high as and close to the neck, to indicate the heart rising in the throat.

Deaf-mutes hold the hands in front, and then shrink backwards and downwards with the body, at same time withdraw the hands and indicate their fear by the expression of the eyes and face.

Afraid of No One. Point with index finger of right hand in several directions, and sweep the flat hand circularly in front of body, then make sign for AFRAID, and sign for NO.

Deaf-mutes make the sign for afraid, then resuming first position and determined expression of countenance, make circular sweep of hand, and shake the head.

After. Conception : Falling behind. Bring left hand, back up, well out in front of body, about opposite left breast, index finger extended, pointing to left front and slightly upwards, others and thumb closed ; bring right hand similarly fixed in rear, little to right, trifle lower than left, so that index finger of right hand shall be parallel to left index, tip of right index just over knuckles of left index ; draw the right hand to right and rear, keeping index finger pointing in same direction. This refers specially to time ; and to convey the idea of a short time after, the right hand would be moved a very little. Long time, longer distance, and for very long time, the right hand is drawn as far as possible to rear, and the left pushed well to the front. Some Indians make simply sign for WAIT. The description of, and remarks made in regard to, BEHIND, apply to *after*.

Deaf-mutes bring the hands closed, with the exception of the thumbs, which are extended and vertical, in front of body, back of left to left, right to right, and the right hand some inches in rear of left ; the left hand precedes the right in taking its position, and the right is brought from the front to the rear of left.

Afternoon. Indicate the position of the sun westward from the zenith with the incomplete circle of thumb and index of right hand, other fingers closed, hand held to the right and above head, and following the path of the sun in the heavens.

Deaf-mutes hold right forearm vertically in front of body, place palm of left hand at right elbow, and then bend the right forearm down to left and front, terminating movement when forearm is about horizontal, right hand extended, back up.

Age. Indicated by denoting the number of winters. There are few tribes, aside from the Cheyennes, Sioux, and Arapahoes, who pretend to keep any account of their individual ages, claiming that ''when young they don't care to know, and when old they don't want to.'' One accustomed to judge can pretty accurately determine the age of Indians from the appearance of the eyes and teeth, as, after middle age, a whitish, filmy ring appears on the iris, and in most cases the teeth become very much worn.

Deaf-mutes denote extreme age by placing side of curved right index, other fingers and thumb closed, against the chin and lowering the head with a tremulous motion.

Agency. Conception: Distributing house for food and clothing. Make sign for HOUSE, for BY ITSELF, for DISTRIBUTE or GIVE, for BLANKET, for FOOD. The sign for *giving* is here used entirely in the sense of distributing ; though the gesture for *by itself* is rarely used : it is always understood. The Indians do not consider the goods a gift by any means, but as a payment for the lands taken from them. Agencies are of course of comparatively recent date, and these signs illustrate very well how gestures are coined to meet emergencies. The issue of supplies of any kind is an important event to the Indians ; to a people who have nothing to do, it breaks pleasantly upon the monotony of every-day life, and, as is usually the case at the time of an issue, if they have been fasting for a day or more, it must add a certain zest to the interest on the occasion of securing something to eat. Issue days are about alike at all agencies, and a description of one at the Shoshone Agency, Wyoming, perhaps will give an idea of the scene that is presented once in seven days at other places as well as there. I was present on October 1, 1881, the issue day for the Indians at that agency for rations. The clouds which had been hovering around us for the few days before had drifted away on the wings of the wind, and the bright, warm sunshine gladdened and beautified everything in that little valley. It was a perfect fall day,—the russet and black of the distant hills, the gray sage-brush, and the brown fields stretched away to the hazy-blue horizon in the east to the delicately-tinted bluffs and sombre-colored mountains in the west. The men lounge lazily around the office and store, smoking, and talking about the latest news; the young bucks, gaudily dressed, gather in small groups, mounted and dismounted ; the women, old and young, at first collect at the window of the office and have the family ration ticket examined and corrected ; ponies are standing about tied and untied ; many dogs, sorry-looking curs, of Indian and other breeds, are following closely at the heels of the women. A few wagons, with dejected-looking ponies attached, are waiting for their loads. The door of the storehouse is opened, and now one can understand why the women have been crowding in so closely, aud waiting so patiently. The issue is then made,—"first come, first served." Flour, sugar, coffee, bacon, tobacco,—whatever the ticket calls for,—is handed out, and is quickly put in the dirty bags, or tied up in the pieces of cloth brought for the purpose. These are carried by the squaws to their ponies, or wagons, packed with skill, and, getting up on top of the load, they jog back to their tepees or over to the corral where the beef is issued. Here this was done at the block, but the offal was just as eagerly sought after as ever. When issued " on the hoof," the young men have quite a good buffalo-hunt running the Texas steers. After witnessing one issue of beef, I have never wondered at the disillusioning of the young officer who had become somewhat infatuated with an Indian girl. One look at their business-like manner of handling the intestines of a freshly-killed beef would have a tendency to disenchant any one not an Indian.   On issue days of warmth or sunshine, and with a dry track, the men, young and old, gather at a short distance from the agency and race their ponies from about noon till dark.   Most of the races are for short distances over a straight course, only a few being for a mile or more. (See RACE.) Gambling is freely indulged in on any race.   A rainy-day issue beggars description.   The old squaws gather in a sombre and drooping way, like a lot of wet ravens, hurriedly clutch in their bony old hands whatever is given them, and, pulling their wet blankets over their heads, vanish in the storm.

Agent.   Indian.   Make signs for WHITE MAN, for CHIEF, for DISTRIBUTE, for FOOD or EAT, for BLANKET, for BY ITSELF.   The Indians frequently call the agent "father," and make sign for *father* who distributes.   Some Indians make signs for *white man* and *mine*, others simply *headman*.

Agitate.   See EXCITE.

Agony.   Physical suffering is expressed by passing the hands over the surface of the afflicted part, making sign for SICK or darting pain, and then sign for BRAVE.   Mental agony would be expressed in some natural way after giving the exciting cause.

Deaf-mutes indicate this by physical contortion.

Ahead.   See BEFORE.

Deaf-mutes indicate this by closed hands, thumbs extended as in *after*.

Aid.   Combine signs for WORK and WITH.   *I want you to assist me* would be, *I want you to work with me.*   Sometimes they will say, *I want you to make a road or trail for me.   Show me the road or trail;* but this refers more to counsel or advice in regard to a plan of action.

Deaf-mutes hold the left forearm horizontally in front of body, place the palmar surface of fingers of extended right hand against it on under side near wrist, and lift the left forearm upwards some inches.

Aim, To.   Conception : From manner of using weapon.   If with bow and arrow, bring hands up in front of face as though drawing arrow to its head ; if with a gun, place hands in position of holding a gun when about to discharge same at an object.

Deaf-mutes make same gestures.

Alight, To.   Indicate from what, and then bring the extended and separated index and second fingers of right hand, others and thumb closed, from above downwards, towards the ground, pointing towards same and about vertical.

Deaf-mutes place the tips of index and second fingers on left palm, latter held horizontally in front of body, other fingers and thumb closed, and this is sometimes also used by the Indians.

Alike.   If to express the idea that two people look alike, pass the hand over the face and then make sign for EVEN or SAME.

Same with deaf-mutes ; but their sign for *even* or *same*, it must be remembered, is like the Indian sign for *marry*, and this caution applies with equal force to all my remarks in regard to the natural signs of deaf-mutes.

Alive. Conception : Walking about. Bring the right hand in front of body at about height of breast, index extended and pointing upwards, other fingers and thumb closed ; move the hand to the right and léft few inches, and at same time turn it from right to left, and from left to right, by wrist action, as the hand passes to right and left. To say that a person was very ill, just alive, the sign for *little* and then this sign, moving the hand but slightly ; or use the sign for RECOVER after partial sign for DIE. In asking a question, such as, " Is such a person alive ?" would be in gesture INTER-ROGATION or QUESTION. Name the person by gesture, and then the sign I have described.

The deaf-mute natural sign for animal life, and from this their sign for animals generally, presents the most radical difference exist ing between the Indian sign language and their gesture speech. They hold the extended hands, backs outwards near the chest and parallel to the surface, hands at same height, index fingers horizontal, fore-arms nearly so, and tips of fingers near each other ; then, mostly by wrist action, move the hands outwards a few inches, repeating motion, to indicate the swelling and contraction of the chest in breathing ; and this same sign is used by the Indian to represent sickness, and to denote the throbbing sensation of an unhealthy pul-sation. The deaf-mute sign for *sick* is to lean the head forward, place palm of left hand on forehead, and palm of right at upper part of chest or against the heart. In case of a brute, the Indian sign would, I think, be the best. A more correct description of the word *alive*, as made by the deaf-mute for a human being, would be to hold the hands as above described, but against abdomen, and the fin-gers slightly separated, the hands then raised (keeping palmar surface against body) with a tremulous motion ; this denotes the flow of blood through the system.

All. Move the right hand, back up, fingers extended and touch-ing, in a horizontal circle from right to left, starting from about op-posite right shoulder, carrying the hand well out to front from that point. Sometimes, after the circular movement of the right hand, both hands are brought together, gently clapping palms two or three times ; this particularly when using it in sense of " all the people of a camp moving,"—it then slides to and fro in the way of indicating that all the people are gathered together for a move.

Deaf-mutes hold both hands near each other, little higher than head, and bring them together again at about the height of waist, each describing a vertical circle as it is brought down, and when hands meet, put back of right on left palm.

All Gone. The Southern Indians usually bring the extended hands, held rather loosely at the joints and wrists, backs outwards, in front of body, right near it, fingers pointing to left ; left opposite and out-wards a few inches from right, fingers pointing to right ; the right hand is moved outwards, the left towards the body, back of right hand striking left palm, and fingers bending as hands pass ; then the motion of hands is reversed, back of left hand striking right palm. The most common sign in the North is to bring the extended hands in front of body, back of left down, right up, and pass the right outwards over the left, palms touching. (See WIPED OUT or EXTER-MINATE.)

Deaf-mutes draw the partially compressed right hand from above downwards through the left hand, pressing it in a clasp with thumb and fingers as it passes, after making sign for ALL.

Alliance. Make sign for PEACE ; and if for war purposes, add signs for GOING TO WAR and TOGETHER or WITH.

Deaf-mutes form two circles with thumbs and index fingers, and link them together, other fingers closed.

Alone. Bring the extended index finger of right hand, others and thumb closed, in front of body, at about height of neck, and pointing upwards. To indicate a movement, carry the hand from right to left, at same time turn the hand slightly by wrist, so as to give a swinging movement to index finger ; the hand is not turned as much as in ALIVE. In an Indian fight nearly always some of the men mount their ponies and ride out in front of their lines up and down between the two forces, sometimes to draw the fire of the enemy, to try and get him to waste his ammunition ; at others, an exhibition of dauntless courage, bravado, or triumph. If any are hit and killed they are sung about, and their bravery extolled long afterwards. I have seen them make a dash along the line within easy range, where hundreds of bullets were sent after the daring individual, and at intervals repeat the operation for hours without getting hit, due mostly, it would seem, to the fleetness of their ponies, and throwing the body from side to side. They, however, attribute their good luck entirely to the power and efficacy of their "medicine." The sign is also used in such sentence as, he rode alone in the thickest of danger. In fact, the gesture is common, and used about as we use the word.

Deaf-mutes use the same sign.

Amatory. Make sign for FOND or LOVE and indicate opposite sex.

Deaf-mutes use the same.

Ambitious. Conception : Must rise above others; must be superior. Make sign for the person, then sign for PUSH or MUST, then bring both hands, palms outwards, in front of body, index fingers extended, pointing upwards, and placed side by side, touching, other fingers and thumbs closed, left hand little higher than right, so that tip of right index shall be at about second joint of left, raise the right hand till tip of right index passes beyond tip of left, keeping sides of index fingers pressed together. This is used rather more in the sense of one rising in rank, power, influence, ability, or bravery above another; and to denote rising above several, or a number, the fingers of left hand are all extended, and the right index placed against left palm and then raised.

Deaf-mutes simply say *a pushing man*, and their sign for *push* or *must* is the same as the Indian gesture ; sometimes they only push the right hand upwards, and add force by the expression of the countenance.

American. Many of the Northern Indians called the people of the colonies, after the establishment of their independence, "Long Knives," to distinguish them from the British.

Deaf-mutes call the Americans proper, *i.e.* the Indians, "the people with rings in nose and ears," and denote them in signs by pinching the cartilage of the nose with tips of thumb and index of right hand, also the lobe of the right ear; the other fingers are closed, and the index and thumb form a circle.

Among. Bring left hand in front of body about height of neck, thumb and fingers extended, separated and pointing upwards, hand slightly compressed; bring extended right index, other fingers and thumb closed, index pointing upwards, and mix it in with fingers of left hand by moving about among them.

Deaf-mutes use the same.

Ancestors. Indians usually simply make sign for *old people;* some specify the kinship by appropriate signs.

Deaf-mutes extend the index fingers of both hands, others closed, and make a rotary motion, one about the other, as they are carried back over the right shoulder. Right hand thrown over the right shoulder means ancient. To express *coming down from ancestors,* they place the hands well back over right shoulder and then revolve them to front and downwards. I should have stated, perhaps, that family pride of Indians is fully as great as with any people; in fact, I think it is much stronger than with the white race.

Angry. Conception: Mind twisted. Bring the closed right hand, back to right, against or close to and opposite forehead, thumb pressing against second joint of index finger, and back of thumb resting against forehead; move the hand slightly outwards a little to left, and simultaneously twist the hand, by wrist action, from right to left. According to Indian belief, all emotions arise in the heart, and cause certain actions. In this instance the heart is irritated, and, as a consequence, the mind is twisted or wrenched. Reverse the operation of the sentence, and it is readily seen that the sign expresses what the Indians invariably say in vocal language when they are angry, viz., "heart is bad;" in fact, many of them make sign for *heart,* and then sign for *bad,* while others hold partially-closed right hand over heart, hand resting against surface of body, the hand being turned and twisted, as in ANNOY. The first gesture I have described is frequently accompanied by a gruff and fierce grunt.

Deaf-mutes clutch the hands in front of and near body, and assume an angry expression of countenance.

Annihilate. See EXTERMINATE.

Annoy. Conception: The heart is disturbed and in a flutter. Make sign for HEART, and then, with right hand in this position, separate and nearly extend the thumb and fingers, and by wrist action twist and turn the hand as it rests against left breast, then turning the hand so that fingers point upwards, raise it with a tremulous motion. These gestures indicate a serious annoyance or trouble.

Deaf-mutes rub the breast with a circular motion of right hand, and perhaps strike the .head ; much depends on the expression of the countenance.

Annuities. Make signs for BLANKET, for FOOD, and for DIS-TRIBUTE. Sometimes the sign for BY ITSELF is made ; this should properly always be added, but as a fact it seldom is.

Another. Bring the right hand, back up, in front of body, about height of breast and near it, fingers extended, touching, pointing to left, hand very slightly compressed, thumb resting on palm ; sweep the hand upwards, outwards, to right, and then downwards or curve, turning hand during movement back down, stopping hand when it is lowered to about waist. This gesture is very much like the one for *other side*, or *beyond*, but the hand is moved more to the right. Frequently the left hand is also held in front of body, the right held just over it ; the above-described gesture made, and then returning hand to first position, carry it to left and front similarly. This gesture is not common, it is very difficult to describe, and by no means easy to execute.

Deaf-mutes bring the right hand, back to right, fingers closed, thumb extended and pointing upwards in front of body, then move the hand on small vertical curve upwards to right, and then downwards, terminating movement when the hand is at same height as when starting.

Antelope. Conception : Pronged horns of animal. Bring the hands, palms toward and alongside of the head near base of the ears, index fingers and thumbs extended and spread, other fingers closed, index fingers pointing about upwards ; move the hands by wrist action parallel to head from rear to front, repeating motion. Some tribes do not move hands. Sometimes signs for *white flanks* are also made. The coarse, brittle hair of the antelope is used for pillows, the tanned skin for the uppers of moccasins, and the shin-bone is made into a pipe. The meat at certain seasons is highly prized, and the liver sprinkled with a little gall is eaten hot ; *i.e.*, before the animal heat has been dissipated after the killing. The brains are usually cooked by roasting the entire head, the horns being broken off before the head is placed on the coals.

Anxious. Make sign for Now, and then bring right hand back to right, fingers curved and touching, thumb resting on index, about one foot in front of body, hand about height of shoulder ; draw the hand inwards and downwards and towards the heart, not bending the wrist. The subject or object is drawn near the heart. Some-times the right hand is placed over the heart and the hand fixed as in *look* or *see*,—the heart is looking or searching.

Deaf-mutes bring the hands in front of face, right near it, back up, left some inches outwards and little higher, back down, fingers par-tially separated, and then an upward look with the eyes, with an intense or expectant expression of countenance.

Apache (Indians). Hold the left hand, back up, in front of the left breast, index finger extended and pointing to front, others and thumb closed ; bring the right hand back outwards, index finger extended, others and thumb closed near left, side of right index resting on back of left near second joint ; move the right hand inwards and outwards, mostly by wrist action, side of the index finger of right hand rubbing against back of left ; repeat motion. I have heard two distinct conceptions for this gesture : the Cheyennes claiming that the sign came from a peculiar musical instrument made from an elkhorn, which produced weird-like sounds by rubbing it backwards and forwards with a stick, and the second (I do not remember what tribe gave me the conception) from a specially good whetstone which the Apaches made and used. This gesture refers to the Apaches living with the Kiowas at the Wichita Agency, Indian Territory. There are several other bands in Southwestern New Mexico and Arizona called by the Indians Wood or Timber, Poor, Long Arrow, Mountain and Hooked or Curved Toe Apaches, and corresponding signs are made for each. Those at Wichita Agency are frequently called Kiowa Apaches. One of the old men of the latter band, in speaking to me of himself and his tribe, said that he was about seventy years of age and was born near the Missouri River, northeast of the Black Hills. He claimed that the Apaches of the extreme Southwest did not formerly understand the sign language, but that they learned it from the Kiowas, who went down there and joined them in raids into Mexico. This band in customs and habits are very much like the Kiowas, with whom they have lived for so many years. They do not have an annual Medicine-Dance, but join the Kiowas when they have theirs. They bury their dead in the ground, and also in caves ; and some of the bands have a special mourning custom of wailing and chanting, just as the sun disappears in the western horizon, for the first time after the death of the person mourned for. The Kiowas, Comanches, and Apaches at the Wichita Agency, as a rule, wear the scalp-lock, but the rest of the hair is often worn loose, and frequently cropped around the neck. Some cut off only one side, and wear the other in a twist or braided, and wrapped with a string of red or blue cloth. They do not, as a rule, use otter-skin for this purpose, as do many other tribes. Ear ornaments and the pipe-clay breastplates are prized, and the use of paint is the same as with the Northern Indians. The Apaches of the Southwest, though poorly armed until within a few years, have gained by their shrewdness, cunning, treachery, cruelty, and active hostility a notoriety second to no other tribe. The country in which they have operated is specially adapted to Indian warfare. The Commissioner of Indian Affairs, in his annual report for 1881, gives the following as the numerical strength of Indians in New Mexico and Arizona :

ARIZONA.

COLORADO RIVER AGENCY.

Mohave	802
Chimehuevis	210

MOQUIS PUEBLO AGENCY.

Moquis Pueblo   2,100

PIMA MARICOPA AND PAPAGO AGENCY.

Pima   4,500
Maricopa   500
Papago   6,000

SAN CARLOS AGENCY.

White Mountain Apache   596
San Carlos Apache   795
Warm Spring Apache   275
Coyotero Apache   819
Tonto Apache   586
Mixed Apache   119
Southern Apache   171
Chiricahua Apache   246
Apache Yuma   309
Apache Mohave   662

INDIANS IN ARIZONA NOT UNDER AN AGENT.*

Hualapai   620
Yuma   930
Mohave   700
Suppai   75

Total population   21,015

NEW MEXICO.

JICARILLA SUB-AGENCY.

Jicarilla Apache   705

MESCALERO AGENCY.

Mescalero Apache   906

NAVAJO AGENCY.

Navajo   16,000

PUEBLO AGENCY.

Pueblo   9,060

Total population   26,665

Although the area covered by Mr. Bancroft as "Apache country" contains several tribes marked by entirely different languages and many different ways of living, habits, and religious beliefs, still the following extract from his work contains much that is pertinent, accurate, instructive, and interesting in regard to these Indians :

"The Apache country is probably the most desert of all, alternating between sterile plains and wooded mountains, interspersed with comparatively few rich valleys. The rivers do little to fertilize the soil except in spots ; the little moisture that appears is quickly absorbed by the cloudless air and arid plains which stretch out, sometimes a hundred miles in length and breadth, like lakes of sand. In both mountain and desert the fierce, rapacious Apache, inured from childhood to hunger and thirst, and heat and cold, finds safe retreat.

---

* Taken from report of 1880.

It is here, among our western nations, that we first encounter thieving as a profession. No savage is fond of work; indeed, labor and savagism are directly antagonistic, for if the savage continues to labor he can but become civilized. Now, the Apache is not as lazy as some of his Northern brothers, yet he will not work, or if he does, like the Pueblos, who are nothing but partially reclaimed Apaches or Comanches, he forthwith elevates himself, and is no longer an Apache; but being somewhat free from the vice of laziness, though subject in an eminent degree to all the vices of which mankind have any knowledge, he presents the anomaly of uniting activity with barbarism, and for this he must thank his thievish propensities. Leaving others to do the work, he cares not whom, the agriculturists of the river-bottoms or the towns-people of the North, he turns Ishmaelite, pounces upon those near and more remote, and if pursued, retreats across the *jornadas del muerte*, or journeys of death, as the Mexican calls them, and finds refuge in the gorges, cañons, and other almost impregnable natural fortresses of the mountains.

"All the natives of this region wear the hair much in the same manner, cut square across the forehead and flowing behind. The Mojave men usually twist or plait it, while with the women it is allowed to hang loose. Tattooing is common, but not universal; many of the Mojave women tattoo the chin in vertical lines like the Central Californians, except that the lines are closer together. Paint is freely used among the Mojaves, black and red predominating, but the Apaches, Yumas, and others use a greater variety of colors. Breech-cloth and moccasins are the ordinary dress of the men, while the women have a short petticoat of bark. The dress of the Mojaves and Apaches is often more pretentious, being a buckskin shirt, skull-cap or helmet, and moccasins of the same material; the latter, broad at the toes, slightly turned up, and reaching high up on the leg, serve as a protection against cacti and thorns. It is a common practice among these tribes to plaster the head and body with mud, which acts as a preventive against vermin and a protection from the sun's rays. In their selection of ornaments the Mojaves show a preference for white, intermixed with blue; necklaces and bracelets made from beads and small shells, usually strung together, but sometimes sewed on to leather bands, are much in vogue. The Apache nation adopt a more fantastic style of painting and in their head-dress; for ornament they employ deerhoofs, shells, fish-bones, beads, and occasionally porcupine-quills, with which the women embroider their short deer-skin petticoats.

"The food of all is similar. Most of them make more or less pretensions to agriculture, and are habituated to a vegetable diet, but seldom do any of them raise a sufficient supply for the year's consumption, and they are therefore forced to rely on the mesquit bean, the piñon-nut, and the maguey plant, *Agave Mexicana*, and other wild fruits, which they collect in considerable quantities. The Navajos, Mojaves, and Yumas have long been acquainted with the art of agriculture, and grow corn, beans, pumpkins, melons, and other vegeta-

bles, and also some wheat.   Some attempt a system of irrigation,
and others select for their crops that portion of land which has been
overflowed by the river.

"Maize soaked in water is ground to a paste between two stones.
From this paste tortillas, or thin cakes, are made, which are baked
on a hot stone.   To cook the maguey, a hole is made in the ground,
in which a fire is kindled ; after it has burned some time the maguey bulb is buried in the hot ashes and roasted.   Some concoct a
gypsy sort of dish, or ollapodrida ; game, and such roots and herbs
as they can collect, being put in an earthen pot with water and
boiled.   As before mentioned, the roving Apaches obtain most of
their food by hunting and plunder.   They eat more meat and less
vegetable diet than the other Arizona tribes.   When food is plenty
they eat ravenously ; when scarce, they fast long and stoically.
Most of them hate bear-meat and pork.   So Jew-like is the Navajo
in this particular that he will not touch pork though starving.

"Their fighting has more the character of assassination and murder than warfare.   They only attack when they consider success a
foregone conclusion, and rather than incur the risk of losing a warrior will for days lie in ambush till a fair opportunity for surprising
the foe presents itself.   The ingenuity of the Apache in preparing
an ambush or a surprise is described by Colonel Cremony as follows :
' He has as perfect a knowledge of the assimilation of colors as the
most experienced Paris modiste.   By means of his acumen in this
respect, he can conceal his swart body amidst the green grass, behind
brown shrubs or gray rocks, with so much address and judgment that
any but the experienced would pass him by without detection at the
distance of three or four yards.   Sometimes they will envelop themselves in a gray blanket, and by an artistic sprinkling of earth will
so resemble a granite boulder as to be passed within near range without suspicion.   At others, they will cover their persons with freshly-
gathered grass, and, lying prostrate, appear as a natural portion of
the field.   Again, they will plant themselves among the yuccas, and
so closely imitate the appearance of that tree as to pass for one of its
species.'

"Household utensils are made generally of wicker-work or straw,
which, to render them water-tight, are coated with some resinous
substance.   The Mojaves and a few of the Apache tribes have also
burnt-clay vessels, such as water-jars and dishes.   For grinding
maize, as before stated, a kind of metate is used, which with them is
nothing more than a convex and a concave stone.   Of agricultural
implements they know nothing.   A pointed stick, crooked at one
end, which they call *kishishai,* does service as a corn-planter in
spring, and during the later season answers also for plucking fruit
from trees, and again, in times of scarcity, to drive rats and prairie-
dogs from their subterranean retreats.

"Although not essentially a fish-eating people, the Mojaves and
Axuas display considerable ingenuity in the manufacture of fishing-
nets, which are noted for their strength and beauty.   Plaited grass

or the fibry bark of the willow are the materials of which they are made.

"The system of enumeration of the Apaches exhibits a regularity and diffusiveness seldom met with among wild tribes, and their language contains all the terms for counting up to ten thousand.

"Ancestral customs and traditions govern the decisions of the councils; brute force, or right of the strongest, with the law of talion in its widest acceptance, direct the mutual relations of tribes and individuals. Murder, adultery, theft, and sedition are punished with death or public exposure, or settled by private agreement or the interposition of elderly warriors. The doctor failing to cure his patient must be punished by death. The court of justice is the council of the tribe, presided over by the chiefs, the latter, with the assistance of sub-chiefs, rigidly executing judgment upon the culprits. All crimes may be pardoned but murder, which must pay blood for blood if the avenger overtakes his victim.

"All the natives of this family hold captives as slaves; some treat them kindly, employing the men as herders, and marrying the women. Others half starve and scourge them, and inflict on them the most painful labors. Nothing short of crucifixion, roasting by a slow fire, or some other most excruciating form of death can atone the crime of attempted escape from bondage. They not only steal children from other tribes and sell them, but carry on a most unnatural traffic in their own offspring.

"They are immoderately fond of smoking, drinking, feasting, and amusements, which fill up the many hours of idleness. Dancing and masquerading are the most favorite pastimes. They have feasts with dances to celebrate victories, feasts given at marriage, and when girls attain the age of puberty; a ceremonial is observed at the burial of noted warriors, and on other various occasions of private family life, in which both men and women take part. The dance is performed by a single actor, or by a number of persons of both sexes, to the accompaniment of instruments or their own voices. All festivities are incomplete without impromptu songs, the music being anything but agreeable, and the accompaniment cornstalk or cane flutes, wooden drums, or calabashes filled with stone and shaken to a constantly varying time. They also spend much time in gambling, often staking their whole property on a throw, including everything upon their backs.

"They make their own spirits out of corn and out of *Agave Americana*, the pulque and mescal, both very strong and intoxicating liquors.

"In the character of the several nations of this division there is a marked contrast. The Apaches, as I have said, though naturally lazy like all savages, are in their industries extremely active,—their industries being theft and murder, to which they are trained by their mothers, and in which they display consummate cunning, treachery, and cruelty."

Apparel. Pass the palmar surface of spread thumbs and index fingers over and near the surface of the body, or such portion as may be necessary to explain the particular clothing which it is desired to describe.

Deaf-mutes pass the extended hands, palms near surface of body.

Appear. Indicate by signs whatever it was, and in what way. A man appearing or coming into view, the extended left hand, back out, fingers pointing to right, is held in front of body at about height of neck; the right hand, back out, index alone extended and pointing upwards, is passed under left hand and beyond, and pushed up till the index rises into view.

Deaf-mutes raise the extended right on a curve slightly towards body.

Apple. Clasp the nearly-closed and compressed right hand with left in front of body, then make sign for TREE, and then hold the compressed and partially-closed right hand, back up, well out and in front of and above right shoulder; drop the hand slightly, raise it, and let it drop again in a little different place, to represent the apples on the trees. To make it more definite, make sign for EAT and GOOD. Peaches and pears are represented in the same way, and the same principle obtains with any fruit growing on trees. These fruits being mostly new to the Indians, there are no well-known and definitely established signs in general use, and to distinguish different kinds, some particular quality of the fruit, manner of its growth, season when ripe, or special use made of it must be noted. Dried apples are represented by first making sign for APPLE, and then CUTTING UP over left palm, then touch the ear to indicate the shape of the dried fruit.

Deaf-mutes indicate the size and shape by clasping closed and compressed right with left hand, and then hold closed left hand at mouth, as though eating an entire apple in that way.

Approach. Indicate by proper gesture the object and manner; for instance, a person, the elevated index of right hand is brought in towards the body.

Deaf-mutes use the same signs.

Arapahoe. The three bands have totally distinct signs. It is claimed by the Northern Arapahoes, those now at the Shoshone Agency, near Fort Washakie, Wyoming, that the sign for their band is *the* tribal sign, and that it was derived from their being the mother of all other tribes; while other tribes, who do not admit this claim as valid, say they got the sign from a famous chief of their band having had the smallpox, his chest being greatly disfigured by the disease. (This conception would seem to be the correct one, as the Prairie Gros Ventres frequently make the gesture opposite the face.) For this band, bring the right hand, back outwards, in front of centre of breast, few inches from it, compress the hand and partially curve the fingers, so that tips of fingers and tip of the thumb shall be near together, tap or strike gently the breast with the tips of the thumb and fingers, repeating motion.

For the Southern Arapahoes, those located at the Cheyenne and

Arapahoe Agency, near Fort Reno, Indian Territory, bring the extended index finger of right hand back to rear, alongside of and touching nose, index pointing upwards, others and thumb closed; raise and lower the hand two or three times; frequently index is held near, but does not touch, the nose.

The third band, located with the Assinaboines, at Fort Belknap, on Milk River, about twenty-eight miles from Fort Assinaboine, are known as Gros Ventres of the Prairie, and the sign for Gros Ventres is made to designate them.

I have seen the sign for *blue cloud* made to denote the Arapahoes, and this is a correct translation of the Sioux word for this tribe, though perhaps a clear sky would be better; and I once saw an Indian rub his forehead with tip of right index as a sign for the Arapahoes; why, I could not learn.

Very reliable tradition locates this tribe in Western Minnesota several hundred years ago, meeting the Cheyennes as they (the Cheyennes) came out on the prairie, and for many years moving and camping with or near them, so that for all practical purposes they were one people, and the history of one relates very closely to the history of the other. (See Cheyennes) In their migration they separated from the Cheyennes after passing the Black Hills (though they frequently came together after this), and pressed on to the head-waters of the Missouri, and then were driven out of that country by the Blackfeet and other tribes, and skirted along and wandered in the mountains and plains to the south as far as the head-waters of the Arkansas. They have been greatly reduced in numbers by disease and wars with other tribes, and, like all broken Indian nations, the fragments have not prospered. What is known as the "Chivington Massacre," near old Fort Lyon, Colorado (the Indian camp was on Sand Creek), was a cold-blooded, dastardly murder of a number of Arapahoes and Cheyennes by the Third Colorado Volunteers. Black Kettle and White Antelope were the chiefs of the Cheyennes, and Left Hand of the Arapahoes, and they, with the greater part of the men, had been lured away from their camp by deception. It was an indiscriminate slaughter of mostly women and children, followed by a horrible mutilation of the dead, the troops showing a ferocity and brutality which the savages themselves have never exceeded.

The Arapahoe men are intelligent and brave, not differing materially (physically or mentally) from the Cheyennes and Sioux, but the standard of virtue for the women is not nearly as high as with either of these tribes. Their vocal language is entirely different from any other I have ever heard, and it is almost an impossibility for a white man to learn to speak it. They are known as among the best in gesture speech, and used it to such an extent that, until recently, it was supposed their vocal language was so poor as to make it necessary; in fact, some people had stated that to such a degree were they dependent on signs that they could not carry on a conversation in the dark. Their vocal language, however, has a rich vocabulary. At neither of the three agencies during the past season was there an interpreter, which, considering the laxity of their morals, struck me as being very singular indeed, and I made special inquiry as to whether white half-breed babies were killed by the mothers, as is done by some tribes, but could find no evidence that such was the case.

Only a few of the young men took part in the Sioux and Cheyenne war of 1876 and 1877, and then only in the Custer affair on the Little Big Horn River, after which many of them enlisted as scouts and rendered most excellent service.

The traditions and myths of the Northern band were elicited by myself, mostly by means of the sign language, and my notes of the Southern band were secured in the same way, Mr. Ben Clarke acting as interpreter. The little that I have in regard to the Gros Ventres of the Prairie I have given under GROS VENTRES. Little Raven, the former war-chief of the Southern band, claimed that the war with the whites in 1868 determined the separation from the Northern band. They were then camped on the Arkansas River, and the Northern band would not join in the war. In regard to older history, Little Raven said, "When we were all together, we roamed from the head-waters of the Platte to the Arkansas, and long ago, farther north, went over the mountains at head of North Platte River. We got tired of war with the Utes, and came out on the Plains. When my father was a child we were at war with the Sioux,—twenty-nine years since he died, and he had seen sixty winters at his death. We afterwards made peace with the Sioux, and sometimes lived with them. The Cheyennes made peace first. The Sioux first saw white men, then the Cheyennes, and I was about twenty when I went with some Cheyennes to the Missouri River, and saw the first white man. About one hundred years ago we were ranging over as far as the Big Horn River. The Great Spirit had taken pity on us a long time before and given us buffalo. A raiding-party from our camp was out, the young men came on the Shoshone Indians, saw ponies, ran off some; these were the first we had ever seen. We used to think there was a force, an unknown power (Great Spirit) in the earth, and we used to pray to it; finally it gave us all the earth could give,—stone implements, corn, etc.; then this force went above. This same power is in the sun and at the four corners of the earth,—everywhere. All of our customs, marriages, dances, etc., are like the Cheyennes, except in burying our dead. Our people always buried in the ground. The Arapahoe custom was to dress the remains in the best clothing,—war-bonnet, best robe or blanket, never putting weapons with remains,—nothing but good clothing, and painted the face with red paint. Before we crossed the Missouri River we used to plant and raise corn. The Arickarees stole the corn and the art of raising it from us. Before we went hunting so much we lived on what we raised from the ground."

I visited the camp of the Northern band, taking with me some flour, sugar, coffee, tobacco, etc., and had a feast made for the old men. They gathered in the sub-chief's lodge, decrepit with age and blighted with disease, some six of the oldest being blind, the result probably of hereditary or acquired scrofula or syphilis. Having no interpreter, and these men being blind, "Sharp Nose," second chief of this band, gave me their stories in the sign language, and in this way I received the following traditions and account of their customs. This band was sent to their present agency in 1878, and finding here evidence of their occupying this country long ago, probably soon after their separation from the Cheyennes, they were inclined to think this was the exact spot where they were created, and, moreover, as this would, in their minds, give them a prior claim to the land over the Shoshones, they, in their shrewd and cunning way, endeavored to press this point with me, and gave all their migrations as roamings from this place. Now in their poverty and degradation, needing the help and charity of others, they lay great stress upon their own generosity in the palmy days of their prosperity.

Wolf Moccasin, though blind and seventy-four years of age, was evidently the brightest and best preserved mentally of any in the council. He stated that when he was a small boy, old enough to remember well the event, however, the Gros Ventres of the Prairie were living in the far north ; subsequently they came over and joined the Arapahoes, when they were camped on the head-waters of Powder River, about fifty-five years ago, and remained with them for some little time,—a few years. They left when the Arapahoes were camped on the Platte River. Their tradition did not go back to the time when they first got ponies. In shaking hands they rub the palm of the hand over the arm and body immediately afterwards, if they have great confidence in and respect for the person whom they were saluting. Their custom was to embrace before meeting the whites. A long time ago they fought the Sioux, but they very soon made peace with them,—a peace which has been always kept. They believed that after death they went to the land of the rising sun ; this land was far away beyond and below all mountains, a level country near the ocean. An Arapahoe killed in battle did not have to travel over this long trail by land, but went though the air easily and com· fortably by the dead man's road, or rather, the road of the warriors killed in battle (Milky-Way). They buried their dead in the ground, laid them away on the breast of their mother, and with the remains never put the weapons, but best blankets, pipe of deceased, and a pony killed for the spirit to ride to the country beyond the rising sun. Those who had died for a time (fainted) had, on their return, stated that they had seen the lodges of their people in that far-off land, and they had plenty of buffalo, antelope, and all kinds of game. There were seven bands of soldiers : Young Men or Boys' band, Medicine Rattle band, Image band, Medicine Lance band, Dog band, Crazy band, and Old Bull band.

War-parties had a partisan who went in advance, and carried a pipe in the hollow of left arm. This chief did not eat or drink from the rising to the setting of the sun, but soon after the shadows of darkness had covered the earth some of the young warriors of the party brought him water and food. He thanked them, and drank and ate. They had a Sun-Dance like the Sioux, but much more severe, the participants not eating or drinking for four days and nights. To the muscles of the back they usually hung shields instead of buffalo-heads, and these shields afterwards possessed the power of protecting them from harm in battle. They also cut off a piece of flesh from the arm and gave it to the God in the sun, praying as they did so that they might live long on the earth, and be spared from sickness and disease. In regard to their dances, Sharp Nose (he had visited Washington) said they had as many as the white people in the East. Their dances were named after their soldier bands, and in all of them they imitated the motions of the animals after which they were named. They never, like the Cheyennes, had the Medicine-Dance. In the Crazy-Dance they all sang a few words in a low tone and then suddenly broke out into a loud and fierce shout. In former times the moccasin was made with a long anklet, which near the top was turned down, making a flap. Porcupine-quill work in circular shape was put on the top of foot near instep, and several rows of the same kind of work ran round the leggings at bottom, the sides of which were heavily fringed, as were the sleeves of the shirt. The girls and women wore the protective string at night, a practice which, judging from appearances in these later times, doe, not seem to have accomplished in any great degree the object of its institution.

They could not explain why it was that there were no half-breed whites and Arapahoes, and insisted that they did not kill the young. At this point they sent out for one, and a little tangle-haired ragged boy of about eight years came into the lodge. He could not speak English, and was looked upon as a curiosity. He had Ute blood, however, in his veins, as Sharp Nose said, "One-third Arapahoe, one-third white, one-third Ute!"

The God of their forefathers gave them paint. It protected them from the heat of summer and the cold of winter, and also gave them good luck. Black paint was used after returning from war, indicating joy, rejoicing; red paint was used in profusion when under the pressure of any excitement, either in war or love,—put on face, hair, and body.

Some of their medicine-men had the power to produce rain or wind to assist them, and had exercised this power. They could also cause the snow to vanish and rain to come; in fact, could control all these elements through means which they tried to explain, but I could only make out that it was a kind of jugglery. They did not have any ceremony when a girl had her first menses. The white buffalo was sacred,—it was created first, and in olden times it was impossible to kill it.

In regard to the creation, they said that long ago, before there were any animals on the earth, it was covered with water, with the exception of one mountain, and seated on this mountain was an Arapahoe, crying and poor and in distress. The gods looked at him and pitied him, and they created three ducks and sent them to him. The Arapahoe told the ducks to dive down in the waters and find some dirt. One went down in the deep waters, and was gone a long time, but failed. The second went down, was gone a still longer time, and he also came up, having failed. The third then tried it, he was gone a long time; the waters where he went down had become still and quiet, and the Arapahoe believed him to be dead, when he arose to the surface and had a little dirt in his mouth. Suddenly the waters subsided, disappeared, and left the Arapahoe the sole possessor of all the land. The water had gone so far that it could not be seen from the highest mountain, but it still surrounded the earth, and does so to this day. Then the Arapahoe made the rivers and the wood, placing a great deal near the streams; he then created a Spaniard and a beaver, and from their union came all the people of the earth. The whites were made beyond the ocean; there were then all the different people the same as at the present day. Then he created buffalo, elk, deer, antelope, wolves, foxes,—all the animals that are on the earth, all the birds of the air, all the fishes in the streams, the grasses, fruit-trees, bushes, all that is grown by planting seeds in the ground.

This Arapahoe was a God. He had a pipe, and he gave it to the people. He showed them how to make bows and arrows, how to make a fire by rubbing two sticks, how to talk with their hands; in fact, how to live. His head and his heart were good, and he told all the other people, all the surrounding tribes, to live at peace with the Arapahoes, and these tribes came to this central one (Arapahoe),— came there poor and on foot, and the Arapahoes gave them of their goods, gave them ponies. The Sioux, the Cheyennes, the Snakes, all came. The Cheyennes came first, and were given ponies; these ponies were "*Prairie Gifts.*" The Snakes had no lodges, and with the ponies they gave them skin tepees. The Arapahoes never let their hearts get tired with giving; then all the tribes loved the Arapahoes.

I have been unable to ascertain why these Indians are called "Arapahoes." They can give no reason for it, and I have not been able to find a similar word in any of the languages of the surrounding tribes. The Northern Arapahoes call themselves by a vocal word, which they claim means *good* or *strong heart.* The Southern band claim the word simply means *men, people,* or *the men, the people.*

Formerly the head chief of the Arapahoe nation was elected by a grand council; this was, however, a mere matter of form, for, as they said, "The man who had led the soldiers to war, had done many brave things, was sure of the election." They also had sub-chiefs, headmen of the soldier bands, and frequently a council or peace chief, who, as a rule, held his position by the power of his persuasive eloquence.

Arickaree (Indian). Conception: Cornshellers. Bring the closed left hand, back to left, in front of body, thumb extended and resting on index finger; bring right hand, back to right, fingers closed,

thumb partially extended alongside of left, placing the ball of thumb
of right hand at back of left thumb near its base ; twist the right
hand by wrist action to the right and downwards, keeping the right
thumb pressed against base of left until in its movement it slips off
with rather of a snap against the index finger of right hand.   Repeat
motion.   Many Indians make the sign for *dirt houses* for these
people.

These Indians are clearly an offshoot from the Pawnees (see
PAWNEE), from whom they first separated longer ago than tradition
gives any account of.   During the past two hundred years they have
made peace and been at war with the Mandans and Gros Ventres
several times, but since about 1838, when they all suffered so terribly from smallpox, the necessity for the alliance to protect themselves from the surrounding hostile tribes has kept them together as
friends.   Though speaking different languages, from intermarriage
and long intercourse they have many habits and customs in common.   From a powerful band, numbering several thousand, they have
been reduced by various causes—smallpox, cholera, chickenpox, and
other diseases new to them, and wars with the surrounding tribes—
to (according to the report of the agent for 1881) only six hundred
and seventy-eight.

Mr. F. F. Girard joined the Arickarees (usually called Rees) in
1849, in the interest of a trading company.   He subsequently married into the tribe and learned the language.   When he found them
they were with the Mandans, located at old Fort Clarke, the Gros
Ventres then having their village at the site of the present agency.
The Rees then called the Mandans *Connit*, from *Conniche*, meaning
stone-people, people who live on the stony hills; and the Gros Ventres *We-tutz-ce-han*, from man and river-people, living on or near
the river ; and they then claimed that they first met them on Knife
River near its mouth.   He thought there were two thousand five
hundred Arickarees at this time, and their social and military organization consisted not of a division into gens, but into bands, as follows :
1, Young Boys' or Fox band ; 2, Young Dog band ; 3, Big Young
Dog band ; 4, Strong Heart band ; 5, Bull band ; 6, Crow band.
The latter composed of all the old men who have passed through
all the bands, and are entitled to a seat in any of the others.   For
police purposes there was a band of soldiers, or black-mouths.
These were appointed for this special purpose, and taken from the
above-named bands.   They blackened the lower part of their faces
as a badge of their authority.   These several bands were, it would
seem, organized mainly for social pleasure, such as dancing, etc.,
and the members passed through the grades by purchase.   As a rule,
each member had to pass regularly through each band, but if ambitious for sudden promotion, say from the *Big Young Dog* to the
Strong Heart band, it could be accomplished by purchase and temporarily giving his wife to the embraces of the chief of the band,
should the young man have one.   The young man was then considered as a son, and could, if he went to war, take one of the

names of his new father. If not married at the time of adoption, he could not marry into the family of his adopted father.

Their dances were, more than with other Indians, of the masquerading, pantomimic order, different animals being represented, closely imitating them in dress and movement. Among other dances they had what was called a *Test-Dance*, which was for the purpose of asserting the virtue of the females, either married or unmarried. If slanderous tongues had falsely accused a wife or daughter, the injured one went to her father or husband, asked him to give a feast and make a dance. When everything was in readiness she took an arrow, and, touching a painted buffalo skull, made a solemn oath of chastity. These dances were to test the virtue of females, and those who could not pass through the ordeal were for the time abandoned to the lusts of whoever might desire them.

They also had a ceremony of giving away one's wife for cause. If the wife of a chief had dishonored him, sometimes the whole camp would be gathered together, and in their presence the wife would be given to her lover with a present of some kind.

Tradition and remnants of their dirt-houses give evidence only of their living on and near the Missouri River, and from their present location as far down as Fort Randall, Dakota.

These three tribes have had their personal appearance, habits, manners, customs, and religious beliefs quite accurately and extensively described by Lewis and Clarke, Catlin and Mathews.

Arise. Hold the right hand, back down, well in front and little to right of right breast, index finger extended, and pointing to front, other fingers and thumb closed, forearm about horizontal; mostly by wrist action, bring the back of hand outwards and index pointing upwards. This would represent one person as arising; repeating motions would indicate several. This gesture can perhaps illustrate the importance of making signs so as to convey a clear idea of the surrounding circumstances; for instance, in such a sentence as *An old man arose slowly*, the sign for an *old man* would be made, and then the index finger would very slowly be brought to a vertical position; but to express the idea of a sudden arising, as, I heard a shot and jumped up, the proper gesture for I *heard a shot* or *discharge of a gun* would be made, and then the index finger would be brought into a vertical position with a jerk, and the manner of doing this—expression of face and attitude of body—would determine the degree of alarm and activity of the startled person. It is a pantomimic language, and animation gives emphasis.

Deaf-mutes carry the right hand well out to front and downwards, extending and separating index and second fingers, back of hand down, index finger pointing to left; then, being extended, left hand, back down, fingers pointing to front, in front of body, and raising right hand from its position, place the tips of index and second on left palm, these fingers vertical.

Arrange. Usually comprises signs for WORK and FIX, frequently signs for WORK or MAKE and ROAD.

Deaf-mutes hold extended hands in front of and equidistant from body, opposite each other, same height, few inches apart, fingers pointing to front, palms towards each other; keeping hands in this position, move them on curve upwards to right, and then downwards to same height as when starting a second motion the same as this, still more to right.

Arrest. Conception: To seize hold of and tie at wrists. Make a grasping motion with both hands in front of body as though seizing hold of a person, and then cross the wrists, hands closed; sometimes the closed left hand, back to left, is held well out in front of and little higher than left shoulder, left forearm nearly vertical; grasp left wrist with right hand and pull it a little distance to right.

Deaf-mutes simply make a grasping movement with hands to front of body, as though seizing hold of a person.

Arrive Here. Hold the extended left hand, back outwards, in front of breast and close to it, fingers pointing to right; carry right hand, back to front, well out in front of body, index finger extended and pointing upwards, others and thumb closed; bring the right hand briskly against back of left, second joints of closed fingers of right hand about on a line with index finger of left hand.

Deaf-mutes use the same.

Arrive There. Hold left hand, back to front, well out in front of body, about height of neck, fingers extended touching and pointing to right; bring right hand, palm outwards, in front of and close to neck, index finger extended and pointing upwards, others and thumb closed; carry the right hand out sharply and strike palm of left, second joints of the fingers of right about on line with index of left hand. The left hand is used in this—in the sign *to arrive here*—and generally to indicate the point or place; and often the hands are so changed in position as to indicate the direction where one came from or was going to, thus making the gesture more graphic and more easily understood in conversation.

Deaf-mutes use the same.

Arrow. Conception: Drawing arrow from left hand. When hunting or fighting and ready for action, one or two extra arrows were carried in the left hand, and usually one in the mouth. Bring left hand, back down, and inclined a little to left and front—*i.e.,* little finger a trifle lower than index—well out in front of left breast, fingers touching and partially curved, thumb curved, forming with index finger nearly a complete circle, space of about an inch between tip of index and thumb, left forearm pointing to right and front; place the extended index finger of right hand, back outwards, and to right, in the centre of the circle formed by thumb and index, other fingers and thumb closed; the index of right hand held parallel to palm of left hand, draw the right hand to right and rear, keeping index finger on line of prolongation of its first position. Some tribes make the sign for Bow, and snap the index fingers to denote the arrow.

Deaf-mutes make motion as though drawing arrow from quiver,

and then thrust the index finger forward to indicate flight of arrow. The Sioux claim that the Cheyennes first had arrows given them by the Great Spirit,—two for hunting, which were black, and two for war, which were red. The Shoshones admitted to me that before they met the whites they used poisoned arrow-heads, and for this purpose they were dipped in a compound made of ants pounded to a powder and mixed with the spleen of an animal. The mixture was then placed in the sun and allowed to partially decay. The result was such a deadly poison that if the arrow broke the skin in touching a person it was sure to produce death. They also said the Plains Indians never used them. The Blackfeet use goose- and eagle-feathers as arrow-guides, while most tribes prefer the feathers of smaller birds.

There is some difference in the feathering, some nations employing three feathers tied round the shaft at equal distances with fine tendons. "The Tonto-Apaches have their arrows winged with four feathers, while some of the Comanches used only two. All have some distinguishing mark in their manner of winging, painting, or carving on their arrows."—*Bancroft.*

"Much labor was also expended in the construction of arrows. The shafts were made from sprouts of dogwood (*Cornus stolonifera*) of a year's growth. After cutting the bark was removed, and the rods were rubbed between two grooved stones, held firmly together in one hand, till reduced to a proper size and smoothness. The head, made of hoop-iron, was then inserted in one end of the shaft and bound in position with sinew. The back end of the shaft was now furnished with a triple row of feathers, attached by means of glue and sinew, and the end notched to fit the bow-string. With a small chisel-like instrument three slight grooves or channels were cut along the shaft between the head and the feathers, and the arrow was complete. Various reasons were assigned for this channelling. Some claimed that it caused the arrow to adhere more firmly in the wound; others that it was simply designed to facilitate the flow of blood. The manufacture of arrows, as of bows, was a slow and irksome process. Three or four were probably the limit of a day's work, even after the rough material was already at hand. So exact were they in making them that not only were the arrows of different tribes readily distinguishable, but even individuals could recognize their own arrows when thrown together with those of others of the same band. Disputes sometimes arose, after the slaughter of a herd of buffalo, as to whose some particular carcass rightfully was. If the arrow still remained in the body, the question was easily decided by drawing it out and examining the make of it. Some Indians made two kinds of arrows, one for hunting and another for war. In the latter the head was so fastened that when an attempt was made to draw the shaft from the wound the head was detached and remained in the body of the victim. The Pawnees never used such. When once he had possessed himself of a good bow and a supply of arrows, the Pawnee was as solicitous in the care of them as a hunter would be of a choice rifle. The bow, if not in actual service, was kept close in its case, and the arrows in the quiver. Great pains were taken that they should not become by any chance wet, and much time was spent in handling them that the bow should not lose its spring and the arrows should not warp. The average length of the former was four feet, of the latter twenty-six inches."

Mr. Belden, in writing of this, says, "Let me teach you how to make a good bow and arrow. And first, we will begin with the arrow. The shoots or rods must be cut in the arrow season, that is, when the summer's growth is ended. They must not have any branches or limbs on them, but be straight and smooth. The Indians cut their arrows late in the fall, when the timber is hardening, to withstand the blasts of winter. The sticks are not quite so thick as one's little finger, and they are sorted and tied in bundles of twenty and twenty-five. These bundles are two or two and one-half feet in length, and wrapped tightly from end to end with strips of rawhide or elk-skin. The sticks are then hung up over fire in the tepee to be smoked and dried, and the wrapping keeps them from warping or bending. When they are seasoned, which takes several weeks, the bundles are taken down, the covering removed, and the bark scraped off. The wood is very tough then, and of a yellowish color. The next process is to cut the arrow-shafts exactly one length, and in this great care must be used, for arrows of different lengths fly differently, and, unless they are alike, the hunter's aim is destroyed. Another reason for measuring the length of arrows is to identify them, for no two warriors shoot arrows of precisely the same length. Each warrior carries a measuring or pattern stick, and it is only necessary to compare an arrow with the stick to find out to whom it belongs. But should the arrows by chance be of one length, then there are other means of identifying them, for every hunter has his own private mark in the shaft, the head, or the feather. Of many thousands I have examined, I never found two arrows exactly alike when they were made by different warriors.

"The shafts being made even, the next work is to form the notch for the bowstring. This is done with a sharp knife, and, when made properly, the bottom of the notch will be precisely in the centre of the shaft. The arrow is then scraped and tapered toward the notch, leaving a round head an inch long near the notch to prevent the string from splitting the shaft, and to make a firm hold for the thumb and forefinger in drawing the bow.

"All the arrows are peeled, scraped, and notched, and then the warrior creases them. To do this he takes an arrow-head and scores the shaft in zigzag lines from end to end. These creases, or fluted gutters in the shaft, are to let the blood run out when an animal is struck. The blood flows along the little gutters in the wood and runs off the end of the arrow. The arrow-head is made of steel or stone. It is shaped like a heart or dart, and has a stem about an inch long. The sides of the stem are nicked or filed out like saw-teeth. Nearly all the wild Indians now use steel arrow-heads, they being a great article of trade among the savages. There are firms in the East who manufacture many hundreds of thousands every year and send them out to the traders, who sell them to the Indians for furs.

" When the shaft is ready for the head, the warrior saws a slit with a nicked knife in the end opposite the notch, and inserts the stem of the arrow-head. The slit must be exactly in the centre of the shaft, and as deep as the stem is long. When properly adjusted, the teeth of the stem show themselves on each side of the slit. Buffalo, deer, or elk sinew is then softened in water, and the wood is wrapped firmly to the arrow-head, taking care to fit the sinew in the teeth of the stem, which will prevent the head from pulling out.

" The next process is to put on the feathers. To do this properly great care must be taken. Turkey- or eagle-quills are soaked in warm water to make them split easily and uniformly. The feather is then stripped from the quill and put on the shaft of the arrow. Three feathers are placed on each shaft, and they are laid equidistant along the stem. The big end of the feather is fastened near the notch of the shaft and laid six or eight inches straight along the wood. The feathers are glued to the shaft, and wrapped at each end with fine sinew. The arrow is next painted, marked, dried, and is ready for use. It takes a warrior a whole day to make an arrow, for which the trader allows him ten cents. . . .

"'To make war-arrows, the Indians manufacture the shafts the same as for game-arrows. The head is then fastened loosely in the wood, and when it is fired into the body it cannot be got out. If you pull at the shaft the barbs catch and the shaft pulls off, leaving the arrow-head in the wound. Some war-arrows have but one barb, and when this arrow is fired into the body, if the shaft be pulled, the barb catches in the flesh and the steel turns crosswise in the wound, rendering it impossible to extract it. Fortunately, but few Indian tribes now use the poisoned arrow.

Arrow-Head. Make sign for ARROW, and then bring left hand, back to left, in front of left breast, index finger extended and pointing upwards, others and thumb closed; place the tip of the extended and horizontal index finger of right hand against index of left at second joint, other fingers and thumb of right hand closed, back of hand up; press the tip of right against side of index of left; raise right hand slightly, moving the right index with snap as it leaves the index finger of left hand. To indicate that it was iron, point to something made of this metal. There is no sign for *iron*, but of late years, however, an Indian has been rarely seen without something about him made of this metal. The length and shape of the arrow-head usually discovers the tribe. (See ARROW.)

Artilleryman. Make signs for WHITE MAN, for SOLDIER, for WITH, and CANNON.

Deaf-mutes make signs for *man* and *cannon*.

Indians, who have seen regular artillery soldiers, add signs to denote the red stripe down the leg of trousers. I have given some of these signs to show the easy and natural manner in which gestures are coined, and to illustrate the easiness of construction of the language, as well as the necessity for its constant growth.

Ascend. Indicate in what way, and what was ascended ; for instance, a bluff; make the sign for this with left hand, and, still holding it in position, bring extended right index, other fingers and thumb closed, near wrist, and pressing inner surface of index against surface of left hand ; raise the right hand slowly till tip of index is higher than left hand.

Deaf-mutes indicate the surface of bluff or hill with back of extended left hand. Their general sign for *ascend* is a simple movement of the right hand upwards.

Ashamed. Conception : Drawing blanket over face. Bring both hands, backs outwards, fingers extended, touching and pointing upwards, in front of the face, few inches from it, right opposite right, and left opposite left cheek ; move the right hand to left, left hand to right, mostly by wrist action, keeping hands nearly parallel to face, and right nearest to it, terminating movement when wrists are crossed.

Deaf-mutes bring the back of the fingers against right cheek, fingers pointing downwards, and with a circular movement of hands rub the cheeks, to denote the blush or color.

Ashes. Conception : Wood reduced by fire to powder. Make signs for TIMBER, for FIRE, then bring right hand in front of body, back upwards, hand compressed, fingers partially curved ; rub the tips of fingers with tip of thumb several times. Usually in conversation this last is the only gesture used, and such abbreviations are frequent in the sign language.

Deaf-mutes make same, their sign for *wood* and *fire* being different.

Assinaboine (Indian). The general sign is the same as SIOUX, but usually add the sign to denote the band, as the Boat or Canoe band at Wolf Point, Montana, Rocky band in the north, etc. The Arickarees call the Assinaboines the people of the North, or cold people. The Crows call them Yellow Legs. Of course corresponding signs are made. This branch of the Sioux family take their name from a Chippewa word.

Mr. Beaulieu, writing to me of them, says, " I made inquiry of some Indians here (White Earth Agency, Minnesota) whether, by tradition, they knew of the Assinaboines, and am informed that as far back as they have any account of them these Indians inhabited the country adjoining that of the Crees, which latter tribe, ' Kinisten-eaux,' they claim as a part of their own (Ojibway), and that they, the Assinaboines, Rees, Crows, Pottowattomies, and Ojibways were always friendly with each other. Boine in Ojibway is the definition for a Sioux Indian. Assin or Ahsin is a stone, so that I should suppose Ahsinaboine or Assinaboine meant ' Stone Sioux,' perhaps ' Rock Mountain Sioux.' Ah-sine-wah-ziew or Assinewah-ziew : ' Rocky Mountains.' Boine, in Chippewa, means, so I was told by one of these Indians, simply *enemy*, and would *in this way only* be, as Mr. Beaulieu says, a definition for the Sioux.

"The Assinaboines separated from the Sioux on account of trouble which grew out of the actions of a faithless wife; the tradition, however, is vague and unsatisfactory. I have heard the Sioux call the Assinaboines Hó-hé, but I always supposed that this referred only to a particular band called the ' Stonies,' and I still think this is the case; but the following appears in ' Snelling's Tales of the Northwest' : The Hó-hé (Hô-hây) are the Assinaboines, or 'Stone-roasters.' Their home is the region of the Assinaboine River, in British America. They speak in Dakota tongue, and originally were a band of that nation. Tradition says a Dakota ' Helen' was the cause of the separation and a bloody feud, that lasted for many years. The Hó-hés are called ' Stone-roasters' because, until recently at least, they used ' wa-ta-pe' kettles and vessels made of birch-bark, in which they cooked their food. They boiled water in these vessels by heating stones and putting them in the water. The ' wa-ta-pe' kettle is made of the fibrous roots of the white cedar, interlaced and tightly woven. When the vessel is soaked it becomes water-tight."

In the "History of Manitoba," by the Honorable Donald Gunn, I find the following: "De Grosselier and Raddison turned their attention to the Northwest, and in about 1666 pushed through Lake Superior, ascended the Kaministgoia River, and fell on the waters that flow northwest through Lake La Plui to the Lake of the Woods, and thence passed through the Winnipeg River into the lake of that name, and finally passed by the river Nelson into Hudson's Bay. These gentlemen were conducted by the Assinaboines to Hudson's Bay, probably by the Nelson or Hay's Rivers, and after having discovered that great inland sea, they retraced their steps, being still guided and protected by their friends, the Assinaboines, as far as Lake Superior, whence they proceeded to the settlements on the Lower St. Lawrence."

We are informed by history that the enterprising Du Luth, during the summer of 1679, visited some encampments of the Dakotas, where no Frenchman had ever been. After his return we find him meeting the Assinaboines and other nations at the head of Lake Superior, for the purpose of settling their difficulties with the Dakotas, and was successful. The Crees, who visited the trading-posts on the shores of Hudson's Bay, and the Assinaboines, who traded in 1678 with Du Luth, at the west end of Lake Superior, were about the same time put in possession of fire-arms, and within a few years thereafter they seem to have made a simultaneous movement,—the former pressing on to the southwest, the latter pursuing their course to the northwest, until they met in the region west of Lake Winnipeg, and on the plains of Red and Assinaboine Rivers. Indian tradition informs us that during the first half of the last century the Mandans occupied the country to the southwest of Lake Winnipeg, and that they had been forced by the united efforts of their invaders to leave their hunting-grounds and retire to the Upper Missouri. But how

long it took these tribes to drive out those whom they found in possession of the country, and what wars they carried on to accomplish
that object, are lost in the mist of years. However, we have had
the evidence of a living witness to the fact that the Crees and the
Assinaboines lived on the plains southwest of Lake Winnipeg for
some years previous to the year 1780, and that they made a preconcerted attack that year on the trading-posts on the Assinaboine.
These small houses were at Portage la Prairie, and represented three
different associations, and had but few men at each. The Indians
had kept their intentions so hid from the whites that the latter were
altogether unprepared to resist the onslaught made by their painted
and feathered assailants, who made themselves masters of two of the
houses, massacred those who defended them, and carried away the
booty. Intoxicated by their success, and confiding in their prowess,
they rushed on to attack the third house, which was defended by a
Mr. Bruce, at the head of a few men. Mr. Bruce was known among the
savages by the formidable name of Ketelie Mink-man ; *i.e.*, Big Knife.
He was evidently known among the Indian tribes for his bravery and
determined courage, and they learned by sad experience on the
present occasion that his fame for valor had not been overrated,
for he not only defended his post, but slew a number of those by
whom he had been attacked, thereby admonishing the survivors
to beat a timely retreat, leaving the resolute and formidable Bruce
in possession of the slain and of the field of battle. How far the
savages intended to carry their hostility towards the traders we have
not been able to learn, but we may presume that their defeat before
Mr. Bruce's little post at Portage la Prairie cooled their military ardor,
and the following year smallpox of a most virulent type attacked the
tribes in the vicinity of Red River, and spread over all the Indian
territories, even to the shores of Hudson's Bay. As late as the year
1815 the bleached bones of those who had become the victims of
the plague were to be seen in great quantities at several points on
the shores of the bay. The Assinaboines were encamped at several
points near the Red River when the disease appeared among them,
and was attended by the most fatal effects, so much so that ten years
after, when the Red Lake Ojibways came for the first time to Pembina
to trade, they found the Assinaboines, or rather, a small remnant of
that once numerous tribe, in that vicinity. After some days had
been devoted to feasting and the mutual interchange of presents, the
Assinaboine orators pathetically deplored the miserable condition
of their people, stating that wherever they went they saw nothing
but the bleached bones of their kindred ; that their former allies, the
Crees, had always been treacherous, and that on the appearance of
the disease they went before it to the west. " We are no longer able
to resist our enemies, the Sioux. Come, then, and live with us.
Let us have one fire and one dish. The country is large and full of
all kinds of wild animals. You need not fear want." After spending some time with their new-made friends, the Ojibways went back
to Red Lake for their families, and returned the following year to

join their allies. Their descendants still occupy the banks of the Lower Red River and the shores of Lakes Manitoba and Winnipeg. The Hudson's Bay Company's servants made their appearance for the first time in Red River in the year 1793. They met the Assinaboines in small groups at different points along the Lower Red River and along the Assinaboine River, as far west as the mouth of the Little Souris, where the English company erected their first trading establishment, to the southwest of Lake Winnipeg.

The stories of their migrations are also meagre and indefinite. They say, however, that they came from the far east and north, and they still preserve memories of the birch-bark canoes, and the use of this bark for other vessels, such as are now used by the Chippewas. Their wars with their own kinsfolk, the Sioux, seem to have been more bitter and unrelenting than with any other tribe. I found it difficult, in fact impossible, to follow the migrations of these people by the same plan as that pursued with success with other tribes and bands. I met at Fort Belknap two old men, eighty years of age ("The Pheasant" and "Many-Shells"). The former said he was born on the Missouri River, not far from the confluence of the Yellowstone, the latter six hundred miles north of the British line, on Big Timber River, north of Saskatchewan. One of these old men said to me, "We came from near the Red River of the North. The country was large, and we got separated. Our forefathers fought the rest of the Sioux. The old people told my ancestors that a voice from above told them that this world was made for them; that there was another world across the great water for the whites, and between these two there was a land where only the dead went after death,—a land to the far east and north, a fair and good country. This voice told them many things of the rain and winds, and what these things would do for them."

So far as any information can now be secured, it would seem that the Assinaboine country in former times was north of the British line, and as far east as Lake Superior. They drifted to the west, and some bands to the south as far as the Missouri, but it was not until about 1870 that they got as far west on our side of the line as their present agencies at Wolf Point and Fort Belknap, Montana. In 1828 some bands of them were camped near old Fort Union, at the mouth of Yellowstone River. Their westward and southern migrations were undoubtedly due to the encroachments on their hunting-grounds of the Chippewas from the east, and Crees from the north, and the bitter hostility of the Sioux. It would seem that they vibrated between peace and war with the Mandans, Arickarees, and Gros Ventres. They were checked in this westward movement by the Blackfeet, Bloods, Piegans, and Prairie Gros Ventres; it being only a few years since they made peace with these tribes. They were also at war with the Crows, Shoshones, Nez Perces, and Flatheads, which stayed farther movement to the South. Present tradition claims that they were always friendly with the Crees, but this goes no farther back than the time when they lived in the Red River country. The Pheasant told me that his father informed him that he could remember when they made knives, and pointed their arrows with the bones taken from the hump of the buffalo.

They are divided into several bands; the principal one at Wolf Point being called the Canoe band, and at Belknap the Whirlwind band. There are also at these two agencies, the Girl, the Canoe tied to the Shore, and the Leggings bands; and north of the line there are also several others. The agent's report for 1881 gives the following as the numerical strength of this tribe:

Wolf Point (Fort Peck Agency, Montana) 1413
Fort Belknap Agency, Montana 900

Total population 2313

The Assinaboine men are inferior in intellect and physique to the Sioux proper, and the women rank about with the Arapahoes in chastity. They trim their shirts and leggings with rough fringe like the Crows, and wear the hair in all kinds of ways, though they claim that in olden times they all wore a scalp-lock and banged the hair over the forehead, similar to the present fashion of the Crows. Like the Indians at Berthold, they seem to have adopted some of the styles of dress from all the tribes with whom they have come in contact. They believe that thunder and lightning is a kind of bird something like an eagle,—the noise is the cry of the bird, the lightning the fire flashing from eyes and mouth in its flight. Their language is a poor dialect of the Sioux, and in their customs they are also like them, but it seemed to me of a lower order. They are lazy and without enterprise even in the ordinary occupations of savages. As a consequence they are poorly armed, are not well provided with ponies, and still use the dog for transportation; have small lodges and little personal property. They bury on scaffolds and in trees, and claim that not very long ago, when a man died, his dogs were killed to accompany him to the spirit-land. They told me that in olden times they had an image carved out of wood representing the Great Unknown, which they worshipped. They gathered round this annually, and with much ceremony made presents and offerings to it. They said that this image represented the Great Spirit, but immediately added, "This same white man's God gave us the bow and arrow, and told us to kill game with it."

Astonish. Bring the palm of left hand over mouth, and draw the body backwards; the manner and expression denote the degree. This gesture is also used to denote great surprise, mingled with great pleasure or intense disappointment.

Deaf-mutes use the same.

Astray. The sign for LOST is the usual sign; but to be led astray, for instance, in such a sentence as "You led me astray," would be in sign, *you, lies, gave me road;* and then holding extended left hand, back up, fingers pointing to front, well in front of body, bring right hand, back up, alongside of left, index finger alone extended and pointing to front; turn the hand by wrist action, so that index points to right and front, and thrust index in that direction.

Deaf-mutes make sign for *mistake*, and then thrust index to front and right as above.

Astride. See, first, description given of PONY or HORSE.

Deaf-mutes make the same sign.

Attack. Make sign for CHARGE, sometimes add sign for HEAVY FIRING. Indian strategy and tactics are based on secrecy of movement and surprise, and so universal is this that the above are the only gestures I have ever seen. (See WAR.)

Attempt. Make signs for WORK and PUSH.

Deaf-mutes make sign for *push*.

Attention. See QUESTION.

Aunt. Indicate the possessive; make signs for FATHER and SISTER. (See KINSHIP.)

Deaf-mutes make arbitrary sign for letter *a*, and then make gesture for *woman*.

Aurora Borealis. Hold both hands, back down, well out in front of body at height of wrist, hands partially closed, ball of thumb pressed against nails of fingers; raise the hands, at same time extend and separate fingers and thumb with a partial snap, to indicate the flashes of light in the northern sky; and, unless in conversation where the sign is readily understood, it is better to face towards the north.

Deaf-mutes use the same. Some Indians make also the sign for *medicine*, calling it the mysterious light or fire of the north; others call it the light of the northern dancers; while still others call it the "white man's fire," or "sacred cloud."

Autumn. Make sign for TREE with both hands, for LEAF, and while the hands are in this position let the right pass slightly to right and downwards, with a tremulous, wavy motion. In the sign for leaf the right hand is held near left finger-tips, and in dropping, it falls as a leaf falls to the ground. *Early* autumn is represented by some of the leaves, one here and there turning yellow; the *middle* by sign for same, after the sign for yellow leaves; *late*, by all the leaves having fallen. In northern latitudes the sign for a little snow would be added for very late fall or early winter.

Deaf-mutes, same.

Avoid. Hold the hands in front of shoulders, index fingers extended and pointing upwards, others and thumb closed, back of right hand to right, left to left, hands at same height; move the hands towards each other, and when near carry the left outwards, and right nearer body as the hands pass. (Indicates an effort made to go around or pass by.)

Deaf-mutes simply bring the hands, holding them well in front of body, backs up, and right more in advance than left.

Awe. Bring the palm of either hand over the mouth and slightly draw back the head; sometimes the sign for HEART, and then bring right hand, fingers and thumb extended and partially separated, in front of and close to breast, thumb nearest body, fingers pointing upwards; raise the hand several inches with a tremulous motion. (The heart is first still, and then flutters into the throat with surprise and astonishment.) This gesture is used at the unexpected meeting of old friends ; at hearing the recital of wonderful deeds of valor, etc. ; or suddenly and unexpectedly meeting a great chief.

Deaf-mutes simply raise the hand and denote the awe by the expression of countenance.

Awl. Conception : From the manner of using same in sewing with sinew. Bring the left hand, back to left, in front of body, hand partially closed and thumb pressed against index, as though holding a piece of leather or buckskin ; make a thrusting motion over and near left thumb and index, at same time turning hand by wrist action.

Deaf-mutes make a boring motion with tip of right index, other fingers and thumbs closed, against left palm.

Axe. Hold left hand, back to left, arm nearly extended and about horizontal, in front of left shoulder, fingers extended touching, and wrist bent down, so that fingers point as nearly downwards as possible ; carry right under left forearm, and grasp it near elbow with spread index and thumb, other fingers closed. The sign for Chop is sometimes added, and is also frequently used by itself. Before the advent of the white race axes were made mostly from the shoulder-blades of large animals, those of the buffalo being specially prized.

Deaf-mutes make the sign for *chopping*, usually first making their sign for *wood*.

B.

Baby. See PARTURITION or CHILD and WRAP.

Deaf-mutes hold nearly extended left hand, back down, in front of body, forearm about horizontal and pointing to right and front; then lay the back of partially compressed right hand on left forearm near wrist.

Baby-Holder. Make sign for PARTURITION, for WRAP; then carry both hands alongside and rather close to rear portion of head, palms towards it, index fingers and thumbs spread, index fingers pointing upwards and about parallel to sides of head, other fingers closed (sometimes the slightly curved hands are used to denote the hood instead of the spread thumbs and index fingers); bring the hands simultaneously to front, keeping hands about same distance from head, terminating movement when hands have passed in front of face few inches; then bring extended left hand well in front of body, back outwards, fingers pointing upwards, hand about height of face; place the back of extended right hand, fingers pointing upwards, against left palm.

The Indian cradle when tied up is a little coffin-shaped sack with a hood-like projection about the head. It is made of cloth or skins of perhaps several thicknesses; always two at the back, and to this a board or stiff piece of rawhide is securely fastened to keep the child's back "as straight as an arrow." Instead of a board covering the entire back, the Cheyennes use two flat pieces of wood about three inches wide and one-half inch thick. The outer cloth or skin in front and on the hood is usually heavily beaded or garnished with porcupine-quills, and sometimes very handsomely worked. Stout strings are used to tie the baby firmly in the cradle, and one fastened to the back piece to hang the cradle up by. I have seen a baby not two days old snugly tied up in one of these little sacks; the rope tied to the pommel of the saddle, the sack hanging down alongside of the pony, and mother and child comfortably jogging along, making a good day's march in bitter cold winter weather, easily keeping up with a column of cavalry which was after hostile Indians. After being carefully and firmly tied in the little cradle, the child, as a rule, is only taken out to be cleaned in the morning, and again in the evening just before the inmates of a lodge go to sleep; sometimes also in the middle of the day, but on the march only morning and evening.

Bachelor. Signs for MAN or MALE, MARRY, and No are made. This, of course, simply means an unmarried man. The rather common acceptation, viz., a man who has passed the average age at which men marry, would hardly apply to Indians, as the men all marry. There is no such thing, I believe, as an "old bachelor;" of course there may be cases, and probably are, where men, because of some physical deformity or injury, have not married ; I have never, however, known of such.

Deaf-mutes, same ; *i.e.*, man not married. Their sign for *not* is different from *no ;* the latter being a shake of the head, while for the former, carry the extended right hand from near the body well out to front and right about horizontally, very similar to the Indian sign for *good*, only hand is carried more to right, and with some is lowered a little in being carried to right and front.

Bacon. Hold the extended left hand, back to left and front, in front of body, fingers pointing to right and front ; bring the right hand, back down, and clasp the base of the little finger between thumb and fingers, using only palmar surface of thumb and fingers to first joints ; rub the sides of the lower edge of left hand several times backwards and forwards. This sign really means anything fat or greasy, and is very much like *thick*, and there is but little difference between *thick* and *thin*. Like all signs of such very recent origin, where there is no striking peculiarity different gestures are made. Sometimes the size of the sides of bacon as issued to Indians is made, and also the sign for *eat ;* and some tribes make the sign for *hog.* All this, of course, depends on what name they have given the substance. The gesture for rooting is common. In some cases it is " white man's bear ;" others, " white man's dog," etc.

Deaf-mutes hold the extended and compressed right hand under the chin, pointing to front downwards and slightly to left.

Northern Indians are fond of bacon, and eat it, with their lean dried meat or bread, raw, or rather, in its partially cured state as shipped to them. When they cook it, they generally put it with other meat or material of some kind.

Bad. Conception : *Suddenly* thrown away. Hold both closed hands, back up, in front of body, hands at same height and equidistant from body ; move the hands outwards, downwards, and simultaneously open them with a partial snap, terminating the movement with the fingers extended and separated. This sign is frequently made with one hand.

The difference between this and *abandoned*, both having the same conception, viz., thrown away, not worth holding, is that in *abandoned* the hands are carried to left and rear before being opened, indicating retention or possession for a time ; while in the sign for *bad* it is instantly thrown away, the movement being similar to what would naturally follow if one were to pick up what was supposed to be a rope and it should prove to be a snake.

Deaf-mutes make sign for *good*, and then turn the hand, back down, as it is thrown down to left.

Bad Lands. Bring both closed hands, backs outwards, in front of body, hands about height of shoulders and about six inches apart, forearms nearly vertical ; raise and lower the hands alternately several times (this represents the broken country, the bluffs or hills) ; then hold left hand, back outwards, about twelve inches in front of body, fingers extended, touching, and pointing to right ; carry right wrist over left hand few inches above it, right forearm nearly horizontal ; bend right hand down from wrist so that back shall be nearly outwards, index finger of right hand extended, pointing downwards and to left, others and thumb closed ; move the hand from left to right several times, commencing with index finger, passing near back of left hand, the tip of this finger starting near and opposite upper part of left wrist ; this tip in being moved to right passes down a little below left hand, and after passing by the hand rising, second time start little farther out, and again farther out at third movement, and so on (this represents the cut banks and ravines). Some Indians merely point to or touch the earth and make sign for BAD.

Badger. Conception : Digging and striped face. Hold right hand, back up, fingers extended, touching, and pointing to front, in front and to right of body at supposed height of badger (this is the manner of representing height of animals generally, height of human beings being represented by the extended right hand held vertically, fingers pointing upwards); then draw the palmar surface of extended and separated index and second fingers, other fingers and thumb closed, from nose upwards over top of head ; then bring hands in front of body, fingers partially curved and touching, hands slightly compressed, left hand little nearer body than right and little lower, hands a few inches apart, back of left hand nearly to front, back of right nearly upwards, the curved fingers pointing towards ground. Execute with both hands a pawing motion, moving hands to right downwards, to left and rear on curve, repeating motion.

Bag. Hold left hand, back to left and front, in front of left breast, fingers touching and partially curved, thumb also slightly curved, forming with left index an incomplete horizontal ellipse, left forearm horizontal ; bring compressed right hand from right and above downwards, fingers of right hand pointing downwards as right hand passes through the partial ellipse, as though latter represented opening of bag ; then hold both arms extended horizontally from shoulders, hands bent at wrists and knuckles so that fingers, which are extended, touching, and pointing upwards, shall be at about right angles with arms.

Bald. Make sign for HAIR, touch top of head with palmar surface of right hand, and make sign for ALL GONE or WIPED OUT. Indians when old have thin, short hair, but I have never seen a bald-headed one (prior to scalping). They claim they never had any, and say the first one they ever saw was a white man, who created great astonishment and surprise among them. They attribute the loss of hair to the wearing of hats or caps.

Deaf-mutes make the same sign.

Band. Make sign for CHIEF, for TEPEE. Indicate the number and add sign for POSSESSION. If to denote a soldier band, indicate chief, name of band, and men belonging to same. (See SOLDIER.)

Bannack. Make sign for SHOSHONE. The Crows call these Indians "the people of bad lodges," and make signs for BAD LODGE to denote them; but the vocal word Bannack, pronounced quite plainly, usually accompanies any gesture made for this tribe. Tribes having the same sign can, of course, only be distinguished by something from the conversation in which the gesture is used, or by some further description, as the country inhabited by them, or some peculiarity of custom or dress.

I have never been able to discover any satisfactory evidence of the time when the Bannacks and Shoshones first met. They have lived with and near each other longer than any tradition gives account of, and have intermarried to such an extent that, so far as the Indians at Fort Hall are concerned, it would be difficult to find a pure-blooded Bannack. Their vocal language is totally different from that of the Shoshones, and fully as difficult to acquire as the Arapahoe. They nearly all, however, speak the Shoshone language, many of them as fluently as their own.

Tihee, the chief of the Bannacks at the Fort Hall Agency, told me that there were five bands, or sub-tribes, who spoke the Bannack language. As given to me by him they are, 1st, Too-he-re-ah-ka, or Black-tailed Deer-Eaters, in Nevada; 2d, Sho-he-ah-gyot-ti-ka, or Salmon-Eaters; 3d, Tah-gand-da-ca, Root-Eaters; 4th, Wah-ra-ree-ca (the interpreter could not make out what this meant); 5th, Wah-wee-otz-so, or Pi-Utes, in Nevada.

This chief also said that all their customs, dances, religious ceremonies, implements, ways of living, lodges, laws, punishments, etc., were like the Shoshones. In regard to the creation, he said his grandfather told him that they had a father who made them. In what shape this father is at present they do not know,—"perhaps a cloud, the sun, or a storm, but at first it was the Big Gray Wolf." He was the father of the Bannacks, and the Coyote was the father of the Shoshones. He said, "The Gray Wolf was a God, our God; and when the Bannacks died they went to where he was. This wolf formerly lived in a rock near Winne mucca,—a huge hollow rock. The trail made by this wolf in going in and out is still visible; the footprints in the solid rock can be seen to-day. A spring of pure water is near the base. At this place the Bannacks were made. The Big Wolf and the Little Wolf were brothers. They both lived there, and hence the Shoshones came from the same place. Because made by these Gods we are poor; have to live on game and roots; cannot learn to read and write; never had these things given to us. This wolf made everything on earth. He showed us how to live; gave us the bow and flint-headed arrow; this long before there were any whites. All the birds of the air were once human beings, changed by the Wolf into birds to give room for us. My grandfather said that once the earth was covered with water, except the highest peaks, and the wind blew so hard that the water washed out the deep ravines which are now seen. This was before any people were made. In olden times we were at war with the Utes, but we made peace before the whites came, and have kept it since. The Washakie Shoshones only made peace recently. Many years ago we were at war with the

Nez Perces. The Blackfeet used to live here (Fort Hall, Idaho); the river and butte were named after them. We drove them out of this country when I was a young man. My father was a Bannack, and my mother a Shoshone. I was born near here, on Snake River, and when a boy went to the Neises Indians, beyond Boisé."

The Bannacks do not keep an account of their individual ages. They claim that the word Bannack came from Pan-ah-ki, a name given them by the Shoshones, and that the Utes, or Utahs, as they called them, speak an entirely different language from either Bannacks or Shoshones, but that nearly all the surrounding tribes knew a little of the latter.

Tihee stated that they learned what they knew of the sign language from the Crows and Nez Perces; that from Fort Hall to the north and east the sign language was well understood, to the west and south it was not. They never ate dogs, but are specially fond of roots and seeds; sunflower-seeds are prized. They bury their dead in the ground, and kill ponies at the death of noted men. The gun placed with remains is usually broken. They locate heaven as beyond the setting sun. Children are not named until they reach the age of ten or twelve years. Sometimes an old man gives his name to a young one, but as a rule the father and mother name the children. They do not often, like the Plains Indians, name them after a dog, wolf, coyote, or fox. Many of the female children are named after different kinds of frogs. Only a few years since they mainly used sage-brush and grass with which to build their lodges. They claim they did not kill one child of a woman who had twins. They call the whites "trade people,"—"Soyape." The first they saw were emigrants, who constantly wanted to trade, hence the name. Tendoy, the chief at Lapwai, is half Bannack and half Snake; many of his band are "Sheep-Eaters."

The Bannack women are more plump, shorter, and better-looking than the Plains Indians, but very filthy. They wear the hair loose, parted in the middle, and falling down over the face a half-bang and very low on the forehead. The men and women use a profusion of red paint, and this is about the only kind they do use. The women as well as the men are greatly addicted to gambling. They manufacture very good matting from rushes, and from rushes and grass make vessels and dishes. The men are fond of white blankets with rainbow-hued stripes. The women wear very short leggings, and their dresses about the same length as the Crows. Porcupine-work is not used, and beads not so much as with other tribes. (See SHOSHONE.)

Barracks. Make sign for WHITES, for SOLDIER, and for HOUSE.

Barren. Make sign for the person or animal, sign for PARTURITION, and for CANNOT or NO.

Deaf-mutes use the same.

Bashful. Similar to ASHAMED, but the head is dropped a little, as though drawing blanket more over head.

Deaf-mutes put tip of index of right hand, other fingers and thumb closed, against teeth, lower the head slightly, and cast down the eyes.

Basin. (Depression in the ground.) Bring the hands, backs nearly up, about eight inches in front of body, same distance apart, same height, and opposite each other, arms extended downwards, about the full length, index fingers and thumbs spread and curved, so as to form an incomplete horizontal ellipse, other fingers closed ; move the hands towards each other a few inches, then, still holding left hand in its position, make motion with partially curved and slightly compressed right hand, as though pawing or scooping out dirt from the space indicated between the spread thumbs and index fingers. To denote a buffalo-wallow, make first sign for buffalo, and then the above. For a vessel or utensil, indicate the shape with the hands.

For a vessel deaf-mutes indicate the shape.

Basket. Make sign for KETTLE, and then interlock the fingers to denote the manner of interlacing the material.

Deaf-mutes hold the left forearm horizontally in front of body, pointing to front, then hold right index against it on lower or under side, at wrist, other fingers and thumb closed ; drop the hand, and carry it on curve backwards, bringing it up again, and placing it against arm near elbow.

Bat. Make sign for NIGHT and for BIRD ; instead of the latter sign the extended hands are brought side by side, at index and thumbs, in front of body, backs up, fingers pointing to front, and the hands given a wavy motion to front, right, and downwards a few inches ; then similar motion is made to left, front, and downwards, indicating the zigzag way a bat flies.

Deaf-mutes use the same.

Battle. Make sign for FIGHT, and for VOLLEY or HEAVY FIRING. Sometimes the hands are held opposite each other, as in FIGHT, and then the sign for shoot made with both hands towards each other.

Bay. (Water.) Make sign for WATER, then bring right hand well out in front of body, index finger and thumb curved and spread, forming a partial horizontal ellipse, other fingers closed, back of hand outwards and to right.

Deaf-mutes make sign for WATER, DUST or DIRT, and then indicate the shape by curving left arm, and passing right hand over it.

Bay. (**Color.**) Make sign for RED. Indians usually call a bay pony a red pony ; sometimes it is called a " common" color.

Deaf-mutes make same sign.

Bayonet. Make sign for GUN, then place the extended index fingers alongside one another, other fingers and thumbs closed, right index projecting beyond left one-third its length.

Deaf-mutes make sign for GUN and make thrusting motion forward with both hands, as though making a thrust with bayonet attached to a gun.

Beads. Hold the right forearm horizontally in front of body, pointing to front, slightly compress the right hand, and allow it to drop by its own weight (held loosely at wrist), shake the hand slightly, giving it a quivering motion to indicate the shimmering of the beads when stirred by the hand or when holding a string up by the hands,—such " strings" as are sold at the Indian stores. Sometimes the tips of first and second fingers are wet by placing against lips, and then put against left palm, the left hand being extended, and, back down, held horizontally in front of body ; then make a motion similar to *sew*, to denote the stringing of the beads on the sinew. These gestures indicate their way of making bead-work. Usually an Indian has some bead-work on his person, and he simply points to the beads. In fact, I never saw the sign I have described used in conversation until I made special inquiry about it.

Lewis and Clarke give an account of finding beads made by the Indians of the Mandan and Gros Ventres tribes, and describe the process as pursued by these Indians in 1804. Beads of Indian manufacture are found in the burial mounds near Devil's Lake and Pembina, Dakota Territory, and from other implements found there it would seem that the art was known and practised long before 1804, and probably by the Mandans in their southern migration.

Deaf-mutes make the sign for METAL, that can be seen through, and then indicate a string round the neck.

Bear. Conception: Rolling motion in running. Bring both hands, backs up, well out in front of body, some distance from it and about six inches apart, little finger extended, others and thumbs closed, forearms nearly horizontal and same height ; lower the hands simultaneously and raise them, mostly by wrist action.

The Crows and some other tribes partially close the hands and hold them alongside of head, palms to front,—from the position of the bear's front feet at times when scouting, or from the ears of animals. The Pembina band of Chippewas add to this a clawing motion, with hands to front upwards and then downwards.

To specify the kind, as gray or grizzly, black, cinnamon, etc., make sign for BEAR, and then sign for HAIR, and give it the proper color, or denote the kind by the locality where found or some peculiarity of the beast.

Deaf-mutes, after sign for ANIMAL LIFE, fold or cross the arms over chest, hands resting on arms just above elbow, and with the fingers execute a clawing motion on arms.

The Crows and some other tribes have been credited with having a peculiar superstition against killing bears, and also against tanning the skins. As nearly as I could find out the first resulted from fear of personal harm from the animal, and the latter, it is claimed, makes sore the throats of the women who work over bear-skins, dressing and tanning them.

Beard. Place backs of hands against cheeks, right against right, left against left, hands slightly compressed, fingers pointing downwards. For chin-whiskers the right hand only is used, back being placed against chin. For side-whiskers the hands are placed farther back on cheeks, at their bases.

Deaf-mutes make motion in front of chin and downwards, as though stroking the beard.

There is no good ground for the belief that Indians would not have beards if they did not pull the hair out. They claim that a beard is no protection against cold, is disagreeable in hot weather, and is troublesome to keep clean. Some tribes pull out the eyebrows and eyelashes as well, and nearly all permit no hair to grow on the body except on the head.

Beautiful. Make sign for HANDSOME or PRETTY, and for very beautiful add BRAVE.

Deaf-mutes describe a circle with tip of right index finger in front of and close to face, other fingers and thumb closed, and then, holding extended right hand, palm towards and near face, bring the tips of fingers and thumb together.

Beaver. Conception : Tail of beaver striking mud or water. Hold extended left hand, back up, pointing to right and front, in front of body, left forearm horizontal ; bring the extended right hand, back up, under and at right angles with left, back of right resting against palm of left hand ; lower the right hand by wrist action, and raise it, back of right striking against left palm sharply ; repeat motion. I have seen Indians, who were not fully conversant with the sign language, make gesture for little animals working in mud and water, gnawing down trees, etc., to denote a beaver.

Deaf-mutes make sign for animal life, and with first and second fingers denote the flat tail moving on the water, and sign for latter.

Beaver Dam. Make sign for BEAVER, for WATER, and for HOLD, —the fingers in latter sign being frequently separated and sometimes interlocked, and some add sign for TREE.

Bed. Hold left hand, back down, fingers extended and touching, and pointing to the right in front of and close to left breast ; bring right hand, back down, fingers extended, touching, and pointing to left and slightly to front in some horizontal plane in front of and close to left ; move the right hand well out to front, a trifle to right, keeping in same plane.

Deaf-mutes indicate the four posts and a covering for the bed, drawing hands back as though spreading same over a bed.

Before. (Sense of time.) Hold the left hand, back up, in front of and few inches from centre of breast, index finger extended pointing to front and slightly upwards, others and thumb closed ; bring the right hand similarly fixed to the front of the left hand, passing close by and over, and stopping a few inches in front of it, knuckles of right hand same height as tip of left index finger, right index in front of and pointing in same direction as left.

Deaf-mutes make the sign for TIME, being a tapping of tip of right index against back of left hand near wrist, other fingers and thumb of right hand closed, and then hold hands as in AHEAD or ADVANCE.

Before. (Animals and comparison.) Bring the left hand, back up, fingers extended and touching in front of centre of breast, fingers pointing to front and slightly upwards; bring right hand, back up, index finger extended, others and thumb closed few inches in front of left hand, knuckles of right hand height of tips of fingers of left, index finger pointing to front slightly upwards, it being in front of centre of left hand. To express a great distance before or in advance, the right hand is put farther to the front. To express higher or highest rank, say of several chiefs, make the proper sign to denote the chiefs, then pointing to one or making sign for him, and then the above sign; this would express that they were all chiefs, but such a one was in advance of them in influence and power. (See also AHEAD and SUPERIOR.)

The sign is of frequent use to express bravery. For instance, a large party of Pawnees went to war; then make sign for any particular one, and then the foregoing sign. This would indicate that he went in advance, rode before all others, fearless of danger. Thus this little sign might convey a higher tribute to dauntless courage than many long eulogies; for a party might pass through a country thick with danger and death, and he who should go single-handed in the midst of it would be worthy of the highest praise so generously given in their Indian songs, and this is a reward rich in honor according to their views of the matter.

Deaf-mutes make the sign for ANIMAL, and then separate hands as explained in AHEAD.

Behind. (Time.) See AFTER.

Deaf-mutes make sign for TIME, and then separate hands.

Behind. (Animals and comparison.) Hold left hand, back up, well out in front of centre of breast, fingers extended, touching, pointing to front and slightly upwards; bring the right hand, back up, in rear of left, index finger extended, pointing to front, slightly upwards, and being in rear of centre of left hand, its tip being at height of knuckles of left hand, other fingers and thumb closed. The right hand is brought from the front over the left to its position.

The remarks made in reference to BEFORE apply with equal force to this gesture; and as the Indians hold bravery the greatest virtue, they necessarily consider cowardice the greatest vice. There are no oaths in any Indian language, but to say that one is a coward, damns the person most completely.

Remarks under BEFORE for deaf-mutes apply to this word.

Below. Fold extended left hand, back up, fingers pointing to front, well in front of body at about height of breast; carry the extended right hand under left some inches, according as is wished to express how far under or below. Simply pointing below with index finger denotes below. (See INFERIOR.)

Deaf-mutes use the same.

Belt. Carry both partially-closed hands to the waist, and a little to rear of body, right on right side, left on left; bring the hands round in front till they meet, as though clasping a belt.

Deaf-mutes use the same sign.

Indian women, as a rule, wear belts; men only the one for cartridges, and the narrow one next the skin for fastening the breechcloth.

Berry. Make the sign for ROSEBUD, and then distinguish by signs for the color, size, use when ripe, manner of gathering, such as striking bush or tree, and catching fruit on blanket spread under same, etc., and also by some description of the bushes. Berries are also distinguished by the animals which are fond of them.

Deaf-mutes denote size by marking off with index and thumb of left hand a small part of tip of right thumb, giving color and size of bushes, etc.

Best. See BEFORE (sense of comparison).

Deaf-mutes use the superlative of good,—*i.e.* good, better, best—by twice raising hand, as in GOOD.

Bet. Conception : From collecting in a pile the articles wagered. Indicate in what way or manner, as with cards, horse-race, game of ball, etc., and then hold partially-compressed hands, fingers pointing downwards, those of right hand slightly to left, of left slightly to right, about eighteen inches to front, slightly to right and left of body, hands little lower than breast ; move the hands simultaneously on curve, upwards to front, and then downwards, terminating movement by bringing hands about three inches apart, and few inches lower than when starting. This represents the two piles of blankets, robes, or whatever may have been wagered. The passion for gambling is strong in the Indian heart. The two most noticeable characteristics are the high stakes for which they will play, and the calm, serene grace with which they will lose all they have in the world.

Deaf-mutes make sign for MONEY, and then throw both hands downwards and to front.

Betray. Make signs for LIE and GIVE, then bring right hand, back up, in front of body, index finger extended and pointing to front, others and thumb closed ; turn the index finger so that it points to right and front, and thrust the hand in that direction ; sometimes the sign for TRAIL is made and this sign,—*you gave me lies, and I went astray from the trail.* The manner and circumstances are usually specified.

Deaf-mutes make sign for DEVIL or WICKED.

Beyond. Hold extended left hand, back up, in front of body about ten inches, fingers pointing to right ; bring extended right hand, back up, between left and body same height, fingers pointing to left ; swing the right hand upwards, outwards, and then downwards on curve, beyond left hand, turning right hand, back down, in movement.

Deaf-mutes use the same.

Big. Bring the hands opposite with palms towards each other, well out in front of body, hands a little lower than shoulders, and few inches apart, fingers extended, touching, and pointing to front ; separate hands, carrying right to right, left to left, keeping them opposite each other. This would seem to denote big in the sense of broad, wide, etc., but I have seen it used frequently in such sentences as the "Big Chief," "Big Horse," etc.

Deaf-mutes use the same.

Big Belly. Bring hands in front of and close to abdomen, fingers touching and slightly curved, palms of hands towards each other, index fingers horizontal, tips of fingers of the hands near each other, wrists well separated ; bring the wrists near together, increasing the distance between tips of fingers of hands. Frequently this sign is made by simply indicating the curved surface of a large belly with extended hands, backs of hands outward.

Deaf-mutes use the same.

Bird. Conception : Wings. Bring the hands, palm outwards, fingers extended and touching above, to right and left in front of shoulders, hands same height; move them simultaneously to front and downwards, repeating motion, imitating the motion of wings; care must be taken to imitate closely. The wings of small birds move rapidly ; those of large ones slowly. Some peculiarity may have to be noted,—the manner of flying or soaring, its habits, and even its tone of voice. A goose would be known by indicating the long, slow motion of its wings and the triangular figure taken by these birds in their flight to the South or distant North, and perhaps indicating the noise made by them. The sign for WOODPECKER illustrates this point.

Deaf-mutes hold right hand, back up, near mouth, thumb and index extended and touching at tips, other fingers closed ; thumb and index represent the bill of the bird.

Bison. See BUFFALO.

Bit. (For animal.) Place palmar surface of spread index and thumb of right hand, other fingers closed, against mouth. The Blackfeet and some other tribes form two circles with thumbs and index fingers, and press same against cheek at corners of mouth, to represent the rings of the bit.

Deaf-mutes make sign for IRON, and then draw index fingers across the mouth, right to right and left to left.

Bite. Bring right hand, back outwards and upwards in front of body, fingers compressed, partially curved and touching, thumb slightly curved, and its tip near tips of fingers ; snap sharply tips of first and second fingers against tip of thumb, repeating motion.

Deaf-mutes use the same.

Bitter. Touch tongue with tip of index of right hand, other fingers closed, and make sign for BAD.

Deaf-mutes touch tongue with tip of right index, and then make wry face.

Bitter-Root. Indicate the shape of root with extended right index, other fingers closed, and the pink blossom about one inch in diameter.

The Flatheads and adjacent tribes are very fond of this ; the root only needs drying for use.

Black. The sign for COLOR with many tribes is used for BLACK, but the more safe way is to point to something black in color.

Deaf-mutes touch the eyebrow with tip of right index.

Blackfeet (Indians). Make signs for MOCCASIN and for BLACK.
The agency for the Blackfeet, Blood, and Piegan Indians is located
on Badger Creek, a tributary of Medicine Lodge, about eighty miles
from Fort Shaw, Montana. The valley is only a small opening in
the foot-hills of the Rocky Mountains, which are about eighteen
miles distant from the agency. The buildings are constructed of
sawed logs and enclosed by a stockade. The soil is fertile, and the
stream furnishes plenty of water for irrigating purposes. There are
several hundred acres of land in the valley adjacent the agency building, which might be utilized for agricultural purposes. Ninety-four
acres are fenced in and under cultivation. There are a few log
houses and canvas lodges, occupied by Indians, scattered about the
valley. The agent in his report for 1881 gives a total population of
seven thousand five hundred Indians, and claims that the majority of
these are Piegans.

I was present at the agency on July 4, 1881. The Indians had
been informed by the agent that it was a great "Medicine"-day for
the whites, and they commenced to gather for what they called a
"horse-and-foot" dance at one P.M. Most of the Blackfeet and
Bloods were away hunting, or were north of the boundary-line,
claiming just at that time to be loyal subjects of the "Great
Mother," and hoping to secure some of the money being distributed
there. Some old men who were to drum and sing first arrived just
outside the stockade ; then came straggling from all directions men,
women, and children. The braves were in full dress,—*i.e.*, with
painted faces and bodies ; full war toggery,—bonnets, shields, guns,
spears ; ponies decorated and painted,—a parade of savage splendor.
The Horse-Dance consisted in circling, charging, shouting, firing
of guns, etc. A small number separated from the main body, and
represented the Piegans, while the larger number represented their
enemies, whom the few, being Piegans, easily routed. The foot-
dancers formed in a semicircle, and in their costume of paint,
breech-cloths, head-dresses, looking-glasses, anklets of skunk-skin,
etc., performed the usual Indian dance. They had made themselves
as hideous as possible, and in this respect had met with perfect success. The old women and children and some men were seated on
the ground in line near by, and in their shrill metallic voices loudly
applauded. Near the end of the dance, after the hard bread, the
coffee in wash-tubs and brass kettles, and the wheelbarrow-loads of
bacon had been distributed and nearly all eaten, an old Indian, bent
with age, a few gray hairs for a beard, quaintly gotten up in his old
finery, a pair of iron spectacles hiding his sightless eyes, was led into
the circle of dancers, where presents were made to him. One young
man gave him a little stick, representing a pony. This occasioned
many shrill cheers from the outsiders and a long speech from the old
man, who, first holding his hands high in the air with the palms
toward the sun, and then placing them on the young warrior, made
his prayer, asking that the blessing of the God in the sun might rest

on the young man. He reminded this God of the gifts and sacrifices he had made to Him, the ponies, beads, tobacco, cloth, skins, pipes, etc., he had given Him, and asked that this young man might be saved from harm, and meet with success in war and in peace. As he finished, the youth turned and passed the palms of his hands over the old man, from his head down over the body, and all the dancers rushed up and did the same thing, in this way asking a blessing, and thanking him for his advice and the good "medicine" made for the generous youth. The old man's gifts were wrapped up in a blanket, which some one had presented him, and he was led away by a little child. As the sun was sinking in the rose and purple light of the sky behind the mountains, they scattered out to the log huts and miserable tepees, or drifted round the agency building. They had had their howl, their dance, and their feast, and in imagination had killed many of their enemies, and in their estimation had especially honored the glorious natal day of the Republic.

I had no difficulty in conversing with these Indians, though not understanding one word of their vocal language. In personal appearance they are, at present, inferior to the other Plains tribes. The women part the hair in the middle, and usually wear it loose. The men usually part it on one side, some few braid it ; but most of them wear it loose, whilst others bang it in front like the Crows. The moccasin fairly distinguishes them from other tribes. It is made like that of the Prairie Gros Ventres ; but the bead-work at the front of the upper terminates in three prongs, to represent the three bands,—*i.e.*, the Blackfeet, the Blood Blackfeet, and the Piegan Blackfeet. Tradition clearly points to a Northern origin for this nation, who call themselves by a word which means "The People."

There is a slight dialectical difference in the vocal language of the three bands. They claim that they got the name Blackfeet from the fact that the black soil of the far North, where they formerly lived, soiled their moccasins. The Piegans were so named from a chief of this band, who wore a robe badly dressed and spotted. The Bloods are called "Kiara," which means old-time people. There is a sub-band of the Piegans whom they call "Bloods." In their migration southward they kept near and parallel to the main divide, and occupied the country as far south as Salt Lake. They were very numerous, very warlike, and were not only able to drive the Snake Indians out of this country, but hold their own against the Mountain Indians to the west and the Plains Indians to the east. Tradition gives the Blackfeet proper the most northern location, the Bloods next, and the Piegans next to the south.

Their myth of creation is that an Old Man who lived in the far North made everything, prairie and mountain, and all that they contain. The chief said to me, "The Old Man of the North. our people saw, and we have seen his works. There is a river in the North called ' The River,' where the Old Man played. There are two huge rocks there, which he used to play with as boys play with pebbles at present. These rocks have worn a deep trail in the solid rock where they have been rolled about." They claim that the Gros Ventres of the Prairie lived with them in peace until 1862, at which time a war-party of Snakes went to a Gros Ventres camp, which was near Bear-Paw Mountain, where they met two Gros Ventres, whom they killed, and got from them a white pony, which, as they returned, they gave to some Piegans whom they met and made peace with. Afterwards, the Gros Ventres, seeing the horse, said the Piegans had committed the murder, and this led to the subsequent war with that tribe and their separation. They have a plurality of wives, and marrying an elder sister gives them certain claims on younger sisters, whom they call wives even before marriage.

The Sarcees, a Northern band or tribe of Indians, are mixed up with the Bloods and Blackfeet, and these three bands are friendly with the Crees. The Piegans, however, do not like the latter, and call them thieves and liars.

In about 1841 they contracted the smallpox from the white people at Benton. They admit that word was sent them not to come there, but they had no other place to trade, and went, and as a result the Piegans, who formerly numbered fourteen bands, each as large as their entire number now, were swept away. Some bands came out of this awful ordeal with only one or two families. Their treatment for this, as well as chickenpox and measles, is almost certain death, viz., hot-steam baths, followed by plunges or being thrown into cold water. These, with such accessories as dirt and constant exposure, leave little ground for wonder that they were so nearly wiped out. They again suffered severely from smallpox in 1868–69.

The belief entertained by these Indians of their ghostly future state, wandering about in the dreary land of sand-hills north of Cypress Mountains, is worthy of special notice, as, with the exception of the Gros Ventres of the Prairie (who, without doubt, derived the belief from them), I know of no other tribes that have similar religious views. The tangible evidence, to them, of this country being inhabited by departed spirits is seen in the little circles of small stones which, they claim, fasten down the invisible tepees. In the centre of these circles are small piles of stones, where the fires are built, and they have heard the talking and singing of the ghostly inhabitants. They also believe that after a time the spirits come back to their former habitations, and this belief has been a source of annoyance to the agent, in that they would not live in a house after a death had taken place there. It also accounts for the destruction of tepees, etc. They gave me two accounts of scalp-taking. Said one, "Long ago, near here, the Snakes and Piegans were about to have a fight. The two tribes approached each other from opposite sides of a river, each reaching the bank at the same time. The stream was swollen with recent rains and the current very swift. The Snakes called out and made signs for the Piegans to select their bravest man, and they (the Snakes) would do the same. These two men would wade into the stream, and by personal combat decide the controversy. This was done, and the Piegan drowned the Snake and swam ashore. As the body of the Snake was floating down the stream, some Piegans ran along the shore, grasped the body by the hair, and cut off the scalp as a trophy,—an evidence of the great fight in the river, and the grand bravery and strength of the Piegans.'' The Indian who told me this, however, did not seem to have perfect confidence in it, for he added, ''We take the scalps to make the war strong ; and when the women and children see the scalps of their enemies their hearts will be glad.'' The second account, and the one to which they ascribe a sacred character, was given me as follows: ''The Old Man who made us, and who created all things, played—*i.e.*, gambled—with a similar Old Man, who made the people on the other side of the mountains. We have seen the huge boulders which they used for this purpose. The Old Man from beyond the mountains won all the mountain-sheep and elk, and left only the buffalo and antelope. After all the game had been lost, our Old Man wagered his head against that of the other Old Man and won, but in consideration of a return of part of the game, he only took his scalp, and when he did this, said, 'When any of your young men kill any of mine they shall take their scalps, and when any of mine kill yours they shall do the same, and this will make them chiefs.' ''

They, however, in common with all other Indians, believe that one killed in battle and scalped goes to the hereafter with all the pomp and glory of a successful war-party returning with the scalps of their enemies, whilst one who dies from old age or sickness goes in a much more inglorious fashion. The Medicine-Lodge-Dance of the Blackfeet takes the place of the Sun-Dance with other Plains tribes, but the details are sufficiently different to justify a description. A woman who has kin at the point of death, or for other reasons similar to those which prompt the men to make the *vow* in the Sun-Dance, makes a promise to the God in the sun, just at sunrise or sun-setting. The vow is made in the winter or early spring, though the dance does not take place until the berries are ripe, about August. The men, when surrounded by danger, can and do promise that they will have some of their women kinsfolk make the Medicine-Lodge-Dance. After the woman has made the promise, and commenced saving buffalo-tongues, her clothes and her travois must be painted red, and her lodge in camp must have fresh green brush put around it at each camp they make. In addition to the original vow, there must be a daily one of purity.

Sweat-Houses are made prior to the Medicine-Lodge, three before locating the camp for the dance, and the last one locates the Medicine-Lodge. The soldier band cuts the willows for what might be properly called the Medicine-Lodge Sweat-House, which is made of one hundred willows. These young men go out for the willows on horseback, and circle about the camp as they return. Any one who may be away from camp, coming across one of these Sweat-Houses, knows at once where and when the Medicine-Lodge-Dance will take place. The Sweat-Houses are made the last four days prior to the building of the Medicine-Lodge. The young men, gaudily decorated, drag the brush with lariats to camp for the lodge, and fire at it as they drag it along. The centre-pole is hauled on a travois, and this is also fired at as they carry it to camp. The centre-pole, as they call it, which corresponds to the Sun-Dance-Pole, is selected, and an old man, who must be able to count four "coups," makes a speech at the foot of the tree before it is cut, and strikes the tree, which is then cut down. During the felling the tree is constantly fired at by the warriors. Some of the young men are selected to go out and get a fresh buffalo-skin, which two of the bravest cut up into strips and tie to the willows at the forks of the centre-pole. A hole is made near the foot of the pole for a fire, and the tail of the buffalo hangs down from the forks of the pole some feet above it. The young man who has stolen the most ponies since the last dance is allowed to put pieces of brush, one for each lot of ponies stolen, on the fire made in the hole, and should he be able with his limited number of sticks to build a fire large enough to burn the tail, he is estimated a great warrior.

The medicine-man has a separate lodge for himself opposite the door and outside of the big lodge, which faces the east. He fasts and dances to the sun, blowing his whistle. He is painted in different colors, and he must have no water, and only after dark can he eat, and then only the inner bark of the cottonwood-tree. In dancing he holds up his hands and has strings, made of the under-wing feathers of an eagle, tied to his fingers. A picture of the sun is painted on his forehead, the moon, Ursa Major, etc., on his body. The dance continues four days, and should this medicine-man drink, it is sure to cause rain, and if it rains, no other evidence of his weakness is wanted or taken. He is deposed as high-priest at once, and another is put in his little lodge as chief medicine-men. Sometimes they allow him a little food, as they say, "Two bites the first day, four the second, six the third, and eight the fourth." He is put in his little lodge with great ceremony, of which dancing and drumming is the principal feature. Inside the big lodge, the young men, gaudily painted and in war costume, dance and charge across towards each other, dividing themselves into two parties, recount their deeds of bravery and valor, make gifts, etc., and those who have made the "vow" dance as the Sioux do in the Sun-Dance, mutilate themselves, etc. Many gifts are made to the sun ; *i.e.*, placed on the Medicine-Lodge. The feasting is principally on buffalo-tongues, of which there are as many as the woman who made the vow has been able to gather. The tongues contributed are all carried to her lodge whole, and are cut by her for drying and packed away in par-flèches. At the Medicine-Lodge each woman is obliged to take a tongue, break off a small portion, give it to the sun and announce her purity. The man who cuts the holes in the breasts of the men who are to be tied to the central pole must have captured a lance from the enemy. A shield is tied to the muscles at the back of shoulder, and, as in the Sun-Dance, they have to dance until they tear themselves loose. Sometimes the medicine-man presses his weight against the victims of self-torture. They have a story that a long time ago a man wandering about was taken up to the sun and cared for, and to him they pray, dance, and make gifts. They also have a Medicine-Pipe-Dance. For this tobacco is saved up, a bundle is made, tied with strings of elk- and deer-skins, and when opened, the sounds made by these animals are imitated. The bundle also contains a pipe handed down from generation to generation, used only for this special smoking and several other kinds of "medicine."

The practice of surgery is rare among Indians, and although these people do occasionally invoke its aid, they hardly seem justified by its results. In one case I learned that two holes were bored in the upper part of a man's chest, who had asthma, for the purpose of blowing out the evil spirit, who had possession and caused the trouble. Another case was that of a woman sick with brain fever. A hole was bored in her head to let the evil spirit out. It is hardly necessary to say that both patients died.

These Indians do not keep an account of their individual ages, and, whatever they may once have been, are now inferior mentally, morally, and physically to the other Plains tribes, and beyond any of them have suffered reduction by wars and disease, but principally the latter, to an extent with which few of the others are comparable.

Blackfeet (**Sioux Indians**). Make sign for SIOUX and for BLACK-FEET. There are several stories told as to the manner in which this band of Sioux Indians, now located at Standing Rock Agency, on the Missouri River, received its name. The first one I heard was to the effect that a chief became jealous of his wife and compelled her to keep the soles of her moccasins constantly blackened with charcoal, so that he could trail her wherever she might go. The second was that a number of warriors started out after the Crow Indians, succeeded in capturing some ponies, but on account of subsequent carelessness allowed themselves to be surprised and some of the number killed, and lost their camp equipage as well as the stolen ponies; returning home, the country had been burnt over, soon their moccasins were worn away, and the blackened stubble mutilated and tattooed their feet. The chief, with the party and his followers, were ever after called Blackfeet. (See SIOUX.)

Blanch. Pass the palm of right hand over face, and make sign for ANOTHER. The face is changed, it is another face, either through fear or whatever may have been the cause. The Arapahoes, instead of saying "a person turned white," say "turned red with fear," and they make the sign for a red color shooting up into the face. I have also seen both hands held in front of face, backs out, fingers extended and separated, and a fluttering motion given to hands.

Deaf-mutes make the sign for WHITE, and then holding closed right hand near face, extend the fingers as the hand is raised, to denote the white color being thrown into the face.

Blanket. Conception: Wrapping about shoulders. Bring the closed hands, palms towards each other, opposite and near each shoulder; move the right hand to left, left to right, terminating movement when wrists are crossed, right hand nearest body.

Deaf-mutes make sign for WOOLLEN CLOTH, and then draw the hands backwards from front, as though spreading blanket over a bed.

Bless You. Raise both hands, palm outwards, to front and upwards, arms fully extended, hands raised towards person, fingers extended, touching, and pointing upwards; lower hands several inches, at same time pushing them outwards slightly towards the person; repeat motion. Sometimes the palms of hands are first held towards the sun, and then towards the earth, and then the above, thus asking, as they say, the blessing of the Father and Mother of all life and power to rest on one.

Deaf-mutes close the right hand over the mouth; then carry the hand outwards and downwards towards person, open the hand, turning it palm outwards.

Blind. Bring both extended hands, backs outwards, in front of and close to eyes, right hand nearest and both hands parallel to face; move right hand slightly to left, left to right. Frequently the palmar surface of ends of fingers are placed against closed eyes, this to denote the physical affliction of blindness, and the former when used in a metaphorical sense.

Deaf-mutes place the palmar surface of index and second fingers over closed eyes.

Blood. Bring right hand, back outwards, first and second fingers extended and separated, others and thumb closed, in front of mouth, tips of first and second fingers pressed against nostrils; move the hand to the right and downwards, giving it a tremulous motion. Sometimes the position of the hand is changed so that the first and second fingers point downwards from nose, and then the hand is moved downwards and to front, and a tremulous motion given it. Some Indians hold the right hand in front of mouth, thumb and fingers extended and separated, pointing upwards and to front, and move the hand upwards to front and then downwards from mouth, indicating the flow of blood from the mouth and nose of a wounded buffalo. I have also seen the extended index of right hand, other fingers and thumb closed, held near leg or thigh, and the hand moved or thrust outwards with a vibratory motion to indicate the spurting of blood from a large vein or artery, and then the sign for RED made.

Deaf-mutes indicate the red color and the flowing.

Blood (Indian). Bring the right hand, back up, in front of mouth, index finger extended and pointing to left, other fingers and thumb closed; draw the index finger horizontally to right, between or just touching lips. (See BLACKFEET.)

Blue. Point at or touch something of that color. Sometimes, but rarely, the sign for a clear sky is made, indicating that the clouds have all passed away. Many Indians do not note any difference between blue and black, and very light blue they sometimes call green.

Deaf-mutes indicate the arch of the heavens for blue.

Bluff. Bring the closed right hand, back outwards, well out in front of body, forearm nearly vertical ; push the hand up slightly for a small bluff, and increase it according to height of hill ; *i.e.*, as high as one could reach in this way would be the highest bluff or mountain. For several bluffs, a hilly country, both hands are used. (See MOUNTAIN.)

Deaf-mutes indicate the surface of hills, bluffs, and mountains with back of nearly-extended hand or hands.

Boat. Conception : To paddle. Bring both closed hands well out in front of body, right hand over left ; swing the hands to the rear, a little to left and slightly downwards, as the hands are carried back in front of body ; place right under left and swing the hands to rear, a little to the right and downwards. These motions are made by elbow and shoulder action, and the hands are held in the natural position when grasping a paddle, viz., back of right nearly to right, back of left to left, when making the motion on left side of body, and the reverse when making it on right side. The birch-bark canoe is indicated usually by above sign, and then hold the curved and compressed right hand in front of body, back down, to denote the curved prow of same.

Deaf-mutes partially curve and very slightly compress the hands, bring lower edges together, and join the tips of little and third fingers,—a scoop-shaped position of the hands denoting shape of boat.

Boil. (Tumor.) Press the little finger of the closed and compressed right hand over and against the part supposed to be afflicted, and sometimes add sign for SICK over this part.

Boil (To). Make sign for whatever fluid it may be, the sign for the vessel, then the sign for SPRING (water).

Bone. Make sign for the animal, for DIE ; lie on the ground long time ; touch part of body or limb corresponding to place of bone in animal, and then point to something white.

Deaf-mutes touch the teeth with index finger.

Bonnet. Carry hands alongside of rear part of head, palms towards it, fingers extended and pointing upwards ; move hands simultaneously to front ; sometimes spread thumbs and index fingers are used, other fingers closed. (See WAR-BONNET.)

Deaf-mutes indicate the string down side of cheeks either with tips of thumbs or tips of index fingers, and also pass hand over head to denote the covering of same.

Born. Conception : Issuing from loins. Bring right hand, back up, in front of centre of body and close to it, fingers extended, touching, pointing to front and downwards ; move the hand downwards and outwards on curve. This sign is used by parents in speaking of their children at any time of life, and is also used in speaking of the young of any animal, as well as to describe the act of parturition.

Deaf-mutes cross the hands as in BABY, and then move them to the front and slightly downwards.

Borrow. Make sign for GIVE (to you or to me), BY AND BY, and then GIVE. There is no such word as loan, but the Indians say, "Give it to me for a time (usually specifying duration), and I will give it back."

Deaf-mutes use the same sign.

Bow. Conception : Bending bow to shoot. Bring left hand, back to left, well out in front and little to left of body, left forearm nearly horizontal, hand about height of left breast ; close the fingers, except index ; place the extended thumb on second finger, press the index finger around end and sides of thumb ; carry the closed right hand, back nearly upwards, thumb extended, and pressing against second joint of index finger, so that back of second joint of this finger shall rest against back of thumb of left hand ; then draw the right hand little to right and well to rear, very slightly upwards.

Deaf-mutes, same.

The material used in making bows depends on the locality. On our almost treeless prairies nearly every species of wood found is brought into service. I was once with a party of Indians, and it was desirable that we should have a bow. There seemed to be no suitable material, but one of them found an old, broken ash wagon-bow lying along side of the road. It was taken into camp, greased, warmed by the camp-fire, trimmed with their hunting-knives, slowly, carefully, and skilfully bent into shape, and quite a shapely and serviceable article was the result. Among the Plains Indians, bows are made from oak, hickory, ash, elm, cedar, osage-orange, one or two varieties of willows, plum, cherry, bull-berry, and other bushes, and from the horns of the mountain-sheep and elk.

"The bow—the weapon so long in use among the different Indian tribes of this continent, so typical of Indian life, and the mere mention of which always associates our ideas with the red men—is made of various kinds of wood, and its manufacture is a work of no little labor. Even at this day the bow is much used, and although an Indian may have a gun, he is seldom seen without his long-bow, and quiver well filled with arrows. The gun may get out of order, and he cannot mend it; the ammunition may become wet, and there is an end of hunting ; but the faithful bow is always in order, and its swift arrows ready to fly in wet as well as dry weather. Thus reasons the savage, and so keeps his bow to fall back upon in case of accident.

"Until the invention of breech-loaders, it is a fact well known to frontiersmen that the bow was a far more deadly weapon at close range than the best rifle. A warrior could discharge his arrows with much greater rapidity and precision than the most expert woodsman could charge and fire a muzzle-loading rifle. . . .

"The Indian boy's first lesson in life is to shoot with a bow. He is furnished with a small bow and ' beewaks,' or blunt arrows, so he will hurt nobody, and with these he shoots at marks. By and by, when he has acquired some skill in handling his weapon, he is given small arrow-points, and with these he shoots birds, squirrels, and small beasts. As he grows older he receives the long-bow, and at last the strong-bow. These strong-bows are powerful weapons, and I have seen them so stiff that a white man could not bend them scarce four inches, while an Indian would, with apparent ease, draw them to the arrow's head. A shaft fired from one of these bows will go through the body of a buffalo, and arrow-heads have been found so firmly imbedded in the thigh-bones of a man that no force could extract them. The parents take great pride in teaching young Indians to shoot, and the development of the muscles and strength of their arms is watched with much interest. A stout arm, ornamented with knots of muscles, is a great honor to an Indian, and no one but those who can handle the strong-bow are deemed fit for war.

"Of all the Indians of the West, the Sioux and Crows make the best bows. The Sioux bow is generally four feet long, one and a half inches wide, and an inch thick at the middle. It tapers from the centre or 'grasp' towards the ends, and is but half an inch wide, and half an inch thick at the extremities. At one end the bow-string is notched into the wood and made permanently fast, while at the other end two notches are cut in the wood, and the string at that end of the bow is made like a slip-knot or loop. When the bow is to be used, the warrior sets the end to which the string is made fast firmly on the ground, and then bends down the other end until the loop slips into the notch. This is called 'stringing' the bow. The bow is never kept strung except when in actual use, as it would lose its strength and elasticity by being constantly bent. When unstrung, a good bow is perfectly straight, and, if properly made and seasoned, will always retain its elasticity. . . .

"When the bow is made of cedar it need not be seasoned; but all other woods require seasoning, and are not worked until perfectly dry. Every tepee has its bow-wood hung up with the arrows in the smoke of the fire, but well out of reach of the flames. A warrior with a sharp knife and a sandstone or file can make a bow in three days if he works hard, but it most generally takes a week, and sometimes a month, to finish a fancy bow. When done it is worth three dollars in trade.

"All the bows differ in length and strength, being gauged for the arms of those who are to use them; but a white man would, until he learned the sleight of it, find himself unable to bend even the weakest war-bow. This has given rise to the impression that the Indians are stronger than white men, which is an error; for, although only a slight man myself, I learned, after some practice, to bend the strongest bow, and could send a shaft as far or as deep as any savage. On one occasion I shot an arrow, while running, into a buffalo so that the point came out on the opposite side; another arrow disappeared in the buffalo, not even the notch being visible. The power of the bow may be better understood when I tell you that the most powerful Colt's revolver will not send a ball through a buffalo. I have seen a bow throw an arrow five hundred yards, and have myself often discharged one entirely through a board one inch thick.

Once I found a man's skull transfixed to a tree by an arrow which had gone completely through the bones, and imbedded itself so deep in the wood as to sustain the weight of the head. He had probably been tied up to the tree and shot. . . .

" When sinew is placed on the back of a bow the surface of the bow is made perfectly flat, then roughened with a file or stone, the sinew being dipped in hot glue and laid on the wood. The sinew is then lapped at the ends and on the middle or grasp of the bow. The string is attached while green, twisted, and left to dry on the bow. The whole outside of the wood and sinew is now covered with a thick solution of glue, and the bow is done. Rough bows look like hickory limbs with the bark on, but some of them are beautifully painted and ornamented. I once knew a trader to glue some red velvet on a bow, and the Indian paid him an immense price for it, thinking it very wonderful.

" The Crows make bows out of elk-horn. To do this they take a large horn or prong and saw a slice off each side of it ; these slices are then filed or rubbed down until the flat sides fit nicely together, when they are glued and wrapped at the ends. Four slices make a bow, it being jointed. Another piece of horn is laid on the centre of the bow at the grasp, where it is glued fast. The whole is then filed down until it is perfectly proportioned, when the white bone is ornamented, carved, and painted. Nothing can exceed the beauty of these bows, and it takes an Indian about three months to make one. They are very expensive, and the Indians do not sell them ; but I once managed to get one from a friend for thirty-two dollars in gold.

" In travelling, the bow is carried in a sheath attached to the arrow-quiver, and the whole is slung to the back by a belt of elk- or buck-skin, which passes diagonally across the breast, and is fastened to the ends of the quiver. The quiver and bow-sheath is generally made of the skin of an ox or some wild animal, and is tanned with the hair on. The quiver is ornamented with tassels, fringe of buckskin, and the belt across the breast is painted or worked with beads.

" To shoot with the bow properly, it must be held firmly in three fingers of the right* hand ; the arrow is fixed on the bow-string with the thumb and forefinger of the left hand, and the other three fingers are used to pull the string. The shaft of the arrow lays between the thumb and forefinger of the right hand, which rests over the grasp of the bow. To shoot, the bow is turned slightly, so one end is higher than the other, and the arrow is then launched." (*Belden.*)

" I once saw an Indian ride alongside of a large buffalo cow going at such speed that it required the best exertions of his very fleet pony to overtake and keep up with her. Leaning forward on his pony, and drawing an arrow to its head, he sent it entirely

---

* This description was evidently intended for a left-handed man.

through the buffalo just back of the foreshoulder, so that it fell on the ground on the opposite side.''

Bow-String. Make sign for Bow, then holding left hand in position, touch the left index finger with tip of extended right, other fingers closed, and carry right hand to shoulder, lowering the hand and then raising it, the index finger passing under left arm ; the left arm here represents the bow, and the index traces the position of the string. Some Indians hold the closed left hand, back down and slightly to left, some eighteen inches in front of left shoulder ; bring the right hand, back up, fingers extended, touching, pointing to front and slightly downwards, in front of right shoulder or height of waist ; move the hand to front and slightly downwards ; repeating motion. These gestures represent the holding of the material in the left hand, and the right twisting the green or fresh sinew. Should this gesture be made when seated, the palm of right hand presses against surface of thigh.

Deaf-mutes make sign for Bow and indicate the string similarly to the first description.

Bowl. Indicate the shape with curved hands, and denote material by proper gestures.

Braid. (Hair.) Carry both hands to right side of head, and make motion as though grasping hair and braiding same.

Brain. Touch the forehead with tips of extended first and second fingers. The brains of animals mixed with boiled liver furnish the Indians with tanning material. (See TAN.)

Brand. (Upon animals.) Close fingers of right hand except index, with it and thumb form a partial circle, there being a little space between tips ; carry the hand to left shoulder, and press the circle formed, as described, against it on the outer side ; this shows the animal branded on shoulder ; press against hip to indicate branded there.

Brave. Hold firmly closed left hand about eight inches in front of centre of body, left forearm horizontal and pointing to right and front, back of left hand vertical and on line of prolongation of forearm ; bring the firmly-closed right hand some six inches above and a little in front of left hand, back to right and front and on line of forearm ; strike downwards with right hand, mostly by elbow action, the second joints of right hand passing close to and about on a line with knuckles of left hand.

Some Indians hold left hand as I have described, but left forearm pointing to right and slightly upwards; and the right hand is carried more round the left and then down, when opposite forearm. Mr. Girard, at Fort Lincoln, who is a fluent sign talker, held that the former was used more in the sense of strong. The distinction is a fine one, and few Indians note it,—using the same gesture exactly, as a rule, for *brave* and *strong*.

The conception of the gesture comes from the signs for HILL, BREAK, and SIT DOWN.

I believe there is no other gesture used by Indians who are thoroughly conversant with the sign language that is as flexible and possesses as much strength and character as this, for when added to other signs it intensifies their descriptive powers wonderfully, adds to many the superlative, gives heroic character to bravery, arrant cowardice to timidity, makes an ordinary meal a feast, and of a fast starvation; pleasure becomes bliss, and care most bitter sorrow. Pointing to a man and making this sign would convey to an Indian's mind the idea that he was *brave, fearless*, and this to them is the highest, most perfect virtue, and creates not only respect, but positive reverence. The gesture, as a rule, is used in this sense, but at times to express opposite or antagonistic ideas. If an Indian visited another tribe, was feasted, given ponies, robes, arms, and other presents, he might finish the description with this sign: "He had a *brave* time;" and Dull Knife, the Cheyenne chief, used it when he told me of his escape from Fort Robinson, and subsequent journey of eighteen days in an arctic climate with only one blanket and a few rosebuds and snow to eat,—"brave" hardships surely. A good time becomes royal, a bad time tastes strongly of wretchedness.

A boy is a swift runner, add this sign, and it intensifies the idea of his fleetness. An old man walks slowly, add this sign, and it conveys the impression that he can only drag his limbs along. This sign is used as frequently with other gestures as it is by itself; it is added to others to complete, perfect, and strengthen them. (See PHRASES.)

Deaf-mutes bring the closed hands sharply against breast, and then push them outwards.

Bravado. Make sign for FIRE, TALK,—*i.e.*, little talk,—STRAIGHT, or TRUE, and NO. One talks *fire*, but there is no truth in it; sometimes, FIRE, TALK, BRAVE WORK, and AFRAID. Talks *fire* bravely but acts the coward; *i.e.*, talking fiercely, but there is no real bravery in it. One Indian gave this to me as, "Behind in everything but lies;" trying to get to be a chief by talk alone.

Bread. Make sign for FLOUR, then bring the nearly-extended hands, palms together, in front of body, back of left down, right up, hands at about right angles; turn the hands with a partial rotary and swinging motion, bringing right under left as the hands are being turned; separate them slightly and join them with a gentle clap; repeat motions.

Sometimes in speaking of loaves of bread as we make them, they add signs for size of loaf, viz., bring both extended hands, palms towards and opposite each other, in front of body, fingers touching and pointing to front, hands about as far apart as the supposed width of the loaf (this sign is general to show the width or breadth of small objects).

The Indians usually mix their flour with water into a dough, sprinkling on some yeast powder, and then fry it; and frequently the signs for this are made to represent bread instead of the one I have given.

Deaf-mutes indicate the working or kneading of the dough, and then holding left hand, back to left, fingers extended and point-ing to front, in front of body ; make motion of cutting off slices of bread with lower edge of extended right hand, held back to right, parallel to left, and some inches from it.

Break. Conception : Breaking a stick held horizontally in the closed hands. Bring both closed hands, backs up, close together in front of body, and at some distance from it, as though holding a small stick horizontally in the closed hands; twist the right hand to right, left to left, as though breaking the stick.

Deaf-mutes make the same sign.

Breech-Cloth. Carry right hand, back outwards, fingers extended, touching, pointing downwards and slightly to rear, below and little in front of crotch ; raise the hand, keeping it close to and about parallel to centre of belly.

Bridge. Bring both hands, back down, fingers extended, touching, and pointing to front in same horizontal plane, in front of body, arms horizontal and nearly extended, hands few inches apart. Fre-quently the signs for STREAM, or whatever is bridged, and TIMBER and WORK are first made.

Deaf-mutes make sign like BASKET, but instead of making the loop under left arm with index, make it with first and second fingers.

Bridle. Bring the spread thumb and index finger of right hand, back outwards, other fingers closed, over the mouth parallel to face ; move the hand upwards, terminating motion when reaching a point opposite the eyes. Sometimes the sign for BIT is made, and then the side pieces are indicated by drawing the tips of index fingers from corners of mouth up sides of face to temples. This latter is about sign of deaf-mutes.

Bring. Move the right hand briskly well in front or to right or left of body, index finger extended, others and thumb closed ; draw the hand in towards the body, at same time curving index finger.

Deaf-mutes use the same sign.

British. Make signs for COAT and for RED. The Northern In-dians call the Canadian or British subjects "Red-coats." Some-times this only means the soldiers or policemen, and gestures for the Queen's people are made to represent the Queen's subjects, calling her the Great Mother.

Deaf-mutes cross the hands over the abdomen to indicate an Eng-lishman.

British Line. (Boundary-line between United States.) The usual signs among Northern tribes are for ROAD and MEDICINE. By such as have seen or heard of the mounds that mark the boundary-line proper signs are made to indicate them. Among the Sioux, Chey-ennes, Blackfeet, Assinaboines, and some others, frequently the gestures for TREES and BLUFF are made, and then the extended index of the right hand, other fingers and thumb closed, is drawn from right to left in front of body, to represent a line ; they calling it the line passing through or near Woody Mountain.

Broad. See BIG.

Brother. Bring the tips of the extended, and touching, first and second fingers of right hand against lips, back of fingers up and horizontal, other fingers and thumb closed ; carry the hand some inches straight out from the mouth, then make sign for MALE. (See KINSHIP.)

Among many tribes there are brothers by adoption, and the tie seems to be held about as sacredly as though created by nature. One cold, wintry morning in the late fall of 1876, while yet the gray shadows of darkness hovered mistily over crag and gorge, some enlisted Indian scouts and regular troops charged down upon a hostile Indian village sleeping in fancied security in a cañon of the Big Horn Mountains. One of these scouts, Three Bears by name, rode a horse which became crazed by excitement and unmanageable, and being wonderfully fleet, dashed with him, ahead of all others, into the very centre of the hostile camp, where men, women, and children were running in wild confusion, where bullets were flying thick and fast, and where the hostiles were making a sharp resistance to protect their families. Feather-on-the-Head, another scout, seeing the trouble his friend was in, dashed after him, urging his own fast pony forward with vigorous strokes of the whip, at the same time throwing himself from side to side of his pony to avoid the shots of his enemies. Thus he followed Three Bears through the bushes and across the stream, down among the tepees, and into the very centre of the village, where Three Bears' horse had fallen dead, shot through the neck. His rider had scarcely touched the ground when Feather-on-the-Head, sweeping past, took him behind himself and bore him safely away out of the valley of death. Feather-on-the-Head had saved Three Bears' life at the risk of his own, and thenceforward the two were much together, and became brothers by adoption. Feather-on-the-Head never seemed to think he had done anything very noble, and never boasted of it ; but keen-eyed, brave, loyal, wiry little Three Bears deeply appreciated the service he had rendered him, and there would have been glad sunshine in his heart if an opportunity had presented itself for him to have reciprocated the gallant action.

With some tribes—particularly with the Cheyennes and Arapahoes —the brother and sister were allowed by social law to have only limited social intercourse ; were not allowed to speak to each other after reaching the age of puberty. If either wanted anything of or from the other, they would ask a third party to make their request.

Deaf-mutes make sign for MALE and same.

Brother-in-Law. Bring the left forearm, pointing to right and slightly upwards, in front of and close to breast, hand back outwards and either extended or closed ; hold the right hand, back outwards, fingers extended, touching, pointing upwards and to left, just in front of left wrist ; strike downwards and to left with right hand, terminating as the right hand passes beyond left elbow. The left forearm is usually pressed against breast instead of being held near it. (See KINSHIP.)

Deaf-mutes make sign for MALE and then hold left hand, back to left, in front of body, fingers extended, touching, and pointing to front; bring spread thumb and index of right hand, other fingers closed (sign for Letter L), and place them against left palm, index horizontal, resting against centre of palm and pointing to front. This is the Indian sign for WITH.

Brook. Make sign for RIVER and SMALL.
Deaf-mutes make sign for SMALL STREAM.

Brulé (band of Sioux Indians). Carry the palm of extended right hand near the right hip; move the hand in small circle parallel to surface; frequently the palm is pressed against surface. The Sioux, of course, do not know this French word, and call this band "Si-Chun-goo," or "Burnt-Thighs."

I have heard several explanations as to how the band gained the name, one being that a chief with quite a number of followers started on the war-path. Securing some whiskey, they all got drunk, and, lying down near the camp-fire, burned their thighs. Another, that some Sioux, including a chief, were, when there was ice on the ground, digging artichokes; brush was spread over the surface and set on fire to melt the ice and thaw the ground, so that they could dig the artichokes. The chief pulled one out of the ground, which was very hot, and he thoughtlessly rubbed it against his thigh (which was exposed), and consequently burned himself; and he and his followers were afterwards called "Burnt-Thighs." The Brulé Sioux are located at Rosebud Agency and at Lower Brulé; the latter on the Missouri River, about fourteen miles from Fort Hale, Dakota Territory. The famous Spotted Tail was the chief of those at Rosebud. Those at Lower Brulé Agency claim that they separated from the others quite a long time ago, and the trouble grew out of a dispute about a woman. (See SIOUX.)

Buffalo. Conception: Horns of buffalo. Bring the hands, palms towards and close to sides of head, index fingers partially curved, others and thumbs closed; raise the hands slightly and carry them a little to the front. This is the sign generally used for buffalo, regardless of sex or age, used as we use the word.

Buffalo Bull. To represent a buffalo bull, make the above described sign, then bring the right hand, back up, in front of centre of belly, close to it, index finger extended pointing to front and upwards, other fingers and thumb closed. (Sign for MALE.) The sign for buffalo bull is also frequently made by bringing the compressed hands from above downwards to near basis of brain, fingers partially curved, so that tips touch tip of thumb, backs of hands mostly up; this represents the large horns of the bull.

Buffalo Cow. Make sign for BUFFALO as first given, and then sign for FEMALE.

Buffalo Calf. Make sign for BUFFALO, for PARTURITION, and hold right hand, back up, fingers extended, touching, and pointing to front, in front and to right of body at supposed height of calf; this latter is general in representing height of all animals. Some Indians represent a buffalo calf by holding hands closed, with the exception of thumbs, which are extended and pointing upwards, close to the ears, back of right hand to right, left to left; by wrist action twist hands simultaneously so that back will be to the front; repeat motion. In using this sign for buffalo calf,—the second described sign for buffalo bull,—the first described sign for buffalo would then represent a buffalo cow.

Some Indians make sign for the horns, and indicate dark or black hair for buffalo.

Deaf-mutes indicate horns as in cattle, and then partially close right hand and bring it, back out, against forehead, backs of bent fingers, between first and second joint, resting against forehead; rub the forehead by circular movement of hand to indicate the curl of hair presumed to grow on the forehead of the animal. (As a matter of fact this hair does not curl; I have seen it a foot in length and straight.)

The great geographical area over which these animals ranged, their countless numbers, their importance and necessity to hostile Indians in the past, and their certain extermination in the near future, have all led me to make close investigation into the uses made of every part of the animal, and in condensed shape I give the result.

It is no exaggeration to say that many millions of buffalo have been slaughtered by white hunters and tourists on the Plains merely for the pleasure of killing these animals to gratify that innate craving for destruction of life which all human beings seem to possess, and at times for the tongues, which are a special delicacy. This wasteful and wicked course has in many instances so irritated the Indians that they have sought revenge by outbreaks and by killing innocent settlers. Though I call the wanton killing wasteful and wicked, still, as a force for the solution of the Indian question and viewed in the accepted light of this necessity, the destruction has accomplished an excellent result.

The Indians universally believe that the buffalo were made by the Creator especially for their use, and certainly when they are plentiful they can get along quite comfortably with very little else. When one considers the uses made by them of the buffalo, both at the present day and prior to the advent of the whites, one is not surprised at the claim and belief. Of the skin they make robes, lodges, lariats, ropes, trunks or par-flèche sacks, saddles, saddle-covers, shields, frames for war-bonnets, gloves, moccasins, leggings, shirts, hats, gun-covers, whips, quivers, knife-scabbards, cradles, saddle-bags, saddle-blankets, decorations for saddles, beds, bridles, boots, a kind of sled for hauling the meat over the snow, and from the thick part of the skin of the neck a glue is made by boiling and skimming.

Ropes and lariats are made from the scalp-lock, or long tuft on the forehead, and pillows from the hair. From the horns, spoons, cups, dishes, powder-horns, arrow-heads, bows, by splitting the longer horns, and the tips are fastened to slender poles which are used in certain games.

From the fascia (thin tendinous covering which supports the muscles, and by the interpreters called sinew), found under the shoulder-blades, the abdominal fascia, the two strips on each side over the hump, and the strip on each side of back, they make thread, bow-strings, rope for softening robes by rubbing, fasten feather-guides to arrows, and stiffen and make bows more elastic by placing on back. From the thick ligament of the upper portion of nape of neck is made a pipe. An instrument used to straighten arrows is fashioned from the centre bone of the hump by cutting a hole in it, and from some of the smaller bones arrow-heads are made, and an instrument for "flushing," or scraping the meat from hides. From shoulder-blades, axes, knives, arrow-points, instruments for dressing robes and smoothing down porcupine-work.

The trachea is used as a sack for paints, etc. The rough papillæ of the tongue for hair-brushes. The brain, liver, and fat for tanning skins. Instruments for shaping bows and small dog-sleds from ribs. From the paunch, water-pipes or sacks, in which meat and blood are sometimes cooked by boiling with heated stones, the latter being dropped into the sacks.

From the thigh-bones, traps similar to our deadfalls. From the tail, knife-scabbards, handles to war-clubs, and medicine-rattles. The udder, dried, becomes stiff and hard, and is used for dishes, tobacco-bags, medicine-rattles, etc. The pericardium for sacks. The gall is sometimes used as a drink, and produces intoxication ; there is also sometimes found in the gall a hard yellow substance, and this is highly valued as a paint for the face.

The amniotic fluid, in which the fœtus floats, is used by them to quench thirst when water cannot be obtained, and is also generally used to cook or boil the fœtus in, the latter being specially prized as a dainty and delicate morsel of food. The marrow is eaten both raw and cooked, being roasted in the larger bones by laying them on the coals.

The teeth are used for necklaces, and are also put in medicine-rattles.

They consider the contents of the paunch an excellent remedy for skin diseases, and in case of frost-bite, if the afflicted member is thrust into the paunch of a freshly-killed buffalo, relief obtains without evil after-effects. A very little buffalo fat is sometimes mixed with the tobacco and red-willow bark for smoking. The liver is often eaten raw, and while still warm with animal heat, the gall-juice being sprinkled over it as a sauce. The kidneys are eaten both raw and cooked. The meat, fat, and most of the intestines are staple articles of food, and are kept for months by being simply dried in the sun ; the hump is considered particularly fine for drying. The contents of the paunch furnish food for ponies, and the liquid in same, cleared by the gall, is prized for drinking, is cool and tasteless ; *i.e.*, devoid of any unpleasant taste.

The "buffalo-chips" are used for fuel, and before the days of flint and steel and matches, were particularly good when dry for making a fire by the friction of wood. These "chips," pounded fine and kept dry, are used to keep the small children warm, they being partially buried in the powdered material. The value of these chips can scarcely be appreciated by those who have not suffered for the want of fuel on our treeless prairies.

The tanned buffalo-skin without the hair furnishes the best material for tepees.

The only systematic effort ever made that I know of to specially utilize the hair of the buffalo, as wool, is described by Mr. Donald Gunn in his "History of Manitoba":

" A new project was set on foot this year (1822), which, to some extent, affected the interest of the infant colony. The plan formed by the projectors was a joint-stock company bearing the novel title of 'The Buffalo Wool Company,' consisting of one hundred shares of twenty pounds each, with provision for increasing their stock at any time. Mr. John Pritchard was placed at the head of the new company. His calculations seem to have been based on the supposition that the requisite articles—wool and hides—could be had for the trouble of picking them up.

" The express objects of the company were as follows :

" 1st. To provide a substitute for wool, as it was supposed, from the numbers and destructive habits of the wolves, that sheep could not be raised nor preserved in Red River, at least to any extent.

" 2d. The substitute contemplated was the wool of the wild buffalo, which was to be collected on the Plains and manufactured both for the use of the colonists and for export.

" 3rd. To establish a tannery for manufacturing the buffalo-hides for domestic use.

" It was the chairman's belief, to quote his own words, that ' to accomplish these important ends neither much capital nor much skill was required ;' but others thought differently of the project, and were assured that much would depend on economy and proper management. Nevertheless, the capital, amounting to two thousand pounds, was no sooner placed to the credit of the new company in the Hudson's Bay Company's books than operations were commenced with great activity and confidence. All the buffalo-hunters were enlisted in the enterprise ; the men were exhorted to strain every nerve to preserve hides, and the women were encouraged to gather all the wool they could find by the promise of a liberal price for all they would bring to the manufactory. An establishment worthy of the Buffalo Wool Company was erected in the heart of the settlement, and the possession of a certain quantity of the requisite materials was judged to be all that would be necessary to insure the success of the enterprise. At the time of which we are writing the buffalo were in great numbers a few miles south of Pembina, and a multitude of people, composed of the various races in the land, had congregated to hunt these animals during the winter months ; and in the spring, when the hunters returned to the settlement, a trifle of wool and a considerable number of hides were delivered at the factory. But it was now found out that wool and hides were not to be had for the picking of them up, for the wool cost something, and the price of a hide ranged from eight to ten shillings sterling, and before the hide could be freed from the wool it had to undergo the different operations of soaking, heating, and pulling. All the available hands in the place, male and female, were called into operation. The men and lads manipulated the hides, and it is well known that an expert hand at pulling the wool could gain from six to ten shillings per day. Even boys thought themselves ill compensated for their labor at anything less than four or five shillings per diem. Female labor was neither overlooked nor undervalued, as all who could spin were invited to the factory to receive wool to make into yarn, for which labor they were paid at the rate of one shilling per pound. Thus we find that the industry of the colony had not only been stimulated, but also turned into a new channel, in which it found money or credit in the Hudson's Bay Company's books, neither of which they could have realized from the produce of their farms. This affair enabled the settlers to obtain a little money at the right time. A small herd of domestic cattle was brought in this summer on speculation, and, arriving at this juncture, were eagerly competed for by the few who had money or credit, and sold at highly-remunerating prices ; good milch-cows sold as high as thirty pounds each, and oxen trained to work sold for eighteen pounds each.

"It may be interesting to observe here that these were the first cattle ever brought from the United States to this settlement, and the first the colonists owned since they left their native hills. Here we must inform the reader that operatives were introduced from England, consisting of wool-dressers, furriers, curriers, saddlers, and harness-makers ; likewise an outfit of goods was procured, and a store opened in the establishment for the convenience of those carrying on the work. Some leather and cloth had been manufactured, but they could not compete favorably with similar articles brought from Europe, and, unfortunately, rum formed a considerable portion of the outfit, and it was well known that drunkenness and disorder prevailed in the establishment to a fearful extent. Hides were allowed to rot, the wool spoiled, the tannery proved a failure, and, although the concern dragged on until 1825, it was apparent to the most cursory observer that its progress was from bad to worse, and when its affairs were finally wound up, it was found that they had not only expended their original stock of two thousand pounds, but were indebted in the amount of five hundred pounds to their bankers (the Hudson's Bay Company). This heavy loss hung for some years over the heads of the stockholders, until the Honorable Hudson's Bay Company relieved them from their responsibilities by cancelling the debt.''

There are many stories told in regard to the buffalo, and prominent among them, from its wide circulation in the North and the general confidence in it, is that of a buffalo cow killed near Slim

Buttes, Dakota, some twenty-five years since.   On cutting her open
to take out the fœtus, an old woman, wrinkled and gray, was found.
All the bands of Sioux, and some of the adjacent tribes, were called
to the spot to see the phenomenon.   I was told that Lean Dog, now
at Standing Rock Agency, was the Indian who killed this cow.   Very
reliable Indians have told me this story, and insisted that they saw
the monstrosity.   The Arapahoes also insisted that a few years ago
they killed a buffalo, about two years old, near the Big Horn Mountains, which had only one eye and that in the centre of its forehead.
Among some tribes the first buffalo killed by a young man was the
occasion for a special religious ceremony and feast.   Mr. Dunbar
thus describes this among the Pawnees :

"The entire animal was carried to the lodge of some prominent
person, who thereby became master of the feast.   He invited in a
dozen or more old men to feast with him and assist in the observance
of the occasion, and other special guests ; they began at sunset ; the
meat was cut in small pieces and set over the fire to boil, except the
heart and tongue, which were carried without the lodge and burned
as a sacrifice.   While the meat was boiling and the sacrifice was
burning, the medicine-bundle was taken from its place, opened, its
contents inspected and placed out in due order, various ceremonies
were performed over them, puffing smoke over them, stroking them
with the hand, talking or praying to them, etc., by members of the
company ; speeches were then made by certain of the old men, the
burden of whose remarks was laudation of the slayer of the buffalo,
the master of the feast, etc., and finally a prayer was offered.   The
meat having thoroughly cooked meanwhile, was apportioned among
all present, each of whom had opportunity to gorge himself to the
utmost.   After the eating, the sacred things were gathered together,
replaced in the bundle, and suspended again in place."

Before the introduction of guns many devices for killing buffalo
were resorted to.   They were lured over precipices by a decoy ; *i.e.*,
an Indian disguised as a buffalo, who, when the herd was stampeded,
would run towards a precipice, the herd following.   Natural en-
closures were strengthened by fallen timber, and the animals driven
into them.

I have seen Indians send arrows entirely through a buffalo, the
arrows passing through the body, just back of the foreshoulders, and
falling to the ground from the side opposite its entrance.   I have
been told that Indians have been known to kill from a herd *three*
buffalo in quick succession with but one small-headed arrow.   The
Indian would ride alongside the buffalo, and, leaning forward from
his pony, drive the arrow to the heart of the animal, pull it out, and
on to the next.   Such a feat, as may be imagined, required nerve,
strength, and activity, as well as a very fleet pony.

Buffalo, White.   This animal has furnished dreamers or medicine-men of the different tribes with the material for many of their
mythical stories, and, though wonderfully rare, it yet does exist,
and is like any other buffalo, except that the hair is of a brownish-

white color. I secured the skin of one in 1879, near Fort Keogh, Montana. In nearly all of their myths in regard to it, the animal is given the power of transforming itself into some other shape,—a white hawk, a gray fox, or, more commonly, a beautiful woman possessed of supernatural powers. The most interesting of these myths to me, perhaps because I knew the Indian who they claimed held the gift of the goddess, was related to me first by a Cheyenne, and afterwards by the Sioux chief at the agency where the sacred pipe possessing the mysterious power was kept.

"Long ago, many years before the Sioux had ponies, many generations before the whites crossed the wide waters, two young men were sent out from the Sioux camp in search of buffalo. In their wanderings they espied a beautiful young woman, who was more fair to look upon than any of the Sioux maidens. One of these young men was wise and good, his heart was brave and strong ; the other was foolish. The latter said, 'Here is a beautiful young girl on the prairie alone ; let us overpower and enjoy her.' The young man of sense said, 'No, that would be wrong ; this is a holy woman.' They were as yet some little distance from her, and she had attracted their attention by singing. After making signs to her she approached, and knowing the conversation which had passed between the young men, she said, 'I am alone and in your power.' In spite of the protests of his companion the foolish young man, crazed by his passion, forced her to the ground, when a great mist or fog suddenly arose, enveloped them, and spread over the prairie, and the air was filled with terrible and hissing sounds. As suddenly as it came the fog lifted, and it seemed to take with it numberless rattlesnakes. Then the wise young man saw the woman standing near him, and between her and himself the ghastly bones of his comrade, from which the flesh had been entirely consumed by the rattlesnakes. The woman then said to the surviving young man, 'You are wise, brave, and good; I have taken pity on you and your people. This young man was wicked, and he has suffered the fruit of his own misdeeds. Go and tell your people that I know that they are poor, and that I will take pity on them.' The young man returned to camp and told what he had seen and heard. A large lodge was pitched in the centre of the camp. The beautiful woman had followed the young man, and as she approached the village she was met by the medicine-men and carried on a blanket. It was noticed that when she was first seen, and while being carried on the blanket, she held a pipe high in the air and pointed towards the sun. A large fire was built in the tepee ; circle after circle of men, women, and children formed outside, and a great circle of fires was also made round the lodge. All eyes were on the beautiful woman. She said, 'I have taken pity on you; have brought you four things which will be good for you, viz., tobacco, red robe, white shield, and war-bonnet of eagle's feathers ; and I have also brought you this sacred pipe, which will tell you by its increased weight when buffalo are near and plenty.' She then presented the pipe to the chief medicine-man of the Sioux, accompanied with much good advice, and at once, from the very midst of the fires and the people, mysteriously vanished from sight.

"This holy pipe, which has been handed down from father to son for so many generations, is now in charge of Elk-Head, a Sans Arcs chief, living at Standing Rock Agency, on the Missouri River. It is kept carefully wrapped up, and few people are allowed to see it.

"The beautiful woman was a white buffalo, who took that shape to give them this pipe. The pipe had, and still possesses, wonderful power to assist in getting buffalo. The first use that the Sioux made of it was to move in a large circle. No animal could cross the magic line thus made, and seven Crow Indians, happening to be within the circle, were killed with the rest of the game; an ear from one of these enemies was cut off and glued on to the stem of the pipe, where it still remains.

"When game is scarce, the ceremony of the white buffalo is even now practised. It is a rude imitation of the original as traced in this story."

Buffalo-Robe. Make sign for BUFFALO and for BLANKET; sometimes sign for HAIR is made before sign for BLANKET.

Deaf-mutes make sign for BUFFALO, for SKIN, and sometimes indicate wrapping about shoulders.

Bull-Berry. Make sign for BERRY, for TREE, and then strike with lower edge of extended right hand towards the tree, as though knocking off the fruit.

Burn. Make sign for FIRE, then represent whatever was destroyed or injured by the fire, and the manner and extent will usually suggest itself. If one wishes to say that he was burned by the fire, say his clothes and flesh, make sign for DO TO ME and BAD; then carry extended hand, fingers separated and pointing in the direction which the flames took, in a wavy, tremulous motion, over the surface of parts where the flames went; and if very badly burned add sign for BRAVE. Sometimes the signs for FIRE and KILL are made when a person has received bodily injury from a fire; the sign for KILL being made, of course, towards the part burned.

Deaf-mutes make sign for FIRE and explain.

Bury. Make sign for WRAP, then make sign for DIG, and drop the compressed right hand, back down, into the imaginary hole; or hold the extended and separated first and second fingers of each hand opposite each other and about six inches apart, in front of body, palms towards each other, tips of extended fingers slightly higher than shoulder; then place the tips of first and second fingers of right against tips of first and second of left hand, holding them horizontally, backs up, keeping left hand in its original position; draw these fingers horizontally to right some inches; then turn the compressed right hand, back down, and lay it on the horizontal lines drawn by first and second fingers of this hand (from finger-tips of first and second fingers of left hand).

Deaf-mutes indicate being laid away and covered over.

In olden times, and to some extent at the present day, four or five skins, robes, or blankets were spread out and the corpse laid on them ; if a child, its childish possessions, toys, and little things were placed by its side ; if a man, his bow and arrows, shield, war-bonnet, rifle, ammunition, paint, some tobacco and pipe, his weapons for the chase and war, and his instruments for peace were carefully wrapped up with the remains, and round the whole stout cords were tied.

Sometimes, if a chief, his favorite war-pony would be led to his tepee just as he was breathing his last, and as the spirit took its flight the pony would be shot, that he might ride to the spirit land. At other times one or more ponies would be led to the grave, and after the remains had been securely fastened to the limbs of some tree, to poles placed in the ground or hidden away in the rocks, according to the manner of burial, the ponies would be killed. As a rule the older men and women of the camp prepare the remains for burial.

The Mandans bury with the head towards the east, and do not kill ponies. The River Gros Ventres bury in the ground, or on poles, according to wishes expressed just before death. They do not take food to the grave.

The Assinaboines usually buried on scaffolds or on trees ; sometimes in a lodge, if a chief. Before possessing ponies they killed dogs at death of prominent persons : frequently all the dogs that belonged to a chief.

The Comanches prepare the remains carefully for burial, and then the funeral cortege must move directly east or west from the camp to the burial-place, which may be a gulch, cave, or a hole dug in the ground. Bow and arrows, knife and whetstone, pipe, tobacco, flint and steel, and a goodly quantity of personal property are buried with the male corpse. With the women are buried their implements for dressing robes, etc. The lodge is burned to destroy the memory of the grief at their loss.

Mr. Clarke, the interpreter at the Wichita Agency, told me that a Comanche chief, called Be-a-repepsa, had, at the time of his death, which occurred in 1865, near North Fork of Red River, an immense herd of ponies, and two hundred and eighty-five white ones were killed for him to journey to the land of the Setting Sun ; and another, called Prairie Fire, who died in 1875, had one hundred and fifty killed for his spiritual herd.

The Caddos bury in the ground, and keep a fire burning at the grave for six days and nights after burial. They carry water and food in small vessels and place them near the grave. They claim that it takes six days for the spirit to get home. They do not kill ponies at the death of chiefs or other persons.

The Apaches also bury in the ground in very deep graves, and in caves, and with the deceased bury some of his personal property. The saddle is excepted, and the remainder of his effects are burned. Relatives cut off hair and fold it with the corpse.

The Kiowas are not particular about the direction of grave from camp, but they dig it twelve or thirteen feet deep. When a Kiowa is killed while out on the war-path, he is not buried in the ground, but is wrapped up and left on the prairie, or, if near timber, is fastened among the branches of a tree. Sometimes, if no near kin happens to be with war-party, and through neglect the remains were not buried, they are afterwards sought out, and, even if nothing but the bones remain, they are wrapped up and placed among the branches of a tree or up on poles. Very rarely, however, the remains are brought to camp and there buried in the ground. These Indians believe that the spirits of their strongest medicine-men return to their camps even years after death, and communicate with the living through their friends. Sometimes the spirit returns as an owl, and imparts information as to the location and intentions of their enemies, gives warning of danger, etc.

The Sacs and Foxes bury in the ground, and in former times used to place the corpse in a sitting posture. They made only a slight excavation, and then built heaps of earth, sods, or stones over it. They admit that very many years ago they often buried in trees. Sometimes a pony, fully caparisoned, was led to near a dying chief's lodge, and the lariat put in his hand. At the death the pony was shot, and the equipments afterwards taken away. They never burned or destroyed personal effects.

The Poncas bury above-ground, and distribute personal property to kinsfolk.

The Nez Perces buried in the ground, in rocks, etc., and sometimes, in travelling, threw the remains in the water.

Among the Blackfeet the remains are buried very soon after death. Those effects which the deceased was fond of are put with the corpse ; whatever is left is seized upon, so "that the kin are only left with their grief."

Buy. Make sign for Money and Exchange.

Deaf-mutes make sign for Money, for Giving, and for Receiving.

By and By. Same as Behind (sense of time). Some Indians make sign for Wait.

Deaf-mutes bring extended right hand, back to right, in front of and close to right shoulder, fingers pointing to front ; move the hand to the front on slight curve.

By Itself. Hold the extended right hand, back down, well in front of right breast, fingers pointing to front ; mostly by wrist action move the hand few inches to left, rather sharply, as though cutting with edge of hand, hand returning to position with life, and repeating motion two or three times.

This is a metaphoric idiom of the language, used in connection with other gestures. A gift with this sign becomes a free gift ; no return gift expected ; sometimes called a "prairie gift." A killing with this sign becomes a murder ; no excuse for the killing. Death becomes fainting, etc. The gesture means also *alone, solitary,* an action uninfluenced by any other action.

C.

Cache. The usual sign is simply to indicate a hiding away, by carrying right hand under left, as in HIDE; but the Mandans and other tribes, who store away the fruit of their agricultural labor in small jug-shaped holes in the ground, carefully concealed and covered over, make in addition the sign for digging a hole, putting something in it and covering it up.

Deaf-mutes make the same sign; their sign for HIDE or CONCEAL being only slightly different.

Caddo. Same as NEZ PERCE.

The agent in his report for 1881, dated at Anadarko (named after a former band of Caddos), Indian Territory, gives the number of these people at five hundred and fifty-two.

From personal investigation among these Indians, I learned that the known migrations of their tribe only show that about the year 1819 they were living in Louisiana, near Natchitoches, on the Red River. From there they moved to Texas, near the Clear Fork of Brazos River, and from there to their present location on the Washita River in 1859. Mr. Dunbar says of them, "At the date of the Louisiana purchase the Caddos were living about forty miles north-west of where Shreveport now stands. Five years earlier their residence was upon Clear Lake, in what is now Caddo Parish. This spot they claimed was the place of their nativity, and their residence from time immemorial. There they had long been known to the French traders, who had a factory among them. Soon after the annexation of Texas they settled upon a reserve provided for them by the government on the Brazos River, just below Fort Belknap. It would seem that their migration from Louisiana, for whatever cause undertaken, must have been slowly accomplished, for they are reported to have tarried upon one of the tributaries of the Sabine River sufficiently long to leave it the name of Caddo Fork. They have a tradition that they are the parent stock, from which all the Southern branches have sprung, and to some extent this claim has been recognized."

They are very dark-colored, and rather below medium height. Formerly wore the scalp-lock, and a large ring in the nose, from which they gained the tribal sign. The Wacos, numbering about two hundred and six; the Keechies, seventy-seven; and Towaconies, one hundred and fifty-one, have for many years lived near the Caddos; in fact, present tradition claims that they *originally* came from the same country. They, however, speak different languages, or at least different dialects. They all use the same conical-shaped grass-lodge as the Wichitas. In regard to their creation, they at present claim to have come out of the ground near

Caddo Peak, Indian Territory.   As one of the chiefs said to me,
" There was an opening in the ground, and as each one came out
a handful of dirt was picked up and placed at this point, and the
mountain was made."   They believe that after death they return to
near the peak, and again go inside the earth : but they travel to this
place by a trail high in the air.   Some of them believe that the journey takes six days, and during this time a fire must be kept burning
at the grave (remains are placed in the ground), and some food and
water must be left in vessels near it.   " Big Man," chief of the
Caddos at the agency, a bright, intelligent, and prosperous Indian,
who dresses in citizen's clothes, has cultivated fields, and a good log
house, told me that, when they lived in the East, they did not understand the sign language, but they learned to talk in this way from
the Prairie Indians.   Said he, " When we first met the Keechies, we
talked partly by signs and partly by vocal language.   They knew
gesture speech first.   As we adopted the signs, of course they are
like the rest ; *i.e.*, like those used by other tribes."

Call. Bring back of index finger of right hand, others closed,
against or near the mouth, back of hand to right and rear, index
finger curved, its tip pressed against thumb, which is nearly extended ; raise the hand upwards and outwards, at same time extending index finger with a snap.   This sign is used in giving the name
of an object called so and so, or to ask the name of an object.   For
the latter, first make the sign for INTERROGATE or QUESTION.   The
conception arises from the custom of calling out names in an Indian
village.   Each camp or band has a crier, who, whenever there is to
be a council, walks about, throws his head back, and calls out very
loudly the names of those who are requested to assemble ; or of any
one man or chief who is wanted ; or when any special information, orders, etc., are to be communicated, it is done in the same way.   The
words are thrown outwards and upwards over the camp.

Deaf-mutes cross the index fingers in front of body, others and
thumbs closed (like the Indian sign for TRADE), and then move their
hands, held in this position, to front on slight curve.   The first is the
sign for NAME, and the movement of hands denotes the action.

Camas. Conception : Curved stick used in digging the root.
Partially curve the index finger of right hand, others and thumb
closed, and make motion downwards, as though thrusting stick in
the ground.   Sometimes signs for EAT, GOOD, and perhaps signs to
denote the blue flower, are made.

This root has been one of the staple articles of food for the Shoshones, Bannacks, Flatheads, and adjacent tribes.   The high moist
mesâs of the Rocky Mountains furnish large tracts of camas prairies,
where these Indians annually congregate, dig, and prepare the root for
use.   Excavations are made in the ground, a fire is built in the hole,
and flat rocks are heated and put on the bottom and sides.   A thin
layer of leaves and grass is put on the rocks, and the hole filled with
camas-roots, which are then covered with grass, leaves, bark, and
stones, and usually a fire is built on the top of the pile.   It requires

about three days to properly cook the roots in this way. The annual gathering of camas occurs in June and July, when it may be considered as ripe. Late in the fall the roots are at times prepared by boiling. This tuber is very nutritious.

Camp. Make sign for TEPEE or LODGE ; then bring both hands about fourteen inches in front of centre of body, hands opposite, and palms towards each other, fingers and thumbs partially curved, fingers separated slightly, forearms nearly horizontal, wrists a little higher than elbows, about two inches space between tips of thumbs and tips of fingers of right and left hand, thumbs and index fingers forming an incomplete horizontal circle ; lower the hands simultaneously and briskly some inches, mostly by elbow action.

To indicate the size of the camp, give the number of lodges, or make sign for TEPEES ; sign for SMALL, if there are few lodges, and MANY, if a large camp. If an unusually large village, add sign for TREES ; the idea being that the tips of the tepee-poles look like a forest.

To express the idea of going into camp, the sign for TEPEE in the first instance is not made, and sometimes only the sign for SLEEP is made. The description I have here given refers to tepees, lodges, tents, or people in camp or bivouac ; and the same sign is used to denote a village or city of white people, the sign for HOUSE being made instead of tepee.

Candid. Make signs for TRUE, for DAY, and GOOD, conveying the idea of openness and clearness like the day; truth and goodness.

Deaf-mutes use the same signs.

Candle. Hold left hand, back to left, well out in front of left shoulder, index finger extended and pointing upwards, others and thumb closed ; make sign for FIRE (at the tip of left index) ; then mark off with lower edge of right hand or with extended right index on left forearm the length of a candle, measuring from the tip of left index.

Deaf-mutes make a similar sign, sometimes also holding the tip of left vertical index near mouth and blowing at it, as though extinguishing the flame of a candle in that way.

Candy. Make sign for SWEET or SUGAR ; then hold left index vertically in front of body, other fingers and thumb closed, and with the tip of right index indicate on left the stripes of different colors.

Deaf-mutes make the same signs.

Cane. Conception : Old man walking with stick. Bring the right hand fixed as, and in the position of, OLD ; then move the hand slightly to front, also raising it a little ; then lower it to about same height as when starting ; repeat motion.

Deaf-mutes make the same sign.

Cannon. Conception : Large gun. Make sign for GUN, and for LARGE.

Sometimes the signs for DISTANT and DISCHARGE are also made ; a second shooting or explosion ; this latter rather indicates a large gun firing shells. Some Indians make an incomplete vertical circle with thumbs and index fingers to denote the bore of the cannon.

Deaf-mutes hold left hand, back to left, in front of body, index finger alone extended and pointing to front; the right hand, index alone extended, is brought over left, right index vertical and tip resting at base of left index; move right hand sharply to front, right index tip pressing against side of left index finger. The signs for size of gun and for iron are sometimes also made.

Cannot. Make signs for Work and for No. The following is a better sign used, not generally, perhaps, but by those who are thoroughly conversant with gesture speech, viz.: hold the left hand, back to left, fingers extended, touching, and pointing to front, well out in front of left breast, left forearm about horizontal; bring tip of extended index finger of right hand, back up, against centre of left palm, this finger perpendicular to its surface, other fingers and thumb closed; then move right hand to right some inches, as though rebounding after tip strikes left palm, keeping index finger about horizontal and in line of its prolongation from first position. This sign is used in the sense of *impossible*, and its conception seems to be, will not go through. Some Indians make sign for Behind (sense of time), drawing hands well apart, and dropping them, as in Tired or Age.

Deaf-mutes hold extended left index horizontally in front of body, pointing to front, other fingers closed, and drop right hand from above down on to it, and as left index is struck it bends and allows right to pass; sometimes only right index drops on left.

Canoe. Make sign for Boat, and then hold compressed and curved right hand, back down, outwards in front of body, to denote the curved prow.

Deaf-mutes make sign for Boat and then signs for paddling same.

Cañon. Conception: High bluffs or mountains on either side. Bring both closed hands, palms towards and opposite each other, in front of body, and little higher than shoulders, forearms nearly vertical, hands about six inches apart. Sometimes signs to denote Cut or precipitous banks are also made.

Deaf-mutes use the same signs. A winding cut through mountains is sometimes indicated by holding extended hands in front of body and opposite, about four inches apart and palms towards each other, fingers pointing to front; move the hands, keeping them at same distance apart, simultaneously to front.

Cards. Hold nearly-closed left hand in front of body; carry right hand near to it, and make motions with right hand as though dealing out the cards to several persons. The king is distinguished from the jack by coloring the head-dress of the former yellow, the latter red.

Indians are passionately fond of gambling and have adopted some of our games with cards, which they play with modifications, the result being that it is generally a mere question of luck, and not of skill.

Deaf-mutes hold left hand in front of body, as though holding a "hand of cards," and then, with right near left, make motion of arranging same; sometimes also making motions of throwing down cards taken from left thumb.

Cartridge. Hold right hand, back nearly up, in front of body, index finger extended horizontal and pointing to front, other fingers closed; thumb pressing against side of index, with tip just back of second joint, represents metallic cartridge now in use. Sometimes signs for GUN and SHOOT are also made.

Cartridge-Belt. Make sign for BELT, and then, fixing right hand as in CARTRIDGE, carry the index finger to right side, and make motion as though putting it in the loops of belt.

Cat. Conception: Flattened or turned-up nose. Bring closed right hand, back to right, in front of face, thumb resting on second joint of index finger, nose touching tip of thumb and second joint of index; twist the hand upwards and very slightly outwards, mostly by wrist action, nose still touching thumb and index. Frequently the size of the animal is added.

Deaf-mutes indicate the moustache, stroking an imaginary one with tips of fingers and thumbs right and left on upper lip.

Cattle. Conception: Spotted buffalo. Make sign for BUFFALO and SPOTTED. Some Indians only indicate straighter horns by not curving the index fingers as much as in buffalo; and some make sign for tame buffalo; *i.e.*, buffalo working side by side under a yoke.

Cavalryman. Make sign for WHITE MAN, for SOLDIER, and for RIDE. Frequently the signs for the yellow stripe on trousers are made.

Deaf-mutes make signs for SOLDIER and RIDE.

Centre. Bring hands in front of body and make a horizontal circle with thumbs and index fingers, other fingers closed; then, still holding left hand in this position, bring right hand from above, and place the tip of extended right index, other fingers and thumb closed, in centre of the horizontal circle first formed; the right index is held vertically and points downwards. (See also MIDDLE.)

Deaf-mutes make the same signs.

Certain. Make signs for I, KNOW, and GOOD. A quick, vigorous, and decisive manner of making the gesture is also necessary.

The sign for TRUE is also made. The latter is the gesture used by deaf-mutes.

Charge. To charge against others. Hold the closed hands, backs up, near the right shoulder; move the hands briskly to front, slightly to left and trifle downwards, at same time opening hands, extending and separating fingers.

Charge. Sense of others charging against or towards one. Hold the nearly-closed hands, backs down, a few inches apart, in front and little to left of centre of body, hands about height of shoulders; move the hands briskly, mostly by wrist and elbow action, in towards the body, turning backs upwards and to front by bending wrists towards forearms, at the same time extending and separating the fingers, having them point at about lower portion of face, tips being a few inches from it at termination of movement. The conception seems to come from gathering together, making a rush, and scattering out. The sign is used to designate troops, Indians, buffalo, or anything that could make a charge, and frequently metaphorically; as, the wind or the water came charging against us. (See ATTACK and WAR.)

Deaf-mutes make a similar motion, but do not close the hands; *i.e.*, start with fingers extended and separated.

Cheat. Explain in what way, and then make signs for KILL, LIE, and STEAL. To cheat is to *win* by lying and stealing.

Deaf-mutes make sign similar to Southern Indians' sign for TRADE, only the right hand passes outside of left and then under it,—"an underhanded exchange."

Cherries. Conception: The fruit hanging on the tree. Make sign for TREE, then hold the right hand, back up, well out in front of and little higher than right shoulder, fingers and thumb separated, hand allowed to drop down by its own weight, held loosely at wrist; shake the hand a little to right and left, giving it the naturally tremulous motion when shaken in that way and held thus loosely. With most signs for FRUIT the gestures for GOOD and EAT are added. The signs for fruit are at times difficult to understand and frequently require explanation.

Deaf-mutes make sign for TREE, color and size of fruit.

Cheyenne. There are two distinct conceptions for the sign for this tribe, and each is supported by evidence. The first conception, and I think the best, or rather the more correct one, is from the custom which formerly obtained, and still exists to some extent, of cutting or slashing the wrists and arms. The second one is from the peculiar manner of striping their arrows.

Hold the left hand, back upwards and slightly to left, in front of left breast, index finger extended horizontal and pointing to the front, others and thumb closed; bring the right hand, back outwards, opposite and little above left, index finger extended horizontally and pointing to left, others and thumb closed, right index pointing to left and upwards, its second joint above left index; lower right hand so that right index rests on left, and then draw the right hand briskly to right and downwards; repeat motion two or three times, sometimes moving right hand after each movement towards body, as though slashing wrist and arm.

Pictographically, the Cheyennes are represented like the Sioux and Arapahoes; *i.e.*, with the hair combed down sides of face, braided and wrapped with otter-skin or other material, and long scalp-lock hanging down behind.

The tribe of Indians known by the name Cheyenne speak an entirely different vocal language from any of the nations surrounding them. The word evidently came from the Sioux Sha-ey-la, or Sha-en-na, and, according to the Indian explanation, was given them by the Sioux because they first met a Cheyenne who wore a robe painted red and had his body painted the same color; *sha* being the Sioux word for red, and *la* simply a diminutive, sometimes used, it would seem, only for euphony. I made a very careful inquiry in regard to the derivation of the word, and obtained only this explanation from the best informed of the Cheyennes and Sioux. In conversation, however, with the Reverend A. S. Riggs recently on this subject, he informed me that the Sioux called any language they understood a *white*, and any they did not understand a *red*, language. In a letter received recently from him he says, "In regard to the red language or red-talkers, I would write Shaw-ee-a-yah, Sha-ee-a-la, Sha-ee-a-na. The third syllable is surely there, though in rapid utterance it may not be plain. Written in Dakota it is

$$\left.\begin{array}{l} \text{Sa; } i.e., \quad \text{ya} \\ \text{Red-talk;} \quad \text{la} \\ \qquad\qquad\quad \text{na} \end{array}\right\}$$ a suffix of not well-determined meaning, *ya* being Santee; *la*, Teton; *na*, Yankton.

This view of the case would seem to derive support from the name given the Crees, though the Teton-Sioux pronounce the word for these Indians *Sha-èya*, as nearly as I can write it phonetically. The usual explanation, and the only one I ever heard of prior to my investigation, viz., that it came from the French word *Chien*, and on account of the Cheyenne soldier being called dog-soldier, is not, I think, correct. I made a special study of the organization of the soldier bands of the different tribes, and found that these Indians gave no greater prominence to this band than do other tribes. (See SOLDIER.) They call themselves Sa-Sis-e-tas, and one Cheyenne claimed that this word meant "the cut or slashed arms;" but I could not confirm this, and was unable to secure any satisfactory explanation of the meaning of the word. It would seem to mean, like most words for tribal names, simply *people* or the *people*. Some of their traditions and myths would seem in a very faint way to point to their location as far east as Niagara Falls, but there is no evidence of migrations westward from any place beyond the head-waters of the Mississippi in Minnesota, near the present site of St. Paul, and nothing in their vocal language or customs which would justify any assertion of a more eastern origin. I was at first inclined to think that the great prominence given to their myths and stories in regard to the first buffalo, some of them commencing with "before we had buffalo," etc., indicated that it must have been at a comparatively recent date that they reached the buffalo country; but as the same stories are told with more exactness, even in regard to the bow and arrow, I was compelled to give up any theory or views I held on the subject and accept as a fact the answer made by a very old man and former chief (he was seventy-nine) to my question as to where they were before they lived in Minnesota: "The Great Spirit made us right there!" Occupying then the country at the head-waters of the Mississippi several hundred years ago, they were slowly forced westward by the Sioux, perhaps southward by the Mandans, the latter being driven from the north by the same power which pressed upon the Sioux, viz., the great Algonquin family, assisted in later years by French arms.

It is more than probable that this migration was due in a measure to and determined by their search for game, as traditional evidence in regard to their relations with the Sioux and Mandans is not clear and conclusive. (Lieutenant Bailey, Fifth Infantry, obtained, from what is considered a reliable source, information which went to show that the Sioux and Cheyennes were never regularly at war, but had frequent misunderstandings and difficulties with each other, and that the Cheyennes met the Mandans two hundred and two years ago, as they —the Cheyennes—crossed the Missouri River. For several years they were at war with the Mandans, after this made peace, and have maintained peaceable relations ever since. Before the whites commenced making war against these tribes they frequently camped together, and many Cheyennes and Mandans intermarried.)

At any rate, they left the wooded country and drifted into the plains, where they were joined by the Arapahoes, and, about two hundred or two hundred and fifty years ago, reached the Missouri, and crossed near the mouth of the Cheyenne or Good River, as they call it. A portion of the Arapahoes, now called Gros Ventres of the Prairie, refused to cross, and going to the northwest joined the Blackfeet. Before commencing this movement it would appear that they lived in permanent villages, contiguous to their cultivated fields, and went out for their annual hunts like the Pawnees, Mandans, and other tribes who live in dirt-lodges. It is impossible to locate the time when they first saw a white man, but I give their tradition for what it is worth. They never had many ponies until after they reached about the present site of Fort Meade, near the Black Hills. The Crows then roamed near the head of the Little Missouri River, and the Powder and Tongue River country. The Kiowas and Apaches were southwest of and near the Black Hills, while the Pawnees occupied the Lower Platte valley. Some claim that the Arapahoes first secured a pony; others, that a Mexican gave one to one of their chiefs. Be that as it may, the Cheyennes, soon after their arrival near the Black Hills, heard of the tribes who had ponies, and of the wild horses on the plains to the south. They gave up farming and apparently went into the business of driving the Crows, Kiowas, and Apaches out of the country, catching wild ponies, and stealing them from the tribes to the south and west who had them. They claim at this time to have had anywhere from three to five thousand lodges. I was informed by an interpreter, who went to the Cheyenne camp some thirty years ago as a trader, that at that time they had about fifteen hundred lodges. Keeping in a northwesterly direction, they drove the Crows before them, took possession of the country, and roamed about near the head-waters of Little Missouri, Powder, Tongue, and Rosebud Rivers, going at times to the mouth of the Rosebud, but not crossing the Yellowstone, except above the mouth of Tongue River. They did not neglect the Kiowas and Apaches, but forced them south, between the Pawnees and numerous other tribes to the east, and the Utes to the west, until they joined the powerful nation of Comanches in the far south. In the mean time the Arapahoes had separated from them (though always remaining friendly and frequently joining them in offensive and defensive warfare), and had gone farther into the mountains. Peace had been made and broken numerous times with the Sioux, but about eighty years ago a permanent and lasting one was effected. As a Cheyenne said to me, "For many years we were at war with the Sioux, particularly the *Wychayélas* (this includes all the bands of the *d* and *n* dialect of Sioux). Peace would be made; they would hold out the pipe to us, and smilingly, and apparently with sincere intentions, say, 'Let us be good friends;' but they time and again treacherously broke their promises. We made a peace, which was unbroken except by one battle about the time we first got guns."

About fifty years since a partial separation of the tribe took place on a tributary of Tongue River, due to a desire of a portion of the tribe to go with a trader who was with them, and also to increase their supply of ponies by trade and theft from the tribes to the south; a permanent separation was not made until some twenty years later. Speaking of their migrations from the Black Hills to the Big Horn Mountains, and from there to the Platte and Arkansas Rivers, Whirlwind, of the Southern Cheyennes, said to me, "We roamed around that country, moving down to the White Earth and Platte Rivers. The time of the great gathering on Horse Creek (near Fort Laramie, Wyoming Territory), when all the tribes got together,—Crows, Snakes, Arapahoes, Sioux,—all up there,—and goods were distributed to us, may be taken as the time when we separated from the Northern Cheyennes (this was between thirty and forty years ago). We drifted apart. We used to come together at times, but not just like one people. We would go north and live with the Northern Cheyennes, and they would come and live with us; but this was only for a short time. We were like two different tribes, only we spoke the same language and had the same habits and customs."

Four chiefs formerly ruled the Cheyenne camp. They were selected for their bravery, wisdom, good judgment, and generosity to the poor. A grand council was called, and a large tent pitched to hold it in; sometimes making this council-lodge out of several common tepees. Four sticks were driven in the ground, inside the lodge, representing the four headmen of the tribe. Four very old men, usually those who at different times had held the position of chief, were selected to go and bring in the four men who were to be made chiefs, if they were not already present. Four pipes were filled and placed on the ground near the sticks; these were taken up and lighted by the old men, and held to the newly-made headmen, who took a few puffs while the pipes were still in the hands of the old men. Should one of the four be killed, die of disease, or, through public sentiment, be, as they say, thrown away, the other three acted, and so on until only one was left, when a council was called, and four others were made. An election, if this can so be named, was never called to elect one or two, but always four. These four decided all matters of minor importance, and they usually selected one of their number to act as head-chief. Any question of vital importance, such as declaring war or making peace, was decided on in a general council. At the election only a few prominent men from each of the soldier bands were present; they had five such bands, viz.: Strong Heart (sometimes called Crazy Dog and Bow String), Dog Fox, Smooth Elkhorn, and Swift's Tail.

Black Pipe, who was bent and withered with the wear and exposure of seventy-nine winters, and who trembled like some leafless tree shaken by the wind, but of sound mind and memory, related to me the following story: " Long ago the old men had a tradition that some disease or disaster killed off nearly all the Cheyennes. Where this happened our tradition does not say; but only a few lodges, some three or four, were left. Our oldest stories located the Cheyennes on a large lake, and a stream running from this fell to a great depth. This waterfall made constantly a loud noise. The stream ran to the east, and was beyond the Big River." (I have some doubt as to whether he meant the Missouri or Mississippi, but am inclined to locate the place as Minnehaha Falls, Minnesota.) " Before falling it was narrow, then suddenly was wide. A great mist rose to the sky, and a loud, rumbling noise was constantly made. One day, when encamped near the lake, two of our young men, handsomely painted and gaudily dressed in skins and furs, approached the camp and said that they had something of importance to communicate, and asked that the camp move to the falls, and put up near the falls a large council-lodge. An unseen force, a mysterious influence, seemed to hang over the camp. The women took down the tepees nervously; the men were restless and impatient; even the dogs were agitated, and gave more trouble in packing than usual. After making the request the two young men disappeared, and were not seen till the camp, laid out in a great circle near the falls, was made. A huge council-lodge was pitched near the falls, and then the two young men, more peculiarly and brilliantly dressed and painted, reappeared. They went to the water's edge, plunged in, and disappeared under the falls,—seemed to go into the solid rock as they vanished from sight,—and the mist rose higher and the noise was louder than before. After some little time of anxious suspense the young men reappeared. They rose up out of the mist and water, and on reaching the shore it was observed that they held their hands closed, and one of the young men had something red in one hand. They repaired to the council-lodge, where, in obedience to the calls of the criers, all the men, women, and children had congregated. The young men asked for large plates (only those made of stone were used at that time), which were brought. One of the young men opened his right hand over the plate, and it was immediately piled high with dried buffalo-meat. The plate was passed round, emptied, and refilled in this way, until all had eaten enough. He then opened his left hand and supplied them with tobacco. The other young man opened his hands. In one was a pipe, in the other seeds of corn, tobacco, melons, etc. After the feast and smoke the young men said that these things had been given to them by an old woman in a cave under the falls, who told them the Great Spirit had left these things with her for their use, and that when they smoked the tobacco they must hold the pipe towards the Great Spirit, who gave it to them, and towards the earth, that supplies the nourishment for the plant.''

Running through all the stories, legends, and myths of the Cheyennes, the number four seems to possess a magical influence for good luck. Four halts are made before they charge in the preliminary march of the Sun-Dance, four times is the covering to the medicine sweat-house raised, and four winters they starved, according to the following story, which was often repeated as a warning against quarrelling: ''Long, long ago an old man and a young man got into a dispute over a buffalo-skin, and the old man knocked the younger one senseless with the leg of the buffalo. Near by was a fire, upon which an old woman had placed a large clay kettle filled with water and buffalo-meat, around which a large number had gathered. When the young man fell the kettle was upset, the water ran out over the fire, creating a great deal of smoke, steam, and dust. During the disturbance the young man disappeared; was not seen again for four winters. At the end of that time he appeared on an eminence near camp, having a buffalo's lower jaw fastened to each heel, and holding a peculiar lance in his hand. As soon as he was discovered he again disappeared behind the hill. In a very short time he appeared on the hill again with a different kind of lance, and a bunch of hair tied to each leg (the long hair that grows on a buffalo). He disappeared a second time, and again reappeared with a small, round war-bonnet, one with no trail, and with a painted stripe across his body, which was naked. He again disappeared, and again reappeared with a different lance in his hand, a buffalo's head for a head-dress, and some of the skin hanging down from this on each side. He then disappeared, and was not seen for four winters. In the mean time gaunt, fierce-eyed, wretched, and cruel starvation seized the Cheyenne camp; all game disappeared; roots and berries did not grow. Some were so hungry that they ate dirt.

''One day in the early spring some little boys were out hunting with hungry eyes, digging with wasted hands for something to eat, and finding some mushrooms, devoured them. Whilst they were eating these the young man appeared to the boys, having in his hand four arrows, and told them that as they were hungry he would give them something to eat. Taking some dried buffalo-chips, he pounded them up and handed the mass to the boys. It was dried meat pounded fine. He then told the boys to go to the camp and tell their people to pitch a big lodge with the door towards the rising sun, and that when this lodge was pitched he would show himself to them; he would go into the lodge and sing to them, and would again bring game into the country about them. The lodge was pitched, the young man appeared, the boys recognized him and cried out, 'There comes the man!' He came towards the lodge, around which the people of the camp crowded, crying and holding their hands up towards the Great Spirit. He walked round the people to the left, and entering the lodge at the door, remained within for four days and nights singing ; at the end of the fourth night he unrolled the arrows which he had in a bundle, and immediately after the buffalo swarmed about camp, bellowing and pawing the earth, some even went into the big lodge, and were there killed. The young man then said that he was going away, but that before he went he wanted a very beautiful young woman who was in the camp. The woman was given to him, and he went away, and has never been seen since. Our people thought he got these sacred arrows from Bear Butte, and that he went back there. Game was plenty, and roots and berries grew in abundance, and many kinds of fruit that before this time we had known nothing about.

"Before going away the young man told us many things, explained to us how to live, and said that, instead of being one of our people, he was a God, and was one of those who had gone into the cave to get the meat, corn, and tobacco. He said that there were people in a far-off country, where the sun rises ; that he made those people, and that they were his ; that after a time we would see and meet with them ; that they would come to our country ; that there were a great many of them, and they would overpower us, would kill our game, eat and destroy our fruit, and finally they would get so numerous that we would find them on every stream. He told us that the big game would come from the north, where it was cold, and ponies from the south, where it was warm. He told us to eat wild fruits and wild game, and in that way we would be healthy and happy. He told us that the people who came from the rising sun would have a different kind of food, and said that this would not be as good for us as what we would find on the prairie."

White Bull, one of the Indians present when the story was told me, here said that it made his heart heavy and sad to think of these things,—the spoliation of his country, the driving away of all the game, and the crowding out of existence of his people. Once they were happy, had a country of their own, game and all that they wanted to make them happy ; now they were poor and broken and separated, and some of their people had been sent away to die in a strange land.

The story of the first white man seen by the Cheyennes, though possessing no special merit, still throws some light upon Indian thought, and gives their version of the treatment the whites received at their hands. "Long ago," said Black Pipe, "the Cheyennes were camped near some lakes beyond the Missouri River ; they made fire with two sticks, which was hard work. The women used porcupine-quills for needles in sewing. We had stone vessels to cook in, stone knives and stone points to our spears and arrows. The Great Spirit had given us the bow and arrow to kill game with. One morning a Cheyenne and his wife, awakening from their sleep, saw a strange creature in their tepee. The woman was frightened, and was about to cry out, but was quieted by her husband, whilst the strange being slowly and feebly arose to a sitting posture. He was so thin that he had scarcely any flesh on his bones, and for clothing had only some moss and grass. He was very near death. This creature looked something like a Cheyenne, but he had a white skin and a strange language. The Cheyenne gave him something to eat, but at first he was so weak and exhausted that his stomach would not hold it, yet after a little while he got stronger. The Cheyenne told his wife to keep the matter a profound secret, as some of the others might kill this strange being, believing he would bring them bad luck ; but, as the camp was moving one day, the others discovered him, and there were a great many talking at once about him and of him. The Cheyenne in whose lodge the man had been found said that he had taken him for a brother, and if any one harmed him he would punish them ; and that he believed the Great Spirit had sent this man to them to do them good. Well! The Cheyenne clothed him, fed him, and so led him back to life. After a time the man learned to talk our language a little, and to make signs so that he could be understood ; and then he told his story. He said he came from the land of the rising sun, and that his people were powerful and numerous, and had many good things which the Cheyennes did not have ; that he, with four others, had started out to trap the beaver, and when on the lake in a boat the wind came up suddenly, over-turned the boat, and drowned the others ; and that he had wan-dered about, living on beaver, until all his clothes had been worn and scratched off, when, in a blind and dazed condition, nearly dead with hunger, he had wandered into their camp and fallen into this lodge. He said his people were fond of beaver fur, and that if we would get some, a number of dog-loads, and give to him, he would go to his people and give them the fur, and get in return needles for the women to sew with, knives to cut with, guns to kill game with, and steel to make a fire with. The furs were given him, and he, with his dog-train, departed, and was gone nearly a year, when one bright, sunshiny day a loud noise, like thunder, was heard near the camp, and on a bluff near the village the white man was seen. He distributed the things he had brought,—knives, needles, steel, and showed us how to use them ; as well as the black powder and hollow iron with which he had made the noise that sounded like thunder. This man wore at the time a red cap and red coat."

At the present time the three bands of Cheyennes are widely sep-arated. There are now about five hundred held as prisoners of war, at or near Fort Keogh, Montana. Some of them are the ones who surrendered there, after the Sioux and Cheyenne war of 1876, and the rest are a part of the band which broke away from their agency in the Indian Territory in the fall of 1878, and were captured in Montana in 1879. These are self-supporting. At Pine Ridge Agency there are about two hundred and fifty, who were recently sent there from the Indian Territory, and at the Cheyenne and Arap-ahoe Agency the agent reports four thousand nine hundred and four for 1881. As a tribe they have been broken and scattered, but in their wild and savage way they fought well for their country, and their history during the past few years has been written in blood. Innocent settlers have suffered cruel outrages at their hands ; women and children have gone down to horrible deaths through their revengeful rage, and burning houses have lighted their pathways of devastation. They in their turn have been hunted like wolves, and shot down like mad dogs, until they are now only a wreck of their former greatness. Perhaps these savage and cruel wars, with their attending horrors, were but the legitimate fruit of bad policy and mismanagement of Indian affairs, or wilful indifference to or misunderstandings of the conditions and circumstances of the Indians, and their relations to the Government, which in times past has too often permitted dishonest agents to be the intermediaries between the Government and them, and through weakness or cowardice has at times paid more heed to the clamors of rapacious miners and settlers of the white race than to treaty obligations and plighted faith with Indians. At any rate, it seems certain that the Cheyennes were at first friendly to the whites, and that they subsequently became one of the greatest terrors of the frontier. The men of the Cheyenne Indians rank as high in the scale of bravery, energy, and tenacity of purpose as those of any tribe I have ever met, and in physique and intellect they are superior to those of most tribes and the equal of any. Under the most demoralizing and trying circumstances they have preserved in a remarkable degree that part of their moral code which relates to chastity, and public sentiment has been so strong with them in regard to this matter that they have been, and are still, noted among all the tribes which surround them for the virtue of their women.

In dress and general appearance they differ but little from the Arapahoes and Sioux. Their vocal language is difficult to acquire, and is noticeable for the rapidity with which orators can articulate in making their speeches and harangues. It literally flows forth a constant and swift stream. I have heard no Indian tongue that compares to it in this respect, except perhaps the Nez Perce. In the degradation of their barbarism, in many of their revolting customs, and in their faith we can find much to condemn, but a close study of their character, at peace and at war, will reveal much to admire. It has often been asserted that the fiendish cruelties and terrible tortures which have at times been inflicted by Indians upon their unfortunate and helpless captives has been, and is, the practice of all Indians. The Cheyennes make war as terrible as possible to their enemies, and when influenced with the passion of revenge, tender infants and pleading women go down before the same war-club that crushed the skulls of dead fathers and husbands ; but there is no good evidence that captives have been burned at the stake, flayed alive, or any other excruciating torture inflicted on prisoners captured by these fierce, war-loving, and enterprising barbarians. Sickening mutilations of the dead have characterized all our Indian wars, and this tribe has, in common with all others, in this way vented their savage and impotent rage.

Chicken. (Domestic.) Make sign for BIRD, sign for RED, and pass the extended right hand over the top of the head, to indicate the comb. The signs for EGG, EAT, and GOOD are also sometimes made.

I have given only a few words of this character, as it will readily be seen that the sign must necessarily be of quite recent origin. Some seem necessary to show how, as well as the ease with which signs are coined and understood.

Deaf-mutes make sign for BIRD, and then scratch left palm with tips of fingers or nails of right hand,—a scratching bird.

Chief. Conception : Elevated ; rising above others and looking down at them. Hold right hand back to right, index finger extended and pointing upwards, others and thumb closed, in front of, higher than, and little to right of right shoulder (hand about on line with front of face) ; raise the hand some little distance higher than head, and as hand is being raised, carry it over in front of face ; when hand reaches highest point, turn index finger so as to bring it vertical, pointing downwards. The index finger is raised, turned and lowered about as an arrow fired straight up in the air would go. The Blackfeet, Flatheads, Crows, and some others raise the index vertically, pointing upwards after the above sign. This movement properly means the head-chief of a tribe. I have seen the signs made for the man who wears the medal to denote the chief, but this only by Indians who were not conversant with gesture speech. Any officer, civil or military, is called a chief ; non-commissioned officers are represented as small chiefs, or by marking lines on arm to denote chevrons. Some Indians claim the conception of this sign to be, " Rising above all others and standing solidly on the ground."

Deaf-mutes swing extended right hand, back up, in horizontal circle in front of body, little higher than shoulder. This means a commander or ruler.

The position of chief was not hereditary, but all other things being equal, the son of a chief secured the position made vacant by the death or age of his father. They elected no one to absolute command, but the general direction was left open to the strongest will and most persuasive voice. Running through every organization was a public sentiment which gave its own tendency to affairs. The government rested upon the popular will, and not upon the arbitrary sway of the chiefs ; but with the Indians as with the Romans, the two professions, " oratory and arms," established men in the highest degree of personal consideration. The form of government necessarily incident to the nomadic and hunter state is that of chief and follower, and formerly the powers of the chief were much greater than at the present day, because they had better opportunities to display the qualities which secured them the position, viz., bravery at war, skill in hunting, and generosity at home ; so that from the position of a leader of braves on the war-path, whose authority extended but little further than to be "foremost in danger, most cunning in strategy, and bravest in battle," they, at times, became despotic rulers of their tribes or bands ; but, even then, excessive indulgence in arbitrary power was sure to be followed by a destructive tide of public opinion, which swept into obscurity or killed the offender. After contact with the whites the tribes frequently had several chiefs for each tribe or band, viz., war chief, trading chief, and council chief ; the war chief being considered as the head-chief. Frequently at the agencies a man is put forward to do the business for the band who really has little influence, and is given the place by the Indians through some real or fancied ability on his part to deal with the agent. I found among all tribes about the same answer to my question as to how one of their number could become a chief, which was, that the greatest warrior, the one who went constantly to war, stole ponies from all the adjacent tribes, got guns and weapons, brought home the trophies of war, was generous, big-hearted, and brave, they would stand in awe of such a person, his word would be law, and all would accord him the position of chief.

Mr. Dunbar says of the Pawnees, that "the government of each band was vested nominally in its chiefs, these ranking as head-chief, second chief, and so on. In ordinary matters the head-chief consulted his own pleasure in directing the affairs of the band. At other times he was assisted by a council called for special deliberation. In the exercise of this authority they were generally mild, but when occasion required, if persons of energy, they could be rigorously severe. Instances have been known where life has been taken to secure obedience. A person persisting in wilful insubordination was pretty sure of at least a sound beating. Many of the chiefs used their influence steadfastly for promoting the welfare of their people, often making great personal sacrifice to that end, and proving themselves in reality the fathers of their people. Such chiefs exerted great power over their bands. On the other hand a chief was sometimes only such in name, being surpassed in actual influence by those of no recognized rank. The office itself was hereditary, but authority could be gained only by acknowledged personal accomplishments. Chiefs, when able, gave presents to their people freely, but were not accustomed to receive any in return. They were also, so far as possible, expected to provide food for the destitute in their bands. Hence a chief frequently had about him a considerable number of persons whom he fed, and in compensation used very nearly as servants. These parasites were usually among the most worthless of the tribe. While under the chief's eye they were tolerable, but in his absence their true nature instantly reappeared. Any stranger who had occasion to visit the tribe was sure on his departure to be waylaid by them, and, if not too strongly guarded, to be, under some specious plea, subjected to heavy tribute ; and, in case of refusal, grossly insulted, and perhaps injured. In such doings their dependence on the chief was used by them as a cloak for most arrant villainies. It is, no doubt, to this class of persons almost entirely due that the Pawnees have acquired so generally among the whites who have been in casual contact with them an unenviable notoriety as a tribe of vagrants and thieves.

"Besides their usual functions, chiefs were often called upon to arbitrate in personal differences between members of their respective bands. Their decision in such cases was accepted as final. The government of the tribe was exercised by the concerted action of the chiefs alone, or assisted by tribal council. Until recently the Xau'-i have held the precedence, their head-chief outranking those of the other bands."

Child. Conception : Parturition and height. Bring the right hand, back outwards, in front of centre of body, and close to it, fingers extended, touching, pointing outwards and downwards ; move the hands on a curve downwards and outwards ; then carry the right hand, back outwards, well out to front and right of body, fingers extended and pointing upwards, hand resting at supposed height of child ; the hand is swept into last position at the completion of first gesture. In speaking of children generally, and, in fact, unless it is desired to indicate height or age of the child, the first sign is all that is used or is necessary. This sign also means the young of any animal. In speaking of children generally, sometimes the signs for different heights are only made.

Deaf-mutes make the combined sign for male and female, and then denote the height with right hand held horizontally.

Indians are very fond of their children, and treat them, as soon as they are able to understand anything, with the greatest respect and consideration. They very rarely whip them, and no children, I firmly believe, are happier than these little dirty, half-clad specimens of humanity.

Indian mothers nurse their children about as long as the child wants or desires this method of nourishment, sometimes until it is four or five years of age, and in the mean time another child may have sprung into existence. This practice accounts, in a measure, for the small number of children usually born to Indian women. Their babies do not cry as much as white babies, as they do not get what they want by simply crying for it. As a rule, they are healthier.

Some tribes have regular story-tellers, men who have devoted a great deal of time to learning the myths and stories of their people, and who possess, in addition to a good memory, a vivid imagination. The mother sends for one of these, and, having prepared a feast for him, she and her little " brood," who are curled up near her, await the fairy stories of the dreamer, who, after his feast and smoke, entertains them for hours. Many of these fanciful sketches or visions are interesting and beautiful in their rich imagery, and have been at times given erroneous positions in ethnological data.

Chippewa. There is no well-known generally-used tribal sign for the Chippewas, but I have seen several different ones employed by different tribes to denote them.

The Assinaboines call them the Bad Talkers, and sometimes the same as the Crees,—" Rabbit People."

The Sisseton Sioux call them " the people by the fast-running water," or, " people who live near the falls," and, as a tribal sign, simply make a wavy, tremulous motion with right hand.

The Uncapapa Sioux call them Sore Faces, and I think the Cheyennes call them " the people who have long hair, and who live in the woods by the lakes."

Appropriate signs for each of these names are made, and the location of the tribe usually added.

Mr. Charles H. Beaulieu informs me that the Chippewas, or, more properly, the Ojibways, received their name " from the peculiar style of moccasins once worn by them, and which were gathered or laced in folds on the face of the moccasin."

The country bordering on the St. Lawrence at the time of Champlain's arrival at Quebec (1607) was occupied by bands of Algonquins, who were engaged in a bitter war with the Iroquois Confederacy. An alliance was made with the French, and by this means the extension of the Iroquois Confederacy to the north was checked. In their emigration westward from La Pointe, on Lake Superior, the Pillager band seems to have been in advance, and they reached Leech Lake, Minnesota, about one hundred and fifty years ago. The name of this band, like most of the others of the Chippewas, is of modern origin ; it means " taking openly," and came from robbing a trader of his goods. The other bands, known as White Earth, Red Lake, Pembina, etc., have received their names from the French, or from the lands occupied by them when treaties have been made.

In their migration westward the Chippewas not only had to contend with the Sioux, but with their relatives, the Sacs and Foxes, who joined the Sioux against them.

" The war between the two tribes was bloody in the extreme, and carried on with all the cruelty of savage warfare. Captives were taken and burnt by fire. This custom originated in the following manner : A noted warrior of the Ojibways was once taken captive by his own nephew, son to his sister, who had been captured and married among the Foxes. The nephew, to show his people his utter disregard to any tie of relationship with the Ojibways, planted two stakes in the ground, and taking his captive by the arm, tied his feet and hands to the stakes, remarking ' that he wished to warm his uncle by a good fire.' He then built up a large fire, and after roasting one side of his victim, he turned the other to the blaze ; when the naked body had been burnt to a blister, he untied him, and letting him loose, told him ' to go home, and tell the Ojibways how the Foxes treated their uncles.'

" The uncle recovered from his fire-wounds, and in a future excursion succeeded in capturing his nephew. He took him to the village of the Ojibways, where he tied him to a stake, and taking a fresh elk-skin, on which a layer of fat had purposely been left, he placed it over a fire until it became one immense blaze, and then throwing it over the naked shoulders of his nephew, remarked, 'Nephew, when I was in your village you warmed me before a good fire ; now I, in return, give you a mantle to warm your back.' The elk-skin, covered with fat, burnt furiously, and crisping, lighted around the body of his nephew a dreadful mantle that soon consumed him. This act was again retaliated by the Foxes, and death by fire soon became customary with both tribes." (*Warren.*)

Their traditions would seem to indicate that at first they were at peace with the Sioux, but, as they say, "trouble commenced about a woman." One was killed,—they cannot say whether by the Chippewas or Sioux,—but it led to a war which was prosecuted with an intense bitterness, even for savages, with scarcely a respite until (a few years since) the Government authorities interfered. As one of the chiefs said to me, "The Great Father finally took notice of our wars, and called a council, not only of the Sioux and my people, but of the Winnebagoes, Sacs and Foxes, and Menomonees, and said we must stop. He set apart our country. Since then there have been wars, but we have gained no benefit. Before this forced peace we secured the country. We have had no wars for about ten years, through the President giving us agricultural implements. He said, ' Lay aside scalping-knives and guns, and take ploughs and hoes and till the soil !' We are pleased with the new life ; we are at peace, and visit one another ' as brothers' !"

Their agency in Minnesota is located at White Earth, though there are sub-agencies and schools at the reservations of Leech Lake and Red Lake. The Pembina band drifted into the prairie country some years since, and adopted many of the ways of the Plains Indians. They are located at present on unceded lands, near Turtle Mountain, and receive, I believe, no assistance from the Government.

The agent in 1880 reported three thousand five hundred acres of land under cultivation, but this, of course, includes land cultivated by the French half-breeds, or mixed bloods, who are very numerous. He gives a total population of six thousand one hundred and twenty-six in his report for 1881.

This reservation possesses greater possibilities in an agricultural way than any I have ever seen.

At Mackenzie, Michigan, the agent reports a total population of nine thousand seven hundred and ninety-five. The Menomonees, at Green Bay, and Chippewas, at La Pointe, Wisconsin, are given at six thousand six hundred and nine.

Colonel C. H. Beaulieu, at present a trader at the White Earth Agency, who was born of Indian and French parentage at Lake De Flambeau, Wisconsin, in 1811, and has spent his life among these people as an employé of the American Fur Company, and in other capacities, informed me that the Ojibway language was spoken from Montreal to the Rocky Mountains, and, spreading north, found a kindred tongue among the Esquimaux. This seems, however, to be a matter of some doubt, as will be seen from the following extract of a letter from a son of Colonel Beaulieu, to whom I sent a partial vocabulary of the Esquimaux language:

"I see no similarity in the words or between the languages of the Esquimaux and the Ojibway Indians, judging from the slip you enclosed, and which I return, excepting in the endings of words, or nouns, in *nah, uk, ok, ing, ick,* and *ock,* and in this list of Esquimaux words those expressing the meaning of an object in one language is entirely different in the other, both in endings and otherwise. The captain of the Red Lake United States Indian Police called on me to-day. He is an Indian who has travelled extensively among the Northwestern Indian tribes. I questioned him as to the various bits of information you were seeking, but have obtained nothing new. He has been to York Factory, on the Hudson's Bay, and has seen Indians there speaking the Ojibway tongue, but so corruptly as to be barely understood by him. He says that the York Factory Indians do not understand the Esquimaux. It may be possible that the Indian language used at the Factory may be a connecting-link between the Ojibway and Esquimaux language.

"There is a branch of the Ojibways living north of the Lake of the Woods, called by these Ojibways 'O-mush-ke-go,' or 'inhabitants of the swamp,' though at no very great distance from these Indians their language, in accent, and in some words, is different. The 'Boisforts,' residing in this State (northeast), are also Ojibways; still their accent is different. As I have remarked before, the endings of some words in Esquimaux are much like others in Ojibway, and it may be possible that Roman Catholic missionaries at York Factory may discover something resembling both the Ojibway and Esquimaux in the language of the Indians among whom they are stationed."

Colonel Beaulieu claimed that they had only used ponies for about twenty-five years. The camp baggage was formerly moved by the women, and when it was impossible to use canoes for this purpose, only six or seven miles would be made in a day. As few moves were made as possible; but the seasons demanded certain changes of their camps,—in the spring, to the maple groves, where the sugar was made; after this to the lakes and streams, for fishing; and in the fall they scattered out to the hunting- and trapping-grounds. Some fishing was, of course, done in winter; but an attempt was always made to provide in advance a winter's supply of food.

These Indians were not only numerous, but were, from training and inherited qualities, good at fighting in a wooded country, and being allies and employés of the French, they had fire-arms long before the Sioux. They admitted the superiority of the latter on the prairie, but claimed an equal, if not greater, advantage and skill on the lakes and rivers in their canoes. As the Ojibways moved westward in search of game and peltries, assisted by the current of French enterprise, and pressed by the Iroquois, they never mixed much with other tribes, but they received a strong infusion of French and English blood, and their present advanced state in agriculture is no doubt in a great measure due to this. They use quite extensively reed matting for the sides of the summer lodge, and birch bark for the roof. The matting can be easily transported, and it is claimed that mosquitoes do not infest these lodges as much as other dwelling-places of either skin, canvas, or wood. Even those who have comfortable frame and log buildings use these lodges in summer, not only as a protection from the flies and mosquitoes, but to force the vermin by starvation from their houses.

The striking characteristics of this tribe seem to be that they make sugar ; are particularly fond of dogs, both as beasts of burden and as meat ; do not pass the pipe when smoking ; possess wonderful skill in the use of birch bark ; have no Sun-Dance ; never kill ponies at the death of an individual, and do not put gun or pipe with the remains ; are especially fond of camping near lakes and streams where they can get fish ; are very skilful in the manufacture and management of canoes ; and are very rich in mythological lore, there being scarcely an object in the animal or vegetable world possessing a marked peculiarity which has not some elaborate explanation.

The following story told of the "diver duck" illustrates this : Nanaboojou, who was conceived by his mother exposing her person to the north wind, was a God (and, of course, in the form of an Ojibway), and could converse with all animate and inanimate objects, and though, according to their belief, he did not exactly create, yet could effect change of forms. Nanaboojou was living with his grandmother, and having only a bow and arrow, was forced to devise many cunning ways to secure game ; so he made a kettle-drum similar to the one now used by the Ojibways, and knowing the birds could not resist its music, commenced beating it. All the water-fowl heard it and flew down into the lodge through the smoke-hole in the top, and seated themselves in a circle round the fire, like so many Ojibways,—geese, ducks, swans, all kinds,—on each side of Nanaboojou and his grandmother. Then Nanaboojou told them that they must dance,—round and round as the Ojibways do now,—but they must keep their eyes closed under penalty of having them forever red. The birds commenced dancing as instructed, and as they passed by Nanaboojou's grandmother she picked out the fattest and best, quickly wrung their necks, and threw them behind her. The little "diver" opened his eyes, saw what was being done, and gave the alarm, when they all flew for the aperture in the top of the lodge. In the rush the little "diver" was knocked down, and attempted to run out at the door of the lodge, when Nanaboojou quickly put his foot on his back, and cursed him for giving the alarm, saying, "For your treachery and disobedience, you and all after you shall have broken backs and red eyes." This God could talk to all things, and they could talk to him,—the bright little flowers softly and sweetly with perfumed whispers, the nodding grasses, the soughing trees,— either gloomily or happily, as the clouds of sadness drearily oppressed, or the glad sunshine brightened and made their hearts happy. The little birds sang to him, and he understood the sentiment of their beautiful songs ; the butterfly's gay summer whisper, the fierce scream of the eagle, and the terrible roar of the Thunder-bird,—these were not merely sounds to him, but language which he clearly and fully understood. The bark of the red willow was colored by his blood ; in fact, all that is peculiar in nature was made so by him,—changed through his pleasure or anger.

There are, I think, few well-authenticated cases of cannibalism on the part of our Indians, but the two following cases of the Ojibways, given by Mr. H. R. Schoolcraft, are worthy of notice : " In 1851 a party of Chippewas returned to their camp near the Winnebago agency, bringing with them five Sioux scalps. The Indians being now assembled, they proceeded with their dance ; the scalps were hung up on sticks set in the ground, and men, women, and children danced around them ; occasionally the women and children would take a scalp and carry it round the ring. This dance was continued for hours with great excitement. One of the Chippewas killed his man with a spear ; finding it difficult to extricate his weapon on account of the barb, he cut out a piece of flesh with his knife and brought it home, still adhering to the spear ; this flesh was cut in pieces and given to the boys, who ate it raw."

Still more revolting and horrible is the story told of the practice in very old times. The account says, " Poisoning in those days was a common mode of revenging an injury. These Indians, on a small scale, have had their ages of Medicis, Borgias, and poisons, as well as the whites, and it is told that it required but the slightest cause for a person to draw upon himself the displeasure of a medicine-man and die of his poison. Instances occurred where the poisoners are known to have dug up their victims and invite the relatives to a feast on the body. This horrid ceremony was got up in utter darkness, and not till the friends of the deceased had received their share of the feast were torches suddenly lighted and they became aware of the nature of the banquet. Fear of the poisoner's power and vengeance would constrain them to eat what was placed before them. This was a usual sacrificial feast to the spirit of the poison."

I have heard of cases in recent years where starvation led some tribes in the North to feed upon their fellows, but I have never been able to find any evidence which would justify the assertion that it was practised at any other times.

These Indians use some few signals, but have no special system or code, and their knowledge of gesture speech is limited.

Deaf-mutes are rare, but with these they claimed that the immediate kinsfolk invented a system of signs, and they also stated that in some instances the deaf-mutes had learned to read their own language from the lips of those who talked to them. Though it cannot be said that there is any perfected gesture speech among them, still many of their signs are so natural that no difficulty is experienced in making ordinary wants known in this way. The peculiar nature of their relations with the Plains Indians, and the great geographical area covered by their own vocal language, has prevented the necessity of perfecting or learning the sign language, etc. Some few bands, like the Pembinas, who have been thrown more with other tribes, are fairly good sign-talkers. The great advantage Indians have in pantomime language is their close observation and excellent memories. As they have no good means of recording events, they cultivate and develop these qualities. As White Cloud, their head-chief, said to me, "We only use a few signs, but have no particular trouble," and illustrated his meaning in this way: "Suppose two Indians of different tribes were seated on the ground and a white man approached them, he would see no difference; but if an Indian approached, he would detect at a glance the difference, and probably know to what tribes they each belonged."

The manufacture of maple sugar seems to be the women's work, and is about the only article which these Indians produce for sale and barter. I saw and tasted some that had been made and put up in their queer-shaped bark vessels, and found it very good indeed. They tap the tree with an axe, use a chip for a spout, and catch the sap in a rectangular-shaped vessel made of birch bark, fastened at the bent-up ends with basswood-bark strings. The water is evaporated from the sap by boiling in kettles, and the sugar is both grained and caked. Formerly the evaporation was effected by dropping heated rocks into stone and bark vessels. As I have stated, birch bark with these Indians takes the place of buffalo-skin, par-flèche, used by the Plains tribes in the manufacture of boxes and vessels of all kinds.

Chop. Bring right hand back to right, and downwards, well out in front of right breast, fingers extended, touching, and pointing to front; strike with the lower edge of the hand, mostly by elbow action, downwards and to left; then carry the hand in front of left breast, palm downwards and to left, fingers extended and pointing to front; strike with lower edge to right and downwards. The hand is held in these motions at about the angle an axe is held when chopping. Sometimes the sign for TREE is made, the left forearm held in a vertical position to represent it, and the right hand is moved towards the left elbow, as though about to cut or chop it with lower edge. Indians also frequently represent the chopping with both hands.

The latter is the deaf-mute sign.

Cigar. Make sign for TOBACCO; then bring extended index fingers alongside of each other in front of body, others and thumb closed, backs of hands about outwards, index fingers horizontal; by rotary motion move the index fingers one about the other. Sometimes the sign for SMOKE is added, and the sign for SMALL to denote a cigarette.

Deaf-mutes place the tip of extended right index in mouth and imitate the smoking of a cigar.

Citizen. Make sign for WHITES. I have also seen the sign for BY ITSELF made after white, seeming to convey the idea of a white man going where he pleased,—nothing to interfere with or obstruct his movements; this by Indians who knew soldiers had to go where they were ordered.

Clean-Handed. Conception: Great Spirit has no blood on hands. Bring extended hands, palms up, high above head, about over shoulders; make sign for BLOOD and sign for No. This movement properly means, clear of the crime of taking human life in violation of their laws.

Close. Conception: Drawn near. Bring right hand, back to right, fingers curved and touching, thumb resting on index finger, well out in front of body, hand about height of shoulder; draw the hand in towards the body and slightly downwards.

Very close, the hand is drawn near the body. Close in the sense of close together, near to one another, crowded together, would be represented by sign for SMALL.

Deaf-mutes hold extended left hand in front of body, back out, holding right, back out, beyond left; bring it near it.

Cloud. Bring the extended hands, held horizontally, backs up, well in front and somewhat higher than the head, sides of index fingers touching; carry right hand to right and downwards on a curve, left to left and downwards on curve, so that hands will in this movement be parallel to vault of the heavens; terminating movement when hands are little lower than shoulders. Frequently only one hand is used.

Deaf-mutes indicate the arch of the heavens, and then rotate the hands one about the other, holding them above head to denote the clouds.

The keen eyes of an Indian can detect by a little scrutiny whether the clouds are rising or falling; if falling, they reason that they will be pressed together, and it will rain; if rising, they will scatter, and the sunshine will break through. Clouds are frequently used metaphorically to represent anxiety or trouble. The clouds press down, the gloom of danger, of trouble, or of loss is near; they rise, fears vanish.

I once heard an Indian say, in regard to a treaty which gave away some of his country, " The clouds pressed down close above me, and the earth seemed to tremble when the first paper was signed."

Coal. Make sign for HARD or ROCK, for FIRE, and for GOOD.

Deaf-mutes make signs for BLACK METAL and FIRE.

Coat. Bring the hands in front of and a little over right and left breasts, palms towards body, index fingers and thumbs well spread, other fingers closed, index fingers nearly horizontal, close to and parallel to breasts; carry hands downwards simultaneously, the inner surface of spread thumbs and index fingers near to body, keeping index fingers nearly horizontal in this movement, and terminating it when at about lower part of waist. This is the general way of representing any wearing apparel; *i.e.*, the spread thumb and index passed over and near surface of body where clothing is worn. Sometimes the other fingers are not closed, and this is the way deaf-mutes represent wearing apparel. In the case of a coat, they also note with index fingers the outline of the garment. The sign I have given also represents a shirt ; usually, however, the color or material is given to determine whether shirt or coat.

Coffee. Conception : Grinding coffee in mill. Hold the extended left hand, back down, in front of body; bring the closed right hand a few inches over left palm, little finger nearest and parallel to it ; move the right hand in small horizontal circle, representing the turning of the crank, which causes the grinding of the coffee.

Some years since, before the general introduction of coffee-mills, the usual sign was to hold right hand, back nearly to right, thumb pressing against first joint of nearly-extended and about horizontal index fingers, others closed, so that thumb-nail will leave little more than tip of index visible. This is the sign for LITTLE, and is used for a grain of any kind also.

I have sometimes, but very rarely, seen the signs for KETTLE, for putting water in it, for fire under it, for drink and good, added. This would hardly be necessary, and I mention it merely to show the ease with which signs can be so elaborated upon as to clearly show their meaning. I have also seen the signs for DRINK, WATER, and BLACK made. Indians are very fond of coffee. The berry is browned, usually in a frying-pan, then pounded up or ground in a mill if they have one, put in the kettle to boil, and sufficient sugar put in to sweeten it. As a rule they do not drink it very strong.

Deaf-mutes make the same signs.

Cold. Bring closed hands in front of and close to body, height of shoulder, and a few inches apart, body slightly bent and shoulders drawn in ; give a tremulous motion to hands and arms, as though shivering from the effects of the cold.

Deaf-mutes make the same signs.

Collect. This is used usually in the sense of gathering together ponies, cattle, supplies of meat, robes, etc., which we would call collecting. The Indians would express it differently, as they do not have much of a leaning towards collecting or accumulating. In regard to buffalo-meat, they would say they made a surround, cut up the meat, packed it into camp, dried it, piled it up in packages (they use folded raw-hide sacks, called par-flèches, to put in or store many articles as well as dried meat), and any other collecting would be explained in some similar way.

Deaf-mutes indicate the gathering together by both hands.

Color. Hold the extended left hand, back up, in front of body, fingers pointing to front ; bring the extended right hand, back up, and rub with inner surface of fingers up to first joints the back of left hand, fingers of right hand pointing to left. This sign is sometimes used for BLACK, but, as a rule, it means simply some color. It is customary to rub the cheek to indicate a red color with nearly all tribes, and for all other colors to point to or touch something the color desired to be represented. Blue is sometimes represented by pointing to clear sky. Gray is denoted by making sign for BLACK and WHITE, and then usually adding sign for MIXED.

Deaf-mutes indicate black by touching the eyebrow ; red, touch the lips ; white, the shirt-bosom ; and for the rest, indicate in the same way as with Indians; *i.e.*, point to or touch something possessing the color.

Column. (Troops.) Make signs for WHITES, for SOLDIER, then bring hands, backs up, in front of body, fingers touching and partially curved, second joints about on line with back of hand, right hand near the body, left in front of right and a trifle higher, hands about six inches apart and edges pointing to the front and slightly upwards ; move the hands to front with gentle jerks. Indians, as a rule, never march in column or in any set or special formation, unless the custom of single or Indian file can be so called.

Though the above sign is used to denote the approach of soldiers, yet generally, in saying the enemy's soldiers are approaching, turn the back of hands outwards, hold the hands farther from body, and bring them in towards it. The hands are here fixed as in KILL.

The coming up of a thunder-storm, the looming up of the dark clouds, is represented in the same way.

Some Indians hold hands, extended fingers pointing to front, back of left to left, right to right, right hand few inches to right and rear of left, and then move the hands to denote a column moving.

Comanche. Conception : Snake. Hold the right hand, back up, well to front of body opposite right shoulder and height of waist, index finger extended pointing to front, others and thumb closed ; draw the hand to rear, and by wrist action give a vibratory or sinuous motion to index finger. The Southern Indians draw the hand to the rear, while in the North they push it to front to denote a Snake, or Comanche.

Mr. Healy, of Montana, a gentleman who has had much practical experience with Indians, claims that for the Comanches the above sign is made, but on its completion the hand is turned over and the same gesture repeated, to convey the idea of *another Snake.*

Vocally, these people call themselves by a word which signifies " People," or " The People," and claim that the name Comanche was given them by the Mexicans. They are divided into five bands, viz. :

1. Pene-teth-kas, Honey- or sugar-eaters.
2. Cas-cho-teth-kas, Buffalo-eaters.
3. No-co-nys, Moving in a circle.
4. Yäp-pä-reth-käs, Root-eaters.
5. Qua-ha-das, Antelope band.

Mr. E. L. Clarke, the interpreter at their agency, furnished me the following information : " The Yäp-pä-reth-käs band of Comanches came from the Rocky Mountains, north of the head-waters of the Arkansas River, about one hundred and fifty or two hundred years ago, which country they inhabited with the Shoshones. They are without doubt of the same origin as the latter tribe. I have not been able to determine from the information thus far obtained the exact area of country these Indians occupied at so remote a time. They are indefinitely located in traditions as north of the head-waters of the Arkansas River.

"There are a few Snake Indians with the Yäp-pä-reth-kās; and one, a very old man, with the Qua-ha-das band.

"Straight Feather, who is about seventy years old, says his father was a Snake Indian, and his mother one-half Pawnee and one-half Pen-a-teth-kas. He was born a short distance south of the Colorado River, in Texas, and is considered as belonging to the Pen-a-teth-kas. At what period of time the Pen-a-teth-kas band of Comanches separated themselves from the main body is not definitely known, but evidently long anterior to the migration of the main body southward, as there is a well-authenticated tradition that the Pen-a-teth-kas had wandered off a great distance and were entirely lost to the other bands, and that long afterwards they were discovered by the Yäp-pä-reth-kās and Qua-had-da warriors, who went to Mexico on raiding expeditions, at which time the Pen-a-teth-kas and No-co-nies bands were together, occupying the same region of country. They were, however, distinct bands, and both were large and formidable.

"The Qua-ha-das occupied a region south of the Yäp-pä-reth-kās, but still in the Rocky Mountain country.

"The original name of that band was 'Quä-he-huk-e,' meaning 'Back shade,' because they inhabited the plains, or a country without timber or trees, where no shade could be had, and during hot weather they shaded their faces by turning their backs to the sun.

"A small band of Comanches, called 'Ya-nim-ma,' or Liver, supposed to have derived their name from their fondness for liver, were also with the Pen-a-teth-kas and No-co-nies in Mexico, and no doubt separated from the main body about the same time with the Pen-a-teth-kas, and were also a separate and distinct band. But few of these are now left, and they are merged with the other bands.

"It is a generally-accepted idea with all or most of the Comanches that they came from the Northwest, and it is highly probable that if the fact could be ascertained, which I have no doubt a thorough research would establish, it would be shown that the Shoshones, Comanches, and Utes were formerly one and the same people,—a conclusion based upon the similarity of their language, habits, style of dress, and physical characteristics,—and upon the undisputed knowledge that these tribes, at no very remote period of time, occupied the same region of country in the Rocky Mountain range.

"The Comanches call the Snake Indians 'Ah,' meaning Hour.

"There was another band of the Comanches, 'Tit-cha-ken-ah,'— which means Sew, as with a needle. This band was originally with the Shoshones, but are now with and form a portion of the Yäp-pä-reth-kās.

"Ta-ba-nau-a-ca and his brothers are descendants of this band, but are known now altogether as Yäp-pä-reth-kās.

"A long time ago the Utes captured a number of women belonging to the Tit-cha-ken-ah band, who afterwards became the wives of their captors, and from whom sprang a band of Utes called 'Yap-pi Utes.' This band is not as large as the 'Sau-nah' Utes, known as the Rosin or Gum Utes.

"I have not had opportunity to make sufficient inquiry to arrive at any satisfactory conclusion as to the time when these women were captured, nor how long the Comanches have been at war with the Utes, but from such as I have been able to make I am led to believe that the capture was long anterior to the migration of the Comanches southward, and that feuds and wars have been of long standing between them and the Utes.

"The Kiowas say that they have been at war with the Utes from time immemorial, and never have had enough intercourse with them to learn anything of their language, and cannot communicate with them excepting by signs and through the medium of the Comanche tongue.

"One of the Comanches, a brother of Ta-ba-nau-a-ca, says he once met a Ute on the prairie, who spoke to him in Comanche, and asked him to make friends, but while they were having this friendly talk the hostile bands of the Utes and Comanches, to which each respectively belonged, came in sight and commenced firing, which put an end to their conversation. This Ute spoke good Comanche. This is not, however, an uncommon or remarkable circumstance, considering the fact that the Comanche language is more or less spoken and understood by other Northern tribes."

The Shoshones or Snakes in the North claim that the Comanches left them and went South in search of game and ponies, but they can give no idea of the time of the separation, while the Comanches claim that the Snakes are an offshoot from their tribe ; but when or where they left they do not know. I do not think the Utes can be classed linguistically with the Comanches.

The Pen-e-teth-kas and affiliated bands first had a reservation in Texas, near the present site of Fort Griffin, on the Clear Fork of the Brazos River. The main body of the Comanches roamed at large, going as far north with their villages as the Arkansas River. They frequently came near Camp Cooper, where they stole stock, killed white people, etc. The Texans charged these depredations to the Indians on the reservation, and the feeling against them became so strong and bitter that, in 1859, they were moved out of Texas under a military escort and brought to the present site of the Wichita Agency, where they were turned over to what was known as the superintendency of Arkansas. Mr. Horace P. Jones, Government interpreter at Fort Sill, Indian Territory, was then a guide with the troops commanded by the late General George H. Thomas, and he informed me that the Caddos, Tonkaways, Wacos, Keechies, a few Delawares, and some Shawnees started from their agency at mouth of Clear Fork of the Brazos River at about the same time, and joined the Comanches on Red River, some fifty miles below the present site of Fort Sill, and went to Wichita Agency. It was not until 1874 that the last of the roving bands of Comanches were finally subdued and placed on a reservation, where many have begun farming.

Mr. Bancroft, in his valuable work, associates the Comanches with the Apaches. In many customs, manners, habits, and in language they are entirely different. I found no evidence that the Comanches ever tattooed the face and breast. They have for many years used the ordinary conical skin lodge ; in fact, have done so since a period antedating all their traditions. The system of enumeration is much the same as with other tribes. In knowledge of the stars and constellations they are about equal to other Indians.

Their division of time corresponds to that of the nations surrounding them, but, like all the Shoshone family, they keep no account of individual ages.

Their form of government is about like that of all the Plains Indians. There is no special form of election to the position of chief ; public opinion, the sentiment of the camp, elevates those specially distinguished in war to the highest position of power. No council is called for this election other than that held on the battle-field. Their councils are held, as with other tribes, to discuss and decide matters of importance. No special laws are made, and no special dignity is attached to the office of the camp-crier, who promulgates the decision of the council, or the orders of the chief, or imparts general information. Their sweat-lodges are made as I have described them. In former times all the Comanches wore the scalp-lock, and considered it necessary as a mark of manhood. Now it is by no means a universal custom. Some of them only tie up one side of the hair, and in battle they frequently allow both sides to drop loosely. They call the sun " The Great Father," and the earth Mother, and consider the former as the source of all power. They do not have an annual Sun-Dance, but do have religious dances to propitiate the Great Spirit in the sun. Mutilation is not practised in these dances. They do not eat dogs. The language is easy to acquire, and may be considered the court language of the Southwest.

The Comanches are considered superior to the other Indians that range over the same areas as themselves, and, though they are proud and intractable in many ways, yet the agent informed me that they were much more reasonable and easy to get along with than the Kiowas and Apaches. They have long been noted for their great skill in riding ; and their war-parties, in former times, scoured the country from the Black Hills, Dakota, to the interior of Mexico. They are a little taller, and have better physiques than their kinsfolk, the Shoshones.

In a conversation we had concerning their beliefs in a future state of existence, one of their chiefs said to me, " The way we know there is a future state is that sometimes a man dies for two days and goes to the land of the setting sun. There he finds a cut bank, and far beyond and below sees the white lodges of a Comanche village. The denizens of the village meet him at the cut bank, and tell him he is not really dead, and on this account cannot enter, but must return ; and they point out where his kinsfolk are camped. He comes back to life and tells where he has been, and what he has seen. Sometimes as the sun is sinking in the west the sky is filled with a beautiful red light. We look at it, and our hearts are made glad, for we know that this is caused by the dust raised by the dead and gone Comanches, who are having a great dance.''

The Comanches were once a very powerful nation, numbering, probably, ten thousand souls; but through wars, smallpox, cholera, and other diseases, they have been reduced in such degree that the agent, in his report for 1881, gives a total population of only one thousand five hundred and one.

With the Cheyennes, Kiowas, and Kiowa Apaches they have been generally at peace during the last seventy-five years, and during that time have made and broken peace several times with the Sioux.

Their most bitter wars have been with the Utes, Pawnees, Sacs, and Foxes, and the whites (including Mexicans). In these wars they have practised the cruelties and hellish barbarities of savages, and yet it is said of them that ''though formal and suspicious to strangers, they are hospitable and social to those whom they consider their friends.'' Among Indian tribes they have the reputation of being brave warriors.

Comb. Bring the right hand, back to right, near upper part and side of head, fingers partially curved and close to hair ; bring the hand down as though combing hair over side of head. The Sioux, Cheyennes, and other Indians used porcupine-tails for combs. It is claimed that the Crows do not use combs, and it is on this account that they are more lousy than other Indians.

Deaf-mutes make the same sign.

Come. Carry right hand, back out, index finger extended and pointing upwards, others and thumb closed, well out in front of body (or towards person you wish to cause to approach, and this should be observed, as a rule, in regard to the imaginary positions of absent persons or objects in all conversations in gesture speech) ; draw the hand rather sharply in towards the body, lowering it slightly. The index finger is usually kept elevated, though it is sometimes curved as the hand is brought in towards body.

The sign is used in the sense of '' come here ;'' '' you go and tell him to come here,'' and emphasis is added by bringing right hand against back of left as in ARRIVE HERE.

Deaf-mutes strike left wrist to call attention, and then make similar motions.

Come Between. The left hand represents the remote object and is held well out ; the right hand passes between left and body. The subject under consideration will naturally suggest the proper signs.

Deaf-mutes indicate similarly. Their sign for BETWEEN, however, is to lay the lower edge of right hand on curved surface between spread thumb and index of left hand.

Come into View. Indicate by gesture whatever may have appeared, and then hold left hand, back out, fingers extended, touching, and pointing to right, about eight inches in front of lower part of face, left forearm about horizontal; carry the right hand under and in front of left, back outwards and downwards, index finger extended, others and thumb closed, index pointing upwards, and by raising right hand place its palm against back of left, the right index appearing above left hand. To say "a man appeared behind a bluff, looked at me, and then disappeared," make sign for BLUFF, then the above sign (still holding left hand as in bluff), then the sign for LOOK; this sign made with right in position outwards from left, first and second fingers pointing towards face; then suddenly drop the right hand. Here the part of right hand seen above left represents the proportion of body exposed, all that can be seen from the position of the observer.

Deaf-mutes make similar sign.

Commence. Make sign for PUSH. This is used in the sense of "commence work," "make an effort," etc., and is used more in the imperative sense than any other sign. As I have stated, the usual way would be to say, "I think it good that you should do so," etc.

Deaf-mutes make a similar sign.

Conceal. See HIDE.

Congress. Make sign for PRESIDENT'S HOUSE, sign for WHITE CHIEF, repeating this several times, sign for BRING, from several different directions, and then sign for SITTING IN COUNCIL.

Most Indians now understand something of our form of government; but, as a rule, they consider that the President calls the chiefs, the headmen of the nation, together, as their chiefs call a council in their own camp.

Deaf-mutes make sign for UNITED STATES and LAW PERSONS.

Cook. Make sign for WORK, for KETTLE, for FIRE, for EAT; sign for AFTERWARDS or BY AND BY sometimes made before EAT, and at times sign for WOMAN is first made.

Indians, as a rule, are more careful in regard to the cleanliness of their cooking utensils than their usually dirty and sometimes filthy personal condition would indicate. In former years stone, clay, and other kinds of vessels were used, many of which would not withstand the action of fire. With these, heated stones were put in the liquid contained in the vessel, and in this way articles were cooked.

Indians now use the large iron camp-kettles issued by the agent and sold by traders, and nearly every article of food is cooked by boiling. Meat is seldom fried. Should they desire a change, or when away from their camps, hunting, etc., the meat is roasted by hanging on a stick near the fire. In this way it retains its juices, and is wonderfully good. Bread is usually cooked by frying in grease. As Indians can get along very well, when in a wild state, on meat dried in the sun, and such berries and roots as they can find, it is easy to comprehend how the Plains Indians can subsist quite comfortably on the treeless prairies.

Copulate. Hold left hand, back nearly downwards, in front of body, fingers extended, touching, and pointing to right and front, thumb extended and pointing upwards ; bring the right hand, index finger extended, others and thumb closed, back of hand to right front and a trifle downwards, and thrust index finger between thumb and index of left hand, side of index touching the hollow between thumb and left index, backs of closed fingers of right hand striking briskly against left palm ; repeat motion two or three times. This is the sign used in describing the act with all animals. There are several others, all suggestive, but this is the most common. Indian men and women talk freely together on all such subjects.

Deaf-mutes place the palm of extended right on back of extended left, or place the palmar surface of right index on that of left, right index back up, left back down.

Corn. Conception : Shelling the corn. Bring the closed left hand, back to left, in front of body, thumb extended and resting on index finger ; bring right hand, back to right, fingers closed, thumb partially elevated, alongside of left hand, placing the ball of the thumb of right hand on back of left thumb near its base ; twist the right hand, by wrist action, to the right and downwards, keeping the ball of right thumb pressed against back of left until in its movement it slips off with rather of a snap against the index finger of right hand ; repeat motion. Sometimes signs for WORK, for "dropping corn in the ground as in planting," for GROW (making this higher), and then hold compressed right hand alongside of and touching elevated left forearm, in one or two positions, to represent ears of corn on the stalk. Ordinarily the first is sufficient, and this used to denote any grain fed to animals.

Mr. Dunbar says of the Pawnees that dried corn was boiled alone, or with beans, forming a sort of succotash ; when thus prepared, buffalo-tallow was put in freely to season it. Matured corn was sometimes boiled as hominy, but more frequently was ground in a mortar and boiled as mush or made into cakes, and baked in the ashes or on hot stones. The corn was sometimes parched before triturating, and by this means the flavor of the food was much improved. Beans and pumpkins, green or dry, were prepared by simple boiling. Nearly all tribes seem to consider corn as one of the articles directly given them by their God. The Arapahoes claim that their God gave them one ear before he went to the "land of the rising sun." The Mandans, Gros Ventres, and Arickarees claim that certain parts of one ear were given to each tribe, but with them all it possesses a sacred character.

Deaf-mutes close the extended index of left hand, other fingers closed, with right hand, and turn latter as though twisting off the grains of corn from the cob.

Corporal. Indians who have on the frontier mixed with the troops represent non-commissioned officers by the chevrons on the arms, making signs for WHITES and SOLDIER, and then with index and second finger of right hand mark the position and shape of the stripe on the left arm.

Corpse. Make sign for PERSON, for DIE, then sign for LIE DOWN, —the person is dead and is lying down ; not yet been buried.

Deaf-mutes simply make sign for DEAD PERSON.

Corral. Conception : A circular space enclosed by interlaced trees. Make sign for TREE, then bring the hands, backs outwards, well out in front of body ; lock the fingers ; *i.e.*, place fingers of right hand between those of left, pressing them together, index fingers and forearms about horizontal ; loosen the fingers and bring the wrists towards each other, throwing the hands, by wrist action, to right and left slightly, at same time slightly curving them so as to make a circular enclosure. To indicate that animals were in the corral, make sign for same, hold left hand in the position above described, and bring partially-compressed right hand and drop it into the imaginary corral, fingers downwards, back of hand to front and upwards.

Deaf-mutes make horizontal curve of the arms and lock the fingers.

Council. Conception : Sitting in a circle and talking. Bring the closed hands, backs outwards, well out in front of body, a little lower than shoulders, lower edges of hands touching ; move the hands simultaneously on a curve towards the body, having them meet close to it, hands forming in movement as nearly as possible a horizontal circle ; turn the hands as they are brought on circle towards body, so that when they meet the backs will be towards the body (the hands can also start in the last position describing a horizontal circle and meet well out in front of body in position first taken above) ; then hold both hands, backs down, fingers extended, touching, and pointing to front in same horizontal plane, well out in front of body, hands about six inches apart and about height of breast ; move the hands, mostly by wrist action, simultaneously a few inches to left, then return to original position, and then move them few inches to right ; carry them backwards and forwards in this way two or three times ; this represents the handing of the words from one to another.

The necessity for sitting in a circle is apparent in a tepee, and the custom seems universal outside of it. When any number of Indians congregate, either to decide on a plan of action, to smoke, to talk matters over, or to gather round a fire, to receive or impart information, in fact, for any purpose whatever, they seem to crystallize instantly into a circle seated on the ground ; the blanket drops down, the overlapping sides are given a roll over the drawn-up knees, which fastens it, and they are quite comfortable.

Every talk of any importance is called a council. If the camp is going to move, if a surround of buffalo is to be made, if they are going to war, or are considering propositions of peace, in fact, any question which affects their welfare, has to be talked over in this way ; and when the matter is one of importance and the camp is large, two or three tepees are pitched, opening into each other for this purpose. An essential and necessary part of a council is the feast (see FEAST) and the smoke. (See SMOKE.) The talk usually comes after; only the chiefs and headmen sit in council, men of years and experience.

With some bands, boys who have "killed their man," or distinguished themselves by some special act of bravery, are entitled to sit in council and have a right to express their views, though they rarely exercise it. Though none are excluded, popular opinion in an Indian camp is not an ambiguous or hidden force, and it is, as a rule, well understood who are expected to sit in council. Frequently the camp-crier calls out the names of those who are expected to meet and discuss matters of importance pertaining to the camp.

Some commence their speech with "My friends!" . . . others, "My soldiers!" . . . or, if a chief has made the feast, then he is addressed personally.

In every large camp and in many small ones there is a council- or soldier-lodge set apart and used only for this purpose, and kept well supplied with food by voluntary contributions from the people of the village. A large village, when making a long march, appoint a number of the headmen from each band to take charge of the movement, determine the length of the marches to be made each day, select the camps, send out scouting-parties, and, if going out for a buffalo surround, take such precaution as may be necessary to prevent the buffalo from being stampeded. Sometimes as many as twenty are selected for this purpose. They march in line in front of the camp, usually on foot, each armed with a pipe, and frequent halts are made and ceremonial smokes taken. No member of the village is allowed in advance of these men, and the chief has no more to say in regard to the movement than any one else. These governors of the march meet each night at the soldier's lodge, receive the reports of the scouts (who have been sent on in advance, if the camping-places are not thoroughly well known, or if there is any prospect of danger), eat a great deal, smoke a great deal, and talk a great deal.

The soldier-lodge is a perfect bonanza for the lazy vagabonds of the camp, who hang round it to pick up something to eat.

Mr. Dunbar says of the Pawnees that councils of a band or tribe could be called by the head-chief on his own motion, or at the prompting of another. If the matter to be brought under deliberation was of great consequence, or involved anything of secrecy, the council was appointed in a lodge, or at a place removed from immediate observation, and no one not personally entitled was admitted. In other cases any convenient place, in-doors or out, that might be named, and those not strictly privileged to sit in the council could, if disposed, attend as spectators. The right to participate in tribal or band councils was a much-coveted dignity. The call and time of assembling were duly published by the herald or crier of the chief. This functionary was one of the most conspicuous in a village. Quite often his voice was heard first in the morning proclaiming the order of the day. If, during the day, the chief wished to communicate to the band any important news or special order, it was made known through this dignitary, who for hours perhaps would promenade the village, or stand upon the top of some convenient lodge, announcing in set tone and phrase the intelligence. While making a proclamation he frequently took occasion to intersperse or append numerous advices and monitory appeals of his own, some of which he addressed to the young men, others to the old men, etc. He naturally, therefore, came to be regarded as a sort of preceptor in general duties. Each chief had his own herald. The council on assembling, after the usual preliminary of smoking, was opened by the head-chief, or by some one designated by him. After his will had thus been made known, the discussion was thrown open to all present as members; but great scrupulousness was observed that there should be no infraction of their rules of precedence and decorum. Rank, seniority, and personal prestige were all carefully considered in determining the order in which each one should speak. The speaker addressed the council as a-ti'-ŭs (fathers), the word being repeated at the beginning of nearly every sentence. The members of the audience, on the other hand, felt perfectly free to accompany any speaker's remarks with expressions of approval, lau! or dissent, ugh! though the latter was more usually indicated by silence. After the discussion of the matter in question was closed, the opinion of the council was gathered, not by any formal vote, but from the general tenor of the addresses that had been delivered in the course of the debate. The result was then made public through the herald.

Counsel. Make signs for TALK, for MAKE, for ROAD. The metaphor of a trail, or road, is a frequent one in regard to the course, or plan of action, to be, or which was, pursued. Men of age, wisdom, and experience are constantly giving advice to the younger and less experienced, and great deference and respect extended, as well as presents made for it.

Count. The system of tens is universally used by our Indians in enumeration. In counting from one to ten, the usual way is to hold the closed right hand in front, and back towards and about height of shoulder, edges of hand pointing up; for one, the little finger is extended; two, the third; three, second; four, index; five, thumb, keeping fingers extended, separated, and pointing upwards; six, bring the closed left hand at same height, equally advanced, and near right, and extend the thumb; seven, extend left index; eight, second finger; nine, third finger; ten, little finger.

For twenty, the closed hands are brought in above-described position and the fingers and thumbs extended and separated twice; for twenty-five, the above for twenty, and then the left hand is dropped and the right curved little more to centre of body, and the fingers and thumb extended and separated; for thirty, the hands are usually opened three times; but above this number an arbitrary sign is usually made by the best-informed sign-talkers, viz., the right hand is brought in front of right shoulder, fingers extended, separated, and pointing upwards, thumb closed, palm of hand outwards, still keeping fingers extended and palm to front; the hand is moved to the left and downwards, tips of fingers describing a vertical curve. (See HUNDRED.)

Some tribes indicate a number of tens by making sign for ten, then hold extended left hand horizontally in front of body, fingers separated and pointing to front and slightly to right, and draw the tip of extended right index from base over the back of each finger to its tip, each motion of this kind representing ten, then holding right hand similarly fixed to left, mark the backs of its thumb and fingers with tip of left index.

In numeration,—*i.e.*, numbering or counting in a limited way,—where there is doubt, such as the number of camps made on a journey, number of people killed in a fight, the left hand is held back down, fingers extended and pointing to front, in front of body ; then, with the tip of extended right index, other fingers and thumb closed, back of right hand up, the little finger of left is pressed back or closed, and frequently held down during the discussion, then the third finger, and so on. After five, the right hand is held back down, with the little finger closed, with index or thumb of left hand for six, and so on, the final result being usually announced in the first-described way for counting. The majority of Indians have no clear conception of any number beyond a thousand, and many not beyond two or three hundred. The fact that in so many instances remote and seemingly unrelated nations have adopted *ten* as their basic number, together with the fact that in the remaining instances the basic number is either five (the fingers of one hand) or twenty (the fingers and toes), almost of themselves show that the fingers were the original units of enumeration. The still surviving use of the word digit as the general name for a figure in arithmetic is significant, and it is even said that our word *ten* (Saxon, *tyn ;* Dutch, *tien ;* German, *zehn*) means, in its primitive, expanded form, *the hands ;* so that, originally, to say there were ten things was to say there were two hands of them.

Deaf-mutes naturally use both hands, but the French method as taught uses a system of fives, and the counting is done entirely with the right hand. The closed right hand, back outwards, is held in front of right shoulder, edges pointing upwards ; for one, index finger extended ; two, second ; three, the thumb ; four, thumb closed and fingers extended ; five, thumb extended, fingers and thumb extended, separated, and pointing upwards; six, press tip of ball of thumb against tip of little finger, others extended ; seven, tip or ball of thumb against third, others extended ; eight, against second, others extended ; nine, against index, others extended ; ten, close the fingers, extend the thumb, and by wrist action give it a jerk to the right ; for twenty, the index and thumb are extended, and a sharp motion, by wrist action, made to right, and so on ; for one hundred, the arbitrary sign for the letter C is made.

Count-Coup. Conception : Striking an enemy. Hold left hand, back to left and outwards, in front of body, index finger extended and pointing to front and right, others and thumb closed ; bring right hand, back to right and front, just in rear of left and little lower, index finger extended, pointing downwards and to left, right index under left, other fingers and thumb closed ; raise right hand, and turn it by wrist action so that end of right index strikes sharply against side of left as it passes.

The matter of counting coups—*i.e.*, relating the stories of their deeds of valor in striking the bodies, either dead or alive, of their enemies in battle—is the pride and pleasure of every Indian warrior. With most tribes, an Indian who first strikes or even touches the body of an enemy in a fight, even after he has been killed, is credited with the killing. The bravest coup is to strike the enemy before killing him, and this, in the days of bows and arrows, was frequently done. They sometimes carry a long, slender stick or pole for this purpose, called a "coup-stick," and in charging a village, if one strikes a tepee he counts coup on it, and the lodge and all in it belongs to him ; and the same rule is observed with the women, ponies, etc., captured. The striking must be done in the fight, in the heat of battle, so to speak. As a wounded Indian settles to his deadliest aim, and mortal wounds only intensify the desire to kill, it will readily be seen that, in many instances, he who counts coup runs the greatest risk ; and the law naturally urges on those who are ambitious. The blow can be struck with a whip, or any kind of a club or stick.

The Cheyennes claim that the old woman in the cave told some of their medicine-men in the "long ago" how to make a medicine coup-stick, and by carrying it, when going to war, the enemy could not hit them. The stick was inherited from father to son, and some few are still in existence. By riding close up to an enemy, shaking this stick and making a peculiar noise, the enemy became paralyzed with fear through the mysterious power of the stick, and was, of course, at their mercy.

Country. The Indians use this word to designate the territory which they hold by physical force, or which they have held in that way for any length of time. In signs, point to the ground, and explain the extent by gesture for the streams or other natural boundaries.

Deaf-mutes use the word as used by use for our country ; they make sign for United States, which is by interlocking the fingers, hold arms curved in front horizontal, and move the hands and arms to right and left horizontally.

Courtship. Make sign for FEMALE, then hold left hand, back outwards, well out in front of and about height of left shoulder, index finger extended and pointing upwards, other fingers and thumb closed, this represents the girl standing ; then make sign for MALE, and hold right hand fixed like left, but with back to right and in front of right shoulder, this represents the male standing ; move the hands by gentle jerks towards each other, and when near make sign for LITTLE TALK, towards tip of left index ; then make with the right hand a grasping motion towards left index. Some Indians make a grasping motion with both hands in front of body as though seizing a person, and then motion of throwing blanket round same, while still others hold hands over face as though hiding same, and by looking over or between them indicate the watching, and then throw out arms as though making an embrace ; perhaps adding sign for HIDE, meaning that the talking, grasping, etc., were done slyly, secretly.

The young men of the Plains Indians do the most of their courting in a standing position. An Indian lover will stand and wait near the lodge where abides the object of his admiration until she appears, when he walks up alongside of her and throws his blanket round her. If she reciprocates the tender sentiment, they will thus stand for hours, his blanket covering both their heads and closely wrapped round both their bodies. I have seen as many as half a dozen young men waiting by the path which led down to the water near a camp, and one after another throw his blanket around a girl as she was going down to fill the water-vessel. While so waiting or standing outside a lodge they usually have the head entirely covered with their blanket, excepting only a little hole for one eye. By not wearing the blanket usually worn it is, of course, improbable that any one will recognize them. If the girl likes to be held, she makes some reply to the first tender greeting ; if she expresses dislike to his advances, the man, by the law of courtship, must at once desist. The embrace under the blanket excites no comment or annoyance from mischievous boys or garrulous old men, and the young man can hug the object of his affection to his heart's content unmolested.

In 1877 it became necessary for the military authorities to know something of the movements and plans of the great war chief of the Sioux, Crazy Horse, and to discover these one of the enlisted scouts suddenly became smitten with the charms of a dusky maiden who lived in the tepee adjoining that of the chief, and as she reciprocated the tender feeling, the scout would stand just outside of Crazy Horse's lodge, holding the girl in a fond embrace, while his quick ears took in every word that was uttered in the lodge. He discovered a conspiracy, which, if it had not been for his cunning shrewdness and prompt and loyal action to the whites, would in all probability have terminated in the murder of a general officer, but which eventually led to the necessary killing of the chief himself.

I was told at White Earth Agency, Minnesota, that the Chippewas practised "bundling," but I am not able to assert this positively. It is undoubtedly a fact that some tribes do allow the young men to go in the lodge where the young girls are sleeping and lie alongside of them outside the blankets. This, in former times, was the last chapter in the story of the courtship with the Flatheads, as they said, "The young man courting a girl would go to her lodge and sleep near her. The family would see him in the morning, and that determined the trade, which was made at once." Before the priests came to these Indians, the custom of claiming younger sisters after marrying the eldest was practised, as it is with the Plains Indians.

Cousin. Make sign for BROTHER or SISTER, and for NEAR,—

nearly a brother or sister. As a rule, the sign for cousin is the same as for brother or sister. (See KINSHIP.)

Deaf-mutes make sign for either sex, and then link index fingers.

Coward. Point to or make sign for the person, and then make sign for AFRAID. Sometimes a trembling motion is given hands and body, as in WINTER,—the person shakes with fear. The rather common impression that Indians are cowards is, I think, erroneous. It is claimed that they will not make a "square, stand-up fight." How silly it would be for them to do so! Their education and training, their social laws and conditions of physical existence, demand a certain order of strategy; and the great vital principle of this is to do the greatest possible amount of damage to the enemy with the least possible loss. There is no pension-list with them, and the widows and orphans are thrown upon the charity of their people. The superstitions which govern their movements, their peculiar method of warfare, and their susceptibility to stampedes, render it difficult for us to correctly judge them in regard to courage or the lack of it, but certainly after middle age their natural caution in many instances becomes rank timidity. As courage is the highest virtue, so cowardice is the lowest vice, taking their standard, of course.

Coyote. Conception : Small wolf. Make sign for WOLF and for SMALL.

Cradle. See BABY-HOLDER.

Deaf-mutes make sign for BABY, and indicate the rocking.

Crazy. Conception: Brain in a whirl. Bring the right hand, back to right and rear, hand slightly compressed and pointing upwards in front of and close to forehead; turn the hand, mostly by wrist action, so that tips of fingers describe a small horizontal circle. Crazy and foolish are synonymous words with Indians, and this gesture is therefore very frequently used.

The size of the circular movement of hand determines degree of foolishness or insanity.

Deaf-mutes use both hands, rotary motion, one above the other, near forehead,—mixed brain.

Cree (Indian). There seems to be no tribal sign in general use for these people. They are poor sign-talkers, and say they have none for themselves. The Blackfeet make signs for SIOUX and LIE. The Berthold Indians make signs for BLACKENED FACES to denote them. The Assinaboines make sign for RABBIT.

The French gave this name to this branch of the Algonquins, but they are called by themselves and other Indian tribes Kenistenos, or Knis-ten-eaux, because of the sanguinary character of the war which they waged northwest of Lake Superior. "This word is derived from the animate (transition?) Chippewa verb *nisau*, to kill. The people are an offshoot of the Algonquin family, the language of which they speak, but with less purity and richness of inflection than the Chippewas." (*Schoolcraft.*)

They were formerly numerous and powerful, and may have possessed many of the superior qualities which some writers claim for them, but those whom I have seen were wretchedly poor, and mentally and physically inferior to the Plains Indians.   For many years they occupied the country lying between Lake Superior and Hudson's Bay, and many of the servants of the Hudson's Bay and Northwest Fur Companies married into the tribe.   They also ranged west from Winnipeg, on the Assinaboine, Mouse, and Saskatchewan Rivers, to the Rocky Mountains, sometimes crossing the British line in search of buffalo, as they have been doing in the vicinity of the Milk River country during the past three years.   Many of them still use dogs as a means of transportation, but those who can afford it have "Red River carts."

An annual dog feast, conducted with great ceremony and much "making medicine," seems to take the place of the Sun-Dance. They have mixed with and adopted the manners of so many tribes that they have nearly lost their identity, so far as dress is concerned. I have perhaps only seen the poorer, more nomadic class.   They seem to have been at war with most of the tribes on our side of the line, except the Assinaboines and some of the Blackfeet.   They are credited with being one of the forces which drove the Mandans out of the country near Lake Winnipeg.

Cross. (Sulky.)   Incline the head slightly forward and rest forehead on left hand, left forearm close to body.   This is used more in the sense of moody, a melancholy frame of mind.   Some Indians make signs for HEART and BAD, others for HEART, for NEAR, and BAD, others, again, for HEART turning and twisting, indicated by right hand placed over heart and turned and twisted.

Deaf-mutes assume a scowling expression, and make a clawing motion with hands in front of face.

Cross. (Decoration.)   Bring both hands in front of body; form a cross with extended index fingers, others and thumbs closed; press the cross thus formed against breast.

Deaf-mutes indicate the shape of a cross on breast with index of right hand.

Cross. (To cross a stream.)   Hold slightly compressed left hand, fingers extended, touching, and pointing to right, about ten inches in front of body; bring right hand, back to right, fingers extended, touching, and pointing to front and slightly upwards between left hand and body; move right hand on curve to front slightly upwards, and then downwards, terminating movement when right hand has passed beyond left; the fingers of right hand here front to front and slightly downwards.

To cross a stream, mountain range, prairie, first make proper gesture to represent the object; then the left hand represents that object, and is crossed over.

Deaf-mutes make the same sign.

Crow (Indian).   Bring extended hands, backs nearly up, in front, a little higher than, and slightly to right and left of, shoulders; move the hands simultaneously a little downwards, slightly outwards and a trifle to right and left, indicating motion of wings.

When the Cheyennes crossed the Missouri River in their westward migration, about two hundred years ago, the Crow Indians occupied the country west of the Black Hills. The Government has since set apart as a reservation for them all the country extending from the 107th meridian to near the 111th on the west, and including all that portion of Montana lying between the Yellowstone River and the Wyoming line. In 1880 the Indians ceded to the Government, by treaty, some two millions of acres of the mineral lands of the southern and western portion of the reservation, still retaining some sixty thousand acres of mountain, prairie, and valley lands. It certainly speaks well for the cunning strategy and bravery of these people that, surrounded as they were by such powerful enemies, they should have been able to have secured or retained possession of such a valuable tract of land, for some parts are rich in mineral deposits, others particularly fine for grazing, and still others seem well adapted to agriculture. The agent, in his report for 1881, gives the number of Indians as three thousand five hundred, and he also reports fourteen thousand head of horses. This, of course, includes the ponies and mules.

The agency is located on a clear, cold mountain stream, a small tributary of the Sweetwater River, some twenty miles from the Yellowstone.

Though admitting that they separated from the Berthold Gros Ventres, many generations ago, over a dispute in regard to the division of the "manifold" (first stomach of buffalo), and giving the location of this separation as on the Missouri River, at the mouth of Heart River, they still claim to have been created in the country they now hold as a reservation. They call themselves Absaraka, and could give me no definition of its meaning other than it meant people,—the Crow people. The surrounding tribes and the whites call them Crows. I have heard three explanations of this. A Cheyenne Indian told me that when they first met this tribe they had a pet "medicine" crow, and on account of the attention and devotion paid to it, they called them Crow people. It is also claimed by some of the Gros Ventres that soon after their separation from the Crows they had a fight with their enemies, the Sioux, and some of the Crows being present, sat on the hills near by and would not come down. A warrior called out to them, and asked, "Why they sat up there like a lot of crows?" and ever afterwards they were called Crows. Running Antelope, a chief of the Uncapapa band of Sioux, and one of the cleverest Indians I have ever met, said to me that the Crows got their name from a corruption of the name for the "manifold," over which they disputed when they separated from the Gros Ventres.

In personal appearance the Crow Indian men are fine-looking, tall, and well formed. The women are small and inferior in appearance, and are not as virtuous as other Plains Indians. They might, however, be considered on a level with the Arapahoes in this respect. Their vocal language is coarse and harsh, and does not seem to have a rich vocabulary. They keep no account of their ages, and are poor in tradition. The men cut the hair squarely off round the forehead, leaving this bang from four to six inches in length, which, when they are in full dress, is made to stand upright by dressing it with clay, which is sometimes made more adhesive by admixture with a sticky substance obtained by boiling certain gummy weeds and bushes. From this custom they are indebted for the pictographical designation, viz., " Hair-straight-upon-forehead." The side hair is at times braided, and the hair on the back of the head separated into several " strips," which are held in place by glue placed at regular intervals. To give them the appearance of having very long hair, hair that has been cut off in mourning, or that taken from their ponies' tails and manes, is glued on to lengthen it out. This, I presume, was what Mr. Catlin saw, and supposed to be their natural hair, when he said, "their hair trails on the ground." They do not pull out eyebrows or lashes. In dress, the men wear the hooded coat made of a blanket, and white blankets striped with black and red are preferred. At the shoulder, wrist of the coat, and down the leggings a coarse fringe is fastened. The women wear the dresses much shorter than do the Sioux and Cheyennes. The Crows have an excellent reputation among other tribes for their cunning, crafty skill, and bravery in war. They have been almost constantly at war with the Cheyennes, Arapahoes, and Sioux since the latter crossed the Missouri River, though they have made peace dozens of times, and have confederated with them against other tribes and the whites. With us, however, as a rule, they have been friendly, and since 1876 have rendered valuable service as enlisted scouts. At present they are better armed and better mounted than any other tribe of Indians. The Cheyennes and Arapahoes forced them out of the Little Missouri, Powder, Tongue, and Little Horn River countries, and, in fact, carried on the war so vigorously that a portion went north of the Missouri, and, joining the Gros Ventres of the Prairie, remained there for some years, and became known as the River Crows. Their status of peace and war with the Sioux, Cheyennes, and Arapahoes represents fairly their relations with the Snakes, Blackfeet, Nez Perces, Flatheads, Assinaboines, and others, though with the Nez Perces, Bannacks, and Snakes they kept to their treaties in a moderately honest way, because it was necessary in order to repel the invasion from the east.

Their low standard of chastity is illustrated by their prevalent custom of rounding out hospitality to a stranger by according him for his night's entertainment the company of some one of the host's female relatives, and wife, sister, or daughter were presented according to the demands of circumstances. A wife's honor was also frequently bartered for a blanket, but it is only fair to say that of late years these customs have become much more infrequent than they formerly were.

From Iron Bull, who, as an agency chief and orator, has obtained some renown, and is probably better known to the whites generally than any other chief of the Crow Nation, I obtained some information in regard to the sign language and the peculiar customs of his people. At the time of the occupation of old Fort C. F. Smith this Indian was of service to the Government troops stationed there, and many of the officers who were so unfortunate as to be present at that time cherish a very kindly feeling for him. He has a rather fine, round, smiling, benevolent face; his manners are pleasant and affable, and his fund of information large. He has visited Washington, and for some years was recognized by the Government as head-chief of the Crow Nation. From him and others I find that the Crows do have a Sun-Dance, but it differs essentially from that of the Sioux and other tribes. The dance originates in a spirit of revenge, and through it they seek to secure the assistance of the Supreme Being in carrying out their plans for vengeance, and in prosecuting their wars and horse-stealing expeditions. In olden times the dance prevailed to a much greater extent than at the present day. It could be held at any time from the first budding of the leaves in the spring to their fall in the autumn. The instigator or prime mover of the dance, the man, in fact, who gave or got up the entertainment, was he who had suffered the loss of kin or friend at the hands of their enemies. This man looked up a camp near a buffalo herd, and a grand hunt and gathering of buffalo-tongues was first made. These tongues were used both for feasting and also as a badge, so to speak, of virtue and bravery. The details and minor ceremonies differed somewhat, according to the power of the imagination of the medicine-men. The poles for the medicine-lodge, in which the dance was to take place, were cut according to some peculiar rule, and from start to finish the ceremony was more or less complicated. Some woman in camp, who had been true to her vows of matrimony, held a buffalo-tongue in her hand, and the men standing near fired arrows or bullets through it. Many of the ceremonies connected with the dance were for the purpose of testing the virtue of the women, the bravery of the men, and their power to endure physical pain. It also gave them opportunities to tell their war stories, give an account of their heroic deeds of valor, and "count their coups." Instead of having one central Sun-Dance pole, to which the victims were fastened, they had several.

The camping-ground was selected by the man who inaugurated the dance. The poles for the medicine-lodge were cut by the women, and hauled by the men riding their ponies to this ground. The camp then moved, all the tepees were pitched in a circle, with an open space to the east. Two men, selected in recognition of their skill as hunters, were detailed to go out and get two fresh buffalo-skins from animals which, for this purpose, must be slain with a single bullet, or, in former years, by a single arrow. Each pole for the medicine-lodge is named after the braves in the camp, about twenty-one being used. The lodge was first pitched with only five or seven poles, which were covered with brush. The pole representing the bravest Indian in camp was cut down by an hermaphrodite (if there were one in camp, and I believe they are more common with this tribe than with any other), and as it fell the young men fired at it with pistols, guns, etc. The preliminary lodge was then taken down and the final one made. First, three poles were tied together as is usual in putting up any lodge, but near the top of the poles the skin of the freshly-killed buffalo was fastened, and as the poles were raised the man who gave the dance took his seat on it and was raised with the poles. He had eagle's wings fastened to his arms, and represented the eagle as rising in the air. The three poles were then fastened, the man came down, and the lodge was completed, the names of the poles being called out as they were put in place. The wood to be used for cooking and for fires was then gathered. Such women as had been loyal and true to their marital relations and some virgins were put up behind the braves, and rode out on their ponies to cut the wood and bring it in. Then some men of similar character were selected to go and get some white clay of which to make a bed or pedestal for the man who gave the dance, and upon this dais he takes his place and sings, whistles, and dances for several, sometimes as many as seven, days. Poles with a fork some eight or ten feet from the ground were then cut and planted round the lodge on the outside, for the dancers who are to establish their bravery, and produce good luck by mutilating themselves after the fashion done in the Sioux Sun-Dance, by fastening themselves to these poles. Several of these poles were sometimes used, and several persons tied to each. They were cut by the kin of the dancers, who were provided with the whistle as in the Sioux Sun-Dance. Some of the young men had buffalo-heads tied to the muscles of the back, and danced through and about the camp at this time.

The following is their story of the creation as related by the old chief:

"Long ago there was a great flood and only one man was left, whom we call 'the Old Man,' because it happened so long ago, and because we have talked about him so much. This God saw a duck, and said to him, 'Come here, my brother. Go down and get some dirt and I will see what I can do with it.' The duck dove; was gone a long time. Coming to the surface, he had a small bit of mud. The God said he would make something with it, and added, 'We are here by ourselves, it is bad!' Holding the mud in his hand till it dried, then blowing it in different directions, there was dry land all about. The duck and the God and the ground were all that existed. He then made the creeks and mountains, and after that they asked each other to do certain things. The duck asked the God to make certain things, among the rest, Indians on the prairie. The God took some dirt in his hand, blew it out, and there stood a man and a woman. A great many crows sprang up at once from this dirt, but they were blind. The first man created pulled open one eye and saw the streams and the mountains, and then the other, and cried out that the country was fine. The first woman created did the same, and they told the rest to do the same, and to this day the peculiar marks about the eyes show the manner of opening them.

The first two then asked the God for something to hide their nakedness. The God told the woman and explained to the man how to propagate their species.

"The God was on a little hill. He called the one who first pulled open his eyes, and said, 'Look! Here are antelope, deer, elk, buffalo. I give you these to eat.' The God killed one buffalo for them. Then he took up a rock, threw it down, broke it, and with one of the pieces cut up the buffalo. He showed the man how to make a bow and arrow, explained the parts of the buffalo, the location of the sinew and its use, the use of the skin for a robe; in fact, all that was necessary. Then he commenced dividing up the people, Piegans, Sioux, Cheyennes, and the rest, and gave them the country to live in. The people asked him if they were to eat the meat raw. The God then took two sticks and rubbed them with a little sand, and said, 'There, my children, is a small fire for you. Get some wood and keep it burning always.' But the first man said, 'Father. No. We want to move around. We cannot pack fire with us. Make it so we can get fire;' and it was done. Then the first man asked for vessels in which to cook and to carry water, and the God showed him how to dig out the black rocks for those purposes. The God then told them how to tan the skins of animals by means of the brain and liver, and how to grain it with the bone of the fore leg of animals. He showed them how to prepare the skins for a lodge, etc., how to take the hair off, how to make the poles, and marked out on the ground the shape to make the lodge. The God then said, 'Name yourselves, children;' and the first man said, 'We will call ourselves after the black bird,—Crows.¹ Then the God said, 'As I made you, I am going to tell you what to do. Cry; and as the tears drop on the ground, you will know what it is.' Then the first man said, 'That is not much to do,—to cry; tell us something else.' The God then said, 'I have made the high mountains for you. Go up there. Cut a piece of flesh out of your arms and give to me. Fast, and you will have visions, which will tell you what to do.' The God explained in regard to the sweat-houses. If this did not cure them when sick they would carry them to some other good hunting-grounds. He then said, 'I have showed you how to make all these things; how to live. Among all the buffalo I have made a few white ones. When you kill one of these sing three songs, place the skin on a hill, give the skin to me. I like them.' He also said, 'I like the black-tail deer-skin and the hawks with white tails. Give me, once in a while, some of these.' The God then told them how to get horses. He told them to go over the hill and not look back. They started. One man was behind the rest. The horses came up behind, whinnying and prancing. The man behind could not resist; he looked back, and the horses vanished. If it had not been for this we would have had many horses. They then went to the Yellowstone River. The God said, 'This is your country; the water is pure and cold; the grass is good. It is a fine country, and it is yours.' He then said, 'I made all this country round you.   I have put you in the centre.   I have put these people round you as your enemies.   They will fight you, and keep fighting you, until you are greatly reduced in numbers, and then I will come and help you.'   He said, ' Kill your enemies ; take their scalps ; blacken your faces with fire-coals ; and when any of your people are killed, let your tears fall to the ground, and cry out in your distress mourning.'   He also said that he would not help foolish people, but would assist those who were good.   He said, ' I have put red paint in places in your country.   Get this and make your faces and bodies red.'   He also said, ' These women may breed too fast ; you will have to destroy some of the young before they are born.'   After this he went to a tree, struck it, and the whites came out like mice out of a hole.   He said, ' I have sent these whites to show you how to make iron.   Do not fight them ; shake hands with them.   At eighty years you will all be pretty old, and at one hundred you will be of no account ; your skin will peel off.   From the time you are born till you are fifty you will be strong and well ; from sixty you will feel the weight of many winters ; will be crippled and go down hill.'   He then said, ' I have given you all these things ; sometimes give me what I have told you to ; and when you make these offerings call on me.   I will hear and help you.'   He then took them all over the country, and at Powder River disappeared.''

Crow.   Make sign for BIRD and for BLACK.

Cry.   Conception : Tears.   Bring both hands, backs outwards, index fingers extended and pointing upwards, other fingers and thumbs closed, in front of and about six inches from face, tips of index fingers about height of eyes ; lower the hands, at same time bend index towards face, repeating motion, tracing the course of tears flowing down face.

Deaf-mutes use the same sign.

Cunning.   Make sign for WOLF.   Sometimes the sign for Fox is made ; a cunning person acts the part of a wolf or fox.

Cutting Up.   Hold left hand, back upwards, in front of left breast, fingers extended, touching, pointing to front, upwards, and slightly to right ; bring right hand, back down, fingers extended, touching, pointing to front, upwards, and slightly to left, about six inches to right, and little lower than left hand ; move the right hand on a curve outwards, downwards and to left, as though cutting with its lower edge parallel to left hand ; repeat motion.   This sign is used not only to express the idea of cutting up game so that it can be packed into camp, but the cutting of meat into thin strips, which after being so cut is placed on horizontal poles and dried in the sun.   Three days of pleasant weather are sufficient to cure it so that it will keep for years, provided it remains dry.   Where there are heavy dews, or when it rains during the process of drying and curing, the meat must be taken into the lodge.   When cured it is packed away in the par-flèche sacks, and is ready for use.   It is generally eaten without any further preparation or cooking.   Sometimes it is roasted a little and pounded up with dry fat; and at other times a kind of stew is made of it.

Deaf-mutes hold extended left hand, back up, fingers pointing to right, in front of body; bring extended right hand back to right, fingers pointing to front and downwards, and place lower edge just at left finger-tips; move right hand to front and downwards as though slicing off finger-tips of left hand. This is the sign used by the Indians for cutting tobacco.

D.

Dakota. See SIOUX.

Dam. Conception: Holding the current. Make sign for STREAM or RIVER, and for HOLD.

Deaf-mutes make signs for BUILD, for WATER, and indicate its rising from the effect of the obstruction.

Dance. Conception: Hopping action. Bring the hands in front of body about height of breast, with lower edges horizontal and pointing to front, palms towards each other, about six inches apart, right hand slightly higher than left, lower edge of same about on a line with centre of left palm, fingers slightly curved and little separated, thumbs extended and pointing about upwards; move the hands briskly upwards and downwards few inches several times, mostly by elbow action. Sometimes the hands are held with fingers pointing upwards.

It is extremely difficult, almost impossible, to describe an Indian dance so that a person who has never seen one can form any correct idea of it. To better understand the matter, however, it is necessary to clear one's mind of the thoughts of the sensuous pleasures of our modern dance, and try to contemplate the subject as it is handed down to us through the history of the ancient Spartans, who, it seems, like our Indians, made the act of dancing an expression of their emotions, relating mostly to religion and war.

The violent physical exertion and mental excitement, with such accessories, in the scalp- and other dances, as blackened faces, painted bodies, full war costumes, weird singing, hideous "tum tums" of the drums, gory scalp-locks held high in the air on slender poles, the wind playing with the straight black locks or lighter-colored tresses, perhaps at night, their wild faces and bodily contortions thrown into a bold and horrible relief by the flickering light of the tongues of flame from a huge fire, all combine to throw the dancers into a state of excitement bordering on frenzy.

There is a great similarity among all the tribes in their dancing, and their motives and objects are also about the same. The Sun-Dance and Medicine-Dance partake the most strongly of a religious character, and of them I have given a brief description separately. (See SUN-DANCE, MEDICINE-DANCE.)

Generally they form in a circle. The music consists of drums and rattles, and from two to four singing-girls, who are located just outside the group, and keep time to the drums in a shrill, nasal, metallic chant. The heels of the dancers are raised from the ground, the weight of the body resting on the balls of the feet. The body is raised, lowered, contorted, sometimes resting on one foot only, and every motion keeping time to the infernal "tum tum" and monotonous singing. Gaudily decked out, half naked, and gorgeously painted, they make a fantastic picture. In most of their dances they first sit down in a circle, and get up at short intervals to participate in the dancing. In some dances, as in the Scalp-Dance, they move round and round in a circle by short sideway hops. In the Grass- or Omaha-Dance, they form in two lines, move forward towards, pass each other, turn, repass, and so on. Some of these dances they can have at any time, others only after certain intervals and upon speci- fied occasions. There are dances for the old men, dances for the old women, for mothers whose sons have gone to war and have met with success, dances for the young men before going to war and after returning, and some which seem to soften down to an æsthetic social character, permitting the young men and women to dance to- gether, and allowing little tendernesses in the way of kissing the girls. Whether this is of late origin, and due to the civilization of the white race, I am unable to say.

Some of the different dances are distinguished by the songs for each, some by the dress, and a few of them by the step. Feasting and smoking, but especially the smoking, either before or after, and sometimes during the dance, is an essential part of all their cere- monies. As a rule, the different dances take their names from the names of the different soldier bands. The Comanches have the Raven, Buffalo Bull, Swift Fox,—all war-dances,—and Dance of Fear, with shields and lances, when they expect an attack; Turkey- Dance, imitating motions of turkeys. The Deer-Dance might be called the juggler's-dance, as the dancers pretend to swallow red beans and then draw them out through the breast.

The Caddos had a Corn-Dance, held when the corn was ripe enough to eat, and, until this dance took place, no one was allowed to pick any of the corn. They also had a Beaver-Dance, in which the medicine-men swallowed large shells.

The Berthold Indians have a special dance for the women, called a White-Buffalo-Dance. They also have the Strong-Heart-, Bull-, Wolf-, and Young-Dog-Dances. They use masks of buffalo-heads for the Bull-Dance, and wolf-skins for the Wolf-Dance.

The Cheyennes have a special war-dance when all the soldiers are wanted for war purposes. A large fire is made in the centre of the camp, where the warriors assemble, mounted and dismounted, but wearing all their war-toggery, weapons, etc. Men, women, and chil- dren join in the dance, and when the excitement has become in- tense, has reached its greatest height, the headmen go among the dancers and pick out twelve of the best and bravest soldiers, and place two lines of six each on opposite sides of the fire. Then the old men and headmen give them advice, telling them that they must be vigilant and brave, and must never run from their enemies, and that their people will, after their return, sing of their brave deeds, but should they be killed on the battle-field, than which there is no more glorious death, they will be great chiefs in the hereafter. Gener- ally speaking, the Plains Indians have the Omaha- or Grass-Dance, by men, old and young, at any time: this is also a begging dance;

Fox-Dance, by young men, at any time ; Wolf-Dance, by those going to war, just before their going; Horse-Dance, once in two years ; a large lodge is pitched in the centre of camp ; the men are in war costumes, and their ponies painted ; they then circle, charge, discharge guns, etc. ; Scalp-Dance, by men and women, after the scalps have been brought home ; those who have been on the war-path have their faces blackened ; Chief- or Short-hair-Dance, mostly by old men, at any time ; Night-Dance, young men and girls, at any time ; Strong-Heart-Dance, young men, at any time ; Spirit-Dance, young men, at any time ; Otter-Dance, young men, using poles with otter-skins, at any time, and is a medicine dance ; Kill-Dance, by mothers whose sons have been to war and met with success.   These do not exhaust the list of dances, but are the principal ones.

Deaf mutes hold extended left hand, back down, fingers pointing to front, in front of body, and place tips of extended and separated index and second fingers on left palm, these fingers vertical, others and thumb closed ; twist and turn the right hand ; the fingers represent person standing, and the movement the gyration of the modern dance.

Dangerous.   This word when used in respect to a person would be expressed by saying that he is *angry*, heart is *bad*, and sign for BRAVE and perhaps KILL.   If of a place, specify in what way or by whom made dangerous.

Deaf-mutes make the sign for letter D alongside of head for a dangerous person.

Dark.   Bring the hands, back outwards, in front of face, about parallel to it, fingers extended and touching, right hand nearest face, palm of left about two inches from back of right, hands crossed so that lower edge of right hand is about on a line with centre of left palm and nearly at right angles with lower edge of left hand, tips of index fingers about opposite centre of forehead ; bring the hands very slightly towards face.   Some Indians make sign for NIGHT and SAME, or hold extended hands in front of and close to eyes.

To travel in an unknown country—*i.e.*, a country where the topography is unknown—would be expressed by saying " one travelled in the dark."

Deaf-mutes use the same sign.

Daughter.   Make signs for PARTURITION and for FEMALE.

Deaf-mutes make their signs for FEMALE and CHILD.

Day.   Hold the extended hands in same horizontal plane, backs up, in front of body, fingers pointing to front, about four inches apart, equidistant from body and at height of breast ; sweep the hands upwards and to right and left, and then downwards on curve simultaneously, turning the palms up ; terminating the movement when hands are about opposite shoulders and in same horizontal plane as when starting.   For *To-day* the sign for Now is first made.

To Indians darkness seems a tangible body.   It covers the earth at night like a huge blanket, and in the above-described sign a part of the gesture for NIGHT is used,—the darkness is folded away, laid aside, opened out for the sunshine. The time of day is expressed by noting the position of the sun in the heavens, and a reference to the sun being at any point above the horizon is sometimes used to express day instead of the sign I have described.

Deaf-mutes indicate the "path of the sun in the heavens" with extended index of right hand.

Daybreak. Hold both extended hands, backs out, in same vertical plane, little finger of right hand resting on left horizontal index; raise the right hand vertically a few inches. The darkness is lifted up a little, leaving a bright space, but no sun as yet is visible. Some Indians bring the right hand, back to right, towards the eastern horizon, arm nearly extended, thumb and index finger curved into an incomplete circle, space of about an inch between tips, other fingers closed; raise the hand slightly, then make sign for LITTLE. Others add to this by holding extended left hand, back out, over right wrist, and then, by bending up right hand, show the incomplete circle formed with index and thumb a little above the horizontal left index.

To-day or this day is expressed by making sign for NOW after gesture for DAY.

Deaf-mutes make about the same signs.

Dead. Make sign for DIE and SLEEP.

The deaf-mute sign for DIE is the Indian sign for KNOCKED OVER or LAID DOWN.

Dead-Shot. Make sign for SHOOT, then hold the left hand, back outwards, well in front of body, index finger extended and pointing upwards, others and thumb closed; bring the right hand, back up, close to breast, index finger extended and pointing to front, towards left index, other fingers and thumb closed, right hand at height of left; move the right hand out, and strike centre of left index with tip of right. To emphasize, sometimes after sign for SHOOT add the sign for BRAVE or STRONG, and then the foregoing sign; then move the right hand twice out, thrusting right index to right and left of left vertical index, and then make sign for NO. It goes to the centre; neither to the right nor left.

Deaf-mutes make about same signs.

Though Indians are not, as a rule, fine shots at a target, yet they are all good field marksmen. They are accustomed to shoot from their ponies at moving objects, are excellent judges of distances, and carefully estimate the effect of the wind.

Tribes like the Nez Perces, who partially subsist themselves on small game, are of course better shots than the Plains Indians, who have depended mainly upon the buffalo.

Deaf. Press the palm of extended right hand slightly against right ear, and move the hand in small circle parallel to and close to the ear. Frequently both hands are used, left being pressed against left ear, of course, and the sign for BAD also made, or the head shaken to indicate that one cannot hear. (See DEAF-MUTE.)

Deaf mutes simply touch right ear with tip of right index.

Deaf-Mute. Make sign for the PERSON, for PARTURITION, for DEAF, and for DUMB.

I have never seen but one deaf-mute Indian, and he was a most accomplished sign-talker. Deaf persons who have lost the sense of hearing by disease or age are more common, though not as prevalent as with the white race. The Indian I refer to as being deaf and dumb is a Crow, and is at present at their agency. Ignorant of all written and spoken languages, nature found a means of educating him through gesture speech. Though his ears are locked against all sound, and his tongue paralyzed, yet through this gift life is made to him not intolerable. He is keen, shrewd, and intelligent, and when I knew him was richer in stock-horses and cattle than any other Indian of the Crow tribe. Ordinarily he talked rapidly in clean-cut signs, using either hand with graceful ease, but when excited his hands seemed to *flash* forth his pent-up emotions ; his air-pictures were strikingly perfect, and true to the subject under consideration.

As I have for comparison with the Indian gestures given a brief description of the natural signs made by deaf-mutes, it appears proper to note something of the present status of the efforts made by the civilized world to rescue these people from the bondage, burden, and darkness under which they, until a comparatively recent date, suffered, as well as note something of the growth of these efforts.

" For educational purposes, those persons who become deaf at so early an age that they have not learned articulate language, or speedily lose all impress of it upon the mind, share the mental characteristics of the congenitally deaf, and are classed with them as true deaf-mutes. Those who retain some knowledge of articulate language acquired through the ear are called semi-mutes. Deaf-mutes are more prevalent than is generally supposed, the proportion in the United States and Great Britain being probably one in two thousand of the entire population. France was the last of the leading European nations to engage in this work. As late as the commencement of the seventeenth century a Père Dumoulin denied its possibility.

" Very little use had been made of the gestures by which the uneducated deaf naturally express their desires and feelings. Diderot's " Lettre sur les sourds et muets" (1751) indeed eulogized pantomime as a means of communication, but to test its capabilities fully and practically was reserved for the Abbé de l'Épée.

" De l'Épée at first followed Vanin in teaching by means of pictures, but soon found that they produced extremely incorrect impressions. He next tried articulation, but was disheartened by the slow and unsatisfactory progress made. Suddenly bethinking himself that the connection between ideas and spoken words was purely arbitrary, he surmised that an association could be equally well established between ideas and *written* words. He observed also that the deaf possessed already a means of communication in gestures, and considered that to teach them one of our conventional languages would be merely a process of translation from this natural language, when it had been philosophically improved and expanded with an exact correspondence with the others. Upon these principles he proceeded, and successfully.

"De l'Épée died in 1789, and was succeeded by the Abbé Sicard. Sicard, while preserving in the main the system of De l'Épée, improved it in many important respects. In nearly all the American institutions an improved French or manual system is employed. Most give more or less instruction in articulation, a special teacher being employed in some.

In writing the history of the art, the terms German, French, and early English are applied to the systems. But geographical boundaries have long ceased to divide them ; all three are now to be found side by side in almost every country.

"The language of signs is based upon the gestures devised by uneducated deaf-mutes, which have been found strikingly similar to those employed by various savage tribes. They are, pointing to objects, expressions of real or simulated emotions, imitations of actions, and representation with the hands of the shape or use of articles." (*American Cyclopædia.*)

From a "Tabular Statement of the Institutions for the Deaf and Dumb of the World, reprinted from the American Annals of the Deaf and Dumb, January, 1882," I make the following extract :

"One of the most interesting items of information is that relating to the methods of instruction now prevailing. There is so much variety among these, however, that it is not easy to present them accurately in the narrow limits of a statistical table. The best we are able to do is to group them into four classes,—*manual, oral, combined,* and *transition.*

"By the *manual* method is meant the course of instruction which employs the sign language, the manual alphabet, and writing as the chief means in the education of the deaf, and has facility in the comprehension and use of written language as its principal object. The degree of relative importance given to these three means varies in different schools ; but it is a difference only of degree, and the end aimed at is the same in all. If the pupils have some power of speech before coming to school, or if they possess a considerable degree of hearing, their teachers usually try to improve their utterance by practice ; but no special teachers are employed for this purpose, and comparatively little attention is given to articulation.

"By the *oral* method is meant that in which signs are used as little as possible,—the manual alphabet is generally discarded altogether,—and articulation and lip-reading, together with writing, are made the chief means as well as the end of instruction. Here, too, there is a difference in different schools in the extent to which the use of signs is allowed in the early part of the course ; but it is a difference only of degree, and the end aimed at is the same in all.

"The *combined* method is not so easy to define, as the term is employed with reference to several distinct methods, such as (1) the free use of both signs and articulation, with the same pupils and by the same teachers, throughout the course of instruction ; (2) the general instruction of all the pupils by means of the manual method, with the special training of a part of them in articulation and lip-reading as an accomplishment ; (3) the instruction of some pupils by the manual method and others by the oral method in the same institution ; (4)—though this is rather a combined *system*—the employment of the manual method and the oral method in separate schools under the same general management, the pupils being sent to one establishment or the other as seems best with regard to each individual case. In this Tabular Statement it is impracticable to distinguish between the first three sub-classes of the combined method : where the fourth prevails the two establishments are designated separately.

"Some institutions which formerly followed the manual or the combined method have decided within the last two years to adopt the oral. In accordance with the recommendation of the Milan Convention, however, the old course of instruction is continued with the pupils whose education was begun before the change was decided upon, while the oral system is pursued with the new pupils. The method of such institutions is designated in the Tabular Statement as *transition*."

LOCATION.	No. of Institutions.	Male.	Female.	Total.	No. of Teachers.	Manual. No. of Institutions.	No. of Pupils.	Oral. No. of Institutions.	No. of Pupils.	Combined. No. of Institutions.	No. of Pupils.	Transition. No. of Institutions.	No. of Pupils.	Not reported. No. of Institutions.	No. of Pupils.
Australia	3	74	59	133	9	...	...	...	...	...	...	...	...	3	133
Austria-Hungary	17	645	446	1,128	60	...	...	17	1,128	...	...	...	...	...	...
Belgium	10	482	382	864	...	...	...	4	285	5	525	1	54	...	...
Brazil	1	32	...	32	3	...	...	...	...	...	...	...	...	1	32
Canada	6	412	398	810	75	1	18	1	171	4	621	...	...	...	...
Denmark	4	150	176	326	41	1	142	2	150	...	...	...	...	1	34
France	60	1,656	1301	2,957	240	5	248	7	330	7	412	9	864	32	1103
Germany*	90	1,042	908	5,608	580	...	...	90	5,608	...	...	...	...	...	...
Great Britain and Ireland	34	1,331	1090	2,421	152	7	582	7	266	13	1256	4	152	3	165
Italy	35	815	676	1,491	237	...	...	34	1,405	1	86	...	...	...	...
Japan	2	37	28	65	7	2	65	...	...	...	...	...	...	...	...
Netherlands	3	256	209	465	40	...	...	1	118	2	347	...	...	...	...
Norway	5	155	128	283	34	...	...	2	70	2	154	...	...	1	59
Portugal	1	7	1	8	1	...	...	...	...	...	...	...	...	1	8
Russia	3	...	...	...	...	...	...	...	...	...	...	...	...	3	...
Spain	7	125	97	222	16	...	...	...	...	...	...	...	...	7	182
Sweden	17	385	265	650	74	2	107	3	68	7	222	...	...	...	...
Switzerland	11	182	198	380	39	...	...	11	380	5	293	...	...	...	...
United States	55	4,034	2985	7,019	444	10	412	12	527	32	5971	1	109	...	...
Total	364	11,820	9347	24,862	2052	28	1574	191	10,506	78	9887	15	1179	52	1716

* The reports from the Prussian institutions do not indicate the sex of the pupils.

The above brief *résumé* seems properly to terminate with the following extract from the "American Cyclopædia," though the men referred to, from the nobility of their efforts and the splendid fruit achieved, are worthy of a stronger eulogy :

"In America, as early as 1793, appeared an essay 'On Teaching the Deaf to Speak,' by Dr. W. Thornton, of Philadelphia. In 1811 one of Braidwood's grandsons attempted to establish a school, first at New York and then in Virginia, but he was unsuccessful. Finally an inquiry into the number of the deaf and dumb in Connecticut was made by Dr. M. F. Cogswell, of Hartford, whose daughter, having become deaf, he was hesitating whether to send her abroad. Discovering an unexpectedly large number, he enlisted the co-operation of several other gentlemen of Hartford in the project of establishing a school there. One of these, the Rev. T. H. Gallaudet, seemed pointed out for the active initiation of the work by his rare talent, force of character, tact and amiability, and deep religious feeling. Accepting the duty, he embarked on May 25, 1815, for England, to acquire the art of instruction. Both at London and at Edinburgh the exorbitant terms imposed by the Braidwood-Watson family repelled him, and having met Sicard and his pupils in London, he finally accepted their invitation to Paris. Here he received every facility and assistance, and on his return, in August, 1816, he prevailed upon Laurent Clerc, one of Sicard's most distinguished pupils and most valued associates, to accompany him. On April 15, 1817, the Connecticut Asylum was opened at Hartford with seven pupils, and within a year had thirty-three. Congress soon màde it a donation of a township of wild land, the proceeds of which now form a fund of three hundred and thirty-nine thousand dollars. In acknowledgment the name of the school was changed to the American Asylum, it being expected that it would suffice for the whole country for a long period. But other schools were soon called for, and the asylum has long been practically limited to the New England States. Gallaudet remained at its head for many years, and when he was compelled by ill health to retire his warm interest and influence were felt until his death, in 1851. A monument was erected to his memory by contributions of the deaf and dumb throughout the country, and from designs by the deaf-mute artists Newsam and Carlin. Two of his sons have devoted themselves to the same work, the Rev. T. Gallaudet, D.D., of New York, and E. M. Gallaudet, LL.D., of Washington. The New York institution was chartered on the very day the Hartford asylum was opened. At first Watson's book was taken as the guide, and articulation was taught, but with such unsatisfactory results that in 1830 a thorough reorganization was effected, and two teachers were obtained from Paris and Hartford to introduce the French system. The French teacher, M. Léon Vaisse, after four years, returned to Paris ; the other, Harvey P. Peet, LL.D., served as principal from 1831 to 1867, and built up the institution into the largest and one of the most efficient in the world. His name is worthily borne by his son and successor, Isaac Lewis Peet, LL.D.

This institution has had among its professors many men since eminent in other walks of life.''

Deceive. Make sign for GIVE, for LIE, or MISTAKE, then bring right hand, back up, in front of breast, index finger extended and pointing to front, others and thumb closed ; thrust the index finger to front and right ; return hand, and thrust it to front and left (through the lies and mistakes given, any way but the straight way is taken).

There are, of course, other ways of noting a deception, such as making a trail in a certain direction, then scatter and go in the opposite direction ; and this would be used, metaphorically, to mislead either mentally or physically. They also frequently express the idea of deceiving one by saying that they had made a fool of the person spoken of.

To deceive in war and take advantage of the deception is not only practised by the Indians, but is considered about as high an order of merit as bravery in battle, for often the fruit of such action is much greater. It might be said that their lives, in the hunter state, are filled with the study and practice of deception, and yet I have found, as a rule, that an Indian's word or promise would be kept. Unfortunately for the race, our opinions of them in many cases are based upon the observation of the vicious habits of those who hang about the immediate presence of portions of our Western civilization, which has, by its rough and rank dissipation, demoralized the barbarian, who usually absorbs the bad and eschews the good, quickly becoming diseased mentally, morally, and physically, and in this debased condition there are few vices or crimes of which they are not capable.

Deaf-mutes make a sign very similar to the Indian sign for TRADE, only carrying the right hand well under the left ; an underhanded changing.

Decrepit. Conception : Bent with disease or age. Hold right hand, back to right, in front of and higher than right shoulder, index extended and pointing upwards, other fingers and thumb closed ; lower the hand several inches, at same time bend index. This is not used very extensively, and usually in connection with OLD.

Deep. To indicate depth of river or of water, generally a corresponding distance is measured off on the legs or body in front with spread thumbs and index fingers, others closed, palms towards body, index fingers horizontal ; and as the hands reach about the neck, raise hands above the head. To emphasize, add sign for BRAVE. To represent depth of water at a ford, the height to which the water would reach on a pony is noted by marking on arms with spread index and thumb.

Deaf-mutes simply point downwards with right index.

Deer (**White-tailed**). Conception : Movement of tail and manner of jumping. Bring right hand, back nearly to right, in front of body, index finger extended pointing to front and upwards, others and thumb closed ; carry hand from right to left several times, hand held a little loosely at wrist, so as to give a swinging motion to index finger, imitating as nearly as possible the movement of the deer's tail ; then bring nearly-compressed right hand in front of and little lower than right shoulder ; carry the hand upwards and outwards on a curve, bringing it down to same height as when starting. Frequently the first sign, representing the movement of the tail, is made with the extended hand instead of index finger, and sometimes something white is touched or pointed at. In giving the gesture for jumping it is desirable to bear in mind the way in which the different animals jump, so as to determine the nature or radius of the curve. The white-tailed deer jumps high and a goodly distance, the mountain lion not so high but longer distance ; the size of the animal has something to do with it, as with a rabbit, where the hand indicates very short jumps. There is one exception to this latter rule, viz., the frog, whose jump is represented as quite long.

Deer (Black-tailed). Conception : Movement of tail and black tip. Make, first, sign for movement of tail as above described for white-tailed deer ; then hold left hand, back nearly to left, in front of body, index finger extended, pointing about upwards, others and thumb closed ; bring right hand, similarly fixed, back up, index about horizontal, and place its tip against first joint of left index ; move right hand slightly upwards, tip of right index pressing against surface of left, rather snapping as it leaves it, and becoming partially elevated ; then make sign for BLACK.

Deer (Red). Conception : Horns and timber. Make sign for ANTELOPE (sometimes the second finger is also extended) and sign for TREE. The sign for the horns is frequently made prior to making either the sign for white- or black-tailed deer.

Deaf-mutes indicate the horns, but like all their signs for animals it is faulty, being the Indian sign for ELK.

Defame. See ABUSE.

Defy. Close the right hand, placing thumb between the index and second finger, and push it out sharply towards a person, frequently accompanied by a sharp, short, gruff grunt. As the interpreter said, an Indian is "fighting mad" when he makes this sign. It seems to concentrate and combine the elements of hatred, detestation, abhorrence, and defiance, as much as to say, "You excrement-eating dog ! Do your worst !"

Deaf-mutes simply shake the closed right hand at person.

Delight. The Crows, Flatheads, Blackfeet, and some others make sign for EXCITE ; the heart is lifted up or disturbed, though from a different cause.

Deaf-mutes combine signs for PLEASED and HAPPY.

Depart. See GO.

Deaf-mutes nearly use the same, but hand is held, back outwards, and more of a swinging motion given to it.

Depose. See ABANDONED.

Deaf-mutes knock down extended left index with right hand.

Destroy.   See EXTERMINATE.

Deaf-mutes use the same sign.

Dew.   Make signs for NIGHT, for GRASS, and then separating and partially extending fingers and thumb of right hand, pass this hand with a tremulous motion over, just above the position of the hands when making sign for GRASS, at the same time the sign for WATER is also made.

Deaf-mutes make their arbitrary sign for letter W near mouth for WATER, and then indicate this over the grass.

Die.   Conception: Going under.   Hold the left hand, back out, well in front of body, fingers extended, touching, and pointing to right; bring right hand, back out, between left and body, and at same height, index finger extended, pointing to others and thumb closed; move right hand downwards and outwards, back of index grazing lower edge of left hand as the right passes index; frequently the slightly-compressed hand is passed under left instead of having index finger only extended, as I have explained.   I have also seen the right hand alone used, passed downwards and outwards, as above, and also swept outwards to front and right, turning palm up in the movement; this latter in the sense more frequently of being *knocked over*, such as the sudden falling of an animal on being shot, etc.

This latter is the deaf-mute sign.

There is no fixed rule or law regulating property inheritance at death, other than that it goes to the kinsfolk, generally distributed, unless there may have been a will made,—*i.e.*, a verbal request,—and the provisions of this are usually sacredly carried out.

The Gros Ventres of the Prairie usually give a dying person a drink of water just before decease, for what reason I was unable to ascertain.   (See BURY.)

Faith in a happy hereafter for all is universal, and, in consequence, Indians are not agonized with fear and doubt at the approach of death.   Nature has given them, in common with all other animals, an innate desire for life, and this in connection with their social laws, which forbid self-destruction, keep them from committing suicide, so that this crime (if it can be so called) is rare.

Mr. Dunbar says of the Pawnees, that if a man died leaving a wife and no children, or only small children, his relatives stepped immediately in and took possession of all his property.   The destitute widow returned to her father's lodge, to be sold away anew.   If too old, she was sometimes cared for, but too often was left to struggle through the remainder of life as best she might.   If there were man-grown sons, they took the property, and the mother with them, who, if not sold away again, remained as in her own lodge.

Dig.   Make first part of sign for BADGER, and similar motion on left side of body.

Deaf-mutes make motions as though digging with a shovel or spade.

Dirt.   Point to the ground with extended right index, or rub tips of fingers and thumb as in Ashes. This latter is the sign used by deaf-mutes.

Disarm. Make sign for Weapon, then of Taken from some one else, not Yourself or your people. Move the right hand, back to right, well out to front of body, index finger extended, others and thumb closed ; draw the hand in towards body, at same time curve index finger : the weapons are taken away ; and the hand is moved out to right and front and left and front, as though taking away from people in circle.

To be taken from you or your people, hold the right hand in near the body, and move it outwards with index finger curved, others and thumb closed : pulled or taken from you.

Deaf-mutes make a grasping motion as though seizing weapons.

Disgust. Make sign for Heart and Tired. The head is sometimes turned to one side, and the idea conveyed by the expression of the countenance.

Dismount. Make sign for Pony, then raise right hand, carry it to right and lower it, index and second finger extended, separated, and pointing downwards ; repeat the motion to indicate more than one dismounting.

Deaf-mutes use the same sign.

Dispatch. Make sign for Write, and then elucidate how it is to come, or has come, how it is to go, or has gone ; *i.e.*, by wire or courier, etc.

Distance. Distance, by nearly all Indians, is measured by so many marches, or so many days' riding (the latter being represented by so many nights). If the pony is fresh, strong, and fleet, a great distance is covered ; if tired, weak, and slow, a small distance, of course. For people who are so nomadic, so constantly wandering from place to place, and frequently going over the same ground, it is astonishing what poor ideas they have of distance, or any standard for its measurement. Of course they at times correctly compare distances ; but, as a rule, not accurately. To do this, they mention some well-known distance, and any portion of this by the time required to cover it, mentioning at what gait, or if moving with lodges, etc. To do this in gesture speech, extend left index and forearm, held horizontally, mark off the entire distance with right index, and then indicate the fraction desired to be represented.

Distant. Bring right hand, back to right, in front of right breast, and little lower than shoulder, fingers curved and touching, ball of thumb resting on side of index, hand close to body ; push the hand to front, raising it slightly. Very distant indeed would be represented by extending arm to full length.

Distribute. Bring the right hand, back to right, well in front and little to right of body, fingers extended, touching, and pointing to front ; move the hand upwards to front, and then downwards ; return hand to first position and make similar motion a little more to left, as though giving to several persons in a circle in front of one. (See Give.)

Deaf-mutes use the same sign.

Dive. Hold left hand, back outwards, well in front of body, fingers extended, touching, and pointing to right ; bring right hand, back out, some inches in rear of and higher than left hand ; fingers extended, touching, pointing downwards and slightly to front ; move the right hand sharply downwards and outwards, back of hand grazing lower edge of left hand, fingers pointing a little more to front after passing index of left hand ; terminate movement when wrist is under left hand.

To express *coming up*, the right hand is turned to point upwards and to front after passing under left hand, and movement continued until tips of fingers are little higher than left index, accomplished by bending right wrist. The signs for RIVER or WATER are frequently first made.

Deaf-mutes bend forward, place the hands above and near head, as is usually done in diving in the water.

Divorce. See ABANDONED.

Deaf-mutes make sign for MARRY, and then indicate a tearing apart.

Mr. Dunbar says of the Pawnees, that the separation of man and wife did not often occur. Infidelity on the part of the latter was almost the only cause that produced final divorcement. Usually, through principle or fear, wives were faithful. If a case of unfaithfulness was discovered, the punishment remained in the hands of the husband. The most common penalty was that the offending wife should be unmercifully beaten, and relegated back to her father's family. I never knew of a guilty woman being mutilated or killed, as is frequent among some of the Southern tribes. The husband might retain the children or not, as he saw fit. Between him and the offending man, unless through the mediation of friends the offence was condoned, a life-long feud generally ensued. Sometimes a man, without assigning any specific reason, cast off a wife, but such conduct was not ordinarily sanctioned. On the other hand, it sometimes happened that a wife left her husband. In most of this kind of instances, if she had not eloped with another man, an understanding was before long effected, and they again lived together. The whole matter of the relation of sexes must be judged with large allowances, for certain ways of thinking, to which they were educated, tended directly to cut away all idea of mutual obligation in it.

Do. To express the idea of one working or doing for another person, or another person working or doing. (See WORK.) For another person working against you, doing evil to you, etc., bring hands, palms towards each other, well out in front of body, hands opposite and about six inches apart, held little lower than breast, fingers extended, touching, and pointing to front ; turn the hands by wrist action, thumbs inwards so that backs of hands shall be towards each other ; then, mostly by wrist action, move the hands on a curve downwards, keeping backs at about same distance as when starting, and at same time bring the hands in towards body, raising them when approaching close to it; then sweep them upwards and to front.

To slightly illustrate, take the sentence, " I think you did me an injury" (mentioning it). Make signs for I, for THINK, point to person, make the above sign, then sign for BAD. In a similar way express a good service done. In such sentences as " you made me poor," they express the idea by saying that " you gave me poverty," and poverty is expressed by the sign for POOR.

Deaf-mutes indicate action by horizontal motion of hands to front.

Do Not. Make signs for Do and No.

Do not, in the sense of some of our peculiar expressions, such as Hold on a moment, Do not go, Wait a moment, Keep cool, Keep quiet, etc., is expressed by bringing right hand, back up, fingers extended, touching, and pointing to front and upwards, in front of body, or towards person, hand a little higher than shoulder and held well out; lower the hand slightly by wrist action, repeating motion.

Deaf-mutes indicate the action, and make their sign for NOT.

Doctor. Make the sign for the person, if an Indian, his name or tribe, or locate him in some way, and then make sign for MEDICINE. If a white man, make sign for WHITES, for CHIEF, and then sign for MEDICINE. (See MEDICINE.)

The Mandans, Gros Ventres, Arickarees, Flatheads, Blackfeet, and some others, simply make sign for WORK, and for BRAVE or STRONG; a mighty worker.

Deaf-mutes feel the pulse in the left wrist with right hand.

Dog. Conception : Wolf drawing travois-poles. Bring right hand, back up, in front of and little lower than left breast, first and second fingers extended, separated, and pointing to left; draw hand to right several inches, keeping index about parallel to front of body.

Some Indians only indicate the height of the animal, and make a barking sound; others sign for WOLF and SPOTTED, and also denote the travois-pole; and I have seen the size noted and motion made of packing, on left index, held horizontal and extended.

The Arapahoes claim that the Indian dog was bred originally from the big gray wolf, the coyote, and the fox. They do not know whether this was the result of a purpose or an accident. Indian dogs certainly seem to possess, in some degree, the characteristics of all three, though now in every Indian camp the strains of our breeds of dogs are plainly apparent. With many of the Plains Indians the dog was used as a beast of burden, as a companion, and for food, and from the importance and value accorded to the animal, I was led to believe that they did not use the expression, "You dog!" etc., which is often, but not commonly, used as an epithet and term of reproach; but a closer investigation discovered the fact that they did so use it. Nearly every tribe has a band of Dog-Soldiers, and a dance named after the band; and the name so used is in a sense the reverse of derogatory.

Comparatively speaking, it is only a few years since the Northern Indians used dogs as a means of transportation (see PONY), and they are now used quite extensively, particularly north of the British line. In the summer of 1879 I saw dogs belonging to Crees, Chippewas, and Half-breeds with small poles attached to their necks, one on each side, comfortably trotting along with about forty pounds weight fastened on the poles, and the Assinaboines, at Wolf Point, Montana, use dogs almost exclusively to haul the water needed at their camp, located at some little distance from the river. The Rocky Mountain range seems to form the western geographical limit of the tribes who eat dogs. The Blackfeet, Crows, Flatheads, Nez Perces, Shoshones, Bannacks, and Utes do not eat dogs, but the Sioux, Cheyennes, Arapahoes, Kiowas, Apaches, and others prize them highly, and for a special feast *dog* is considered better than anything else. The meat combines the flavors of bear and pork, and is wonderfully nutritious; one can undergo a great deal of hard work, especially hard riding, after a hearty meal of dog, without inconvenience, and I verily believe could go longer without special desire or need for food than after a meal of almost any other substance.

Mr. Dunbar says of the Pawnees that a fatted dog constituted a most delicious repast. Formerly, a Dog-Dance, accompanied by a dog feast, was a frequent occurrence; now it is become rare, and is observed quietly, apparently that it may not attract the attention of the whites. Till recently, since the Government has undertaken to subsist the tribe, they were very rigid in refusing to touch pork in any form; but this scruple has now entirely disappeared.

Deaf-mutes slap the right thigh with right hand, and snapping motion with thumb and fingers.

Dollar. Make sign for MONEY, and hold up index finger to denote one.

Deaf-mutes use the same sign.

Door. Make sign for TEPEE or for HOUSE; then hold left hand, back outwards, well in front of breast, fingers extended, touching and pointing to right; bring palmar surface of extended and touching fingers of right hand against left palm, fingers pointing upwards; turn the hand, by wrist action, to the right, as though turning a door, with little finger as a hitch, till back of right rests against left palm.

The skin or cloth covering the orifice in a lodge for ingress and egress is called a door. The cloth or skin is simply fastened to two crossed sticks.

Deaf-mutes make the outline with hands.

Doubt. See PERHAPS.

Deaf-mutes make their signs for THINK and PERHAPS.

Dream. Make signs for SLEEP, for SEE, for GOOD, and KNOW; sometimes for NIGHT, SLEEP, WORK.

Indians place great confidence in their dreams or visions, and this is shadowed forth in the gesture. They do not think, but they see and know. Not only are the dreams of a natural and healthy sleep prized, but artificial means are constantly resorted to to secure these visions,—the sweat-bath, solitude and prolonged fasting, mutilation, etc. Some Indians have only their dreams for their "medicine" or charm to protect them from evil, as is the case with Little Wolf, a chief of the Northern Cheyennes. The Sioux chief Crazy Horse had a most remarkable dream some ten days before he was killed. While walking on the prairie near his camp one day he came across a dead eagle. He went to his tepee and gloomily sat there for many hours afterwards. Being asked by some of his people as to what was the matter, he said "that he had found his dead body on the prairie near by," and a night or two after this he dreamt that he was on an elevated plateau riding a white pony. He was surrounded by his enemies and big guns (cannon), and he was killed, but not with a bullet. He had always claimed that he bore a charmed life, and could not be killed by a bullet. In putting him in the guard-house he attempted, with his knife, to cut his way to liberty though surrounded by about twenty soldiers, and was bayoneted in the attempt. A white pony was held by one of his friends just outside the circle of soldiers, and some howitzers were standing a few yards in front of the guard-house.

Dreamer. See MEDICINE-MAN.

Dress. Pass the spread thumb and index finger over the part of body which it is desired to represent as covered. As a rule, the dress of an Indian discloses his tribe. Mr. Dunbar says of the Pawnees that boys were allowed to go without any dress, other than such bits of clothing as they might pick up, till about six years old. Girls, after three years, were covered with a skirt. The dress of both sexes was quite simple. That of the men consisted of a girdle about the loins, to which was attached the breech-cloth, and from which depended the buckskin leggings covering the thighs and legs. On the feet were moccasins. In winter the body was wrapped in a buffalo-robe or blanket; in summer a light blanket or a thinly-dressed skin was worn. But in warm weather they often went without either of these. Moccasins and breech-cloth alone were considered indispensable; the former, because without them travelling on the prairie was impossible, the latter from considerations of modesty. The dress of the women consisted of moccasins, leggings, tightly laced above the knee and reaching to the ankles, a skirt covering from the waist to below the knee, and a loose waist or jacket suspended from the shoulders by straps. The arms were bare, except when covered by the robe or blanket. The garments of the women, other than the moccasins, were made, if the wearer could afford it, of cloth, otherwise of some kind of skin dressed thin and soft. The making and keeping in repair of moccasins was a ceaseless task. The last thing each day for the women was to look over the moccasins and see that each member of the family was supplied for the ensuing day.

The full-dress toilet of a young brave was a matter of serious and protracted study. His habiliments might be few, but the decoration of his person was a slow and apparently not unpleasing process. With his paints mixed in a dish before him, and the fragment of a mirror in his left hand, he would sit for hours trying the effect of various shadings and combinations on his face and person, wiping off and reapplying the pigment with seemingly inexhaustible patience when the effect was not satisfactory. No devotee of fashion ever labored more assiduously to produce striking results in dress than some of these Pawnee braves. Quite a common recreation, after a self-satisfying adornment had once been secured, was to ride leisurely about the village or camp and complacently permit those of the common throng to lose themselves in admiration.

Deaf-mutes pass extended hands over the part of body which it is desired to represent as covered.

Dried Meat. Indicate what kind it is by proper signs for animal, and then make sign for Cutting Up, and then denote the putting or spreading same on the poles to dry.

It seems a little strange, but the Indians have no sign for the word Meat.

Deaf-mutes pinch the muscular tissue between the thumb and index of left hand between the ball of thumb and index of right to denote meat.

Drink. Conception: Drinking from the curved right palm. Compress and curve the right hand as though holding water in its palm; then carry to the mouth from slightly above, downwards, as though in the act of drinking water in that way; continue movement till hand has passed below chin. Sometimes motion is made as though dipping the hand in water, and then above gesture.

Deaf-mutes make motion with closed right hand, as though drinking out of a bottle.

Drive. (Sense of driving a herd, or running of a herd.) Bring hands, palms towards each other, in front of breast, index fingers and thumbs spread, curved and horizontal, others closed, hands opposite each other and same height, about an inch between tips of thumbs, right index pointing to front and left, left index to front and right; move the hands simultaneously to right and left, or front, keeping hands in same relative position. The hands are, of course, moved in the direction in which the herd is supposed to be driven. (See To Herd.)

Deaf-mutes simply indicate the driving of a team by imitating the holding of the reins.

Drouth. Make sign for Long Time, for Rain, and sign for No. Sometimes add signs for Grass, for Wiped Out, for Same, and for Fire.

Deaf-mutes indicate rain not, ground dry.

Drown. Make sign for Water, and express its status, whether river, lake, etc., and usually the way the person or animal went into it, and then make sign for Die.

Drum. Hold the hands as in first motion for Kettle; then, still holding left hand in its position, strike downwards several times with nearly-closed right hand, back up, hand held over the imaginary drum, and imitating their way of beating it. Usually this last part is all the sign that is made for drum, either to denote the instrument or the action.

Deaf-mutes imitate the civilized way of beating a drum.

Drunkard. Point to or make sign for the person, make the sign for WHISKEY, sign for DRINK, repeating this several times, and frequently using both hands, and sign for MUCH. Sometimes they seem to combine the sign for WANT with the sign for DRINK, by fixing both hands as in WANT, and then bring the hands, by rotary motion, round each other, close to mouth.

Dry. To express that *a stream is dry*, make sign for STREAM, for WATER, and ALL GONE.

Deaf-mutes indicate that a person is dry by holding crooked index across mouth.

Duck. The usual signs are for BIRD and WATER. Sometimes the gestures for flat bill, the color of legs, shape of feet, manner of flying are made, and the quack! quack! sounds imitated. Portions of the skin of the head and neck are used to decorate the medicine-pipes of the Indians, not only on account of the beauty of the feathers, but also from the important and sacred part assigned this bird in many of their myths of creation.

Deaf-mutes make their sign for BIRD, and imitate with both hands the waddling motion of the bird in walking.

Dull. Hold left hand, back down, in front of left breast, fingers extended, touching, and pointing to right and front; bring lower edge of right hand into palm of left, fingers of right hand extended, touching and pointing to left and front; move the right hand backwards and forwards several times, as though trying to cut or saw with its lower edge. Sometimes the sign for BAD is added.

Dumb. Press the palm of right hand over the mouth, or make sign for LITTLE TALK and for No.

This first gesture is also used to express the idea of keeping silent, taking no part in the conversation, etc. (See DEAF-MUTE.)

Deaf-mutes simply touch lips with right index.

E.

Eagle. Conception : Wings and black tips of tail-feathers. Make sign for BIRD ; then hold extended left hand horizontally, back up, in front of left breast, fingers pointing to front and right ; lay the lower edge of extended and vertical right hand, back to right and outwards, fingers pointing to left and front, on back of left, about on knuckles ; move the right hand outwards and to right, then make sign for BLACK ; this represents the black ends of the tail-feathers, and sometimes the sign for TAIL is made before this sign.

The bald-headed eagle is represented by signs for BIRD and BALD HEAD. The Berthold Indians sometimes add signs for CROOKED BILL ; and the Blackfeet for SOARING HIGH IN AIR.

The tail-feathers from the "chief of all birds," as they call the golden eagle, are highly prized, and are the chief and talismanic decoration of war-bonnets. These feathers are fastened in the hair, and also in the manes of their war-ponies. Some tribes only allow a man who has killed some one in a fight to wear a feather of this kind on the head ; *i.e.*, stuck in the scalp-lock. Should two or three be worn there, they indicate the number of people killed by the wearer. Some Indians claim that this bird was created and given them by God for its beauty, for decorating themselves, and as a special charm in battle. The Indians, as did the ancients, regard the golden eagle as an emblem of strength and courage. "Its extraordinary powers of vision, the great height to which it soars in the sky, the wild grandeur of the scenery amidst which it chiefly loves to make its abode, and its longevity, have concurred to recommend it to their poetic regard, inspired them with hope and confidence of success and victory." (See WAR-BONNET.)

The wings of the bald-headed eagle are prized for fans, and the large bones of eagles' and hawks' wings are used for whistles. (See WHISTLES.)

Deaf-mutes make their sign for BIRD, and then indicate a crooked bill, or beak.

Early. If early in the morning is meant, make signs for DAY-BREAK and LITTLE ; if early in the evening, make signs for SUN PASSING BELOW WESTERN HORIZON and for LITTLE.

Deaf-mutes indicate the first by holding right forearm under left wrist, back of hand down, and bending it up, so that it will appear a little above left hand ; for early evening, the right wrist is put over left and the hand bent down ; the left forearm is held horizontally in front of left breast in both cases.

Ear-ring. Conception : Long narrow pendant. Hold the extended index fingers, pointing downwards, others and thumbs closed, alongside of ears, backs of hands towards head ; shake the hands slightly so as to give a tremulous motion to index fingers.

I have seen ear-rings worn by Indian women a foot long and about an inch wide, made of little shells about an inch in length. Strips of bright-colored shells are much sought after for this purpose. Sometimes a large ring is fastened to the ear, and pendent from the ring there will be rectangular-shaped decorations.

The ears of male and female children are cut usually by the medicine-man of the camp at some religious festival. They are not pierced, but *slit;* sometimes three or four holes are made, and a fringe of pendants hung from them.

Deaf-mutes form a circle with the index and thumb of right hand, other fingers closed ; pinch the lobe of right ear between tips of thumb and index, and then lower the hand slightly, with tremulous motion to indicate the pendant.

Earth.   Point with the right index finger to the ground.

Most of the tribes call the earth Mother or Grandmother. A Sioux chief said to me, " The earth is God's wife. She was created, and had inside of her all that was necessary for our existence, and we to-day call her mother because we get from her all that we want, as an infant is nourished from its mother's breast. The Great Spirit went to the sky as the Great Father. He told us to pray to him, and said his soldiers should be the Thunder-Bird and Rivers. These soldiers would give to his obedient children the rain and the moisture, and would punish the wicked by drowning and by the lightning-stroke. Man learned from the Thunder-Bird to make bows and arrows. The Great Spirit is now called Grandfather, and the earth Grandmother."

Eat.   Bring the tips of the fingers of nearly-compressed right hand, in front of, close to, and little over mouth, back of hand to left and front, fingers pointing towards face and a little downwards ; by wrist action move the hand downwards, tips passing a little below and close to mouth. To represent eating rapidly, or eating a great deal, as at feasts, or many people eating, both hands are used, left being fixed similarly to right, hands passing round each other by rotary motion.

The Jesuit priests have certainly obtained a great influence over the Flatheads, Nez Perces, Kootenays, Pend d'Oreilles, and other Indians, who partially subsist themselves on fish, berries, roots, etc., while they have not over the Plains Indians.

It has been supposed that the meat diet of the latter makes them more hardy, energetic, and warlike, more restive against restraint of any kind, than are those who subsist only on fish and vegetables, and I have thought that the peculiar nature and many of the characteristics of the Ute Indians were due to their meat diet. Deer, elk, etc., have been and are still very plentiful in their country, and are their principal subsistence ; but after reasoning all this out to my entire satisfaction, I came across an article on Hindu Households, by William Knighton, in the *Fortnightly Review* for June, 1881, which somewhat qualifies my opinion. He says, "Among the higher castes the food consists chiefly of wheat and maize, flour, grain, pulse, clarified butter or ghee, milk and sweets; fish and meats, particularly mutton and fowls, are not objected to by the lower castes if they can procure them, but beef is an abomination as coming from a sacred animal, and pork is abhorred as vile and as containing the germs of disease,—only outcast Hindus partake of these last.

"Like the Buddhists, the higher castes of Hindus reverence the sanctity of life. They are warned by their religious writings against shedding blood, against the infliction of pain, against the taking of life. They hold every living animal as sacred as a human being. In Bengal, however, fish is very generally used as an article of diet by all classes, in contradiction to their religious tenets. Nor does this abstinence from animal food impair the physical strength or warlike vigor of the best classes of Upper India. The Mahratta cavalry have been praised for endurance and courage by all our writers, and the Gurkas and Telingas are admitted to make first-rate soldiers,— wiry, obedient to discipline, ready to endure fatigue and hardship, and by no means deficient in energy or courage."

Mr. Dunbar claims the Pawnees have a saying that "even the dogs, it is well (for them) to eat in peace," which seems to indicate that to the Pawnee eating was an act which claimed something of deferential respect. Without inquiring whether the apparent spirit of this maxim was always observed, it may at least be truly said that the question of what he should eat was perhaps as potent as any other that influenced him during life. It demanded ever his serious thought, provoked his ingenuity, taxed his energy, and largely controlled his movements during the entire year. When travelling they had but one meal a day, at the close of the day's march, but when at home they cooked and ate as often as hunger prompted. The ability and readiness to eat whenever occasion offered was in their estimation an exponent of health, and if an invalid failed to take food at all, hope of recovery was immediately relinquished.

Their food was in the main coarse, but wholesome. The staple articles of daily fare were buffalo-meat and corn. The flesh of smaller game, and when on the hunting-grounds that of the buffalo also, was eaten fresh, but for the greater part of the year they had only the dried flesh of the latter. Dried meat was frequently eaten raw, a mouthful of lean and of fat alternately, to facilitate mastication and deglutition, and in case of exigency fresh meat was so taken, but usually both were cooked. The more common way of preparing was by boiling; hence one of the most important articles of household furniture was a large vessel for this purpose. Prior to coming in contact with the whites they used rude pottery of their own manufacture. Such ware was in use in cooking with the poorer portion of the tribe till quite recently. Their favorite method was to boil the meat alone, or with corn and beans, till the whole was reduced to a pulpy mass, and eat it as a thick soup with spoons. If time or appetite did not permit this, it was simply boiled. Fresh meat, and sometimes dried meat if sufficient fat adhered, was also broiled by being held in suitable pieces over coals. Another usual way of preparing the former was to cover large pieces in a bed of coals till sufficiently cooked. This method was in high repute, as it preserved most of the native juices in the meat and rendered it especially palatable.

There were a number of wild plants, the root or fruits of which afforded a partial subsistence at certain seasons. The poorer people were sometimes obliged to live almost entirely upon food of this kind. Among the edible roots were the wild potato (*Ipomœa pandurata*), wild turnip (*Arisacma triphyllum*), pomme blanche (*Psoralea esculenta*), ground-bean (*Apios tuberosa*), cucumber-root (*Medeola Virginica*), a sort of artichoke (*Helianthus doronicoides*), and some others that I was never able to determine. A species of mushroom growing freely in some localities on the prairies was sometimes gathered in considerable quantities. The umbels of the large milkweed (*Asclepias cornuti*) were cut when in bloom, with the tender extremities of the stalks, and boiled as a relish. When travelling in the summer they often picked and ate, as a preventive against thirst, the fruit of the ground-plum (*Astragalus caryocarpus*). Various wild fruits, as strawberries, plums, cherries (especially the sand-cherry), and grapes were gathered in their season and eaten fresh, or dried for preservation. In the latter state they were much used in flavoring other dishes.

Breakfast is the only regular meal with Indians ; or rather, the only meal taken at a regular hour each day. Meals are prepared at other times whenever they are hungry, and whoever may be present when it is ready is asked to partake.

Deaf-mutes use same signs for EATING.

Eaten Enough. Conception : Filled to throat. Make sign for EAT ; then bring spread thumb and index finger of right hand in front of and close to breast, index and thumb horizontal, other fingers closed, back of hand to left and front ; move the hand upwards till about height of chin. To emphasize, "making a royal meal," add sign for BRAVE.

Deaf-mutes make same sign, not using BRAVE, of course ; sometimes knocking the back of extended right hand against under side of chin.

Effort. Conception : Making a push. Hold both closed hands in front of and close to breast, left hand nearest body, back nearly to front, back of right hand nearly to right, hands same height, right few inches in advance and about ten inches to right of left hand ; push the hands firmly and determinedly to front.

This sign is used in many ways, and might, perhaps, more properly have been described under MUST or PUSH.

Egg. Make signs for BIRD, and such additional gestures as will identify it, for PARTURITION, and represent the size of the egg by clasping with left hand the compressed and partially-closed right, in front of body.

Deaf-mutes hold the hands, with index and second fingers extended and touching, other fingers and thumbs closed; cross these fingers as in the Indian sign for TRADE, and then from this position turn the hands, by wrist action, so that these fingers point downwards.

Elk. Conception: Horns. Bring the hands alongside of head, palms towards it, fingers and thumbs extended, separated, and pointing upwards; move the hands by wrist action to front and rear two or three times, keeping them about parallel to sides of head.

Deaf-mutes make signs for LARGE DEER.

Elope. To induce a woman to elope is to STEAL her, and the proper signs for this are made. (See COURTSHIP.)

Encamp. Make sign for CAMP without making sign for TEPEE. This is the general sign for going into camp or bivouac.

End. Conception: Cut off. Hold left hand, back to left and front, in front of left breast, fingers extended, touching, pointing to front and right; bring right hand, back to right and front over and in front of left, fingers extended, touching, and pointing to left and front; strike downwards with lower edge of right hand; the right hand is held so that palm will just graze finger-tips of left hand as it is moved downwards. The sign for FINISHED is also used.

Deaf-mutes make the same sign, frequently holding the left forearm horizontal and moving right hand over it, lower edge resting on it, and then as it reaches the finger-tips, is dropped down sharply.

Enemy. One's enemy or enemies would be expressed by the sign for PEOPLE or MEN against whom one went to war, or people one did not shake hands with; signs for FRIEND and NO.

The Mandans, Gros Ventres, and Arickarees simply make sign for SIOUX.

I have also seen signs for want to fight or go to war against them made for ENEMY, and rarely gestures for a person of another kind, or on the other side.

Deaf-mutes hold the hands as in their sign for FRIEND, and then suddenly draw the hands apart several inches, carrying right to right, left to left, and extending index fingers, others and thumbs closed, right index pointing to left, left to right.

Energetic. To say a man is energetic would be expressed by saying he is a *pushing* man; and to emphasize it, add sign for BRAVE,—bravely energetic, strong in his efforts.

Enlist. Make sign for WORK or MAKE, and sign for SOLDIER. This is used only, I believe, where enlisted scouts have been employed.

Enough. There is no general sign for this. I never saw it used, except in the sense of eaten enough, and this is very rare. The sign for FULL is sometimes made, but hardly in this sense.

Enter. (To enter a lodge or house.) Conception: Stooping position in entering a lodge. Make sign for LODGE or HOUSE; then hold partially-compressed and slightly-curved left hand well out to the front and centre of body, back of hand upwards and slightly to front, fingers pointing to right; bring the partially-compressed right hand a little higher and nearer the body than left hand, back of hand up, fingers pointing to front and downwards; move the right hand downwards and outwards, back touching left palm and lower edge as it passes under. To express the idea of some one's entering a lodge in which you were, or of some one coming into your lodge, hold left hand in above-described position, but nearer the body; carry partially-compressed right hand in front of and little lower than left, back of hand nearly outwards, fingers pointing upwards and towards body; move the hand in towards body, slightly upwards, so that back shall graze lower edge, and slightly touch left palm as it passes. Continue movement till right hand passes above left, between it and body.

The opening to a lodge being a small triangular-shaped hole, apex above it, it is necessary to stoop to enter, hence the sign. The gestures for entering and making one's exit from a lodge are about the same; but, as a rule, the right hand turns up more in the latter sign after passing under left.

Deaf-mutes make the same sign.

Equal. Conception: Even race. Bring hands in front of breast, backs up, index fingers extended, pointing to front, other fingers and thumbs closed, index fingers about two inches apart, and in same horizontal plane; move the hands simultaneously to front, keeping index fingers in same relative position, tips opposite. This is part of the sign for RACE, and represents the two horses or men as "coming out exactly alike," "just even."

I have also seen the hands moved upwards and to front, and place the index fingers side by side. This more particularly in regard to the influence and power of two chiefs, and similar expressions.

Deaf-mutes bring index fingers together, as in Indian sign for MARRY.

Escape. Cross the wrists, hands closed, separate them sharply by swinging right to right and upwards, left to left and upwards; then make sign for Go. Sometimes the sign for LOST is made before Go, and then the latter made beyond left hand, combining signs for LOST and Go.

Deaf-mutes wrench hands apart, and then make their sign for Go.

Evening. Make gesture for sun sinking in western horizon, signs for NIGHT and for LITTLE,—the beginning of night.

See EARLY for deaf-mute gesture.

Every Day. Make sign for DAY, and repeat it several times. This is difficult to express accurately by gesture. I have also seen signs for DAY and OFTEN made.

Deaf-mutes hold the closed right hand, back to right, thumb extended and pointing upwards, in front of right shoulder (sign for DAY); then move hand to front by gentle jerks (day after day).

Exchange. The usual sign in the North is to bring the hands in front of body, index fingers extended, others and thumbs closed, back of right hand to right and front, back of left to left and front, right hand some inches higher than left, right index over left ; lower the right hand, crossing index fingers at right angles between first and second joints, side of right index resting on left.

In the South the more common gesture is to hold hands in front of shoulder, back of right to right, left to left, index fingers extended and pointing to front and upwards, other fingers and thumb closed; move the right hand to left and downwards on curve, left to right and downwards on curve, right hand passing above but close to left ; terminate movement when wrists are crossed.

The above signs are used for TRADE, BUY, SELL ; in fact, any exchange ; and I have seen both used in the North as well as the South, but the first is the more common one in the North, and the latter in the South. I at first thought that the Southern sign was used more in the sense of an uncompleted act of exchange, buying, etc., but this distinction, though sometimes made, is not usually observed.

Deaf-mutes make signs to denote GIVING and RECEIVING, holding closed right hand near breast and reaching well out with left with a grasping motion ; the left hand is then brought in towards body, right carried out over left, and when well out, opened.

Excite. Conception : Heart flutters. Make sign for HEART ; then turn the hand, by wrist action, so that back shall be to right and front, fingers extended, slightly separated and pointing upwards; raise the hand, giving the fingers a tremulous, wavy motion ; one is alarmed, excited, or frightened, his heart flutters up in his throat, and joy sometimes produces the same action.

I have also seen both hands used, as though the whole body was in a tremor. Sometimes sign for HEART is made, and then a vibratory motion given with right hand, to indicate throbbing; then a motion with both hands, to denote a lifting up of the heart, and an excited respiration indulged in.

Deaf-mutes indicate an increased flow of blood, or a palpitating action of the heart, by holding extended left hand some inches in front of heart, placing extended right between it and body, and striking left palm with back of right.

Exterminate. Conception : Wiped out. Hold left hand in front of body, palm up, fingers extended, touching, pointing to front and right ; bring palm of extended right hand just over left wrist, fingers extended, touching, and pointing to left and front ; move the right hand outwards and to right, pressing palms together ; terminate motion after right hand passes some inches beyond left. This is as though "wiped out with one blow, one effort," etc.

Frequently to indicate a more complete action, to emphasize, the palms are pressed together, and a circular motion given to each. This gesture is much used. If a village is surrounded and destroyed, if disease kills a portion, if there is no grass, no wood, no water, the same sign is used. (See ALL GONE.)

Deaf-mutes make similar sign.

F.

Faint. Make sign for DIE and for RECOVER. Sometimes the sign for BY ITSELF is made before recover.

It is difficult to see the force of the metaphoric idiom used in this connection, but it seems to indicate a peculiar manner of dying; death alone, not the final departure of the spirit and decay of the body, but death disassociated from any and all of these influences. I have seen other signs made, such as SICK, LYING DOWN, and RECOVER, and others indicating an excessive trembling.

Deaf-mutes indicate the white color coming into face, and lie over, as though sleeping.

Fainting is universally, I believe, looked upon as death, and whilst in this condition the belief prevails that the soul visits the abode of departed spirits. The following story told me by the Sioux orator and chief Running Antelope is typical of all such accounts:

"A young man, an orphan, called Little Fox, died, and went to the Happy Hunting-Ground in the South, where he found all his kinsfolk. When he returned to life, he said that he had only come back for a time; that he was going to return—*i.e.*, go back to the land of the dead—the following winter. He said the people in the spirit-land were the same as when living here. Those who had killed enemies had their faces blackened and the feathers on the head to show it. They told him that there was no use in his staying here, where there was only a remnant of his people, but to come there. A cousin of this young man had been killed in battle with a war-bonnet on, and he was scalped, but the young man saw him, dressed just as he was when killed, and an old man was singing his praises. This old man told Little Fox that he ought to have come in the way that his cousin did, as a chief, because he had been killed in battle like a brave man."

Running Antelope said he got this account from Little Fox in person, and that the young man was dead for twenty-four hours, and the following winter died for good and all; just as he had said he would.

Fall. (Season.) Indicated by leaves falling from trees. (See SEASON.)

Deaf-mutes use the same sign.

Fall. (Water.) Make proper signs for STREAM, and then hold left hand, back out, in front of body, fingers extended, touching, and pointing to right; bring right hand, palm down, fingers extended, slightly separated, and pointing to front, in rear of and little higher than left hand; move the right hand to front, and as fingers pass over left index turn them down and give them a tremulous, wavy motion; terminate movement when right hand has passed left. This gesture is very suggestive,—the left hand represents the wall of rock or other material; the right, the water moving, breaking at the fall, and the quivering motion as it goes down.

Deaf-mutes indicate the fall of the water with rotary motion of hands.

Fall (To). Hold right hand, back up, in front of centre of body, several inches from it, fingers extended, touching, pointing to left and front; sweep the hand on a curve upwards, outwards, and to right, and then downwards, at same time turning hand palm up, terminating motion when arm is pretty well extended and a little lower than when starting. This is used in such expressions as "shooting a person and have him fall off his pony;" or "striking him and have him fall off;" "riding against anything and falling off;" "shooting anything and have it fall over," etc.

Deaf-mutes hold the tips of the extended and separated index and second fingers of right hand perpendicularly on left palm, other fingers and thumb closed, and then, by wrist action, turn the hand and lay these fingers down on left palm.

Fame. An Indian glories in his war achievements, which bring him about all the glory he knows of or cares for. Therefore, to express fame, or the idea that a man was famous, you would say he was a CHIEF, BRAVE. His tribe knew it, and the adjacent tribes knew it, and perhaps add that they were AFRAID of him. Wise in council! Brave in war! These are their highest eulogies.

Deaf-mutes make their sign for TALK with both hands, moving the hands well out to right and left,—one's words spread out over the country.

Farm. Make signs for CORN and for WORK. This is the general sign. To particularize, state what was planted. Some tribes hold hands as in ROAD, and then to front as though scooping up something, and add signs for PLANTING, and sometimes the growing of whatever is planted is indicated.

Deaf-mutes make their sign for PLOUGHING.

There can be no question, I think, but that the Indians farmed much more extensively before the advent of the white race than they ever have since. Improved weapons and ponies for transportation have caused them to abandon agricultural pursuits and become nomadic. The history of the Mound-Builders, so far as is known, illustrates this point forcibly.

Farther. In speaking of two places, and to express the idea of one being farther away than the other, mention the nearest place and make sign for CLOSE; then the other place, and make sign for DISTANT.

Deaf-mutes use the same signs.

Fast. Conception: Pass by. Hold left hand, back to left, in front of body, fingers extended, touching, and pointing to front; bring right hand back to right, several inches in rear of and slightly to right of left, fingers extended, touching, pointing to front and downwards; carry right hand swiftly past left and close to it, and as it passes, by wrist action raise the hand so that fingers will point upwards and to front.

Deaf-mutes make about the same gesture.

Fat (Animal's). For a human being, say the person has a BIG BELLY. For the brutes, bring the closed hands well out in front of breast, edges pointing to front, backs about upwards, knuckles of index fingers touching, knuckles of little fingers somewhat higher than those of index (this represents the back of the animal); then separate the hands, moving them on slight curves, right upwards to right and downwards, left upwards to left and downwards. To express the idea that they were getting in good condition, growing fat, move the hands rather slowly and with slight jerks (growing round). (For FAT, GREASY, see BACON.)

Deaf-mutes hold hands as in Indian sign for BACON, and then drop the right, repeating motion, to denote the dripping.

Father. Bring the compressed right hand, back nearly outwards, in front of right or left breast, tips of fingers few inches from it; move the hand, mostly by wrist action, and gently tap the breast with tips of fingers two or three times; then make sign for MALE. Some Indians tap right breast for father and left for mother.

Deaf-mutes make sign for MALE, and then holding hands fixed as in their sign for BABY, but a little higher, move the hands to front and upwards.

Father-in-Law. Make sign for wife's or husband's FATHER.

Deaf-mutes make sign for FATHER and for "L."

Feast. Make signs for WORK, for two or three KETTLES in a row, for BRING (from several directions), first part of sign for COUNCIL, and for EAT (this latter several times or with both hands).

Deaf-mutes simply make sign for EATING with both hands.

Feasts are of daily occurrence in a large camp and form an essential part of every ceremony, either of business or pleasure. The materials for the feast are prepared by the women, and are left in the lodge in the several kettles, etc. The men gather, usually bringing their dishes, and one or two of the young warriors serve the food. As a rule, the women are not allowed in the lodge during any ceremonial or important feast. Something in the manner of grace is said by each man before and after eating, such as "I am a soldier! I am a chief! all the strong hearts join." Seated in a circle, broken at the entrance to the lodge, the man at one end begins with one of the above remarks, and each one in succession repeats it after him around to the other end. If any one is not able to eat all that is placed before him, and no one alongside will "help out," a present must be made, either to the giver of the feast or to some of the poor of the camp. Among the Cheyennes, after everything is ready and before commencing to eat, the oldest man in the party solemnly fills a pipe, and holding it towards the heavens, says, "You gave me this pipe to smoke, now I will fill it and give you the first puff of smoke from it. I want you to help me, and my ears are open to hear you." Then a small portion is taken from each dish of the different kinds of food. At least six pieces are selected and given, one to each of the four winds, one to their Grandmother the earth, and one to their Grandfather the God above; whilst holding the latter up the old man says, "I offer this to you: I am going to eat to-day, and I give you first a portion of it. I hope that what I eat may not hurt me but do me good, and that what I give you may do you good. I ask you to give health to me and to my children, that my children may all grow up to be men and women. Give us plenty of buffalo to kill and plenty of grass on the earth for all animals to eat."

Sometimes a man makes the feast in order to gain popularity, or something may be, as their phrase is, "troubling him," and he says to the Great Spirit, "I will make a feast for my people, and you, and they, and myself will eat it."

At some feasts guests are permitted to take home some small portions for their children as sacred food, especially good for them because it came from a feast.

Among the Cheyennes and some other tribes a murderer is not allowed to attend any of the ceremonial feasts.

Mr. Dunbar says of the Pawnees, that during their stay in the villages or encampments, if food was plenty, much of the time of the men was spent in feasting. Any one was at liberty to make a feast as he had the means. These entertainments were usually had in the early part of the day; still, they might occur at any hour. It was not infrequent that guests were called from sleep in the dead of night to attend a feast, and seemed to participate with unimpaired zest. When a man had resolved to give a feast, he ordered his wife to hang the kettle over the fire, and fill it with corn and beans, or meat, and water sufficient for boiling. This was done in the evening. If several courses were to be served, the viands were all set to cook in different kettles. Early the following morning he called in two acquaintances, who were to serve on the occasion. After smoking with them, he bade one to go and invite the first chief of the band, or, in his absence, the second. The chief was expected to bring his pipe and a supply of tobacco. After all had smoked, the host communicated his intention to the chief, who thereupon directed the two apparitors to go about the village and invite such persons as he named. The kettle (or kettles) was now taken from the fire and placed in readiness near the entrance of the lodge. All women and children were dismissed, not to return till the guests were all departed. When the apparitors returned, after smoking together again, they were sent out to borrow dishes, if the host had not sufficient of his own. These dishes were usually calabashes made from large gourds, and each containing a gallon or more. As the guests arrived each remained standing just inside the entrance till his place was assigned by the chief, who acted as master of the feast. If numerous, they were seated in two circles, one immediately about the fire, and the other nearer the wall of the lodge. Sometimes if those invited already proved not enough, more were called in. After these preliminaries, the master designated those who should make speeches, a number of which were expected on every such occasion. Frequently two or three old men were allowed to be present, with the understanding that they should do most of the haranguing. One of them began by making a speech in commendation of the entertainer, the chief, and other guests, and if there was any business to be transacted, he closed by stating it, and expressing his views concerning it. He was followed by the master of the feast, and after him by any distinguished person who chose to speak. After the laudation was finished and the business dismissed, an old man made a prayer, and the talking was ended. The company was then counted, to determine into how many portions the food should be divided, and some one appointed to distribute the contents of the kettle equally in the dishes. One dish filled was dispatched as a present to some one of the medicine-men. Another was placed before the master of the feast, who, carefully raising a spoonful, drained it, and returned the spoon to the person making the distribution. He refilled the spoon from the kettle, covered it with one hand, reverentially raised it toward the entrance or east, stepped across to the opposite side, directly in front of the master, and poured the contents in two places on the ground, in one place three-fourths, in the other the remainder; the larger portion an offering to the buffalo, the smaller to Ti-ra-eva. From the time of assembling, thus far the pipe and tobacco of the master were kept busily circulating. The dishes, all filled from the kettle, were now distributed to the guests, one to each, or one to every two, as proved most convenient. The contents were soon devoured, and the distribution repeated till the courses were all served. The dishes were then collected by the apparitors, and such as were borrowed returned at once to their owners. The company expressed their compliments to the entertainer and withdrew. Not infrequently it was arranged that two or more feasts should succeed each other, the guests passing from one directly to another. Several series of such feasts might also be going on at the same time under the conduct of different chiefs.

It was a usage that a guest should eat or carry away all that was set before him. The latter alternative, however, rarely occurred, as a Pawnee's digestive capacity was quite equal to any such requirement, or an accommodating friend seated near, of greater powers, would kindly devour whatever a guest might for any reason be compelled to leave uneaten. Once in a while, when going through a series of feasts, a guest might be seen sedulously endeavoring to settle the contents of his already overloaded stomach by placing his clinched left hand closely against the lower part of the breast, and striking heavily upon it with the right, shifting the position of the left hand during the process from side to side across the gastric region. By means of this pounding it was imagined that room might be secured for further indulgence. Such was an ordinary social feast. The routine could be varied somewhat, according to circumstances or the choice of the master, but the general features remained identical. The religious and cere-

monial feasts had each a character peculiarly its own. One or two
may be sketched briefly as illustrations.

One of the most important and generally-observed feasts was held
annually immediately after returning to the villages from the winter
hunt. The aim of it was to secure a healthful season, good crops,
and success in all enterprises. Both old and young men participated
in this feast, and its celebration was usually observed in several lodges
in each village at the same time. From ten to thirty men were assembled in each lodge early in the day. Several of them were sent
through the village by the master of the feast to collect dried buffalo
hearts and tongues, and from thirty to sixty of each were brought in.
The sacred bundle was taken down, its contents inspected, and
placed out in order. In its proper place with them was set the skull
of an old buffalo bull. Some red paint was prepared in a dish with
tallow by some one appointed for the purpose, and handed to the
master, who proceeded to paint his face, breast, arms, and legs. He
then divided the paint in two dishes, passing one to his neighbor on
the right, the other to the neighbor on the left. They decorated
themselves in like manner, and passed the paint to those next, and
so on till all were painted. Some one was then designated to paint
the bull's skull. The person named to this office took his place behind the skull, passed his hand, smeared with the pigment, three
times from its nose back over the central part of the forehead. One
hand was then passed on either side from the corner of the mouth
back to the base of the horn, and thence to its tip. Five rods about
a yard long were now whittled out and painted. To the end of
each was attached a fragment of the scalp of an enemy as large as a
twenty-five-cent-piece. Four of the rods were taken out and set
in the ground outside of the lodge, one toward each cardinal point
of the compass, with the bit of scalp at the top. The fifth was set
up inside, directly in front of the painted skull. Next came the
ceremony of smoking the sacred pipe. The smoke from it was
puffed up toward the sky, down toward the earth, to the four points
of the compass, upon the sacred things, upon the bull's pate, etc.,
by the master and all others present consecutively. Two persons
were then named to offer a sacrifice. One of them took up a buffalo
tongue and heart and passed out, bearing also the sacred pipe ; the
other followed with a bundle of fagots. They went to one of the
rods before set up, arranged the fagots in a pile before it, and, after
placing upon them the heart and tongue, set the pile on fire. The
same rite was repeated at each other rod. The man bearing the
pipe then returned to the interior, while the other continued without
till the piles were entirely consumed. During these services several
speeches were delivered by different persons within, and a prayer
offered. The proceedings thus far would occupy till noon. To
preserve interest meantime, the contents of two large kettles of
boiled corn, or corn and meat, were at convenient stages distributed
among the guests. A portion was also each time set before the bull's
skull. When the corn was at last all eaten, the hearts and tongues

were cut up, boiled, and dealt out, being about as much to each as a man should eat in two days. After feasting thus gluttonously, the sacred things were packed up and put in place, and the company dispersed. The proceedings lasted commonly till late in the afternoon.

Feather. Conception : Feather in wings. Bring right hand, back to front, and upwards, fingers extended, slightly separated, and pointing to left shoulder ; sweep the hand to left downwards and outwards over left arm. For a feather in the head, or one feather worn as a decoration, make signs for BIRD, for TAIL, and hold extended index finger of right hand, pointing upwards, at back of head, base of index finger resting on crown of head.

Deaf-mutes make motion of picking a feather from left arm with index and thumb of right hand, and then bring hand in front of mouth and blow it away.

Female. Conception : Hair falling loose on each side of head. Bring both hands, palms towards, close to, and parallel to sides of head, fingers extended, touching, and pointing upwards, tips about on a line with top of head ; lower the hands, at same time curving fingers as though combing with them the hair down over the ears and cheeks. This is the sign for WOMAN, and also the female of any animal. Sometimes the signs for COPULATE are made to denote the feminine gender.

Deaf-mutes indicate the bonnet-strings with right index or thumb, other fingers closed.

" Reared as these people are, surrounded by so much that to them is incomprehensible, is it strange that the seeds of blind faith should find in their untutored minds a fertile soil wherein to germinate, burst, bud, blossom, and yield a fruitful harvest of superstitious fancies ? The squaws were cooking at most of the camp-fires, around which, lounging in indolence or seated cross-legged on the ground, the older braves were smoking their pipes and discussing in low, guttural tones the events of the day, whilst the young men wooed their sweethearts in the shadows of the lodges, or strolled and stalked through the village in quest of such entertainment as the occasion afforded. Everywhere the observer was struck with the servitude to which the female was subjected, and could not fail to draw the parallel between her status in the two conditions of barbarism and civilization. In the social world of the former she is a veritable hewer of wood and drawer of water, and in her subdued looks, shrinking mien, and poor apparel is read the story of toil, drudgery, and degradation. Neither in feature nor person can she compare favorably with her lord and master, for she is a striking example in her savage state of that law of nature by which, of every created species, whether the human race or the fish of the sea, the male is made the model of beauty for its kind. Female beauty is undoubtedly the product of civilization, and the estimation in which woman is held is and will always be the best proof of its quality and the excellence of its institutions. Man has taken from her hands the rougher implements of labor, has clothed her in fine raiment, and bedecked her with jewels; has lavished upon her kindness and affection.   She, all the while, like some wild flower that, transplanted to a more generous soil and softer atmosphere, grows each succeeding year in fragrance, delicacy of texture, and richness of tint, has gone on increasing in loveliness of feature and graces of person till, long since ceasing to be but the mother of his children, she has become the ornament of his home and the object of his respectful adoration.

"What a contrast is presented by the old, withered hag before the fire! As she kneels, supporting the upper part of her body on her left hand, and clutching with the long, bony, talon-like fingers of the right a stick, at the end of which is cooking a piece of meat for the lazy vagabond behind her, there is much in her attitude, the hanging breasts, the expression of the eye, and the beak-like shape of the nose to fix one's faith in Darwinism.   Can it be possible that the common ancestors of us all moved upon all-fours, and that from such a root was evolved the beautiful flower of womanhood?"   (*Payne.*)

Few.   Conception: Compressed; occupying a small space.   Hold the partially-closed hands, palms towards each other, in front of body, lower edges pointing to front, hands opposite, but lower edge of right hand height of index of left, hands about eight inches apart; move the right hand to left, left to right, terminating movement when right is nearly over left.   This is also used for CLOSE, CROWDED, NEAR, etc.

Deaf-mutes hold closed right hand, back down, in front of body, extending fingers one after the other, commencing with index.

Fight.   Bring partially-closed hands, palms towards each other, well out in front of body, thumbs towards body, hands about height of shoulders and about three inches apart; bring right hand in towards body few inches, at same time move left out about same distance; then carry right out, and bring left in, repeating these motions two or three times, making them by wrist and elbow action.

The hands are fixed as in sign for KILL, and seem to indicate a killing by rubbing together.   I have seen the fingers extended and separated, and then close the hands, and represent shooting right towards left hand, left towards right.

Deaf-mutes hold the hands, backs up, same height, in front of body, fingers extended, separated, right fingers pointing to left, left to right, hands few inches apart; move the hands horizontally to right and left simultaneously.

In olden times the individual combat of two Indians frequently determined the success or defeat of large parties.   It was told by Berthold Indians that what is now known as Skull Butte, about forty miles below Fort Stevenson, took its name from a famous fight between the Mandans and Sioux.   "The Sioux came in large numbers, and we went out to meet them; but they were too strong for us, and drove us back towards our village, when one of our young men dashed out from our side, rode straight for the Sioux medicine-man, grasped the reins of his pony, struck the man twice with his coup-stick, and then killed him. This filled the hearts of all our men with confidence and courage, and our enemies with fear and distrust. Our people made a grand rush, charged, and drove the Sioux back, killing over one hundred of them. We afterwards put the skulls in a large circle, and in smaller circles inside the large one, which was as large as this lodge." (About fifty feet in diameter.)

Finished. Bring the closed hands in front of body, thumbs up, backs of hands nearly outwards, second joints of fingers touching; separate hands several inches, moving right to right, left to left. The sign for END is also made, though this is more common in the North for both words.

Deaf-mutes only make the sign for END.

Fire. Conception: Blaze. Carry the right hand, back down, in front of body, and well down, arm nearly extended, fingers partially closed, palmar surface of thumb resting on nails of first three fingers; raise the hand slightly, and snap the fingers upwards, separating them, repeating motion.

Deaf-mutes hold the hand in same position, but fingers about extended and separated; the hand is raised, giving a wavy motion to fingers.

In olden times fire was made by the friction of two sticks, one held vertically and given a rapid rotary motion by means of a string and bow (similar to some of the hand-drills now used). The end of the vertical stick was placed on a dry piece of wood, sometimes a little sand sprinkled on it, and rotten wood or pounded buffalo-chips placed at the foot.

When they met the whites, they learned "to knock it out of certain stones," as they express it, and now they have matches, though there are few camps of Plains Indians without a flint and steel.

In olden times a fire once started was seldom allowed to die out, they carrying the burning brands with them on all their shorter marches. It must be remembered that before they had ponies their marches were, as a rule, very short, and their villages much more permanent than after their acquisition.

Fire. (Discharge of weapon.) See SHOOT.

Fire Volleys. (Heavy firing.) Bring the extended hands, palms towards each other, in front of body, hands at about right angles; clap them together sharply several times. This is used to express heavy firing in a fight; volleys fired in battle; and has come into use since the introduction of gunpowder. A single loud clap is made to denote the sound of the discharge of a cannon.

Firm. This would usually be expressed by sign for BRAVE, with such modifications as would be necessary to express the nature, character, or necessity for the firmness. Some Indians make sign for HEART and HARD to denote firmness.

Fish. Make sign for WATER; then hold right hand, back to right, in front of right shoulder, about height of waist, fingers extended, touching, and pointing to front; move the hand to the front sinuously.

Deaf-mutes same, with the exception of usually marking length of fish on right forearm with left hand, as the hand is moved to front.

Fix. Hold left hand, back to left, outwards and slightly upwards, several inches in front of left breast, fingers extended, touching, and pointing to right and front; bring right hand, back to right and front, fingers extended, touching, and pointing to left and front, and place little finger on back of left hand near base of thumb; move the right hand outwards and to left and little downwards, as though cutting left hand with lower edge of right, at same time turn left hand slightly, by wrist action, so as to bring back up. This sign is frequently used with sign for WORK. I will fix it for you; I will arrange matters; being, I will work and fix or arrange it for you.

Flag. Hold right hand, back to right, in front of and little higher than right shoulder, arm pretty well extended, forearm horizontal, fingers extended, touching, and pointing to front; place palmar surface of extended, touching, and vertical fingers of left hand on right wrist, tips on line with upper surface of wrist; move right hand by wrist action to right and left several times, representing waving motion of a flag when exposed to the breeze. Frequently the left hand is not placed against right wrist.

Deaf-mutes make same sign.

Nearly all the tribes understand the white flag to be a flag of truce, and if they have not been deceived, and do not fear treachery, will respect it. The Cheyennes say that they learned from the Mexicans to put up a cross for the same purpose.

Flathead (Indian). Press the upper part of forehead and head with palms of hands, fingers extended and touching, tips of fingers touching above head.

The Fort Belknap Indians touch the head and then make sign for FEW or SMALL. The Flatheads and contiguous tribes usually only touch right side of head or hat with right hand, palm towards head, hand extended.

The agency for the Flatheads, Pend d'Oreilles, and Kootenays is located on a small tributary of the Jocko River, about twenty-eight miles from Fort Missoula, Montana, at the base of the "backbone" of the world, as Chief Michelle called the range of mountains which rise abruptly in sombre grandeur about one mile in rear of the agency buildings. The latter are frame cottages, painted white, and many of the yards have fine growths of flowers, strawberries, and garden vegetables.

Mr. Peter Ronan, the agent, gives the following description of the adjacent country in his report for 1878: "The mountains are covered with a dense forest of fir, pine, and tamarack, which grows very large and furnishes excellent lumber. In the lofty range, and in close proximity to the agency, are several clear mountain lakes abounding in speckled trout, and from one of these lakes a waterfall, or cataract, over one thousand feet high, of great beauty and grandeur, falls into the valley, about eight miles northwest of the agency, forming one of the tributaries of the Jocko. The valley is formed in a sort of triangular square, about five miles in breadth and twelve in length. Along the river and tributaries there are some excellent farming lands, cultivated mostly by Flatheads and half-breeds, but a large portion of it is rocky and gravelly. Following down the Pend d'Oreille River the valley closes, and for a few miles the Jocko rushes through a narrow gorge, but before joining its waters with the Pend d'Oreille the valley again opens into a rich and fertile plain, where a large number of Indian farms are located. Good log houses and well-fenced farms, with waving fields of grain, give evidence of husbandry and thrift. Leaving the Jocko Valley to the left, and passing through a narrow cañon over a low divide, devoid of hills, which forms the north side of this valley, the road leads to Saint Ignatius' Mission, seventeen miles from the agency, where the Indian school is located, and is taught by Sisters of Charity. The Missoula Valley is a broad and fertile plain, well watered by the streams which flow from the ranges of mountains that rise on both sides of the valley, and from the Missoula to the Flathead Lake—a distance of some thirty miles—are scattered Indian farms and habitations.

"*Flathead Lake.*—This beautiful sheet of water is forty-eight miles in length, and has an average width of ten miles. Around the foot of the lake, and amid the most delightful scenes that the mind can well picture, is grouped another Indian settlement, where houses and crops give evidence of thrift. Crossing the lake by canoe or boat, and following a northeasterly direction to Dayton Creek, you will find the homes of the Kootenays, living mostly in lodges, but this spring they have commenced the erection of a few houses. The Kootenays live mostly by hunting and fishing. A large prairie in the vicinity of their village furnishes them with camas and bitter-root, which they dig and dry in the spring for winter's use. In brief, it is hardly possible in any country to surpass the natural resources of the Jocko Reservation as to agriculture, grazing, timber, and water-power. The fishing is excellent in all the rivers, lakes, and mountain streams, and the hunting is good in the surrounding country."

The mission is in charge of Father Van Gorp, of the Society of Jesus, one of " those soldiers of the cross who shrink from no difficulty, are appalled by no dangers, and are as much at home in the wild wilderness, amid the painted heathen, as they are in the halls of the Escurial or the sacred precincts of the Vatican. There is something absolutely fascinating, soul-compelling, about this celebrated mysterious order, which the kings of the earth, including even the royal Pope himself, have at times persecuted and expelled. Bigotry, prejudice, what may be called the fanatical superstition of a predetermined unbelief, have all aided to invest the Society or Order of Jesus with attributes that partake of the lights and shades of romance in its grandest and gloomiest forms. The poet, the painter, the moralist, the orator, all have at times lent their genius and their renown to portraying the Jesuits in heavenly or demoniacal shapes, as power or education or belief might prompt them. Having about equally the praise or blame of mankind, and alike indifferent to both, the great order has held, in spite of all opposition, from the powerful Pope to the pigmy preacher, its own in Christendom as in heathendom, and has planted the cross in the desert before which the pagan has knelt in worship, and beheld himself transfigured in the splendor of salvation.'' In addition to this mission, started by Father De Smet in 1854, the society has St. Joseph's, at Yakema and Lapwai ; De Smet, at Cœur d'Alene ; St. Francis Regis', at Colleville ; St. Mary's, at Bitter Root ; St. Peter's, at Blackfoot Agency ; while the spiritual welfare of the Crows is attended to from Helena. Father De Smet first started St. Mary's in 1841.

I found here (at St. Ignatius') two boarding-schools. The boys are taught by the Fathers, and the girls by the Sisters, industrial arts being included in the instruction given them. They utterly condemn the day-school system. This mission is supported by the products of the soil and an annual allowance of four thousand dollars made by the Government for the education of the children. This, of course, has to pay for their clothing, food, purchase of books, etc., and is supposed to be one hundred dollars for each child, but they have some sixty children at the schools. The church was much like all Catholic churches, but the long, low building adjacent, called the '' Sisters' building,'' or Convent, built of logs, clapboarded, and painted white, contained, in addition to the Sisters, some twenty young girls. I was much impressed with this school. The dresses of the girls, the floors, tables, everything, was the perfection of neatness. The Sisters in their black and white caps and plain, coarse dresses, with the narrow band of white crêpe across the forehead, the beads hanging at their sides, the resigned and placid expression of their faces when in repose, the look of thorough renunciation of all worldly pleasure which veiled their eyes, the sweetness and gentleness and purity of their lives, cannot help exercising a great influence for good on these minds emerging from barbarism. One of the Sisters had just died after seventeen years of patient toil at this mission. The yard in rear was enclosed by a board fence, and in it was a luxuriant garden of bright, beautiful flowers, which perfumed the afternoon air. Pinks, sweet-williams, mignonette, pansies, and roses looked up to the apple- and plumtrees loaded with fruit. Some of the Indian girls had been at the school eleven years, and the chirography of several of them was excellent.

I have given some of the peculiar customs of these people under PEND D'OREILLE, a band of the Flatheads, but the following interview with Father Antoine Ravalli, whom I visited at Stevensonville, shadows forth some of the habits, beliefs, and laws of this nation. (He has since died.)

I found the father lying on his bed, partially paralyzed from the hips down. His mind, however, was still bright and his memory good. Speaking of Indian languages, he considered them similar in construction ; a word sometimes expressing an idea and conveying as much as a sentence in English. Some thirty-five or forty years since he prepared a work on the sign language, but the means for having the same printed were not at hand. Some of this manuscript was left at his former station on the Columbia River ; a part he had had here, but all had been lost. This mission was called St. Mary, and was established in 1842 by Father De Smet, and in 1844, Father Ravalli came here. He says that Lewis and Clarke, in 1804–5, found probably near here a band of Chenook Indians, who tied their young to a board and fastened to this board a second one to compress the frontal bone of the infant, which by constant pressure flattened the skull. The Flatheads, so called, never had this custom.

The Nez Perces used to wear a bone in the cartilage of the nose ; the Pend d'Oreilles, a large ring in the ear, hence the names. The Flatheads, the Pend d'Oreilles, Spokanes, Cœur d'Alenes, Colleville, and several other small sub-tribes of this nation speak nearly the same language. These people are called Shellis, those near Colleville are called Kalispel.

Father Ravalli said, "I do not believe there exists at present a pure-blooded Flathead. Their mixture with other tribes,—these tribes coming into and living in this particular locality,—has led to their all being called Flatheads. Even before the coming of the priests, and subsequently the whites, there were some Iroquois among these people who gave them the idea of the Great Spirit. These Iroquois were brought as servants of the Hudson's Bay Company, and afterwards located among the Flatheads. They, the Flatheads, seemed to have an idea in old times that some spirit inhabited the highest mountain. Their medicine-man sometimes took an animal —a beaver, a prairie-chicken—to represent the spirit, which they would worship as their personal guardian spirit. This came to them as a vision, when they, after climbing to a high mountain and fasting, were addressed by this spirit, and sometimes the animal was wrapped up and carried by them as their medicine,—a sort of guarantee of good luck, and a safeguard against evil. The most of my time has been spent with these people. I came into the country *via* the Cape and Vancouver. I was born in Italy in 1812.

"The Chenook language is a very difficult one ; I think something like the Nez Perce. It is a rich language, and has a profuse vocabulary. The Chenook jargon is very easily acquired, and though it contains only a very limited number of words, one has no trouble in expressing by means of it any ordinary ideas. It is a mixture of French, English, and Chenook.

"The sign language was much used by the Flatheads and kindred tribes when meeting others who did not use the same vocal language, or when too tired or indolent to talk with the tongue. It is a conventional language, the same among all tribes, with perhaps some slight differences ; in general it must be the same. When we first came, the Indians practised polygamy, but they were well disposed, and gave up this custom readily. The Blackfeet have not been so tractable.

"They had two kinds of dances, one to move the spirit to stir the people up to war. In this dance they were naked to the waist, painted, beating a small tambour, only warriors participating. Then after the war or expedition, another dance, in which both sexes participated. This was usually a Scalp-Dance, celebrating their victory. They had one particular gathering or dance annually, like the Blackfeet and some other nations. They had a general idea of a hereafter, a happiness agreeing with their material ideas of the present. They had a large number of ponies when I first came, but now are comparatively poor. Their riches consisted in horses. The rich went naked like the poor, but their ponies represented their wealth. Their agency was at this place, established about 1852 or '53, and only remained here three or four years. In 1849 the Blackfeet made an attack, and attempted to kill me. My house was where the old fort is now. A small boy who was serving me was killed. One man and some twenty old women were there at the time. The Blackfeet also killed a white man who was with me on Snake River. I once made two gallons of splendid alcohol from about three bushels of camas by fermenting, and with the aid of a zigzag worm of tin for a still. I took great care that the Indians should not know of this, so as to learn the art. There are many eatable roots in this country. There is a root called slocum, having a taste like hazelnut, and when cooked a taste of chestnut, rather aromatic. The second bark of the poplar-tree is sweet and good. In fact, they find many things on which they thrive and do well where a white man would starve. Some of the things are not very palatable, but they sustain life. I have had to live on these things. There is a water-plant which furnishes a kind of potato, and is very nutritious. The Flatheads never had the custom of cutting the nose for adultery. They never ate dogs.

"Surgery was mostly limited to the fixing of broken limbs, binding up wounds, etc. They had some very good roots which they used for medicine, and did not rely altogether on jugglery and superstition for cures.

"They always used skin lodges here, but farther down the river they used bark and certain reeds. When I first came they arranged themselves in rows. They had a few shot-guns, which they fired, and shook my hand so cordially, and seemed so heartily glad to see me, that I was moved to tears.

"Many reminiscences of ancient times come to me now and then, but they quickly vanish. I was in constant danger from the hostility of the Blackfeet. Lewis and Clarke were the first white men these people saw, and after them Colonel Bonneville."

The evidence of Father Ravalli, and of Chief Michelle, of the Pend d'Oreilles, would seem to support the assertion that the Flatheads, so called, never practised flattening the skulls, but that this, to us repulsive custom, was limited to the Chenooks and kindred tribes. It is a well-known fact, however, that the custom of flattening the foreheads was common to many Indian tribes. It was at a remote period of time the usage of the Choctaws, and Du Pratz says it was the practice of many other tribes in the South. Dr. Foster states in his valuable work, "The Prehistoric Races of the United States," that he has but one skull showing signs of artificial compression, and that was found in Indiana. He claims in this book to have discovered a special type of crania, which he calls the skull of the Mound-Builders, "a type so distinct that it must have belonged to a wholly distinct race, a type so degraded that it must have belonged to a very early stage in the development of man." This is a matter of importance worthy of extensive and searching investigation, as it will readily be seen that once established it must tend to dispose of the many fanciful theories concerning the origin of the American Indians.

One-half the energy and learning which have been expended in searching for proof of a foreign origin of these people would probably have established beyond question that they are indigenous to this continent, and this "type of skull, so degraded that it must have belonged to a very early stage in the development of man," may prove a key to what writers have insisted on making a great mystery. Accepting the theory of evolution, I never could understand why the evolvement could not have taken place here as well as elsewhere.

Flint. Conception: Striking with steel. Hold left hand, back up, in front of left breast, close fingers except index, the ball of extended thumb resting on side of second finger; press index finger round end and sides of thumb, latter pointing to right and front; bring right hand, back nearly up, some inches above and to right of left hand, fingers closed except index, which is curved, thumb pressing against its first joint; strike down with right hand, tip of thumb and back of curved index grazing side of left index and back of thumb. These gestures represent left hand as holding FLINT, and the right striking down with a steel held between forefinger and thumb.

Deaf-mutes make about the same gestures.

Float. Indicate the water, river, lake, etc., by proper gestures, and then bring extended left hand, back up, in front of left breast, fingers pointing to front; place palmar surface of extended right hand on back of left; move the hands with a wavy motion horizontally to right.

Deaf-mutes use the same sign.

Flood. Conception: Rising and charging. If a river, make sign for it; then hold the extended hands, backs up, near each other and little to right of body, hands in same horizontal plane, and height of waist; raise the hands till little higher than shoulders, then close the hands, carry them over right shoulder, and make sign for CHARGE. If from cloud, frost, or other cause, make signs and proper position of hands to indicate the rushing waters.

Deaf-mutes simply indicate the rising waters.

Flour. Hold right hand, back to right, in front of body, and rub tips of fingers with tip of thumb, then point to something white and make sign for BREAD.

Deaf-mutes make their sign for WHITE, and then rub the palms of hands together, like the Indian sign for EXTERMINATE, to denote the grinding.

Flower. Make sign for GRASS, holding hands a little higher ; then hold left hand, back to left and front, in front of centre of breast, index finger and thumb curved forming a partial ellipse, space of about an inch between tip of thumb and index, other fingers closed ; bring right hand similarly fixed to right of left index, and thumb little more spread, so as to clasp with palmar surface of tips of thumb and index the outer surface of thumb and index of left hand at first joints, the right thumb in this position pointing to left and downwards ; turn the hands, by wrist action, bringing thumbs to point nearly upwards, and the little fingers close together. (This represents the opening out or unfolding of the flower from the bud.) The bud is sometimes first represented—*i.e.*, after sign for GRASS—by the compressed and partially-closed right hand being placed back down, at height of the supposed stalk.

Deaf-mutes make their sign for GROWING, indicate the stalk with extended left index, and place the right hand near nostrils, as though inhaling the perfume.

Fly. Make signs for WINGS, as in BIRD, for LITTLE, and then describe the kind by some peculiar property or habit, as seen in bee, mosquito, etc.

Deaf-mutes swing the right hand sharply over left horizontal forearm, closing hand in movement as though catching a fly.

Fly (To). Make sign for WINGS, as in BIRD.

Deaf-mutes use the same sign.

Fog. Make sign for WATER ; then hold hands, backs out, well in front of and little higher than face, fingers extended and separated, right hand little nearer face than left, fingers crossed ; bring hands towards face and slightly downwards, so that spread fingers shall be rather close to and in front of eyes (one can see through, but not far and clearly ; called by some, as these signs would indicate, "smoky water," "rain"). Sometimes prior to bringing hands down in front of eyes, make motion of mixing hands and sign for not seeing well or far.

The Cheyenne Indians have a metaphoric idiom for fog, both in their vocal and gesture speech. They call it a *tortoise,* and make sign for it ; meaning one in a fog cannot see farther than a tortoise.

Deaf-mutes make sign for FINE or POWDERED RAIN, and sometimes add a similar sign to the one here first described.

Fond. Conception : Pressed to the heart. Cross wrists little in front and above the heart, right nearest body, few inches from it, hands closed and backs out ; press right forearm against body, and left wrist against right. This expresses regard, liking, fondness, affection, love, etc.

Food. Make sign for EAT.

Deaf-mutes have a gesture for things, which is a sinuous motion of right hand nearly extended, held to right of body, and move to left. They make this sign and then sign for EAT.

Fool. Make sign for CRAZY. For unwise, indiscreet, foolish, etc., add sign for LITTLE.

Idiots are rarely met with ; in fact, they claim they have none, and state that it is due to their strict laws forbidding marriage of near relations. I have seen many thousand Indians, and never saw an idiot among them.

Deaf-mutes bring right hand near right side of forehead, index finger and thumb extended and pointing upwards, other fingers closed, and move the hand to left, just in front of forehead.

Footprints. Make signs for WALK, for SEE, fingers pointing towards ground.

Deaf-mutes simply make sign for WALK.

Foot-race. Make signs for RUN, and for EQUAL or EVEN ; or, if you desire to say one came out ahead, move one hand to the front faster than the other, indicating by proper gestures that the finger going to front represents the winner.

Deaf-mutes make sign like the Indian one for FAST after their sign for RACE or STRUGGLE, which is, bring closed hands in front of body, equally advanced, back of right to right, left to left, hands height of breast and few inches apart ; bring right hand towards body and carry left out ; then carry right out and bring left in, making motions firmly and sharply, as though with great effort and determination.

Forage. Make sign for CORN, proper gesture for the animal, and sign for EAT. Hay is represented as *cut grass*.

Ford. Make proper signs for STREAM, and indicate the nature of the bottom by spreading the hands out horizontally in front of body ; then make sign for HARD or SOFT, and indicate depth of water ; if it is to be waded on foot, as in DEEP ; and if on horseback, mark on left arm the depth of water with extended right hand, back up, index finger resting on the arm ; the left arm represents the legs of the horse or pony.

Deaf-mutes indicate simply a walking through the water.

Forelock. Curve the fingers of right hand from second joints, backs of fingers from second joints on line with back of hand, and place back of wrist against centre of forehead, edges of hand pointing upwards.

This sign is used to describe the manner in which the Crows, Gros Ventres, Nez Perces, and some others wear their hair. It is sometimes used in connection with the sign for the tribe, and is used pictorially to represent them.

The hair is "banged" and kept standing straight up by means of a sticky clay.

Deaf-mutes grasp a lock of the hair over forehead.

Forest. Make sign for TREE ; then draw left hand to rear some inches, and carry right to right and front, extending right arm to full length (trees stretching out a long distance).

Deaf-mutes simply indicate many trees by repeating sign for TREE.

Forever. There is no well-defined and well-known gesture for this, and a very long time in the future is the nearest approach to it. Make signs for MY or MINE, CHILD; repeat same several times, and then make sign for BEYOND, meaning beyond my children's children, etc. I have seen metaphors used, such as "while grass grows," "while the mountains stand," etc. Some simply point with extended right index to front and upwards, extending arm to full length.

Deaf-mutes describe a vertical circle in front of body with tip of right index, other fingers and thumb closed.

Forget. Make signs for HEART, for No. Frequently the sign for KEEP is made, and after holding left index for an instant, let left hand drop (can't hold on to it).

Deaf-mutes hold extended right hand, palm against forehead, fingers pointing to left; swing the hand to right, outwards and downwards.

Forks. (Of river or trail.) Make sign for RIVER, ROAD, or TRAIL; then hold the left hand, back up, in front of body, index finger extended and pointing to front and slightly to right, other fingers and thumb closed; bring right hand, similarly fixed, and place tip of index of right against side of left index finger, fingers making such an angle as the streams or trails make. This is used to represent one stream emptying into another, the right index usually representing the smaller stream.

The forks of a trail or stream are also represented by bringing the hands, backs up, in front of body, and placing them side by side, touching at knuckles of index fingers, index fingers extended and horizontal, others and thumbs closed, right index pointing to right and front, left index to left and front. Sometimes the left hand, back up, is held in front of body, and the forks represented by extended and separated index and second finger, other fingers and thumb closed.

Deaf-mutes indicate the current flowing with both hands, and then separate the hands, denoting a separating of currents.

Fort. Conception: White soldiers' house. Make sign for WHITES, for SOLDIER, and HOUSE.

Deaf-mutes indicate an embankment or enclosure, and cannon.

Found. This is represented by I SAW IT, PICKED IT UP, or CAUGHT IT.

Deaf-mutes use the same signs.

Fox. Indicate size of animal, and the long, large tail with white tip; also color of hair, and the jumping-sideways motion in running.

Fragrant. Conception: Smells good. Bring right hand, back nearly up, in front of lower part of face, first and second fingers extended, separated, nearly horizontal, and pointing towards face, tips close to chin; move the hands upwards by wrist action, nose passing between tips of fingers; then make sign for GOOD.

Deaf-mutes pass the open right hand from below up past nostrils, palm towards face.

Indians are not only fond of, but apparently think there is some charm in many of the sweet-smelling roots, herbs, and grasses, and frequently have tiny sacks filled with something of the kind tied to the hair or fastened to a string round the neck. It is simply wonderful how many sweet-smelling grasses they will find in a country where a white man would fail to find any. Being thus fond of sweet smells, it is strange how indifferent they are to many foul ones. Most Indians have a personal exhalation, a sort of characteristic halo or atmosphere, entirely unlike that which marks a negro, but in its way just as strong, though less offensive, and which a Government mule will tremblingly detect at a great distance. It is a pungent, musty odor, something like that of combined smoke and grease.

Freeze. Make sign for COLD, and then add explanatory signs : if of water, that ice is forming ; if of body, that the cold *kills* the part.

Deaf-mutes make their sign for WATER, and then hold hands, backs up, in front of shoulders, fingers extended, separated ; curve the fingers slightly.

Freeze Over. Conception : Ice closing over a stream. Make sign for COLD, for WATER or STREAM ; then hold the extended hands, backs up, in the same horizontal plane, in front of and little lower than shoulders, fingers pointing to front ; move the hands towards each other, index fingers meeting and sides touching in front of body. This represents the ice formed on the surface of the water.

Deaf-mutes make their sign for WATER, FREEZE, STRONG, and WALK OVER.

Friend. Conception : Brother, and growing up united, together. The most common sign in the North is to hold the right hand in front of and back towards neck, index and second fingers extended, touching, pointing upwards and slightly to front, others and thumb closed ; raise the hand, moving it slightly to front at same time until tips of fingers are about as high as the top of head. (Sometimes the index finger of each hand is used, and the hands raised similarly.) The hand is fixed as in BROTHER, and raised as in GROW.

The Southern Indians frequently link index fingers in front of body by bringing left hand, back out, well in front of breast, index finger extended and pointing to right, other fingers and thumb closed ; bring right hand, back to rear and right, index finger extended and pointing upwards, other fingers and thumb closed, and place palmar surface of right against left index, curving and linking them firmly. This evidently comes from clasping hands, and some tribes make this sign for friend.

The Berthold Indians make sign for BROTHER. The Flatheads use both index fingers as I have explained, whilst the Apaches, Kiowas, and Comanches link the index fingers.

Deaf-mutes link index fingers twice, first holding left hand back down and then turning it back up.

The men of some tribes have friends or "partners" in their own tribe, or sometimes in other tribes with which they may be thrown, or among the whites. This characteristic is specially seen among the Arapahoes. They really seem to "fall in love" with men, and I have known this affectionate interest to live for years, surviving lapse of time and separation. The adoption is about the same as explained under BROTHER.

Frighten. See EXCITE.

Deaf-mutes throw up the hands and draw back the body, as though cowering before danger.

Frog. Make sign for WATER; then compress the right hand, hold it back to right, in front of and little lower than shoulder; move it to front on a curve upwards to front and downwards, imitating motion of frog jumping.

Deaf-mutes indicate the jump with right hand, but extend first and second fingers, others closed.

Frost. Make sign for COLD. Sometimes add signs for GRASS and KILL.

Fruit. It is necessary to specify the kind; no general sign.

Funeral. Make sign for BURY.

Future. It is necessary usually to specify time. The hands are drawn apart frequently as in BY AND BY, to denote an indefinite future time.

Deaf-mutes make their sign for TIME, and then push right hand, index finger alone extended, well to front.

G.

Gall. Hold compressed right hand against surface of body over location of gall ; then rub the tips of fingers against left palm, extended left hand held horizontally, back down, in front of body ; then point to something yellow.

Frequently the signs for LOSE and BAD are also made, to indicate the bitter taste of the liquid. I have referred to the hard yellow substance sometimes found in the gall-bladder, and highly prized for medicine-paint, under BUFFALO, and also the uses made of the liquid.

Gallop. Make sign for RIDE ; then bring the hands in front of centre of body, back of right to right, left to left, fingers extended, touching, and pointing to front ; left hand near the body, right in front of and little to right of left, tips of fingers of left hand opposite right wrist ; move the hands simultaneously up and down several times by wrist action, the tips of the fingers describing vertical curves. To indicate galloping a long distance rapidly, the hands are from above-described position moved to the front, after making the gesture with a wavy, tremulous motion, introducing the idea of going like the wind. Sometimes the hands are held as RIDE, and then the left hand moved as above described.

This latter is the deaf-mute sign.

Game. Specify whatever kind it may be.

Gap. (Mountain pass, or depression in bluffs.) Hold the left hand, back out, in front of breast, index and thumb spread, others closed, thumb pointing upwards and to left ; pass the extended right hand, palm towards left thumb, lower edge resting on left hand between the spread thumb and index. (This indicates going through, or the possibility of going through the pass.)

It would perhaps be well to first make sign for MOUNTAINS or HILLS.

Deaf-mutes indicate a mountain-pass.

Gender. See signs for MALE and FEMALE.

Generous. Make signs for HEART, and for BIG or GOOD.

Deaf-mutes make their sign for GOOD with both hands.

There are few people so generous as the Indians, in fact, liberality is so largely developed that it crowds out gratitude, as we know and understand the word. Generosity is one of the essential steps to chieftainship, as I have stated, and stingy Indians are rare. They are nearly always held in great disfavor, and are thoroughly condemned by public opinion for their meanness.

In their religious and war ceremonies, at their feasts, festivals, and funerals, the widows and orphans, the poor and needy, are always thought of ; not only thought of,—for this is done by the kneeling crowds in our gilded palaces, rich in ornament, called churches, where the softened and beautified light, coming through stained glass, falls like a true halo from heaven, crowning each bowed head with tints of rose and violet,—but their poverty and necessities are relieved. The hearts of our outcasts and poor are not, commonly, very much gladdened or their burdens lightened by hearing that we are to have a great supper or a grand ball, or some impressive religious ceremony. But with these wild and barbarous people, in torrid and arctic climates, these gatherings mean also gifts for the needy and suffering. These gifts are made with as much ostentation as possible, and are called "prairie gifts," or a gift "by itself," meaning that nothing is seen but the gift; no reward or return is in sight or is expected; and for days after the camp-crier and the women of the camp sing their praises of the donor,—his feats in war, his bigheartedness in peace.

I have seen white men reduced to the last "hard tack," with only tobacco enough for two smokes, and with no immediate prospect of anything better than horse-meat "straight." A portion of the hard bread was hidden away, and the smokes were taken in secret. An Indian, undemoralized by contact with the whites, under similar circumstances, would divide down to the last morsel. This characteristic may be accounted for both by his nature and his training. He finds a thousand ways to support life where a white man would starve; and a firm confidence in himself stifles fears for the future, assuages the pangs of hunger, and begets a lively faith that Nature will furnish him with food. The "taking no thought for the morrow," generosity, liberality, and hospitality have all been obstacles to their advancement in civilization, and will continue so to be until they can learn and practice something of the thrifty economy of our friends, the Jews and Chinamen.

Ghost. Expressed by the gesture for one who dies and walks about at night; adding also signs for seeing him, and his looking like something white.

Frequently the index fingers and thumbs are curved into a circle, other fingers closed, and their circles placed over eyes, to denote the big eyes which ghosts are supposed to possess.

Deaf-mutes make signs for White, for Wrapping Up, and for Spirit.

Indians say that they sometimes hear and frequently see ghosts; and physical afflictions are often attributed to their malign influence. Wonderful and thrilling stories are told of men who have been killed while out from camp with a war-party, and long before the party returned, or any news was heard of it, the family lodge would be entered by the spirit of the deceased.

The belief that the spirits of deceased persons who die away from home return to their village before starting for the Happy Hunting-Ground, and by ghostly footsteps and weird, windy whisperings give information of their own deaths to their kinsfolk, seems to be quite common.

Girl. Make sign for FEMALE, and hold right hand, back out, in front of and to right of body, index finger extended and pointing upwards, others and thumb closed, holding hand at supposed height of girl. Sometimes signs to indicate " not married" are made.

Deaf-mutes make their sign for FEMALE, and indicate height.

Give. Hold right hand, back to right, fingers extended, touching, pointing to front and upwards, in front of body at about height of shoulder ; move the hand outwards and downwards. If giving to more than one, make the motions as though persons were in your front in a circle. Some Indians use both hands.

For a *free* gift, when nothing is expected in return, make, first, the sign for BY ITSELF. Sometimes this is called a prairie gift,— nothing in sight but the gift ; and this expression is always used in reference to gifts made to the poor.

Deaf-mutes hold closed right hand near body ; move it outwards and open it.

Give Me. Bring the right hand well out in front of body, about height of neck, back of hand nearly to left, lower edge nearest to body, fingers extended, touching, and pointing upwards ; draw the hand in towards the body, at same time lowering it slightly. In bringing hand in towards body keep it as nearly as possible in same vertical plane.

Deaf-mutes hold the open hand well out in front of body, close it, and bring it in close to body.

Give Name To. Make signs for CALL and for GIVE.

A young man, after making his maiden effort on the war-path, if he has met with success, "sheds" his boyish name, and is given frequently the name by which some of the old men in his tribe have always been known. (See NAME.)

Glad. Conception : Daylight or sunshine in the heart. Make sign for HEART, and then carry left hand out to position for DAY ; carry right hand simultaneously out from position over heart, sweeping it to right, and moving palms up as explained in DAY. Carrying hands into positions on curves thus, gives grace and beauty to movements. Some Indians make sign for HEART, and then make sign for LIGHT ; and others indicate the heart as fluttering, as in EXCITE, while others simply make signs for HEART, GOOD, and BIG or BRAVE.

Deaf-mutes hold palm of extended right hand against surface of body over heart, patting same for pleasure, and moved circularly for happy, pleased, etc., meaning *glad.*

Gloomy. Conception : Clouds are close. Make sign for CLOUDS, and with the hands in this position lower them to near head. (The clouds press down upon one.) This is a very common metaphor. The clouds are close, the world is dark and gloomy. (See also CROSS, SULLEN.)

Deaf-mutes hold extended right hand, back out, in front of face, fingers pointing upwards, hand few inches from face ; lower the head and hand at same time.

Glove. Pass the spread thumb and index of right over left hand. This, of course, would mean any covering for the hands. Deaf-mutes use the same sign.

Glue. Conception : Fastening feather-guides to arrow. Make sign for ARROW, and then hold left hand, back to left, in front of body, index finger extended and pointing upwards, other fingers and thumb closed ; carry the extended index of right hand to front and downwards, other fingers and thumb closed, as though dropping or dipping it into some vessel ; then bring right hand up, and rub side of left index with palmar surface of right index near end. Indians made and still make a very good glue from the thick muscles and muscular tissue found on each side of the neck of a buffalo bull or bull elk. This is boiled in water for two or three days, and when of a thick, sticky consistency, or, as they say, "when it gets right," a small stick with notches on the end is twisted and turned in the contents of the vessel, until a large amount adheres to it ; this hardens on cooling and exposure to the air, and the glue is kept in this way for long periods of time. Sometimes the scrapings of an elk-horn are boiled with the muscular tissue, but it is not necessary. When used, a small portion is chipped off and gently heated in water ; the amount of the latter being regulated, of course, by the amount of glue needed. It is used for fastening the feather-guides to arrows, fastening sinew on the back of bows, fastening the hair on the feathers of a war-bonnet, etc. ; in fact, used when glue or cement would be necessary or desirable, and possesses the qualities of both, though in an inferior degree. It is whitish in color, unless stained or colored, as is sometimes done, with ochre.

Go. Hold right hand in front of body, back to right, fingers extended, touching, pointing to front and downwards ; move the hand to front, at same time, by wrist action, raise the fingers, so as to point to front and upwards. The hand can, of course, be held to right or left of body, making the motion to indicate the direction, and is usually so made. "I am going," make sign for I and above sign. "Going to and reaching a place," is expressed by the signs for ARRIVE THERE.

Deaf-mutes wave the right hand outwards from body, back outwards and upwards.

Go Away. If speaking to a person with you, simply make sign for Go ; but if to tell people who are approaching to "go away," the right hand, palm out, is waved from the body outwards and to right.

Go Near. To illustrate, take the sentence, "I am going near the Sioux camp," make signs for I, for Go ; then sign for ARRIVE THERE ; but right hand stopping little short of left hand for SIOUX, and for CAMP.

In sentences of similar construction, the signs for Go and ARRIVE THERE are frequently combined. This sign for Go being indefinite, needs other gestures to fully establish its meaning.

Goat. Conception : Horns, and long hair under chin. Bring the hands alongside of head, index fingers extended and pointing upwards, other fingers closed, hands held just over ears; then place the back of right wrist against under side of chin, hand partially compressed, fingers extended, slightly separated, and pointing downwards. Some Indians add also the signs for WHITE HAIR.

Deaf-mutes use same sign.

God. Make sign for MEDICINE and point to zenith, or add sign for GREAT and point to the zenith with extended index of right hand; frequently the signs for WHITES and for CHIEF are made. The Flatheads and Crows make the sign for the OLD MAN IN THE EAST, but the more common name is, as I have given it, the Great Mystery, or Medicine Chief, or Great White Medicine Chief above.

Deaf-mutes raise the right hand, to full extent of the arm, in front of body, index finger alone extended and pointing to zenith; then lower the hand, at same time extending the fingers and thumb.

I once asked a very intelligent Indian, one who keenly and bitterly felt the loss of his country and the fall of his people, why it was he made the sign for a white God in the heavens? why not a Cheyenne, Crow, Sioux, or Pawnee God? To which he replied, "Long ago my people had two Gods above to whom we prayed,—one was in the North, who was the God of the snow and cold winds, as well as of the large game; the other, the God of the warm sunshine and growing grass, was in the South, where all the birds go in winter. The white people came among us, scatteringly at first, and then like a flood; they drove away our game in the name of God, who was above; lied to us in His name, robbed us of our country in His name, and, I think, He must be a white God!"

Keokuk, chief of the Sacs and Foxes in the Indian Territory, said to me in answer to my questions in regard to the story of the creation of his tribe, "God made the Indians—the Sac of yellow, the Fox of red, clay. He then made woman out of man's rib. The beaver wanted it always night, God's son always day; so God made it half daylight and half darkness." This, he insisted, was the Sac and Fox account long before they met the whites.

Questioning the Assinaboines at Fort Belknap, I found that they formerly had an image cut from wood, which represented the Unknown above. To this they made presents and offerings, and at stated intervals all gathered round it. They also said, "The same white man's God, which this image represented, gave us the bow and arrow and showed us how to kill game. Afterwards the white man showed us how to use the medicine iron."

It will thus be seen how difficult it is to get any correct idea of the original beliefs of our aborigines about what the interpreters call the "Great Spirit." There is nothing in the vocal word, but the gesture does give a clue. It is *the white man's God*, and a close investigation into such religious ceremonies as have been preserved from the corroding influences of time and the alterations of our own beliefs, leads me to assert that the Indians were limited pantheists,—if I may use such expression as meaning that they did not believe that the universe, taken as a whole, was God, but that every-thing in the world had its " spiritual essence" made manifest in the forces and laws of nature.   They were also limited polytheists, in that they deified the oldest people of their tribe whom tradition gave any account of.   These two were united, in most cases, by the shadow, hardly the substance, of fetichism ; something akin to the superstitious feeling which many of our own race still have in regard to the influence exercised on our fortunes by a horse-shoe nailed over the door or fastened to the wall ; though the Mandans, in their worship and sacrifice to the spirit of wood, pass beyond the shadow and reach the substance.

One who knew nothing of our religious views might be led into error by seeing a Catholic solemnly counting his beads, and rev-erently bending the knees and bowing in worship before a cross. And so the sight of a savage piously whispering his prayer to a painted stone, or devoutly pointing his pipe and humbly making his petition to the white skull of a buffalo, might lead one to form erroneous opinions.

The belief of the Indians, though something like that of the ancient Greeks, had not crystallized into such shape that names were given for a definite number of superior, and an indefinite number of in-ferior, gods, but the forces of nature worked for them good or evil ; *i.e.*, good luck or bad luck.

It is as difficult to obtain a definite and clear understanding of the Indian's view of the "spiritual essence" propitiated by their sacri-ficial worship as it is to define our own ideas of God ; and in this connection the following extract from an address recently made by an eminent divine, Professor David Swing, may be appropriate :

" What a calamity to the religious nature of man were we all com-pelled to find only one import to words, and to live and die with one interpretation !   The Creator of man having made him to be of broad and varying taste, did not forget to make equally the realm where he must pass his life.   An unlimited mind demands an un-limited objective and subjective world.   The wings of an eagle be-speak for it the open air.   It, therefore, comes to pass that all can-not and need not think of the very foundation of religion, the Deity, with the same thoughts.   He may appear before one in the likeness of man, His raiment glistening in excessive light, His hair white as wool, with the wisdom and dignity of eternal years.   To another He may seem as broad as all space, as omnipresent as the sweet ether, as invisible as music.   To another He may seem within all life, the soul of all that lives, while others may say in humility, ' who by searching can find out God !' "

The Indians are essentially a religious people, or more correctly, a superstitious people, and as bats thrive best in darkness, so do super-stitions in barbarism.   Therefore it seems natural that they should believe in the direct agency of superior powers, and consequently their sacrificial system is the natural result of their belief ; and their vision-seeking, through steam-baths, fasting, and self-mutilation, the only means of ascertaining the will and wishes of these mysterious powers, as well as to gain their assistance.

Morality has no place in superstitious worship, and hence we find that the morals of the Indians are not sensibly controlled or regulated by any religious views they may have. Crime is not a violation of the laws of any of their mysteries or Gods, but an infraction of the material laws which they find necessary to their physical existence as a people or tribe. The sweet promises of future rewards, or the dire threats of future punishments, are totally and entirely eliminated, except so far as virtue in bravery is concerned. Those killed in battle go to the hereafter by the starry trail in the heavens (Milky-Way), and are met in that "far-off land" with songs and feasts and made chiefs.

In addition to the general mysteries which all Indians hold in common superstitious awe, individuals frequently have a personal mystery, which exercises a direct influence upon all the more important events of their every-day life, and from whom information is received by means of visions or inspirations, in the shape of warnings of danger or advice, which will secure success. This personal God may always appear in the same form, and directly foreshadow coming events, or may cause the Thunder-Bird to flash forth an omen, an owl in the stilly darkness of the night to solemnly hoot an admonition, the toes of moccasins thrown in the air to fall pointing in a certain direction, so that the flight of a bird or the direction of the wind has determined the course and result of many war expeditions.

Gold. Make sign for MONEY, then point to something yellow in color.

Deaf-mutes hold right hand as in their sign for little Y; give it a trembling motion, and then make their sign for METAL.

Good. Conception: Level with the heart. Hold the extended right hand, back up, in front of and close to left breast, fingers extended, touching, and pointing to left (index finger usually rests against breast in this position); move the hand briskly, well out to front and right, keeping it in the same horizontal plane.

I have seen Chippewas make the sign for GOOD with the left hand, and sweep it well round to the left. The Utes pointed to something good; and, for a person, used sign for TRUE or STRAIGHT. The Yankton Sioux sometimes sweep hand out from heart, turning, back down, as in DAY.

Deaf-mutes place palmar-surface ends of fingers of extended right hand on lips, fingers pointing upwards, wave the hands outwards little to right and downwards, turning palm up. This is also used for "Good-day," "Good-by," "Thank you," etc.

Goose. Make sign for BIRD (remembering the long swinging motion made by the wings of a goose in flying), then make a sound as closely as possible imitating that made by a goose. Instead of the sound, the peculiar triangular shape taken by flocks of these birds in their migrations, or some of the habits of the bird, are sometimes represented.

Grandfather. Represent by proper signs the father of mother or father. Many tribes call "God" grandfather in their vocal language, instead of the "Great Mystery," or, as it is translated, "Great Spirit." Many tribes also call the sun grandfather.

Deaf-mutes make their sign for FATHER, repeating motion of moving crossed hands to front.

Grandmother. Represent by proper signs the mother of mother or father. The Indians call the earth mother or grandmother,—she provides nourishment for her children. Many Indians simply make signs for OLD MAN or OLD WOMAN for grandfather or grandmother.

Deaf-mutes make sign for MOTHER, and then move the crossed hands to front second time.

Both the signs for grandfather and grandmother are sometimes indicated by making sign for FATHER or MOTHER, and then sign for BEYOND, as is the usual way of representing former generations.

Grass. Hold the hands, backs downwards, well down, arms extended to full length, in front of or to left or right of body, fingers and thumbs well separated, slightly curved, and pointing upwards, right hand close to and little in advance of left, hands about same height, little finger of right hand near to fingers of left hand ; separate the hands some inches, moving right more than left and to front (considering edge of left hand as determining this direction).

Deaf-mutes hold right hand in sign for letter G, give trembling motion to it, which is sign for GREEN ; then make their sign for GROW, and indicate stalk with extended index finger.

Gratitude. There is no general single sign for this, but it is expressed usually by, "You have taken pity on me ; I will remember it, and take pity on you." (See PHRASE.)

Deaf-mutes hold the right hand near heart, thumb and index nearly extended, and palmar surface near ends pressed together, other fingers closed ; move the hand outwards (represents drawing something from the heart, and means "thanks") ; then make their sign for GIVE with both hands.

There are many well-known cases on record of Indian gratitude surviving the lapse of years, the trials of a burdened life, and keeping pure and strong in the midst of treachery, ingratitude, and deception dealt out to them ; and I have no doubt there have been many individual Indians who have possessed a warm, friendly feeling for a benefactor ; in fact, I have seen decided exhibition of this sentiment. But a feeling of thankfulness, a keen, lively sense of gratitude, can only live in an atmosphere of selfishness, can only be kept alive by contrast, and illiberality is a product of civilization, not of barbarism. I use the word selfishness here mostly in the limited sense of greed, or of a hope of gain, a desire for the accumulation of worldly goods, and gratitude mostly in the sense of an appreciation for gifts received to relieve physical wants. An Indian is stricken with a great grief ; death takes away his wife or his child ; all of his possessions are given away ; he and they all knowing that in a short time gifts will be made to him which will perhaps more than counterbalance the goods distributed. A young and ambitious warrior, returning from a successful horse-stealing foray, presents the fruit of his efforts to the poor of the camp. He and they all feel that his reward has been paid by the high estimate public opinion places on his merits and the advantages which will result from such public estimation.

Grave. (Burial-place.) Make signs for DIE and for BURY.

Deaf-mutes make motion as though digging with spade or shovel, and then sign for DEAD.

Gray. Conception : White and black. Point to something white in color, and make sign N, or point to something black. Sometimes sign for LITTLE is added to each sign.

Deaf-mutes indicate white and black mixed.

Grazing. Conception : Cropping grass. Make sign for ANIMAL, and frequently sign for GRASS ; then hold right hand, back up, fingers partially extended, slightly separated, pointing about downwards, well out in front of body ; lower the hand, at same time compress the hand,—*i.e.*, bringing tips of thumb against tips of fingers ; raise the hand and repeat motion in different places in front or to right or left of body.

Greasy. Make sign for FAT. Some Indians rub inner surface of extended fingers of right hand over blanket for this word, and only use the gesture given under FAT to indicate thick or thin, according as the left hand drops down between thumb and finger of right.

Great. Bring the extended hands, palms towards each other, well in front of breast, hands opposite, few inches apart, and fingers pointing to front ; separate hands, carrying right to right, left to left.

To indicate an object as high as well as broad, the extended right hand held horizontally, back up, is raised in front of body.

Deaf-mutes make sign for letter G, and then the above.

Green. Point to something green. Sometimes sign for GRASS is made to denote the color.

Deaf-mutes make sign for letter G, and then give a trembling motion to hand.

Grieve. Make sign for CRY, and also indicate that the hair is cut off.

Grizzly. Same as GRAY.

Gros Ventre (Indian). The Crows make the sign for BIG BELLY to denote the Gros Ventres of the Prairie, and sign same as for ARICKAREE, or for DIRT HOUSES, to denote the Gros Ventres at Berthold, while the latter frequently hold the nearly-closed right hand, back to right, near mouth, back of thumb touching lips ; twist and carry the hand to left, as though twisting something with this hand to facilitate biting it off,—the gesture meaning bitten or cut off. There is also a band of Ogalalla Sioux, Little Wound being the chief, which has the same sign ; they are called at the agency (Pine Ridge, Dakota) the Cut-off band. The Gros Ventres claim that this name (Big Belly) was given them by the whites. Neither this tribe nor the Gros Ventres of the Prairie have larger abdomens than other Indians. The agent at Fort Berthold, Dakota, where this tribe is located, gives the number as four hundred and forty-five, in his report for 1881, so that only a remnant is left of a once-powerful nation numbering several thousands. I visited the agency in June, 1881, and gathered most of the following data from the chief, Poor Wolf, whom I found to be a venerable, professor-like-looking old fellow, dressed in an army-blue coat and trousers which, in true professor-like style, were a little too short, a pair of old-fashioned iron spectacles rested uneasily on his nose, a calico shirt, a paper collar, and black "fly" cravat, which was, of course, askew, completed his toilet. He was sixty-one years of age, and was born near the mouth of Knife River. He informed me that the Gros Ventres call themselves Hidatsas, which was an abbreviation of the words for Red Willow village. They migrated towards the Missouri River from the North, and here first met the Mandans. The Arickarees were then below Fort Pierre.

In olden times, before the Crows left, there were three chiefs who controlled and regulated all the affairs of the camp. Crossing the Missouri, they camped on both sides of Heart River. An arrangement or agreement had been entered into in regard to the buffalo killed on each side of this stream, Heart River; a dispute arose over one killed in the stream, which led to angry feeling and a separation. They formerly had an annual Sun-Dance, which was peculiar in that the person who made it was forced to secure a large number of buffalo-robes, seventy or eighty, have them carefully dressed, garnished with porcupine-work, before he notified the headmen, who then had the crier formally announce the information to the camp. At the dance these robes were given away. The ceremony seems to have differed but slightly from that observed by the Sioux, a mock battle being fought over the Sun-Dance pole, and then they hauled it to camp with their lariats. In addition to the ordinary mutilation, they frequently cut off the little fingers in this dance. The old man claimed that they had "corn, tobacco, and beans when they came out of the ground, and since then the whites had given them potatoes, melons," etc. They bury their dead mostly above-ground, in trees and on scaffolding, but this depends on the wishes expressed by the person just before death. The widow inherits the property. No food is taken to the grave. The "Happy Hunting-Ground" is located as beyond the rising sun.

They did not eat dogs in olden time, and never, until recently, wore the scalp-lock. They have a special dance when the corn has ripened sufficiently to be eaten; this was commanded by their God when He first gave them the corn. The women wear their dresses quite short, and do not use a "protection string." Poor Wolf, though not absolutely vouching for the truth of the story,—in fact, to do him justice, he said he did not know whether it was true or not, but said the tradition had been handed down to him by his forefathers,—gave me the old, old story of the origin of the Hidatsas, including, of course, the Crows. Formerly, said he, they lived in a world under the earth, when one day a man, by the aid of a root or vine, climbed above, out from that inner or lower world to this fair earth. He remained some time, and then, by this same ladder of destiny, returned to his people, told them of the better and more beautiful country above, and they made, by means of the root or vine, the ascent ; not all of them, however. Half of the tribe had made good the ascent, when a fat old woman, large beyond description, and additionally heavy with her unborn child, started, sailor-like, up the vine ; it broke, and the rest were doomed to remain in their lower world. This story is carefully and definitely located at Devil's Lake, Dakota.

The part of the tribe who had thus fortunately come upon this beautiful earth soon suffered the inconvenience of a flood, and many were drowned. They were still numerous and strong, were divided into three bands, then into two, and camped separately, and located imaginary geographical lines of possession, so far as the game was concerned. This led to the trouble which finally separated them from the Crows. Their known migrations are limited to the Missouri River Valley, and from Knife River up to their present village, and I am quite convinced that the Mandans moved from the North and joined them, crossing the Missouri River for that purpose.

Mr. Morgan claims that "they carried horticulture, the timber-framed house, and a peculiar religious system into this area, and adds, "There is a possibility that they are the descendants of the 'Mound-Builders.'" Their permanent dwellings have always been, so far as known, the dirt and frame lodge, as described under TEPEE. In their hunting excursions they, like other tribes, used the skin lodge. The time of the separation of the Crows from them cannot be definitely ascertained. As one old man said to me, " They separated from us a long, long time ago ; my father did not know when, his father did not know, but his grandfather did know of the time. The languages are something alike. The young men get new words, and change the pronunciation of the old ones; in this way our languages have become separated."

The dirt lodges are fast giving way to log huts, covered and chinked with mud, the roof being made similarly to the roof of the lodge. The dirt lodges last about seven years, are dark, moist, and perfect nests for vermin. The use of the "bull-boots" and active cultivation of corn are marked characteristics.

In his valuable and interesting Hidatsa Grammar, Dr. Washington Matthews says of these Indians and their allied tribes, the Mandans and Arickarees : " On the plain, between the cemetery and the village, may be seen some half-dozen tall, forked logs, erected at distances of a few hundred feet apart. They are evidently of different ages ; one looks quite fresh, as if recently taken from the woods, some appear older, others are rotten at the base and ready to fall, and a few of the oldest are now lying on the ground. Each year one of these forked logs is set up. On the day when it is determined to commence their annual religious ceremonies the men of the Hidatsa tribe, dressed and mounted as for a war-party, proceed to the woods. Here they select a tall, forked cottonwood, which they fell, trim, and bark; to this they tie their lariats, and by the aid of their horses drag it toward the village. In the procession, the man who has most distinguished himself in battle, mounted on the horse on whose back he has done the bravest deeds, takes the lead; others follow in the order of their military distinction. As they drag the log along they fire their guns at it, strike it with their sticks, and shout and sing songs of victory. The log, they say, is symbolical of a conquered enemy, whose body they are bringing into the camp in triumph. When the log is set up, they again proceed to the woods to cut and bring in willows. A temporary lodge of green willows is then built around the log, and in this lodge for four days and four nights is performed the *dah' pike,* or yearly ceremony of the Hidatsa. The most remarkable features of the ceremony are the voluntary and self-imposed fasts and tortures, which rival, and perhaps excel, in their barbaric cruelties, those of the more famous ' Okeepa' of the Mandans.

"Unlike the Hidatsa, the Mandans and the Arickarees perform their annual religious ceremonies in houses erected especially for religious purposes, and which may properly be called temples, although usually designated by the whites as ' medicine-lodges.' In front of each of the temples is an open space or plaza. The objects of veneration in the Arickaree plaza are a painted boulder and a dead cedar-tree. The ' medicine' of the Mandan plaza is a small circular palisade, which is emblematic of the ark in which the Noah of Mandan mythology was saved from the flood. Within the temple and around the palisade is still performed the Mandan *Okeepa,* which Catlin so accurately describes in his ' North American Indians.'

"When Lewis and Clarke ascended the Missouri, in 1804, they found four tribes of agricultural Indians, numerous and prosperous, inhabiting the Upper Missouri Valley west of the Dakota nation. They had eight permanently inhabited towns, several of which they lived in temporarily, and a number more which they had abandoned and allowed to go to ruin. They are spoken of in Lewis and Clarke's journal as the ' Ricaras,' ' Mandans,' ' Minnetarees,' and ' Ahnahaways.' All that are left of the four tribes are now gathered together in this one village, at Fort Berthold, which does not probably number over two thousand five hundred souls. The last-named tribe, the Ahnahaways or Amahauris, ceased long ago to have an independent existence. After the smallpox epidemic of 1838, the few that were left joined the kindred tribe of the Minnetarees, accepting the chief of the latter as *their* chief, and adopting the traditions, myths, and ceremonies of the Minnetarees as their own. Almost the only evidence we have of their former existence is the mention made of them by early travellers, and the few orphan words of their language which have been adopted into the Minnetaree tongue. There are but few white men, even among those who have dwelt for years in the country, who know that such a people ever did live, and the Indians of Fort Berthold are always referred to as ' the three tribes.' The remains, now nearly obliterated, of their old towns may to-day be discovered by sharp-sighted observers on almost every prairie terrace adjacent to the Missouri, along six hundred miles of its course from the mouth of the Lower White Earth to the Little Missouri. To the philologist it is an interesting fact that this trio of savage clans, although now living in the same village and having been next-door neighbors to each other for more than a hundred years, on terms of peace and intimacy, and to a great extent inter-married, speak nevertheless totally distinct languages, which show no perceptible inclination to coalesce. The Mandan and Gros Ventre (or Minnetaree) languages are somewhat alike and probably of a very distant common origin, but no resemblance has yet been discovered between either of these and the Arickaree ('Ricara'). Almost every member of each tribe understands the languages of the other tribes, yet he speaks his own most fluently, so it is not an uncommon thing to hear a dialogue carried on in two languages, one person, for instance, questioning in Mandan, and the other answering back in Gros Ventre, and *vice versa.* Many of them understand the Dakota tongue and use it as a means of intercommunication, and all understand the sign language. So, after all, they have no trouble in making themselves understood by one another. These Indians must have excellent memories, and even 'good capacity for study,' for it is not uncommon to find persons among them, some even under twenty years of age, who can speak four or five different languages.''

Gros Ventre of the Prairie (Indian). It is claimed that this tribe received its name from the custom they had of running from one lodge to another to get something to eat,—always having their bellies full; and so were called Big Bellies. They are called Gros Ventres of the Prairie to distinguish them from the Gros Ventres at Fort Berthold, being an entirely distinct tribe, different in language, customs, and beliefs from the latter. These Indians are clearly an off-shoot from the Arapahoes, and, mistily and imperfectly, tradition tells of their remaining with this tribe in their southeastward migration until they met the Cheyennes, near the Red River Valley, then moving with the Cheyennes and Arapahoes westward until they reached the Missouri River, when they separated from the others and went to the northwest, joining the Blackfeet, remaining with them for a long number of years. Louis Reve, seventy-eight years of age, whom I met at Fort Assinaboine, Montana, in June, 1881, said that he came to Fort Marias, at the mouth of the Marias River, Montana, in 1829. At this time the Gros Ventres were living with the Blackfeet, and numbered some three or four hundred lodges. There were about two thousand lodges of Blackfeet, including the Bloods and Piegans. In 1833 or 1834 smallpox broke out in the Gros Ventres' camp, and swept away large numbers of them. The other Indians were farther north, and did not have the disease. The old men of the Gros Ventres, at this time, claimed that they came from the far North, across some wide body of water, and moved right through the other tribes and joined the Arapahoes. In

1831 the Arapahoes were on the Arkansas River, and the Cheyennes and Sioux were together.   These Gros Ventres worshipped the sun, or the Supreme Power, which they located in the sun, and sacrificed their bodies to this power.   They believed that after death they went to some lonesome land in the North, and claimed that when there, they had seen spirits about them.   They had at this time (1829) very few ponies.   When they left the Arapahoes they fought their way through the tribes, with the exception of the Rees and Mandans, who were friendly to them.   In this way they were stripped of all their property, including, of course, the ponies their kinsfolk, the Arapahoes, had given them.   They were at this time considered very brave, and fought well.   This visit, which was made about sixty years ago, and which lasted some time, has been an obstacle in the way of gaining correct information of the migrations of this tribe, as well as the date of the separation of the two bands. For this visit they joined the Arapahoes near the Big Horn Mountains, moved and camped with them until they reached the Platte, or, as some claim, the Arkansas River; and undoubtedly Little Raven, of the Southern Arapahoes, referred to their leaving at this time when he said to me, "They separated from us (Northern and Southern Arapahoes) fifty-two years ago.   We had ranged together up to this time as far south as the Arkansas.   They left us when we were camped on the river, and went north, on account of a war between the Kiowas and Comanches; these two tribes joined together against us.   Before this we had been friendly."   The agency for these Indians and some of the Assinaboines is located at what is called Fort Belknap, near the forks of Milk River, twenty-eight miles from Fort Assinaboine, Montana.

I visited them in June, 1881, and found that I had been able to gain much more reliable information in regard to their migrations from the Cheyennes and the Arapahoes than I could from them. They do not keep an accurate account of individual ages.   Their traditions are not reliable for more than three generations, and are poor at that.   They could give no reason for the separation from the Arapahoes, and were inclined to think it took place near the headwaters of the North Platte River.

They have an original Sun-Dance, and hold the torture in high esteem; claim that they "suffer to please the God in the sun, and also the white man's God."   Among other dances, they have the Strong-Dance for women,—intended as a support to their chastity. The Buffalo-Dance is also a religious ceremony to propitiate the power, force, or God in the sun,—a prayer for the sun to take pity on them, and give them buffalo.   In this dance the participants wear buffalo-bonnets or head-dresses.   The Manhood-Dance is also an annual dance held late in the summer, when lodges are made; this is for young men old enough to take on themselves the responsibility of a family.

They bury their dead mostly in lodges, and believe that after death they go to the Lonesome Land north of Cypress Mountain.   They said one died (fainted), went there, and came back and told them. They were formerly at war with the Flatheads and all the tribes in that part of the country. For many, many years they were friends of the Blackfeet, Bloods, and Piegans. Their pleasant relations were ruptured, they claim, by the killing of the wife of one of their chiefs, who went to visit a Blackfoot camp; this led to war, which lasted for some years; only recently made peace again. They were also formerly at war with the Assinaboines.

These Prairie Gros Ventres seem rather inferior to other Plains Indians. In dress they resemble the Crows and Blackfeet; are fond of the coarse fringe at the shoulders, wrists, and down the seams of the leggings. They have no one particular style of dressing the hair, going through all the grades from the stiff, upright bang of the Crows to the plain braid and scalp-lock of the Cheyennes. The women are lighter colored than the Arapahoe women and dress like the Crows,— short skirts and short leggings, not reaching to the knees. Their vocal language is unmistakably Arapahoe. They have few myths, and keep no pictorial history of the tribe. Their several Medicine-Dances seem to look more to the sun as the seat of their God than with the surrounding tribes, and they could, with more propriety, be called sun-worshippers. When I was at the agency most of the lodges were away hunting; the poor, old, and lazy hung about the agency buildings, which are small log huts with dirt roofs, surrounded by a stockade.

The cultivated fields looked well, about one hundred and fifty acres in all under cultivation; wheat, oats, corn, and garden vegetables looked thrifty.

Grow. Hold right hand, back down, index finger extended and pointing upwards, other fingers and thumb closed, in front of body, hand held near the ground; raise the hand by gentle jerks.

Deaf-mutes indicate the growing of persons similarly, but for the vegetable world they hold the partially-closed left hand in front of body, and force the compressed right hand from below upwards between the thumb and fingers, and as the fingers appear above the index and thumb of left hand, the fingers are spread, opened out.

Guide. Make signs for Go, for WITH, for LOOK, for ROAD or TRAIL, and for GOOD.

Deaf-mutes make signs for SHOW and LEAD; for the former hold the extended left hand, palm out, in front of left shoulder, fingers pointing upwards, and place tip of extended right index against left palm, other fingers and thumb closed; for the latter, hold extended left hand, back to left, fingers pointing to front, in front of and close to left side; join left finger-tips with tips of fingers and thumb of right hand, and draw the left hand to front.

Gum. Hold the compressed left hand in front of body, back to left, fingers pointing upwards; bring the closed right hand near left, and place ball of right thumb against base of thumb of left hand, and, by wrist action, twist the right hand to right and front; then make a chewing motion with the jaws.

Gun. Conception : Flash and smoke. Hold the right hand, back out, some eight inches in front of neck, hand partially closed, palmar surface of thumb pressing against the nails of first three fingers, edge of hand pointing upwards ; elevate hand some inches, at same time extend and separate fingers and thumb with a snap. Some Indians hold the hands in position of aiming a gun to shoot, and this latter is the deaf-mute sign.

Gun-Cover. Make sign for GUN ; then hold left hand, back down, several inches in front of body, fingers touching and slightly curved, pointing to right and upwards, thumb slightly curved and pointing upwards ; bring compressed right hand between left hand and body and thrust it towards left and beyond, hand passing left thumb and index, and the lower surface and forearm touching left palm as the movement is made ; terminate movement when elbow rests on left palm ; represents thrusting the gun into the cover.

Gunpowder. Make sign for GUN, and then rub the tip of thumb against tips of fingers, as in ASHES or DUST. Sometimes sign for BLACK is also made.

Deaf-mutes make sign for DUST and BLACK, and then holding extended left hand, palm down, in front of body, place the nearly-closed right on its back, and suddenly raise it, extending the fingers, to indicate the flash or explosion on ignition.

H.

Hail. Make signs for RAIN, for COLD, and indicate size of hail-stones with curved index and thumb of right hand.

Deaf-mutes make signs for FROZEN RAIN.

Hair. To denote hair of human being, touch hair of head ; for brutes, hold left forearm horizontally in front of body ; separate and partially curve the thumb and fingers of right hand ; carry it to and place back of fingers against left forearm, near elbow ; move the hand from elbow to wrist, finger-tips little higher than upper surface of left forearm.

Deaf-mutes simply touch the hair of head.

The manner of dressing or wearing the hair in former years usually determined the tribe, the style in each being different. The practice of pulling out the beard and hair from all parts of the body except from the head was common to all tribes, and was only at first used as a means of keeping the body free from vermin. It obtained the color of sacredness only from being an old custom.

Half. Hold left hand, back to left and front, in front of breast, fingers extended, touching, and pointing to front and right, thumb extended, pressing against side of and same height as index ; lay lower edge of right hand on upper edge of left, resting at about knuckle of left index, back to right and front, fingers extended, touching, and pointing to left and front; move the right hand to right and outwards.

To illustrate : "I give half to you and half to him," make sign for I, above sign, and sign for GIVE (moving hand towards you in sign for GIVE) ; then bring right hand back to its position on left, move it to left and rear, and make sign for GIVE (towards him). This sign indicates cutting anything in two equal parts (in the illustration, one part given to one, the other part given to the other).

Deaf-mutes hold extended left index in front of body, and lay extended right on it at right angles, at middle point from knuckle to tip, other fingers and thumbs closed.

Half-Breed. Conception : Half of body one kind, half of another. Bring right hand, back to left and downwards, in front of centre of breast, fingers extended, touching, pointing upwards and towards body, little finger and lower edge of hand near breast or resting on it ; move the hand to left until it passes beyond body, return hand to its first position, and move it to right until it passes body, making before the first gesture the sign for whatever *breed* it is desired to represent one-half of, and after the motion to right, the other breed.

To illustrate : To represent a half-breed of the white and Sioux races, make sign for WHITES, then for the half to the left, as above described ; then make sign for right half, and then sign for SIOUX.

Similarly executed for all animals. Sometimes the right hand is held opposite the face. Deaf-mutes make their signs for WHITE and MIXED. I am indebted to Mr. J. J. Hargrave, of Winnipeg, Manitoba, for the following in regard to the half-breeds of British North America:

"The half-breeds of British North America are the descendants of the traders, who have lived in the country and formed connections with native Indian women. Previous to 1763, when by the peace of Paris the country was ceded by France to England, these traders were Frenchmen, who, under licenses of trade, granted by the Government, pursued their calling in a desultory and adventurous manner throughout the country north and west of Lake Superior. Between 1763 and 1784 the trade slackened, but in the latter year the formation of the Northwest Company of Montreal gave it renewed impetus. The latter company was well organized, and, between the year of its inception and that of its coalition with the Hudson's Bay Company in 1821, had succeeded in organizing its posts as far north as Lake Athabasca, and as far west as the Pacific Ocean.

"In this enterprise it drew its best instruments from among the half-breed race, who, having been born in the country, and familiar from their earliest years with its hardships and its savage industries, formed the connecting link between the Indian and the white man.

"After the coalition between the Hudson's Bay and Northwest Companies had taken place in 1821, even until the present time, the services of the half-breeds as boatmen, hunters, and plain carriers have been held in great esteem by the former corporation.

"The white servants of the Northwest Company consisted of Scotchmen and of Frenchmen, engaged in Montreal; while the European servants of the Hudson's Bay Company were mainly Orkneymen and Scotchmen engaged in Europe, and until 1821 stationed in the immediate neighborhood of Hudson's Bay.

"Until some years after the formation of the Canadian Confederation in 1870, when emigrants began to enter the country, there was an almost total absence of white female population. For about a century, therefore, there had been a gradual increase in the number of half-breeds, as the Europeans employed in the fur trade married with women purely Indian during the earlier decades, and subsequently in increasing numbers with the daughters and descendants of their predecessors.

"From the European point of view there are two classes of half-breeds, usually known as English and French half-breeds; the former being descended from an English-speaking, and the latter from French-speaking, ancestry. There is a well-defined difference between these, and they have not much amalgamated. They all agree in an intimate speaking acquaintance with their Indian mother-tongue. The French half-breeds, however, are a race of hunters and travellers, who have never taken very kindly to agricultural pursuits in the various settlements which have been established in the Indian country, while the English half-breeds have as a class been mildly successful agriculturists, and in the Red River country and on the Saskatchewan, have become comfortably established as settlers.

"The influx of population into the Northwest Territory and the consequent disappearance of game, more especially of the buffalo, have disposed the French half-breed population to retire before the advancing wave of whites. The buffalo, in fact, formed their great staff of life. While these animals still occupied the prairie country west from Red River, spring and autumn expeditions were organized to hunt them, and the results in the shape of pemican and buffalo-robes furnished the hunters with the necessaries of life for the remainder of the year.

"Those half-breeds who were too poor to purchase the necessary outfit to enable them to hunt the buffalo, would engage as voyageurs during the summer months, and the high wages obtainable during the five months of open water would enable them to tide over the winter months.

"Improvidence has been a prominent characteristic of the French half-breeds more particularly. While plenty abounds with them they live amid waste, but when the evil day of want arrives they sustain privation with amazing fortitude.

"In point of religion the French half-breeds are chiefly Roman Catholics, and the English mainly Protestants. Their improvement has been for many years one of the chief objects of the labors of missionaries of all creeds in the Indian country.

"As a class the half-breeds have no special written laws, conforming themselves in this respect to the habits of the Indians while in the Indian country, and to the laws of the whites among whom they live on the frontier. While actually in the field chasing the buffalo, however, they are under a very strict discipline, administered by a captain and staff of assistants, whose office is by general election of the camps.

"From the Indian point of view the half-breed race belongs to no special tribe or nation, members of this class being descended from every tribe among whom whites have traded, from the Chinooks of the prairie to the Iroquois of the Atlantic coast.

"They reside throughout the whole Northwest Territory, but there are certain localities where settlements of more or less pretensions have been formed, such as Red River settlement in Manitoba, and Prince Albert on the Saskatchewan.

"The enormous increase in the value of land which has taken place in the former locality within the last two years has enriched many members of this class, by enabling them to exchange their lands for money. The general result can scarcely be estimated, but it will end in a western emigration of individuals, and the ultimate 'survival of the fittest' to cope with new conditions created by the advent of the locomotive."

What are known as the Red River half-breeds are, as I understand it, mostly of white and Algonquin extraction ; *i.e.*, Chippewa and Cree. I have seen them this side of the British line on their hunts and in their winter quarters, and they are veritable gypsies.

Their carts, which they use for transporting their possessions, are known as Red River carts, and their sleds, which they use in winter, are as simple in construction. Mr. Hargrave, in his interesting book on Red River, thus describes these carts:

"They are constructed entirely of wood, without any iron whatever, the axles and rims of the wheels forming no exception to the rule. Although this might at first sight appear a disadvantage, as denoting a want of strength, yet it is really the reverse, because in the country traversed by these vehicles wood is abundant, and always to be obtained in quantities sufficient to mend any breakage which might take place. The only tools necessary, not only to mend but to construct a cart, are an axe, a saw, a screw-auger, and a draw-knife; with these the traveller is independent, so far as regards the integrity of his conveyance. Indeed, the cart may be described as a light box frame poised upon an axle connecting two strong wooden wheels. The price of such an article in the settlement is about two pounds sterling. The harness is very rude, and is made of dressed ox-hide. Each cart is drawn by an ox, and in cases where speed is an object a horse is substituted. The horses used on the plains for draught purposes are usually the wiry little 'Indian ponies,' one of which, with a load of four or five hundred pounds in the cart behind him, will overtake from fifty to sixty miles a day in a measured, but by no means hurried, jog trot. Horses are, however, generally used only when men travel 'light,' and time is an object, in which cases the bulk of the loads consists of the canteens, bedding, and personal luggage of the passengers."

Of late years ponies have been used extensively on this side of the line. In marching the carts follow each other, and in camping they are halted as each one comes up, so as to form a circle, and the tepees are pitched just outside and within a few feet of the carts. This forms an excellent corral for the animals, which are driven inside for the night, or during any emergency.

The men dress in civilized clothing, but all wear moccasins, and a sash (usually red) around the waist for ornament and to sustain the trousers. The women also wear the ordinary dress of civilization, usually made of calico. The men and boys are fine horsemen, ordinarily using for a saddle merely a pad stuffed with hair, often handsomely beaded. The stirrups are small, made of iron or leather, and are attached to the pad with a narrow strap. The women ride in the carts.

During the winter they select some wooded and well-sheltered place for their camps, and construct log houses. If their fall hunt has been successful, and they have a sufficient supply of dried meat and pemican, in addition to that sold for sugar, coffee, and flour, to last them during the winter, and they can secure a few barrels of whiskey, they seem to be perfectly happy. Many of them are fair musicians, and they all seem fond of such sounds as they can worry out of their cracked and seedy violins.

Unlike the full-blood Indians, the men perform their share of the work, and as the women do not suffer such great privations and hardships, which limit the lacteal period, and ride in the carts, it is not infrequent for them to bear from eight to fourteen children.

There are several thousand of these people who might very properly be classed as a band or tribe, and the Red River Half-breeds are the only ones who, so far as I know, form a genuine tribe. Of course at each of our agencies there are usually found mixed bloods, and I think, properly speaking, as the gestures would indicate, Indians whose parents belonged to different tribes should come under this head, but it is not customary to so class or consider them. The capture of women and children by war-parties, or the meeting of different tribes when waging war or at peace, has led to quite a number of these Indians. As a rule, they seem to possess great linguistic ability, and it is a remarkable fact that many of our most noted Indian chiefs were of mixed Indian blood. Logan's father was a Cayuga, his mother a Shawnee. Tecumseh's mother was a Creek, his father a Shawnee. In more recent times, Chief Joseph's father was a Nez Perce, his mother a Cayuse. Washakie's father was a Shoshone, his mother a Flathead. Little Wolf's father was an Arapahoe, his mother a Cheyenne.

Halt. Hold extended right hand, palm outwards and downwards, in front of body, fingers extended, touching, and pointing upwards and to front, hand about height of shoulder ; move the hand sharply to front and downwards, stopping it suddenly.

In a similar manner any one coming from right, left, or rear would be halted or stopped. This gesture, repeated, means also *keep quiet, wait a moment*, etc., though not made so sharply or decidedly.

Deaf-mutes strike the left palm with lower edge of right hand sharply, left hand extended, back down, right hand at right angles to left.

Handsome. Conception : Looking in mirror and good. Hold extended right hand, back outwards, in front of and few inches from eyes, fingers pointing to left ; drop the hand down till opposite breast, then move it out horizontally, back up, to the front and right.

Hang. (To describe hanging a person.) Hold right hand, back up, near right side of neck, index and thumb spread, other fingers closed ; move the hand well upwards and little to right with a partial jerk, at same time closing index and thumb.

Deaf-mutes place ball of right thumb under chin, little finger extended, others closed, making a push up against chin.

Hang (To). (As pendant.) The left index is extended and held horizontally in front of body, other fingers closed, and the right curved and hooked to it.

Indians have a special aversion and horror of death by hanging. I have heard the Sioux say that a person who committed suicide in this way had to go through the next world dragging whatever object the rope had been attached to. Death by violence, such as shooting, stabbing, etc., is so common that they have become accustomed to it ; and in the songs and praises of the bravery of the deceased much of the distressing bitterness of the affliction is forgotten ; but at the thought that one has died like a dog, been choked to death with a coward's rope, barbarism is sickened into silence.

Happy Hunting-Ground. There is no general well-known sign, but the proper gestures are used to denote country *beyond* death and living; *i.e.*, DIE, point to ground BEYOND, and INHABIT are usually made. As the Comanches and some others think they go to the West, the Flatheads, Crows, and others to the East, the Sioux and others to the South, the Blackfeet and Prairie Gros Ventres to the North, and the Caddoes and others inside of the Earth, the Cheyennes rather inclining to the zenith, it will be readily seen there could be no general sign, as with deaf-mutes, for HEAVEN.

It is impossible to learn positively at this late day what may have been the belief of the Indians prior to our advent, but I am inclined to think that they did in olden times as now, picture a hereafter. One reason for this belief is that our missionaries have as earnestly sought to convince them that there is an eternal hell which may swallow up their souls in endless torture as that there is a heaven of endless bliss, and though they are free to admit that the whites may and probably will all go to hell, I have yet to see an Indian who in his heart of hearts believed any Indians would go there.

Some years since a commission was sent by the President of the United States to investigate a very treacherous and cowardly slaughter, —the Chivington massacre. With the commission was a Methodist clergyman, who at that time (and perhaps does now) believed in a literal and physical hell of fire and brimstone, where the souls of wicked transgressors would writhe in eternal torture. Being not only anxious to spread the good seed, but curious as well to learn from the lips of the wild Indians their views of the hereafter, he asked the chief to tell him what were his beliefs in regard to the life after death. The chief gave him the usual picture of the pleasant fields, white tepees, clear waters, and abundance of game in the Indian's heaven, and then in turn asked the minister to describe the white man's heaven, which was done in glowing colors. The streets of gold, the gates of pearl, were duly depicted, but not stopping there, he went on and pictured the flames of hell, and described the lot of the transgressors who would surely go there. The Indian stopped him and asked "if it was really true that all the whites who played cards, swore, drank whiskey, lied, stole, etc., would surely go to this place?" When answered in the affirmative, he stopped further discussion with laughter, and by saying "that in the next world they would not be troubled with any whites; they would all be burnt up, for the minister had included all those whom he had ever seen or heard of."

It would please me if I could honestly say that each and every Indian I have met possessed a clear tradition of the original knowledge or belief in one God, and that a rich heirloom of perfect faith in the life beyond death had for ages been handed down from father to son; but no such arch of rainbow-hued comfort can truthfully be given. Some of the Indians claim to have seen the Happy Hunting-Ground during fainting fits; they calling these swoons death, and believing that the spirit temporarily leaves the body (see FAINT), and describe it on recovery as rich in all that barbarians could desire or hold precious : good lodges, fresh grass, cold pure water, plenty of timber, large quantities of game, fast ponies, etc. ; but unfortunately for a more complete understanding and perfect knowledge, "just as they are asked to a feast" they come to life again. Many of the Indians trouble themselves very little about the subject, think little and care less ; but the medicine-men, the dreamers, build strange fabrics out of their vague and misty ideas, and these pass as the current coin of Indian beliefs. It is safe to say that they are not whipped into any action by the bitter lash of fear of future punishment, but are held to good deeds by the inherent attraction of the good in them, and the social and moral laws which govern their physical existence. They are then, so far as any faith of future life goes, firm in the conviction that they will all go to the happy land beyond death. No cloud of doubt ever casts a shadow on mind or heart. They do try to mete out punishment for crime and misdeeds here, the penalty falling quickly on the heels of the offence, but the facts constituting a crime or offence are, of course, judged according to the code of morals found in barbarism, not by ours. The warmth of the South is in the story told me by Ta-ba-nan-a-ca, one of the chiefs of the Comanches; and the dreary coldness of the North is felt in the story of the desolate region of sand-hills, where roam the dead and gone Blackfeet and Gros Ventres of the Prairie. Forming their ideas, then, from the vagaries and visions of swooning men and dreamers, it is not strange that they should believe in a future physical life similar to that which they are now passing through ; and, as courage is their greatest virtue, it is not to be wondered at that the warrior killed in battle goes easily over the starry trail, and on reaching his destination is hailed as chief. The magical touch of fancy washes away the blood, heals the wounds, restores the scalp and streaming war-bonnet, and thus bravely decked out in all his savage finery, the spirit is materialized. The pictures are not all rose-colored. Among the Indians of the far North there are only sad beliefs of a future life too intangible for description. The Blackfeet appear to expect in the great hereafter nothing better than a dreary, ghostly existence.

Some tribes believe that withered old age is transformed into the flush of youth, and that the maimed and deformed are freed from the heavy burdens of their afflictions, whilst others claim that the young are young, the old are old, the infirm are infirm, and the diseased are diseased ; in fact, that the future is a perfect reproduction of their present existence. (See GOD.)

Hard. Hold left hand in front of left breast, back to left and slightly to front, fingers extended, touching, pointing to front and slightly to right ; strike with the back of fingers, from second joints to knuckles, of firmly-closed right hand the left palm two or three times, drawing right hand back from left only few inches, back of right hand nearly to front, and forearm about horizontal. This sign is used in such sentences as a "hard man to trade with," "a high rocky mountain," and also sometimes in the sense of firm, determined, brave, etc.

Deaf-mutes hold closed left hand, back up, in front of body, and strike knuckles of same two or three times, with short, sharp blows, with second joints of closed right hand.

Hard-Bread. Make sign for BREAD, and then hold extended left hand, back nearly downwards, in front of body, fingers pointing a little to right of front; lay the lower edge of right hand on left wrist, fingers extended and touching, hands at right angles. Sometimes the sign for HARD is made.

Deaf-mutes make sign for HARD, and then cut back of extended left hand, fingers pointing to right, with lower edge of extended right hand held beyond left, fingers pointing up and towards body.

Harlot. Conception: Crazy or foolish female. Make sign for FEMALE, and CRAZY or FOOLISH.

Deaf-mutes make sign for FEMALE and SHAME.

Among some of the tribes the women, as a rule, are virtuous, while with other tribes the rule is reversed. These conditions obtain with tribes that for years have had most intimate relations with each other, and have nearly all their customs and laws exactly alike. This is instanced in the case of the Cheyennes and Arapahoes, the former being noted for the chastity of its women, whilst the latter is equally notorious for their lewdness.

In former times, among many of the tribes, adultery on the woman's part was punished by cutting off the cartilaginous portion of the end of the nose. Indian women do not treat their sisters, who may have yielded their virtue by reason of passion or necessity, with that fine scorn, contempt, hatred, and loathing which civilized women so cheerfully accord under similar circumstances, and social ostracism and punishment does not necessarily follow through her entire life a woman who may have "loved not wisely, but too well."

According to the stern laws of some tribes, if a woman cannot pass the test of purity, or virginity, she is at the mercy of any or all the men in the camp, and there have been many cases where the horrible brutality of savage lust was wreaked with fiendish and hellish delight. But in barbarism a woman can step at any time from the paths of folly into the ways of purity, and be assisted in her efforts by those of her own sex.

The ceremony for testing the purity of the women usually occurred once a year, and was accompanied by a dance or feast. If a woman was accused falsely, she could have some of her kinsfolk make a feast, confront the slander with denial, and silence unjust insinuations or open charges with her oath of purity.

Hat. Bring right hand, back outwards, in front, close to, and little above head, index finger and thumb spread and nearly horizontal, other fingers closed ; lower the hand until thumb and index are about opposite the eyes, spread thumb and index, passing down close to forehead, index to left, thumb to right.

Deaf-mutes indicate shape, and then make motion as though putting same on head with right hand.

Hawk. Make sign for BIRD ; then hold the partially-compressed right hand in front of and little higher than right shoulder ; move it to front and downwards, finishing on a slight upward curve, imitating the manner in which a hawk "dives" through the air after smaller birds, swooping down after its prey.

Headache. Make sign for SICK, holding hands near head, and then frequently add the sign to denote darting pain.

Deaf-mutes make their sign for SICK near forehead.

Heap. Indicate the shape with both curved hands.

Deaf-mutes use the same sign.

Hear. Hold the right hand, back to right, near right cheek, about on a line with front of face, index finger and thumb spread, other fingers closed, index pointing upwards ; move the hand back, mostly by elbow action, so that ear will be in about centre of space between thumb and index. Sometimes the sign for LITTLE TALK is made (the index finger snapped opposite right ear and close to it) ; then holding hand little farther out, extend index finger, point it towards the ear, and when tip of index approaches it, move the hand sufficiently to front to pass the face, indicating that the words not only struck the ear, but went through the head. This gesture implies an earnest attention to what one has heard ; that one is inclined to listen ; that the ears are open to receive advice or instruction ; and that a decided impression or conviction had been the result. The words go through the head.

Sometimes the hand in the first sign given is held in rear of the ear and brought forward.

Deaf-mutes hold the right index horizontally opposite and pointing towards right ear.

Heart. Bring the compressed right hand, fingers slightly curved, so that tip of thumb is near tips of fingers, against left breast, index finger and thumb resting over heart and pointing downwards.

Deaf-mutes describe a small circle on surface over heart with tip of extended right index.

The heart is understood to be the seat of the emotions, the abiding-place of tenderness and anger, love and hatred, pleasure and pain, of joy and sorrow, and of courage and fear. All the influences which color life directly affect the heart. In distress it is weighted to the ground,—pressed down and covered with clouds. In happiness it is light,—lifted up into the sunshine. In anger the heart is *bad*. In love it is *good*. In homesickness it looks wearily towards the land of nativity.

Heaven. Point upward with right index. (See HAPPY HUNTING-GROUND.)

I have also seen gestures made to denote father, mother, and old people dying, and their arrival there, to indicate the land beyond death.

Deaf-mutes indicate the arch with both hands held curved, backs up, above head, tips of fingers touching ; then move right to right and downwards, left to left and downwards ; then holding left in first position, make sign for ENTER with right passing under left.

Heavy. Conception : Cannot hold up. Hold hands, backs down, in front of body, fingers extended, touching, and pointing to front, hands same height and few inches apart ; raise the hands slightly, and then let them drop several inches.

Deaf-mutes use the same sign.

Help. Make signs for WORK and WITH.

Deaf-mutes hold left forearm horizontally in front of body, and placing palmar surface of extended fingers of right hand under left forearm, lift up slightly the left arm.

Herd (To). Conception : To hold. Hold the hands opposite each other, at same height, in front of body, index fingers and thumbs spread and horizontal, index fingers pointing about to front, hands about six inches apart ; move them simultaneously to right and left, keeping them same distance apart. The signs for ponies, cattle, or whatever are herded, are usually first made ; and to represent the animals as bunched together, as in a herd, partially compress the hands, fingers slightly curved and little separated ; bring the hands near together in front of body, back of right hand to right front and upwards, left to left front and upwards, fingers pointing downwards and outwards, tips of thumbs and fingers near each other, hands height of the shoulders and equally advanced ; move the hands slightly downwards and outwards ; bring hands a little nearer each other.

Indian ponies of a large camp, when turned out to graze, amicably settle into small groups. Sometimes one group belongs only to one family ; at other times to several families who have lived near each other for a long time, or are kinsfolk. An Indian boy can run out, lasso one of the ponies, and easily drive his group through a large herd, either to water or into the camp. I have seen this done frequently where there were several thousand ponies, and the other groups were not disturbed.

Here. Make sign for SIT.

Deaf-mutes make sign similar to Indian sign for PLACE or FROM.

Hermaphrodite. Conception : Half male, half female. Make sign for MALE, then hold lower edge of right hand against breast, fingers extended and touching, back of hand nearly to left ; move the hand to right, then make sign for FEMALE, and holding hand as above, move it to left.

The Crow tribe of Indians seem to have had several well-authenticated cases of hermaphrodism.

Hide (To). Hold the left hand, back to left and upwards, well out in front of left breast, fingers extended, touching, and pointing to front and right ; bring the right hand, slightly compressed, back up, and fingers pointing to front, several inches to right of left ; move the right to left, and when approaching left, lower it, having it pass under and little to left of left hand. This is also used to express "secretly," "privately," "confidentially," "a talk under a blanket," "lost," "hidden away," etc.

Deaf-mutes close the right hand, and place back of thumb against left, then move that hand under, the left held as I have described in the Indian sign, the back of right thumb grazing left palm as it passes under.

Hide. (Skin.) There is no general sign ; explanatory signs must be made.

Deaf-mutes hold extended left hand, back up, in front of body, and with the thumb and forefinger gather up, with a pinch, the loose skin on the back of left hand.

High. Hold right hand, back nearly up, fingers touching, about extended, and pointing to front, in front of right shoulder ; raise the hand according to the height desired to be represented.

Deaf-mutes hold right a little in front and to right of right shoulder, index only extended and pointing upwards ; raise the hand by gentle jerks.

Hill. See BLUFF.

Deaf-mutes indicate the shape of surface with extended hands, backs up.

His or Hers. Make sign for the person, and then sign for MY or MINE.

Deaf-mutes push the palm of extended right hand, fingers pointing upwards, hand held in front of right shoulder, to left or towards person.

History. Hold left hand, back outwards, well in front of face, fingers extended, touching, and pointing upwards ; with partially-extended thumb and index, other fingers closed, make motion of sketching something on left palm. This in conversation would be sufficient, but to further elucidate (as the same sign is used for photograph or picture and nearly the same for writing), explain that by looking at it one would know where they were many years ago.

Deaf-mutes make the signs for PAST HAPPENINGS. (For HAPPENINGS, hold the hands in front of shoulders, backs up, index fingers only extended, right pointing to left, left to right, hands same height and opposite ; by wrist and elbow action turn the hands with a jerk, so that backs are about towards body. For PAST, hold right hand, back to right, well in front of right shoulder and little lower, thumb extended pointing upwards, fingers closed ; move the hand directly back by elbow action, so that thumb points over right shoulder.)

Some of the tribes (especially the Sioux in the North and Apaches in the South) have a hieroglyphical history or chart, extending back some hundred years or more ; a species of picture-writing on a partially-tanned skin ; the years being represented by pictures of the most important events which occurred to them during the year.

I have never seen one representing more than a hundred years, and the only history which can now be obtained from them consists of vague and unsatisfactory traditions, handed down from father to son. These are in many cases unreliable, and at best reach back only two or three hundred years.

The Santee Sioux claim that formerly their old men kept a record of events by tying knots in a long string. By the peculiar way of tying them, and by other marks, they denoted the different events, fights, etc., and even smaller matters, such as births of children, etc. I once saw a slender pole some six feet in length, the surface of which was completely covered with small notches, and the old Indian who possessed it assured me that it had been handed down from father to son for many generations, and that these notches represented the history of his tribe for over a thousand years ; in fact, went back to the time when they lived near the ocean.

Hobble. (For animals.) Bring closed hands, backs up, well out in front of body, hands opposite, few inches apart, and at same height, forearms held as nearly as possible parallel, pointing to front and downwards ; clasp the right wrist with thumb and index of left hand ; return left hand to position, and clasp left wrist with thumb and index of right hand, and return to position ; other fingers in these movements closed, and as the hands resume position the wrists are slightly bent downwards.

Ponies are hobbled by means of a short thong or rope tied to the front pasterns, fettering the legs, the length of the rope between the legs being usually about one foot. This prevents the animals from straying too far, places an obstacle in the way of a stampede, and causes a delay in that pleasant amusement known as "running off the stock," which tribes at war practise on each other so constantly.

The young men of a war-party or horse-stealing expedition travel so as to leave no trail, winding through the dry beds of streams, ravines, and low places, thus keeping concealed day and night ; they frequently, and especially in the winter, going on foot, and with wonderful craft and cunning creep up to within a short distance of the camp or herd of ponies they are after. Then watching their opportunity, some of their number, with knives in hand, crawl around among the animals, cut the hobbles and lariats, and then with a shout make a dash at the herd, accomplishing the stampede.

It is rarely the case that after attaining such success the marauders are overtaken, as from the stolen herd they can select plenty of relays.

Hog. Indicate the height, then form a circle with thumbs and index fingers, others closed, and hold it some inches in front of lower part of face, to denote the snout ; and then extended and compressed right hand, back up, against chin, fingers pointing to front and downwards, make motion to imitate the rooting.

Some tribes call the hog the "bear-antelope," some the "white man's bear," and many simply make sign for FAT, as in BACON, to denote the animal.

Deaf-mutes indicate the rooting with extended right hand under chin.

Hold. Hold the extended hands, backs out, well in front of body, fingers of left hand pointing to right, of right hand to left, backs of fingers of right hand resting against inner surface of fingers of left, index fingers horizontal, forearms nearly so ; move the hands, held in this position, slightly to right and left, by elbow and shoulder action. (See SOLDIER.)

This sign is used to express soldiering ; *i.e.*, holding a camp ; to hold or detain a person as prisoner ; to keep, hold, or detain anything.

Deaf-mutes clasp extended left index pointing upwards, other fingers and thumb closed, with right hand.

Hole. Form a circle with the thumbs and index fingers of both hands, others closed, and, still holding left hand in position, pass the compressed right through the imaginary hole.

Deaf-mutes form a circle with left index and thumb.

Homely. Pass the palmar surface of extended right hand over face, and make sign for BAD.

Deaf-mutes make a jerking motion of closed right hand in front of face.

Homesickness. Make sign for HEART and for LOOK, the right hand in LOOK held close to heart, and fingers pointing in direction of home. Sometimes simply sign for SICK over the heart is made. I have also seen the signs for MANY NIGHTS LOOKING TOWARDS CAMP or COUNTRY and HEART SAD made, and also signs for HEART TIRED after the sign for LOOK and COUNTRY. The heart looks or longs for this country, and becomes tired or worn out with the weary watching and waiting ; hope has died out in the heart.

Deaf-mutes make signs for WISH and HOME ; one wishes for home (for WISH they hold the hands well out in front of body, backs down, fingers partially separated and slightly curved ; the hands are drawn in slightly towards the body, motion repeated ; for HOME make sign for HOUSE, EAT, and SLEEP or BED).

Honest. (See TRUE.) Some Indians make signs similar to DAY, and add GOOD,—a person is open, clear, and good.

Deaf-mutes make their signs for TRUE and RIGHT.

Honey. Make sign for FLY ; indicate, by pinching the skin on back of left hand, the fly that bites, and then make sign for defecate. Sometimes the sign for SWEET is also made. Honey is usually called bee-excrement.

I have also seen signs made to denote a large tree with a hole in it, the bees going in and out. The wasp and bee are frequently called the " chiefs of fly-biters," and at other times the " fly with one arrow in his quiver."

Deaf-mutes make signs for BEE and SWEET.

Horse. The most common sign, and one used almost entirely in the North, is to hold the left hand, back to left, in front of left breast, fingers extended, touching, and pointing to front ; bring the right hand, back about outwards, and place first and second fingers astride the left index. This represents one of their horses or ponies.

To represent what they call an " American horse," make sign also for WHITES. The conception of this is, of course, from riding.

The Southern Indians frequently use what they call " the Caddo sign," which is to hold the right hand, back nearly outwards, well in front of left breast, fingers extended, touching, and pointing to left, hand a trifle bent at knuckles ; move the hand horizontally to right and a little to front, terminating movement when hand is about opposite right shoulder. The conception for this is from the curved neck of the animal in grazing (see WILD) and its height.

The Utes hold right hand, back up, well out in front and little to right of right shoulder, index and little fingers extended and pointing upwards and little to front, other fingers and thumb closed. They claim the conception of this from the horse's ears.

I have also seen the sign for MEDICINE-DOG made, as it corresponds to the vocal name applied to the animal by some tribes. (See PONY.)

It will readily be seen that in conversation some other sign than the one for riding is desirable, as the two would frequently fall together in gestures, and might be confusing.

Deaf-mutes hold the hands alongside of head, near and just above ears, backs of hands to rear, index and second fingers extended, touching, and pointing upwards, other fingers and thumbs closed ; by wrist action move the fingers to front ; repeat motion.

Horseback. See RIDE.

Horse-Race. Make sign for HORSE, for RACE.

Deaf-mutes make their sign for HORSE, and denote the STRUGGLE, as in race.

Hospital. Make sign for HOUSE and MEDICINE,—a mysterious or sacred house.

Deaf-mutes indicate friends visiting in hospital.

Hostage. This would have to be explained. One could say, we will hold one of the number, or, putting it stronger, imprison the person ; then, if certain things are done, he will be set at liberty, etc.

Hot. Conception : Rays of sun pressing down. Hold the hands, backs nearly up, above and in front of head, fingers nearly extended and slightly separated, tips of fingers of right near left, fingers of right pointing about to left, left about to right, hands few inches apart ; bring the hands down and slightly in towards head. (The heat presses down from the sun.) I have also seen signs made for the SUN RISING, ABOVE, for FIRE, and SAME.

The heat from a fire is expressed by making sign for FIRE, and then qualifying it by proper gesture. That anything was hot, the natural gestures will suggest themselves.

Deaf-mutes indicate the heat of day from the sun by drawing crooked right index across forehead from left to right ; that anything was hot, or a hot fire, by holding nearly-closed right hand, back out, at mouth ; suddenly throw the hand out, and extending the fingers, at same time make motion with mouth as though the hand was blown on by the breath.

House. Conception : Corners of the log huts and houses. Bring the hands in front of body, and interlock the fingers near tips, fingers at nearly right angles and horizontal. Some tribes do not link fingers, but bring hands in same position, as though about to do so, and then throw or move the hands by wrist action to right and left a few inches, bringing wrists near together. This gesture indicates the shape of the house.

Deaf-mutes indicate the usual shape of the roof by joining the tips of extended fingers, hands held in front of body.

How. Make sign for YES, usually moving hand downwards and to left, giving in this way emphasis, a pronounced or decided *yes*.

The Indians have learned this word from us, using it as a salutation, and also as an expression of consent and approval. They have no such expression as " Good-morning," " Good-evening," or anything very similar, but instead they usually say, " Fill up the pipe ; let us smoke," which supplies the want and redeems their meetings, on entering each other's lodges, from an appearance of sulkiness or gruffness.

After a long absence, or a special favor given and received, Indians frequently embrace. In parting with their husbands, brothers, fathers, and sweethearts, the women usually pass the palms of the hands down from the neck over the breast of the man, and accompany this pathetic blessing with sobs and tears and piteous wailings. The man stands apparently unmoved during this affectionate demonstration, and particularly is this the case if other people witness the separation.

How Many. Hold the left hand, back down, edges pointing a little to right of front, in front of left breast, fingers partially separated and slightly curved ; hold right hand, back nearly outwards, to right and slightly in front of left hand, index finger extended and pointing to left and front ; move the right hand, mostly by wrist action, briskly towards the body, repeating motion, end of index striking first little finger, and then the others in succession, and as these fingers are struck or bent back, they remain more curved, nearly closed.

Deaf-mutes assume a questioning look, and hold closed right hand in front of body, opening fingers, one after the other, commencing with index.

How Much. Usually expressed by How MANY. How much money? would be how many dollars, etc., and could only be done by comparison, interrogating as to whether little or a great deal.

Hump. Make sign for BUFFALO ; then partially compress right hand and pass it over right shoulder, and hold it as nearly as possible between shoulder-blades.

Hundred. Expressed as ten tens by many tribes, but the Arapahoes, Cheyennes, Teton Sioux, and some others usually bring the hands, palms out, in front of right shoulder, fingers and thumbs extended, separated, and pointing upwards, hands in same vertical plane, tips of thumbs touching ; move the hands well out to left and downwards on vertical curve, keeping in same vertical plane.

Deaf-mutes hold up index finger and make sign for letter C.

Hungry. Conception : Cuts one in two.   The Southern Indians bring the lower edge of extended right hand, back down, against the epigastrium, fingers pointing to left, pressing edge of hand against body ; move it to right and left, as though cutting or sawing with edge.

I never saw this sign used in the North, the usual way being to say that "one wants something to eat," by the signs for EAT, NO ; touch abdomen, and then sign for POOR.

Deaf-mutes partially close the right hand, and make a clawing, scratching motion on front of body.

Indians can certainly go longer without food than white men, and suffer less from the fast, but the ordinary cases, where comparison is possible, are hardly fair tests, as they find many things, such as roots, berries, etc., to eat where a white man finds nothing.   There can be no question, however, that their powers of endurance in the deprivation of food are far exceeded by their enormous capacity for gorging themselves when they are plentifully supplied.   There have been many occasions when scouts have consumed their several days' rations in a single night, spending the entire night in cooking, singing, beating on their drums, and eating.

Hunt.   Make sign for SEARCH, or SCOUT, or LOOK FOR, and specify what for.

Deaf-mutes partially close right hand, and hold it well out to front and right of body, back to right, and move it to the left, about horizontally, as though ready to grasp something.

Mr. Dunbar says that the Pawnees made yearly a summer and winter hunt ; the former from the last of June till the first of September, the latter from the last of October till early in April.   The general direction of the hunting expeditions was to the southwest, into Western Kansas, but sometimes the summer hunt was confined to Western Nebraska.   The entire distance travelled on an expedition varied greatly (from four hundred to nine hundred miles), according as the game proved plenty or scarce.   The exact time of departure from home was generally fixed by a tribal council.   Prior to starting, all goods that they did not choose to take along were carefully cached, and every man and beast called in.   When the day for setting out arrived, all articles not previously disposed of were packed upon horses, each family, as it was ready, fell into line, and the bustling villages were left utterly desolate.   They travelled in Indian file, and of necessity the line was often several miles in length.   The men rode in advance and upon the flanks, keeping a diligent lookout over the country through which they were passing. The women and children walked in the trail, each leading one or more pack-animals.   Children too small to walk were carried by their mothers, or bestowed upon some convenient horse.   It occasionally happened that an animal became frightened or restive, broke away from its leader, kicked about till it had freed itself completely from its load, and galloped away at full speed.   The unfortunate woman who had it in charge must then follow it till caught, bring it back, gather together the scattered load, replace it upon the horse, and regain her place in the line, if indeed it was not already in camp. All the recompense she had for the fatiguing exertion was, quite probably, a severe chiding from her husband, who, perhaps, had witnessed the whole occurrence and made sport of it.

The aged and infirm were obliged to travel with the line and worry along as best they might. Such persons were accustomed to start earlier than the main body, so that they might arrive in camp in good season. Old age and decrepitude with the Indians was the dark day of life. While at home they were tolerably cared for, but on these hunts they endured extreme hardship and privation. Instances have been known where persons, who felt unable to accompany their bands, chose to remain or were left behind in the villages. A supply of provisions was given them, which in summer they might easily supplement by gathering wild fruit and various edible roots. Those in this condition, however, were almost sure to fall victims to prowling Dakotas, who regularly, during the absence of the tribe, visited the villages to perpetrate whatever maliciousness they could see their way to.

In winter the daily march did not ordinarily begin early, but in warmer weather they set out at dawn or sooner, and advanced till from eleven to four o'clock, as circumstances dictated. The distance daily traversed was from eight to twenty miles. For two or more hours after the advance had halted the line would continue to pour into the camp, which was fixed where wood, water, and forage were plenty. As soon as a family arrived the women unpacked the horses and turned them loose to graze, while they themselves pitched the lodge (a work in which they were so expert that but few minutes were required for its performance), brought wood and water, and prepared the daily meal. Sometimes they travelled all day, reaching the place selected for camp just at nightfall. On such occasions the scene which transpired beggars description. The horses were unruly, the children hungry and petulant, the women vexed and weary, the men ill-natured and imperious. Horses whinnied and pranced, dogs yelped and snarled, children teased and cried, women scolded and men threatened; no one heeded and everything went wrong. Tongue and ears at such a time were of little avail.

As soon as they arrived on the buffalo-grounds the greatest circumspection was exercised in their daily progress. Men regularly appointed, known as la-rĭ-pŭk′-us (soldiers), were kept constantly on the watch, and when a herd was discovered all its movements were cautiously watched. After the camp had been moved as near as might be from the lee side without alarming the game, a council was called to determine whether all indications were favorable to an instant hunt. In these councils the ku′-ra-u (doctors or medicine-men) played a prominent part, and sometimes postponed action for several days with no further reason than the bare assertion that *it was not good*. If, however, the result of the deliberation was favorable, the proclamation of a hunt was duly made by a herald. All who

wished to participate in the sport caught their fleetest horses and
equipped. A number of the soldiers were assigned, whose business
it was, in conjunction with the chiefs, to have charge of all the preliminaries, as also of the final chase. Two of them, curiously painted
and wearing a variety of fantastic accoutrements, rode out, bearing
the soldiers' escutcheon, and took position, with about a dozen armed
attendants, upon some convenient eminence till the body of the
hunters had assembled. They then moved forward, and the hunters
followed. Two old men with rattles and medicine-bags ran on foot
in front, singing and shaking the rattles. A person who should have
the temerity now to dash ahead of the soldiers, would scarcely escape
with life. He would at least secure to himself a most merciless flog-
ging, even rank not availing to avert the penalty. This regulation
was so strict that it would not screen from summary punishment a
person who should go out and kill a buffalo, and alarm the herd
before the regular hunt, were he even to plead in extenuation that it
was done to save his family from starving. This was a wise usage,
though it may seem uselessly severe. In this manner the troop proceeded till they were come as near as possible without startling the
herd. The hardly-repressed excitement at this moment was intense.
Halting, the hunters were quietly drawn up in line facing the game,
so that all might have an equal chance. The word was given, and
with a loud cry they sped away, each urging his trained steed to the
utmost, that he might first overtake and secure a victim. The horses
in these charges were guided by the knees of the rider, his hands
being busied with bow and arrows. In a few minutes each hunter
might be seen nearing the animal that he had selected. (Till the
buffaloes were two and a half years old there was little choice between the sexes. After that age the flesh of bulls became distasteful,
and was rarely taken, unless in a time of great scarcity. It was
owing to this fact that bulls were in excess in many herds.) Just
before coming abreast of it he discharged an arrow, endeavoring to
strike it high in the flank, between the projecting hip and ribs, so
that the shaft should take a course obliquely forward toward the
vitals. A single arrow sent with skill and force in this direction,
even if not immediately fatal, caused such distress as to soon bring
the buffalo to a stand-still. If one did not suffice, others were used.
As soon as the animal ceased running the hunter passed on to another, and sometimes a third, fourth, and even a fifth was brought
to by one man in the course of half an hour. The entire number
slaughtered in a single chase frequently exceeded three hundred.

The Pawnees seldom resorted to a surround, attacking from all
sides at once. This method was more tedious and dangerous, and
was regarded as less huntsmanlike. When the chase ended the hunter
returned upon his track, and dispatched the wounded buffalo that he
had left on the way, if indeed they were not already dead from loss
of blood. If still alive, they were usually found lying down, but on
being approached would instantly rise and show fight. The carcasses
were now skinned, cut up, packed on spare horses that had been

brought up meantime by the women, and conveyed to camp. There a scene of the greatest activity ensued. The hides were stretched upon the ground with pegs to dry. The meat was carefully cut in thin strips or sheets suitable for drying, and laid upon a frame-work of poles over a slow fire. When the exposed side became dry enough to cause the meat to begin to roll, or crumple, it was placed upon the ground and trampled or beaten with billets of wood till completely flattened out. The other side was then exposed, and the process repeated till the meat was dry. The design of the trampling or beating was to preserve the meat in the best form for packing in bales for transportation. Sometimes it was dried in the sun alone, but was not then so good. Several days were usually required for drying the meat of one slaughtering. No salt was used in either case, but with proper care the meat could be preserved without apparent deterioration for years.

The Pawnees were excellent horsemen, and in the buffalo-hunt their consummate equestrianism was displayed to the finest advantage. Without hesitation they would rush at full speed, over the roughest ground, into the midst of masses of buffalo which were surging along in the wildest confusion, single out and separate their victims, and repeat the manœuvre at pleasure. But sometimes accidents of the most distressing nature happened. In an unguarded moment a hunter might be overtaken by a charging buffalo, or a horse going at full gallop might step into the burrow of some animal, and, with its rider, be hurled headlong. In many places on the prairie the ground is so cut up by the burrows of the prairie-dog (*Cynomus Ludovicianus*) that a person cannot ride over it at an ordinary pace without great care, while at a rapid gait necessary precaution is impossible. Mishaps from one of these sources, not infrequently resulting in death, were almost inevitable in every chase.

The weapons employed in this hunting, as already stated, were the bow and arrow. The facility with which they could be managed on horseback, and their much greater efficiency in the work of destruction, were unanswerable recommendations. A buffalo wounded with a ball in a vital part might run a great distance. On the other hand, a single well-directed arrow, securely lodged, so sickened and distressed the animal as to bring it soon to a stand. An arrow could be sent with such force as to pass entirely through a buffalo, in case it did not encounter a bone, and stick in the ground on the other side ; but the aim was rather to lodge it firmly in the body, as its effect was then more marked, and also the presence of the shaft would serve to indicate to whom the carcass rightfully belonged.

In the winter hunt they killed what meat they needed as soon as might be after arriving on the hunting-ground, before the buffalo became poor. They went into winter quarters in some place where water, wood, and unburnt grass in abundance for the horses were to be had. Here they remained till forage became scarce, when another place was sought. If grass could not be found in sufficient quantity they cut cottonwood-trees, and subsisted the horses on the bark and tender twigs. The return to the villages did not take place till young grass was started in the spring. In the summer hunt they remained away no longer than was necessary to procure the requisite supply of meat. By the time this was accomplished their corn was ready for drying, and required immediate attention. As their calendar was not very exact, they were sometimes in doubt as to just when was the proper time to return home. In such cases they were accustomed to examine the seed in the pods of the large milkweed. A certain maturity in these was thought to mark roasting-ear time.

They also hunted other game, as elk, deer, and antelope. While the buffalo was hunted mainly as an indispensable means of subsistence, these smaller animals were sought rather for their skins. Though their flesh was eaten, that of the buffalo was preferred ; but for the manufacture of articles of clothing, as moccasins, leggings, and shirts, buck-, elk-, or antelope-skin was far superior. They were taken by still-hunting or stalking with bow or fire-arms. As they had opportunity and inclination, beaver and otter were sought for their pelts, which were used in making fancy articles of clothing. Bears, when to be found, were eagerly hunted for their skins, flesh, and claws. Panthers were also in constant request. A bow-case and quiver of panther-skin was a coveted possession. Skunks were esteemed for their flesh and skins. The latter, after being taken off as nearly entire as possible, was buried in loose earth for two or three days to divest it of the native odor. It was then dressed and used as a tobacco-pouch or medicine-bag, the mouth of the animal serving as the opening. The boys were very expert in capturing prairie-chickens and quails. When one of these was started up on the prairie, the exact spot of its lighting was noted. Armed with a withe five feet long, a boy cautiously crept up to within a few feet of the crouching bird, and then darting forward, struck it down with a well-directed blow as it attempted to rise on the wing.

Though referring especially to the Pawnees, the above description gives a most excellent idea of the arrangements and operations of all Indian tribes on their hunting excursions. With some of the Eastern bands of Sioux, as well as with other tribes, a very ostentatious and elaborate display and feast were made over the first animal killed by a boy, and in olden times the boy frequently gave a small portion of some particular part to his personal God ; and ever afterwards this same part of any animal he might kill would be sacrificed, an offering which was in fact a prayer and pledge,—a prayer for good luck, and a pledge of future good faith on his part.

An old Cheyenne once said to me in regard to the first fruit of a boy's effort in hunting and the encouragement given to him in consequence, that "when I was eight years of age I killed a goose with a bow and arrow, took it to my father's lodge, leaving the arrow in it. My father asked me if I had killed it, and I said yes ; my arrow is in it. My father examined the bird, fired off his gun, turned to an old man who was in the lodge, presented the gun to him, and said, 'Go and harangue the camp; inform them all what my boy has done.'

When I killed my first buffalo I was ten years old. My father was right close, came to me and asked if I had killed it. I said I had. He called some old men who were near by to come over and look at the buffalo his son had killed, gave one of them a pony, and told him to inform the camp."

This Indian was eighty years of age when he told me the story, and the memory of the pride and pleasure which he experienced at this recognition of his boyish skill as a hunter was still fresh and gratifying to him, and it must be remembered, to fully appreciate the compliments and recognition given him, that a gun and pony were much more valuable to the Indians seventy years ago than they are at present.

Hurry. Conception: Lift up quickly. Hold nearly extended hand, backs down, in front of body, equally advanced, same height, and few inches apart, fingers pointing about to front; move the hands sharply, by wrist and elbow action, upwards a few inches, repeating motion. Some Indians make signs for WORK and FAST.

Deaf-mutes hold right hand, and snap thumb, as boys do in firing marbles.

Husband. Make sign for MALE and MARRY.

Deaf-mutes make their signs for MAN and MARRY.

I.

I. (Myself.) Touch the centre of breast with tip of extended thumb of right hand, fingers closed, and back of hand to right, hand held few inches in front of centre, and moved horizontally towards body. Some Indians touch the nose with extended index of right hand. Sometimes, for emphasis, the breast is struck vigorously with right fist.

Deaf-mutes use the first-described gesture. A thrusting of right index finger towards centre of breast means boasting.

Ice. Make signs for WATER, for COLD, and bring hands together as in FREEZE OVER.

Deaf-mutes make their signs for WATER and FREEZE.

Icicle. Make signs for WATER, for COLD, and hold right index vertically in front of body, pointing downwards.

Deaf-mutes make their signs for WATER, FREEZE, and then holding right extended index in front of body, pointed downwards, pass left index over it, to represent water running down its sides.

Impossible. See CANNOT.

Deaf-mutes hold left hand in front of body, index finger extended and pointing to front, others and thumb closed; then bring right hand above left, index alone extended, pointing to left; lower right hand, right index striking left, and knocking it down.

Imprison. Conception: Seizing hold of. Hold closed left hand, back to left, in front of and little higher than left shoulder, forearm about vertical; seize left wrist with right hand, and carry or drop it to right some inches; then cross the wrists in front of body, hands closed, thumbs up, right wrist above and resting on left.

Deaf-mutes indicate the "prison bars" by crossing the extended and separated fingers in front of body, and then cross wrists to indicate being bound.

In. In the sense of "in my house," if for person, make sign for HOUSE and SIT; if an inanimate object, sign for LIE, in the sense of *laid down.* "Going in" would be expressed by ENTER.

Deaf-mutes thrust compressed right into partially-closed left hand.

Incite. Expressed by saying "a fire was built among them by talking," etc.

Deaf-mutes make gesture for to TEMPT and to REBEL. For first, touch the lips with right index, with an upward entreating expression of eyes. For latter, the right arm is raised as though to ward off a blow, hand closed, and more of a twist or turn given to arm, holding forearm about horizontal.

Increase. The manner or nature of the increase would naturally suggest the sign, but the usual one is to hold the hands, palms towards each other, well out in front of body, hands at same height, opposite each other, a few inches apart, fingers pointing to front; separate the hands, moving right to right, left to left, by gentle jerks. A vertical increase is indicated in a similar manner.

Deaf-mutes indicate the increment similarly.

Indian. Specify the tribe by giving the tribal sign.

Deaf-mutes make sign for AMERICAN.

This word, growing out of a mistake, has been perpetuated apparently by the mere force of the error, until, for us, it has become a necessity in all descriptions relating to our aborigines, who vocally, as well as by gesture, always specify the tribe.

Infantry. Make signs for WHITES, SOLDIER, and WALK.

Inferior. (In rank or influence.) The inferiority of one person to another, as, for instance, of one chief to another of the same tribe, is represented by the index fingers extended side by side and pointing upwards, other fingers and thumbs closed; one index, representing the inferior, is held a little lower than the other. If it be wished to represent several persons as inferior to one, the right index is placed alongside and higher than the extended fingers of left hand.

Sometimes the sign for BEHIND is made.

Deaf-mutes fix both hands as in their sign for CHIEF, and then holding them in front of body, lower the one representing the inferior person.

Inhabit. Conception: Alive and moving about in a certain part of the country.

Hold right hand very slightly compressed, fingers and thumb extended, separated, and pointing upwards, well out in front of body; hand about height of face; mostly by wrist action turn the hand from right to left two or three times, rather slowly.

Deaf-mutes indicate home of person.

Injure. Conception: Doing evil to. If with reference to another person, make sign for WORK and BAD. If with reference to one's self, make sign for DO TO ME and for BAD.

Interpreter. This is expressed by naming person, or saying he or she talks whatever language it may be, and one's own; using for talk the sign for LITTLE TALK. If talking or speaking of the ability of a person to interpret, and it is desired to explain that he or she will interpret for my people, or for us, use the sign for TALK or SPEAK, in the sense of handing words from one to another. (See COUNCIL.) The lack of honest and efficient interpreters has been one of the great causes of all our trouble with the Indians, one of the greatest obstacles to a thorough understanding of the Indian question, and the greatest source of false impressions of their abilities, laws, customs, habits, moral and immoral qualities of character. It has fettered civilization, retarded Christianizing influences, held the Indians in the close embrace of barbarism, cost billions of money, made corruption and theft not only possible but easy, stained the soil of every State with innocent blood, and led the race to the threshold of extermination.

Interrogate. Hold right hand, palm outwards, well out in front of body, about height of shoulder, fingers and thumb extended, separated, and pointing upwards. If the person is close, turn the hand slightly, by wrist action, two or three times, moving it also a trifle to right and left. If the person is distant, hold the hand higher, and move it well to right and left.

If a person be riding or walking past, and one makes to him this sign, it asks him, "Where are you going?" "What are you going for?" etc. When two persons meet, one may ask with this sign, "What news have you?" "What do you want?" etc. It accosts, interrogates, questions, and investigates.

Deaf-mutes hold the left forearm horizontally in front of body, and sharply strike upper surface near wrist with palmar surface of fingers of right hand.

Iron. When I first asked about this sign, I was told that there was none, that the only way was to point to it, and my informant added, "You will never see an Indian without a piece of iron in some shape." This is generally true. He always has his knife, gun, arrow, head-buckle, or something made of the material.

The sign for HARD is, however, frequently made, and from its connection is generally understood. It can also be expressed by describing something made of iron or steel (which are the same to them).

Island. Bring hands well in front of body, palms towards each other, and form an incomplete horizontal circle with index fingers and thumbs, space of about an inch between tips, other fingers closed; then bring wrists near each other, separating tips of index fingers by wrist action, throwing right hand slightly to right, left to left; then holding left hand in its position, make sign for WATER; then compress right hand, and move tips of fingers just above left hand, outside the circle first formed.

Deaf-mutes indicate land surrounded by water.

Itching. Scratch left palm with nail of right index, or indicate by scratching with nails of right hand the location of the sensation.

Deaf-mutes use the same signs.

J.

Jealous. Conception : Elbowing to one side. Hold the closed hands near right and left breasts; move the right elbow a little to rear and to right, then left elbow a little to rear and to left, repeating motion ; if it is desired to express active jealousy, constant elbowing to one side. Some Indians indicate a twisting of the heart, while others make signs for BAD and SECRET, considering a jealous person as one who works evil secretly. Some make sign for ABUSE, and the left hand is held as in HIDE ; and still others make signs for HEART, BAD, and ABUSE. I have also seen gestures to denote two people as "picking" at each other.

To one ignorant of the principles of gesture speech, the several signs above given would be ample and sufficient proof to establish the fact that there are as many different signs as vocal languages among our aborigines, but a brief examination of the gestures shows that they are but the lights and shades necessary to express ideas. The first would be used in such cases as where one was envious of the position of others and endeavored to elbow himself into a better one. The second, the doubts which cause a young person to question the sincerity of the object of adoration ; his jealousy twists and turns his heart. The third indicates a person vexed at the success, jealous of the renown of some one, and though there was evil in him, yet it was hidden. The fourth indicates a jealous person talking badly of one "behind his back" ; and the fifth, as having, through jealousy, a wicked heart, and throwing lies or mistakes against one or his reputation on account of this ; whilst the sixth indicates two jealous persons picking at each other, or tearing down each other's reputations.

Joke. Hold the right hand, back down, in front of mouth, fingers separated and partially curved ; move the hand to front and upwards. This sign is not common, and there is no general sign in use for the word. I have seen also the sign for MISTAKE MADE, and then LITTLE TALK, and then sign for LIGHT (not heavy).

Deaf-mutes grasp the nose with right hand ; move the hand to front and downwards, and at same time incline the head to the front.

Joyous. Make signs for HEART, for LIGHT (or GLAD) ; sometimes adding sign for SING. Many Indians make signs for HEART FLUTTERING, as in EXCITE.

Jump. Hold nearly compressed right hand, back to right, in front and close to right shoulder, fingers pointing to front ; move the hand briskly to front, upwards, and then downwards on a vertical curve.

15

Deaf-mutes hold extended left hand, back down, in front of body; place tips of separated and extended first and second fingers of right hand on left palm, other fingers closed, then move the right hand to front, upwards and then downwards.

Junior. This is usually expressed by the sign for BEHIND. For two persons or officers it is frequently indicated as in INFERIOR; the tip of one index lower than the other, and the distance determines the difference in the rank,—a very little below, about equal, etc.

K.

Keep. Hold right hand, back to right, in front of body, fingers extended, touching and pointing to front; carry left hand, back to left, index finger extended, others and thumb closed, and place index in centre of right palm, index pointing upwards as it strikes right palm; close right hand, holding index firmly, and move hands slightly to right and left.

This gesture is frequently used in the sense of having held on to the promises made, etc. Sometimes used in sense of remember. (See HOLD.)

Deaf-mutes use their sign for POSSESS, and then fixing hands as in LOOK, lay little finger of right on base of thumb of left, index and second finger of right hand pointing to left and upwards, index and second of left pointing to right and upwards,—guarding with double eyes.

Keep Close. Expressed by signs for GOOD and NEAR, or, perhaps, I HOLD and GOOD and NEAR, or, making it more imperative, sign for MUST or PUSH and NEAR.

Deaf-mutes make their signs for STAY and NEAR.

Keep Quiet. Hold extended right hand, palm outwards and downwards, well in front of body, fingers extended, touching, pointing to front and upwards, hand about height of shoulder; move the hand rather sharply outwards and downwards few inches, repeating motion.

Frequently both hands are used, and after second motion the hands gently lowered. This is also used in sense of *fear not, do not be anxious, quiet down*, etc.

Deaf-mutes about same.

Kettle. Form an incomplete horizontal circle in front of body with index fingers and thumbs, other fingers closed, little fingers down; then, still holding left hand in its position, carry partially-closed right hand back to right and downwards over the imaginary kettle, as though about to lift it by the bail.

Deaf-mutes indicate shape, make their sign for the material out of which made,—*i.e.*, iron, tin, etc.,—and then sign for FIRE.

Kidney. Hold compressed hands against surface of body over the location of kidneys.

Deaf-mutes use the same sign.

Kill. Bring right hand, back nearly up, in front of body, about height of shoulder, hand very nearly closed, ball of thumb pressing against second joint of index, second joints of fingers nearly on line with back of hand, back of hand making a slight angle with wrist; *i.e.*, knuckles higher than wrist; strike to the front, downwards and little to left, stopping hand suddenly, and giving it a slight rebound. In descriptions of personal combats, which in former times were frequently resorted to by the medicine-men of contending parties, the result determining the victory of one or the other of the parties, I have usually seen the left palm struck with the lower edge of extended right hand, though at times the ordinary sign for KILL would be made. The first-described gesture is common, and is used metaphorically in many ways. To win in gambling is to *kill* the person to the extent of the amount won. If any part of the body is frozen, the cold has *killed* the part. A severe storm *kills*. Indigestion *kills*. To get decidedly the worst of an argument is to be *killed*. To win a girl's affection is to *kill* her, etc.

Deaf-mutes hold left hand, back to left, in front of body, index finger extended and pointing to front, other fingers and thumb closed ; bring right hand similarly fixed, fingers back to left, between left hand and body and little higher, index finger pointing to front and trifle downwards ; thrust the index finger of right hand to front, its tip grazing side of left index, and then sweep hand into position by their sign for DIE.

Kinship. Conception : Near or distant from one source. Bring the tips of extended and touching first and second fingers of right hand against lips, back of fingers up and horizontal, other fingers and thumb closed ; carry the hand some inches straight out from the mouth ; then make sign for DISTANT or NEAR, according as it is desired to represent distant or near kinship.

I have also seen the sign for BROTHER-IN-LAW made, and the sign for DISTANT or CLOSE added over left arm.

Deaf-mutes cross the index fingers at right angles, thus denoting halves.

The nomenclature of kinship of the Plains Indians generally is illustrated by the saying of an Indian to me, " Suppose the man beside me married my daughter, his and my daughter's children would call me grandfather ; all the children would call this man's brothers *fathers,* and his sisters *aunts ;* they would call my daughter's sisters *mothers,* and her brothers *uncles ;* they would call all this man's brother's children *brothers* and *sisters,* all of his sister's children *cousins ;* they would call all the children of my daughter's sisters *brothers* and *sisters,* and all of her brother's children *cousins.*"

Mr. L. H. Morgan asserts that the various tribes of Indians were formerly divided into several different *gens,* each of which determined for its members inheritance of property and power as well as the marriage relations. He says that in Latin, Greek, and Sanscrit, the word *gens* and its synonyms have alike the primary signification of *kin.* A gens, therefore, is a body of consanguinity descended from the same common ancestor, distinguished by a gentile name, and bound together by affinities of blood.

" Where descent is in the female line, as it was universally in the archaic period, the gens is composed of a supposed female ancestor, and her children, together with the children of her female descendants through females in perpetuity ; and where descent is in the male line, into which it was changed after the appearance of property in masses of a supposed male ancestor and his children, together with the children of his male descendants through males in perpetuity. The family name among ourselves is a survival of the gentile name with descent in the male line, and passing in the same manner ; the modern family, as expressed by its name, is an unorganized gens with the bond of kin broken, and its members as widely dispersed as the family name is found.''

It is safe to state that among the majority of the tribes of Plains Indians, and I think Western Indians generally, no such organization exists at present, and, judging from their laws of inheritance and marriage customs, never did. The Mandans and Poncas, however, do show a trace of it.

Mr. Dunbar says of the Pawnees, that ''the family organization and degrees of kinship were not so fully developed by distinct terminology as in some Indian tribes. The only attempt hitherto made to exhibit the Pawnee system of relationship is to be found in ' Morgan's Systems of Consanguinity and Affinity.' '' He then proceeds to illustrate by appropriate words in the Pawnee language the status of their views in regard to kinship, and adds :

'' From this exhibit it will be observed that, even in designating the simpler degrees of relationship, the terminology becomes in certain cases undeterminate. Some of the terms given are not names at all, but descriptive phrases, seeming to indicate that even in some of the most usual relations there is an almost entire lack of reflective generalization. Much more will this be the case when they attempt to trace out the remoter degrees. The answers made by the most intelligent Pawnees, when questioned concerning degrees, direct or collateral, remoter than those given, are conflicting and altogether unsatisfying. Hence it is self-evident that a considerable number of the terms given by Morgan are of no special value.''

Kiowa (Indian). Hold the right hand, back nearly down, in front of right breast, about height of and near shoulder, fingers touching and slightly curved, lower edge of hand pointing to left and front ; by wrist action give a rotary motion to hand, keeping palm up, finger-tips describing an ellipse. Some Indians hold the hand near right cheek.

I was given two conceptions for this tribal sign, both plausible, though not very pertinent. One Indian said they were called ''Crazy-Knife people,'' and another, '' Prairie people,'' constantly rising up. This latter does possess the radical parts of the gestures sometimes made for the prairie and for arise.

Tradition locates the Kiowas near and to the southwest of the Black Hills, Dakota, and without doubt they had previous to that time lived near the Missouri River. The Apaches with whom they are now associated were at this time with them. The Cheyennes crossed the Missouri River, moved to near Bear Butte, and drove the Kiowas and Apaches to the southwest. They were forced south between the Pawnees to the east and the Utes to the west, and evidently made no successful resistance until they reached the Comanch country and joined this tribe. They subsequently made peace with the Cheyennes and Arapahoes. In fact, the Comanches, Crows, Kiowas, Apaches, Sioux, Cheyennes, and Arapahoes confederated together against their common enemies the Utes, Pawnees, and other tribes, but the confederacy was tied together by a "rope of sand," and in the last one hundred and fifty years they have been alternating between peace and war.

Though preserving their language and some of their customs still, from long intercourse and intermarriage these three tribes, the Kiowas, Comanches, and Apaches, have much in common, and in dress it would be difficult to distinguish them.

They do not have a Sun-Dance, but an annual Medicine-Dance, which is observed with great ceremony. Their bury their dead in the ground, in graves twelve or thirteen feet deep. Their peculiar idol worship has been noticed (see GOD), as well as their organization of ten priests'or medicine-men.

They have four bands, called Elk, Shield, Cut-Off, and Black. Some claim five, the Apache Kiowa band.

The Kiowas not only eat, but are fond of dog-meat.

In 1874 some sheep were given them, purchased by the money received from the sale of their ponies, taken from them by the troops. These flocks have mostly disappeared, they admitting that they ate some of them, but claim that "wolves, starvation, and cold weather killed off the majority," so that the effort to change them from hunters to herdsmen failed.

In personal appearance, intelligence, and tenacity of purpose I consider the Kiowas inferior to the Comanches.

In his report for 1881, the agent gives the total population of this tribe as eleven hundred and forty-five. Wars, and new diseases peculiar to civilization, have greatly reduced them in numbers.

Knife. Conception: Cutting a piece of meat held with left hand and with teeth. Hold right hand in front of and close to face, back outwards, lower edge just over mouth, fingers extended, touching, and pointing to left and upwards; move the hand upwards and to left two or three times, as though trying to cut or saw with lower edge of hand. Frequently left hand is held in front of and a little higher than right and close to it. I have also seen length marked on left forearm, and then motion made like CUTTING UP.

Indians in eating meat usually take a piece in the left hand, and conveying it to the mouth and grasping an end with the teeth, with a dexterity almost alarming sever the bit to be masticated from the chunk by means of a butcher-knife, one or more of which are always carried by a wild Indian in a sheath attached to his belt on the left side. These knives are only sharpened on one side, which seems to make them better for skinning, and, for some reason not well understood, to cut better and retain a fine edge longer than when sharpened on both sides, as is our custom. I have seen them cut up a deer, going right down through the backbone, cut or chop open the skull to take out the brains, and scarcely impair the edge of an ordinary knife costing about fifty cents. This seems incredible, but is absolutely true. It is possible that the metal of the blade on the surface is better tempered, and therefore makes a better cutting edge than the central portion.

Deaf-mutes hold first and second fingers of left hand extended and touching, other fingers and thumb closed, in front of body, and, with right hand similarly fixed, with side of second make motion of "whittling" side of left index.

Know. Hold right hand, back up, close to left breast; sweep the hand outwards and to right, turning hand by wrist action, palm nearly up, thumb and index extended, other fingers closed, thumb and index about horizontal, index pointing nearly to left, thumb about to front. This seems to combine the sign for THINK, drawn from the heart, and then the thumb cuts it off.

Sometimes, for emphasis, both hands are used, the left being swept to left as the right is to the right. Some Indians touch right ear with right index. The Utes thrust the index towards ear, as in HEAR.

Deaf-mutes place the palmar surface of extended fingers of right hand against forehead. They make a distinction between know and understand; Indians do not.

Know Not. Make sign for KNOW; then from this position, only stopping the hand for an instant, open the hand, sweep it still farther to the right, upwards and outwards, on curve as in NO.

Deaf-mutes make their sign for KNOW and NOT, both of which are very different from the Indian gestures.

Koutenay (Indian). There is no well-known tribal sign. Some call them the "White-tailed deer people," making proper gestures for this expression.

These Indians, numbering, according to the agent's report for 1881, three hundred and ninety-five, are located on the Flathead Reservation, Montana. They migrated from north of the British line, and made peace with the Flatheads, about eighty years since. After this peace they annually visited this part of the country for the fishing and hunting, and then returned north. When the treaty was made with the Flatheads and Pend d'Oreilles they were included with the rest, and were given the same rights and annuities as the others. Their vocal language is totally different from the Flatheads, and they also differ in some of their customs. In dress they are about the same, only a more beggarly-looking lot, and seem, more than other Indians, to be afflicted with ophthalmia.

L.

Lacota. See SIOUX.

Lake. Conception : Water and shape. Make sign for WATER ; then bring the hands in front of body, palms towards each other, and form an incomplete horizontal circle with index fingers and thumbs, space of about an inch between tips, other fingers closed ; then bring the wrists near each other, at same time separating tips of index fingers.

Deaf-mutes indicate water surrounded by land.

Lame. Conception : Limping motion of animals. Hold closed right hand, back up, about twelve inches in front of right breast ; move the hand slightly to front, and at same time, by wrist action, bend the hand downwards and to left ; repeat motion.

Deaf-mutes hold index fingers pointing down in front of body, other fingers and thumbs closed, one hand held lower than the other, and imitate motion of walking, with one leg being shorter than the other.

Lance. (See SPEAR.) For a " medicine lance" the sign described for SPEAR is made, and then the crooked right index is held in front of and higher than right shoulder, other fingers and thumb closed, back of hand to rear. This seems to indicate a lance not to be used in war, but one made only, or used only, to bring good luck to the possessor.

Large. Make sign for BIG, and if necessary add sign for HIGH.

Deaf-mutes spread the thumbs and index fingers, bring the hands in front of body near each other and same height ; separate the hands, carrying right to right, left to left.

Lariat. Make sign for ANIMAL ; then clasp the right side of the neck with spread thumb and index held about horizontally, and then make sign for ROPE.

Lariats are about twenty-five feet long, and are usually made of untanned buffalo- or elk-skin, from which the hair has been carefully scraped. They are generally braided with three strands, and have a small loop at one end. After braiding they are stretched taut and pinned to the ground, and after becoming thoroughly "set" or dried, are then greased and rubbed until soft and pliable. Made in this way, they possess the merit of great strength and durability ; are light and pliable in dry weather, but not so satisfactory in wet weather ; and unless care is used in drying, are liable to become stiff and vexatious to use.

Deaf-mutes make their sign for ROPE, and motion to indicate lassoing an animal.

Lasso. Make sign for ROPE or LARIAT, then hold right hand, back about to right, little to right of and higher than right shoulder, index and thumb spread, index pointing about upwards, other fingers closed; move, or rather, throw, the hand well to front upwards and downwards; then draw the hand back quickly a short distance, at same time closing index and thumb.

The lasso, with the Indians, is simply the lariat formed into a noose at one end by passing the other end through the small loop made in the lariat. Though the Indians are not as dexterous as the Mexicans in throwing a lasso, yet some of them exhibit great skill; and I have seen Indian boys run with a herd, and with a lasso catch any pony they wished.

Last. See BEHIND.

Deaf-mutes hold extended left index in front of body, and bring extended right index from left forearm and place it on left index, other fingers of hands closed.

Last Year. Make sign for WINTER and BEYOND. This is the general sign. (See SEASONS and TIME.)

Deaf-mutes make their sign for YEAR, and then point with extended thumb of right hand, fingers closed, over right shoulder.

Lead (To). Conception: Leading pony with lariat. Hold closed right hand, back to right, in front, close to, and little higher than right shoulder; move the hand some little distance to front by gentle jerks.

In going to war on horseback, if they possess or can get them, each Indian takes two ponies. The best and fleetest, or, as we have named it, "war pony," is not ridden until an emergency arises. Indians keenly and thoroughly appreciate the value of a fresh animal, either for a dash and pursuit after their enemies, should they come suddenly upon them, or as a means of escape. An Indian mounted on an animal which he considers better than that of his enemies does not fear to penetrate into their very midst, and as a scout will be apt to do excellent service; but let him once feel that his mount is less fleet, less enduring, than are those of his enemy, and he is worthless,—will take no risks where a white man might be persuaded to at least do his best; and this characteristic has given rise to divers opinions as to the courage and worth of not only the Indians of different tribes, but oftentimes of individuals. (See SCOUT.)

Deaf-mutes hold the extended left hand, back to left, near left side; grasp ends of fingers with thumb and fingers of right hand, and draw the left to the front.

Leaf. Make sign for TREE, and then hold right hand well out in front of body and little higher than shoulder, index and thumb curved, space of about an inch between tips, other fingers closed, back of hand nearly to right, lower edge pointing to front and upwards; give a tremulous motion to the hand to represent leaf on the limb of a tree.

Deaf-mutes rest right wrist on tip of extended left index in front of body and wave the extended right hand.

Leggings. Pass the hands from well down on legs up towards hip-joints, right hand over right, left over left leg, thumb and index spread, other fingers closed, backs of hands about outwards.

Leggings are universally worn, and for men are now made of both cloth and tanned skins, reaching from the ankle to the hip, terminating there in a V-shaped point. They are fastened to the belt worn around the waist, the seam being down the outer side. The cloth or skin sometimes projects beyond the seam one or two inches, and this with some tribes, as with the Crows, is cut into a fringe.

The leggings for the women are made close-fitting, either wrapped or buttoned, and are usually worn only about as high as the knee. With some tribes, as with the Utes and Apaches, the leggings are fastened to the moccasins, forming a part of them.

Lend. See Borrow.

Liar. Make sign for the person and for Lie.

Liberate. Make sign for Hold and Go, or sign for Prisoner; then, throwing hands well out to right and left, make sign for Go.

Deaf-mutes cross the wrists, hands closed, and then wave the hands outwards and to right and left.

Lie. Conception: Two tongues or forked tongue. Bring right hand, back out, a little in front and to right of mouth, index and second fingers extended, separated, and pointing to left, other fingers and thumb closed; move the hand to left past mouth, index finger passing a little higher than mouth, after passing of which the hand is lowered a little, index and second fingers pointing to left and slightly downwards. Some Indians only pass extended index across mouth, and I have seen the index and second to the front from mouth. This is also the sign for Mistake.

Deaf-mutes pass extended index of right hand across mouth.

It is extremely difficult to get an Indian to make a positive promise. He usually adds some saving clause, and as the latter is not usually mentioned by the interpreters, they have gained the reputation of being great liars. My experience does not justify any such assertion; in fact, I have found that as a rule they are much more truthful than they have usually been accredited with.

It is a matter of vital importance to any one who wishes to gain influence over them that no mistakes should be made,—no promises made unless with the certainty of fulfilling them. This is just as necessary in little matters as in great, for from these minor affairs they form their opinions, and confidence once destroyed is rarely or never restored or regained. Where confidence is reposed their trust and credulity are boundless.

In time of war, of course, deception is considered not only justifiable but praiseworthy.

Lie Down. Hold extended right hand, back up, in front of body, fingers pointing little to left of front; move the hand upwards, outwards, and to right, at same time turning hand, by wrist action, palm up, when hand is little to right of body; the hand, moving on a curve, is swept into position. Many Indians incline the head to the right, and rest it on palm of hand or hands. Sometimes the index finger is held vertically, and then laid over horizontally.

Deaf-mutes incline head on hand, or lay extended and separated index and second finger on palmar surface of fingers of left hand, sometimes first holding them vertically on left palm.

Light. (Not heavy.) Hold extended hands, back down, in front of body, hands same height, equally advanced and few inches apart, fingers pointing to front; raise the hands briskly, mostly by wrist action. This is also used in sense of HURRY, HASTEN, etc.

Deaf-mutes use the same gesture.

Light. (Not dark.) Make sign for DAY.

Deaf-mutes hold extended hands, backs up, in front of and higher than head, tips of fingers touching; move the right to right and downwards on curve, left to left and downwards on curve.

Lightning. Conception : Zigzag flash. Hold the right hand well in front of and higher than head, index finger extended, others and thumb closed, back of hand nearly up, index finger pointing to left, front, and upwards; move the hand to right, rear, and downwards, giving to index finger a wavy, tremulous motion, imitating the zigzag flash. Sometimes the signs for RAIN and THUNDER are first made. I have also seen fingers fixed as in MEDICINE, and the hand raised instead of lowered.

Mr. E. L. Clarke, the interpreter at the Wichita Agency, Indian Territory, kindly furnished me the following :

"I have been unable to trace the existence of any such custom among the Wichitas as the Medicine-Dance to produce rain. They say they have no dance for rain at all ; but that individuals who claim to understand and control the rain carry small flint arrow-heads tied in their scalp-locks, which they claim is a 'thunder charm,' and who believe that one of these flints comes down with each stroke of lightning.'"

Some tribes claim that a certain species of sage will prevent the lightning from doing any harm. At times individual Indians become possessed and harassed with the belief that they are going to be killed by the lightning,—the result of some dream,—and they can only dispossess themselves of the fear by making some special *medicine; i.e.*, sacrificial worship.

Many claim that they were first instructed in the use of the bow and arrow by the Thunder-Bird. (See THUNDER.)

Like. (Comparison.) Make sign for EQUAL. Sometimes the left hand is held back to left, about eighteen inches in front of body, index finger extended and pointing to front, others and thumb closed ; bring right hand, back up, near breast, little higher and in rear of left hand, index finger extended, pointing to front and slightly downwards, other fingers and thumb closed ; move right hand to front and slightly downwards, so that tip of right index touches the back of left index as it passes over it. This is used in such sentences as "one exactly like the other." It is also used for TRUE, STRAIGHT, HONEST, etc. ; LIKE in the sense of pleased with. (See FOND.)

Listen. Hold right hand, back to right, near right ear, index and thumb spread, other fingers closed, ear in space between thumb and index, latter pointing upwards ; turn the hand slightly, by wrist action, from right to left, and from left to right. (See HEAR.) The index would be thrust towards ear and past face when wishing to say, " I listened to what you said," or, " I will listen ;" meaning that you not only heard but would act on what had been said ; and I have seen the open left hand held near left ear, and then closed, as though grasping on to what had passed through the head.

Deaf-mutes hold extended right hand, back to rear, fingers pointing upwards, just back of ear, index touching it.

Little. Hold right hand in front of body, about height of shoulder, back nearly to right, end of thumb pressing against inner surface of index, so that only about the end of index is seen beyond thumbnail, other fingers closed. This is used in the sense of very little of anything. Little in the sense of FEW or small is expressed by sign for FEW. Little in the sense of a little animal is frequently represented by holding partially-compressed right hand, back up, near the ground, in front and to right of body. For a little man make sign for SHORT.

The above sign is used in such expressions as "little talk," "heard a little news," " know but little," " know only a little part of it," "many lies and little truth," etc.

Deaf-mutes clasp the right thumb near end with thumb and index of left hand.

Live. See ALIVE, also RECOVER.

Liver. Place extended hands on surface of body over location of liver, and then, holding them in front of body, give them a tremulous motion.

Lock. Hold extended left hand, back out, in front of body ; bring thumb and index of right against left palm, right hand closed, as though holding a key, and turn the right hand as though turning a key in the lock. This belongs to the somewhat long list of very recent gestures, as Indians never or very rarely, even now, use locks, except when with white people.

To lock up a person the wrists would also be crossed.

Deaf-mutes use the same gestures.

Lodge. See TEPEE.

Long. Make sign for AFTER in the sense of time. This is used in regard to animals as well as time. For inanimate objects it is expressed in some manner similar to LONG KNIFE.

Deaf-mutes hold the hands fixed as in Indian sign for AFTER, but carry right hand back over left arm.

Long Knife. Make sign for KNIFE, and then carry hand well up and to left.

Long Time. Make sign for AFTER, drawing the hands well apart. Frequently the hands are partially closed, tips of thumb and index of each pressed together, other fingers closed, left hand held well in front of body, back about up, tips of right thumb and index brought near left, and the right hand drawn to right and rear. Sometimes the extended right hand, back to right, is brought close to right ear, fingers pointing upwards; by wrist action move the hand to front and rear two or three times. This seems to express the idea of, before we had ears (long ago).

Deaf-mutes make their signs for Long and Time.

Look. Make sign for See.

Lost. See Hide.

Deaf-mutes place hands as in Indian sign for Hold, and then wave hand outwards.

Louse. Scratch the head with the finger-nails of right hand, and then closing the nails of index and thumb as though one had seized a louse, carry the hand to the mouth as though eating same.

Some tribes are very lousy, but there is a great difference in this respect. With such as have these parasites, the heads of the children are frequently scouted over by the mothers, who, seated on the ground with the child's head in her lap, captures the lice and eats them; and I have seen stalwart lovers stretched out on the young grass in the enervating days of early spring, their heads resting on the laps of their sweethearts, whilst the latter cleverly and tenderly ran down and devoured the game. I have also seen Crow scouts in the field showing this little attention to each other.

This disgusting habit is more common with the Crows than with any tribe I have been thrown in contact with.

Love. Make sign for Fond.

Deaf-mutes press extended hands over left breast, right above left.

Low. Hold extended right hand, back up, in front of and to right of body, fingers pointing to front, hand few inches from ground or floor.

To express how *low*, make sign for some animal or object whose height is well known, and then hold hand to represent that height, then hold hand to represent height desired to be expressed; comparing the objects, one lower or higher than the other.

Deaf-mutes use the same sign.

Luck. See Medicine.

Lung. Hold right hand, fingers nearly extended and separated, over breast.

Deaf-mutes make gesture like Indian sign for Sick.

M.

Mad. See ANGRY.

Mail-Coach. Make signs for WRITE and WAGON.

Deaf-mutes make their signs for WAGON, and indicate that it is covered; and then holding the head back, carry the nearly-closed hand from mouth outwards and upwards, to indicate the horn formerly used.

Make. Conception: Hands move to make anything. (See WORK.)

Deaf-mutes bring closed hands in front of body, right resting on left; by wrist action, turn the right to left slightly, and left to right slightly, at same time separate hands about an inch, lowering left, raising right, bring hands rather sharply together, repeating motion several times.

Male. Conception: Organ of generation. Hold the right hand, back nearly up, in front of centre of body, index finger extended, pointing to front and upwards, other fingers and thumb closed.

Deaf-mutes make motion as though grasping the visor of cap with right hand.

Man. Make sign for MALE.

Deaf-mutes make motion with right hand, as though grasping lock of hair on forehead, and then hold right hand out to right of body to denote height.

Mandan. Conception: Tattooing chin and lower sides of the face. These Indians are usually indicated by the same sign as that made for the Arickarees; but the proper tribal sign is to partially compress the right hand, bringing tip of thumb near tips of fingers, and tap the chin and lower part of face several times with tips of thumb and fingers.

The Crows form two circles with thumbs and index fingers, and hold same alongside of ears, to indicate big holes in the ears, made for wearing ear-rings.

I was told by Mr. Girard that tattooing was practised when he first came among these people in 1849. The women had a line on the chin and a small spot on the forehead tattooed by the medicine-man, whom they paid roundly for the work. The chiefs only, of the men, were tattooed, and on one side, or one-half of the breast, or one arm and breast. This was part of the ceremony when they were elected or made chiefs. They call themselves by a word which signifies "people of the east," but claim that this refers only to the position they at first occupied in the village. Tradition, among these Indians, gives no definite account of their migrations, other than the movements of their villages on the Missouri River, not, of course, considering the myth of their subterranean origin at Devil's Lake, Dakota. The Cheyennes, who are clearer in their traditions than most tribes, claim that the Mandans came from the North. Mr. Donald Gunn, in his " History of Manitoba," says, " The Crees who visited the trading-posts on the shores of Hudson's Bay, and the Assinaboines, who traded in 1678 with Du Luth at the west end of Lake Superior, were about the same time put in possession of fire-arms, and within a few years thereafter they seemed as if by mutual consent to have made a simultaneous movement ; the former pressing on to the southwest, the latter pursuing their course to the northwest until they met in the region west of Lake Winnipeg, and on the plains of Red and Assinaboine Rivers. Indian tradition informs us that during the first half of the last century the Mandans occupied the country to the southwest of Lake Winnipeg, and that they had been forced by the united efforts of their invaders to leave their hunting grounds and retire to the Upper Missouri. But how long it took these tribes to drive out those whom they found in possession of the country, and what wars they carried on to accomplish that object, are lost in the mist of years. However, we have had the evidence of a living witness to the fact that the Crees and the Assinaboines lived on the plains southwest of Lake Winnipeg for some years previous to the year 1780, and that they made a preconcerted attack that year on the trading-posts on the Assinaboine.''

I am inclined to think that this statement is in the main correct, but believe that the Mandans were driven out of this part of the country (adjacent to Lake Winnipeg) at an earlier date, for we find them located on the Missouri in 1772, with evidences of their having been there for many years. " Information given to the late General William Clarke in his expedition up the Missouri denotes that the Mandans have suffered greater vicissitudes of fortune than most of the American tribes. About a century ago they were settled on both banks of the Missouri, some fifteen hundred miles above its mouth. They were then living in mire villages, surrounded by circular walls of earth without the adjunct of a ditch. The ruins of one of the old villages, observed in 1804, covered nearly eight acres, and denoted a comparatively large population. Two of these villages were on the east and seven on the west side of the Missouri. They were first discovered and made known to us in this position in 1772. (Mitchell's letter herewith.) They appear to have been a hated tribe to the Dakotas, or Sioux, and Assinaboines, who, from the earliest traditionary times, carried on fierce war against them. Finding themselves sorely pressed by this war, and having experienced the wasting inroads of the smallpox, the two eastern villages united into one, and migrated up the river to a point opposite the Arickaree, fourteen hundred and thirty miles above the mouth. The same causes soon pressed the other seven western villages, reducing them to five ; they also afterwards migrated in a body, and joined their tribesmen in the Arickaree country, and concentrated and settled themselves in two large villages. Here they dwelt for a time, but were still subject to the fierce attacks of their enemies ; and deeming the position unfavorable, they removed higher up the river, and took possession of a precipitous and tenable point of land formed by an involution of the Missouri, where they formed one compact village in 1776. The eastern Mandans had settled in two villages, but finding the attacks of the Sioux hard to be resisted, united also in one village. The two divisions of Mandan villages were still separated by the Missouri River, but seated directly opposite each other about three miles apart, including lowlands.

"The position is estimated to be sixteen hundred miles from the junction of the Missouri with the Mississippi. There they were visited by Lewis and Clarke on the 27th October, 1804. This was a memorable and an auspicious event in their history, as these intrepid American explorers determined to pass their first winter in this vicinity. They built Fort Mandan, a few miles distant, on a heavily-wooded piece of bottom-land, which yielded trees of sufficient size for erecting quarters for themselves and the men. They immediately opened an intercourse with the Mandans and established a friendship with them, which was strengthened by the incidents of a winter's residence." (*Schoolcraft.*)

The following is an extract from Mr. Mitchell's letter referred to: "The early portion of their history I gather from the narration of Mr. Macintosh, who, it seems, belonged to or was in some way connected with the French Trading Company as far back as 1772. According to his narration, he set out from Montreal in the summer of 1773, crossed over the country to the Missouri River, and arrived at one of the Mandan villages on Christmas-day.

"He gives a long and somewhat romantic description of the manner in which he was received, and dwells at some length upon the greatness of the Mandan population, their superior intelligence, and prowess in war. He says at that time the Mandans occupied nine large towns lying contiguous, and could at short notice muster fifteen thousand mounted warriors.

"I am inclined to think that the statistics of the author whom I have quoted are somewhat exaggerated, and at the time he visited the Missouri the Mandans were not so numerous as he represents. There are, however, the ruins of five villages in the neighborhood of the present village, which were evidently at one time occupied by the Mandans; and, judging from the space which these 'deserted villages' cover, they must have been powerful communities, at least as far as numbers could make them powerful."

Whatever may have been their population, there is no doubt that the Mandans suffered more severely from the smallpox than any of the other tribes, and were, in fact, nearly exterminated by it. Mr. Girard says that when he joined them in 1849 the memory of the terrible ravages made by the disease was still fresh in their minds, and they stated that only thirty-five survived the terrible ordeal. He thinks that the disaster overtook them in 1832 or 1833, when there were five villages of from sixty to two hundred and fifty lodges each, in all about one thousand lodges, averaging some thirteen persons to a lodge. I am inclined to think he is mistaken in regard to the date, and that they had the smallpox in 1837 instead of in 1832–33. School-craft, speaking of this, says, "Surrounded as the Mandans were by active enemies, and doomed, as they appear to be, to extinction, they might have resisted this course of depopulation a long period had it not been for the *reoccurrence* of smallpox among them in the summer of 1837. By this fatal calamity their numbers were reduced in a few days to less than one-sixteenth of their whole number. One of the reports of the disaster reduced the survivors to thirty-one, another to one hundred and forty-five."

The agent, in his report for 1881, gives the total population as two hundred and twenty-three.

They maintained their individuality as a tribe and increased their numbers by stringent marriage laws. They did not allow their women to marry into other bands or tribes unless the man would re-nounce his tribal relations, join them, and agree that the children should talk the Mandan language, and be reared in their customs and beliefs.

The physical peculiarities of many of the Mandans, viz., their blue eyes and light hair, have led to the wildest kind of speculation in regard to their origin, some claiming that they were a lost Welsh colony, and that their language supported this theory. It is hardly necessary to say that this has no foundation in fact. Some of the children also have gray hair, but this probably "only denotes a mor-bid state of it, analogous to that which supervenes in albinoes." This peculiarity is not limited to the Mandans, the Arapahoes having fully as many children who have gray hair, it being seemingly an inherited quality in certain families. I have also seen the same thing in other tribes. In regard to the light hair, one of the old men said to me that when God made them, He, as a special mark of His pleasure, took the silky tassel of the corn with which to make their hair. As a matter of fact this peculiarity is of recent date. Since 1804, when Lewis and Clarke spent their winter with this tribe, their liking for the white men of their party is a matter of record, and particularly of one or two of the men who had red hair and blue eyes.

They place calico and other cloths round the posts in their lodges as gifts to the God of timber, to satisfy him for the spoliation, be-lieving that it hurts a tree to be cut down ; *i.e.*, gives it physical pain. The tree is alive, and its destruction is the destruction of life, but by giving something to God,—making a sacrifice,—it pleases Him, and gives them good luck. This is a curious peculiarity of their religious belief, which is shared by no other tribe that I have ever met. Near the village and cultivated fields I saw poles fifteen or twenty feet long planted in the ground, with bundles of female clothing tied to these poles near the top. On inquiry, they told me that these were gifts to the three Mandan medicine-women who kept lodges for the sun,—one where the sun rises, one at the zenith, and one where the sun sets. These women never die, and the sun stops at their lodges to smoke. "By watching closely," said the old man, "you can see that the sun stops for a short time just as he rises, the same at meridian, and he stays with the third at night. We were told never to forget these women, and we make these gifts to them so that they will say a kind word for us." Their oath is made by the moon or sun.

After death they believe they go to the east, and claim that a man killed in battle is better treated, better liked, in the hereafter, than one who dies of disease. They cling tenaciously to their old beliefs, customs, and habits, and though they have adopted some of the manners of the Sioux, and their own allies, the Arickarees and Gros Ventres, they are bitterly opposed to the ways of the whites. In speaking of their language, Mr. Mitchell says, "I always contended that Mr. Gallatin was in error in supposing the Mandans and Sioux descended from the same stock. Mr. Kipp, who has been well acquainted with both tribes for upwards of thirty years, and speaks both languages with great fluency and correctness, fully concurs with me in opinion. There are a few words that are somewhat similar in sound; but this Mr. Kipp accounts for by the fact of the Sioux and Mandans having been neighbors from time immemorial, and, during intervals of peace, visiting and intermarrying with each other." Many of them now speak the Sioux language, and though I consider their vocal language as distinct and different from all others, still, high authorities, at present, class it with the Sioux; that is, being of the same *stock*.

The "bull-boat," though sometimes used by the other tribes, is considered as specially belonging to these three allied tribes, now living at Fort Berthold. The frame of this boat is made of a wicker-work of strong willows, each about two inches in diameter, over which the skin of freshly-killed domestic cattle or buffalo is stretched whilst still green. The boat is circular in shape, about five feet in diameter, deeper at the centre than at the sides or edges. In the centre it is about two feet deep, and at the edges eighteen inches, a cross-section of the bottom being an ellipse. One of these little tubs is capable of carrying six persons. The women make and navigate them, and after crossing the river, carry them to their lodges on their backs. They are held in position by two straps, one over the breast and one over the forehead. Nearly all the Mandans, Arickarees, and Gros Ventres are conversant with the sign language, and use it constantly in their daily intercourse with each other, and with the surrounding tribes.

Many. Hold the hands well in front, and to right and left of body, fingers slightly curved, separated, and pointing about to front, back of right hand to right, left to left; move the hands towards each other on vertical curve downwards; move them slightly upwards, as though grasping hands, terminating full movement when hands are a few inches apart and opposite each other. This is also sign for MUCH. Sometimes the hands are closed and opened several times in succession, rapidly, indicating more tens than can be counted.

Deaf-mutes open and close the hands several times in quick succession, hands held in front of body about height of shoulder.

Many Times. Hold left forearm horizontally in front of left breast, pointing to front and right; touch forearm several times with the side of tip of extended index of right hand, other fingers and thumb closed, back of hand nearly to front, commencing near left wrist and moving hand towards elbow. This is also used in sense of REPEAT and OFTEN.

Marry. Conception: Trade or purchase, and lying together united. Make sign for TRADE, and then bring hands, backs up, in front of body, and join extended index fingers side by side, other fingers and thumbs closed, index fingers pointing to front. Sometimes the signs to denote the "stealing of a female" are made.

These are the signs made by the men; the women, I believe, usually only use that portion relating to being united, and this is also used for SLEEP WITH in the sense of cohabiting.

Deaf-mutes clasp the hands in front of body, back of left down, right up, edges of left pointing to front and very slightly to right, edges of right at right angles with left.

Among the Pawnees, as related by Mr. Dunbar, the children of both sexes associated indiscriminately till about seven years of age. Most of their time was spent in various childish sports; the girls made dolls, the boys rode sticks; both amused themselves fashioning all sorts of objects from mud, and aping the different phases of maturer years. After that age their occupations diverged. The boys began watching horses, learning to use the bow, hunting the smaller kinds of game, etc. At the age of sixteen or eighteen they aspired to appear as men, and as soon thereafter as their means warranted married. The girls were also busily engaged, under the tutelage of their mothers, learning the manifold details of their future life of drudgery. They rarely appeared abroad unless under her immediate care, or with some elderly female in charge of them. They attained puberty at about thirteen, and were usually married soon after. The qualities most desired in a young woman by a suitor were that she should be of good family, and that she should be well versed in household offices, and in the manifold other duties of woman's life. Personal beauty, though it had its place and value, was of less consequence. The considerations most dwelt upon by the woman were the personal prowess, rising influence, skill in hunting, and fine form of her lover.

When a young brave had decided to enter the married state, he put on his robe with the hair side out, drew it over his head so as to almost entirely conceal his visage, and in this guise walked to the lodge of the intended fair one, entered and sat down. No one addressed him, nor did he utter a word; but his object was sufficiently understood by all concerned. Having sat thus in silence awhile, he arose and passed out. After the lapse of a few days he ventured to repeat his visit, wearing his robe as before. If on entering the bearskin or other seat of honor was made ready for his reception, he was at liberty to disclose his face and be seated, for such a welcome indicated that his addresses were not unacceptable; but if he met with no such preparations he might retire, as his attentions were not regarded favorably. If he was received, the young woman soon appeared and took her seat beside him. Her father also made it convenient to be at home. Between him and the suitor a conversation ensued, in the course of which the latter found occasion to ask his mind in regard to the proposed connection. The father replied guardedly that neither he nor his family had any objection to his becoming a son-in-law. He, moreover, advised the young man to go home, make a feast, invite in all his relatives, and consult them concerning the desirableness of the proposed alliance, adding that he would call in and deliberate in like manner with his daughter's kindred. It sometimes happened that the young woman was herself disinclined to the match, either because of a previous attachment, or from personal aversion to the wooer. If he was a man acceptable to her relatives, they usually made endeavor to overcome her repugnance by persuasion, in some cases even resorting to violence, cruelly beating her with their fists or sticks till consent was extorted. On the other hand, opposition might originate with the kin on either side. The personal and family history of each was sought out and fully canvassed by the relatives of the other. Those of the suitor might fail to find her family of sufficient position, or conclude her qualifications inferior; while her relatives were equally free to decide that he was not of desirable family, that he was not wealthy, or that some personal stigma was attached to him. In either case the matter was dropped, or further proceedings suspended till the objection was obviated. Sometimes, in such cases, if the two young people were really lovers, they ventured to take matters into their own hands and eloped, going to another band, or to some friend, with whom their stay had been before arranged, and there remaining till a reconciliation was effected. If, however, after due inquiry, no cause of objection was raised on either side, the two families then proceeded to settle upon the price that the young man should pay. This custom of paying is almost universal among Indian tribes. The question has been raised as to whether the property that passes from the wooer to the father of the woman is really a price paid, or rather of the nature of a free gift. I wish I might assert the latter. But so far as I have been able to learn, the facts all mark the transfer as purely commercial. The transaction is spoken of among the Indians themselves as buying, and the amount of property is always carefully determined beforehand,—from one to six horses. The union then followed without further ceremony, other than a final feast given by the wife's father. The husband went to the lodge of the father-in-law, and lived there with his wife. A particular part of the lodge was allotted to him, and henceforth he was a member of that family. Such was the case with the eldest daughter. The others were given by the father to the son-in-law as they became marriageable, the father receiving a horse or two in return for each successive one. Hence the son-in-law usually spoke of his wife's sisters as wives, though they might yet be small children. The eldest sister was the principal

wife, and ruled the younger, who seemed to be little better than domestic slaves, as it was a general rule among the Pawnees that, rank
being equal, the younger should obey the elder. A younger wife,
however, if a favorite with the husband, escaped most annoyance
from this source.

Such was the ordinary course; but a man need not necessarily
confine himself to one family in taking wives. If his wife had no
younger sisters, or from choice, he might look elsewhere. The only
positive restriction as to where a man should marry was kinship.
The rule was that relatives by blood could not marry; still, ties of
consanguinity were so intricate and confused oftentimes that the
regulation became practically inoperative. In case a man did take
an additional wife from a new family, the wooing was conducted the
same as in the first instance, and at its consummation she went to
her husband's home. Marriages of this kind, however, were not so
favorably regarded, and, in fact, did not usually conduce to domestic
quiet. Discord and quarrels between wives were frequent enough
under the best circumstances, and experience seemed to indicate that
sisters were more likely to live peaceably together than strangers.
When quarrels did occur between wives, they might end with mere
wrangling, or proceed to blows and tearing hair, unless the husband
was disposed to interfere and restore quiet. A man rarely had four
wives; three were not uncommon; many had two, but by far the
larger number had only one. Long mentions one Pawnee with
eleven wives, and a friend of mine knew a Ski'-di with eight; but such
cases were exceedingly rare. From the fact that they were obtained
by purchase, the number of a man's wives was, in a certain sense,
an index of his wealth,—*i.e.*, of the number of horses he owned,—
and with some men this was a provocative to take a new wife as often
as opportunity presented. Still, there were frequent exceptions;
men of rank and in good circumstances who seemed to be living
perfectly contented with only one wife. In such instances husbands
have been known to evince a real affection for their wives, not deeming it too much to be found assisting them in their various labors;
and this for an Indian is a great deal.

From personal observation, I am of the opinion that there are
more female than male children born to Indian mothers; but be this
as it may, for of course it is a mere matter of opinion, polygamy
was a necessity to the Indians. In their tribal wars many of the
men were killed, and from their manner of living the lives of the
males were often jeopardized, and, as a necessary consequence, the
number of females greatly exceeded the number of males.

Through the efforts of the Jesuit Fathers, the Flatheads, Pend
d'Oreilles, Koutenays, Nez Perces, and some other tribes near them
have abandoned polygamy, and are regularly married by the priests.

The marriage customs of the Indians have, I think, hardly had
justice done them by different writers. The women have been represented as so much merchantable property, as much so as a dog or a
horse. I imagine, in some instances, this partial mistake grew out

of the questions of the observers, who would say to the interpreter, "I want to know about the marriage customs; suppose, now, I should want to marry a squaw, how would it be done?" etc. When white men marry Indian women it is a genuine sale, growing out of greed of gain or some benefit, real or imaginary, which will accrue personally to the interested parties; and the dusky, dirty maiden may go to the nuptial couch with tears and protestations of a most violent nature, afterwards becoming a faithful slave.

Though in Indian marriages the affair savors strongly of a commercial transaction, and a wife is usually spoken of as being secured through purchase or theft, still, as a rule, there is quite an expenditure of sentiment and affection prior to the business part of it. The social laws which regulate this vary somewhat in the different tribes, but whatever the form in olden times, as well as at the present day, men wishing to marry laid siege to the affections of the girl; and very rarely, if they did not meet with success, made another effort to secure her. But if they could "kill" all opposition on her part, —and this was comparatively easy if one had gained renown as a warrior,—a friend took ponies, blankets, etc., in number and value according to the wealth of the would be bridegroom and the social standing of the girl, and sent them to some of the kin of the girl, usually to the father.

The animals were tied near the lodge, and the friend informed the kinsfolk of their presence and meaning. A family council was held, calling in perhaps friends and headmen to take part. If the girl was willing and other things satisfactory, the presents were accepted; if not, the ponies were turned loose. In the former case the girl went to the man's lodge; and were she the daughter of a wealthy or renowned chief, she was sometimes carried on a blanket, and a greater number of ponies and richer gifts were sent with her as a dower. Sometimes the young man was poor and proud, and not having the requisite or conventional number of ponies, would not ask his father for them; in this case, had he met with success in winning the girl's affection, he, as they expressed it, "stole" the girl; arranging, in fact, an elopement. This sometimes turned out pleasantly, for the father of the young man would, perhaps, send the presents, and the girl's father would send the dowry; but unfortunately, or fortunately, in many cases the parents objected, and the girl's mother took her by force, if necessary, back to her lodge.

Marriage is prohibited between blood relations. The tracing of this is kept by oral tradition. There seems to be no special distinguishing mark or name which would materially assist in the matter; even admitting that some of the tribes have been divided into gens, and still preserve the laws in regard to prohibition of marriage in the same gens, as claimed by Mr. Morgan (see KINSHIP), I do not see that this would be of any special value after several generations.

The peculiar custom, mentioned by Mr. Dunbar, of the proprietary interest secured in younger sisters by marrying the eldest of several daughters, is common to many tribes, but it is not common for the man to go to the lodge of his father-in-law ; the Pawnees being an exception to the general rule in regard to the law prohibiting social intercourse with the mother-in-law.

Marvellous. See MEDICINE.

Deaf-mutes hold extended left hand in front of body, back out, fingers pointing to right hand about height of shoulders ; bring the extended right from below upwards and near left quickly, back out, fingers pointing upwards ; right hand passes between left and body, back nearly touching left palm, and passes few inches higher.

Match (Lucifer). Fix the right hand as though holding a match between thumb and index, and rub with quick motion the tips of thumb and index against left forearm, as though scratching a match.

Deaf-mutes use the same sign.

Mean. Conception : Compressed heart. Make signs for HEART, for SMALL. This expresses a compressed, contracted heart, narrowed by selfishness or avarice, etc.

Deaf-mutes indicate a pulling in, or grasping after, money ; sharp dealing.

Measles. (See SMALLPOX.) All eruptions of the skin have about the same sign, adding some descriptive gesture to denote the mildness or violence of the disease.

Meat. Strange as it may appear, yet it is none the less true, that among the Indians who have so greatly perfected gesture speech, and who lived mainly on animal food, yet they have no generally well-known and commonly used sign for meat in the abstract. The gesture for the animal must be made, and appropriate signs for the part and its condition.

Deaf-mutes clasp with the ball of right thumb and index finger the flesh between the spread thumb and index finger of the left hand.

Medal. Form an incomplete circle with thumb and index of right hand, space of about an inch between tips, other fingers closed, and place little finger on centre of breast. To such an extent were medals prized, and so great was the authority conferred by them, that some tribes, like the Ojibways, use this sign for chief.

Deaf-mutes clap right palm against left, and with right index indicate size of medal worn on breast.

Medicine. Hold right hand in front of and close to forehead, palm outwards, index and second finger extended, separated, and pointing upwards, others and thumb closed ; move the hand upwards, at same time, by wrist action, turn the hand from right to left, so that tips of extended fingers will describe a spiral curve. I have also seen signs made to denote beating on a drum, shaking a rattle, and WORKING made ; and sometimes the sign for BRAVE finished the description.

Some claim that the first-described sign came from the use of the rattle, others from the lightning.

Deaf-mutes hold the extended right index near forehead, others and thumb closed, and move the hand to right, upwards and front; by wrist action turning hand so that tip of index describes a spiral curve.

The Indians use this word to indicate the mysterious and unknown. God is the Great Mystery rather than the Great Spirit, as it is usually translated. We have no one word which can convey the meaning of "Medicine" as used by the Indians. Sometimes it shadows forth holiness, mystery, spirits, luck, visions, dreams, prophecies, at others the concealed and obscure forces of nature, which work for us good or evil.

When they first saw a pony, some tribes called it a "medicine-dog;" a gun, "medicine-iron."

They attempt the cure of disease in many cases mainly by an appeal to the "unknown," and try to propitiate this power, as in the Sun-Dance. They have "medicine-men" who claim to have visions, to prophesy, to cure the sick by remedies known only to themselves, and which, they insist, were learned from the whisperings of some animal to them while they were asleep. If success crowns their efforts their medicine was *good;* and defeat, suffering, death, are all the legitimate fruits of *bad* medicine. They live close to nature, and are impressed and awed by her wonders and mysteries; and anything which is beyond their comprehension they call "medicine." Their faith in their medicine to secure their personal protection from physical harm, as well as to promote their general happiness, is simply marvellous. (See WAR-BONNET.) Whirlwind's belief in the efficacy of good medicine is by no means exceptional, but he will illustrate his faith in his story of the great fight which took place twenty-four winters ago between the confederated Kiowas, Comanches, Snakes, Arapahoes, Cheyennes, and Sioux, and the Sacs and Foxes, where his allies witnessed the storm of bullets which swept away the feathers of his war-bonnet. The manner of the old man was impressive as he said, "I was not wounded in the fight; I never was hit. I had such 'medicine' made for me that it was impossible for my enemies to hit me, and this was a little hawk holding my medicine, which I wore on my war-bonnet. When all the feathers were shot away the hawk was not hit : balls went to the right and left, above and below me. I was mounted, and the Sacs and Foxes were dismounted in a hollow like a buffalo-wallow. It was the Great Spirit and the hawk which protected me."

This personal medicine may be a tiny sack worn on a string around the neck, a piece of shell tied in the scalp-lock, and I have seen a Crow Indian who, in battle or under any trying circumstances, wore a roll strapped to his back about five feet long and six inches in diameter, which he said their medicine-man had given him. This was kept carefully wrapped in blue cloth, and I could not learn what it contained.

Medicine-Dance. Make signs for MEDICINE and for DANCE.

The following dance partakes strongly of a religious character, and is designed to perpetuate game. Though some other tribes practise it, it is particularly a Cheyenne dance.

Two large lodges are pitched near together, and from the sides of the open space between them two wings are made of brush and trees, extending some distance out. The old men gather in the lodge, where they feast themselves, smoke and sing, whilst nearly all the rest of the camp perform a huge pantomime, representing the birds of the air and the beasts of the field. Here a herd of buffalo are quietly grazing, there a band of elk or deer, and prowling about are the wolves and foxes,—the men representing the males and the women the females, whilst the children take the part of the young.

The hunters go out, fire, shout, and stampede the herds; they creep up at another point, fire, and the animals drop, imitating the death-agonies of the slaughtered.

They do all this that game may be preserved for their use. A rude, wild, savage form of worship, and a strange way of petitioning the forces or Gods of nature.

Medicine-Man. Make signs for MAN and for MEDICINE.

The medicine-man is a self-constituted physician and prophet. No man gave him his authority, and no man can take it away. His right is his own, and his influence depends upon himself.

As a rule, there is no limit to the number, but the Kiowas claimed that they had only ten of these priestly doctors, and each had a sacred sack (given the Kiowas by the Great Spirit), handed down from one generation to another, but never opened. Should this sacrilegious thing be done, a flood or some disaster would be sure to overtake them.

I have been told by Indians that they did not practise amputation because they had so little knowledge of surgery. As a rule, there is a strong prejudice against it, death being usually preferred.

Mr. Dunbar says of the Pawnees that all knowledge of the art of healing was believed to be vested in the guild of Doctors (Ku'-ra-u-rŭk-ar'-u), a secret order. To become a recognized member of the fraternity a certain period of probation was required. A person might assume the dignity of doctor without submitting to the prescribed routine, but unless he could achieve some remarkable success, he was generally regarded as a pretender and discountenanced. The duration of the pupilage varied according to the candidate's aptitude in mastering the mysteries of the craft. A considerable initiatory fee was demanded, and an additional fee at certain stages of the course. The convocations of the fraternity, or members of it, were shrouded in the most impressive secrecy, and so strictly was this secrecy maintained that I never knew of one not a member being admitted. The principal business of these conclaves seemed to be the concocting of drugs, comparing and discussing certain curatives, interspersed with sundry ceremonial performances. Their great ordinance was the Medicine-Dance, celebrated with the utmost formality at certain seasons, and continuing from one to four days. So far as may be judged by appearances, the great object of this dance, with its numerous ritual details, was to reassure themselves and awe the people. Candidates who had passed the requisite preparation were formally admitted to the body on these occasions.

The distinctive mark of a doctor was the wearing of the robe with the hair side out, and the ever-present medicine-bag, curiously wrought and ornamented. In it were carried his nostrums, and it was often claimed to be possessed of healing properties which might be imparted by touch. Doctors were quite numerous in the different bands, and as a matter of course most of them were arrant knaves. So far as concerned any insight into the real nature of disease, they knew nothing. The general theory was that sickness was caused by malign spiritual influences. Occasionally, after pretending to discover the location of the disturbing spirit in the body of the patient, the only remedial agency employed consisted in incantations for exorcising it. The following is a correct account of the treatment administered to a man who had been badly burned:

The sufferer was brought home in the evening, and a doctor summoned at once. For some reason he delayed answering the call till the ensuing morning, quite possibly to add something of impressive importance to his coming. He was accompanied by another doctor. On entering the lodge they did not deign to notice any one, and sat down in silence, and remained motionless till a pipe was filled and handed to them. The elder received it, held it up at arm's length over his head for a moment, muttered some unintelligible sounds, lowered it, carefully took from the bowl with his thumb and forefinger a small portion of the tobacco, and placed it on the edge of the hearth before him. One of the family then held a brand from the fire to the pipe till it was lighted. The doctor slowly puffed the smoke two or three times upward, downward, and toward each of the cardinal points, and taking the pipe by the bowl, passed it to his companion, who went through the same form, and this was repeated till the contents were consumed. The pipe was then handed to the one who had lighted it. He emptied the ashes upon the hearth, so that they should entirely cover the particles of tobacco before taken from it and deposited there. He then touched the tips of his fingers to the ashes, and passed his hands in succession over the pipe from the bowl to the end of the stem, and returned it to the owner, who did the same. The doctors now proceeded to inspect the patient's injuries, and after the examination was completed began their practices. One of them took a mouthful of water from a calabash placed beside him, groaned, beat his breast, crept backward and forward on his hands and feet, took up some dust from the ground, rubbed it in his hands, made various intricate gestures, and then pretended to vomit the water, which all the while had been in his mouth, upon the hearth. Again he filled his mouth, and after going through an even more elaborate *rôle*, parted the hair upon the head of the patient, blew the water in small quantities upon the scalp, breast, and other parts of his body. This was repeated several times. He then applied his mouth, previously filled with water, to the sick man's head, and with groans seemed to be endeavoring with all his might to suck something from it. When this had continued some minutes, all at once he started back, and approaching the hearth, squirted the mouthful of water upon it, as if drawn from the invalid's head. The same operation was repeated on several parts of his body. He then took up some of the ashes emptied from the pipe, rubbed them in his hands, and blew them upon the patient's head, breast, and wherever the suction had been tried. After all this operose detail, he took a minute quantity of dark powder from his medicine-bag, sprinkled it on the burns, and departed. During all this performance the other doctor was busily shaking his rattle, parading his medicine-bag, and dancing with great violence over the sufferer, the occupants of the lodge looking on in profound attention and awe. These absurdities were repeated twice a day so long as the unfortunate man lived. The night he died, four days after receiving the injuries, when he was actually in *articulo mortis,* the doctors were sent for, and with redoubled fury began their elaborate parade of juggling, and by the noise and confusion to all appearance expedited dissolution.

This will serve as a fair specimen of their therapeutic treatment. Though the producing cause of the ailment was not directly recognized as spiritual, the appliances were essentially the same. In case of ordinary disease, suction, and whatever other applications were made, was directed to the part of the patient's body in which the disturbing spirit was claimed to be located,—usually where the most pain was felt. The doctor would often, after long sucking, expectorate a pebble, a fragment of bone, or even an arrow-head, which he pretended to have drawn from the spot. Sometimes violent friction, pressure, or a sort of kneading of the ailing parts was tried. At other times they attempted to frighten away the disturbing spirit by noises, as muttering, yelling, barking, or growling, or by strange posturing, as of a wolf, a buffalo, or bear, or by angry demonstrations, as brandishing a war-club or a tomahawk, and threatening to strike the affected part.

This system of jugglery may well enough be called senseless ; but to the mass of the Indians it was otherwise. The mere physical effort on the part of the doctors was often so intense as to provoke in themselves profuse perspiration, and so protracted as to induce complete exhaustion. The uninitiated regarded all their ceremonies with the most deferential awe, and so strong was this feeling that it sufficed to invest the persons of those who had performed any (pretended) remarkable cure with a sort of glamour which enabled them to assume an almost unlimited authority in the general affairs of their bands. It was believed that some of them could, if they chose, exercise powers of witchcraft over any who had incurred their displeasure. They could negative a contemplated war-party, and when on a hunt, though thousands of buffalo might be immediately about the camp, they could delay a chase indefinitely, assigning no other reason than that it was not good.

It has been asserted that remedies were never administered internally. It may be true to a large extent, but as an absolute statement it is certainly a mistake. Just what the simples were I never learned, as the doctors were very chary of saying aught concerning the secrets of the profession unless they were liberally paid. Of external treatments other than that already described, a few means may be specified. Cauterizing was not infrequent. It was done by inserting a bit of the stalk of the *Achillea maillefolium*, about an inch long, in the skin, setting fire to the exposed end, and allowing it to burn down into the flesh. Sometimes several pieces were inserted near each other at once. Blistering was produced by rubbing the skin with the bruised leaves of an acrid plant, the name of which I never knew. Blood-letting was accomplished by applying the lips directly and sucking the blood through the skin, or the skin was scarified with a knife, and the blood drawn by means of a horn prepared for that purpose.

In treating wounds, contusions, and sprains, such as are of frequent occurrence, some of the doctors were quite skilful. The same ceremonies as already described were, of course, had, but the subsequent treatment seemed to be more intelligent. Amputation was unknown ; in fact, there was a deep-seated superstitious prejudice against maiming of any kind. Broken bones were sometimes well set. Probing and the extraction of foreign bodies from wounds were not much practised. Major North, who commanded for several years the Pawnee scouts in the service of the Government, and is in all respects well qualified to pronounce an opinion, while expressing unbounded contempt for their general clinical practice, stated to me that he would prefer. the treatment of a good Pawnee doctor for a wound to the care of an ordinary surgeon. Among others he related the following remarkable cures effected by one of these doctors :

In July, 1867, the horse of one of his Indian scouts fell while running a race near Fort Sedgwick, on the Upper Platte. The rider was thrown violently, his thigh broken and hip dislocated. He was at once sent to the military hospital and kept under treatment for several weeks. The dislocation could not be restored, nor was the fracture healed, and the case was given over as hopeless. The thigh was then swollen to enormous size and badly inflamed. At the invalid's urgent request Major North sent him by railroad home to the Pawnee Reserve to die,.as he supposed. But in the ensuing December the man returned to the command and resumed his duties, with no mark of his injuries except a slight shortening of the leg. In June, 1869, while serving in General Carr's command, on the Republican, the hand and forearm of another scout were badly shattered by the accidental discharge of a carbine. The wound was cared for by a surgeon, who advised amputation. To this the Indian would not consent. In the hardships of active service the hurt could not be properly treated ; in a short time the patient began to decline, and the wound filled with maggots. This man also was sent home, in an army-wagon to Fort McPherson, and thence by railroad, to all appearance to die. The following November, however, he had recovered, with the practical loss of the use of three fingers. Both these men were restored by Pawnee doctors after the cases were pronounced hopeless. One further instance will illustrate the usual surgical quackery prevalent among the doctors : In 1874, Pit'-a-le-shar-u, head-chief of the tribe, was wounded in the thigh by a revolver. The physician at the agency did not consider the hurt dangerous, and under his care the chief was progressing favorably. But, unfortunately, one of the doctors advised that the treatment must be changed. The chief consented, and he at once proceeded to plaster over the affected part with a heavy coating of moist clay. This, of course, stopped suppuration and brought on a fever, from the effects of which the chief soon died. Examples of such malpractice were only too common.

The materia medica of the doctors was nominally quite extensive. Considerable time was apparently spent in searching for and preparing their drugs. Fossil bones of certain kinds were carefully sought and preserved. The *Artemisia Ludoviciana, Acorus calamus, Monarda fistulosa* and *punctata, Mentha Canadensis,* and many other herbs and roots were esteemed for their real or fancied virtues. Some herbs were generally known and used outside of the profession as specifics. Artemisia and monarda were in general use as disinfectants and cosmetics. In the latter use they were bruised or macerated, and rubbed over the person. Decoctions of the artemisia were also drunk by women at certain periods. The sedative property of the *Argemone Mexicana* was known, and they were also familiar with the cathartic qualities of some plants.

The charges made for treatment, if not previously stipulated, depended somewhat upon the issue. If successful, and the head of the convalescent's family was able, the charges were sometimes quite exorbitant, amounting in the aggregate to several ponies. If unsuccessful, they were moderate, and sometimes nothing at all was received. Doctors occasionally became very wealthy by their practice. This fact was no doubt a provocation to some to endeavor to enter the profession as an easy method of securing a living.

Women spared no effort in caring for their husbands and children during sickness. Each morning and evening in pleasant weather they would carry them out of the lodge to enjoy the sunlight, assist them in changing positions, endeavor to gratify every momentary caprice, and prepare any delicacy they could to tempt their appetite. There is no doubt that this last often aggravated sickness. Children, particularly when ailing, were kept alternately stuffing and vomiting to their manifest detriment. As long as an invalid could eat there was supposed to be hope, and so there was a natural tendency to keep offering, and even urging, food. Women, as a rule, did not when sick receive as solicitous attention, though instances were by no means wanting of men showing tender attention to invalid wives. It has been charged that men have been known to drag away sick wives when helpless and leave them in out-of-the-way places to languish unattended; but this, if true, is only of recent occurrence. Aside from this consideration of affection, there was some reason for a husband receiving more care in sickness than a wife; for to a wife the death of her husband might entail the temporary loss of home, while the husband might expect easily to replace a deceased wife.

Some of the foregoing details, as their proneness to indulgences of the appetite, and the extreme facility with which they suffered themselves to be duped by the shallow trickery of the merest charlatans, are not attractive traits in Pawnee character. They are, however, not peculiar to the Pawnees alone, but are common to all forms of Indian life; and the only wonder is that when controlled to such extent as they were by these practices, they should have succeeded in developing and retaining the many nobler traits that they possessed.

Meet (To). Hold the hands opposite each other, well out to right and left of body, back of right to right, left to left, index fingers extended and pointing upwards, others and thumbs closed; bring the hands towards each other, and as they approach incline index fingers, so that tips will meet and touch. This, by itself, would really mean two persons approaching each other and meeting; the hands would be held so as to represent the direction each party came from.

Deaf-mutes make same gesture, but do not incline index fingers.

Memory. Make signs for HEART and for KNOW.

Deaf-mutes indicate a continued knowing.

Menses. Make signs for PARTURITION and for BLOOD. They are sometimes also called woman's mystery or medicine.

During menstrual periods Indian women are considered as unclean for several days, and are not allowed in the general lodge, a temporary one being made for them outside.

These little lodges are wretched affairs, usually not large enough to admit of a fire, and as dreary and comfortless as it is possible to imagine. The cruel custom has been fast dying out during the past few years. Some tribes had a special ceremony at a girl's first courses, which was in effect an announcement to the village that the girl was ready for marriage. Sometimes this publication was made known by the criers, and a dance or feast or general gathering followed. I saw the latter in the camp of the Sioux chief Crazy Horse. The daughter of a prominent man had the day or night previous her first menstrual flow. The camp-criers announced the fact to the entire village and requested all the people to visit the lodge. A crowd of men, women, and children gathered, the lodge was thrown open, and the girl, gaudily and handsomely dressed, was seated on a bundle of skins and blankets back of the fire. An old man was haranguing her and the crowd, and, as nearly as I could gather, was giving her good advice, pertinent to girls just entering upon the threshold of womanhood, and calling attention to the sacred and mysterious manner in which nature had announced the fact that she was ready to embrace matrimony. The old man had been given a pony, and several others were distributed whilst I was present. The prospect of a gift, it seemed, was the attraction which had drawn the crowd to the lodge, and I was told that at times upon such occasions all a man's worldly goods would be given away.

Metal. There is no general sign for this unless that for HARD be considered one. Something made of metal must be touched or pointed at. Sometimes the gesture for an armlet is made, or signs to denote a vessel for culinary purposes.

Deaf-mutes hold extended left hand, back up, in front of body, fingers pointing to front, and pound the back of it with lower edge of right fist, with a sliding motion to front as the right hand strikes back of left.

Meteor. Make sign for STAR, and with hand in that position make sign for FIRE, and then let it drop with a wavy, tremulous motion. Meteors and comets cause great uneasiness in Indian camps. Guns and arrows are sometimes fired at comets, and pieces of flesh, cut from the arm of the man who is firing, are placed with the bullet, or attached to the arrow, as gift or sacrifice to the mysterious power. Some disasters having followed soon after the appearance of comets and meteors, they look upon them in superstitious dread as the harbinger of bad luck.

Deaf-mutes indicate a hard hot substance that comes down from the skies.

Mexican. There is no general sign. Some tribes make signs for WHITES, and indicate a chin beard, and that they come from the South.

Deaf-mutes link index fingers, others and thumbs closed in front of and close to the neck.

Mid-day. Indicate that the sun is directly overhead, or make sign for DAY and MIDDLE.

Deaf-mutes indicate position of sun.

Middle. Hold the left hand, back to left, well in front of left breast, index finger extended and pointing to front, others and thumb closed ; hold right hand in front of right breast, raise and lower it as in CHIEF, bringing tip of right index down over left index and resting on its centre. This is used in such expressions as middle of summer, middle of winter, etc. Some tribes indicate half one way, half the other, and then lower hand at initial point to denote the middle.

Deaf-mutes make their sign for BETWEEN, which is to lay the lower edge of extended right hand on surface between spread thumb and index of left hand, fingers of left hand extended, touching, and pointing to front, those of right extended, touching, and pointing to left.

Midnight. Make signs for NIGHT and for MIDDLE.

Midwinter. Make signs for WINTER and for MIDDLE.

Migrate. If of birds, indicate their flying far to the south, or far to the north. Any other migration is simply a movement.

Milky-Way. (Ghosts' or dead men's road.) Make signs for
DIE, for ROAD or TRAIL, and then sweep the right hand high above
the head on curve parallel to the luminous zone in the heavens.
Some tribes call it the "mysterious road," and others the "wolf's
road," and of course make signs accordingly.

Deaf-mutes indicate the multitude of stars forming a path of
light.

Some tribes believe that the Milky-Way is the trail made by those
who, killed in battle, go by this easy road through the air to the village of the dead. The Arapahoes are strong in this belief, and yet
they locate heaven towards the east.

Whether the Blackfeet and others, who call this luminous zone the
"wolf's road," mean it in the sense of "God's road" or not I am
unable to say. I am inclined, however, to think that they do, for
nearly all with whom I have talked on the subject considered it sacred.

Mingle. Hold hands near each other, in front of body and height
of lower part of face, fingers and thumbs extended and pointing upwards, hands slightly compressed ; move hands one about the other,
surfaces touching.

Minneconjou (Sioux Indian). Conception : Farming by the
water. Make signs for SIOUX, for FARM, for CLOSE, and for WATER ;
this latter is usually made as river or stream. Like nearly all the
names given to tribes and bands, the origin is uncertain and obscure.
At some period in the history of the Sioux nation some chief and
his followers farmed (or, as they usually express it, planted corn)
near some body of water, and were, in consequence, called Minne-
conjous, or planters by the water. I have heard stories locating this
all the way from Lake Superior to the Missouri River. Pictographically, the land is represented by a stream of water and a few ears of
corn rudely sketched near it. (See SIOUX.)

Mirage. Hold right hand, back outwards, well in front of and
little higher than left shoulder, fingers separated and pointing to left ;
move the hand horizontally to right, giving it a wavy, tremulous motion. This sign is not very generally understood. I have seen gestures made describing different objects seen in the distance, and then
for ARRIVE THERE ; then that the same objects were seen still ahead,
or had entirely vanished.

Mirror. Hold extended right hand, back outwards, fingers pointing upwards, a few inches in front of face.

Mislead. Make sign for ROAD or TRAIL ; indicate a departure
from this, as in DECEIVE.

Deaf-mutes make gesture to denote a deceitful leading.

Miss (To). Make sign for AVOID.

Deaf-mutes use the same sign.

Mistake. Make sign for LIE. Sometimes signs for WORK and
ASTRAY are made.

Deaf-mutes close thumb, second and third fingers, extending index
and little fingers, and place back of closed fingers, from second joints
to knuckles, against under side of chin.

Mix. If it is wished to refer to animals, objects, etc., see Mingle. To mix as by stirring, imitate the motion.

Deaf-mutes hold the hands in front of body at same height, backs out, fingers extended and separated, right nearest body and fingers pointing to left, fingers of left pointing to right; bring left in towards body and carry right out, fingers passing between spaces of left and right hands; repeat motion.

Moccasin. Pass spread thumbs and index fingers over feet and toes to ankles, right hand over right, left over left, palms of hands towards and close to feet. This, of course, indicates a covering for the feet, but to denote a shoe, the sign for Whites is made, and for a boot signs are made imitating the manner of pulling them on. In former times the moccasins of the different tribes were made so differently that for an Indian to see the moccasin was to know the tribe; and even now, in its shape, construction, or garnishment, it is the strongest characteristic mark of each tribe, so far as any clothing or covering is concerned.

The moccasin is the last thing an Indian gives up as he travels towards civilization, and the first thing adopted by the whites who, as hunters, trappers, traders, or "squaw-men," mix, mingle, and live with the Indians. It possesses many advantages in hunting over a boot or shoe, and in dry weather is comfortable and serviceable, but it is utterly demoralized by moisture, so that an Indian in crossing a stream, going through the dewy grass, or in the mud and melting snow of spring, takes off his moccasins, and goes with bare feet.

From Mr. Clark, the interpreter, through Colonel Hunt, the agent at Wichita Agency, I received the following description of the moccasins worn by the tribes there, and as it is more complete and perfect than my notes made when visiting these Indians, I give it in full:

"The Comanche moccasin is composed of a sole cut (from rawhide) as near the shape of the bottom of the foot as practicable, tapering rapidly from its greatest width at the little toe to a point at the big toe.

"The upper part is made from buckskin, cut generally in one piece, having but one seam at the heel, although sometimes each side is cut separately, with a seam in the middle on top of the foot; on each side of seam is a row of beadwork, and on the outside of foot, near the beadwork, there is attached a row of short fringe, composed of buckskin strings, ornamented with pieces of German silver.

"They are generally cut low at the sides, with turn-down flaps about two inches wide, finished with beadwork around the edges; and some of them are made with a narrow piece set in the front part, forked at the upper end, and finished with beadwork to match the flaps or pieces turned down at the sides. The upper part when finished is sewed fast to the raw-hide sole with sinews, and finished with a row of beadwork around and near the seam. A bunch of fringe of buckskin strings, about five inches long, attached to the heel completes the moccasin.

"The Kiowa moccasin is made of same materials, and is cut out very much in the same manner as the Comanche, perhaps a little wider at the point of the large toe. The main or distinguishing features of the Kiowa moccasin are the elaborate beadwork, generally covering the entire front part, the flap at the side lined with red flannel, with greater amount of beadwork on its edges, the fringe of buckskin strings shorter and less in quantity.

"The Apache moccasin is in all respects the same as the Kiowa.

"The Caddo moccasin is altogether made of buckskin, cut with one seam up in front part of foot, and one at heel, sewed and drawn together at the toe to fit the foot. The turn-down flap at the sides, about two inches wide, lined with red or black cloth, and finished on the edges with beadwork. The front part of the moccasin has a cluster of beadwork, and near this are attached small bows of ribbon.

"The Wichita moccasin may be described as similar to the Comanche, excepting there is not quite so much beadwork, and the fringe at the heel not so long."

The Otoe moccasin is sewed down in front, around right side, and up heel, with anklet flap falling on sides and front. A sole is sewed on after the bottom becomes worn, and this is usually the case with moccasins where the moccasin is made whole, or where the bottoms are made of the same material as the uppers.

The Kickapoos sew their moccasins down in front, have wide side anklet flaps, and, apparently to give a better fit, sew the moccasin around the sides for a sole, though the moccasin is made of one piece.

The Flatheads sew their moccasins on the right side, sole and upper of same material, and frequently use anklet flaps of bright-colored fur.

The Blackfeet make their moccasins with anklets and long tongue, the anklets being frequently of colored cloth, and sometimes in front of the tongue the partial ellipse of blue or red cloth is sewed in and edged with beads, or horse-hair stained or colored, like the Chippewas and others, but three prongs from the apex run fan-shaped to the toes, marking this tribe, and each prong represents a band,— "Blackfeet, "Bloods," and "Piegans."

The Assinaboines and Gros Ventres of the Prairie make their uppers very much like the Blackfeet, have anklets, but usually have a raw-hide sole sewed on.

The Bannacks and Snakes make their moccasins in one piece, have anklets, use but little beadwork, and make the moccasins for men and women alike ; this is unusual, the "squaw moccasin" being, as a rule, made differently. There is scarcely any difference between the Sioux, Cheyenne, and Arapahoe moccasin. The uppers are made of tanned deer, young elk, or antelope skins, the soles of heavier material and usually untanned. The men's moccasins have no anklets, while those for the women do. The little tongue to the

Sioux moccasin is usually a separate piece sewed on, while the Cheyennes cut this tongue as a part of the uppers.

The Crows make their moccasins of one piece sewed at the heel, though some have separate soles.

Mr. Peter Ronan, agent for the Flatheads and other tribes at the Jocko Agency, furnishes me the following in regard to the Indians at this agency:

"The Flathead moccasins are made plain, there being no cloth or ornaments upon the instep, and are made neatly to fit like a glove.

"The Pend d'Oreilles make their moccasins with black or red cloth covering the instep.

"The Koutenays make theirs similar to the Pend d'Oreilles, except to decorate the instep with beads or porcupine-quills.

"These Indians know a Crow at once by the handsome manner in which their moccasins are beaded."

Mr. Charles H. Beaulieu says of the Chippewas,—

"There is no difference between the moccasins worn by the men and women, except that, as a rule, the latter are not ornamented. The moccasin is made from a square piece of leather, which is gathered so nicely in folds in working on the tongue that the folds are not noticeable. The tongue is ornamented with bead-, ribbon-, or silk-work, and porcupine-quills in all manner of designs. The more the person is thought of who is to wear them the more work will be put on the moccasins. The hose or anklet is made of cotton or dressed skins, and this and the moccasin carefully fastened to the ankle and foot with strings."

Mr. Belden states in his notes: "It is no difficult job to make a moccasin, and a squaw will cut out and sew up a plain pair in half a day. If they are beaded, however, it takes a week or more to finish them, and those ornamented with porcupine-quills require a month of patient labor. In the winter season the moccasins are made of buffalo-hide or the skins of fur-bearing animals, the hair being turned inwards.

"The Indians never wear stockings, but the leggings are an excellent substitute when one has fur shoes to cover the feet."

He also says that each Indian tribe made their moccasins of different shape, so that an expert frontiersman could readily tell to what tribe Indians belonged by seeing their tracks. This is true in a limited sense only. The Chippewa track could be told from the Sioux, but the latter could not be distinguished from the Cheyennes or Arapahoes.

The dress of an Indian quickly reveals his tribe to another Indian. The manner of cutting, making up, the beadwork, etc., are so characteristic as to be unmistakable.

Money. Hold right hand, back to right, in front of right breast, index and thumb curved, forming an incomplete circle, space of about half an inch between tips, other fingers closed. This represents money generally. Latterly, since the use of paper money, they frequently make proper signs to denote this. The Indians say that they first saw silver dollars, *white metal,* then gold, *yellow metal;* and from the shape came the sign. For paper money I have seen the above sign made, and the size of one of the notes marked off on the palm of extended left hand, or motions made imitating the counting of a number of bills.

Deaf-mutes lay the back of right sharply on left palm, left held well in front of body, back down.

Monkey. Conception: Half white man, half dog. Pass the spread thumb and index finger of each hand, other fingers closed, over and near surface of body from waist upwards, palms towards body, then make sign for Whites, then pass the hands similarly from waist down, and make sign for Dog; the upper portion like white man, lower like dog.

Deaf-mutes "scratch" the ribs with finger-tips of right hand.

Month. Conception: Moon dies. Make signs for Moon and for Die. Sometimes only the sign for Moon is made, and at other times instead of the sign for Die the sign for Wiped Out is made.

Deaf-mutes hold left index finger in front of body, pointing to front, back of hand to left, other fingers closed; close fingers and thumb of right hand, and place tip of extended right index against side of left near tip, right hand over left, right index vertical; draw the right hand to rear, right index finger-tip passing alongside of left index, stopping movement when tip has reached knuckle.

Moon. Conception: Night sun. Make sign for Night, and then partially curve the thumb and index of right hand, space of about an inch between tips, closing other fingers; then raise the hand in a direction a little to south of zenith, and well up, the plane of the circle formed with index and thumb perpendicular to the line of sight, from the eye through the incomplete circle of thumb and index to the position in the heavens where the moon is supposed to be.

Some Indians, in making the circle which represents the moon, use the index fingers and thumbs of both hands.

I have seen a half-month represented by forming a crescent with thumb and index, and usually the moon is represented as full, gibbous, half, and crescent by indicating such and such a portion as dead or wiped out.

Deaf-mutes partially curve the right hand, and place thumb and index round right eye.

Some tribes have twelve named moons in the year, but many tribes have not more than six; and different bands of the same tribe, if occupying widely-separated sections of the country, will have different names for the same moon. Knowing well the habits of animals, and having roamed over vast areas, they readily recognize any special moon that may be mentioned, even though their name for it may be different. One of the nomenclatures used by the Teton Sioux and Cheyennes, beginning with the moon just before winter, is as follows:

1st. The moon, "the leaves fall off."

2d. The moon, "the buffalo cow's fœtus is getting large."
3d. The moon, "the wolves run together."
4th. The moon, "the skin of the fœtus of buffalo commencing to color."
5th. The moon, "the hair gets thick on buffalo fœtus;" called also "men's mouth," or "hard mouth."
6th. "The sore-eyed moon" (buffalo cows drop their calves).
7th. The moon, "the ducks come."
8th. The moon, "the grass commences to get green, and some roots are fit to be eaten."
9th. The moon, "the corn is planted."
10th. The moon, "the buffalo bulls are fat."
11th. The moon, "the buffalo cows are in season."
12th. The moon, "that the plums get red."
Lieutenant Scott gives the following as the nomenclature used by the Sisseton and other Eastern bands of Sioux :
January. Called "very hard to bear."
February. "The month the coons come out, or Coon's Moon."
March. "Sore-eyed month."
April. "The month the geese lay eggs."
May. "Planting month."
June. "The month the strawberries ripen."
August. "Harvest moon."
September. "The wild rice becomes ripe."
October.
November. "Deer-rutting month."
December. "When deer shed their horns."
I obtained the following from the Bannacks :
1st. "Running season for game."
2d. "Big moon."
3d. "Black smoke" (cold).
4th. "Bare spots along the trail" (no snow in places).
5th. "Little grass, or grass first comes up."
They have no names for moons after the season gets warm.
Deaf-mutes have three months cold, three months green, three months hot, and three months falling leaves.

Moose. Generally the sign for ELK is made, but I have seen the sign for ELK made, and then, holding left hand still in its position, carry right in front of and touching it ; move right to front, and left to rear, separating hands a few inches ; this to denote the great width of the horns.

Mosquito. Conception : Blanket-biter, or bites through blanket. Make sign for BLANKET, touch the nose, and holding extended left hand, back out in front of body, strike palm with tip of right index, thumb and other fingers closed (the biting is done with the nose).

Some call mosquitoes the pointed or sharpened noses.

Many Indians make signs for little fly, and represent the sting or bite by nipping some part of the body or hand with tips of right thumb and index, adding, at times, a sound to represent their singing.

Deaf-mutes indicate the bite in some way, and then sharply slap the part with palmar surface of right hand.

Indians are not so much troubled by these pestiferous insects as white people are. The smoky state of everything about the lodge, and their own smoky and greasy condition, afford them a fair protection. All people cease to be irritated by them to the same degree after having lived for a time, without protection of nets, etc., in an atmosphere dense with mosquitoes.

Mother. Bring partially-curved and compressed right hand, and strike with two or three gentle taps right or left breast, and make sign for FEMALE ; though in conversation the latter is seldom necessary.

Deaf-mutes make sign for FEMALE, and cross hands as in their sign for BABY, and move them to front and upwards.

Mother-in-Law. Make sign for HUSBAND or WIFE, and then sign for MOTHER. Sometimes the sign for OLD is also added.

The Blackfeet and some others make sign for ASHAMED ; this, undoubtedly, from custom of "never seeing her face."

The Gros Ventres make apparently half of the sign for ASHAMED for both, mother-in-law and father-in-law, viz., holding right hand opposite left cheek.

Deaf-mutes make sign for MOTHER, and place spread thumb and index of right hand against left palm.

The Arapahoes claim that formerly they held strictly to the custom of never seeing a mother-in-law's face. They told me that the Arapahoe God, their Creator, gave them this law, viz., that they must be bashful and have nothing to do with their mothers-in-law.

The majority of the tribes formerly held, and still largely hold, to the social law of never having anything to do with their mothers-in-law ; as they express it, "Never see her face." Should she be in a man's lodge when he returns to it, if his approach is known, she leaves before he enters ; knowing her to be there he will not enter, and if entering he finds her there he steps outside, draws his blanket over his head whilst she leaves, drawing her shawl closely over her head as she passes out of the lodge. About half of the tribes do not have and never had the custom. The only reason I could ever get for the origin and practice of the custom was given me by an old Cheyenne, who said that when young people are first married they were more or less bashful ; in addition to this, if they should address their mother-in-law, they might be too familiar.

Mound. Slightly curve the hands, and bring them, backs up, alongside of each other in front of body ; separate the hands on curves, carrying right to right and downwards, left to left and downwards.

Mountain. Push the closed hand out as in BLUFF, but raise it higher ; then make sign for HARD or ROCK. Use both hands to represent a mountainous country.

Deaf-mutes simply indicate slope of surface with extended hands, and then make their sign for ROCKY.

Mountain Lion. Make signs for CAT, indicate a long tail, and sign for JUMP. The Crows and some others hold hands as in BEAR, without moving them, then make signs for MOUNTAIN and JUMP.

The skin of this animal has been highly prized by all tribes to make quivers, and the Utes are very fond of them as a sort of riding-pad, the skin being thrown loosely on the pony's back.

Mourn. Conception : Cutting off hair and crying. With extended and separated first and second fingers of right hand, back up, make motion of cutting off the hair round the head horizontally, just below ears, first on right side, then on left ; then make sign for CRY. Sometimes gestures to denote cutting and slashing of body and limbs are also made.

The mourning customs differ somewhat among the different tribes, but cutting off the hair seems to be a common way of marking one's grief; this both for men and women. The women of some tribes mutilate themselves horribly, cutting off fingers and gashing the lower limbs. Barbarism abandoned to sorrow seems to find physical suffering a relief from mental agony.

With the Blackfeet, and some others, as soon as it becomes known that an Indian has died, his lodge is invaded by the relatives, and all the effects of the deceased appropriated.

Among the Sioux, should a man lose his wife or child, he frequently gives away all his possessions ; but through gifts from others he will in a short time be as rich as ever. Saddened and angered by sorrow, it is a common thing for the men, at loss of friend or kin, to announce the fact that their heart is bad, and start at once on the war-path. The howling, wailing, and chanting of the females in an Indian village over the remains is distressingly impressive, and at the death of a famous chief the whole tribe prostrate themselves to their woe.

Mouse. Hold right hand close to ground or floor to represent height, and with partially-compressed right hand imitate its movement in running. Make sign for NIGHT, and represent its nibbling with thumb and index of right hand, nibbling two or three times the leg or some other part of body.

Deaf-mutes imitate the animal's way of eating, holding right hand near mouth and making short, quick motions of jaw.

Move. (To move camp.) Make sign for TEPEE, then, with hands in this position, lower them, at same time, by wrist action, bend right to right, left to left, indicating taking down the lodge-poles; then make sign for WORK, for PACK, and for ADVANCE, or GO. The hands are sometimes held extended, fingers pointing to front, back of right to right, left to left, right hand few inches to right and several to rear of left, and then the hands are moved with gentle jerks to front. This is used more in the sense of moving after having started with the camp, as, " We took down our lodges, packed up and moved off ; while travelling along many ponies became exhausted and were abandoned."

We took down our lodges, packed up and moved off, would be expressed by signs as explained above ; then the expression " while travelling along" would be expressed by this sign, though the signs given under ADVANCE would do nearly as well, and are used as often as this.

Mowing-Machine. Make signs for GRASS, for WAGON, and then hold extended right hand, back down, in front of right shoulder and little lower than waist ; move the hand sharply to left, mostly by wrist action, a few inches, two or three times, as though cutting with edge.

Deaf-mutes indicate motion of the scythe with extended and separated fingers of right hand placed on back of left.

Much. Make sign for MANY. I have also seen a grasping, clutching motion made with both hands to indicate MUCH.

Deaf-mutes sometimes indicate a piling up.

Mud. The usual sign is SOFT. I have seen for "muddy water" the sign made for LIFTED UP, or RAISED QUICKLY. As a necessary consequence to sudden rising of waters they must be muddy. Sometimes indicated by signs for STIRRED UP, which is similar to that for WHIRLWIND.

Deaf-mutes make sign for DIRT, and drop compressed right from above down through left.

Mule. Hold extended hands alongside of ears, palms to front, fingers pointing upwards ; by wrist action move the hands to front and rear, representing motion of mule's ears.

Deaf-mutes use the same sign.

Murder. Make gestures to represent person, add signs for KILL and BY ITSELF. A murder is a "prairie killing," or "killing by itself ;" no cause or reason for the killing ; nothing seen but the killing ; alone inexcusable. This is the peculiar metaphoric idiom spoken of under "a free gift," "fainting," "accident," etc. I have also seen signs for KILL, NIGHT, MAN, KNOW, and NO,—no one knows who did the deed.

Deaf-mutes express the killing, and have to explain.

Murder is considered a grave and serious crime. The nature and extent of the immediate punishment following the offence is determined by the friends of both parties. Should an attempt be made to arrange matters by presents, which is frequently done when public opinion partially justifies the killing, a large lodge is pitched, and a feast made by the friends and kin of the person who committed the offence. Four sticks are driven in the ground just back of the fire, each two like the letter X, and at a distance apart equal to the length of a pipe-stem. The medicine-pipe is filled and laid on these crossed sticks. The friends of the deceased are brought to the lodge, frequently on ponies, which are led, and, after a talk and the distribution of many presents, the pipe is lighted and passed to the kinsfolk and friends of the murdered man. If they are satisfied and are willing to take no further action they take a whiff at the pipe, but if not satisfied they have a perfect right to take vengeance into their own hands. There is no doubt in my mind but that this custom has been the cause of the breaking up of tribes ; murder followed by assassination leading to the division of the nation and years of bitter, unrelenting warfare.

The Bannacks claimed that they had no way of arranging matters. A murderer must suffer the penalty of his crime, viz., " death at the hands of some friend or kin of the murdered person."

Among some tribes, after a man has murdered one of his own people, he is not allowed to smoke one of the large pipes, but usually has a small one, made of bone, for his exclusive use.

Muskrat. Make signs for WATER, move right hand as in FISH, for TAIL, and holding extended index of left hand in front of body, other fingers and thumb closed, rub it with thumb and index of right hand, to indicate the hairless tail. Frequently the sign for STINK is added.

All fur-bearing animals are more or less known by the use which they make of them, and the color of the hair.

Must. Make sign for PUSH.

My or **Mine.** Hold closed right hand, back to right, in front of neck and close to it, thumb extended, ball pressing side of index at second joint and pointing upwards ; move the hand slightly to front, at same time, by wrist action, turn it so that thumb will point to front, back of thumb up. Frequently both hands are used, left usually being under right and fixed like it, given same movement, and often the breast is simply touched, as in I.

Deaf-mutes press extended right hand against left breast.

N.

Name. Make sign for CALL, and indicate possession by sign for YOURS, HIS, or MINE, as the case may be.

Deaf-mutes make a gesture like the Indian one To TRADE, but extend with index finger the second.

An old Cheyenne explained to me in regard to the way in which they were named, as follows:

"When a child is first born, whether a boy or girl, it is called a baby,—a girl baby or boy baby,—afterwards by any childish name until, if a boy, he goes to war; then, if he 'counts a coup,' he is named from something that has happened on the journey, from some accident, some animal killed, or some bird that helped them to success.

"Or, after returning, some one of the older men may give the young man his name. When I was small I was called 'Little Bird.' When I first went to war and returned to camp, the name of 'Long Horn' was given me by an old man of the camp. Then the traders gave me the name of Tall-White-Man, and now, since I have become old, they (the Indians) call me Black Pipe. This name was given me from a pipe I used to carry when I went to war. I used to blacken the stem and bowl just the same as I did my face after these trips, and was especially careful to do so when I had been successful."

In the earliest savage state, according to Spencer, "metaphorical naming will in most cases commence afresh in each generation,—must do so, indeed, until surnames of some kind have been established. I say in most cases, because there will occur exceptions in the cases of men who have distinguished themselves. If 'the Wolf,' proving famous in fight, becomes a terror to neighboring tribes, and a dominant man in his own, his sons, proud of their parentage, will not let fall the fact that they are descended from 'the Wolf,' nor will this fact be forgotten by the rest of the tribe, who held 'the Wolf' in awe and see some reason to dread his sons. In proportion to the power and celebrity of 'the Wolf' will this pride and this fear conspire to maintain among his grandchildren and great-grandchildren, as well as among those over whom they dominate, the remembrance of the fact that their ancestor was 'the Wolf'; and if, as will occasionally happen, this dominative family becomes the root of a new tribe, the members of this tribe will become known to themselves and others as 'the Wolves.'"

This very plausible reasoning is not, I think, founded on fact to any great extent among the American savages, so far as any testimony can be obtained at the present time, as a chief's son does not necessarily inherit the authority and power of his father. The sons must become famous by their own deeds, their own bravery in battle, and their own crafty vigilance in stealing ponies from their enemies. Long before their father has passed away they may have made a name for themselves about which there shines the lustre of as great deeds performed in war as ever illuminated his; and besides the pride in the name made famous in their own and the surrounding tribes by their own efforts, they frequently believe there is a special luck or medicine in the name itself. There are some cases where one son may be named after his father, or rather, where a father may, as they say, give one of his sons his name. This was the case with "Crazy Horse" and "Young-Man-Afraid-of-his-Horses." Both of these names, by the by, have been improperly interpreted. The first should be "His-Horse-is Crazy," the second, "His-Horse-is-Afraid." (See SIOUX.)

The Bannacks and some other tribes do not give names after either a dog, wolf, coyote, or fox. The fathers and mothers name the children, as a rule, but names are sometimes given from some peculiarity or some action of the child. The frogs furnish many names for the girls.

A very peculiar custom obtains with most of the tribes in regard to the men telling their names. When asked to do so, an Indian asked will not tell his name, but the one alongside of or with him will do it for him. The Arapahoes say, in explanation of this, that a long time ago a man would not speak his name, and they were raised in this way. The custom may possibly have grown out of modesty. Being named for a brave deed, in speaking it he appeared to boast; if named because of some deformity or peculiarity, he was ashamed to mention it.

I have sometimes thought the custom grew out of the fact that all Indians of any importance in a camp are well known by name, and to ask it is to question his standing. The same diffidence or reluctance is seen in young men relating their experience when sent on any important mission,—they tell their story in a low tone to some older man, who relates it to the listener.

Mr. Dunbar says that the Pawnee children were named by their parents soon after birth. In the selection of names they did not seem to be particularly solicitous, usually taking such as most readily suggested themselves,—Turtle, Fox, Beaver, etc.; or from some peculiarity early noticed,—Blackey, Whitey, etc.; or after some distinguished person. A great many names were originally mere nicknames, suggested by some physical mark or deformity,—Big Nose, Redhead, Humpback, etc. Many of these names were so appropriate that they lasted through life, though the person might have another name familiar to all.

After performing any special exploit, a man had a right to change his name, if he preferred. Names were sometimes thus changed several times during life. The first such occasion was a great event with a brave. The new name might be chosen as commemorative of the exploit performed, but not necessarily. For instance, a chief succeeded in stealing a number of horses. As it happened several of the horses were spotted, accordingly he took the name Spotted Horse. Sometimes the name was derived from an individual characteristic, as Black Warrior, Angry Chief, etc. But quite usually the new name was selected from mere caprice or with an idea of its special personal fitness, as Shooting-Fire, Gray Eagle, Chief-of-Men, etc. When the name was finally decided upon, in order to have it, as it were, officially sanctioned, a crier was hired, by the bestowal of a horse or other adequate compensation, to proclaim throughout the band that the person in question (giving his old name) should henceforth be known as (giving the new name). The formula used in making the announcement was quite prolix, and but few of the criers were able to go through it correctly.

Narrow. Make sign for FEW.

Navajo (Indian). Make sign for WORK or MAKE, for BLANKET, and for STRIPED.

In their flocks of sheep and goats, herds of ponies, cattle, and mules, in their fruit orchards, in their manufacture of blankets and other wearing apparel, and in their extensive cultivation of the soil, they present a remarkable contrast to the surrounding tribes. They may be said to have reached an advanced state or period of barbarism, and still they stubbornly insist on going their own way, obstinately holding to their own customs, habits, and beliefs.

They number, according to the agent's report, some sixteen thousand, and have ever been credited with being intelligent and warlike. They have had so much intercourse with the Mexicans that nearly all of them understand and speak the Mexican language.

The blankets manufactured by them are highly prized by the Plains Indians, who have ever been ready and willing to pay a large price for them. The country they inhabit is well adapted to a defensive warfare, and their offensive operations against the Mexicans in former years were carried on with such energy and savage cruelty that they may be said to have created a reign of terror in that region. They also committed many depredations against the Pueblos and New Mexican settlers.

Their myth in regard to their origin, like the Mandans, claims that they came out of the earth. Tradition would indicate that they migrated from the northeast. They are considered a branch of the Apache tribe, their language being nearly like the Jicarilla Apaches. "They do not live in houses built of stone, as has been represented, but in caves, caverns, and fissures of the cliffs, or in the very rudest huts, hastily constructed of branches of cedar-trees, and sometimes of flat stones for small roofs." These huts are abandoned as their flocks and herds change their grazing-ground, and then are rebuilt and reoccupied by the herders of the next flock or herd which appears.

Before New Mexico became a part of the United States little or nothing had been done to subjugate these people. Their depredations led to an expedition against them in 1846, another in 1849, and Colonel Sumner established a post (Fort Defiance) in the midst of their country in 1851, which has exercised a great influence for peace. They will not occupy a lodge or house where a person has died, but destroy it by fire. There are many wealthy Navajos who have numerous servants or dependants, and they formerly held their captives as slaves.

Near. Make sign for CLOSE, if meaning not far off, or sign for FEW or SMALL, if expressing near each other.

Deaf-mutes hold extended left hand in front of body, fingers pointing to right. Hold extended right hand, fingers pointing to left, some inches beyond left; draw the right hand so that its palm will be near back of left.

Needle. Make sign for SEW.

Deaf-mutes use same sign. They also sometimes imitate motion of threading same.

Negro. Conception: Black white man. Make sign for WHITE MAN and then sign for BLACK. Sometimes, with tips of fingers and thumb of right hand, motion of kinking hair by twisting is made, usually on right side of head.

There is no prejudice against the colored race, and some tribes are quite fond of them; particularly is this the case with the Crows. This feeling may date from the time when one became quite a chief among them. Indian women seem specially fond of negroes, and they have no trouble in getting Indian wives. They have, however, mixed but very little with the Plains Indians.

Deaf-mutes press nose with index of right hand. (Flattened noses.)

Nephew. Make signs for brother's or sister's son.

Deaf-mutes make sign for letter N at right side of face.

New. Make sign for CLOSE or NEAR.

Deaf-mutes make a sign very like their sign for WONDERFUL, only do not raise right hand so much.

Next Year. It is necessary to indicate the season. Suppose one speaking in the winter wishes to say "next summer," make signs for WINTER, for FINISHED, and for GRASS, holding hands pretty high, so as to indicate the grass as at full length or height. If one is speaking in the summer, make signs for AUTUMN, WINTER, and FINISHED, then denote the season. (See YEAR.)

Deaf-mutes make their sign for YEAR, then carry right hand over left, and place palmar surface against back of left for NEXT.

Nez Perce (Indian). Hold right hand, back to right, in front of right cheek and close to it, index finger extended and pointing to left, its tip little to right of and little lower than nose, other fingers and thumb closed; move the hand to left, back of index passing under and close to nose.

The above is the usual gesture, and so generally used that it can properly be called the tribal sign; but I have also seen the cartilage of the nose seized with the thumb and index finger of the right hand to denote the tribe, and the Blackfeet sometimes make the sign for POWDER, on account, as they claim, of their excessive use of a bluish-black paint. They are also known as fish-eating people by the Plains Indians. The Pierced-Noses, so named by the French, on account of nasal ornaments worn by those first seen, call themselves Sahaptins. The custom of piercing the nose and wearing a ring as an ornament has long since died out, and there is a great deal of doubt whether it was ever generally practised by this tribe. The Sahaptins and the confederated tribes known as Flatheads marked, geographically, the western limit of the buffalo range in former times, and they also might be considered as the advanced guard, to the east, of the fish-eating Indians of the Pacific slope; they subsisting themselves both by hunting and fishing.

For many years these tribes regularly crossed the mountains and went down on the plains once or twice a year to hunt buffalo. Since the advent of the whites their own country has not abounded in large game, and their constant practice in hunting small animals made them excellent marksmen. Roots and berries formerly formed no inconsiderable portion of their food. The men usually did the hunting and fishing, while the women dug the roots, picked the berries, prepared the food; in fact, did about all the rest of the work. The Nez Perces, with their high cheek-bones, straight black hair, and copper-colored complexion, come much nearer the typical Indian of America as pictured by early writers than any I have ever met. They mark the line where Indian tribes held slaves,—none of the Plains Indians proper, except it be the Comanches, ever practised it. They have for many years been noted, even among the surrounding tribes, for the number and fleetness of their ponies.

"In character and in morals, as well as in physique, the inland native is almost unanimously pronounced superior to the dweller on the coast. The excitement of the chase, of war, and of athletic sports ennobles the mind as it develops the body; and although probably not by nature less indolent than their western neighbors, yet are these natives of the interior driven by circumstances to habits of industry, and have much less leisure-time for the cultivation of the lower forms of vice. As a race, and compared with the average American aborigines, they are honest, intelligent, and pure in morals. Travellers are liable to form their estimate of national character from a view, perhaps unfair and prejudiced, of the actions of a few individuals encountered; consequently qualities the best and the worst have been given by some to each of the nations now under consideration. For the best reputation the Nez Perces, Flatheads, and Kootenays have always been rivals. Their good qualities have been praised by all, priest, trader, and tourist.

"Honest, just, and often charitable; ordinarily cold and reserved, but on occasions social and almost gay; quick-tempered and revengeful under what they consider injustice, but readily appeased by kind treatment; cruel only to captive enemies, stoical in the endurance of torture, devotedly attached to home and family, these natives probably came as near as it is permitted to flesh-and-blood savages to the traditional noble red man of the forest sometimes met in romance.

"It is the pride and boast of the Flathead that his tribe has never shed the blood of a white man. Yet none, whatever their tribe, could altogether resist the temptation to steal horses from their neighbors of a different tribe, or in former times to pilfer small articles, wonderful to the savage eye, introduced by Europeans. Many have been nominally converted by the zealous labors of the Jesuit fathers or Protestant missionaries, and several nations seem to have actually improved in material condition, if not in character, under their change of faith." (*Bancroft.*)

The Nez Perces maintained peaceable relations with the whites from their first discovery until 1877. Lewis and Clarke were kindly received by them in 1805, and Captain Bonneville was cordially welcomed in 1832–33. In 1835, Governor Stevens concluded a liberal treaty with these people, giving them an immense tract of country for a reservation; this was confirmed by the United States Senate. In 1863 the encroachments of the whites made it necessary to throw open a portion of this country to settlement. This action created a diversion among the Indians; those who would not agree to this new treaty were called Non-Treaty Indians, and these, led by Chief Joseph, made an outbreak in 1877. The remnant of his followers, those left by defeat in war and disease in peace, are located at what is called a sub-agency, on Sha-kas-kia Creek, some twelve miles from the Ponca Agency, Indian Territory. The Indian account of this war and its results is pathetic beyond description.

Night. Conception: Earth covered over. Bring extended hands, backs up, well out in front of body, fingers pointing to front, right hand very little higher than left, hands about height of breast and several inches apart; move the right hand to left, left to right, turning hands slightly by wrist action, so that fingers of right hand point to left and front, left hand to right and front, terminating movement when wrists are crossed. Darkness, as I have said, seems to be considered a material thing by Indians; it spreads over the earth like two huge blankets. I have also seen sign made to denote sun setting for night.

No. Hold extended right hand, back up, in front of body, fingers pointing to left and front; move the hand to right and front, at same time turning hand, thumb up, so that back of hand will be to right and downwards; the hand is swept into its position on a curve.

Deaf-mutes shake the head.

Noon. Indicate the position of the sun.

Notify. Make sign for TELL, or TALK, or CALL.

Deaf-mutes swing right hand under left from mouth; make then sign for ATTENTION, and also for SPEAK.

Now. Bring extended index finger of right hand, back to right and pointing upwards, other fingers and thumb closed, in front of face about eight inches, and, without stopping, carry it a little to front; then stop with trifle of a rebound. Sometimes sign for HURRY is made.

Number. See COUNT.

O.

Oath. Pointing to the zenith and the earth imposes the obligation of an oath with many tribes. Thus, swearing by the Great Spirit and the earth, and even holding up the right hand, is very generally understood at the present day. The latter would be called "the white man's way" by the Indians.

The Comanche oath is by the sun and earth, and sometimes, to make it very strong, the oath is made early as the sun is rising, and a knife is put in the ashes and drawn between the lips. If the man is swearing falsely, there will be blood on the knife as it is drawn through the second time.

The Mandans swear by the moon or sun.

Some tribes have no special way of adding sacredness to the given word. The special ceremony gone through to receive the report of scouts sent for game or look after the enemy partakes strongly of the character of an oath. (See SCOUT.) Some tribes swear by the sun, the earth, and then kiss any sharp instrument, like an arrow-head or knife. If the truth is not told, death is inflicted with whatever is kissed.

Deaf-mutes pass extended right index from mouth to front, and then hold extended right hand well above head, to front and right.

Obey. Make sign for LISTEN, usually indicating the passing of the words "through and through." Very many Indians use a form of expression illustrated by these sentences: "I will obey you" is rendered by "*I will listen to your words;*" "They refused to do as you ordered," by "*They would not listen;*" or might sometimes say, "*They had no ears.*"

Ocean. Make signs for WATER and for WIDE or BROAD, and sometimes spread out the hands, as in PRAIRIE.

Deaf-mutes use about the same signs.

Officer. Make sign for CHIEF.

Deaf-mutes touch right shoulder with right hand for an army officer; make sign for SHIP in addition for naval officers; indicate the badge for a police officer, etc.

Often. Hold left forearm horizontally in front of left shoulder, height of breast and pointing to front; touch left forearm several times, commencing at wrists with side of extended right index, other fingers and thumb closed, back of right hand outwards, right index raised and lowered at about right angles to left forearm.

Ogalalla (Band of Sioux). Conception: Throwing dirt, dust, or ashes in the face. Make sign for SIOUX, for DUST, DIRT, or ASHES, and then hold closed right hand, back out, well out in front of face; move hand towards face; at same time extend and separate with a partial snap the thumb and fingers. Very frequently the sign for DUST, DIRT, or ASHES is omitted.

There are several stories told of the manner in which this powerful branch of the Sioux family received its name. The most reliable is that two chiefs disagreed on some subject under discussion, when one told the other that if he persisted he would throw some dirt or ashes on his face. Holding to and still expressing his views, the dirt or ashes were thrown, and his followers were ever after called "those who had dirt or ashes thrown in their faces," frequently simply "Bad Faces." The word means "throwing at or into." Nearly all of the band, several thousand in number, are at Pine Ridge Agency, Dakota. (See SIOUX.)

Ojibway. See CHIPPEWA.

Old. Conception: Walking with stick. Hold closed right hand, back to right, about twelve inches in front of right shoulder, about height of breast ; move the hand a little upwards, to front, downwards and back into its first position on small curve, repeating motion. Sometimes the gesturer bends or stoops a little in making the gesture, but not commonly. The Flatheads and Blackfeet make the gesture with both hands, bringing left near right, and holding hands quite near body in making the motion, as though both hands grasped a cane and used it in this way. Among many tribes the old people are treated at times with indifference and neglect. The old women particularly lead a hard and cruel life, and are little, if any, better than beasts of burden, and seem to take it as a matter of course that they should labor constantly. The hard work, constant exposure, and reckless disregard of any precaution to protect them from the inclemencies of the weather cause them all to grow prematurely old and withered, seamed, wrinkled, wretched. They usually look forward to death with feelings more of pleasure than of pain. I have heard many of the men express regret that they had not been killed in battle while still young. A very old man of the Blackfeet nation once said to me that he thought the Great Spirit must have forgotten him.

As age approaches they abandon the war-path, give up horse-stealing, and seek what little comfort they can get in eating and smoking. In some rare cases Indians reach a very great age, but as a rule the average is not equal to that of the white race. I saw an Arapahoe woman who was one hundred and fourteen, and a Red River half-breed woman who was one hundred and thirteen. The latter, when I saw her, was building a fire with which to cook her supper, and though wrinkled and bent was yet quite active and strong. The comforts and respect which cluster about the gray hairs of an honorable old age in civilization are rarely found paralleled in barbarism. Never having accumulated sufficient property to maintain them, or having given away what they had, they become a burden upon the charity of their kinsfolk, and, as a rule, death is a most welcome visitation, relieving them from the most wretched condition of hunter life. Though, as I have stated, it seems to be the universal sentiment that it is better to be killed while young, yet the most of them, notwithstanding this constant assertion and apparent belief, take great trouble and care to reach old age; and I have noticed that, as a rule, the more chances an Indian has taken where he risked his life, the more anxious he is not to take any more. I mean by this, that though perhaps brave and rash when young, a little age entirely corrects the evil, if it can be so called.

Opposite. Hold extended index fingers opposite each other, in front of body, at same height, other fingers and thumbs closed; the right index here represents one object, left another; hold the hands so as to convey the relative position of the objects, and in all conversations in the sign language this is a general rule which should be carefully followed, accurately representing objects and movements.

Deaf-mutes use the same sign.

Osage (Indian). Conception: Shaved heads. Bring backs of extended hands, fingers pointing to rear and slightly upwards, alongside of head; move hands downwards, as though cutting hair with lower edges of hands; repeat motion. Frequently only right hand is used. This is the general sign for Osages, Sacs and Foxes, and other tribes who shaved off the hair, except a tuft near the crown.

Otter. Conception: Dressing or decorating hair. Hold right hand, back about outwards, little to right of right cheek, index, second finger, and thumb extended, thumb resting against inner surface of index and second fingers, others closed; lower the hand, tips of extended fingers describing a small spiral curve. Some Indians add sign for LONG TAIL OF ANIMAL, and the Crows make a gesture very like that for FISH. There is a general custom among nearly all Plains Indians, and some of those who live in the mountains, like the Utes, in regard to the use of the otter-skin. Strips are worn round the wrists, around the body, over the shoulder, twisted into the hair and scalp-lock, put on quivers, and among many tribes it is used by nearly all the men to wrap the braids of hair that fall down on each side of the face. So common has this become that from it the sign for the animal has been derived.

Sometimes so great is the attachment and so powerful the superstition in regard to a particular piece, that it is handed down from father to son for many generations as a special charm.

There is an old tradition among the Arapahoes that a young man went to the top of a high bluff, fasted for several nights and days, and was rewarded with a vision or dream, which told him that if he would go down to the stream which wound about the base of the hill, he would find an animal whose skin, if worn, would protect the wearer from harm. He went, found the animal, killed it, and ever since they have worn strips of this skin, as a charm to paralyze bad and strengthen good luck. Not only is the otter-skin used for its supernatural power, but because it looks well, is the fashion, is prized, and a young man would hardly consider himself well dressed did he not have his hair wrapped. So great is the demand for these skins for this purpose that many Indian traders have them in their regular invoice of goods from the East.

The Comanches and Kiowas do not use the "otter-skin twists" so much, priding themselves more on ear-ornaments, pipe-clay, breastplates, and the artistic use of paints.

Outside. Make proper sign for the object which is to be represented as outside of the tepee, house, camp, or whatever it may be; then the proper sign for either of these; and then, still holding the left hand in position, make the sign for SITTING, STANDING, or LYING, with right hand, near left, but outside of the tepee, camp, etc.

In making the sign for an object, the object is supposed to be where the air-picture marks it, and it is thus easy to establish the relative position of things.

Deaf-mutes make a general outline, and then note outside of this.

Over. To cross over, see CROSS. On the other side, over the river, etc., see ACROSS.

Deaf-mutes use about the same signs.

Overtake. Hold left hand, palm outwards, well out in front of body, fingers extended, touching, and pointing upwards and slightly to front (represents party or object in advance); bring right hand near body, palm outwards, index finger extended pointing upwards and slightly to front; move the right hand out till it touches left.

Deaf-mutes make the same sign.

Owl. Conception: Big eyes. Make sign for BIRD; then bring the curved index and thumbs of both hands over and around the eyes, other fingers closed. Sometimes the extended index fingers are held up alongside of temple to denote the horns, and I have also seen the sign for NIGHT, and the hooting of the owl imitated.

Deaf-mutes use the same sign.

P.

Pack. Hold partially-compressed left hand, back to left, in front of body, fingers pointing to front, thumb extended and side pressed against palmar surface of index ; bring partially-compressed right hand and place palm against left thumb, fingers pointing to front ; raise the right hand and place palm against upper part of back of left, inner surface of fingers of right hand resting against back of these of left ; raise hand and carry to first position, then raise and carry to second ; these motions are executed briskly. The left hand here represents the animal, right the packs or bundles placed on each side, as well as the throwing of them into position. This sign is also used to express the idea of saddling an animal.

Deaf-mutes indicate the putting of things into a trunk or bag.

Long before the Indians had ponies the women packed their dogs, and the knack may almost be called an inherited quality. It requires great skill to properly pack an ordinary Indian load on any pony, and even with the greatest care sore-backed ponies are common.

Packing is woman's work, and as a consequence the men are not very proficient.

Paddle. Make sign for BOAT.

Deaf-mutes use the same sign.

Paint. Rub the cheeks and front of face with palm of right hand, fingers extended.

Deaf-mutes rub or stroke the left palm with palm and back of extended right hand, much as a paint-brush is used in painting wood-work.

The Indians have, without much doubt, been called red men on account of the universal custom of painting their faces and bodies, and for this purpose they used fine clays containing different oxides of iron. Since the establishment of their trading stores they purchase these ochres to a great extent, but usually have some of a similar character which they have themselves found. Some advantages are claimed in the use of these paints as a protection against the rigors of climate, both the icy winters of the North and the torrid summers of the South, but it is also used because of their superstitions in regard to it, viz., that it is conducive to good luck, and that its original use was in obedience to the direct command of God. In applying it, an Indian puts a little ochre and grease in the palm of the hand, and then the palms are rubbed together to thoroughly mix and obtain the proper consistency ; this is used for the "flat tints," and the stripings and fancy touches are put on afterwards. Some Indians take more kindly to a particular color, imagining that it gives better luck than another. When the paint is rubbed on the face the eyes are closed, so that the lids may have their full share, and it may be for this reason that some tribes pull out the eyelashes, as these, by holding an extra allowance, might cause irritation of the eyes. The skin of many Indians' faces, especially that of the nose, often becomes full of little holes, caused, no doubt, by the paints used. The squaws ordinarily use red for the cheeks, and a bright vermilion does add to their beauty, or rather, in a way, hides their ugliness; a perpetual atmosphere of smoke, grease, and dirt, with such accessories as long and fatiguing rides, severe work, and rough food, is not conducive to female beauty. War-paint, so called, is only an excessive use of any color. After returning from an expedition most tribes paint the faces black of those who have been out, that being the color for rejoicing. Frequently these ochres are rubbed over the uppers of moccasins and on clothing, and at their dances horseshoe-marks are painted on the body or on the clothing, and the pony is also decorated in this way. If one has been wounded, the place of the wound is glaringly represented by red paint on their historical pictures.

The Cheyennes claim that they received their orders in regard to the use of paint direct from the "old woman" in the cave, who gave them corn, tobacco, etc. When painting for war they use many stripes and rings of different colors, but on returning only black-colored paint is used. For courting, they claim that they paint themselves as handsomely as possible.

Michelle, chief of the Pend d'Oreilles, said to me, "I do not know exactly why we use paint. When I was young many kinds were used, —black, yellow, red, etc. We know that by its use when it is hot we do not feel the sun so severely, and when cold the winds are not so keen and painful. The priests tried to stop its use; I asked them if it was any worse to paint the face than it was to paint the church, and if the church would last longer by being painted, why would not an Indian? I think God made all things to be used,—the paints for the Indians; and this is why we use all kinds of color on face and hair when we go to war."

The different colors are produced in different ways by different tribes. The Sioux use bull-berries, a shrub something like sumach; moss on pine-trees for yellow paint. Generally speaking, *black* means joy; *white*, mourning; *red*, beauty; and an excessive use of any of these or other colors, excitement.

Mr. Girard informed me that the Arickaree youngsters were not entitled to stripe the face until after they had passed through the initiating ceremony of the Calumet-Dance. Mr. Dunbar says of the Pawnees, "Paint was an important part of the toilet, particularly with men. Young women sometimes used vermilion quite freely on the face, but with men in full costume paint was indispensable. There was no special guide other than individual fancy in its use for personal ornamentation. Sometimes the entire person was bedaubed, but more usually only certain parts, especially the face and breast. When painting the whole body, frequently the nails, or the notched edge of a sort of scraper, were drawn over the body, producing a peculiar barred appearance. Sometimes the figure of certain animals, as the totem of the family to which the person belonged, was conspicuously painted upon the body. In the religious and ceremonial dances various kinds of fantastic and grotesque designs were exhibited. After killing an enemy the lower part of the face might be painted black. The paints used were vermilion, or, if this was not procurable, a kind of clay was burned till it assumed a bright red hue, and then pulverized. Red ochre was also obtained in certain localities on their hunting-grounds. Sometimes a white clay was also used. A yellow paint was gathered from the flowers of a species of solidago. All paints, when used on the person, were prepared with buffalo-tallow; when for ornamenting robes, they were mixed with water.''

Palsy. Bring hands, back up, in front of and close to breast, hands slightly compressed, held loosely at wrists; shake the hands slightly, giving a quivering motion, to imitate the tremulous and shaky condition of weakened or suspended functions.

Deaf-mutes use the same sign.

Parade. Make sign for WHITES, for SOLDIER, and then hold the nearly-closed hands, backs of hands nearly up, well in front of body, hands close together, same height and equally advanced; separate hands, carrying right to right, left to left.

Deaf-mutes make their sign for SOLDIER, and then hold hands, backs out, in front of body, fingers extended, separated, and pointing downwards, hands in same vertical plane; move the right to right, left to left, separating hands several inches.

Part. If *one-half*, indicate it as in sign for that word; if less, hold the right hand nearer end of index, according to portion desired to be represented.

Deaf-mutes denote HALF or less.

Partisan. Make signs for WAR, GO, CHIEF, and for PIPE, and then lay back of right hand in the hollow of left arm.

With most of the tribes in former times the chief of a war party carried the pipe, or, as they expressed it, ''owned the pipe''; and with some tribes he was not allowed to eat or drink until the sun had set, then food and drink were carried to him. With the Flatheads this chief went far ahead of the party, and frequently his medicine became bad, and the whole party turned back. These were the men who, by personal combat, frequently determined the result of a battle.

Partner. Make sign for BROTHER. Some Indians make sign for FRIEND.

Indians rarely enter into a partnership to conduct any business, but frequently adopt a man as friend or brother, forming a partnership of danger, etc. (See BROTHER.)

Deaf-mutes make their sign for PERSONS united and BUSINESS.

Parturition. Bring extended right hand in front of and close to body, back of hand outwards, fingers pointing downwards and slightly to front; move the hand downwards and outwards on curve.

Many of the Indians have separate lodges for the women at childbirth, and such attention as they may get is extended by the old women, though the medicine-men sometimes assist. The woman is usually put in a kneeling posture, the umbilical cord is wrapped around the finger of the attendant, left about six inches long, cut, and the little coil slipped off the finger and placed against the abdomen of the child, and fastened with a bandage, which goes around the body.

With the Shoshones and Bannacks medicine-men are not allowed to assist, and the woman sometimes goes away to the solitude of the brush or timber, and there alone passes through the pains of childbirth, though it is customary for some of her women kinsfolk to go with her. Sometimes the absence is prolonged from four to six weeks. Frequently a little lodge is pitched adjacent the large one, and used for this purpose. It is about as cheerless and uncomfortable as the one used during the menstrual periods.

With the Cheyennes, when a woman feels the pains of approaching childbirth, an old medicine-man is sent for, and also an old woman. The man prepares the medicine, usually a liquid decoction made from herbs and roots, and the woman takes immediate charge of administering it, and assists in cutting the umbilical cord. Sometimes when an unmarried woman has a child she kills it; if the child is raised, there is no prejudice against it, and it receives the same consideration as other children. The mother has a perfect right to kill the child; it is hers, she can throw it away if she wants to, and it is not considered any crime or even an offence to do so.

Mr. Dunbar says of the Pawnees "that accouchment was generally very easy. No special preparation seemed to be made, the woman continuing about her ordinary duties till the moment actually arrived. In travelling she simply fell out of the line, near water, if possible, and in the course of two or three hours resumed her place, carrying the infant on her back. If in the village, she retired to some secluded spot near a stream alone, as before. Sometimes, at the birth of the first child, the mother was attended by a woman acting as midwife; but the principal part of her service consisted in busily shaking a rattle,—a gourd containing a handful of shot. After birth the infant was immediately washed, bandaged, and fastened to the baby-board, where it remained most of the time for the first twelve or fifteen months of life. As soon thereafter as they could begin to walk they were loosened from the board and allowed more freedom."

I have known of cases where Indian women died in labor, and some from the effects of parturition; but as they are strong and usually healthy, and having never had their bodies distorted by artificial means, it would be absurd to suppose that they suffer as much as their white sisters.

Pawnee. Conception: Wolf. Hold right hand, palm outwards, in front of, little higher than, and close to right shoulder, first and second fingers extended, well separated, and pointing upwards and slightly to front, other fingers and thumb closed; carry hand slightly upwards and to front, and bend the hand down slightly, so that fingers point nearly to front.

The agency for the Pawnees is located on Black Bear Creek, some nine miles from its mouth. Near the Cimarron the country is heavily timbered, then it opens out into rolling prairie-land, the streams being fringed with timber and the higher hills covered with scrub-oak.

These Indians came to their present location numbering any-where from two thousand to two thousand five hundred. The agent, in 1881, was issuing to thirteen hundred and forty. They have thirty thousand dollars per year perpetual annuity: one-half of this in clothing, the rest in money.

Rations were also issued them once in seven days. Very few of the men or boys now roach the hair. Some wear citizens' dress, and live in log houses, some in tepees, and some in sod houses. These latter are like the dirt house described by Mr. Dunbar. They are making haste very slowly towards civilization. They claim that the Cheyennes gave them the name of "Wolf," and this corroborates the story told me by the Cheyennes some years since. The Cheyennes also told me that they called them wolves because they were such adroit horse-thieves, disguising themselves as wolves, and it will also be remembered that a scout or Indian going into an enemy's coun-try is called a wolf. They told me that they were not as healthy as when north, that they did not work with a good strong heart as they did when in Nebraska. They have about six hundred and fifty acres of land under cultivation, some four hundred of corn and wheat.

Mr. John B. Dunbar, in the *Magazine of American History* for April, 1880, has given such an excellent account of the Pawnee family that I copy at length from this paper:

"The Pawnee family, though some of its branches have long been known, is perhaps in history and language one of the least under-stood of the important tribes of the West. In both respects it seems to constitute a distinct group. During recent years its extreme Northern and Southern branches have evinced a tendency to blend with surrounding stocks, but the central branch, constituting the Pawnee proper, maintains still, in its advanced decadence, a bold line of demarcation between itself and all adjacent tribes.

"The members of the family are the Pawnees, the Arikaras, the Caddos, the Huecos or Wacos, the Keechies, the Tawaconies, and the Pawnee Picts or Wichitas. The last five may be designated as the Southern or Red River branches.

"The earliest ascertainable home of the Huecos seems to have been upon the Upper Brazos River. The land just mentioned as a reserve was part of their territory. From kinship and proximity they were always specially intimate with the Wichitas. About 1830 a large portion of the band took up their residence with the Wichi-tas, north of the Red River, and continued there for more than twenty years. From this long-continued intimacy they contracted much of the roving character of the Wichitas. Of the early history of the Keechies and Tawaconies very little is known. The home of the latter, prior to their settling upon the Fort Belknap Reserve, was upon the Upper Leon River. The earliest known residence of the Keechies was upon the Trinity and Upper Sabine Rivers. So far as I have been able to learn they were never induced to settle upon the reserve with the forementioned bands, but preferred an irresponsible life, and gradually wandered away across the Red River, and as early as 1850 were living upon the Canadian River, near Choteau's Landing.

"In 1804 the relative numbers of these bands were estimated to be: the Caddos, 100 warriors; the Huecos, 80; the Keechies, 60; the Tawaconies, 200; the Wichitas, 400. Just before that date the Caddos, and probably some of the others, had suffered severely from the smallpox. In 1820 they were estimated as follows: the Caddos, 300 warriors; the Huecos, 300; the Keechies, 200; the Tawaconies, 150; the Wichitas, 300. They were then living in a sort of tribal confederacy. At the head of this confederacy were the Caddos, whose first chief held a commission as colonel in the Spanish army. During the continuance of this alliance, which was probably brief, the Wichitas are said to have removed to the vicinity of the Brazos River, and lived with or near the Huecos. It was no doubt on the return of the Wichitas to their old home beyond the Red River that the part of the Huecos already mentioned withdrew from their own band and accompanied them.

"While living upon the Brazos Reserve the Caddos, Huecos, and Tawaconies are said to have been intelligent, peaceable, quiet, industrious, and disposed to adopt many of the usages of civilized life. Unfortunately, however, a feud was engendered between them and certain of the more lawless white settlers of the vicinity, which resulted toward the close of 1858 in the murder of several unoffending Indians by the latter. The mutual distrust and uneasiness resulting from this wanton act caused the Indians to begin to move in straggling parties across the Red River into the Choctaw country, where a remnant of the Caddos was already residing. The five bands are now all gathered upon a reserve secured for them in the Indian Territory by the Government. Their numbers by the census of 1876 were: the Caddos (including about 100 incorporated Delawares and Iowas), 580; the Huecos, 70; the Keechies, 85; the Tawaconies, 100; the Wichitas, 215. In many respects, in their method of building lodges, their equestrianism, and certain social and tribal usages, they quite closely resemble the Pawnees. Their connection, however, with the Pawnee family, not till recently, if ever, mentioned, is mainly a matter of vague conjecture. I find one record of the Caddos early in this century speaking of the Pawnees as friends (if indeed this does not refer to the Wichitas; *i.e.*, Pawnee Picts), but no allusion is made to any kinship. Gallatin, in his essay (1835), classes them as entirely distinct. Catlin, who visited the Wichitas in 1833, is very emphatic in denying any relationship between them and the Pawnees, claiming that in stock, language, and customs they are altogether different. Gallatin mentions them as presumed, from similarity of name (Pawnee Picts), to be related to the Pawnees. On the other hand, the Wichitas and Pawnees, ever since the acquisition of their territory by the United States, have uniformly asserted their kinship, and maintained constant intercourse. Professor Turner, in volume iii. of the ' Pacific Railroad Explorations' (1853), gives brief vocabularies of the Hueco and Keechie as probably of Pawnee stock. Of the Caddo he gives only a few words, noting some close resemblances to the Pawnee, but expressing no opinion as to any relationship. In the ' Report of the Commissioner of Indian Affairs' for 1876, the fact of any kinship between any of the five bands and the Pawnees is utterly ignored, and the assertion is even hazarded that the Southern branches themselves belong to three distinct stocks: the Caddos speaking one language, the Huecos, the Tawaconies, and the Wichitas another, and the Keechies a third. This is certainly a late and unwarranted contradiction of a fact that has been recognized for nearly a century.

"Of the one Northern branch, the Arikaras, our information is much more satisfying. The reason of their separation from the Pawnees is not certainly known. There has, however, been an old tradition among the Pawnees that they drove them from the once common settlement on the Platte River. The exact date of the movement of the Arikaras northward from this region is also unknown ; but we may safely conclude it to have been quite ancient, from the fact that their migration up the Missouri River must have been before the occupying of the country along that stream by the powerful Dakota tribe, one hundred and fifty years ago. This view is sustained by the remains of various villages built by them at different stages of their progress. The lower of these present the appearance of considerable antiquity. Lewis and Clarke, in 1804, found the Arikaras about latitude 45°, above the mouth of the Cheyenne River. Twenty years before they were reported to have been living below the Cheyenne, on the Missouri. From this latter place they had moved up to the Mandans, with whom for a time they lived in alliance, but later had withdrawn to where Lewis and Clarke found them. At that time they were very favorably disposed towards the United States, and remained so for some years. In 1820 they had become bitterly hostile. This radical change has usually been attributed to the intrigues of the Northwest Fur Company, which, through its factors, was making strenuous effort to divert the traffic of this region from the Missouri Fur Company. In 1823 the Arikaras made an attack upon some boats of the latter company, killed thirteen men and wounded others. In consequence of this act an expedition under Colonel Leavenworth, aided by the company and by six hundred friendly Dakotas, was sent from Council Bluffs, Iowa, against them. In August of that year, after a desultory action at their lower village, they were induced to sue for peace. Nine years after, Catlin, while ascending the Missouri, found them living at the mouth of the Cannonball River, still so hostile that individual intercourse could not safely be had with them. In 1833 they made a visit in a body to the Pawnees on the Platte, and continued there with the *Skï'-di* band two years. To all appearance their intention was to take up their permanent abode with their old-time associates ; at least so it was generally understood. But some of their usages and traits, especially their hostility to the whites, proved so undesirable to their kinsmen that they were finally sent away. On receiving this dismission they returned to their Northern home, where they have since remained. They are now upon a reserve with the Mandans and Minnetarees, near Fort Berthold, Dakota. Their present number is about seven hundred.

" Like the Pawnees, they regard the Dakotas as their natural foes, and wars with them have been ceaseless. Scarcely any other evidence can be needed of their valor than the fact of their having sustained the unequal struggle for so many generations. Their visit to the Pawnees, already noticed, is explained by some on the ground that they were dispossessed and expelled by the Dakotas, but this is incorrect. The real cause of their attempted migration was in some degree the cessation of traffic with them in consequence of repeated aggressions by them upon the traders. But to this should be added their alleged reason,—the partial or entire failure of their crops for several years. To a tribe as agricultural as they seem to have always been, this was no trifling casualty. In the late troubles with the Dakotas they furnished the Government with a considerable number of scouts, who are reported to have done excellent service.

" Of all the branches thus far mentioned the Arikaras most nearly resemble the Pawnees. In personal appearance, in tribal organization and government, in many of their social usages, and in language they are unmistakably Pawnees.

" Of the central branch, the Pawnee proper, the special subject of this monograph, our sketch will be more extended. The name Pawnee is most probably derived from pa'-rïk-i, a horn ; and seems to have been once used by the Pawnees themselves to designate their peculiar scalp-lock. From the fact that this was the most noticeable feature in their costume, the name came naturally to be the denominative term of the tribe. The word in this use once probably embraced the Wichitas—*i.e.*, Pawnee Picts—and the Arikaras. The latter is evidenced by the name Pa-da'-ni, applied by the Dakotas to the Arikaras. Pa-da'-ni is not a Dakota word, but simply their pronunciation of Pa'-nï (it will be observed that throughout this paper I use the common, but evidently incorrect form, Pawnee), and would scarcely have been applied by them to the Arikaras had not the latter, when they first met them, been known as Pa'-nï. The name Arikara is derived, I am inclined to think, not from the Mandan, as is sometimes claimed, but from the Pawnee ür'-ïk-ï, a horn ; with a verbal or plural suffix, being thus simply a later and exact equivalent of Pa'-nï itself.

" The Pawnees themselves have no tradition of ever having occu-

pied or claimed territory north of the Niobrara, though they sometimes hunted there. That region, before the westward movement of
the Dakotas, was held by the Cheyennes, Arapahoes, and Kiowas.

" The true Pawnee territory, till as late as 1833, may be described
as extending from the Niobrara south to the Arkansas. They frequently hunted considerably beyond the Arkansas; tradition says as
far as the Canadian, and sometimes made considerable stays in that
region. Irving ('Tour on the Prairies') mentions seeing in 1832 the
remains of a recent Pawnee village on the Cimarron. On the east
they claimed to the Missouri, though in Eastern Nebraska, by a sort
of tacit permit, the Otoes, Poncas, and Omahas along that stream
occupied lands extending as far west as the Elkhorn. In Kansas
also, east of the Big Blue, they had ceased to exercise any direct control, as several remnants of tribes, the Wyandots, Delawares, Kickapoos, and Iowas, had been settled there, and were living under the
guardianship of the United States. In 1833 the Pawnees, by treaty,
finally relinquished their right to the lands thus occupied. (In 1848
the remains of a considerable village were plainly discernible near
where Wolf River empties into the Missouri in Northeastern Kansas.
The Iowas, then occupying the region, assigned these remains, no
doubt correctly, to the Pawnees. This fact would sufficiently indicate that their control of this locality was once real.) On the west
their grounds were marked by no natural boundary, but may perhaps
be described by a line drawn from the mouth of Snake River, on the
Niobrara, southwest to the North Platte, thence south to the Arkansas. The boundaries here named are not imaginary. In designating
them I have consulted Pawnee history. Messrs. Dunbar, Allis, and
Satterlee, who were laboring as missionaries with the Pawnees, accompanied the different bands on their several semi-annual hunts in 1835,
1836, 1837, and on those hunts the tribe roamed at will over a large
part of the territory within these limits. This territory, comprising
a large portion of the present States of Nebraska and Kansas, formed
a tract which for their purposes was as fine as could be found west of
the Mississippi. The region of the Platte and Upper Kansas, with
their numerous tributaries, was a favorable mean between the extreme north and warmer south; the climate was healthful, the soil
of great fertility, and game, such as buffalo, elk, deer, and antelope,
in abundance to more than supply their utmost need.

" It is not to be supposed, however, that they held altogether undisturbed possession of this country. On the north they were incessantly harassed by various bands of the Dakotas, while upon the
south the Osages, Comanches, Cheyennes, Arapahoes, and Kiowas
(the last three originally Northern tribes) were equally relentless in
their hostility. In fact, the history of the Pawnees, as far back as
we can acquire any knowledge of it, has been a ceaseless, uncompro-
mising warfare against the several tribes that begirt them, and no
more convincing evidence of their inherent energy and indomitable
spirit could be furnished than their having up to that date (1833)
maintained their right over this garden of the hunting-grounds essen-

tially intact. Their enemies were, it is true, making constant forays upon it, and in some instances inflicting severe loss upon them, but in no case had they succeeded in wresting from the Pawnees and retaining any portion of their territory. On the contrary, within the limits named the Pawnee remained the proud master of the land. In 1833 the Pawnees surrendered to the United States their claim upon all the above-described territory lying south of the Platte. In 1858 all their remaining territory was ceded, except a reserve thirty miles long and fifteen wide upon the Loup Fork of the Platte, its eastern limit beginning at Beaver Creek. In 1874 they sold this tract and removed to a reserve secured for them by the Government in the Indian Territory, between the Arkansas and Cimarron, at their junction.

"The traditions of three of the bands, the Xau'-i, Kit'-kĕ-hak-ĭ, and Pit-ă-hau'-ĕ-rat, coincide in stating that the Pawnees migrated to the Platte River region from the South, and secured possession of it by conquest. The period of this migration is so remote that they have failed to retain any of its details, except in a very confused form. The language affords some evidence that their residence in the valley of the Platte has been of some duration. O-kŭt-ŭt and okŭ-kăt signify, strictly, above and below (of a stream) respectively. Now their villages have usually been situated upon the banks of the Platte, the general course of which is from west to east. Hence each of these words has acquired a new meaning,—*i.e.*, west and east. So, also, Kir'-i-ku-ruks'-tu, toward or with the Wichitas, has come to mean south. Such developments are perfectly natural in the history of a language, but require time. The Wichitas, I am told, have a tradition that the primitive home of themselves and the Pawnees was upon the Red River, below the mouth of the Wichita. This would place them in close proximity with the Caddos. The Wichitas also attempt to explain their own southern position by alleging that, having had reason to be dissatisfied with the migration or its results, they attempted to return to their old home. The Pawnees also state that the Wichitas accompanied them on the migration, but left them long ago, and wandered away to the south, though silent as to the reason. This much may be safely claimed, that the separation must have occurred long since, as is indicated particularly by the marked divergence of the Wichita dialect. There are certain facts which may be referred to here as affording something of *vraisemblance* to the tradition of this migratory movement from the South: 1. The Pawnee has always been remarked among the Northern tribes for his fondness for and skill in the use of horses. It was a great ambition with each of them to be the owner of a drove of them. His wealth and, to some extent, his social standing were determined by the number he possessed. For the increasing of his stock he made frequent predatory incursions upon neighboring tribes, especially upon those towards the south, and sometimes these expeditions were extended to a great distance. Personal names were often derived from successful exploits of this kind. 2. The Pawnee warrior always preferred a bow of *bois d' arc,* and besides the bow in actual use he would often have in his lodge a stick of the same material, which at his leisure he would be working into shape as a provision against possible exigency. Bows of this wood were rarely traded away. *Bois d' arc,* however, was to be obtained only in the South, and for the purpose of procuring it a sort of commerce was kept up with certain tribes living there. Now in both these respects—his fondness for horses and his preferences for the *bois d' arc*—the Pawnee is remarkably at one with the tribes of the Southern plains; and though they may not be cited as proof of his Southern origin, they are at least indications. The Pawnee usually locates the Mississippi to the southeast, and the sea to the south. This is perfectly natural, if his present indistinct knowledge of them is the remnant of a more intimate acquaintance that he once possessed in the South.

" The original inhabitants of the conquered territory the three bands already named claim to have been the Otoes, Poncas, Omahas, and Ski'-di. It is in the subjugation of these tribes that the Pawnee finds his heroic age. The tradition is that the Otoes and Omahas were entirely expelled from the country, but, after a long absence to the northward, returned, or rather, were driven back by the Dakotas, and were allowed by sufferance to occupy lands adjacent to the Missouri, as the Poncas had continued to do since the first conquest. From that time they have remained wards of the Pawnees. This much at least is true : the Pawnee always spoke of the Otoes, Poncas, and Omahas as subjugated tribes ; and when together in council, on war or hunting expeditions, though generally acknowledging their prowess,—especially that of the two former,—he still treated them as dependants ; and in times of impending danger from the common foe, the Dakotas, they uniformly looked to him for succor.

" There is an interesting document that may be mentioned in this connection. The Pawnee has a song, constituting the finest satirical production in the language, relating to an attempt that the Poncas are said to have once made to recover their independence. Their warriors in a body, so the account states, made a pretended visit of peace to the village of Xau'-i, at that time the head band of the Pawnees. After lulling to rest, as they supposed, the suspicions of the Xau'-i, according to a preconcerted plan, they made an attack upon them, but were signally discomfited. In commemoration of the victory then achieved the Pawnees composed this song, and the presumption is that such a remarkable production would not have originated and maintained its position permanently in their minds without a good historic basis.

" As regards the Ski'-di, the traditions of the other three bands are very positive in affirming that they are the remnant of a once separate tribe, that has been subdued and incorporated into the Pawnee family. The only statement they give as to the time of this conquest is that it was long ago. Of the exact spot where the event transpired they say nothing. They further claim that once the Ski'-di attempted to reassert their independence, and to this end surprised and badly defeated the Pit-ă-hau'-ĕ-rat band while it was out on a buffalo-hunt. But the two other bands immediately rallied about the survivors of the rout, and having entrapped the Ski'-di, inflicted upon them a severe retribution ; and since then they have been content to remain quietly in their place as one of the four bands. All this the Ski'-di deny. They, however, agree with the other bands in saying that there have been hostilities between the two parties. In 1835 old men were still living who had borne part in a struggle of this kind, probably during the closing quarter of the last century.

" The historic basis of this may be somewhat as follows : In the migration of the Pawnees from the South the Ski'-di preceded the other bands perhaps by nearly a century. With them were the Arikaras. These two bands together possessed themselves of the region of the Loup. When the other bands arrived they were regarded as intruders, and hence arose open hostilities. The result of the struggle was that the two bands were forced to admit the newcomers and aid in reducing the surrounding territory. Subsequently the Arikaras seem to have wandered, or more probably to have been driven, from the confederacy, and to have passed up the Missouri. Later the Ski'-di, in consequence of some real or fancied provocation, attempted to retrieve their losses, but were sorely punished, and henceforth obliged to content themselves with a subordinate position in the tribe.

" The known facts upon which this interpretation is based are these : 1. The remains of the old Ski'-di villages in the valley of the Loup are more numerous, and many of them much more ancient than those of the other bands. 2. The names of several of the Ski'-di sub-bands are local and still retain their meaning ; a fact that would seem to indicate that they were first bestowed in this locality. 3. Since the tribe has been known to the United States the Ski'-di have always acknowledged the precedence of the other bands. Though they have been frequently remarked as more intelligent, as warriors they are inferior. 4. They claim to be more nearly related to the Arikaras than to the Pawnees proper. They, also, do not speak pure Pawnee. Their speech, while Pawnee, is dialectic, and forms an intermediate link between the pure Pawnee and the Arikara.

" Their population is a matter of the greatest uncertainty till 1834. I find an estimate of them in 1719 (attributed to Mr. Dutisné) at about twenty-five thousand, probably of no special value. Lewis and Clarke, in 1805, estimated three bands,—Xau'-i, Kit'-kĕ-hak-ĭ, and Ski'-di, at four thousand. They speak of the tribe as formerly very numerous, but at that time broken and reduced. Major Pike, in 1806, estimated the entire tribe at six thousand two hundred and twenty-three. Major Long, in 1820, gives their number as six thousand five hundred. Thus far only three bands seem to have been known. The authorities in either case were only hearsay, and the estimates are not above suspicion. In 1834, Major Dougherty, the Pawnee agent, and well versed in the affairs of the tribe, estimated them at twelve thousand five hundred. Messrs. Dunbar and Allis, while travelling with the tribe during the three years following, thought this too high, and placed them at ten thousand.   In 1838 the tribe suffered very severely from the smallpox, communicated to them by some Dakota women captured by the Ski'-di early that year.   During the prevalence of the epidemic great numbers of children perished.   The mortality among the adults, though great, was not so excessive.   About a year and a half after this scourge Messrs. Dunbar and Allis made a careful census of the tribe as circumstances would permit, and found them to be six thousand seven hundred and eighty-seven, exclusive of some detachments then absent.   These would have probably raised the total to about seven thousand five hundred.   The conclusion at which they arrived was that their previous estimate may have been quite near the true number.   In 1847 the number was not far from 8400.   In 1856 they diminished to 4686 ; in 1861, to 3416; in 1879, to 1440.

"The causes of this continual decrease are several.   The most constantly-acting influence has been the deadly warfare with surrounding tribes.   Probably not a year in this century has been without losses from this source, though only occasionally have they been marked with considerable disasters.   In 1832 the Ski'-di band suffered a severe defeat on the Arkansas from the Comanches.   In 1847 a Dakota war-party, numbering over seven hundred, attacked a village occupied by two hundred and sixteen Pawnees, and succeeded in killing eighty-three.   In 1854 a party of one hundred and thirteen were cut off by an overwhelming body of Cheyennes and Kiowas, and killed almost to a man.   In 1873 a hunting-party of about four hundred, two hundred and thirteen of whom were men, on the Republican, while in the act of killing a herd of buffalo, were attacked by nearly six hundred Dakota warriors, and eighty-six were killed.   But the usual policy of their enemies has been to cut off individuals, or small scattered parties, while engaged in the chase or in tilling isolated corn-patches.   Losses of this kind, trifling when taken singly, have in the aggregate borne heavily on the tribe.   It would seem that such losses, annually recurring, should have taught them to be more on their guard.   But let it be remembered that the struggle has not been in one direction against one enemy.   The Dakotas, Crows, Kiowas, Cheyennes, Arapahoes, Comanches, Osages, and Kansas have faithfully aided each other, though undesignedly in the main, in this crusade of extermination against the Pawnee.   It has been, in the most emphatic sense, a struggle of the one against the many.   With the possible exception of the Dakotas, there is much of reason to believe that the animosity of these tribes has been exacerbated by the galling tradition of disastrous defeats which Pawnee prowess had inflicted upon themselves in past generations.   To them the last seventy years has been a carnival of revenge.

"One important fact should be noted in this connection.   The treaty of 1833 contains no direct provision that the United States should protect the Pawnees from the Dakotas on the north, and the Comanches and other tribes on the south.   But, unfortunately, the

Pawnees distinctly understood that this was the case ; *i.e.*, that so long as they did not molest other tribes, such tribes should not be allowed to trouble them. Accordingly, for several years, they scrupulously refrained from any aggressive hostilities, though meantime suffering severely from their various enemies. It was only after a final declaration from the Government, in 1848, that it had no intention to protect them that they at last attempted to reassert their prestige. Thus, during this period, while they stood in need of the utmost vigilance, the general influence of the Government was to lull them into fancied security, and centre upon them the intensified efforts of their hereditary foes.

"Another cause has been the locality of the Pawnees, directly in the pathway of trans-continental travel during the last half-century. This great highway has lain along the Platte Valley, directly through their territory. Special diseases, as cholera, syphilis, and certain infantile epidemics, have in this way been freely communicated to them. Modified ailments of a syphilitic nature have been quite prevalent, and have no doubt done much towards undermining their native vigor. It is claimed by some that not a member of the tribe for a generation or more has been entirely free from scrofulous taint, but this is an exaggeration. In addition to these the Indian's great terror, the smallpox, should be mentioned. Lewis and Clarke state that the Missouri tribes had suffered from a visitation of it just before their expedition. About 1825 the Pawnees suffered terribly from it, again in 1838, and also in 1852. There have been lighter visitations from it on several other occasions.

"The history of the tribe since the accession of Louisiana may be passed over briefly. Lieutenant Pike, in 1806, found the Kit'-kĕ-hak-ĭ band somewhat under Spanish influence. A short time before his arrival an expedition from Santa Fé had visited them, intending to form a treaty with the whole tribe, but for some reason returned without fully accomplishing its purpose. The intercourse between the Pawnees and the Spaniards thus revealed seems to have been of long standing. Salmeron refers to them as known to the Spaniards as early as 1626. There is also mention by old writers of an expedition to them from Santa Fé in 1722, but it did not reach its destination. So far as I can ascertain, the continuance of this intercourse in the early part of this century was in consequence mainly of the frequent incursions of the Pawnees into the province of New Mexico for the purpose of stealing horses. These raids were a source of great detriment to the people of that province. Till quite recently horses or ponies bearing Spanish brands were common in the tribe, and were frequently traded in considerable numbers to the Arikaras. The Spaniards not succeeding in protecting their property by force, had recourse to repeated negotiations, hoping, apparently, in this way to conciliate the friendship of the Pawnees, and thus avoid further losses. In 1824 a treaty to this end was formed, and is mentioned as occasion of great rejoicing to the people of New Mexico They thought themselves relieved from a long-continued anxiety and annoyance. The treaty, however, seems to have produced little, if any, amelioration, for, in 1834, emissaries thence again visited the Pawnees, but with no satisfactory results.

"On the other hand, their relations with the United States have always been friendly. Instances might be catalogued, no doubt in considerable number, in which they have committed outrages. But if against these should be set a list of the wanton provocations that they have received at the hands of irresponsible whites, their offences would be probably sufficiently counterbalanced. One incident may be given in illustration of this statement. In the spring of 1852 the Pawnees were reported to have flayed a white man alive. The facts were these: In a small California emigrant-train was a young man, who repeatedly made boast that he would kill the first Indian that he met. One evening, as the train was halting for the night, on a small tributary of the Elkhorn, a Pit-ä-hau'-ĕ-rat squaw, from a village near by, came into the camp begging. Some of the emigrants carelessly rallied the hapless boaster as to the opportunity thus afforded to redeem his threat, and finally, in sheer bravado, he shot and killed the woman. When the band, on the following day, learned of the murder, the warriors pursued and overtook the train, and by their superior numbers compelled the surrender of the young man. After a council, they ordered the train back to the scene, and there, in the presence of his comrades, did flay the unfortunate man as reported. The stream on which this horrible transaction took place is still known as Raw-Hide Creek. One Indian who participated in this summary retribution is still living, and from him I gained this account, which has been sufficiently corroborated from independent sources. During the last fifteen years a battalion of Pawnee scouts, under Major Frank North, have been employed a large portion of the time by the Government against the hostile Dakotas, and in every campaign have won high encomiums for their intrepidity and soldierly efficiency.

"In 1834 the villages of the tribe were located, the Xau'-i on the south side of the Platte, twenty miles above the mouth of the Loup. The Kit'-kĕ-hak-ĭ village was eighteen miles northwest, on the north side of the Loup; the Pit-ä-hau'-ĕ-rat, eleven miles above it, on the same side. Five miles above the last was the Ski'-di village. The sites of these villages were changed from time to time, as convenience or other special consideration might prompt, the average continuance in one place being not over eight or ten years. The Xau'-i and Ski'-di villages were never moved to any considerable distance from the locations named. The Ski'-di village, it is worthy of note, has always been situated to the west of the others, and they have a superstitious belief that this relative position must never be altered. Hence the term tŭ'-ra-wit-u, eastern villages, applied by them to the other bands. The Pit'-ä-hau'-ĕ-rat village, for a considerable portion of the time, both before and since the date named, was upon the Elkhorn, some distance east. The Kit'-kĕ-hak-ĭ, as already shown, from their first discovery till Pike's visit, were settled on the

Republican. This has given rise to the theory that in the northward movement of the tribe they stopped here, while the rest continued on. But there is reason for believing that before occupying this region they resided with the rest of the tribe on the Platte. They have the same tradition as the Xau'-i and Pit'-ă-hau'-ĕ-rat concerning the conquest of that country. There has been a tradition also that after the conquest they moved south for the strategic purpose of keeping the Kansas and Osages from the hunting-grounds of the Upper Kansas River. Their associations with the other bands during the time of the separation were always intimate ; their interests and motives were one, and their speech identical. The exact date of their return to the Platte is not known, but in 1835 men of the band, apparently not more than thirty-five years of age, stated that it occurred while they were children ; probably about 1812.

" One of the most important events of later Pawnee history was the missionary work among them during the years 1834–47. In the first of these years Messrs. Dunbar and Allis, already mentioned, visited the tribe with the intention of establishing a mission in it. Finding the immediate realization of their plan impracticable because of the absence of the Pawnees from their permanent villages for a large part of the year on their semi-annual hunts, they deemed it best, rather than altogether abandon the enterprise, to accompany them for a time on their various wanderings, with the double purpose of acquiring the language and familiarizing themselves thoroughly with Pawnee usages and character, and also of exerting whatever influence they might to induce the tribe to adopt a more settled manner of life. Mr. Dunbar travelled with the Xau'-i band, Mr. Allis with the Ski'-di, Dr. Satterlee, who joined them some time later, travelled with the Kit'-kĕ-hak-ĭ. In February, 1837, he made a visit to the Cheyennes on the Upper Arkansas, hoping to be able to bring about a treaty of peace between them and the Pawnees, and on his return in March was killed by a lawless trapper. After two and a half years spent with the tribe in this way, they were finally induced to accept the encouragements offered by the Government and missionaries, and seemed to evince a sincere desire to enter upon a more regular and fixed mode of living. A spot on Plum Creek, a small tributary of the Loup, was accordingly chosen in 1838 as the site of the mission and Government establishment. Disturbances intervened immediately after, and prevented the execution of the design till 1844. In that year the Government establishment and mission were begun at the place chosen ; a large farm was opened, mission buildings erected, and a considerable number of the Xau'-i and some of the other bands induced to fix their residence in the vicinity. The tribe all displayed a very friendly disposition, and so far as they were concerned the effort to advance their condition towards civilization was progressing most favorably. But, unfortunately, the entire enterprise had awakened the jealous suspicions, and in the end roused the most persistent hostility, on the part of the Ogalalla and Brulé Dakotas. Each year they invaded the region in full force, usually taking advantage of the absence of most of the Pawnees on their hunts, killing where they could, and destroying corn-patches and all other property that they might discover. These continued depredations finally compelled the abandonment of the mission and farm in 1847, and the Pawnees forthwith reverted to their former life.

"The tribal mark of the Pawnees in their pictographic or historic painting was the scalp-lock, dressed to stand nearly erect, or curving slightly backwards, somewhat like a horn. This, in order that it should retain its position, was filled with vermilion or other pigment, and sometimes lengthened by means of a tuft of horse-hair skilfully appended so as to form a trail back over the shoulders. This usage was undoubtedly the origin of the name Pawnee. In the sign language of the tribe and other Indians of the Plains the Pawnee is designated by holding up the two forefingers of the right hand, —the symbol of the ears of the prairie wolf. The precise origin of this practice is a matter of some uncertainty. They claimed that the wolf was adopted of choice as the tribal emblem because of its intelligence, vigilance, and well-known powers of endurance. Their enemies, on the other hand, interpreted it as a stigma upon the tribe because of their alleged prowling cowardice. The emblem probably originated from the name of the Ski'-di band. They being in advance of the other bands in the northern migration, became known to the tribes about them as the wolves, and as the other bands arrived the sign was naturally made to include them also, and in this enlarged use was at length accepted by the Pawnees themselves. The Ski'-di, however, insist that their name has no etymological connection whatever with Ski'-rik-i, a wolf. Their explanation is that the Loup—*i.e.*, Wolf River—was long ago so designated from the great abundance of wolves in its vicinity. (Wolf River is not an infrequent designation of streams with Indians; as Wolf River in Kansas, also in Wisconsin.) From the fact of their location upon it they became known as Wolf (River) Indians. Finally, to most of the Pawnees themselves the real distinction between Ski'-di .—*i.e.*, Ski'-ri—and Ski-rik-i was lost. This is unusually close Indian reasoning, but not altogether conclusive.

"The tribe, as already indicated, consisted of four bands: Xau'i-, or Grand; Kit'-kĕ-hak-ĭ, or Republican; Pit ă-hau'-ĕ-rat, or Tapage; Ski'-di, or Loup. The English names given are all of French origination. The first was applied to the Xau'-i as being the head band, and also the most numerous. The exact origin of Republican, as applied to the second band, I never learned. There has been a tradition that it was first suggested by the semi-republican system of government observed among them when first known ; but this feature was no more marked with them than among the other bands. It is also said to have been applied to them because of their having formerly resided upon the Republican River ; but, *vice versa*, the stream was in all probability so named from the band (the Kansas River from the Kansas Indians, the Osage from the Osages, etc.). Tapage (also Tappage and Tappahs) is of unknown origin. In the treaty of

1819 they were designated as the Noisy Pawnees, which I presume was then the supposed meaning of the name Pit-ă-hau'-ĕ-rat. In the treaty it is spelled Pit-av-i-rate. Tapage is the French substitute for Noisy. Forty-five years ago they were known as the Smoky Hill Pawnees, from having once resided on that stream in Western Kansas. In the summer hunt of 1836 they pointed out to Mr. Dunbar some of their old villages. The name Loup is already sufficiently explained.

"These bands were all further divided into sub-bands and families, each of which had its appropriate mark or token. This was usually an animal, as the bear, the eagle, the hawk, the beaver, etc. ; though sometimes other objects, as the sun, the pipe, etc., were adopted. The separate lodges, and even articles of individual apparel, were usually marked with the token of the family to which the owner belonged. These subdivisions have now entirely disappeared, except as partially retained among the Ski'-di.

"The men were generally of excellent physique, of good stature and robust muscular development. The upper part of the body was frequently large in proportion to the lower extremities, but not so much so as to occasion deformity. The feet, as also the hands, were small, and in walking they were intoed. Obesity was not usual, unless in advanced life. Congenital malformations were rarely seen. This might in part be due to the fact that sickly children, who would be most likely to present such peculiarities, did not survive infancy. The hair was dark, coarse, and straight ; the eyes rather small, black, and inclining to the lack-lustre type. The features, ordinarily well proportioned, were frequently of a very marked character and power. The mouth was a little large perhaps, and the lips thin. These, with the eyes, are the expressive features of the Pawnee face. Hence their proverb, 'If you wish to know whether a man is brave, watch his eye ; if you wish to learn whether he speaks the truth, watch his lips.' The teeth were usually regular and remarkably good. I have seen old men, the crown of whose teeth was worn quite away, and yet they had not lost one. Toothache was scarcely known.

"Their endurance was astonishing. Cases were numerous of sustained effort, which must seem incredible to those not personally conversant with the fact. Runners have been known repeatedly to travel over one hundred miles in twenty-four hours, or less, without stopping on the way for sleep or nourishment. Their gait at such times was a swinging trot. Their power of abstinence was equally marked. Mr. Dunbar, while travelling with them, has known them in many instances to go without food three days, and utter no complaint, nor remit perceptibly anything of their wonted activity. On such occasions, to still the gnawings of hunger, they were accustomed to wrap a thong several times tightly about the waist. It should be added, however, that all such seasons of special exertion or denial were invariably succeeded by periods of recuperation, in which full compensation was made.

"The women were considerably smaller than the men, those who would be remarked as large (by our standard) being extremely few. This was due, no doubt, in some degree to early marriage and child-bearing. Their life was one of constant toil. From early dawn till late at night they were incessantly at work. A Pawnee woman with nothing to do would be a strange anomaly. They cut and adjusted the wood used in constructing lodges and building horsepens ; built the stationary lodges ; pitched and took down the portable lodges ; tanned the skins used in covering the latter (a work both tedious and painful), sewed them together and fitted them to the lodge ; dressed the robes, which were many, both for home use and for trade ; bridled, saddled, packed, and led the horses on the march, and unpacked them on going into camp at night ; made and kept in repair all articles of clothing, mats, bags, bowls, mortars, etc. ; cut and brought all the wood for fires, much of it from a distance, on their own backs; made fires, did the cooking, dried the meat, dug the ground, planted, hoed, gathered, dried, and stored the corn. In short, whatever was done, other than grazing, watering, and bringing in the horses (which were generally done by smaller boys), and going to war, killing game, smoking, holding councils, and giving feasts (which belonged to the men), they did. When with the men in the lodges, they occupied the most inconvenient part ; in the winter the men enjoyed the fire, while they sat back in the cold. In girlhood many of them were quite good-looking, active, and bright, and when together in their work they were very loquacious and facetious ; but their toilsome life and harsh treatment frequently rendered them ill-favored and morose.

"The average duration of life was much less than with the whites ; decrepitude began much earlier, and decline was more rapid. Probably few were to be found in the tribe who were really over sixty years old, though many had the appearance of it. Rheumatic complaints with the aged were frequent and very severe.

"A friend, who has had much experience with the Indians of the Southwest, informed me that he is inclined to believe that the Lipans of Mexico are of Pawnee stock. They have, in times past, exchanged frequent hospitalities with the Wichitas, or Pawnee Picts, and the two understand each other's dialect readily. The name Lipans he explains as Li-pa-nis; *i.e.,* the Pawnees. This derivation is interesting, and, so far as a single word can afford evidence, is very satisfactory. The clue at least deserves careful investigation, and may lead to important results in determining the remoter ethnological relations of the Pawnees. Unfortunately, I have not been able, after repeated efforts, to obtain any vocabulary of the Lipan language by which the worth of the conjecture might be finally judged. If such kinship does really exist, though the Pawnees themselves made no such claim, it would suffice to explain the fact of their apparent familiarity with the geography of the country toward Mexico."

Paymaster. Make sign for MONEY and CHIEF. Sometimes it is also necessary to make sign for WHITES.

Peace. Clasp the hands in front of body, usually back of left down. The sign for SMOKE is also frequently made.

Indians are at peace with those whom they smoke with. To make peace is to smoke. Some Indians clasp the hands by interlocking the fingers, holding forearms vertical.

Deaf-mutes make the Indian sign for QUIET, to denote a state of peace; and they also make their signs for FIGHTING, STOP, and QUIETING DOWN.

The ceremony of making peace varies somewhat with the different tribes, but a necessary and essential part with all is the *smoke,* and with the sacred pipe.

The Cheyennes hold up the pipe before it is filled, pointing to near where the sun rises. The pipe is then filled, sometimes adding to the tobacco some sacred root or sweet-smelling grass; then, before lighting it, the palms of extended hands are held up towards the "four winds,"—a petition that the peace may not be blown away; then the tobacco is lighted, and the smoke of peace taken. They claim that they feared some disaster or disease would overtake them if they did not keep a peace made in this way. The grass and crops would not grow, an epidemic would break out, the snow would fall to such a depth as to occasion great distress, the burden of some affliction would surely fall upon them. They also claim that the two Gods who went into the cave and brought out, among other things, the pipe, told them that the pipe was " good medicine," and instructed them to use it in a friendly way; to smoke it in making peace with their enemies. They think they are the first people who had the pipe given them. To make it very impressive, sometimes the left hand is held high above the head towards the sun or the zenith, as though clasping the hand of God.

The preliminaries to the talk and the smoke were usually determined by circumstances; the pressure of the necessity for an immediate peace often cuts all these short. If the two tribes had been at such bitter war that it was not safe to openly approach within speaking or signalling distance, some tobacco would be secretly left near the camp, or, in the absence of this, rude hieroglyphical figures would be drawn on the rocks, on a piece of par-flèche, or on bark, and left where it would be sure to be found. If the tobacco was taken, that was an open and sacred avowal of a desire for an interview, and negotiations were at once entered into. The inherited habits of many generations could not be wiped out by talking and smoking, and so the peace made between many tribes often only lasted during the existence of the absolute necessity which brought the two tribes together.

When the Sioux chief Crazy Horse came in and surrendered in 1877, he formed all of his warriors in line, in advance of the women and children; then, in front of this line, also mounted, he had some ten of his headmen; and then in front of these he rode alone. I had been sent with Indian scouts to meet him. He sent me word requesting a similar formation on our part, and asked that I should ride on in advance alone. Then we were to dismount and first shake hands, while seated on the ground, *that the peace might be solid.* After all this had been done his headmen came up, the peace-pipe was produced, and we solemnly smoked. One of his headmen put a scalp-jacket and war-bonnet on me, and presented me the pipe with which peace had been made. Some tribes, when they wish to say that the peace has not been kept, express it by saying "the pipe is broken."

Peak. Compress the right hand, and bring the ends of fingers and thumb as nearly together as possible, throwing the hand into as near a cone-shape as one can ; then hold the hand well out in front of body, hand well raised, and back outwards.

Deaf-mutes make the cone with both hands.

Pemican. Hold extended left hand, back down, fingers pointing to right, in front of body ; strike several times the left palm with lower edge of closed right hand ; then rub the hands together to denote the mixing ; then hold both hands, palms up, in same horizontal plane in front of mouth, little fingers touching, and blow on the palms. These gestures represent the pounding of the dry meat, mixing it, fat and lean, and after this fat is melted with marrow, blowing away the scum which rises to the surface of the vessel before the contents are poured over the powdered meat. In choice pemican great care is used in the selection of the meat when drying it, and a great deal of fat and marrow is used. This food is prized very highly, and, carefully put up in bales, remains sweet and good as long as it is kept dry. The Red River half-breeds deal in this extensively.

Pend d'Oreille. There is no well-established tribal sign. Some call them the "Boat or Canoe people" ; some indicate a large ring in the ear, and others often give for them the same sign as for FLAT-HEADS.

The custom of wearing especially large ear-rings, if it ever existed, has long since passed away. The custom of flattening the skull is not now practised, and tradition does not say when it was. Mr. Bancroft claims that it pertains to tribes nearer the Pacific coast, and agrees with Father Ravalli in locating the custom with the Chenooks. He says, "It is about the mouth of the Columbia that the custom of flattening the head seems to have originated. Radiating from this centre in all directions, and becoming less universal and important as the distance is increased, the usage terminates on the south with the nations which I have attached to the Chenook family, is rarely found east of the Cascade Range, but extends, as we have seen, northward through all the coast families, although it is far from being held in the same esteem in the far North as in its apparently original centre. The origin of this deformity is unknown. All we can do is to refer to that strange infatuation incident to humanity which lies at the root of fashion and ornamentation, and which even in these later times civilization is not able to eradicate. As Alphonso the Wise regretted not having been present at the creation, for then he would have had the world to suit him, so different ages and nations strive in various ways to remodel and improve the human form. Thus the Chinese lady compresses the feet, the European the waist, and the Chenook the head. Slaves are not allowed to indulge in this extravagance, and as this class are generally of foreign tribes or families, the work of ethnologists in classifying skulls obtained by travellers, and thereby founding theories of race, is somewhat complicated ; but the difficulty is lessened by the fact that slaves receive no regular burial, and hence all skulls belonging to bodies from native cemeteries are known to be Chenook. The Chenook ideal of facial beauty is a straight line from the end of the nose to the crown of the head. The flattening of the skull is effected by binding the infant to its cradle immediately after birth, and keeping it there from three months to a year. The simplest form of cradle is a piece of board or plank, on which the child is laid upon its back with the head slightly raised by a block of wood. Another piece of wood or bark or leather is then placed over the forehead, and tied to the plank with strings, which are tightened more and more each day until the skull is shaped to the required pattern. Space is left for lateral expansion, and under ordinary circumstances the child's head is not allowed to leave its position until the process is complete. The body and limbs are also bound to the cradle, but more loosely, by bandages, which are sometimes removed for cleansing purposes. Moss or soft bark is generally introduced between the skin and the wood, and in some tribes comfortable pads, cushions, or rabbit-skins are employed. The piece of wood which rests upon the forehead is, in some cases, attached to the cradle by leather hinges, and instances are mentioned where the pressure is created by a spring. A trough or canoe-shaped cradle, dug out from a log, often takes the place of the simple board, and among the rich this is elaborately worked, and ornamented with figures and shells. The child, while undergoing this process, with its small black eyes jammed half out of their sockets, presents a revolting picture. Strangely enough, however, the little prisoner seems to feel scarcely any pain, and travellers almost universally state that no perceptible injury is done to the health or brain. As years advance the head partially but not altogether resumes its natural form, and among aged persons the effects are not very noticeable. As elsewhere, the personal appearance of the women is of more importance than that of the men, therefore the female child is subjected more rigorously and longer to the compressing process than her brothers. Failure properly to mould the cranium of her offspring gives to the Chenook matron the reputation of a lazy and undutiful mother, and subjects the neglected children to the ridicule of their young companions, so despotic is fashion. A practice which renders the Chenook more hideous than the compression of his skull is that of piercing or slitting the cartilage of the nose and ears, and inserting therein long strings of beads or hiaqua shells, the latter being prized above all other ornaments.

Tattooing seems to have been practised, but not extensively, taking usually the form of lines of dots pricked into the arms, legs, and cheeks with pulverized charcoal. Imitation tattooing with the bright-colored juices of different berries was a favorite pastime with the women, and neither sex could resist the charms of salmon grease and red clay. In later times, however, according to Swan, the custom of greasing and daubing the body has been to a great extent abandoned. Great pains is taken in dressing the hair, which is combed parted in the middle, and usually allowed to hang in long tresses down the back, but often tied up in a queue by the women and girls, or braided so as to hang in two tails tied with strings."

In reply to some inquiries of mine, Father Ravalli wrote me a letter, from which I make the following extracts:

"Our three nations, Flatheads, Pend d'Oreilles, and Koutenays, never adored the sun, but, before the light of the gospel, they had their Monton or Medicine, some worshipping one kind, some another kind of small animals, and bringing them with themselves when travelling; so they had not any 'Sun-Dance.' They had, however, two kinds of dances particular to them, one called Estuenchy and the other Eftionly. The dance Estuenchy was performed only by men, and that before going to war, to excite themselves to battle. When they do that, all men, half naked and curiously tattooed and painted, gather in a great lodge, then singing the warrior song and beating the tambour or any noisy article in perfect time and cadence. With the song they do a little jumping, always remaining in the same spot. I have seen it several times, and it is truly electrifying and diabolical.

"The other dance (Eftionly) is performed only by the women after a victory in the battle. These women stand in circles in the centre, and the men make a peripheral circle concentric. Then the men beat the tambour and sing, and the women walk around and around, in slow progression, till this kind of dance is to an end.

"The inquiries here certainly have no reference to the actual manner of dressing of the Flatheads, Pend d'Oreilles, and Koutenays,—being the objects of our daily observation,—but rather to the manner of dressing before the coming of the whites, and in that I can say something, having been with them many years before the immigration altered their customs. Only to be better understood, we must observe that in the actual dressing of the Indians (Pend d'Oreilles and Koutenays have, and had always, identical dressing with the Flatheads) they wear generally not pants as the whites, but long stockings, protecting the legs and femurs, consisting of a hose, the upper extremity of which is overlapping to a string or belt at the loins. They wear also moccasins, and a blanket or a buffalo-robe, which is particularly characteristic of an Indian. What I remark here is a part of their ancient custom of dressing only, instead of artificial stuff they used skin for material. When I entered among them nearly forty years ago, besides the underlaying garment already mentioned, they had, men and women, over all, a kind of long shirt, simply composed of two skins, sewed in their longitudinal side by means of fibres and of tendons of the animals. Moreover, two small skins, connected at the proper place to the two big skins and wised in the shape of sleeves, covered the arms of men, and the women had the same thing as men but not sewed, and so loose as to be able to present the breast to their babies. The ornaments of men were generally a kind of necklace, made of various fantastic things, as claws of bears, feet of elk or human feet, little bundles of human hair from the scalp of their enemies, sea or river shells, and the like ; and always each man had a small mirror and a pair of tweezers hanging from the neck, and a knife at the left side. The mirror and tweezers they were using when encamped to pluck the points of the beard, and the knife for any occasional need, principally for skinning animals in their hunting. Ornaments of beads or grains of enamel, though they used them moderately, yet was a thing particular to women. The dressing of the women was longer, covering to their feet. At their waist the women had a belt, ornamented generally with brass buttons or with beads. They had short leggings, ornamented with beads, similarly were the moccasins ornamented.

"When first I came among the Flatheads there was the custom to gather in the lodge of the dead many old women and friends, and there was a lugubrious lamentation, or rather a wailing, according to a proper tune and cantillation. I believe it is yet observed in some camps of Nez Perces not Catholics. Now, having laid aside the custom, they gather in a lodge and pray all night, of course receiving there the night-meal. Some days after the burial the nearest relatives of the deceased congregate all the willing people of the tribe to pray in an appropriate lodge, and, after praying, they make a common dinner for all the people present. Moreover, they have a custom to distribute all personal property of the defunct to the poor, or to some other person in need, according to their notions, commonly retaining aside the animals, if any, in benefit of the children or nearest relatives.

"The Flatheads, Pend d'Oreilles, and Koutenays have the same customs, and being Catholics, bury their dead in a Christian manner. They pray and sing over the corpse, and bury it in a coffin, enshrouded and wrapped in the best blanket or richest garment the relatives can procure.

"To have an illustrated history and records of a nation supposes a degree of civilization and an advancement in the knowledge of its utility which cannot be dreamed of in the actual state of the Indians, in whom the knowledge of the existence of people of different color, of long afar habitation, of their number and doing, is dated only since our coming among them.

"I have, we have, oftentimes interrogated them to know whether they maintained some ancient tradition, but mine and our inquiries were always fruitless, as they are a people of the present moment, as every one may perceive from their actual manner of doing. They do not care for the past, and less for the time to come. Another point for which they have a kind of impossibility—to conserve records of their forefathers—was the continued wars with the neighboring nations, in which annually was a decimation. Regarding their number of men killed in battle, etc., no one conserved an oral history of their vicissitudes. To have from them any illustrated record it is evident that it cannot be, and the illustrations, which willingly I would have performed, were checked by our inability to obtain information from them of any kind about the things in reference.

"The hair of men, as that of women, was left growing, with the Flatheads, Pend d'Oreilles, and Koutenays, according to nature, only some men were cutting the hair before their front on account of the vision, others having a lock descending upon their nose, and the eyes were appearing between such lock and the hair of the temple.

"The Flatheads had their bows made with great accuracy. The Blackfeet and their associates had them bare. In fact, after choosing a proper branch from which to make the bow, and having split it and polished with stone and equisetum, they covered the back of the bow with the two sinews found near the spinal column of big animals, as buffalo, elk, etc. They glued them to it, by reducing the skin of fish to a thick jelly by boiling, and they completed the work by protecting all that with the skin of a rattlesnake or other serpent glued to it. Such operation, besides improving the appearance of the bows, contributed in a great measure to the elasticity and strength of the article.

"It is a real misfortune for the Flatheads that, partly from necessity, partly from stubbornness and love of liberty, they should continue the nomadic life as of old. The loss in their temporal and spiritual welfare is immense by such depreciated custom. But in the condition in which they are they must, by necessity, be well versed in the sign language, otherwise they could not have any conversation with the other nations when travelling. I am not acquainted with the manner of manual talking of the Sioux or Crows, but by a natural and obvious inference, I must say that the dumb language of all tribes must be the same for all, otherwise how would they understand each other?"

The head-chief, Michelle, informed me that they were not formerly called Flatheads or Pend d'Oreilles, but as they—the present so-called Flathead band—killed one another, they were called "know-nothing people." Kalespel (meaning good) people at present only includes the Pend d'Oreilles.

It is about one hundred and forty years since these Indians first saw ponies.

The vocal language is noticeable for the gl and cl sounds.

Polygamy has, through the efforts of the priests, been abolished. The women do not wear a protection string. The men usually bang the hair in front like the Crows, braid it on each side, and allow the portion at back of head to grow to its full length and to fall loosely.

Michelle, in speaking of their beliefs and customs, said to me, "The old, old people, a long time ago, believed that a good man—a chief —was in the far East, and they said that as he was good he took pity on them when they prayed to him. There was another old man in the far West, and they prayed for him not to see them. When the priests first came they asked us if we prayed, and, if so, to whom ; asked if we prayed to the sun, and we said, No ; we pray to a good man, a great chief in the far East. They told us not to do this, and instructed us to pray to other Gods and saints. In olden times we thought that after death, if we had been good, we went to the East, and if wicked, to the bad man in the West. Some five hundred years ago there was a man named Weosel, and he climbed a tree, and as he climbed the tree grew, until finally he was raised into the far heavens, and saw the world and people there. He came back, told his story, and died here. The old people said the good man of the East made the world, and everything in it. When the whites came they called this man a God, and said he was above ; but we knew all about this before they came."

At the time of the Nez Perce war, in 1877, there was great turmoil and intense excitement at this agency, and even the agent feared that his Indians might be persuaded to join their old friends, and so fearing was about to remove his wife and children from the danger, when Michelle went to him and said that he and his warriors would protect the agent's family from all harm, and if they left it would cast the shadow of an unjust suspicion on his friendship for the whites. The agent was so deeply impressed with the loyalty of the old chief that he concluded to trust the lives of his wife and little ones to the care of these Indians, and in telling me the story was visibly affected.

In this connection it seems proper to say that some fifteen years ago a white man, a miner, was killed some eight miles below Missoula, and the murder was attributed to the Indians. Michelle's son was found near the place the next day, arrested by the enraged whites and speedily hung. Before his death his father saw him, and the young man swore that he was innocent ; but his father told him that he could only be saved, or his death avenged, by a disastrous war with the whites, and asked him to sacrifice his life for the good of his people ; told him to go bravely to death. There was good evidence afterwards to show that the murder had been committed by members of another tribe, and that the boy was, as he claimed, innocent of the crime.

People. Push the extended index finger of right hand, back out, other fingers and thumb closed, out to front and right of body at different heights, index finger pointing upwards.

People are also represented, of course, by proper signs for men, women, and children.

Deaf-mutes form the letter P with each hand, and then raise and lower the hands in front of body.

Pepper. Make sign for FLOUR, for BLACK ; then hold extended left hand, back down, in front of body ; move the right hand, back up, over left in horizontal circle, rubbing tips of fingers and thumb as though sprinkling with pepper. Indians rarely use pepper, and I give the sign more to show how these gestures are coined than for its practical value.

Deaf-mutes make their sign for BLACK, and shake right hand, as though shaking pepper out of a box on something in front of one.

Perhaps. Conception : Two hearts. Bring side of right hand, at base of thumb, against breast over heart, back of hand up, first and second fingers extended, separated, pointing to left and front, other fingers and thumb closed ; by wrist action, turn the hand, so that back of hand will be about to front ; then back to first position, repeating motion. I have also seen both hands used. This sign is much used, nearly always when there is any doubt in the matter, and in making a promise to an Indian it is of vital importance, as it is next to impossible to explain a mistake (which they call a lie). A promise once made, however trivial it may be, should be kept most sacredly to the full spirit and letter. When it is desired to express many conflicting emotions, or many doubts, as to different plans of action, all the fingers and thumb of right hand are extended and separated, held in the above-described position, and the hand turned in the same way.

Deaf-mutes hold the nearly-extended hands, back down, in front of body ; lower one and raise the other like a pair of balance-scales.

Picket. (To picket animal.) Conception : Driving stake in the ground. Make sign for TIMBER ; then hold closed left hand, thumb up, in front of body, and strike it two or three times with closed right hand, imitating the motion of driving pin in the ground. This sign would, of course, mean driving any stake in the ground if used separately ; but would be understood from its connection ; *i.e.*, the signs for the animal, LARIAT, etc.

Piegan (Indian). Partially close the right hand ; *i.e.*, keeping backs of fingers from second joints to knuckles about on line with back of hand, ball of thumb resting on second joint of index ; hold the hand close to lower part of right cheek, back of hand to right, edges pointing upwards ; move the hand, mostly by elbow action, in small circle parallel to cheek. (See BLACKFEET.)

Pipe. Conception : From manner of smoking. Bring hands, backs down, in front of neck, left hand about height of chin and few inches from it, right in front of left several inches and a little lower, index fingers curved, others and thumbs closed ; move the hands simultaneously to front and downwards few inches ; repeat motion. Frequently only the right hand is used, and either left or right can be placed in front, where both are employed. Sometimes the hands are closed as though grasping the long wooden stem usually used by Indians.

Deaf-mutes indicate the shape, and then make a puffing motion with the lips. They sometimes indicate the long German stem with extended thumb and little finger of right hand, other fingers closed, carrying hand from mouth well down and slightly to front.

Professor J. D. Butler, of Madison, Wisconsin, states "that prehistoric pipes being found all over our country show dealings of all sections with Minnesota, being made of a red stone which, it is said, can be quarried only in or near one single county of that State, now fitly named 'Pipe-stone.'"

Mr. James W. Lind gives the following legend of the quarry: "The Pipe-Stone Quarry is a place of great importance to the Sioux. From it they obtain the red-stone clay—Catlinite—of which their pipes and images are formed; and a peculiar sacredness is, in their minds, attached to the place. Numerous high bluffs and cliffs surround it; and the alluvial flat below these, in which the quarry is situated, contains a huge boulder that rests upon a flat rock of glistening, smooth appearance, the level of which is but a few inches above the surface of the ground. Upon the portions of this rock not covered by the boulder above, and upon the boulder itself, are carved sundry wonderful figures,—lizards, snakes, otters, Indian gods, rabbits with cloven feet, muskrats with human feet, and other strange and incomprehensible things,—all cut into the solid granite, and not without a great deal of time and labor expended in the performance. The commoner Indians, even to this day, are accustomed to look upon these with feelings of mysterious awe, as they call to mind the legend connected therewith.

"A large party of Ehanktonwanna and Teetonwan Dakotas, says the legend, had gathered together at the quarry to dig the stone. Upon a sultry evening, just before sunset, the heavens suddenly became overclouded, accompanied by heavy rumbling thunder, and every sign of an approaching storm, such as frequently arises on the prairie without much warning. Each one hurried to his lodge expecting a storm, when a vivid flash of lightning, followed immediately by a crashing peal of thunder, broke over them, and, looking towards the huge boulder beyond their camp, they saw a pillar or column of smoke standing upon it, which moved to and fro, and gradually settled down into the outline of a huge giant, seated upon the boulder, with one long arm extended to heaven and the other pointing down to his feet. Peal after peal of thunder, and flashes of lightning in quick succession, followed, and this figure then suddenly disappeared. The next morning the Sioux went to this boulder and found these figures and images upon it, where before there had been nothing; and ever since that the place has been regarded as wakan, or sacred."

Though this stone undoubtedly furnishes the best material for Indian pipes, yet the Comanches, Utes, Bannacks, and Shoshones use a rather soft stone of greenish color. Whether they cannot obtain stone of sufficient size, or do not care for such large pipes, I do not know, but as a matter of fact their pipes are quite small.

The Utes, Bannacks, and Shoshones prefer and use cigarettes more than they do pipes, and the two latter smoke but little, usually after meals, and some of them only just before going to sleep. The stem of the medicine-pipe is usually decorated with porcupine-work, bright-colored skin of duck's head or neck, and a scalp-lock or horse's tail and some ribbons.

In explanation they say that all these articles represent things that are good to have; that they make the stem look well, and when they pray to God with a pipe, it is good to have these things to offer him. The skin of the duck is undoubtedly used on account of the association of this bird with the myth of creation.

The most mysterious pipe, or one possessing the strongest medicine, is that of "Elk-Head's," spoken of in the story of the White Buffalo.

Through all the stories and histories of the Indians the pipe has been the emblem of peace and friendship, and has always played an important part in their religious, war, and peace ceremonies. To smoke "the pipe of peace" was essential to the perfection of every compact of friendship or treaty entered into by these people, and they usually have a pipe made and used only for this purpose, the stem or tube being from two to three feet long, one half-inch in thickness, and from one and one-half to three inches wide, and decorated with duck-skin, eagle-feathers, brass tacks, horse-hair, etc. (See SMOKE.) A pipe captured from an enemy is highly prized.

The partisan of a war-party, in former times, was the pipe-bearer; but "Washakie," chief of the Shoshones, told me that on account of so much treachery being perpetrated it was finally abandoned.

In addition to the stone pipes the tibia of the deer and antelope were hollowed out at the largest end and used for pipes, but they were not very durable. The thick muscle at the neck of a buffalo bull or bull elk, twisted and dried, was also used for a pipe.

Pistol. Make sign for GUN, and hold up right hand, fingers and thumb extended; and left hand, thumb extended, fingers closed,—a "six-shooter." Sometimes the sign for GUN is made, then the length is marked off on left forearm with lower edge of right hand, left hand extended and slightly compressed.

Deaf-mutes denote a short gun, and then hold out right hand as though firing a pistol.

Pity. (To pity some one else.) Conception: Cry or shed tears for. Hold hands, palm downwards, in front of and near body, hands few inches apart, equally advanced and same height, index fingers extended and pointing upwards, other fingers and thumbs closed; move the hands outwards and slightly downwards, or towards person.

Deaf-mutes make gesture like Indian sign for "bless you."

Pity. (Sense of others taking pity on one.) Hold hands well out in front of body, as described above, but with backs out; bring them towards body, slightly raising them. When saying "God takes pity on one," hold hands higher than head, lower them when bringing towards body. This only illustrates what I have said in regard to position of place of person taking pity, etc. Some Indians make signs for POOR and LOVE, asking that such an interest be taken, that one shall be fond of them; and then, of course, action will be taken to relieve distress.

I have also seen signs made for "I am poor; give me something."

Plan. Make sign for WORK or MAKE, for SEARCH or LOOK, and for ROAD or TRAIL. A good plan or project is a good trail or road; it is easy to travel in it, etc.; and a bad one begets all sorts of trouble and distress.

Deaf-mutes touch forehead, and then hold tips of extended and separated first and second fingers on left palm, back of left hand down; the right hand is turned so as to give different position to the vertical fingers. (These latter probably are intended to indicate measurement with a pair of dividers.)

Plant. Make signs for CORN, for WORK, and then hold the compressed right hand, back up, near right shoulder; move the hand little to front, and then lower it (as though dropping seed in the ground); raise the hand, move it farther to front, and again drop it as before.

Deaf-mutes hold partially-closed left hand in front of body, and drop the compressed right hand into left from above.

Poison-Vine. Make sign for VINE, and then indicate that wherever it touches the body it *kills* the part.

Deaf-mutes indicate the vine, and then denote a swelling of the part touched.

Ponca (Indian). I have seen the forehead tapped with the right hand fixed as in ARAPAHOE, and I have also seen signs for "sitting-down soldier" and "shaved heads" made to denote them. I do not think there is any distinct and well-known tribal sign in general use by surrounding tribes.

The Poncas claim that the Omahas, Osages, Kaws, and two or three other tribes, a long time ago, lived with them and spoke the same vocal language. I could not trace definitely their migrations. Big Bull, one of the headmen, said his grandfather told him that in olden times, when the above-named tribes were with them, they lived near the Atlantic Ocean, and in their westward migrations became separated. They started on this movement from near Washington, District of Columbia, the Kaws and Osages coming across to Kansas, and the Poncas and Omahas going farther north, to Northeastern Nebraska. They claimed that the Poncas were at one time where the present city of St. Louis now stands. These several tribes have about the same customs, manners, and habits, and differ but slightly from the Pawnees. They call the sun God, and the earth Grandmother, and pray to both when making supplication. They formerly roached the hair, but after meeting the Plains Indians let it grow, and wore it like them.

There are five hundred and ten Poncas at the agency in the Indian Territory, and one hundred and twenty-five on their old reservation at the mouth of Running Water, in Northeastern Nebraska.

The agency buildings are located near numerous springs of fresh water, two and one-half miles from the mouth of Salt River, on a high mesa formed by a bend in the river. The buildings are new and in good condition. There are seventy-nine small log and board buildings, about twelve feet square, scattered out over the reservation, and near these ten acres of land have been laid out and fenced with wire and one board. The land was broken mostly by agency employés. The agency is well supplied with all that the Indians need in the way of agricultural implements. The soil is fine, the country a rolling prairie, well adapted to grazing, and if the rain supply does not fail, good crops can be raised.

Pony. (See HORSE.) The hardy little animal known as the Indian pony is justly entitled by its royal blood to all of the best qualities with which it has been accredited, viz., speed, endurance, and docility. The thoroughbred barb-horse, of kindred origin with the Arabian, cultivated by the Moors of Barbary, and introduced by them into Spain, was the animal brought to America by the early explorers ; also used by the Spanish cavalry which landed on the shores of Mexico with Cortes, Narvaez, and others, and sent as presents to the natives by the Spanish authorities. At that time horses were not gelded, and mares and stallions were used indiscriminately, and from this source are descended the wild horses of America, and the immense herds owned by the Indians. The natives, who were awe-struck and terrified by the sight of the first horse and discharge of the first gun, soon overcame their fears and greedily seized upon both. Lashed into the travois, and made to carry heavy burdens when very young, close in-breeding, and change of climate, all these have been potent factors in reducing the size of this horse, which, however, never was very large, though superior in this respect to the Arabian.

The English and Dutch who colonized the present Eastern States were poor. The French in Canada found the water-ways better suited to their purposes than the use of horses overland, but in the South, from Florida to California, climate and conditions were favorable for the reception and propagation of this animal. The present traditions of the Indian tribes are clear and positive in regard to the introduction of the horse among them, and so far as the great plains are concerned, what the railways have done for us this animal did for them ; in fact, it developed the Plains Indians. The average height of an Indian pony is a little over thirteen hands, weight about seven hundred pounds, clean flat limbs, small sound feet, fine nostrils, excellent eyes, and broad foreheads. Those in daily use with the Northern tribes become very thin and weak during the winter months, but quickly fatten on the early spring grasses. In winter, near the large villages, the grass is soon eaten off, even if the deep snow has not buried it beyond the reach of the pony's power of pawing, and then the animal is subsisted mainly on cottonwood bark, large trees being felled by the squaws for this purpose ; and when through fear of having the ponies stolen, or to guard against their straying off, they are picketed in the camp at night, each one is provided with a large bundle of limbs, and the bark from these sticks is cleanly gnawed off. This bark is very nutritious and healthy.

Poor. (Possessions.) Hold left hand, back to left, in front of body, index finger extended, pointing upwards and slightly to front, other fingers and thumb closed; bring right hand, back to front and upwards, little above and slightly nearer body than left, other fingers and thumb closed; lower and raise the right hand two or three times, mostly by wrist action, and as hand is lowered the sides of index fingers rub against each other. To emphasize, turn the left index by rotary motion, and press the side of right hand against it as it passes down. Here the left index represents a person standing, and the motion of right indicates that the clothing is rubbed off,—not removed, but torn away by the friction of ill fortune,—and this condition represents the poverty under which the person is suffering.

Deaf-mutes hold left forearm horizontally in front of body and clasp the sleeve on under side with thumb and index, dropping hand as though indicating that same was torn into strips or rags.

Poor. (Emaciated.) Conception: Flesh clawed off. Bring hands, palms towards body, in front of and close to breast, hands same height, fingers curved, edges horizontal; move right hand to right, left to left, curving fingers a little more. The hands are moved as though clawing off flesh from ribs; the flesh is scratched off by the claws of sickness or starvation.

Deaf-mutes "draw a long face," and pass the spread thumb and index of right hand down over cheeks, pressing them in slightly so as to add to the hollow cheeks.

Porcupine. Hold right hand, as explained, to represent size of animal, then make sign for HAIR, the fingers more elevated, back of hand resting on forearm. Frequently sign for SEW is made. Some Indians make signs for eating bark, for TAIL and SHOOTING, to denote this animal.

Indian tribes as far west as the Rocky Mountains used in former times the quills for garnishing moccasins, leggings, in fact, nearly everything that is worn. They have the art of staining the quills in many brilliant colors, and the work is not only beautiful but wears well. The quills were used about as lavishly as beads are at present. They were assorted and dyed by placing in fairly hot water which had been colored in some cases by ochre of the desired tint and a plant containing a great deal of resinous, sticky, gummy substance. This plant looks a little like sage, but has a yellow flower. The quills after being softened by the water are taken out, flattened, and are ready for use. The tail is used for a comb or stiff hair-brush.

Portrait. Hold left hand as in MIRROR, and make motion with right, as though sketching something on left palm with pencil, held by index and thumb.

All signs of this character are of course of very recent origin, and such articles being rare among them, would not be readily understood, and would usually require further explanation. The necessity for this is evident when it is remembered that this gesture is the same as the one for HISTORY ; it means a picture.

Deaf-mutes draw the crooked index of right hand down over centre of forehead and face, over nose. This for picture, and usually add signs for FORM for portrait.

Possession. Hold closed right hand, back to right, in front of neck and few inches from it, thumb extended and ball pressing side of index at second joint, and pointing upwards; move the hand slightly to front, at same time, by wrist action, turn it so that thumb will point to front, back of thumb up. Both hands are frequently used, the left being under right, its back to left, hands about in position of clasping and holding a stick vertically. Make the sign for person, and this sign added would express belongs or belonged to the person ; point to person and make this sign, would express yours, his, hers, mine, theirs, etc.

Deaf-mutes push the extended right hand, palm out, to front, fingers pointing upwards.

Powder. Hold extended left hand in front of body, back down, and rub tips of fingers and thumb of right hand just over left palm. (See GUNPOWDER.)

I once saw an Indian make motion with right hand, as though pouring powder out of a horn into left palm.

Prairie. Bring the little fingers of extended hands, palms up, alongside of each other, in front of body, fingers pointing to front ; separate the hands, carrying right well to right, left to left. Sometimes the extended right hand, back down, is held well in front of and lower than right shoulder, fingers pointing to front ; move the hand a few inches, mostly by wrist action, to left two or three inches ; repeating motion, as though cutting with edge,—all obstacles, hills, etc., are cut away. This is also the sign for BY ITSELF, and is used in free-gift, fainting, murder, accident, etc. Some Indians, after making sign for LEVEL COUNTRY, make sign for TREE and for No.

Deaf-mutes use the first-described gesture, holding backs of hands up.

Prairie-Dog. Hold the right hand well down in front and to right of body to denote height of animal ; then make sign for HOLE ; then hold partially-closed left hand, back out, in front of body ; bring compressed right hand from below up against left palm, and when thumb and index are above left index, snap them as in LITTLE TALK. This denotes the chattering noise made by these little animals. Sometimes after the height of the animal the right hand is bent back at wrist to indicate a little animal sitting on end, and then the sign for LITTLE TALK, made generally several times to denote the chirping.

The prairie-dog, owl, and snake live in the same hole. This little owl is called the dancing-owl by the Indians, and kills the snake by watching when he comes out of the hole, seizes him by the back of the neck and chokes him to death. The Arapahoes claim to have seen half-eaten snakes, and they also claim that the snake eats quite goodly-sized prairie-dogs, and about this they were very positive. They call the smaller species, found through the Rocky Mountains from the British to the Mexican line, the black-eyed or black-browed prairie-dog, in distinction from the larger species found on the Plains between the same lines. The difference in size strangely corresponds to the difference in stature of the Plains and Mountain Indians.

" The prairie-dogs, peaceable citizens and the only rightful owners of the homes which their own industry had provided them, are joined by two squatters,—the snakes and the owls. The dogs being socially disposed, not only allowed them to remain undisturbed, but in visiting each other at their respective homes, left their babies unprotected in their nests at home, not suspecting danger. The rattlesnakes, taking a mean advantage of their simple-minded neighbors, devoured one or more of the little innocents during their absence, and as prairie-dogs can't count, and as their families are usually numerous, they remain ignorant of the foul crimes daily perpetrated in their midst. The owl now appears as an actor in this little tragic drama. He feeds upon vermin, moles, etc. ; but I am informed upon reliable authority that this owl is also very fond of baby rattlesnakes, and returns the compliment of Mr. Snake for his kind attention to the prairie-dogs by eating up the young snakes; thus swift retribution is dealt to this base and ungrateful wretch, who so unworthily occupies his squatter's quarters in the burrow of the unoffending prairie-dog. I suppose the real truth is that nature has grouped them together so that they may prey upon one another, and thus prevent the too rapid increase of these troublesome animals."

The Arapahoes give four species of prairie-dogs : the two above mentioned,—*i. e.*, Plains prairie-dog, the one found in the mountains in the higher altitudes,—the marmot, and the large squirrels.

Pray. Indians make vocal petitions to the God or force which they wish to assist them, and also make prayer by pointing the long stem of the pipe. The Poncas call the sun God or Grandfather, and the earth Grandmother, and pray to both when making supplications. Running Antelope, a chief of the Uncapapa band of Sioux, said, in regard to pointing the pipe-stem, that the mere motion meant, " To the Great Spirit : give me plenty of ponies, plenty of meat ; let me live in peace and comfort with my wife, and stay long with my children. To the Earth, my Grandmother : let me live long ; hold me good and strong. When I go to war give me many ponies, and let me count many ' coups.' In peace let not anger enter my heart.''

The four winds towards which the pipe is pointed frequently are, first, to the southwest (place where ponies come from) ; second, to the southeast (place where there are many people) ; third and fourth, to the northeast and northwest, whence come deep snows and buffalo.

It seems a startling assertion, but it is, I think, true, that there are no people who pray more than Indians. The God or force to which they appeal is in their regard as omnipotent as all the forces of nature ; as invisible as music ; as indefinite and intangible as all space, and both superstition and custom keep always in their minds the necessity for placating the anger of the invisible and omnipotent power, and for supplicating the active exercise of his faculties in their behalf.

Deaf-mutes place the palms of extended hands together in front of body, fingers pointing to front and upwards, and incline the head.

Predict. There are naturally many ways of expressing this, as in the relation of the dreams and visions following the sweat-bath, the Sun-Dance, or prolonged fasting in solitude ; and then the signs for DISTANT, TALK, and GOOD would be made. (See well into the future.)

Frequently the sign for LITTLE TALK is made opposite and close to right ear, and then sign for DISTANT ; coming events cast not their *shadows* but their *sounds* before, and many Indians pretend at least to hear the whisperings.

Deaf-mutes hold extended left hand in front of face, fingers pointing to right ; carry right fixed as in SEE or LOOK under left. (Seeing under left hand, seeing things partially hidden.)

President. Make sign for WHITES, for CHIEF, for BIG or GREAT, and frequently point in direction of city of Washington ; or, make sign for SIT in that direction.

Sometimes the signs for chief standing high above all others in the East are made, and at times the right hand is swung circularly around, before the signs for BIG and CHIEF are made. (The big chief of all.) I saw among the Blackfeet the sign for ASHAMED made,—the idea seeming to be that he was too great a chief for one to look at face to face. I never saw this but once.

Deaf-mutes make their signs for CHIEF RULER and for UNITED STATES.

Pretty. (See HANDSOME.) Sometimes both hands are held in front of face, and then the sign for GOOD is made, as though face seen in a mirror.

Prickly-Pear. Form partial ellipse with thumb and index of right hand, other fingers closed ; hold this hand near the ground or floor, the plane of the ellipse being at an angle about such as the fleshy plant frequently assumes ; then with the extended index of right hand, other fingers closed, make one or two thrusts near foot, to indicate the action of the spines of the plant when one accidentally hits or touches it.

Priest. Conception: Black-robed. Make signs for COAT, carrying hands well down, and for BLACK ; usually sign for WHITES is first made. Very frequently called MEDICINE-MAN, and by some OLD MAN, establishing in this way a sort of kinship with the God who made them.

The Crows, Piegans, Bloods, Blackfeet, Koutenays, Pend d'Oreilles, Flatheads, and some others call the God who made them the "Old Man." This was explained to me, however, on the ground that, as he had been talked about for such a long, long time, they gave him this name to simplify matters and avoid descriptions. The black-robed, the white-robed, the long dress, the old man, and the man who talks to the medicine-chief in the sun or the heavens, are the names by which priests and ministers generally are known. For the Jesuits, sometimes the index fingers are crossed on breast.

Deaf-mutes make the sign of the cross on the breast, and touch the tips of fingers above head, hands extended, palms towards head.

Prisoner. Conception: Bound at wrists. Close the hands, and cross the wrists, in front of body, usually right resting on left, thumbs up.

Deaf-mutes use the same sign.

The Southern and Eastern tribes have in times past perpetrated many fiendish cruelties on their captives, but it must in justice be said of the Plains Indians that they have not, as a rule, tortured their prisoners,—I mean reserve them for death by torture; particularly has this been the case with the Sioux, Cheyennes, and Arapahoes.

In their inter-tribal warfare the men were killed at once, the women and children adopted into the tribe.

Private. (To talk to a person privately, secretly.) Hold extended left hand, back up, in front of left breast, fingers pointing to front and right; make sign for LITTLE TALK, under and close to left palm. This represents a confidential talk; the idea being that the conversation will be hidden away from the rest of the world.

Deaf-mutes close the right hand, thumb extended, ball pressing against second joint of index; place the back of thumb against lips, and then push the right hand under left, held as explained in the Indian sign.

Proud. This is used by Indians mostly in the sense of vain. Make signs for PAINT, DRESS, and after each sign for GOOD, and perhaps for FOND. (Fond of fine dress, vain of personal appearance.)

Deaf-mutes close the fingers of right hand, and pass the tip of extended thumb up over centre of breast.

Pueblo. Make sign for MEXICAN, for WORK or MAKE, for BLANKET, and STRIPED.

All the Pueblo Indians are called Mexicans who make the striped blanket. This is the general sign in the North.

Mr. Ben Clarke, the able interpreter and reliable scout at Fort Reno, Indian Territory, said in regard to this, "The Indians here have no sign for the Lipans, unless you include them in the same lot with the New Mexico Indians, south of the Utes, the Mescalero Apaches, and Pueblos; they make sign for tying hair behind the head for all of them."

Push. Firmly close the hands, and hold them near breasts, holding hands and forearms rigid; move them to the front as with an effort.

This gesture is also used for MUST.

Deaf-mutes use the same sign.

Q.

Quarrel. Hold extended index fingers, pointing upwards, opposite each other and several inches apart, in front of body, tips little lower than shoulders, other fingers and thumbs closed, back of right hand about to right, left about to left, hands equally advanced ; by wrist action move tips of index fingers, first right tip towards left index finger, then left towards right, repeating motions, and executing them sharply. This is also used for scolding ; the two fingers represent two people, figuratively speaking, flying at each other. Some make signs for TALK and BAD, and still other Indians use the sign for ABUSE.

Deaf-mutes hold the extended index fingers horizontally, tips about four inches apart ; the hands are moved to right and left, keeping same relative positions.

Queen. Make signs for FEMALE, for CHIEF, and BIG.

Sometimes they call the Queen of England the Great Mother, and of course make signs accordingly.

Quench. Make sign for FIRE ; then hold extended right hand, back up, over the point where sign for FIRE was made, and lower the hand ; then make sign for WIPED OUT.

This gesture is used metaphorically a great deal ; a disturbance or outbreak frequently being represented as a fire.

Question. See INTERROGATE.

Deaf-mutes point the extended index of right hand, other fingers closed, and then crook or curve same.

Quick. Make sign for HURRY.

Deaf-mutes make same gesture.

Quiet Down. Hold extended hands, backs up, in front of body, at about height of shoulders, fingers pointing to front ; lower the hands slowly.

Deaf-mutes use the same sign.

Quiver. Carry partially-closed and compressed right hand a little above and slightly in rear of left shoulder ; then move the hand upwards to front and right, as though drawing an arrow from a quiver supposed to be carried upon the back.

"The Pawnee bow-case and quiver are made of skin, dressed to be as impervious as possible to moisture. The usual material was elk-skin. Indians who could afford it sometimes made a quiver and case of the skin of an otter or panther. In removing a skin which was to be used for this purpose from the carcass, care was exercised that every particle of the skin—that of the head, tail, and even the claws—should be retained, and appear in the case when finally made up. Cases of this make, with their heavy coating of fur, were virtually water-proof, and were very highly prized." (*Dunbar.*)

Whatever fur or skin may be used for the arrow-quiver and bow-case, the hair is usually left on in tanning. The mountain-lion skin is prized most highly for war purposes. Extremely handsome ones are made by the Crows, mainly of otter, and that portion of the strap by which the quiver is carried, passing across the breast, being heavily beaded and fringed with ermine. This particular style of quiver is as much a specialty of the Crows as the blanket is of the Navajos.

R.

Rabbit. Indicate the height, and then make sign for JUMP, moving the hand on short curves, repeating motion three or four times.

Raccoon. Indicate height ; make signs for TAIL.

Race. Indicate what with, and then move the index fingers to front, as in EQUAL.

Deaf-mutes make their sign for STRUGGLE or EFFORT, and then sign like Indian gesture for FAST.

Racing is one of the standard amusements of all tribes, and so often and thoroughly are the horses and young men tested that their relative speed is known to within a few feet, but I never knew that any of their races partook of a sacred character until I received the following from Mr. E. L. Clark :

"There is a custom, however, still kept up among them (the Wichitas), which sometimes obtains credence with others, for being performed to produce rain, but which is really perpetuated through a belief that if the practice is discontinued their existence will soon come to an end,—a belief that is vitalized in the same way that other traditions are kept alive among the wilder tribes, such as the Sun-Dance, etc.

"This is their annual run or foot-race, of about five or ten miles distance, in which all their able-bodied men engage, and takes place every spring."

In their foot-races any advantage which one runner can secure over another by trickery is not only considered proper and fair, but is commended, and the same principle obtains in their pony-races, the latter of which are usually for short distances, four hundred yards being the favorite. The animals, as a rule, receive no special preparation, and rarely are any precautions taken in regard to feeding them before the race. The boys ride without a saddle, and if behind, usually whip from the first jump to the end of the course, legs and arms flying ; but his perfect seat, harmony of motion of horse and rider, does not allow this to interfere as much with the stride and speed as one would imagine or naturally expect.

Usually, whatever is wagered is placed in a pile at the winning-post, and very rarely is there any dispute over the result of the race, and at times so reckless is the betting that they are reduced from comparative wealth to abject poverty.

Railway. Make signs for WAGON, for FIRE, holding right hand in front of and higher than head, and then sign for FAST. Frequently only signs for WAGON and FAST are made.

Deaf-mutes indicate the iron rails and movement over same by holding extended and separated index and second finger in front of body, pointing to front, other fingers and thumb closed ; then bring right hand similarly fixed, and place tips of index and second finger on knuckles of index and second of left hand, back of right hand outwards, fingers vertical; move the right hand to front, tips of index and second passing over and touching backs of index and second of left hand.

Rain. Conception: Falling from clouds. Hold closed hands, backs up, in front of body, about height of head, the hands near each other, equally advanced and same height; lower the hands slightly, mostly by wrist action; at same time open, nearly extend, and separate fingers and thumbs; in this position fingers point about downwards; repeat motion two or three times.

An Indian once said to me that as the clouds settled they were pressed together and the water was forced.

Deaf-mutes make their sign for WATER, and then holding extended hands, backs up, in front of body, at about height of head; lower the hands, at same time rubbing tips of thumbs and fingers.

When I was at the Wichita Agency, in the Indian Territory, I was told some remarkable stories by a Mr. Spooner, the trader, in regard to the power of the Wichita and Caddo "medicine" for rain. He was an honest, sensible, practical man, reliable and trustworthy, yet the necromancy of these Indians had made a great impression on his mind,—so great, that it fell little short of conviction that they could really produce rain. His experience extended over several years, and on two or three occasions, after a drought, when it seemed as though the crops would certainly be destroyed, the Indians had gone through the religious ceremony of their Medicine-Dance for rain, and rain it did. Once he said he was specially impressed. For weeks there had been no rain, the earth was parched and burnt; the heat had been intense; day after day the same brassy, cloudless sky; when one evening, as the sun like a great ball of fire was sinking in the west, one of the Indians came to his store and told him that it was going to rain the next day. There was not a cloud to be seen, not a sign which indicated anything of the sort, and questioning the Indian, he ascertained that they had been having the Medicine-Dance for three days, and that afternoon their medicine-man had assured them that their prayers had been heard, and that it would rain the next day,—and it did.

I endeavored to investigate the matter, and meeting "Big Man," chief of the Caddos, asked him about it. He pointed out the place where they had their medicine-house for rain, and explained that it was only used for the purpose of bringing rain through their dance, which was a religious ceremony, in the efficacy of which they had perfect confidence. "Big Man" was suspicious, and refused at first to tell me anything of the ceremony (I was conversing with him in gesture speech), saying he was afraid of me. They have been forced to give up so many of their superstitions, so many of their beliefs have fallen before the aggressive warfare of the advocates of the Christian religion, that he feared they would be forced to give this up if he explained it to me; and having perfect confidence and absolute faith in its power to bring rain, one can readily understand how reluctant he would be to take any chances against its loss. I succeeded in gaining his confidence, and he briefly said that some thirty or forty men gathered and danced under the immediate supervision of the medicine-man, each one having a rattle filled with red beans, and the dancing continued from four to six days. The squaws brought cooked provisions for them, and the supply was, as a usual thing, very bountiful, and was usually brought before the dancing commenced. He said this dance was similar to the one practised by the Wichitas for the same purpose.

At Fort Berthold I was told the following story in regard to rain, elicited by my question as to who they thought made the rain:

"Long, long ago there was a famous Gros Ventre hunter. He prided himself on the great amount of game he killed, and if a day passed without some success on his part he was sad and dejected. His fame was very great. One day, after killing a large amount of game, he lay down and fell asleep. The four eagles—golden, bald, spotted-tail, and brown—seized him and carried him to the Thunder-Bird's nest, which was on a high bluff with perpendicular sides of rock. He tried in every way to find a trail down, but failed. In looking for the trail he discovered the young eagles and young Thunder-Birds, who told him why he had been brought there, viz., 'That an immense snake, with two heads and long horns, came from the adjacent lake and ate them.' The eagles returned, confirmed the story, and asked him to kill the snake. One foggy day the snake came as usual, and expected to have a feast of the young birds, but the hunter fired his arrow at it, and wounded it, and then, with a long knife he had, he cut it in two parts, and then each of these into four, and then, at the request of the eagles, he cut these parts into small pieces. Then they called all the birds of the air there for a feast, and at this feast he discovered that the birds made the rain."

Rainbow. Make signs for RAIN, for FINISHED; then pass the right hand, back up, above head, parallel to arch of heavens. Some Indians also make sign for MEDICINE, and say it belongs to the rain and thunder. Some tribes call it the Great Spirit's fish-line, and say it is "big medicine to drive away the rain." It is also called "the rain's hat." Some tribes have vulgar names for it. If seen in the east, it is considered as a sign of bad weather; in the west, good.

Deaf-mutes use spread thumb and index to "span the heavens."

Rapids. Make sign for STREAM or RIVER, for ROCK, and then hold right hand, back up, near breast, fingers extended, separated, and pointing to front and downwards; move the hand swiftly to front and downwards, giving it a tremulous motion, mostly by wrist action.

Deaf-mutes indicate water (not deep), and by a wavy, tremulous motion of hands indicate the current.

Rash. Make sign for FOOLISH or CRAZY. Some indicate it by saying, "A person went along without looking." This amounts to the same thing, as an Indian would be considered crazy who would do this.

Deaf-mutes indicate careless or foolish bravery. For *careless* they pass the right hand from right to left in front of forehead, index and second finger extended. For *foolish* the little finger and thumb are extended.

Rattle. Hold the closed right hand in front of and higher than right shoulder; shake the hand as though holding and shaking a rattle.

The rattle is made from gourd-shells, birch-bark, par-flèche, etc., and from four to ten inches in diameter. The handle is short, usually about one foot in length. Inside the gourd, or whatever is used, are inserted small pebbles, bits of deer-hoof, or something that will make a sound. The Plains Indians use mostly the rattle made of untanned skin, and attached to the handle is a scalp or buffalo-tail, or the long hair from the forehead of the buffalo. The rattle is not ordinarily used in dances, but possesses a sacred character, and is used mostly by the medicine-men, and to such an extent in sickness that it might fairly be considered the doctor's badge of office. The noises made are certainly disagreeable enough to drive away anything or anybody that could go; and disease being a malign spirit that has invaded the body, the Indian doctor rattles, gurgles, and shouts till the spirit leaves.

Rattlesnake. Make sign for SNAKE; then hold right hand in front of right shoulder, index finger extended and pointing upwards; shake the hand, and give a sharp vibratory motion to index. Frequently a hissing sound is made to imitate the noise made by the rattles.

Deaf-mutes make their sign for SNAKE, and then hold right forearm horizontally in front of body; place left hand near elbow, left index extended and pointing upwards, other fingers and thumb closed; give a vibratory motion to left index.

Ravine. Indicate the cut banks, or describe the character of the formation.

Reach (To). See ARRIVE THERE.

Recover. Hold right hand, back up, in front of right breast, index finger extended and pointing to left and front; raise the hand, at same time turn it, mostly by wrist action, back to front and index pointing upwards; one is near death by disease; this is used to denote the recovery; one is in great danger, barely escaped. The gesture is also used to denote the fact that one lives, and is used metaphorically in regard to the remainder left after spending a part of one's money.

Deaf-mutes indicate a flow of blood and rip palms of hands.

Red. Conception: Paint used on the face. Rub the right cheek with palmar surface of first joints of fingers of right hand, fingers extended, touching, pointing upwards; circular motion of hand.

Deaf-mutes touch lower lip with tips of fingers of right hand.

Refresh. Explain the cause and make sign for RECOVER.

Relieve. Explain in what way. To illustrate: suppose a sentinel on a butte, and you are ordering one out to relieve him, point to or make sign for person, and signs for GO and BLUFF; with left hand for ARRIVE THERE; right hand moved out to left for TELL or TALK, for SOLDIER, for SIT, holding left hand as in BLUFF and right resting on left; for arrive or come here, point to or make sign for person, for SIT, and for SEARCH or LOOK. This would order a person to go out to the bluff, tell the soldier there to come in, and for the person to stay there and look, or watch the country about the bluff.

The manner in which our troops are sometimes posted as sentinels or pickets is a matter of amusement and derision to Indians. A vidette is placed on the highest point near camp and marches up and down his "beat" regularly, and can be easily seen by these keen-eyed people miles and miles away; they don't have to be close enough to recognize the dress, the movement is sufficient; it is a man, and surely no one but a white man, for an Indian would only have his head above the crest of the hill, and even that concealed by some brush, rock, tree, or tuft of grass.

Our method has one advantage. If any one is lost from camp, he has a good landmark to find his way back, and this is the best that can be said of it.

Remain. Make sign for SIT. Sometimes, but not often, the sign for WAIT is made.

Deaf-mutes close the fingers of both hands and extend the thumbs; then cross the thumbs, placing ball of right on left thumb-nail.

Remember. Make signs for HEART and for KNOW. Frequently the sign for KEEP is made in such sentences as, I will remember; I want you to remember.

I have also seen the signs for NOT LOST and HEART KNOWS BY AND BY made.

Deaf-mutes place palmar surface of extended fingers of right hand on forehead, and then cross thumbs as explained under REMAIN.

Repeat. Make sign for OFTEN.

Deaf-mutes make sign for AGAIN, and repeat same; for AGAIN, they place the tips of fingers of right hand, held partially com-pressed, on left palm, latter held in front of body, back down.

Restrain. Make sign for HOLD and for KEEP QUIET.

Deaf-mutes hold left hand well in front of body, clasp it with right, and draw it back.

Retreat. Indians or troops driven back; or warriors charge and repulse, etc. The attack is indicated as in CHARGE, and then the hands are turned, mostly by wrist action, so that fingers point to rear, and the hands moved quickly or slowly according to the nature of the retreat. With Indians a scattering is also usually indicated.

Deaf-mutes denote the marching of soldiers by holding hands in front of body, fingers extended, separated, and pointing downwards, one hand few ir ches behind the other; the retreat is indicated by moving hands to rear. They also sometimes make their sign for OVERCOME.

Rich. There is no one gesture ; must be explained. To say that one had many ponies would express riches, however.

Deaf-mutes indicate a great deal of money.

Ride. To ride an animal, hold hands as in HORSE, and then move hands to front on short vertical curves.

To ride on a *wagon* or other *vehicle*, make sign for same, and then sign for SIT on left palm ; extended left hand held in front of body, fingers pointing to front.

Deaf-mutes use the same signs.

The Comanches and Utes are considered by many Indians the best horsemen, and the Nez Perces and Cayuses as having the best or fastest ponies. The Southern Indians perform more daring and difficult feats on horseback, and are more expert in the use of the lasso than the Northern. Nearly all Indians I have seen use very short stirrups in ordinary riding, but on an emergency not only strip themselves, but ride their ponies "bare-back" ; this not only in fighting, but in swimming dangerous streams, etc. In covering long distances, such as with war-parties, etc., a fast, "scuffling" walk or slow trot are the usual gaits, making about five miles an hour, and a halt made at noon, the animals unsaddled, and turned out to graze, or picketed close by the little fire made for cooking.

Ridge. Bring closed hands, backs out, close together (edges touching) in front of body, hands about height of shoulder ; separate hands, moving right to right, left to left. Sometimes one extended hand is used, held in front of body, forearm and index finger horizontal.

Deaf-mutes use the same sign.

Ring. (Finger.) Hold extended left hand, back up, in front of body ; touch back of one or more of the fingers, just in front of knuckles, with tip of right index, other fingers closed.

The hands could change position. The exchange of a ring between the sexes has at the present time a very strong and tender significance. The men seem even more fond of wearing finger-rings than the women. I have been told that special importance has been given to rings since they have had intercourse with the whites. A young man may be going to war, meets his sweetheart, tells her he is going away, and says, "I want to marry you when I come back from war," pulls off a ring and gives it to her, and if she receives it the action signifies her consent ; and when he is away, by looking at it she is reminded of her absent lover.

Rising Man. Make sign for or point to person ; then hold left hand, palm nearly outwards, in front of body, about height of neck, index finger extended and pointing upwards, others and thumb closed ; bring extended index of right hand alongside of the left, but lower, other fingers and thumb closed ; raise the right hand slowly, right index pressing lightly against side of left. The right index represents the "rising man," and frequently the left some well-known man of eminence; he being mentioned, and the gesture showing that the other was attaining an equal, if not greater, eminence. Sometimes the right index is raised by itself, then sign for BY AND BY and CHIEF made.

River. Conception : Water flowing or moving. Make sign for WATER ; then from this position carry hand little to left of face, close to it, and height of neck, index finger extended and pointing to left, other fingers and thumb closed ; move the hand to right until about opposite right shoulder, keeping index horizontal. This means any stream of water.

Deaf-mutes make their sign for WATER, and then indicate its flow by passing extended right hand from left to right in front of body.

Road. (Wagon.)   Make sign for TRAIL and for WAGON.   Some Indians add sign for WHITES, and I have seen the backs of the hands up in TRAIL.

Deaf-mutes hold the hands several inches apart, palms towards each other, fingers pointing to front, in front of and close to body ; then move the hands to front.

Rock.   Make sign for HARD.   Sometimes indicate shape.

Deaf-mutes hold the closed left hand, back up, in front of body ; close the right hand, and with second joints strike two or three times the knuckles of left hand.

Images are carved on the sandstone rocks by some of the medicine-men, and the kind and groupings of the figures are suggested to them in a dream or vision. They sometimes repair to the rocks, and remain seated and lying on top for four nights and days fasting, —neither water nor food during this time,—and if blessed with a vision of some special remedy to cure disease, or the location of the camps of their enemies, and if afterwards by a happy use of the remedy satisfactory results ensue, or the war expedition is successful, the images receive a rude worship ; and in some cases sacrifices and gifts are made to them long afterwards as the Indians pass by. A famous rock of this kind is located on Painted Rock Creek, near the Big Horn Mountains, a stream emptying into the Big Horn River. The fissures of the rock and the ground near its base are strewn with beads, bits of clothing, etc.,—gifts or sacrifices for good luck.

At times this same practice obtains near old battle-grounds where a signal victory was secured, and figures carved on the rock receive the same sacrificial worship.

Rope. Hold hands as in AFTER, then, as right hand is drawn to rear, by wrist action, make tip of index describe a spiral curve.

Deaf-mutes bring left hand, back up, in front of body ; place as nearly as possible the second finger on back of index, its tip rather hooked on to the tip of index.

Rose-Bud. Hold partially-curved and slightly-compressed left hand, fingers little separated, back to left and front, in front of body, index finger horizontal and pointing to right and front ; bring right hand similarly fixed to right and front of left, and make motion with right as though picking or pulling off berries from tips of fingers of left hand.

Rotten. For wood, make motion of striking it, and then sign for DUST or POWDER. For rotten meat, indicate smell, etc.

Rough. Same as BAD LANDS, without making sign for CUT BANKS.

Deaf-mutes move the right hand on short curves to front, to indicate the rough surface.

Run (To). Make signs for WALK and for FAST; or hold hands, backs about outwards, in front of body, with right nearest to it, index fingers extended, right pointing to left, left to right, other fingers and thumbs closed, tip of right index opposite base of left; raise right hand, and carry it to front briskly, right index passing horizontally above left; when beyond it, lower right hand slightly; as right hand stops, carry left to front similarly, and bring right back to its first position, right index passing under left as it is brought back; repeat motion two or three times. The wrists are held a little loosely, so as to give a vibratory motion to index fingers as the hands stop; the hands stop rather suddenly; in fact, the motions are executed briskly by jerks.

Run Against. Hold extended left hand, back out, well in front of body, fingers pointing to right; hold extended right hand, back about outwards, near body, fingers pointing downwards, knuckles height of left index; move right hand out briskly, back of fingers of right hand striking sharply against left palm and inner surface of left fingers. This is used to represent both mounted and dismounted persons running against anything; to denote also a falling off or over, make above sign, and then sweep right hand outwards beyond to right, and lower than left, turning palm up, and fingers pointing to front.

Deaf-mutes hold extended left hand well in front of body, back out, fingers pointing to right; the extended right hand, back to right, fingers pointing to front, is thrust out so that tips of fingers strike left palm.

S.

Sabre. Make sign for LONG KNIFE, and sometimes add motions for drawing sabre from scabbard.

Deaf-mutes make this latter sign.

Sac (**Indian**). Make sign for SHAVED-HEAD.

This branch of the Algonquin family, known as the Sac and Fox tribe, formerly occupied the central and eastern portions of Wisconsin. The coalition of the two bands is known to have taken place as far back as 1712, and perhaps long before that. By intermarriage and other influences they have coalesced, and can now only be considered as one band or tribe. Their wars with the Chippewas were, like all family quarrels, of an intensely bitter and savage nature. Their relations with the Sioux to the Northwest were those of both peace and war,—the latter predominating in later years. With the Winnebagoes they were generally at peace. Forced to the Southwest from Fox River by their enemies, they occupied the Rock River Valley until 1804, when they ceded that country to the United States by treaty, but with the proviso that they could use it for hunting-ground until it was needed by white settlers. It was to regain possession of this valley that the Black Hawk war of 1832 was undertaken. This war was inaugurated by the murder and mutilation of their agent, a Mr. St. Vrain, at Rock Island, where they then had their agency. The Indians had promised to move and remain west of the Mississippi, but in the spring of that year Black Hawk moved his entire village to the east side, and announced his intention of planting corn in the valley of Rock River,—the announcement undoubtedly being meant as an excuse for his action. Messages had been sent to the Chippewas, Iowas, Sioux, Winnebagoes, and other tribes, and though they sympathized with the uprising, yet none but the Winnebagoes became entangled in the war and suffered by the subsequent defeat. In 1820 they occupied the Mississippi Valley between Prairie du Chien and Rock Island. There is now a small remnant in Iowa and a few in Nebraska, but the majority of the tribe are in the Indian Territory, having gone there under the treaty of 1867. Their agency is located on Deep Creek.

Though the soil in the bottom-lands there is rich, yet the uncertainty of rain and consequent frequent failure of the crops has been very discouraging to those Indians disposed to engage in agriculture. They have, however, made some progress.

Keokuk, the present head-chief, a son of the old chief Keokuk, was born at the mouth of Rock River in 1825. He has adopted the "white man's road," lives in a small brick house, has a white woman for a wife, possesses a goodly herd of cattle and cultivated fields, wears citizen's dress, and has so far progressed in Christianity that he occasionally preaches in the little chapel at the agency. He claims that his tribe learned the sign language from the Plains Indians, and that vocally the Kickapoos, Shawnees, Ottawas, Pottowattomies, Chippewas, Menominees, Sacs and Foxes, all speak about the same tongue, with some slight dialectical differences, which do not prevent them from understanding each other.

About the creation he said, "God made the Sacs out of yellow, and the Foxes out of red, earth."

They now bury their dead in the ground much after the manner of the whites, though they formerly placed the remains in a sitting posture.

They have one annual Medicine-Dance, usually held just after the budding of the leaves in spring, and to participate in this one must, with much ceremony, be initiated into the medicine-lodge.

At the death of a member of the fraternity a dance is held, and an election takes place to fill the vacancy.

The agent, in his report for 1881, gives the population of this tribe as four hundred and forty, and thirty-two of the Missouri Sacs and Foxes.

Sacred. See MEDICINE.

Sacred Arrow. Make signs for ARROW and for MEDICINE.

Some of the tribes claim that their God appeared in person, and gave them, among other things, arrows. These they kept most sacredly, and handed them down from father to son for many generations. Nearly all these arrows are now gone, being swept away by the vicissitudes of war and the trials of their nomadic life. Only a few years ago the Cheyennes had a sacred bundle which contained these arrows. The myths and traditions of the Plains Indians all seem to show that they believed there was a time, and not so very many generations ago, when they did not have the arrow to kill game with ; but these stories are all silent as to how they did kill it.

Sad. Conception : Heart laid on the ground. Make sign for HEART, and then sweep the hand from this position to the right, front and downwards, turning palm up, and partially compressing the hand, as though the heart were physically laid on the ground.

Deaf-mutes hold palm of right hand near face, fingers extended, separated, and pointing upwards; lower the hand slightly, at same time partially close it, and incline head.

Saddle. Hold both closed hands, forearms vertical, several inches apart, in front of body, hands equidistant from body and about height of shoulders, back of right to right, left to left, hands same height; bring the elbows nearer each other, and at same time, by wrist action, bend back the hands, right bent to right, left to left, so that backs of hands are nearly downwards.

Deaf-mutes indicate the animal and shape of the saddle.

Saddle (To). Make signs for ANIMAL, for SADDLE, for first part of SADDLE BLANKET. Sometimes signs are made to denote the fastening of girth, but not often.

Deaf-mutes imitate motions of grasping saddle and throwing it on animal's back.

Saddle Blanket. Make sign for BLANKET; then hold extended and slightly-compressed left hand, back up, in front of left breast, fingers pointing to right and front; hold right hand similarly fixed, but with fingers pointing to front and left, to right of and a little lower than left hand; carry right hand on curve upwards to left and downwards, and place its palm on back of left hand, hands at right angles. If a pad or piece of skin is used instead of blanket, of course it would be indicated by proper signs.

Safe. I have never but once seen a gesture to express this state or condition. It is, however, such a good one that I give it: Hold nearly-extended left hand, back down, in front of body, and place tip of extended right index, held vertically, in centre of left palm, other fingers and thumb closed. This would hardly be generally understood; the particular circumstances why safety was doubtful would have to be explained. The gestures for WORK or MAKE, for BAD and NO, would be understood, and would indicate that no harm would be done to a person.

Sage. Conception: Growth of bushes in bunches. Hold compressed right hand, bringing tip of thumb and tips of fingers near each other, in front of right shoulder, height of breast, back of hand down, fingers pointing upwards; move the hand to front, right and downwards; then resume first position, and lower it in another place.

There are several species of sage, and in some sections the bush grows sufficiently large to make very good fuel. The tridenta and a smaller white species are used for making a tea, which is administered in fevers, and used for fumigating. There is also one species which, by rubbing between the palms of the hands, emits a pungent smell, and is said to be excellent for producing wakefulness. It is used by Indian scouts in passing through an enemy's country, where sleeplessness is the price of success.

It is also believed by some tribes that the white species, fastened to the poles of a tepee, will preserve the lodge from being struck by lightning. For this reason, and its well-known medicinal properties, it is held in the hand in the religious ceremonies called the Sun- and Medicine-Dances.

I have been told that sage-tea possesses some of the properties of absinthe.

Salt. Touch the tongue with tip of extended right index, other fingers and thumb closed, and make sign for BAD. Sometimes the tips of finger and thumb are rubbed as in PEPPER, and sign for WHITE made.

Deaf-mutes hold left hand, back up, in front of body, index and second fingers extended, touching, and pointing to front, other fingers and thumb closed; with right hand similarly fixed, tap or strike the backs of index and second fingers of left with palmar surface of index and second fingers of right hand.

The Plains Indians have not generally acquired the taste or liking for salt, and use but little, and so far as I have been able to learn, they never used any substance of a similar character for seasoning their food.

Same. See EQUAL.

Deaf-mutes hold right hand, back up, little finger alone extended, in front of right breast ; then move hand over to front of left breast, advanced at same distance from body as first position.

Sans-Arc (Sioux Indian). Make signs for SIOUX, for BOW, and for WIPED OUT.

This French translation of the Sioux word for this band has clung to them with rather singular tenacity. Several stories have been told me as to the manner in which they first received the name. In the segregation of the larger Indian nations, made necessary by their manner of subsisting themselves, it was a matter of convenience to name the sub-tribes and bands, and this name usually resulted from some accident or peculiarity pertaining to the chief or the band. It is claimed by many that a long number of years ago a sub-chief started out with a war-party against the Crow Indians, but before reaching the Crow camp they were surprised by their enemies, routed and stampeded, and in their fear and flight threw away their bows, not having fired an arrow. In consequence they were ever afterwards called " No Bows." Speaking of this, an old Indian stated to me that one time long ago this band were suddenly deserted by all their dogs, and as this was before they had any ponies, it was a very serious matter. The medicine-man informed them that the dogs would return if they would place their bows on the tops of the lodges. This was done, and the dogs did return; but being suddenly attacked by their enemies, they did not have time to get their bows, were forced to flee without them, and were, in consequence, called " No Bows." (See SIOUX.)

Satisfy. There is no one special sign. The sign for GOOD would ordinarily be made ; though the gestures for AN ABUNDANCE OF PONIES are sometimes used. (See EATEN ENOUGH.)

Saw. Imitate the motion of using the instrument.

Deaf-mutes use the same sign.

Scalp (To). Point to scalp-lock, and move the left hand out to front and downwards, as though grasping hold of object (scalp); make sign for CUTTING UP, under left hand held in this position.

I made a special investigation in regard to this custom among the following tribes : Cheyennes, Arapahoes, Sioux, Comanches, Kiowas, Apaches, Wichitas, Pawnees, Sacs and Foxes, Otoes, Iowas, Kickapoos, Utes, Blackfeet, Bloods, Piegans, Arickarees, Gros Ventres, Mandans, Shoshones, Bannacks, Nez Perces, Pend d'Oreilles, Koutenays, Caddos, Poncas, Shawnees, Seminoles, Chippewas, Crows, Gros Ventres of the Prairie, and Assinaboines, and in no case could I find that there was any superstitious belief or fancy that scalping a person in any way detrimentally affected his soul after death.

The custom of taking scalps grew out of and became necessary because of false claims made to the honor of killing their enemies.

It is simply a proof of the killing; evidence beyond cavil or doubt; and no superstition exists that by scalping or other mutilation the progress of the spirit towards the happiness of life after death is thereby interfered with. The error of the very general belief that such is a part of an Indian's religion has probably been perpetuated by the fanciful statements of unreliable men, and the daring deeds performed by Indians to keep the bodies of their fallen comrades from falling into the hands of their foes. These actions arise from the fact that bravery of this kind always brings a man's courage into bold relief; his action is observed by many; and the natural desire all human beings have of saving the remains of comrade, friend, or kin from mutilation. It should be distinctly understood that however mutilated a person may be who has been killed in, or who dies from the effect of wounds received in battle, he (as an Indian said to me) "goes by the most direct and easiest trail through a country rich in the freshest grass and purest water to the Happy Hunting-Ground." (See MILKY-WAY.)

The Blackfeet Indians claim a sacred origin for the custom (see BLACKFEET), and I have heard the Cheyennes say that there was a scalp with the medicine-arrows given them by their God, and that in consequence it was also a religious duty to take the scalps of their enemies; but even these admitted that the main objects were to obtain proofs of the killing, and to give their friends the pleasant opportunity of glorifying the deeds of the warriors and to dance over the scalps of their fallen foes.

I was told that the leader of a war-party among the Mandans was in former times entitled to the hair of the scalps taken by the party to adorn a scalp-jacket, and at his death the jacket was buried with his remains; so that a war chief took with him his insignia of rank beyond the grave. Many tribes have used scalps to decorate their shirts and leggings, but they must be for each individual scalps of his own taking. As they expressed it, " When a man was dressed in this way he wore his badge of bravery,—of courageous deeds performed; he walked a chief."

In former years the Sioux Indians, if they had time, cut off the heads of their slain enemies and took them to their first camp after the fight, where the entire scalp was taken off. To make it particularly fine, they kept on the ears with the rings and ornaments. In case a woman had lost some of her kin by death, and her heart was, as they say, "bad," she was at times allowed to go with the war-party, remaining in the camp made near the point of attack. The head of a slain foe would be given to her, and, after removing the scalp, she would make her heart "good" by smashing the skull with a war-club. Hands would be also cut off and taken to her; these she dragged on the ground, with a rope, back to the main village.

In olden times—in the days of the bow and arrow—there were very many hand-to-hand combats, and then many Indians were scalped and not killed. It is claimed that the Fort Berthold Indians had near their village what were called "scalped men's houses." These men were disgraced, and were not allowed to be seen in the main camp or to live with their families; but I could not absolutely confirm this.

Scalping is not necessarily fatal. Mrs. Jane Johns was scalped by the Seminole Indians in Florida and survived. The attending physician, Dr. Welch, states, "I measured the extent of the skull divested of natural integument, which was from the upper part of the forehead (leaving at its commencement only a few hairs) to the occiput nine inches and one-half, from above one ear to the opposite side nine inches."

On the 28th day of April, 1868, Thomas Cahone and Willis Edmonston, freight conductors of the Union Pacific Railway, were fishing in a small stream near Sidney, Nebraska. They had no arms. Indians had been coming and going about the place, and no danger from them was anticipated, or even thought of. The terminus of the road was at Cheyenne. There was a small company of infantry at Sidney, under command of Lieutenant (now Captain) Bubb, U. S. Army. Suddenly a small party of mounted Sioux swept down on the fishermen, in plain sight of the post and the town. The Indians had just before tried to run off a small band of horses, and been foiled in the effort by the herders and others, who fired at them. The Sioux had separated into two parties, one going down the track near which the men were fishing, the other circling after the stock. There was no escape for the men, as they were caught between the two parties. The Indians used only arrows, but riding up alongside of these men, they put eight into and through Cahone, one of which passed entirely through his body; it entered under the point of the right shoulder-blade, and the point of it protruded an inch or two from his breast. Four arrows were fired into Edmonston. Some of the arrows going through Cahone's lungs, caused a great flow of blood, and he fell on his right side. The Indian in advance dismounted and took his scalp proper; the second one cut off the scalp from the left side about seven by four inches. Edmonston was not scalped. The soldiers and citizens hurried out, and the Indians took to flight. The wounded men were brought in to the station, where the arrows were cut out. The one that went through Cahone's body was easily enough extracted, the arrow-head being cut off and the shaft pulled out. The rest were more difficult, but were extracted. At no time did Cahone lose consciousness, and he told me that when he was being scalped he closed his eyes, and expected each instant to have his skull crushed, or feel the knife plunged into him. In October last I met him near Ogden, as the passenger conductor running east, and he informed me that he was in excellent health; that he now never suffered from his wounds or from the scalping. Edmonston was the passenger conductor at this time running west from Ogden. Cahone was twenty-five years of age at the time of his wounding and scalping, and had served during the war of the Rebellion in a Pennsylvania regiment.

Scalp-lock. Touch with tips of fingers of right hand the top of the head, just back of the crown. (See HAIR.)

Deaf-mutes use the same sign.

The majority of the Plains Indians braid that portion of the hair contained in a circle, about two inches in diameter, at the crown of the head. The braid is formed of three strands, and the circle is marked by pulling out the hair, and this little circular path is painted, usually with red ochre. The hair of the head is parted in the middle, and the parting extends to this circle. The scalp-lock seems meant to be a mark of manhood and defiance, a sort of "take it if you dare and can" idea. It is marked out and braided when a boy reaches the age of about five years, and covers the space called the crown or curl of the hair, so that any one can readily tell when he sees a scalp whether it is genuine; *i.e.*, only from this portion of the head. Mr. Dunbar says of the Pawnees that the heads of the men were close-shaven, except the scalp-lock. This was 'dressed as before described. (See PAWNEE.) The beard and eyebrows were kept carefully pulled out. The instrument used for this purpose was a spiral coil of wire, about an inch in diameter and two inches long. It was held closely against the face, and by pressing the coils together the hairs were caught and pulled out. Much time was spent in this work, and great pains taken to prevent the beard or eyebrows from showing at all. The hair of the women was allowed to grow long, and usually hung in two braids at the back. The part of the hair was kept smeared with vermilion, especially by girls and young women. Men, and women also, sometimes wore a handkerchief or other cloth tied about the head like a turban.

Mr. Charles H. Beaulieu, the gentlemanly and accomplished clerk and interpreter at White Earth Agency, writing me in regard to scalping, said, "I learn that when the troubles first commenced between the Sioux and Ojibways, disputes among Ojibway braves arose about personal bravery, and in many instances arrant cowards claimed to be brave, therefore it was made a proof of bravery to take a scalp, four pieces from a single head being a limit, or four persons taking scalps from one head, the 'choice cut' being the topknot, and all ranking according to the order in which each of the four removed his portion of the scalp. These persons were mentioned in the Scalp-Dance song, and were thenceforth looked upon as braves and leaders, and to be depended upon in times of danger.

"The cutting off of the head, mutilating the bodies, and removing the scalps of slain foes seemed also to irritate the relatives of those killed."

Scarce. Make sign for WHERE. This indicates only here and there one. Sometimes the sign for WIPED OUT is also made.

Deaf-mutes make their sign for FEW, opening the hands very slowly.

Scatter. Hold the closed hands, backs up, near each other, and close to breast; move right hand well to front and right, left well to front and left; at same time extending and separating fingers and thumbs.

Deaf-mutes use the same sign.

Scent. Make sign for FRAGRANT, usually omitting sign for GOOD. Deaf-mutes pass the palmar surface of extended fingers of right hand over and close to nose and mouth, from above down, fingers pointing to left.

School-House. Make sign for HOUSE, for WHITES, for LOOK, fingers pointing towards left palm, and for KNOW.

Deaf-mutes clap left palm with right, both hands extended and at right angles, and then make sign for HOUSE.

I was particularly struck with the importance of, and the possible results which might be achieved by, sending Indian children to school when I was visiting the Pawnee Agency, Indian Territory, where the following notes were made:

"*Friday evening, April* 29, 1881, 11 P.M.—I attended a so-called 'collection' of the Pawnee students this evening; Rev. Mr. Heyworth presiding. The agent and teachers were present, and some one hundred boys and girls, attentive and bright looking, with hair cut short and wearing citizen's dress, were in the room. They sang 'Hold the Fort,' 'Sweet Bye and Bye,' and several other hymns quite well; with a metallic nasal twang to be sure, but they entered into it with spirit and evident understanding of the sentiments conveyed by the words, and their pronunciation was good. Treaty obligations require the Pawnees to keep their children at school from seven to seventeen years of age. The Government has not kept to its part of the obligation entered into. The buildings cannot accommodate all, in fact, not more than one-third of the children at the boarding-schools; but the prospect to-night seems quite fair and bright for these little people to make a rapid advance along the 'white man's way' in the near future. The start is made early enough to do some good. The breech-cloth and blanket, and all the habits and customs that go with them, are discarded before the damage is done, before their characters are formed; in brief, before they acquire the art of being expert barbarians. Instead of learning to take advantage of every little knoll, ravine, or tuft of grass to creep up on game; instead of learning how to shoot and ride, and becoming fondly attached to all these ways of barbarism, they are learning how to take care of themselves, how to conduct the affairs of life on a higher, better, and more prosperous plane than did their ancestors. Clothed and fed at the school, the impressions received there will abide with them during their lives, and there are enough of them to have some influence on the entire tribe. Eastern schools take them after their characters are formed. They may cut off the hair, abandon paint and wear citizen's dress, but their hearts long for the days when they were happy little children tumbling about an Indian camp; so when they get out of school they go quickly back to the old pleasures; the old longings overcome them, the hair grows, the paint appears, the breech-cloth is tied on, the blanket is wrapped about them, the pony is mounted, and the deprivation of all this for a length of time only lends a keener pleasure, and we have a savage only sharpened and brightened by his association with the whites. Eastern institutions could follow boarding-schools at the agency, just as our colleges do the common schools scattered all over our land, without which we should ourselves soon be in the embrace of barbarism.''

Scold. Make signs for QUARREL or ABUSE, or for TALK and BAD.

Scout. Make sign for WOLF.

Great care is taken in the selection of the young men who are sent out to gain and bring in information of the movements and condition of the enemy, or of the location of game; and, if there is time, many ceremonial forms are gone through with in the selection and in giving instructions to them prior to their departure. The essential qualifications of a good scout are courage, good sense, truthfulness, and a thorough knowledge of the country.

Suppose four are wanted. They are selected in council, and then sent for; some of the headmen going for them, and leading them to the council-lodge, where, after much solemn and prayerful smoking, perhaps some speeches about the importance of the occasion,—dilating on the benefits that will accrue to the entire people in case of success, and the evils and disasters that may befall them through defeat,— the special instructions for the service to be required, as well as the general instructions which all Indians know by heart, are given them by the chief. These general instructions are usually to the effect that they must be wise as well as brave; to look not only to the front, but to the right and left, behind them, and at the ground; to watch carefully the movements of all wild animals, from the movements of buffalo to the flight of birds; to wind through ravines and the beds of streams; to walk on hard ground or where there is grass, so as to leave no trail; to move with great care so as not to disturb any wild animals; and, should they discover anything important, to return with all possible speed and bring such information as they may find.

Frequently before starting the medicine-man makes medicine for them,—prayers and sacrificial worship to the sun, moon, Thunder-Bird, rivers, bluffs, and winds. The sun and moon are to furnish light, the Thunder-Bird is to spare, the rivers to offer no impediment, the bluffs to furnish points of observation, and the winds not to blow harshly; all nature is asked to assist.

Of late years, in addition to their arms, the scouts carry a mirror and field-glass, which are furnished by friends if they do not themselves possess them. One or two only are sent in the same direction, —a larger party could see no more, and its size alone would increase the danger of discovering them to the enemy. The safety and value of a scouting-party lies not in their fighting qualities, but in their keen-eyed, crafty, shrewd cunning and watchfulness.

Suppose the scout is seen returning, his story is nearly told by his movements or by his mirror long before he has approached near enough for vocal communication. If, when he is near enough for the sound of his voice to be heard, he imitates the howl of a wolf, he has seen the enemy. The main party meanwhile gather in an incomplete circle, with the opening towards the direction from which the scout is coming, and at the opening place a pile of buffalo "chips," or spread out a blanket upon four sticks. When the scout reaches them, if the enemy is too close, or immediate action is necessary, so that there is not time for the story to be told in the ceremonial way, he kicks down the blanket or scatters the chips, as an oath that he is telling the truth, and briefly and hurriedly tells his story. If there is time for a smoke, the pipe is filled, lighted, and the interrogator points the stem to the zenith, sun, earth, and four winds, and then holds the stem to the scout's mouth, who takes four whiffs; again the pipe is pointed as before, and again four puffs are taken by the scout; this is repeated four times, when the interrogator says, "You know all the hills, valleys, and streams in this country; you were born and grew up in it; now tell us what you have seen."

The scout divides his story into four parts, which are told at intervals. At each interval the smokes are repeated, and the interrogator adds, perhaps, to his question, "Tell us, and your people will have glad hearts; they will praise you, and raise your name up among them." On the completion of this ceremony the entire story is usually told continuously without interruption.

This is, as I have said, the custom when there is plenty of time. Usually the return of a scout sent on in advance of a war-party creates the wildest excitement, and all forms and ceremonies are ignored or forgotten.

Scout (To). Make sign for WOLF; then bring right hand, back up, well in front of body, about height of lower part of face, first and second fingers extended, separated, and pointing to front, other fingers and thumb closed; mostly by wrist action turn the hand so that these fingers will point to right, to left, and downwards.

Some tribes use the extended index fingers, others and thumb closed, of each hand, backs up, one held parallel to and little in rear of the other. If left were in front it would be advanced several inches more than right, and about four inches to left.

We have in these gestures, first, the sign for WOLF, then sign for SEE or LOOK, then looking or searching in different directions, and on the ground for trails, etc. Descriptive gestures usually accompany the above, such as going on ahead, creeping up to the crest of hills, etc.

Deaf-mutes hold the partially-closed right hand well out to right and front of body; then move the hand to left on small curves. This more in the sense of *searching* for something.

As I have stated under TRAIL, Indians are bred up to trailing, scouting, and horse-stealing, until, like game-dogs, their natural and instinctive powers are wonderfully increased.

The object of scouting is to see and not be seen. An Indian, if mounted, carefully and slowly rises to the crest of every hill, and by a keen, searching, sweeping glance takes in all the country stretched out below and beyond him.   In ascending, if mounted, he dismounts just before reaching the top, and rises to the crest behind some rock, tree, or tuft of grass, and in going between divides, he moves as rapidly as possible.   In bivouacking, if it be not considered necessary to change camp after dark, the scouting-party moves over an eminence before going into camp, then any one who may be following their trail will naturally be exposed to view before reaching the camp.   Should a fire be used, and it is feared that it may expose them to the enemy, it is made of dry wood, which burns with little smoke, and in a ravine, so that what smoke is made will be dissipated before it reaches the altitude of the sides; and then after dark the party moves on and camps without a fire.   Unless well away from the enemy and confident of their ground, they do not build fires. (See Scout, Trail, and Lead.)

Search. See Scout.

Season. The usual nomenclature for the seasons is Winter, Spring, Summer, Fall,

Deaf-mutes indicate three months cold, three months growing, three months hot, and three months falling leaves.

The particular season is also frequently denoted by the condition of something in nature which reaches a particular state about the same time each year, such as grass large, buffalo bulls fat for summer; late in the summer, choke-cherries ripe and buffalo cows fat; fall, plums ripe and leaves fall off; late fall, first snow.   (See Moon.)

See. Bring right hand, back up, well in front of lower part of face, first and second fingers extended, separated, and pointing to front, other fingers and thumb closed.   The hand can, of course, be held a little to right or left of body, and the fingers should point in the direction one is represented as looking.   Some tribes use both hands as I have explained under Scout, and sometimes before either gesture the tips of fingers touch eyes.

Deaf-mutes hold right hand in front of face, back out, index and second finger extended, separated, and pointing upwards; move the hand to front.   They make a difference between *see* and *look;* Indians do not.

Indians are certainly remarkable for power and keenness of vision, which are inherited qualities, and they are greatly aided in detecting the presence of game by their intimate knowledge of the movements and habits of animals.

Seize. Move the open hands out in front of body, close them suddenly, and draw them in briskly towards body, as though seizing hold of an object.   Sometimes the left forearm is held vertically, and the right hand clasps wrist and draws the arm to right.

Deaf-mutes use the same signs.

Sell. See Exchange.

Deaf-mutes raise hands in front of body, as though holding up a piece of cloth for exhibition.

Separate. Hold the hands, backs up, near each other or touching, in front of body, index finger extended and pointing to front, other fingers and thumbs closed; by wrist action turn the hands, so that right index points to right and front, left to left and front; move the right hand to right and front, left to left and front.

Deaf-mutes bring the closed hands together in front of body, back of right to right, left to left; separate the hands, carrying right to right, left to left.

Sergeant. Make sign for WHITES, for SOLDIER, and then with index of right hand mark the position, extent, and number of stripes on the arms. Instead of this latter, sometimes the signs for LITTLE and CHIEF are made.

Sew. Hold extended left hand, back to left, in front of body, fingers pointing to front, thumb extended, its back a little lower than side of index and pressing against it; bring tip of extended right index just over thumb, index pointing to left, other fingers of right hand closed, thumb extended, and its inner surface pressed against inner surface of index; move the right hand slightly to left, and by wrist action turn back of index down, so that nail of right index just touches side of left index as it passes it; repeat motion two or three times, moving right hand trifle to front each time.

A small bone from near the ankle of a deer was formerly used as an awl in sewing; other bones which were capable of taking a high polish were also used to make holes in leather, through which the sinew was drawn. I have heard it stated that porcupine-quills were also used for the same purpose after being filled and stiffened.

Shackle. Lean forward and clasp the ankles with the hands. Deaf-mutes use the same sign.

Shadow. The shadow of a person is represented by making sign for person; then hold right hand, palm to front, little to right and slightly to rear, and higher than right shoulder, fingers separated and pointing upwards; lower the hand with a wavy, tremulous motion. Sometimes make sign for SUN on one side, and then outline the object on the other.

Deaf-mutes make a sign very like that made for darkness, and then indicate a drawing off from left palm with right hand.

Shake Hands. Clasp the hands in front of body. Some hold forearms vertical and lock the fingers. I have been told by the Indians that they in former times only clasped hands on concluding a treaty, making peace, or other matters of a similar nature and great importance. The most of them now in their intercourse with the whites observe the custom, but not among themselves.

Sharp. Make sign for whatever instrument one may wish to speak of; then hold extended right hand, back down, in front of right breast, fingers pointing to front; touch lightly the lower edge of right hand with palmar surface of ball of left thumb, as though testing the edge of a tool, and then make sign for GOOD.

Deaf-mutes hold left hand, back up, in front of left breast, index and second finger extended, touching, and pointing to front; with right hand similarly fixed touch lightly side of left index with palmar surface of index and second of right hand; right hand suddenly drawn back to right.

Sharp's Rifle. Conception: Movement of breech-block. Make sign for GUN; then hold extended and slightly-compressed left hand in front of body, back of hand to left, fingers pointing to front, thumb extended and pressing against index, forearm horizontal; bring nearly-closed right hand just under and touching left wrist (as though grasping the lever which moves the breech-block); move the right hand downwards and outwards.

Shaved-Head. Bring the back of extended hands, fingers pointing to rear and slightly upwards, alongside of head; move the hands downwards as though cutting hair with lower edges of hands. Frequently only right hand is used. This is the general sign for all those more Eastern tribes who formerly shaved or burned off the hair, except a tuft near crown.

Deaf-mutes extend the thumb and little finger of right hand, close the other fingers, and make motion as though shaving head with side of thumb.

Shawl. Make sign for FEMALE, and then sign for BLANKET.

Deaf-mutes indicate size and shape, and then make motion as though throwing same around the shoulders.

Sheep. (Mountain.) Conception: Horns. Compress and slightly curve the hands; bring them in front and above the head; carry them on vertical curve parallel to and close to sides of head, hands passing just back of and stopping a little below the ears, backs of hands towards head. The hands pass on curve similar to that made by the horns of the sheep.

Softened by boiling and steaming, dishes were formerly made from the horns of the mountain sheep, and even now some Indians will not eat out of any other dish, believing it would bring them bad luck. The horns were also split and made into bows; this required great skill and much labor, but a very superior bow was made in this way.

Sheep. (Domestic.) Make signs for MOUNTAIN SHEEP, for WHITES, and for WITH. Sometimes curly hair is indicated, as well as the operation of shearing.

Deaf-mutes indicate a shearing motion with index and second fingers of right hand over left forearm.

Sheep-Eaters (Shoshone Indians). Only a few years since there were found in the Rocky Mountain region, between parallels 42° and 47° north latitude, Indians who lived at some of the highest points of these mountains. They subsisted mostly on mountain sheep, and on this account were called "sheep-eaters."

They were supposed by many authorities to be a separate tribe, differing in language, habits, and physical peculiarities from all the tribes which surrounded them, while others claimed that they were offshoots from the Shoshones, Bannacks, Flatheads, Pend d'Oreilles, Nez Perces, Crows, and Blackfeet, and that their poverty alone forced them to this peculiar life apart from their tribe. Of course, all the tribes living near the mountains where the big-horn are found devote more or less time to hunting them, but a careful investigation among the tribes named has convinced me that the sheep-eaters proper were Shoshones, and I think their origin as a separate band was due to the invasion of the Blackfeet from the North. (See SHO-SHONE.) Seeking refuge from their enemies in the mountain fast-nesses, they discovered new ways of living, and adopted the peculiar habits of life which characterized them. They dressed in furs and skins long after other tribes near them had obtained blankets and clothing from white traders, and they dwelt among the rocks and in caves. In this they did not differ greatly from the rest of the Sho-shones and Bannacks, as these tribes were noted among the surround-ing Indians for their miserable lodges. Long after their own and other tribes had ponies, the "sheep-eaters" apparently made no efforts to secure them, and they also exhibited a corresponding lack of enterprise in obtaining fire-arms. In hunting the big-horn they used dogs. The sheep, on being pursued by the dogs, fled to the high and isolated points, and were then approached to within close range by the Indians, and killed by the bow and arrow. There are quite a number of these Indians at the Shoshone Agency, Wyoming ; at Fort Hall and Lemhi Agencies, Idaho ; but they have now adopted the customs and ways of living of the bands they are with. In physique, mental qualities, and religious beliefs they are and always have been very much like the Shoshones.

Shell. Conception : Neck ornament. Shells worn as ornaments are represented by forming an incomplete circle with curved thumb and index of right hand, space of about an inch between tips, other fingers closed ; bringing the hand in front of breast, little finger resting against centre, back of hand to left and downwards.

For shell, generally, the partially-compressed hands are brought together in front of body, sides of thumbs and lower edges of hands touching and pointing to front ; mostly by wrist action turn the hands as though hinged at lower edges.

Deaf-mutes hold left hand in position above described, make a strike downwards past and close to left palm with lower edge of right ; then bring hands into the position explained, and turn in same way.

Shield. Form an incomplete circle with curved index and thumb of right hand, space of about two inches between tips, other fingers closed ; hold left forearm horizontally in front of body, pointing to right and front, left hand closed ; place little finger of right hand on left arm, just above elbow, back of hand nearly to front, plane of incomplete circle nearly vertical, as though the shield were hanging on left arm. Sometimes the circle is formed with index and thumbs of both hands, and the hands held to left of left breast.

In the days of the bow and arrow and spear the shield formed an indispensable part of a warrior's equipment. Made from the un-tanned thick skin of a buffalo bull's neck, and usually of double thickness, it was a great protection; and in addition to the physical power of resistance, they were frequently accorded supernatural qualities. When in camp, they were hung on a pole to the east of the lodge, or cluster of tepees, as a charm to ward off danger or harm.

With the introduction of the modern long-range breech-loading rifle, and the consequent uselessness of shields, sentiment and superstition concerning them have nearly passed away. Some few camps still have them, perhaps one or two in a band or tribe, but they are no longer carried in battle, and are used solely for the good luck they may bring the camp.

Indians are quick to adopt new and improved weapons, and equally prompt in abandoning worthless impedimenta.

Shoe. Make sign for MOCCASIN and WHITES.

Deaf-mutes thrust the right hand, as far as the knuckles, into the partially-closed left, left clasps right.

Shoe (To). Make sign indicating the animal to be shod; then hold closed left hand, back to left, in front of body; strike with the lower edge of closed right hand, back down, the second joints and exposed palm of left hand several times, as though driving in the nails to fasten on an iron shoe to the foot, left hand representing the hoof of the animal.

Deaf-mutes make their sign for SHOE, and then indicate the nailing on in a similar manner.

Shoot. Hold nearly-closed right hand, back up, in front of breast, nails of first three fingers pressing against palmar surface of thumb; move the hand outwards, very slightly downwards and little to left, at same time extending and separating fingers and thumb with a snap. (See also HEAVY or VOLLEY FIRING.)

Many Indians make a difference in the gestures for the firing of a gun, and the discharge of an arrow from a bow. For the latter they hold the hands as in Bow, and after separating them, extend the index fingers with a snap; then to indicate an object as hit by the arrow, the extended left hand is held well out in front of left breast, fingers pointing upwards, and the right index thrust out and passing between fingers of left hand. (See DEAD-SHOT.)

Deaf-mutes hold hands as though aiming a gun, and then crook right index as though pulling the trigger.

Nearly all Indians are good shots, and though a "team" for long-range target-firing could not probably be found at even the larger agencies without special instruction and practice, still they would make an excellent record against game or any moving objects. In firing from their ponies when at full speed they are, at times, wonderfully expert.

Short. Hold slightly-compressed right hand, fingers pointing upwards, to right and front of body, hand at height desired to be represented.

Deaf-mutes hold hand, back up, fingers pointing to front.

Shoshone (Indian). Hold the right hand, back to right, in front of right shoulder at about height of waist and near it, first and second fingers extended, touching, and pointing to front, others and thumb closed ; move the hand several inches to front, and, by wrist action, give a wavy, sinuous motion to extended fingers. Frequently only the index finger is extended. I have also seen signs made for BAD or BRUSH LODGE to denote these people.

The Shoshone or, as they are usually called, Snake Nation formerly occupied with the Bannacks an immense geographical area, including what is now known as Southeastern Oregon, Idaho, Western and Southern Montana, the northern portion of Utah, Nevada, and Western Wyoming.

In my investigations I was unable to ascertain positively why they were called Snakes, but one of their old men claimed that it was because they formerly ate serpents. I consider these Indians inferior, physically and mentally, to the Plains Indians proper, or to the Nez Perces north of them. Many of the bands living in the interior formerly had only the rudest kind of lodges,—at times only a pile of sage-brush to shelter them from the wind,—and they subsisted on reptiles and insects, in fact, whatever they could find alive, and such roots, seeds, and berries as grew on the alkaline deserts and in the mountains. With them rabbits were considered large game. Some of the bands living near the streams and lakes abounding in fish subsisted mostly on them, and they exhibited some skill in the manufacture of grass nets, and still others were energetic enough to secure ponies and hunt large game. With this nation is first found the deification of the wolf and coyote. In former times it is claimed that on account of their myths and superstitions in regard to these animals they did not kill them. Such is not the case now, and when pressed by want it is doubtful if they ever held any animal as sacred.

In their myth of the creation, the Gods who created them and instructed them in the ways of life are represented as two brothers, the Wolf and Coyote. The cohabiting of the Wolf with a fair young girl, whose creation, however, they do not take the trouble to explain, produced the Snake and Bannack nations. They locate definitely the den where the Wolf and his brother, the Coyote, lived, and claim that their tracks, leading from a spring of water to their den, can yet be seen in the solid rock. They are represented as possessing all the attributes of humanity as well as having supernatural powers. All that is good, from a Shoshone stand-point, they created, and all their ways of living are the direct result of these Gods' special and personal instruction.

The men of the Shoshone nation are below medium height. The women are also short in stature, with round faces, and for Indian women have rather well-rounded limbs and plump bodies; they allow the hair, which they part in the middle over the head, to fall loosely down on the face, usually cutting off the ends squarely. They do not wear a protection-string. The men wear the hair in all kinds of styles, imitating the Crows, Flatheads, and Sioux. They are not as much given to wearing armlets and other charms as many other tribes. They keep no account of individual ages. Their tradition

22

of the first white man seen by them evidently refers to the party of Lewis and Clarke in 1804, who found them near the source of the Jefferson Fork of the Missouri River. They secured their first ponies from their kinsfolk the Comanches. They claim to have first had smallpox, and to have lost many of their people by the disease, about the time they first saw the whites, and that large numbers have been swept away by it since then. They do not use porcupine-work in garnishing robes, moccasins, etc.

They have waged a defensive warfare for a greater number of years than their traditions reach to with the Blackfeet, Sioux, Cheyennes, and Arapahoes, and with the tribes immediately surrounding them they have been at both peace and war. What is known as the Washakie band broke with the Utes in 1834, over a dispute in regard to some stolen ponies, and only within the last few years have they had any friendly relations since that time.

The agent's report for 1881 gives in Idaho, at Fort Hall, eleven hundred and twenty-eight Shoshones and five hundred and two Bannacks; at Lemhi, seven hundred and seventeen Shoshones, Bannacks, and Sheep-Eaters; at the Shoshone Agency, Wyoming (Washakie band), eleven hundred and fifty; and in Nevada, at the western agency, thirty-eight hundred; making a total population of seven thousand two hundred and ninety-seven.

Sick. Hold extended hands, backs out, in front of and close to breast, hands in same vertical plane, space of about two inches between ends of fingers of right and left hand, fingers of right hand pointing to left, left to right; move the hands outwards few inches several times, mostly by wrist action. This represents throbbing, and of course, to locate the sickness, hold hands similarly fixed over the affected part, palms towards and parallel to it.

Deaf-mutes place the left hand on the breast, and incline the head forward, resting forehead on the right hand.

The general idea of sickness among the Indians seems to be that an evil spirit has entered the person, and that when it is exorcised all will be well. The efforts of the medicine-men are principally directed towards casting out this malign and mysterious presence.

Sign Language. Hold extended left hand, back up, in front of body, fingers pointing to front and right; touch the back of fingers with palmar surface of extended fingers of right hand; then hold extended right hand, back up, fingers pointing to left and front, and touch the back of fingers with palmar surface of fingers of left hand; then make sign for TALK.

Deaf-mutes make their sign for TALK.

I have, in the introductory, given my views in regard to the origin of this language,—stated something as to its extent and use. The gestures—the motions of hands and arms I have described—only coldly outline the force and expression which this vehicle of communicating ideas is capable of.

The human countenance speaks in the most exquisite shades of significance; "the soft, silent wooings of love, the frantic fury of hate, the dancing delirium of joy, the hungry cravings of desire, the settled melancholy of dead hopes,"—all these emotions are vividly pictured. The blanched cheek and skulking figure may express at times a wonderful amount of fear and cowardice, while a noble bearing, flashing eye, and determined expression of face may exhibit a dauntless courage. A haughty, cold, and cruel manner may convey more scorn, contempt, and hatred than could be expressed in words, while a glance, a smile, a tender pressure of the hand may convey a whole world of sympathy and love. The gestures I have described only, as I have said, awkwardly outline the picture ; the coloring and beauty and force of expression must be filled in by the manner of making the signs.

I found, in my special investigation, that the evidence of the Indians as to its existence or non-existence in other tribes was not worthy of implicit confidence. Many of them stated to me that in former times this language was the one common and universal means of communication between all the tribes of American Indians who spoke different vocal languages. As they expressed it, " the *old people* of all the tribes used it."

Little Raven, the former head-chief of the Southern Arapahoes, said to me in regard to the use of gestures, " I have met Comanches, Kiowas, Apaches, Caddos, Snakes, Crows, Pawnees, Osages, Mescalero Apaches, Arickarees, Gros Ventres, Nez Perces, Cherokees, Choctaws, Chickasaws, Sacs and Foxes, Pottawattomies, and other tribes, whose vocal languages, like those of the named tribes, we did not understand, and we communicated freely in sign language. The summer after President Lincoln was killed we had a grand gathering of all the tribes to the east and south of us. (Little Raven was at his agency near Fort Reno, Indian Territory.) Twenty-five different tribes met near old Fort Abercrombie on the Wichita River.

" The Caddos made a different sign for HORSE, and also for MOVING, but the rest were made the same by all the tribes."

From personal investigation, I found subsequently that some of the tribes named had scarcely any knowledge of the sign language used by the Arapahoes. The Kickapoos, Shawnees, Otoes, and Iowas, as well as the Caddos, Delawares, Wichitas, and others, claimed to have learned such gestures as they used from the Plains Indians.

Chief Joseph, of the Nez Perces, said that his tribe learned the language from the Blackfeet some forty years ago, and yet it is a well-known fact that these Indians used gesture speech long before this time. Nichelle, chief of the Pend d'Oreilles, said, " All the tribes talk in signs when they meet, if they cannot understand each other's vocal language. The Blackfeet, Crows, Flatheads, Koutenays, Pend d'Oreilles, Cœur d'Alenes, Spokans, Nez Perces, Yakinus, Pelouses, Cayuses, and others, all make the same signs. When I was a young boy, my grandfather told me that a long, long time ago, when two tribes met who did not speak the same vocal language, they always talked in signs."

Father Ravalli, whom I met at Stevensville, rather confirmed this, as he informed me that some thirty-five or forty years since he prepared a work on the sign language, and claimed its extensive use when he first came among these people. (See FLATHEAD.) And still there is no doubt but that the Chenook jargon, compounded from English, French, and Indian languages, has long been and is still used by the numerous small tribes on the Pacific slope in the extreme Northwest, just as Spanish, or rather Greaser Mexican, has been used by the Pueblos, Navajos, Southern and Uncompahgre Utes, Apaches, and some other tribes in the Southwest.

The remarks made by White Cloud, head-chief of the Chippewas, are worthy of special consideration, and shed a great deal of light on this subject, viz. :

"Indians had no particular trouble in communicating ideas by means of signs. If two Indians of different tribes were seated on the ground, and a white man approached them, he would see no difference, but if an Indian approached them, he would discover at a glance the difference, and would probably know to what tribes they belonged." So in gestures, one Indian described some article of wearing apparel to another, and the tribal identity is revealed.

I do not think it can properly be said that any gesture speech, which can be called a language, exists among the majority of the Ojibways or the Algonquin family north of the British line, who, occupying a country which stretches from the Rocky Mountains to the mouth of the St. Lawrence River, speak the same language or dialects easily understood. The peculiar nature of their relations with the Plains Indians and other tribes, and the great geographical area covered by their own vocal language, has obviated the necessity for their developing or learning gestures. Some few, like the Pembina band, have been thrown more with the Plains people, and are fairly good sign-talkers. It can, however, be said of these Indians, as well as of the Indians of other tribes, who are not at the present time fully conversant with gesture speech, that such signs as they do make are in the main similar to the gestures used by those who are proficient.

There is, of course, sufficient variation in each tribe, and between tribes, to establish individual and tribal identity, and there are a few words and expressions the signs for which are made totally different. It is natural to suppose that in the majority of cases the conceptions would be the same with people who are in the same stage of development, and whose surroundings, occupation, dress, and habits are similar ; and again, the main object of the language, viz., intercommunication between tribes having different vocal speech, would have a great influence, particularly as its other objects, such as instruction of and communication with the deaf, a check against inefficient or corrupt interpreters, with hunting- or war-parties when the use of oral language would discover them to the game or to their enemies, and when persons are separated by a distance greater than the voice can reach, would not be interfered with.

Silent. Place palmar surface of tips of fingers of right hand over lips, and usually incline the head slightly to front.

Deaf-mutes place tip of index on lips and incline head.

Silver. Make sign for MONEY and point to something white.

Deaf-mutes use the same sign.

Since. See AFTER.

Sinew. Hold right hand in front of body, back to right, inner surface of thumb and index touching, other fingers closed; rub the thumb and index as though twisting a thread held by thumb and index; then make sign for the animal from which taken. This should, I suppose, be called fascia, as it is the thin tendinous covering which supports the muscles. It furnishes thread of superior strength, and admits of division, so that it is easy to secure any desired size or thickness. It is universally called "sinew" by the interpreters.

Sing. Hold right hand, back to right, in front of face, index and second finger extended and separated, others closed, tips a little higher than and close to mouth; mostly by wrist action, move the hand briskly, so as to describe with tips of fingers a small horizontal circle.

Deaf-mutes hold the extended left hand well in front of body, fingers pointing to right; then wave right between left and body, as though keeping time to music.

Sioux. Conception: Cutting off heads. Hold right hand, back up, in front of left shoulder, height of throat, index finger extended and pointing to left, other fingers and thumb closed; move the hand horizontally to right, index passing near throat. Sometimes the extended hand is used instead of index finger, or the side of index is drawn across the throat.

To denote the Sioux (other than the Assinaboine branch), the Gros Ventres of the Prairie, Blackfeet, Flatheads, and some other tribes, in addition to above, bring palms of extended hands against top of head and move them down the sides, to indicate parting the hair in the middle and combing it down over sides of head. The tribal sign undoubtedly originated from the custom the Sioux formerly had of cutting off the heads of their enemies slain in battle. (See SCALP.)

Why, when, and by whom these Indians were first called Sioux is not positively known; however, there seems little doubt but that they received the name from the French voyageurs. They call themselves Dakotas, or Lakotas, the latter being the Teton dialect, and say that this word means people who speak one language, or are united by a common tongue.

The Rev. E. D. Neill, in his "History of Minnesota," states, on the authority of French voyageurs, that by the Algonquins they were called Nadowee Sioux, which signifies enemies, and that the name Sioux was taken from the last part of this word. The Algonquin word, however, for enemy is bohn or boine, as is seen in ASSINABOINE.

In answering some inquiries of mine, Mr. Charles H. Beaulieu says,

"The Ojibways called the Iroquois 'Naw-do-way,' or 'Naw-do-way-see.' On further inquiry I gain no information other than I have written before on this subject, with the exception that a certain species of snake found in the States south of this one (Minnesota), not so poisonous, or, as they say, not so cross, as the 'she-she-quay' (rattlesnake), was called naw-do-way. Old men here remember Naw-do-way-see-wug (plural) used as an exclamation on the approach of enemies, but it is now only used to denote the Iroquois. It would seem to me that Indians east, speaking the Ojibway tongue, could give the origin or definition of the word. Sioux cannot be traced to any Ojibway word. Half-breeds now living here remember hearing it first used by early French voyageurs, and may have had its origin from Naw-do-way-see-wug (plural) for Iroquois."

The French called these Indians Nadowrissioux as far back as 1685. Cadillac, writing to Count Ponchartrain, under date of August, 1703, says, "Last year they sent M. Boudor, a Montreal merchant, into the country of the Sioux to join Le Sœur. He succeeded so well in the trip that he transported thither twenty-five or thirty thousand pounds of merchandise with which to trade." It will thus be seen that the use of the word is of long standing.

In speaking of their language, Mr. Riggs says, "The Dakota language, as spoken by the various bands, is the same ; but yet there are considerable dialectic differences. The *n* of one dialect becomes *h* or *k* or *g* in others. In the Teton or Prairie village dialect *l* is extensively used, which sound is not heard among the Eastern branches of the nation."

In writing to the Rev. John P. Williamson I mentioned the *d* and *l* dialects of Sioux. In reply he said, "Your nomenclature of dialects is hardly, I think, distinctive as far as the Santee and Yankton are concerned. To make it entirely satisfactory the Santees should say *deda* (very), but they say *nina*, same as Yankton. They should say *midi* (water), but they say *mini*, same as Yankton.

"I think a better distinction is *hd, gl,* and *kd.* This distinction is perfect. There is not an *hd* in the Santee language but what is changed as above for the other dialects. Santee *hda,* go home. Teton *gla,* go home. Yankton *kda,* go home. Your distinction is more simple than this, and perhaps if I had time to compare more fully I might, with certain restriction, like it, but with my observation the double consonant gives a better idea of the dialect."

Leaving to the philologist the study of the "common stock," which, according to some, embraces Winnebago, Osage, Kaw and Quapaw, Iowa, Otoe, Missouri, Omaha, Ponca, Mandan, Hidatsee, and Crow, we find there are four dialects in the Sioux language, viz., Santee, Yankton, Assinaboine, and Teton,—the latter differing from the first three much more than they differ from each other.

The best authorities in the *hd* and *kd* dialects give the meaning of Teton as derived from Tinta, prairie, and Tonwon, village ; hence Prairie village ; and this would seem to derive support from the location and manner of living of the Tetons for a number of years past. I am strongly of the opinion, however, that this is not correct, and the dialects prove conclusively that the separation must have taken place a very long time ago, and probably when they were living in a wooded country east of the prairies, all the bands subsisting themselves in a similar manner.

The story I first heard in regard to the name and separation was that a chief with a few followers left the main camp or village, and was subsequently joined by others, so that it was a common question, ' How many tepees has he?' In rapid conversation they will say to-day for how many tepees, Te-tona, and I, therefore, believe that Teton is derived from this expression, instead of that for Prairie village.

Of the seven bands of the Teton branch, viz., Ogalalla, Minneconjou, Sans-Arc, Uncapapa, Brulé, Two-Kettle, and Blackfeet, the meaning of the Sioux words Ogalalla and Uncapapa have been most distorted. I have endeavored to correct this under the proper words.

The language is more easily learned than most Indian tongues, and the *gl* or Teton dialect seems more euphonious than the others. There is scarcely a tribe in the Northwest which does not have one or more who speak Sioux quite fluently. To such an extent is the language used in the intercommunication by tribes that it may be considered the court language of the Northern nations.

From oral tradition, pictured and written history, as well as from the stories told by the Sioux and Indians of the surrounding tribes, the Lacotas, or Dakotas, as they call themselves, reached the limit of their eastern migration when they inhabited Northwestern Wisconsin and Eastern Minnesota. Imagination and conjecture have placed them much farther east, and the extent of this is so shown in a little pamphlet published by Mr. A. W. Williamson, that I make the following extract:

"This paper is a preliminary result of my father's dying request to complete an article he was preparing, showing that the Dakotas are of European origin. Some fragments as to mythology and tradition I hope at a future time to publish. I close by giving the conclusions to which he was led by forty-five years of observation. Dictating these was his last work before he went to his home above.

"Concerning the origin of the Dakotas and those speaking kindred languages: Their ancestors landed on this continent near the Gulf of St. Lawrence about the same time, probably at least three thousand years ago. The Dakotas were and continued to be on the north side of the St. Lawrence and great lakes, and the climate being unfavorable to agriculture, soon abandoned it, and depended for subsistence wholly on the chase and fishing. Thus they had no permanent villages, and as there was no allotment of the territory to any part of the people, all hunted freely over every part of the territory the entire tribe could defend and hold as their own, which caused frequent intercourse. Besides, at certain seasons of the year, they would assemble at the best fishing-grounds, and there remain for weeks together. These all continued to speak the same language. At some remote period the most westerly portion reached and entered the prairies, whence their name Titon,—dwellers on the prairies. From that time their mode of life changed, the buffalo became a chief part of their game, they ceased to have much intercourse with their eastern neighbors, and so developed a dialect which differs from the Santee and Yankton far more than they differ from each other, and from the Assinniboine. As it is certain that the separation of the Assinniboines must have taken place nearly three hundred years ago, and perhaps yet more remotely, and as the Assinniboines have been wholly separated, the Titons but partially, I think that this separation could not have been less than six hundred years ago, and was probably much more remote.

" As was said before, I think the tribes speaking kindred languages were south of the St. Lawrence River. They doubtless found the coasts of New England occupied by the Algonquins or others, who would not suffer the intruders to remain near the valuable fisheries. They had probably lost very little of the knowledge of agriculture which their fathers had brought from Europe when they reached the valley of the Ohio River. Here, finding a beautiful agricultural country, they settled in villages and built the mounds and earth-works concerning whose origin there has been so much speculation. The extent of these works is such as to show that the builders must have lived chiefly by agriculture, for it would be impossible for hunters to subsist at one point the number of men sufficient to build or hold them. Many have asserted that these mounds must have been built by a different and superior race, because none of the Indians found in this country by our ancestors had skill to construct them. But this has no foundation in fact. The Indians have as much constructive talent as ourselves. If they did not build better houses it was because they felt no need of them. None of our best mechanics can, with the Indian's tools, make a dug-out canoe nearly as good as the Santees living on the Mississippi made thirty years ago, and very few of them can, with his best tools and the Indian's canoe for a model, equal it. The Indians, in like manner, excel in making arrows, as may be seen by any one who witnesses the whole process. I have no doubt that the Indians of Dakota stock who lived in the Ohio Valley possessed the requisite skill to construct any earth-works and mounds found in that State. These villages being widely scattered, and those inhabiting them living by agriculture, they had little intercourse with each other, and thus arose the various kindred languages. The development of these languages must have occupied at least one thousand years, and probably very much longer, unless we suppose that they were separated into strongly-marked dialects before they reached the Ohio Valley, which does not seem to me to be probable.

" At some remote period, probably about the time of Columbus's discovery of America, the Algonquins or Iroquois began a war of extermination against these inhabitants of Ohio. Hunters have ever been prone thus to war on their agricultural neighbors, and unless the latter have a well-organized government, seldom fail to be the victors. The contest was probably a long and severe one, and many, perhaps much the greater part of the mound-builders, were slain. Their enemies, finding them no more, naturally supposed that they were exterminated, yet many of them escaped to the west. The Winnebagoes removed to the west shore of Lake Michigan, where their persecutors probably never found them. The Iowas and Otoes fled to the prairies of Illinois, where they built many earth houses, the ruins of which still remain, and may be seen by examination to have once been human dwellings. Satisfactory reasons could be given for the difference in size. The Omahas, Osages, and other Southern bands migrated to the southwest of the Missouri, and when first visited by white men were living in earth houses, the ruins of which are now similar to many of the mounds in Ohio."

In justice to the author, it must be noticed that he observes " concerning the origin of the Dakotas, and those speaking *kindred languages.*" The earliest reliable history, as I have stated, locates the villages of the Sioux proper on the lakes and streams near the headwaters of the Mississippi River. Powerful and war-loving, they waged successfully offensive and defensive warfare against the surrounding tribes, until the Algonquins, with the assistance of the French, pressed them to the west and south. There seems little doubt but that many, if not all of them, in olden times used the dirt lodges in their permanent villages, something after the manner of the Mandans, Pawnees, and other tribes, and had their cultivated fields near them. In their early intercourse with the whites they were generally friendly, looking upon the pale-faces at first in superstitious awe, and then hailed them as benefactors who brought to their people many useful and ornamental articles. The officers of the Northwest Fur Company bore testimony to their uniform friendship, and stated that it was the boast of the Sioux in every council for thirty-five years that their hands had not been stained with the blood of the white man, but the seemingly inevitable irritation which ensues under our system when savagery and civilization are brought in contact was realized, and to many of these people every white man became a foe, and every white woman legitimate prey. This feeling culminated in what were known as the Spirit Lake massacre in 1857, and the Minnesota massacre in 1862, the latter of which, in extent, brutality, beastly atrocities, and sickening mutilations, scarcely finds a parallel in the whole history of our border warfare. The Sioux had just cause for complaint, but their fiendish action wiped out all sympathy for the wrongs they had suffered.

In mental, moral, and physical qualities I consider the Sioux a little lower, but still nearly equal to the Cheyennes, and the Tetons are the superior branch of the family. In some of their customs and beliefs the Eastern bands differ from the Western as much as they differ from other tribes. The Western bands do not have the same custom of naming their children, which with those of the East is to call the first-born son Chaské, the second Hârpam, the third Hâpéda, the fourth Châtun, the fifth Hârka. The first-born daughter is called Winona, the second Hârpen, the third Harpstina, the fourth Wâska, the fifth Wehârka. Sometimes these names are retained through life. A close study of different Indian tribes has convinced me that all people in the same plane or period of savagery or barbarism possess about the same ideas of religious worship, and are greatly alike in other respects. Of course, climate, food, and occupation cause many physical and mental characteristics, but still the barbarian of the North, dwelling in his house of ice and subsisting on oils and fats, is not so very different from the barbarian of the South, who, basking in the sunshine, needs no house, and subsists on the tropical fruits with which nature bounteously supplies him.

The Sioux were a very numerous and powerful people, and had they possessed a greater and closer community of interests they would have been able to have dictated terms to the surrounding tribes, and offered a more dangerous resistance to the advance of our western civilization ; but the Santees and Yanktons were latterly only anxious to repel the advance of the Ojibways, preserve the lands of their forefathers, and continue in the old life ; while the Tetons were restless hordes, drifting about on the vast prairies beyond, subsisting mainly on the buffalo. They were the typical Plains Indians, and with them the sign language grew into a more perfect development than with any other branch of the Sioux family. Their mode of life developed them physically and mentally, and being beyond the reach of missionaries, their old religious beliefs were better preserved. In their organization of soldier bands—in fact, what might be called their form of government both in peace and war—they were also superior to the Eastern bands.

With this tribe, as with many others, the position of chief was not necessarily inherited or secured through election. (See CHIEF.) Their laws and ceremonies for the preservation of the chastity of the women were severe, searching, and comprehensive ; but it would appear that except in cases of adultery the man was not liable to punishment. Among some bands the " virgin feast" was held annually, and all the unmarried females of the camp were subjected to this test of virtue. With others, any girl whose reputation had been assailed by slander could demand that the sacred fires be lighted (at these feasts it was customary to light or make a new fire, either by friction or with flint and steel), and that the accusers be brought to the sacred circle and the truth or falsity of the accusation established. The accused was allowed to testify in her own behalf, and it is stated that on one occasion, among the Santee Sioux, a maiden having been falsely accused by a young man of the tribe, took the following oath : " Hear me, Spirit of Good, in Thy presence and in that of all these present, I pronounce this man a baseful liar, and whichever of us has this day desecrated by falsehoods this sacred circle, dedicated to virtue, may the curse of that Spirit rest upon the family of the liar ; may they sicken and die one by one. By this knife, emblem of retribution, I ask may they be stricken from earth, and may the cause of this linger to the last and perish miserably.'' Those who were not able to vindicate their honor were frequently, for the time, abandoned to the lusts of the camp ; but many of these, after being thus brutally debauched, became respectable wives and mothers. The law, apparently growing out of public opinion, which prohibits the marriage of blood relatives, is strictly enforced ; but so far as I have been able to learn there is no division of the tribe into gens as explained by Mr. Morgan. Blood relationship was, however, only kept by oral tradition.

The mythology of the Sioux is not very extensive, and varies with the different bands much according to the visions, vagaries, and imaginations of the medicine-men, who manufacture stories to please their own people or satisfy the cravings of some enthusiast of the white race who may be gleaning the fields of the savage. It is safe to say that nearly all their myths have now become greatly colored, —seriously entangled with the stories told them by the missionaries and others.

The Commissioner of Indian Affairs, in his report for 1881, gives the following as the population of the Sioux at the different agencies :

IN MONTANA, AT FORT PECK AGENCY.

Assinaboines	1413
Yanktonnais Sioux	4814
Total	6227

FORT BELKNAP AGENCY.

Assinaboines	900

IN NEBRASKA, AT SANTEE AGENCY.

Santee Sioux	767
Santee Sioux, at Flandreau, Dakota Territory	306
Total	1073

IN DAKOTA—CHEYENNE RIVER AGENCY.

Blackfeet Sioux	259
Sans-Arc Sioux	346
Minneconjou Sioux	537
Two-Kettle Sioux	759
Total	1901

CROW CREEK AGENCY.

Yanktonnais Sioux	1061

DEVIL'S LAKE AGENCY.

Sisseton Sioux	422
Wahpeton Sioux	403
Cut-Head Sioux	241
Total	1066

LOWER BRULÉ AGENCY.

Lower Brulé Sioux	1509

PINE RIDGE AGENCY.

Ogalalla Sioux	7202

ROSEBUD AGENCY.

Brulé Sioux	3566
Loafer Sioux	1564
Wahzahzah Sioux	1164
Two-Kettle Sioux	384
Northern Sioux	500
Mixed Sioux	520
Total	7698

SISSETON AGENCY.

Sisseton and Wahpeton Sioux	1377

STANDING ROCK AGENCY.

Lower Yanktonnais Sioux	895
Upper Yanktonnais Sioux	493
Blackfeet Sioux	728
Uncapapa Sioux	521

Hostile Indians added July 28, 1881 (surrendered from those who fled north of frontier line in 1876–77) :

Minneconjou Sioux	753
Brulé Sioux	170
Sans-Arc Sioux	524
Uncapapa Sioux	703
Ogalalla Sioux	556
Blackfeet Sioux	107
Total	5450

YANKTON AGENCY.

Yankton Sioux	1998
Making a grand total, including the Assinaboines, of . .	37,462

These Indians are nearly all what are called blanket or wild Indians, supported by Government at their different agencies. Some of them have made feeble efforts at agriculture, a few have stock cattle, and some of the children are sent to school, but the great mass are scarcely any further advanced in civilization than they were when they first met the white race.

Sister. Make sign for FEMALE, and then place the tips of extended index and second finger against lips, extended fingers horizontal and backs up, other fingers and thumb closed ; move the hand horizontally several inches to front. (See KINSHIP.)

Deaf-mutes make sign for FEMALE, and then join index fingers as in Indian sign for MARRY.

Sister-in-Law. Make signs for BROTHER, for HIS, and for WIFE.

Deaf-mutes make sign for SISTER, and then place spread thumb and index of right hand against left palm, left hand in front of body, fingers extended, touching, and pointing to front.

Sit. Hold closed right hand in front of and a little lower than right shoulder, back of hand about to right ; move the hand downwards several inches. This is also used for resting, stopping, to be at a place, abide, stay, remain, etc.

Deaf-mutes use the extended right hand, back up, fingers pointing to front. Sometimes they use both hands.

Skunk. Represent height of animal ; then hold right hand, back to rear, little to right of right shoulder, index finger curved, others and thumb closed ; move the hand to front several inches by gentle jerks ; then make sign for STINK.

Sometimes the following is made, instead of the curved index, which represents the manner of carrying the tail, viz. : Hold extended left hand, back up, in front of body, fingers pointing to front ; draw the tips of extended first and second fingers of right hand, back to front, pointing to front and downwards, others and thumb closed, from ends of left fingers to rear, over the back of left hand ; then point to something white. This represents the white stripes on back of animal.

Deaf-mutes indicate a little animal that stinks ; some indicate this by drawing tips of index and second finger up over face and top of head.

Sled. Hold the hands, backs down, in front of body, same height, equally advanced, and several inches apart, index fingers curved, other fingers and thumbs closed ; move the hands simultaneously to the front,—represents the runners of the vehicle.

Deaf-mutes use the same sign.

Sleep. Bring the extended hands, backs down, with a sweep, so as to lower them slightly into the following position : left hand in front of right breast, fingers pointing to right, right hand several inches to right of left, fingers pointing to front and right, and as the hands are lowered to this position, incline the head to right. Sometimes the right hand is held nearer the head, and with those not conversant with gesture speech, the head is inclined to right, and rests on right palm.

Deaf-mutes carry open hand to front of face, palm towards and near it, incline the head slightly to front, close the eyes, and partially close the hand. They also sometimes incline the head to right, and rest side on palm of right hand.

Sleep (With). Make sign for SLEEP (above) and for WITH ; or if with a female, place the palm of extended right index on left, left hand back down, fingers pointing to front.

Deaf-mutes use the same signs ; *i.e.*, SLEEP and WITH.

Slow. Make sign for WAIT, or signs for FAST and NO.

In speaking of a village, or party moving slowly, indicate many camps,—move a little distance and then camp. Some metaphor is usually employed ; languid or slow gestures also indicate the slow movement. For a slow pony I have seen gestures made to denote whipping same, and he, instead of going forward, nearly stops, with a tendency to lean back.

Small. If an animal, indicate the height. In such sentences as "a small number of lodges," small quantity of anything, make sign for FEW.

Deaf-mutes bring the hands near each other in front of body.

Smallpox. Conception: Marks made by the disease. Compress and curve the right hand, and tap the face and chest, sometimes adding SMELL and BAD.

Deaf-mutes use the same signs.

The Northern Cheyennes claim that they never had the disease, but many were swept away by the cholera in 1849.

Mr. F. F. Girard told me that in 1852 or 1853 he went up the Missouri River from Berthold to Fort Union (mouth of the Yellowstone). He passed an Assinaboine camp of some three hundred lodges. They told him that they then had the smallpox in camp. In the spring he returned and found this camp literally a camp of the dead ; not one had escaped the scourge.

I have heard many sickening stories told of the ravages made by this disease. The Shoshones and Bannacks said they suffered from it some thirty years ago ; they moved to Bear River, where the disease appeared in the spring, and by the fall nearly one-half of the entire camp had perished. I was told at the Blackfeet Agency that it was some forty years since they had the smallpox, which they caught from the whites at Fort Benton. The people there sent the Indians word not to come in, but they had no other place to go to trade, and went. As a result, the Piegans, who formerly numbered thirteen or fourteen bands, each as large as their entire number now, were nearly swept away. Some bands came out of this awful ordeal with only one or two families. Their treatment for it, as well as the kindred diseases, "chicken-pox" and "measles," is almost certain death, viz., hot steam bath and then a plunge into cold water. With such treatment, living in filth and exposed to cold winds, it is little wonder that they were nearly wiped out of existence.

Professor Schoolcraft speaks of this scourge as follows: "No disease which has been introduced among the tribes has exercised so fatal an influence upon them as the smallpox. Their physicians have no remedy for it. Old and young regard it as if it were the plague, and, on its appearance among them, blindly submit to its ravages.

"This disease has appeared among them periodically, at irregular intervals of time. It has been one of the prominent causes of their depopulation. Ardent spirits, it is true, in its various forms, has, in the long run, carried a greater number of the tribes to their graves ; but its effects have been comparatively slow, and its victims, though many, have fallen in the ordinary manner, and generally presented scenes less revolting and striking to the eye.

"This malady swept through the Missouri Valley in 1837. It first appeared on a steamboat (the St. Peter's), in the case of a mulatto man, a hand on board, at the Black-Snake Hills, a trading-post, sixty miles above Fort Leavenworth, and about five hundred miles above St. Louis. It was then supposed to be measles, but, by the time the boat reached the Council Bluffs, it was ascertained to be smallpox, and had, of course, been communicated to many in whom the disease was still latent. Every precaution appears to have been taken, by sending runners to the Indians, two days ahead of the boat ; but, in spite of these efforts, the disease spread. It broke out among the Mandans about the 15th of July. This tribe, which con-sisted of sixteen hundred persons, living in two villages, was reduced to thirty-one souls. It next attacked the Minnetarees, who were living in that vicinity, and reduced that tribe from one thousand to about five hundred. The Arickarees, numbering three thousand souls, were diminished to some fifteen hundred.

"The disease passed from these to the Assinaboines, a powerful tribe of nine thousand, living north of the Missouri, and ranging in the plains below the Rocky Mountains, towards Red River of Hud-son Bay, whole villages of whom it nearly annihilated. This tribe had their principal trade with Fort Union, at the mouth of the Yellowstone.

"The Crows, or Upsarokas, extending west from this point across the plains to the Rocky Mountains, who were estimated at three thousand strong, shared nearly the same fate, and lost one-third of their numbers.

"It then entered and spent its virulence upon the great nation of the Blackfeet, who are known under the various names of Blood In-dians, Piegans, and Atsinas. They have been estimated at thirty thousand to fifty thousand. The inmates of one thousand lodges were destroyed. The average number in a lodge is from six to eight persons.

"Granting everything that can be asked on the score of excite-ment and exaggeration, not less than ten thousand persons fell be-fore this destroying disease in a few weeks. An eye-witness of this scene, writing from Fort Union on the 27th of November, 1837, says, 'Language, however forcible, can convey but a faint idea of the scene of desolation which the country now presents. In what-ever direction you turn nothing but sad wrecks of mortality meet the eye ; lodges standing on every hill, but not a streak of smoke rising from them. Not a sound can be heard to break the awful stillness, save the ominous croak of ravens and the mournful howl of wolves, fattening on the human carcasses that lie strewed around. It seems as if the very genius of desolation had stalked through the prairies and wreaked his vengeance on everything bearing the shape of humanity.' "

Another writer says, "Many of the handsome Arickarees, who had recovered, seeing the disfiguration of their features, committed suicide, some by throwing themselves from rocks, others by stabbing and shooting. The prairie has become a graveyard ; its wild flowers bloom over the sepulchres of Indians. The atmosphere, for miles, is poisoned by the stench of the hundreds of carcasses unburied. The women and children are wandering in groups, without food, or howling over the dead. The men are flying in every direction. The proud, warlike, and noble-looking Blackfeet are no more. Their deserted lodges are seen on every hill. No sound but the raven's croak or the wolf's howl breaks the solemn stillness. The scene of desolation is appalling, beyond the power of the imagination to conceive.'"

Smell. Bring the right hand, back nearly up, in front of lower part of face, first and second fingers extended, separated, nearly horizontal, and pointing towards face, tips close to chin; move the hand upwards, mostly by wrist action, nose passing between tips.

Deaf-mutes pass the palmar surface of the extended finger of right hand from above down over and close to nose and mouth, fingers pointing to left.

Smoke. For distant smoke, like a signal-fire smoke, make sign for FIRE, and continue raising hand till higher than head.

For smoke in a lodge or house, make signs for FIRE, for BAD, and bring extended and separated fingers and thumbs, backs out, in front of and little above eyes; lower hands slightly, and bring them a little closer to face than in FOG. This is also used for a smoky atmosphere,—one cannot see well through it.

Deaf-mutes give a rotary motion to the hands, one about the other, as they are raised from a position about in front of waist, hands open, fingers slightly separated.

Smoke. (To smoke a pipe.) Hold closed left hand, back to left, in front of body; bring palm of extended right hand about three inches over left hand, and strike with this palm left index and thumb briskly two or three times, then make sign for PIPE. This really means fill up the pipe.

Deaf-mutes make their sign for PIPE, and then make motion with lips and cheeks as though puffing at same.

Indians have no salutation like ours on meeting or separating, but it is the custom with many tribes to say on meeting, "Fill the pipe; let us smoke." There are few people who smoke as much as the Plains Indians, and certainly few who give to it in so great a measure a religious character, making of it a social pleasure and prizing it highly and sacredly as a mark of friendship. We are told that, "in the belief of the ancient worshippers, the Great Spirit smelled a sweet savor as the smoke of the sacred plant ascended to the heavens; and this homely implement of modern luxury was in their hands a sacred censer, from which the hallowed vapors rose; as fitting propitiatory odors as that which perfumes the awful precincts of the cathedral altar amidst the mysteries of the church's high and holy days."

As I have stated, the Indians of the majority of the tribes, on the slightest provocation, seem to crystallize into a circular group seated on the ground. If the circle is large, more than ten or twelve, two or more pipes are used. Suppose a group of six or eight; the pipe is filled and passed to the medicine-man, if there be one in the group, if not, then to the eldest or acknowledged headman, who lights it, takes a whiff or two, then points the tube or stem to the

God or force in nature which he wishes to propitiate or supplicate, accompanying the movement frequently with an oral petition ; then points the stem towards the earth, and perhaps to the *four winds;* then the pipe is passed around, each man making his prayer by pointing the stem as in the first case ; the pipe is handed back to the right, and not smoked on the passage. The pipe is pointed to the earth, that it may hold them good and strong ; to the "four corners," that no harsh winds may blow against them, meaning not only the physical action of storms, but trouble and distress ; to the sun, that they may have light to see their way clearly ; the sun is specially smoked to just before going to war, that they may see their way clearly, so as to avoid danger and death. All of these motions are not made each time they smoke, but some of them are. The Chippewas do not pass the pipe in smoking, unless in making peace or some other impressive ceremony ; socially, each man has his separate pipe.

The Bannacks and Snakes do not smoke nearly as much as the Plains Indians, many only cigarettes after eating, and some take a smoke just before going to sleep. The Utes also use cigarettes more than they do pipes.

Smooth. Make sign for PRAIRIE, and to emphasize add signs for ROCK or BLUFF, and ALL GONE, or WIPED OUT.

Deaf-mutes rub back of extended left hand with palmar surface of fingers of extended right.

Snake. Conception : Motion. Hold right hand, back to right, in front of right shoulder, about height of waist, first and second fingers extended, touching, and pointing to front, others and thumb closed ; move the hand several inches to front, and, by wrist action, give a wavy, sinuous motion to extended fingers. Frequently only the index is extended.

Deaf-mutes give a rotary motion to the hand, so that tips of extended fingers describe a spiral curve, and on terminating movement hold the extended and separated fingers pointing to front and upwards.

Snow. Make sign for RAIN, and from this position lower the hands some inches, backs up, fingers touching and pointing to front, —falls like the rain, but lies on the ground.

Speaking of snow, a Mandan Indian said to me that the Gros Ventre God and Mandan God had a dispute about this, one claiming that it was better to have it always pleasant and warm, bright sunshine and flowers ; but the other said no, that their health demanded cold weather ; so they made snow, gave us moccasins, and showed us how to make all our clothing to protect us from the cold.

Deaf-mutes make signs for WHITE, RAIN, and lower the hands very slowly in latter gesture.

Snow-shoe. Trace the size and shape with index of right hand ; make sign for WALK, SNOW, and GOOD.

Deaf-mutes indicate a long SHOE, WALK, and SNOW.

Soap. Bring hands in front of body, and rub them against each other, as is done in washing them.

Deaf-mutes indicate size of cake, and then make same sign.

Soft. (Sense of miry.) Hold left hand, back to front and left, well in front of right breast, index and thumb curved, forming about half of a horizontal ellipse, other fingers closed ; bring closed right hand and pass it from above downwards through this ellipse (consider the right arm as the foreleg of an animal, and let left thumb and index mark off the extent which it is supposed the animal does or would sink) ; then hold right hand similarly fixed opposite left breast, and execute similar movement with left hand and arm.

For SOFT in any other sense, use signs for HARD and No.

Deaf-mutes close and open hands, as though pressing something between fingers and thumbs.

Soldier. The conception for this sign seems to be drawn from several gestures: IN LINE, BOW, STOUT, or STRONG, holding a fiery horse. Bring closed hands, backs up and slightly to rear, well in front of body, hands at same height, equally advanced, touching at thumbs and index fingers ; separate the hands several inches, carrying right to right and left to left.

The Crows and some other tribes usually make the sign for HOLD. At certain times the members of an Indian village are forced to keep together, held, or, as they say, "soldiered," hence this sign.

The Berthold Indians touch something black and draw palm of extended right hand from left to right across lower part of face. In olden times these Indians had a police force regularly detailed to look after the camp, and their insignia of authority was the blackened face.

White soldiers are sometimes represented as WHITES with a peculiar visor to cap, as marching in column, as whites with sharp instrument on end of gun, and whites who fight.

Deaf-mutes hold the closed hands against left breast, right several inches above left.

The origin of the word " Cheyenne" having been given as derived from the French word "Chien," and this applied to a tribe of Indians, because the men of the tribe were known as "dog-soldiers," and the organization of certain tribes into phratries and gentes, as given by Mr. L. H. Morgan, led me to make careful inquiry in regard to the present organizations, and, so far as tradition goes, what had been the form of government in times past.

Mr. Morgan broadly asserts that the plan of government of the American aborigines commenced with the gens, and ended with the confederacy ; the latter being the highest point to which their governmental institutions attained. It gave the organic series, *first*, the gens, a body of consanguinity having a common gentile name; *second*, the phratry, an assemblage of related gentes, united in a higher association for certain common objects ; *third*, the tribe, an assemblage of gentes, usually organized in phratries, all the members of which spoke the same dialect ; and, *fourth*, a confederacy of tribes, the members of which respectively spoke dialects of the same stock language.

I cannot help feeling that Mr. Morgan's careful study of the form of government of the Iroquois League colored his writings in regard to all other Indians; certain it is that no trace now exists of such organization among many of the Plains Tribes. The very nature of the warfare carried on by these predatory hordes for hundreds of years, as well as the character of their social gatherings, prevented any such structure. Among the larger tribes, like the Sioux and Comanches, we find several different bands in each tribe known and recognized under the tribal name, and yet specially designated by the name for the particular band; but, all the men being warriors, it seems only natural that we should here find a special crystallization, formed through necessity and pleasure. There were many influences at work which gave special names to the soldier bands.

The Southern Cheyennes gave me the following six bands as their organization: 1st, Fox; 2d, Dog; 3d, Bow-String; 4th, Bull; 5th, Medicine-Lance; 6th, Chief; and they informed me that the prominence and numbers of each band depended in a great measure on the leader. For instance, the Dog-Soldier band led all others in 1869, but when "Tall Bull," the chief of this band, was killed by General Carr's command in the spring of that year, this band declined in prominence and numbers from that time. In the summer of 1868 "Roman Nose" led the Medicine-Lance band, and this band was more numerous and ranked higher in bravery than any other; but he was killed in General Forsyth's fight on the American Fork of the Republican River in 1868, and then this band lost its prestige and wasted away in numbers.

The Southern Arapahoes have seven bands: 1st, Fox; 2d, Fool-Dog, or Rattle; 3d, War-Club; 4th, Medicine- or Crooked-Lance; 5th, Crazy, or Fool band (meaning that they knew or paid no attention to danger); 6th, Dog; 7th, Old Chief.

The Comanches have five bands, and claimed that the difference is in the dances prior to getting up a war-party. They are named: 1st, Swift Fox; 2d, Gourd; 3d, Raven; 4th, Buffalo Bull; 5th, Afraid-of-Nothing.

The Kiowas have five bands: 1st, Raven Soldiers (black leggings); 2d, Sheep; 3d, Feather-Head; 4th, Horse; 5th, War-Club.

The Caddos have four: 1st, Wolf; 2d, Bear; 3d, Panther; 4th, Beaver.

The Kiowa Apaches have only three bands, viz.: 1st, Big Horse; 2d, Raven; 3d, Swift Fox.

The Sacs and Foxes have no regular soldier bands, but claim that long ago they had a soldier band, which camped separately from the main village.

The Arickarees have eight bands, viz.: 1st, Fox; 2d, Thief; 3d, Basket; 4th, Shaved-Head (one side shaved); 5th, Big Dog; 6th, Bull; 7th, Crow; 8th, Black Mouth.

The tribes at the Flathead Agency seemed to have a very meagre organization. In former times they claimed to have had one or two men called "dog-soldiers," and when a war-party started they went in advance of the rest without arms, only taking their medicine and their rattles. As the old Indian who told me the story, said, " They went right into the enemy's camp or ranks, and, if killed, the rest turned back."

It was claimed that they also had a band of club-soldiers, forty or fifty in a tribe, who executed the orders of the chief, and were apparently a police force to preserve order in the camp (my informant here sang for me a beautiful and inspiriting war-song, suitable for a dog-soldier, at least he seemed to think so).

The Eastern bands of Sioux do not seem to have a very perfect organization of soldier bands. The Teton Sioux have eleven bands, viz. : 1st, Strong Heart ; 2d, Prairie-Dog ; 3d, Crow (carry a lance) ; 4th, White Breast-Strap ; 5th, Shield ; 6th, Night Brave ; 7th, Night-Owl Head-dress ; 8th, Badger-mouth Prairie-Dog ; 9th, Tall Brave ; 10th, Orphan ; 11th, Warrior.

Son. Make signs for PARTURITION and MALE.

Deaf-mutes make sign for MALE, and hold hands as in BORN, only a little lower.

Sorrel. Touch something yellow in color, and make sign for LITTLE.

Most Indians call a sorrel horse a yellow horse, and a dun-colored the color of an elk.

Deaf-mutes use the same signs.

Sour. Touch tongue with tip of extended index of right hand and make sign for BAD.

Deaf-mutes touch tongue and assume a scowling expression of countenance.

Source. (Stream.) Make sign for STREAM or RIVER ; then hold closed left hand, back to left, in front of body ; carry the extended right index, other fingers and thumb closed, to front, the right and place tip against fingers and exposed palm of left hand, right index horizontal.

Deaf-mutes hold left hand extended, fingers pointing upward, and place tip of right index against left palm.

Speak. See TALK.

Spear. Bring right hand, palm outwards, in front of and close to right breast, index finger extended and pointing upwards, others and thumb closed ; raise the hand to arm's full length, and, by wrist action, give a tremulous motion to index finger.

Deaf-mutes hold closed right hand near right shoulder, and move it briskly to front, as though using a spear.

Spider. The Cheyennes vocally call a spider by the same name that they do a white man, and of course make the same sign.

I have seen added to this an imitation of biting with tips of thumb and index of right hand, other fingers closed, and then the sign for ROPE made.

Spoon. Make sign for BUFFALO ; then touch the right hand with finger-tips of left as right is in position, and make sign as though dipping into some vessel with right hand, and carry it to mouth.

From the buffalo-horn were made nearly all the spoons used by the Plains Indians in former times.

Deaf-mutes move the right hand, with index and second finger extended, as though dipping into some vessel, in front of body, and then carry same to mouth.

Spotted. Hold left arm about horizontal and pointing to front; separate and slightly curve fingers of right hand, hold it some inches above and to right of left wrist, the fingers and thumb point about to left, and their ends are just over left forearm; lower right hand, ends of fingers and thumb touching left forearm, as the hand passes; raise the hand, then lower it, moving it each time little towards elbow, tips of fingers and thumb touching left arm in upward and downward movement.

Deaf-mutes tap in different places the back of extended left hand, held palm down, fingers pointing to front, with tip of curved index of right hand, other fingers and thumb closed.

Spring. Conception : Grass coming out of ground. Make sign for GRASS and LITTLE.

In the North, where the snow disappears about this time, sometimes the signs for SNOW and WIPED OUT are made, and I have also seen signs for COLD and FINISHED made.

Deaf-mutes make their sign for GROW.

Spring. (Water.) Make sign for WATER ; then form a horizontal circle with thumbs and index fingers, in front of body, other fingers closed; then carry right hand, back down, just under the circle, nails of first three fingers pressing against thumb; raise the right hand slightly and nearly extend the fingers with a slight snap; repeat motion ; to represent the bubbling and boiling up of the water.

Deaf-mutes use the same sign.

Springfield Rifle. Conception : Throwing open breech-block. Make sign for GUN ; then hold extended and slightly-compressed left hand well in front of body, back of hand to left, fingers pointing to front, thumb extended and pressed against index, forearm horizontal ; bring nearly-closed right hand, and place side of right thumb on base of left ; move the hand upwards and to front, as though throwing open breech-block.

Spy. Make sign for WOLF. To spy about is to act the wolf. This metaphor comes not only from the sneaking, prowling habits of the animal, but a wolf-skin cap was frequently used by scouts and spies in approaching a camp, or rising above the crest of a hill. The disguise was a good one, and the howling of a wolf easily imitated.

Stand. Bring right hand, back out, well in front of, little to right and little higher than, right shoulder, index finger extended and pointing upwards, others and thumb closed. This is used to represent anything as standing upright.

Deaf-mutes hold the extended left hand, back down, in front of body, fingers pointing to front, and place the tips of extended and separated index and second finger on left palm, other fingers and thumb closed, fingers vertical.

For a column, or any inanimate object, they indicate its shape.

Standing Rock. Make signs for STAND and ROCK. Standing Rock Agency, on the Missouri River, derives its name from the small rock which stands on a slight eminence near by, and which is an object of awe and reverence to the Arickarees and Sioux.

The myth in regard to it is, that an Arickaree woman, with a baby in a blanket at her back, in grief and anger left her lodge and went to this little knoll and remained all night. In the morning when her people went to look for her, they found only this rock, which they have since considered sacred, as it is the woman and child changed to stone. They painted and dressed it; made sacrificial offerings of beads, paint, arrows, etc., to it. Some years after the Arickarees had moved farther up the river, a Sioux war-party finding it so decorated, one of the number tore off the clothing, rubbed away the paint, scattered the offerings, and scornfully said, "It is only holy for the Arickarees." The war-party went on, and soon after had a fight with the Arickarees, in which the scorner was the first one killed. In this way it became sacred to the Sioux as well, and they have since kept up the custom of decorating and making offerings to it.

Star. Make sign for NIGHT; then form an incomplete circle with index and thumb, space of about half an inch between tip of index and thumb; raise the hand upwards towards the heavens. To represent many stars, sometimes both hands are used, and pushed up in different directions. To denote any star of particular brilliancy, such as the morning star, the hand is held towards the direction where the star is supposed to be, and then the tip of index pressed against the ball of the thumb and snapped two or three times to denote the twinkling.

Deaf-mutes rub the extended index fingers placed alongside of each other, other fingers closed.

The Arapahoes have just enough knowledge of astronomy to name some of the stars and constellations.

They call the *Big Dipper* "the broken back."

Mars, "big fire star."

Jupiter, "morning star." When Jupiter is an evening star, "the lance." Some call it "the winter star."

Pleiades, "the bunch."

Venus, "day star."

The Hyades, "the hand."

The Plains Indians have special names for a greater number of stars and constellations than some of the mountain tribes.

The Snakes and Bannacks speak of the morning star and evening star; but, so far as I could learn, have no name for any constellation.

Start. Make sign for GO.

Stay. Make sign for SIT.

Steal. To steal from others. Hold extended left hand, back up, to left and front, well in front of left breast, fingers pointing to right and front; carry right hand under and close to left hand, so that right wrist will be under and close to left palm, index finger of right hand extended, pointing to left and front, other fingers and thumb closed; draw the right to right, rear and slightly upwards, at same time curving, nearly closing index finger.

This combines signs for FETCH or BRING, and SECRETLY.

Deaf-mutes hold left hand similarly, and carry right under left in the same way, but make a grasping motion with right hand instead of index finger.

Public sentiment so thoroughly condemns theft, that among themselves Indians have but little trouble on account of thieves. Having no locks or keys, honesty in this respect is a necessity. The personal possessions of Indians are so well known in their camps that it would be extremely difficult for an individual to steal any article, retain possession of it, and not have it known.

Steamboat. Conception: Fire-boat. Make sign for BOAT; then sign for FIRE, holding the hand in front of and little higher than head. Sometimes a puffing sound is also made with the mouth.

Deaf-mutes make their sign for BOAT, and then hold hands to right and left of body, and give them a circular motion to denote the wheels.

Stingy. Make sign for HEART and for FEW. The heart is narrow, compressed.

Deaf-mutes make same signs as for MISERLY.

Stink. Make sign for SMELL and BAD.

Deaf-mutes use the same sign.

Stop. See HALT.

Deaf-mutes strike palm of extended left with lower edge of extended right.

Store. Make sign for HOUSE and for TRADE.

Deaf-mutes make their signs for HOUSE and SELL.

Straight. See TRUE.

Deaf-mutes pass lower edge of extended right across palm of extended left, edge touching palm, hands at right angles.

Strike. Hold extended left hand, back down, well in front of left breast, fingers pointing to front and right; raise the extended right hand in front of and higher than right shoulder; strike the left palm sharply with lower edge of extended right hand. This is usually used to represent a blow given with a weapon. Indians—men and boys—do not fight; *i.e.*, have recourse to fisticuffs. Public sentiment has never allowed this manner of settling disputes. The women do sometimes pull hair like their white sisters.

Deaf-mutes strike the left palm with closed right hand.

String (Protection). Make sign for ROPE, LITTLE, FEMALE; then bring the knees together and imitate motions of tying a string around them.

Among many tribes, young girls, just before and after reaching the age of puberty, use at night what is called a protection-string. This is a small cord which they tie around the legs, just above the knees, before going to sleep at night. The liberty and license of an Indian camp make this necessary, for some young man in the village may mark the position in a lodge where a girl sleeps, and, when the inmates are sleeping soundly, cautiously and carefully creep in at the door, or quietly pull up one or two lodge-pins near where the girl lies, crawl in and feel her person if she has not tied herself.

Public opinion makes this string sacred, and to untie or cut it would be regarded as a heinous offence, much as rape is considered with us. This string is also used by married women when their husbands are away, and with the Cheyennes some women keep the same string from early youth to old age.

Striped. Hold left arm as in SPOTTED, and then draw palm of extended right hand from left to right across the left forearm in different places.

Deaf-mutes draw the right hand down over and around surface of body.

Strong. Make sign for BRAVE. Sometimes sign for MUST or PUSH is used ; in such sentences as " I want you to be strong in your efforts," "strong in your work," etc.

Deaf-mutes bring the clinched fists down from about height of and opposite shoulder to height of waist, and assume a determined expression of countenance.

Sugar. Touch the tongue with tip of extended index of right hand. Sometimes sign for GOOD is also made.

Deaf-mutes hold tips of extended index and second finger against lips, and make motion with jaws as though eating.

Sumach. Make sign for LEAF, for RED, and rub tips of fingers of or lower edge of closed right hand against left palm.

The leaves of the sumach are dried, then, broken up by rubbing in the palm of the hand, and mixed with tobacco, are used for smoking.

Sometimes the signs for SMOKE and GOOD are also made.

Summer. Make sign for GRASS, holding hands quite high. Sometimes sign for HOT is also made. I have also seen signs made to denote the sun as passing directly overhead, and HOT.

Deaf-mutes make their sign for HOT ; *i.e.,* drawing crooked index across forehead from left to right.

Sun. Form an incomplete circle with index and thumb of right hand, space of about an inch between tips ; hold hand towards eastern horizon, and move it on a nearly vertical curve towards the west. The right hand fixed as above, and pushed up towards any one position of the sun, is all that is usually done. This sign is frequently used to denote the time of day, which is determined by the position of the sun in the heavens.

Deaf-mutes raise the right hand towards an imaginary position of the sun, index finger extended and pointing at this sun ; mostly by wrist action describe a small circle with tip of index, then, extending and separating fingers, move the hand downwards tremulously, to denote the rays of heat.

Sun-Dance. Make signs for DANCE and for WHISTLE. Some add signs for the enclosure, and putting of skewers in muscles of breast.

The Sun-Dance is a religious ceremony, the fulfilment of a vow made to some mysterious force in nature. If an Indian be surrounded by his foes, he promises the God in the sun or the Great Spirit that if he be delivered from the hands of his enemies he will, when the time comes (usually full of the moon in June), dance the Sun-Dance. If some friend or kin is at the point of death, he makes the same vow: if the Great Spirit will restore his friend or kin to health. In time of sore need he calls on the greatest and most mysterious force of nature for aid, and promises that he will subject himself to physical suffering and torture, fasting and mutilation, if succor is accorded him.

This dance partakes as strongly of a religious character as any custom which the Indians have preserved since the invasion of the white race; and to my mind, gives evidence that before our Christian religion was disseminated among these people by the missionaries they worshipped the sun more than anything else in nature. This view seems to have support in the fact that to-day, after some hundreds of years of contact with our religious views, they still worship the mysterious and unknown in nature.

I attended the Sun-Dance in the camp of the Sioux war chief Crazy Horse, in 1877, and I give the details, briefly, as I observed them there. The tepees were formed in a circle, with an open space towards the east. The Sun-Dance pole was selected by the medicine-man of the camp; a cottonwood one, about eight inches in diameter, and thirty feet long from the butt to where it forked. It was located in a ravine about two miles from the village, and a day was devoted to cutting and hauling it to camp, a labor in which the entire village united, men, women, and children. Spring was radiant in her beauty, and the savages decorated themselves and their ponies with crowns and shields of wild clematis and other foliage. A group of old women gathered near the foot of the tree selected and danced, chattered, and howled.

The sides of the ravine were thickly lined with painted and decorated savages. The man who had performed the bravest deed during the past year advanced and hit the tree a light blow with an axe, and gave two sticks to the old women, who chanted and danced more vigorously and hideously than before. These sticks were tokens, good for a pony apiece. Then two or three more followed suit,—struck the tree and gave something away to the poor. Two virgins, gaudily gotten up in dresses worked with beads and elk-teeth, cut down the tree and trimmed it. It was then carried by the sub-chiefs and headmen a short distance towards camp (they refraining as much as possible from touching it with their hands, handling it with ropes), where it was put on a wagon. This troubled the soul of an old man, who, sitting near me, said he was afraid the Great Spirit looking down would see it, and would not like it; it was a deviation from a good old custom, which was to have it carried by the headmen to the camp. Four halts were made going to camp, and at each halt the God in the sun was prayed to, through their way of smoking. The last halt was made when this strange and wild procession was about half a mile from the lodges. The warriors here formed in a line, and charged, with shots and shouts, for the centre of the space enclosed by the tepees. The one who first struck the place where the Sun-Dance pole was to be planted, was supposed to be the one who would "count the first coup" in case of a war-party going out. They charged and recharged across this open space, and as I saw it I thought of another scene which must have been somewhat similar, and which occurred only one short year before,—the field of the Little Big Horn River, where General Custer and his three hundred men went down so speedily to death, surrounded by this horde, and where this very chief had two ponies shot and killed under him, as he rode in his demon-like way into the very midst of the soldiers, firm and fearless in his conviction that he could not be killed by a bullet.

The pole was laid on the ground, and all repaired to their lodges for a feast, which, however, did not include those who were to dance the Sun-Dance. They must fast until after it was over. These included the few who had made the vow long before, and those who had agreed to join in the trial. The last had not made a promise, but they would arouse their courage, show their power to endure bodily suffering, join their friends and kin in worship.

In this camp of about six thousand only three had made the vow, and yet, I think, ten fasted, were mutilated, took part in this horrible worship called a Sun-Dance.

The second day was devoted to planting the Sun-Dance pole, making a circular shed or enclosure around it, fastening the " medicine-bag" to the forks of the pole, etc. The early part of the third day was devoted to cutting holes in the ears of the babies. These little wretches were laid at the foot of the pole, and their ears pierced with a knife by the medicine-man.

Those who were to dance only had for clothing a wrapping about their loins ; sometimes, I was told, they only wore a breech-cloth. They each had an attendant, who painted him, filled his pipe, rubbed the palms of his hands with sage and other green herbs, and talked encouragingly to him. They seemed to need the encouragement, for they were faint and weak from fasting and the fear of the horrible torture awaiting them. Around them were feasting and laughter. The circular shed was filled with people, who had brought huge kettles of food. Later the women kinsfolk, wives, sisters, and sweethearts, came in singing, and had their arms slashed by the medicine-man's knife, thus endeavoring to support with their suffering the pain and torture being undergone by the men. Finally one of the dancers was laid with his head near the foot of the Sun-Dance pole, and two holes were cut in the muscles of his chest, through which two sticks or skewers were thrust. To each of these sticks a string was fastened ; then the victim was lifted up, and the strings were fastened to a lariat hanging from the pole. The victim now blew on a whistle made of the bone of an eagle's wing, looked at the sun and its course from its rising to its setting, and until he could free himself by tearing out the flesh and muscles, dancing, whistling, praying for deliverance, and making other requests. Sometimes strings are tied into the muscles of the back and a buffalo-skull fastened to them. I saw one Indian throw himself back with all his force and might, but he could not tear himself loose ; he had to wait for a slight decay of the muscles. One or two were very weak-kneed, heart-sick with fear and fasting ; and if ever I saw regret, it was on their painted faces. The most of them stood it stoutly enough. After breaking loose, if they are exhausted, they are carried off on a blanket, and kindly and carefully cared for.

It would take many pages to describe this horrible ceremony in detail, I have only tried to give some of the salient points. I was told by a Sioux that the enclosure was a church ; their Grandmother (the Earth) was represented by the grass and sage, and a cross was made at the foot of the pole to represent the sun and stars.

The Shoshones call this dance the "Dry-Dance," and hold it about June, when green grass has "come up pretty well." Some one in the camp gives the dance ; *i.e.*, gets it up, and asks the others to join. Those who participate do not eat or drink for four days and nights during the continuance of the dance. The prolonged fasting, excitement, and physical exertion sometimes produce fainting ; and any visions had while in this condition are highly prized. There seemed, from the description, but little difference between this and the Sioux Sun-Dance. The promise does not originate in the same way, but is more the result of religious zeal. A buffalo-skin is hung on the pole at the forks instead of a medicine-bag, the head is left on the skin, and by continually looking at this some vision is hoped for and expected. They plant one pole in the centre, and have ten in the outer circle ; and instead of constantly looking at the sun, they look at the buffalo-head.

The Comanches told me that they did not have a Sun-Dance, but did have dances of a religious character to propitiate the force or Great Spirit in the sun.

The Poncas have a Sun-Dance like the Sioux ; and at the one held in 1880, when they were suffering great sadness at the loss of their country and many were dying of nostalgia, under the pressure of the excitement and religious fervor one was thrown into such a state of desperation that he had the medicine-men make the incisions in the muscles in his chest very deep,—so deep that he could not free himself, and he finally directed them to hitch a pony to his legs and drag him away from the Sun-Dance pole, which was done. Another cut off his little finger and ate it.

The Nez Perces have no Sun-Dance, but a yearly dance is held in the winter.

Sunday. Make sign for DAY and MEDICINE.

A Sioux, who was not thoroughly conversant with gesture speech, in answer to my question as to what sign should be made for Sunday, said, "Work," "No," "White," "Dress," "Good;" indicating that Sunday was a day of rest and fine dressing for the white people.

Deaf-mutes denote a day of rest, or a holy day. For rest they fold hands on breast.

Sun-Dog. Conception: Fires to warm the sun. Make sign for SUN, and then with both hands make sign for FIRE, holding hands on each side of and close to position of right hand when making sign for SUN. The Shoshones call this phenomenon "the sun's winter ear-ring," and of course make signs accordingly.

Deaf-mutes indicate a small sun near the sun.

Superior. In comparing two persons or objects the extended index fingers are placed side by side, other fingers and thumbs closed, and the index held highest represents the superior person or object. One superior to several or many, extend the thumb and fingers of left hand, fingers pointing upwards, and place the extended index of right hand near but higher. The right hand is placed a little or great distance above left, according to the degree of superiority.

Deaf-mutes fix hands, as in their sign for CHIEF, and hold one higher than the other.

Surround. Hold hands well out and to right and left of body, hands equally advanced, same height, palms towards each other, lower edges pointing to front, index fingers and thumbs curved, spread and horizontal, other fingers closed; bring hands towards each other, and form a horizontal circle with thumbs and index fingers, in front of body.

To make a surround of buffalo, make sign for BUFFALO, the above sign for SURROUND, sometimes adding signs for KILL, BRING (with both hands), CUTTING UP, and PACK.

For BRING, move the hands outwards after the horizontal circle is made, extending index fingers to front; then draw the hands horizontally in towards the body, at same time curving index fingers as though hooking on to something; repeat this latter motion in different directions. In former times buffalo were, of course, more numerous; but the absence of weapons or their inferior quality rendered it necessary to take great precaution against disturbing the herd. The camp was carefully moved as near the herd as possible without disturbing it, and, before they had ponies, a favorable location was selected, where the topography of the country needed but a few fallen trees to make a pen, into which the buffalo were driven and killed. There seems to be no doubt that they secured many by stampeding herds over precipices. After they got ponies the herd was attacked from all sides by the men and a large number killed. Then there would be no more hunting until the meat and skins had been taken care of by the squaws, when another surround would be made.

Sweat-Lodge. Make signs for MEDICINE and WICKEY-UP.

Sometimes signs for MEDICINE, WORK, ROCK, FIRE, WICKEY-UP, and motion of throwing stones into the wickey-up are made.

The use of the sweat-bath by means of heated air and steam seems common to all tribes, and with all it is used not only to cure physical disease, but as a form of worship and supplication.

Mr. Dunbar says of the Pawnees, that "they had one hygienic usage (as also many other tribes) that no doubt did much to counteract the prejudicial influences of their uncleanly mode of life. In slight indisposition, and frequently in health, the vapor-bath was resorted to. A small frame-work of withes, about six feet in diameter and four in height, was built. Several of these might at any time be seen in different directions in a village. Whenever any one wished to enjoy a bath, several large heated stones were placed in one of these frames, and the frame-work covered heavily with blankets or skins. The person then crept within, taking along a vessel full of water. By sprinkling this slowly upon the stones the interior was soon filled with dense steam, which might be enjoyed as long as desired. The frequent use of these sudatories produced most beneficial results in maintaining and stimulating the activity of the secretory system.

Sitting Bull, the Sioux chief, gave me a very elaborate description in signs for the sweat-lodge, or sweat-house, as the interpreters usually call it. He made signs for wickey-up, for the covering of same with blankets and skins, heating the stones, pouring water on them, talking to them, making requests, hoping the Great Spirit would listen and make them live long on the earth, give them plenty to eat, furnish them all they wanted, give them success in war, and protect them in peace.

The frame is usually made of green willows, about an inch and a half in diameter at the large ends, which are stuck in the ground. The smaller ends are then bent over and fastened, forming an elliptical-shaped frame-work. The number of willows used varies greatly, frequently being determined by a dream of the man who makes the bath-house.

The Arapahoes use any number from fifteen to one hundred and seven, and a special sweat-lodge is made just before the annual Medicine-Dance. I had heard so much of this bath, had seen the abandoned little frames at so many temporary Indian camps when they were on the march, had seen the same kind of a little house used by so many tribes who in all other customs varied so much, and was able to find out so little in regard to it, that in August, 1881, being at Fort Keogh and a Cheyenne camp near by, I concluded to take one with the Indians. I spoke to the chief and made an appointment. I had no interpreter, and could only talk with the Indians in the sign language, but at about two o'clock one afternoon I rode to the camp. The tepees were located on the bank of the Yellowstone River in the midst of some stately cottonwood-trees. The atmosphere was smoky, and a filmy veil of blue mantled the not distant Bad Land bluffs. A lazy hush had settled on this straggling little Indian village on this hazy day, which so gently heralded the near approach of autumn. I arrived before the preparations were made, and so had the benefit of witnessing all that was done. The squaws turned out to cut some wood, and soon a pile was ready near the sweat-lodge, which in the mean time was covered, first with some untanned buffalo-skins, leaving only a small entrance, and then with canvas and blankets. This lodge was made of twelve willows, four on each side and two at each end, placed in the ground nearly in the shape of an ellipse, then bent over and fastened, so that the frame was not quite four feet high. The ground inside had been smoothed off and strewn with leaves and grass. In the centre was a circular hole about eighteen inches in diameter and twelve deep; this was carefully cleaned out, so that only fresh dirt remained. The squaws laid down a row of sticks a few feet outside the entrance to the lodge, and then placed a row of small stones, about six inches in diameter, on these sticks, then some more wood and then stones, till a crib about two feet high and three feet wide and four long was made, which was then set on fire.

In the mean time I had gone into some tall weeds and thick bushes near at hand, which formed a perfect screen, and arrayed myself, by means of a borrowed strap and towel, in a breech-cloth, and stepped forth dressed for the bath. My appearance created some merriment on the part of the squaws. The chief brought his pipe, tobacco, medicine-rattle, and much of his war outfit, which were first placed inside. He, with the little stick used for cleaning the Indian pipe, drew the figure of a man without arms or legs in the dirt at the bottom of the hole. A buffalo-skull, white with age, was placed just in front of the little door. We had crowded in, and were seated tailor-fashion on the ground. The chief filled his pipe, putting a little tobacco in the hole, and mixing with the tobacco some sweet-smelling dried grass. He lighted the pipe and pointed the stem to the zenith, to the figure in the hole, to the painted buffalo-skull outside, and to the four winds, at the same time muttering a prayer. After taking a few puffs, or rather inhalations, he passed the pipe to me. When we had finished smoking the stones had reached a red heat, and about this time we were joined by five other Indians, so that we were pretty closely packed in. The squaw passed in one of the stones, using a forked stick, which was placed in the centre of the hole, and upon it the chief dropped a few bits of the sweet-smelling grass, which, as it burned, gave out a pleasant fragrance. His rattle and other trappings were then handed outside. One of the medicine-bags was placed on the buffalo-skull, and the rest were laid on the roof of our little house. The other stones were then handed in, and when carefully piled in the hole reached about a foot above the surface of the ground. The skins and canvas were then let down over the door, and we were suddenly in total darkness. The heat became intense. There was a report like a pistol-shot, but from the sounds I knew the chief had taken some water in his mouth and spouted it out on the stones. Waves of hot air and steam passed over me, which seemed more like liquid fire than steam and air. A hand touched my right arm and was moved down to my hand, and

I then felt a wooden bowl of water handed me. I supposed it was intended that I should take a swallow, which I did, and passed it to the Indian on my left. I was sitting upright, and my head touched the roof of the little house. My hair was so hot that I could hardly touch my hand to it. I was becoming dazed and dizzy with the heat. The perspiration ran off my body in huge drops.

I could not talk to the Indians, as I did not understand half a dozen words of their vocal language, and in the intense darkness signs could not be used. Of course, with a slight effort I could have raised some of the skins which formed the covering to the lodge, as they were only fastened to the ground by a few stones, but my pride would not let me do this. I felt that I was being physically and mentally cooked. The chief, who was also a medicine-man, from time to time sang in a weird, chanting way. Suddenly the covering to the lodge was raised at the door and opposite it, and the sunshine blazed in, and the cool air swept gratefully over me. The copper-colored forms of the Indians were all bowed, the heads near the ground at their bent knees.

This was not in worship, but merely to avoid the extreme heat of the top of the little lodge ; it brought their heads nearer the hot stones, but still the heat was not nearly as intense as at the top. I also noticed that the hair of the Indians was wet. Instead of swallowing the water they had held it in their mouths for a moment, and then spouting it into the curved hands, had saturated their hair with it. I at once poured some water from the bowl on my head, thoroughly saturating my hair, and it seemed to clear my brain as from a hot mist. The covering of the lodge remained up some moments, and was then closed as before. This time I held my head down, and my hair being wet, I experienced no uncomfortable sensations. A mouthful of water only was blown upon the stones as before. (Sometimes a little musk or something of the kind is held in the medicine-man's mouth, so that a pungent odor is emitted as this water is blown upon the stones.) The covering was raised and lowered four times, and then quite a quantity of water was poured on the stones, filling the little house full of hot steam. We all then went to the river and plunged in, and felt greatly refreshed. Had I understood the necessity of wetting my hair and keeping my head near the ground, I do not think I should have experienced any ill effects from the bath ; as it was I was half ill for three or four days, and I attributed it to the overheating. I am accustomed to taking Turkish and Russian baths, and have been in a hot room for some time when the thermometer indicated one hundred and seventy degrees, and gone from this through different stages to nearly ice-water, but I have never experienced anything like the cooking I got in that Cheyenne sweat-lodge, and I am confident it was their ordinary bath. Women and little children join the men in these baths.

The spring of the year, just as the snow is disappearing, seems to be a favorite time for the Cheyennes to indulge in this bath ; and at this time they " make medicine" for a speedy disappearance of the snow, quick growth of the grass, and prompt fattening of all animals. I once saw an old man, seventy-six years of age, walking around on the snow perfectly naked, except for his breech-cloth, both before and after taking one of these baths. When vision-seeking, the dreamers do not, I believe, have the skins *raised*, but try and secure supernatural knowledge by enduring the hot air and steam for prolonged periods.

These baths are also taken by persons who are greatly angered or depressed by the loss of friend or kin by death. I know a Sioux chief whose little son, the pride and joy of his heart, was taken suddenly sick and died. His sorrow and anger made him a dangerous creature to meet. His friends put him in one of these baths and "washed his grief away."

Briefly, then, as an Indian once said to me, the sweat-lodge is made as a " medicine," to ask of the Great Spirit anything we want. If one is sick or has anything the matter with them, they go in and ask the Great Spirit to heal them ; and all go to ask for assistance and guidance.

I afterwards learned that the figure in the bottom of the hole indicated what was specially wished and prayed for,—a figure of a man without limbs indicated a wish to kill an enemy; a pony-track, to steal ponies. It is considered specially good luck for the medicine-man to take the bath with others, and he is master of ceremonies.

As they lived mostly on buffalo, the head was placed in front of the sweat-lodge that they might pray to it ; might not forget to petition the Great Mystery of the universe to perpetuate the buffalo and have them always near their villages.

Sweet. See SUGAR.

Swim. Make sign for WATER ; then strike out well to front with extended hands, backs up, as though swimming ; moving first right hand, then left. Indians do not swing the hands so much to right and left as the whites in swimming, but make more of a pawing motion to front.

Deaf-mutes imitate our method of swimming.

Syphilis. Lay compressed hands on groins. The Arapahoes claim that they caught this disease from the Indians to the South. They express it, "When a man has caught the disease, that a woman has broken his thigh with her six-shooter."

T.

Tail. Carry right hand, back nearly up, to rear of centre of body, index finger extended pointing to rear and downwards, others and thumb closed.

Deaf-mutes use the same sign.

Take. To take from some one else : Carry right hand well out in front or to right or left of body, index finger extended and pointing to front, right or left, others and thumb closed ; bring hand briskly in towards body, at same time curving and nearly closing index finger.

If taking from a number of persons, repeat motion in different directions, as though they were in a semicircle in front and to right and left.

To have some one else take from you : Hold hand as explained above, but turn the wrist and arm, so that index finger will point towards body, thumb and index of hand up, back of hand about vertical ; carry hand well in towards body, curve the index, and move the hand briskly outwards, as though hooking on to something. This is also used in the sense of taking from one's people, etc.

Deaf-mutes make a grasping motion with hand.

Talk. There are two distinct signs for this, which are, however, used in different senses. A little talk, a short speech, a few words, or " one person talking to another," would ordinarily be expressed by holding right hand, back up, and slightly to rear, in front of, close to, and a little lower than mouth, hand closed, with nail of index pressing against thumb ; move the hand slightly to front, at same time extend index with a snap (the words are thrown out) ; repeat motion three or four times. This is talking or speaking a little to another person.

For some one else talking : Hold right hand fixed in same way, back out, and snap fingers towards face or ear, hand held well out or opposite right ear ; in the latter case rather close to it.

A slight sound made at a distance, and only faintly heard, would also be expressed in this way.

To illustrate this sign, and give an idea of the manner of establishing the relative positions of objects : suppose two persons standing and talking to each other. Represent the two persons by the extended index fingers pointing upwards, other fingers and thumbs closed. Suppose the persons were standing twice their height apart, hold the index fingers twice their length apart, and then make the above sign for TALK, holding hand so that words are snapped from the position of the person talking towards the tip of the extended index.

For a council, " to speak at length," to " talk a great deal," etc., would be expressed by holding extended right hand, back down, in front of, close to, and little lower than mouth, fingers pointing to left ; mostly by wrist action move the hand outwards few inches, repeating motion two or three times. This is speaking or talking to some one. To be spoken to or talked to in the above sense : Hold the right hand fixed as above, well out in front about height of chin ; move the hand in towards body few inches, mostly by wrist action, repeating motion three or four times.

To represent a number of persons as talking or speaking in council : Make sign for Council, then hold extended hands, backs down, at same height, equally advanced, well in front of shoulders, about height of breast, fingers pointing to front ; move the right hand, mostly by wrist action, towards left, fingers in this position, pointing to left and front ; carry hand back to its first position, at same time execute a similar motion with left hand towards right ; repeat these motions rather briskly three or four times. In this sign the words seem handed back and forth.

The distinction I have made in the two signs is not always strictly observed, but I am convinced that it is correct, and should be. Sometimes after each of the signs, particularly after the first one, the sign for Little is made. Frequently the first-described sign is made with both hands and repeated several times, to denote several persons talking, or one person talking very much.

Deaf-mutes make a circular motion of extended right index in front of mouth.

Tall. Fix, move, and hold right hand as in Stand, but higher, nearly full height of extended arm.

Deaf-mutes use the same sign.

Tan. Bring the hands in front of body, fingers partially curved and touching, hands slightly compressed, left hand a little nearer the body than right and a little lower, hands a few inches apart, back of left hand nearly to front, back of right hand nearly upwards, the curved fingers pointing towards the ground ; bend forward slightly and execute a pawing motion by moving hands downwards and to right and rear on a curve. The position of the hands is sometimes reversed, and movement made to left and rear,—this represents cutting or scraping the meat from the skin ; then bring the closed hands in front of body, equally advanced, same height and few inches apart, back of right to right, left to left ; move the hands about horizontally, briskly past each other two or three times ; this represents rubbing to soften the leather. Sometimes a motion to indicate putting tanning material on the hide is also made.

In the process of dressing and tanning buffalo-robes, the fresh skins are first stretched very taut on the ground by means of pins driven through the edges, or the hides are lashed to the lodge-poles of the tepee or fastened to frames, in which positions they are left until thoroughly dry. The fatty matter and a portion of the hide are removed in thin shavings by means of some sharp instrument,— usually, at present, a piece of steel fastened into a piece of horn. A thin coating of the tanning material, which is a mixture of about one part of brains to two parts of well-cooked liver, with a little fat added, is then spread over the inner surface of the hide, which is then rolled up and allowed to remain two or three days, when the tanning material is washed off. Sometimes the hide is dipped three separate times in brain and liver water. A small rope made of sinew is tied to a tree or stake at an angle with the ground of about forty-five degrees, and the robe rubbed over it until it is dry and soft. In tanning deer-, antelope-skins, etc., the skin is soaked in water and the hair scraped off, after which they are treated as described for buffalo-hides and then smoked.

Their process of tanning and dressing skins and robes is very laborious and slow, and in view of the work expended, it is wonderful how cheap their produce of this kind is.

For tepees, buffalo- and elk-skins are considered the best, the hair, of course, being removed before tanning. Buffalo-hides used for this purpose, and for the soles of moccasins and par-flèches, are usually from animals which are killed when the fur is worthless.

Tangled. The hands are moved one about the other, usually having fingers slightly separated.

Deaf-mutes same.

Taste. Touch the tongue with tip of index of right hand, other fingers and thumb closed.

Deaf-mutes use the same sign.

Tattoo. Compress the right hand, bringing tips of thumb and fingers near together, and tap with ends of fingers the portion of body which has been marked in this way.

Deaf-mutes use only tip of index to denote the marks.

Two tribes, the Mandans and Wichitas, take their tribal sign from this peculiar way of decorating themselves. The Plains Indians generally do not practise it ; but the Apaches in the Southwest and many of the tribes in the extreme Northwest do.

Tea. Make sign for TREE, sign for LEAF, sign for DRINK, and sign for GOOD. Sometimes the signs for KETTLE, putting the leaf in it, and for MAKE are also made.

Deaf-mutes form a horizontal circle with index and thumb of left hand, other fingers closed, and move index and thumb of right hand,—placed on this circle,—as though stirring something in a cup.

Colonel J. W. Mason informed me that the Indians with him (Shoshones) found a shrub on the mountains near the National Park which, when boiled in water, made a drink possessing the characteristics of tea,—the same in taste and effect ; the entire shrub was used. This was found at an altitude of about eight thousand feet, and near by it the Indians also found a bulbous root which made excellent soup.

Telegraph. Make sign for WRITE ; then hold extended left hand, back out, in front of body ; strike with lower edge of extended right hand upper edge of left, allowing hand to slightly rebound, and then sweep hand into the position of GO, making this latter sign quite briskly.

Latterly, since the Indians have seen telegraphic instruments working, they frequently make sign for WRITE, then tap the left palm several times with tip of curved index of right hand, other fingers and thumb closed. Sometimes sign for IRON, STRIKE, and TALK are made.

The telegraph wire is represented by first making the above sign, then drawing extended index of right hand horizontally from left to right, well out in front of body, about height of head, other fingers and thumb closed.

Deaf-mutes hold left hand, back up, in front of body, index alone extended and pointing to front ; tap with tip of curved right index, other fingers and thumb closed, the knuckle of left index, and then move the right hand sharply to front, tip of right index touching back of left.

Many stories have been told about the Indians considering the telegraph line as particularly "bad medicine" ; and I even heard that this special aversion grew out of a most violent shock one got from the current of electricity when he was cutting the wire.

I do not think they have any special feeling about it one way or the other ; they know that it is beyond their comprehension,—they do not understand it ; and hostile Indians seldom interfere with it, because in many instances their interference has discovered their presence and led to pursuit and punishment. In addition to this there is nothing to be gained by the destruction,—*i.e.*, no material benefit accrues to them,—and to take any risks Indians must see something to be gained,—some advantage to be secured.

Tepee. Bring tips of extended index fingers together, forming an angle ; tips of index fingers about height of breast and several inches from it, other fingers and thumbs closed, back of right hand up and to right, left hand back up and to left, index fingers in the same vertical plane.

Sometimes the index fingers are crossed at first joints ; and I have also seen both compressed hands brought tips together and forming a cone.

Deaf-mutes make their signs for INDIAN, HOUSE, and WHITE.

From fourteen to twenty-six poles are used in a lodge, and one or two for the wing-poles on the outside ; these latter for adjusting the wings, near the opening at the top of the lodge, for the escape of smoke ; the wings are kept at such angles as to produce the best draught. The best poles are made from the slender mountain-pine, which grows thickly in the mountains. The squaws cut and trim them, and carefully peel off the bark. They are then partially dried or seasoned, and are first pitched for some time without any covering of canvas or skin. By being thus slowly cured they are kept straight. The length depends on the size of the lodge of course, and varies from sixteen to thirty feet.

Mr. Dunbar says of the Pawnees, that "their lodges were of two patterns, so utterly unlike in appearance and construction that it would scarcely seem possible that they should both be the work of the same tribe.   There was the ordinary skin lodge used while on their hunts.   The frame consisted of from twelve to twenty smoothly-dressed poles, sixteen feet long.   After a good set of these poles had once been secured, they were carried on all their travels, just as any other necessary furniture.   When a lodge was to be pitched, three of these poles were tied together near the top and set up like a tripod.   The cord with which these three poles were tied was sufficiently long for the ends to hang to the ground.   The other poles, save one, were successively set up, the top of each resting against the first three, while the lower ends formed a circle, from twelve to seventeen feet in diameter.   The tops were then bound together securely by means of the pendent cord.   One edge of the covering was now made fast to the remaining pole, by means of which it was raised up and carried round the frame-work, so as to envelop it completely.   The two edges of the cover were closed together by wooden pins or keys, except three feet at the extreme top, left open for a smoke-hole, and an equal space at the bottom for an entrance.   The spare pole was attached to one edge of the cover at the top, so that the smoke-hole might be closed or opened at will.   The skin of a bear or some other animal was fixed to the outside of the lodge, immediately above the entrance, so as to hang down over the latter as a sort of door.   Inside, the fireplace occupied the centre of the lodge.   About it were spread mats, which served as seats by day and couches by night.   All furniture not in actual use was packed on the outside next to the lodge walls.   The covering of the lodge was one continuous piece, made up of buffalo-skins nicely fitted together.   In tanning, these skins were dressed so thin that sufficient light was transmitted into the interior even when the lodge was tightly closed.   When new they were quite white, and a village of them presented an attractive appearance.   Sometimes they were variously painted, according to the requirements of Pawnee fancy.

" The other was the large, stationary lodge found only in their permanent villages.   The construction was as follows: The sod was carefully removed from the area to be occupied by the lodge.   In the centre an excavation, three feet in diameter and five inches deep, was made for a fireplace.   Lieutenant Pike states that the entire area was excavated to a depth of four feet.   This is a mistake.   The accumulation of loose soil immediately about the lodge, during the process of construction and subsequently, did, however, sometimes produce an apparent depression inside.   The soil taken from the fireplace was carefully placed in a small ridge immediately about its edge.   The entire area as thus prepared was then repeatedly beaten with mallets or billets of wood prepared for the purpose, in order to render it compact and smooth.   About the fireplace, at a distance of eight feet from the centre, a circle of six or eight strong posts, forked and rising twelve feet above the surface, was set firmly in the ground.   Outside of this circle, at a distance of nine feet, was set another circle of posts similar, but standing only seven feet high, and the same distance from each other.   In the forks of the posts of the inner circle strong poles were laid, reaching from one to another. Similar poles were likewise laid on the posts of the outer circle. Two feet outside of this circle a small ditch, two inches deep and three wide, was now dug. In this ditch, at intervals of four inches, were set poles two or three inches in diameter, and of sufficient length to just reach the poles on the posts of the outer circle. These inclined poles formed the frame-work of the walls of the lodge. Poles of like size and at equal intervals were now laid from the lower cross-poles to the upper, but reaching so far beyond the latter that between the upper extremities of these poles a circular orifice, about two feet in diameter, was left as a skylight and smoke-hole. These poles formed the support of the roof. Willow withes were then bound transversely with bark to these poles at intervals of about an inch. At this stage the lodge had some resemblance to an immense basket inverted. A layer of hay was now placed upon the frame-work, and the whole built over with sods, the interstices in the sod-work being carefully filled with loose soil. The thickness of the earth upon the roof was about nine inches, on the walls considerably more. The external appearance of a lodge as thus finished was not unlike a large charcoal-pit. The entrance was through a passage twelve feet long and seven wide. The sides of this passage, which always faced the east (as did also the entrance of a skin lodge), were constructed exactly as the walls of the lodge ; the top was flat and heavily covered with turf. Over its inner extremity, where it opened into the lodge, was hung a skin as a sort of closure. The lower part of this was free, so that it might be easily thrown up by those passing in and out. Inside, till a person became accustomed to the dim light, all seemed obscure. Near the fireplace was a forked stake, set in an inclining position, to answer as a crane in cooking. The ground about the fire was overspread with mats, upon which the occupants might sit. Next to the wall was a row of beds, extending entirely around the lodge (except at the entrance), each bed occupying the interval between two posts of the outer circle. The beds were raised a few inches from the ground upon a platform of rods, over which a mat was spread, and upon this the bedding of buffalo-robes and other skins. Partitions made of willow withes, bound closely together with bark, were set up between the ends of adjacent beds ; and immediately in front of each bed a mat or skin was sometimes suspended to the poles of the roof as a sort of curtain, to be rolled up or let down at pleasure. Furniture, as arms, clothing, provisions, saddles, etc., not in use was hung upon different parts of the frame-work, or variously bestowed about the interior.

Several families usually lived in one of these lodges. Though each family had its particular part of the dwelling and the furniture of each was kept separate, anything like privacy in conversation or life was impossible. What one did all knew. Whenever a member of any one of the families cooked, a portion of the food was given to each occupant without distinction of family. They were also very accommodating, borrowing and lending freely almost any article they had.

The dimensions given in the preceding description are those of an average lodge. The actual proportions of one taken as of ordinary size were: Diameter, thirty-nine feet; wall, seven and one-half feet high; extreme height of roof, fifteen and one-half feet; length of entrance, thirteen feet; width, seven feet. Some of these figures might be considerably larger or smaller. One lodge measured was only twenty-three feet in diameter; another was fifty-six feet. Among the remains of an old Skï'-di village on the Loup, one of the lodges seems to have been two hundred feet in diameter. The tradition is that it was a medicine-lodge.

As may be readily inferred, the building of one of these fixed lodges was an undertaking involving much labor. The timber quite frequently was procurable only at a distance, and with their facilities its adjustment was a tedious process. And yet, after all the outlay necessary in its construction, it was occupied a comparatively small part of the year, probably not over four months. The remaining eight months they were absent on their semi-annual hunts. Still, these fixed residences were of great benefit to them. They preserved alive the idea of home, and were undoubtedly one cause of the tribe's retaining a sort of fixity and regularity in their yearly life which otherwise might have been relinquished long ago. On sanitary grounds their brief yearly continuance in these dwellings was no doubt fortunate. The ventilation in them was very defective, and continuous occupation would in all probability have been a fertile source of wasting disease.

This large lodge was also used among the other branches of the Pawnee family, though in the South its construction was somewhat modified. Catlin represents the Arickaree lodges as conical, with no projecting entrance. This is a mistake. Their lodges were essentially the same as those of the Pawnees. Among the Southern branches the frame-work was similar, but instead of a covering of turf they were heavily thatched with straw or grass. Marcy, in his "Exploration of the Red River," gives a cut of a Wichita village, in which the lodges are represented as conical. This pattern was in use, but the other was the more common.

I give the following description of the Chippewa tepee, kindly furnished me by Mr. Charles H. Beaulieu:

"The conical-shaped wigwam is used altogether when camp is moved every day or so, and which can be hastily put up by first making use of three poles, placed together very much on the principle of the stacking of arms for infantry; other poles are then placed equidistant on the ground, their tops resting on the forked tops of the three poles first placed in position. The number of poles and their length depends on the size of the wigwam required to accommodate the family. The poles are placed on the ground from twenty to twenty-four inches apart. This style of wigwam is also altogether used in the winter-time, its conical shape and birch-bark covering reflecting heat of a moderate fire built in the centre. The outside of the wigwam is banked with snow to the height of one and one-half feet, preventing a draft or the cold from coming in at the bottom. The door-way is generally well closed with a blanket or two. A cross-piece is tied on to two poles opposite each other, upon which a piece of green wood, crotched at both ends, is forked to hang kettles or pots when cooking; one end of this piece of green wood is forked on to the cross-piece, the other holding the bail of the kettle.

"The material next the ground in these wigwams, and upon which matting is placed, is boughs of balsam, fir, or cedar. Hay is also used. The covering of these wigwams is always of birch-bark. Being in a country where timber is abundant, the poles are not removed on moving camp. The frame of the wigwam used by the Chippewas in the summer-time, when permanently located, are of any kind that are pliable, are placed securely in the ground and bent to the shape required, each pole having its mate on the opposite side of the lodge. Wherever these poles meet or cross one another, they are securely held with inner bark of basswood; other and smaller poles encircle those stuck in the ground. Raised platforms about fourteen inches high are made on each side of the wigwam as one enters the door-way. These are made of any size, and have sometimes two door-ways, which are always in any wigwam opposite each other. The average size will accommodate from ten to fifteen persons. Cooking is generally done outside, except in rainy weather. When mosquitoes are unusually numerous, smudges are built in the wigwams; but they are generally remarkably free of those pests.

"This style of dwelling is never used in cold weather. There is another kind of summer residence built very much in the shape of an ordinary white man's house; average size thirteen by eighteen feet; sides four and one-half feet high, and four and one-half feet roof; side of tamarack, Norway pine, or cedar-bark; birch-bark roofing.

"Sugar-camps or wigwams are always of this shape, with birch-bark sides or mats of stitched rushes. These wigwams are seldom without two entrances, and have the raised platforms as mentioned in number two. In placing birch-bark on wigwams of any description, it is laid on as siding would be on a house, sufficient lap being allowed to prevent drifting in of snow or leaking in rainy weather. The birch-bark covering for wigwams is cut from ten to twelve feet long and about four wide. The bark is gathered in June. A tree a foot in diameter will produce bark a yard wide. In removing bark from trees, it is done according to the use for which it is needed; consequently for wigwams it is removed in lengths of four feet. All the rough parts on outside are removed, and it is then sewed with a certain root of a tree found in damp places, or the inner bark of basswood. After the strips are sewed together, slender cedar or pine sticks are fastened at each end, to which strings are attached to tie the bark in place, or tie up the bundle when the bark is rolled up.''

I think that red-elm and ash-bark are also used for tepees as well as birch-bark.

There. To represent a person as going to a place, the left hand usually represents the place, as in ARRIVE THERE. The sign for SIT is frequently used, moving the hand well out from body.

Thick. Hold extended left hand, back to left, fingers pointing to front, in front of body ; place the right palm against lower edge of left hand, right hand at right angle with left ; bend up the fingers and clasp the left hand between thumb and fingers, tips of fingers and thumb at middle of left hand ; move the right to front two or three inches and back, repeating motion.

Deaf-mutes use the same, only the fingers do not touch back, or thumb palm of left hand.

Thief. Make signs for person and for STEAL.

Deaf-mutes use the same gestures.

Whipping and taking away property are the punishments which thieves have to undergo, but public sentiment is so strongly against this class that the Indians experience but little trouble from them. Many of the tribes will, however, steal anything they can carry away, from any strangers who may be with them, or from neighboring tribes, even though they may be at peace with them.

Thin. The best way is to point to something thin, but I have seen the extended left hand brought in front of body, fingers pointing to front ; then rub the lower edge with tips of thumb and index of right hand, other fingers closed, ball of thumb resting against first joint of index, index and thumb pointing upwards, edges of hands at angles with each other, back of index to left, back of thumb nearly to right.

Deaf-mutes use the same sign.

Think. Conception : Drawn from the heart. Hold right hand, back up, against left breast, index finger extended and pointing to left, others and thumb close ; move the hand horizontally outwards and to right eight or ten inches.

The Crows and some other tribes seem to combine signs for TRUE and THINK, holding hand as above described, but when moving to front allowing index to drop so as to point to front and downwards.

Deaf-mutes place tip of extended index against centre of forehead, other fingers and thumb closed ; move the hand so that tip of index describes a spiral circle.

Thousand. Make signs for HUNDRED and TEN. (See COUNT.)

Deaf-mutes make their signs for the letter M and ONE.

Thread. Rub inner surface of tips of thumb and index as though twisting thread ; make sign for SEW, and in this gesture carry right hand well beyond left, as though pulling a thread through the material.

Deaf-mutes make motion of sewing.

Thunder. Make signs for BIRD and for FIRE, holding hand in front of and little higher than head. Usually the sign for RAIN is also made.

Some Indians make signs for BIRD and MEDICINE ; and I have also seen both closed hands held in front of and close to mouth ; the hands thrown outwards, upwards, and to right and left, at same time opening them to denote the noise. Some Indians accompany the gesture with a vocal sound.

Thunder is called both the " shooting" and " fire bird."

Some consider that immense wings cause the rumbling, reverberating noise, and that the flash comes from the " shooting." This latter would seem to be of late origin,—since the introduction of gunpowder.

I have also been told many times that the noise was the crying or angry growl of the bird, and the lightning, the fire flashing from its eyes and mouth.

The interpreters tell me they call it a God. It is one of the few mysteries that they have a name for, and it is certain that they pray to and make offerings to it.

A Bannack Indian said to me, " The thunder asked the mosquito why he was so full of blood, and where he got it. The mosquito said he got it out of the pine-trees. He would not tell that he got it out of animals ; and so the thunder believed it, always striking and destroying the trees. I do not know what the lightning is, I only know it can kill, and we have no way of preventing it. A Bannack Indian once tried to escape from a storm,—ran his pony before it ; but as he reached camp, and just as he dismounted, the horse was killed."

Timber. See TREE.

Time. In reckoning the age of a person, or in speaking of past or future time, the general custom is to say "so many winters." " This year" would not necessarily be " this winter." (See YEAR.)

For time of day make sign for SUN, holding hand toward the point in the heavens where the sun is at the time desired to be represented. To specify any length of time during the day, mark space the sun passes over.

Time, as I have observed, is reckoned by the Indians,—days, by nights ; months, by moons ; and years, by winters.

Our expressions which convey ideas of present time are expressed by the Indians by *now,* or more frequently, *to-day.*

It may very truthfully be said that Indians care very little about time ; they seem to have more of it than anything else.

Deaf-mutes hold left hand, back up, in front of body, tap back of left hand near knuckles with tip of slightly-curved index of right hand, other fingers and thumb closed.

Timorous. Make signs for COWARD and LITTLE.

Deaf-mutes make their sign for AFRAID, drawing back only a little, however.

Tired. Hold hands, backs up, well in front of body, hands equally advanced same height and several inches apart, index fingers extended and pointing to front, others and thumbs closed ; lower the hands a few inches, and at same time draw them very slightly towards body. This is used in the sense of worn out, exhausted, etc.

Sometimes before making above sign, the thighs are touched with hands.

Deaf-mutes hold the hands, backs up, near each other, in front of body ; move the hands on small curves, right upwards to right and downwards, left upwards to left and downwards, at same time turning hands backs down ; as the hands turn downwards on the curves, let the hands drop by a sudden relaxation of the muscles, as though paralyzed.

Tobacco. Hold extended left hand, back down, in front of body ; place the lower edge of closed right hand on left palm ; rub with the lower edge the left palm by giving circular movement to right hand. This is the general sign for whatever is smoked in a pipe, and frequently the sign for SMOKE is added. What is usually called "plug tobacco" is represented by above sign, and then hold extended left hand, back to left and downwards, fingers pointing to front, well in front of and lower than left shoulder ; place lower edge of extended right hand on left wrist, at right angles with left hand (this makes the size), then hold left hand back to left and front, in front of body, fingers pointing to front and right ; hold extended right hand just in front and little higher than ends of fingers of left hand, hands at right angles, lower edge of right hand pointing to front, left, and downwards ; move the right hand to front, left, and downwards, right palm grazing left finger-ends as though cutting them off with its lower edge, repeating motion.

"Plug" is the kind of tobacco now commonly used by the Indians for smoking (they very rarely chew it), mixed in the proportions of one part tobacco with four parts of red-willow bark, the leaves of a vine called laube, or the leaves of sumach. The inner bark of the red willow is the portion used, and is prepared by scraping it off in long shavings (first carefully removing the outer bark), drying or breaking or cutting up into small particles.

In smoking they inhale the smoke into the lungs, and eject a great portion of it through the nose, sometimes blowing it in a thin column towards the God they may be making a prayer to.

The bark and leaves have rather a mild, pungent taste and pleasant odor, and the tobacco is so diluted as to relieve it from any very pernicious effects, even in the first attempts at smoking.

Many of the women smoke. The boys begin when about eight years old. The exceptions to the habit are rare ; but the Sioux chief "Spotted Tail," by far the ablest Indian I have ever known, was one ; while "Little Wolf" of the Cheyennes is constantly smoking and chewing, rarely, however, using an Indian pipe, and he does not dilute the tobacco with leaves or bark, preferring a strong cigar to a pipe. I have never seen more than half a dozen Indians who chewed tobacco.

Deaf-mutes hold closed hand near mouth and hoist the hand to right, as though twisting off a " chew."

Tobacco-Bag. Make sign for TOBACCO ; then hold slightly-curved hand, back to left, in front of body ; bring compressed hand from right and above, and thrust it downwards between spread thumb and index of left hand.

Together. Make sign for WITH.

Tomahawk. Hold left forearm in front of body, pointing upwards and to right, and lay the extended right hand on the hollow of the left arm. This is not a common sign.

Sometimes it is indicated by simply striking forward and downwards with right hand.

To-morrow. Make sign for NIGHT, and, continuing motion, make sign for DAY, and usually represent the sun rising in the east.

Deaf-mutes throw right hand to front from right shoulder, back of hand to right, thumb alone extended and pointing upwards.

Tornado. Conception : Wind charges. Make sign for WIND, and, continuing motion, make sign for CHARGE.

Tortoise. Hold right hand, back up, in front of and lower than right shoulder, hand near body, hand nearly closed, but back of fingers from knuckles to second joints nearly on line with back of hand ; move the hand horizontally to front, at same time, by wrist action, twist the hand to right and left.

Some Indians make sign for WATER, shape of the animal, and move the hands to imitate motion of its feet.

Deaf-mutes hold slightly-compressed left hand in front of body, edges pointing to right ; place right under left, touching palm, thumb extended and projecting above back of left hand.

Track. Make sign for WALK and point to the ground.

Deaf-mutes use the same sign.

Trade. Make sign for EXCHANGE. I have found among some tribes that the Southern sign as used by the Comanches—*i.e.*, hands passing each other—was taken to mean the incompleted transaction, and the other as the bargain or trade concluded.

Deaf-mutes indicate a giving and taking.

Mr. Dunbar says of the Pawnees, that " trade was never very extensive. Their implacable warring with neighboring tribes necessarily precluded any general commercial intercourse. Their trade was confined, therefore, to the few tribes with whom they were on terms of amity ; *i.e.*, the Arikaras, the Mandans, and Wichitas. From the latter they obtained horses and *bois d'arc;* from the two former eagles' feathers, a commodity in great demand among the Pawnees, and red pipe-stone. The articles given in exchange to the Arikaras and Mandans were horses, salt from the plains of the Upper Arkansas, and to the latter sometimes corn. To the Wichitas they bartered pipe-stone, and to some extent eagles' feathers. With the whites also their trade was limited, never having been sufficient to induce the establishing of a permanent trading-post among them. The nearest stated establishment of this kind was at Bellevue, on the Missouri, and here their dealings were comparatively light. Perhaps there is no instance of another tribe equally large whose trade in all directions was so restricted. The isolated condition in which they lived, shut in on all sides by unforgiving foes, seems in a considerable measure to have disused them to the thought of any such relations, and taught them to rely only or chiefly upon themselves."

Trader. Make signs for WHITES, CHIEF, and TRADE. Deaf-mutes make the sign for person, GIVE, and TAKE.

Trail. Hold the extended hands, backs down, in front of body, hands equally advanced in same horizontal plane, lower edges a few inches apart; move the right hand to rear a few inches; at same time carry left to front; then bring left to rear, and move right to front, repeating motion two or three times. This is used more in the sense of a heavy, well-marked trail, made by tepee-poles or wagons.

For a tepee-trail, first make above sign, then cross the extended index fingers at first joints, others and thumbs closed, index fingers forming an angle little less than a right angle and held horizontally, hands held close to body; move the hands to front and slightly upwards.

For a wagon-trail or road, make first sign as above, then sign for WAGON.

For a slight trail made by a person or beast, make sign for WALK. (The footprints are left only.)

I met in the Indian Territory a Kickapoo Indian, who made for pony-tracks horizontal and incomplete circles with thumbs and index fingers, and then the motion I have described under WALK.

Trail (To). Make sign for TRACK or TRAIL, and sign for LOOK, the fingers pointing downwards towards ground and moved well about. Something akin to the rigidity of muscles which comes upon a pointer or setter dog when he scents a game-bird is seen in some Indians when discovering and following a trail and fresh "signs" are seen. There is, of course, great difference in the capacities of individual Indians as trailers, some being no better than many white men, whilst others are astonishingly capable, and become famous in their tribes for their ability. In 1878 troops were sent out from Fort Keogh, Montana, to intercept some Cheyennes, who had been reported by an officer as crossing the Yellowstone below the post. After the troops had been two days out from the garrison, a Cheyenne scout, called "Poor Elk," was sent out with dispatches. He had ridden all night, and his pony was very tired, when he joined the column at about ten o'clock in the morning, but he managed, with much whipping, to keep his pony alongside the troops. The country had been overrun by great herds of buffalo, the grass had been eaten and broken down, and there was a perfect labyrinth of buffalo-paths. Some excellent white and Indian scouts were with the command, but nothing had been discovered until, suddenly, "Poor Elk" stopped (he was riding abreast of the middle of the column), and going a little distance to the right, to more thoroughly scan the country, came back at a shuffling tired gallop, and reported that he had found the trail of the Indians.

It crossed the direction of the troops at right angles, and one-half of the command had already passed over it. "Poor Elk" followed it for about a mile to where the pursued party had camped. He brushed away the ashes from the dead fires, and felt of the earth underneath; examined the droppings of the animals, counted the number of fires, and noted, by the marks made by the pins, the size of the lodges; carefully scrutinized some moccasins, bits of cloth, etc., that had been thrown away; noticed that the moccasins were sewed with thread instead of sinew, and were made as the Sioux make theirs; discovered that the calico was such as is used at agencies; found a bit of hair-braid, such as Sioux Indians fasten to the scalplock. A sweat-lodge had been built, indicating that they had remained in camp at least one day, and the droppings of the animals determined that the stay had been but one. The position of the camp, the tying of the animals near the tepees and wickey-ups, the number of lodges, the care taken by the Indians in leaving,—all these things furnished evidence as to the number of Indians and animals, and the number of days since they had camped there. Though moving stealthily, yet they were in no special hurry; were Sioux and not Cheyennes, as stated; had recently left an agency; had not crossed the Yellowstone at the time reported, but two days previously; were evidently a party of Sioux who were on their way to join the Indians north of the British line. In fact, the record left by these Indians was as complete as though it had been carefully written out.

In following the trail of animals, the knowledge of their habits and peculiarities is of the greatest assistance. Troops frequently go through or across country. Indians take the line of least resistance, and war-parties keep concealed. A broken blade of grass, a bead or feather dropped, a moccasin-track, and the story is told.

White horse-thieves on the frontier frequently disguise themselves as Indians and "run off" stock; but, as a rule, they make a trail which can be easily detected. The Indian whips and other articles, which they drop, are placed where they are sure to be seen by the pursuers. Their moccasin-tracks are made in the snow or soft earth, where they will be distinctly outlined. In fact, they overdo the business, and yet they have deceived many good white trailers.

Trap. For iron and steel traps, touch or point to something made of iron or metal, then hold hands equally advanced, at same height, in front of body, back of right to right, left to left, index fingers, slightly curved, pointing to front, other fingers and thumbs closed; raise the hands on curve, and bring index fingers side by side, touching, with a jerk,—to represent action of jaws of trap.

The traps made and used by Indians, such as the "deadfall" and others, are described by natural signs.

Deaf-mutes make same gestures.

Travois. Make sign for TEPEE, for animal which hauls the poles; then bring both hands, backs up, opposite each other at same height, well out in front of body, index fingers extended, pointing to front and slightly upwards; draw the hands to rear and slightly downwards, terminating movement when hands are near body; keep left hand in this position, and bring extended right hand, back up, just over left, fingers pointing to left; draw the right hand horizontally a few inches to right. The first sign represents the tepee-poles, the second their position when fastened to the animal, and the third the skin or blanket fastened to the poles upon which the person or load is placed.

The tepee-poles are fastened at their smaller ends by a rope or rawhide thong, which passes over the pony's withers, and the large ends of the poles drag on the ground. The poles become shafts, and behind the animal the load is fastened. Small children are frequently placed in a wicker-work basket fastened to these poles; and for transporting the sick and wounded the skin of a freshly-killed animal, a robe or blanket, is fastened to the poles, forming a bed upon which the sick or wounded persons recline, two poles only, as a rule, being used for this purpose.

Treaty. One tribe with another, signs for WORK or MAKE, for SMOKE and SHAKE HANDS, are made. With the whites, SHAKE HANDS and WRITE.

Deaf-mutes make their signs for FIGHT, STOP, TALK, AGREE, and PEACE.

Tree. Make sign for GRASS, holding hands a little higher than shoulders. This represents timber,—trees. For one tree make above sign, separate the hands but slightly, and then hold up extended right index.

Deaf-mutes hold left forearm vertically in front of left shoulder, fingers extended, separated, and pointing upwards; place right hand at left elbow. This represents one tree; for more, move the hands and arm thus fixed into different positions.

Trot. Make sign for the beast, and then bring closed hands, backs up, in front of body, same height, equally advanced and few inches apart; strike to the front and downwards on a curve, first with one hand and then with the other, repeating motions briskly; imitating as nearly as possible the action of an animal's front feet in trotting.

Deaf-mutes use the same sign.

Trouble. Make sign for HEART; then hold right hand as in PERHAPS, having all fingers extended as explained in latter part of that description, and turn the hand as there described. Troubled, unsettled, worried with a feeling of fear, would also be expressed by this sign, and sign for EXCITED. Heart also in a flutter and rising into the throat.

Deaf-mutes move the hands in front of face or forehead.

True. Conception: One way, or tongue straight. Hold right hand, back up, in front of and rather close to neck, index finger extended pointing to front, others and thumb closed; move the hand to front. Sometimes the sign for LIKE is made; indicating but one way; does not deviate to right or left; straight from heart and tongue.

Deaf-mutes hold right hand, back to right, in front of neck, extended index and vertical, other fingers and thumb closed; move the hand to front, tip of index describing a circle, so that when hand stops it points to front.

Trunk. Hold the closed hands, backs down, equally advanced, same height, and about opposite shoulders, well out in front of body, forearms horizontal. Sometimes indicate size.

An Indian trunk is made of a large square- or rectangular-shaped piece of untanned skin, the hair carefully scraped off, and the hide folded into shape when green and wet. They are usually decorated with different colored paintings, are used for packing dried meat, clothing, etc., and are called "par-flèches."

Deaf-mutes indicate size and shape, and make motion of putting something in same.

Try. Make sign for Push.

Deaf-mutes use the same sign.

Turkey. Conception : Beard. Make sign for Bird, and then hold compressed right hand under chin, close to breast, fingers pointing downwards; shake the hand slightly, which is held loosely at wrist. Sometimes only index of right hand is extended.

Deaf-mutes hold right index on bridge of nose, to denote the wattle of the turkey-gobbler.

Turtle. See Tortoise.

Tweezers. Nearly close right hand, inner surface of tip of thumb and index pressed together, index and thumb nearly extended, hand fixed as though holding a small pair of tweezers ; carry hand to face or eyebrows, and jerk it away as though pulling out hairs.

Deaf-mutes use the same gesture.

These are in constant use by the Indians in pulling out the beard, eyebrows, eyelashes, and hair of the body generally.

Twinkle. Make sign for Star ; then, still holding hand in this position, snap the index and thumb as in Little Talk. To indicate the brilliancy of a diamond or anything that twinkles, make sign for the object, sign for Same, and above signs.

Twins. Lay the palmar surface of extended and separated index and second fingers on abdomen, other fingers and thumb closed ; then make sign for Parturition. I have also seen sign for Parturition made, closing thumb, third, and little fingers.

Deaf-mutes indicate sex and a growing up equally, as well as same mother and one birth.

There is but very little doubt in my mind that some Indian mothers who have twins born to them destroy one. Twin children are very rare. Sitting Bull has had twins born to him by each of two wives.

Two-Kettle (Band of Sioux Indians). Make signs for Sioux, for Kettle ; repeating these motions as though another kettle was alongside of the first.

There are several stories told as to how this band of Sioux Indians first gained this name. One of the most plausible is that a certain chief insisted on having a certain part of the buffalo cooked in one kettle, and certain other parts in others. They belong to the Teton branch. (See Sioux.)

U.

Ugly. Pass the palmar surface of extended right hand circularly in front of and close to face, and then lowering hand from this position, make sign for BAD.

Deaf-mutes hold the hands at same height in front of and close to face, back of right hand to right, left to left, balls of thumbs resting on sides of index fingers, which are slightly curved, other fingers closed, right hand near right cheek, left near left; move the right hand out a few inches, and the left in towards face; then carry left out and right in repeating these motions.

The sign is not a common one with Indians, and while I have seen the gesture for handsome, pretty, or beautiful often made, I have seen this very rarely indeed.

Uncapapa (Band of Sioux Indians). Conception: Ends of incomplete circle. Make sign for SIOUX, for ENCAMP, and then form an incomplete horizontal circle, with thumbs and index fingers in front of body, other fingers closed, tips of thumbs touching, space of about an inch between tips of index fingers; then, still holding left hand in position, place the tip of extended index of right on first joint, other fingers and thumb of right hand closed, index nearly vertical, and move the hand outwards, tip of index of right touching side of left from first joint; then place right hand in its place in forming the horizontal circle, and move tip of left index similarly out over side of right from first joint.

It appears that this band of the Teton Sioux was named from the position they occupied in the camps. A favorite way for Indians to encamp was in an incomplete circle, with an open space,—this open space being usually towards the east,—and this band occupied the ends of the incomplete circle. The word, according to the Indians, was derived from, or, more properly speaking, is a corruption of Hun-ka-péa, which means ends or outlet. Running Antelope, one of the headmen, and the most noted orator of the tribe, located on the Missouri River, at Standing Rock Agency, Dakota, told me that he could remember when there were in the band eight hundred and fifty lodges. They had four chiefs, he being one of them. These four chiefs met whenever occasion required, and decided what the band was to do, where they were to move, etc. The soldiers were young men, and promptly obeyed the crier, who gave the orders of the chiefs to them and to the camp. (See SIOUX.)

Uncertain. Make signs for KNOW and NO, or for PERHAPS.

Deaf-mutes use the same gestures.

As I have before stated, this sign is of frequent use and great service; and where any shadow of doubt exists it should always be employed. A mistake is a lie. A broken promise destroys confidence, and, unless confidence is instilled and retained, the fruits of the best and noblest efforts are almost sure to be of the Dead Sea order.

Uncle. See KINSHIP.

Deaf-mutes hold right hand near right side of head, as in their sign
for letter U, index and second finger pointing upwards, lower hand
with a wavy, tremulous motion.

Understand. See KNOW.

Deaf-mutes place tip of right index at centre of lower part of
forehead, back of hand to right, other fingers and thumb closed ;
move the hand up and down a few inches two or three times, tip of
index touching forehead as the hand is moved up.

Unite. Make sign for WITH.

Deaf-mutes bring closed hands together in front of body, back of
right to right, left to left, hands touching at backs of fingers between
first and second joints, and expand palmar surface.

Unlucky. Make signs for MEDICINE and BAD.

Deaf-mutes make their signs for HAPPENINGS and BAD.

Ursa Major. Make signs for STAR, and denote the position of the
constellation, called by some the " Seven Stars."

Deaf-mutes indicate in the same manner.

The Sioux say that these stars represent a band of foxes ; their
king was killed in the Bear's tepee (a circular cluster of stars to the
left of the Dipper). The four,—Alpha, Beta, Gamma, and Delta,—
which form the quadrilateral, are carrying the dead king in a blanket.

Epsilon is the medicine-man, Zeta is the woman with a baby on
her back (the little star near this is the baby), and Eta is the woman
with the dried meat. The stars of the tail or handle to the Dipper
have, however, different names ; some calling Eta simply dried
meat, and Zeta water for the dead king.

Some Indians, in smoking, point the stem of the pipe to these
stars, and make a petition for their release ; praying that they may
be permitted to proceed on their journey, and no longer be held
under the malign influence which forces them to wander in the same
circular trail.

Ute. Make sign for BLACK, and rub the face as in RED.

The Ute Indians have, as far back as history and tradition go,
occupied or roamed over the mountains and small valleys of the
country between parallels 37th and 41st north latitude and the
105th and 113th meridians. With the Snakes and Bannacks they
have, as a rule, had friendly relations, with the exception of what is
known as Washakie's band, and with this band, until quite recently,
they have been more than " half at war" since 1834. With the
Plains Indians they have ever been at war. With the Mountain Indians to the southwest, and with the Navajos and Pueblos, both war
and peace have obtained at intervals, the latter predominating.

Many years ago Mexican traders went among them, and from intercourse with them, and with the Navajos and other tribes who spoke
that language, many of them learned to speak Mexican quite fluently.

In 1844 the Mexican who had charge of the trading-post on the
Uncompahgre River was killed by these Indians and the goods appropriated to their own use.

In stature and appearance these Indians combine, one might say, the qualities of the Plains Indians to the east with those of the mountain tribes to the west and south ; in stature, between the Bannacks and the Sioux. They are shorter than the Bannacks and taller than the Sioux. They dress the hair like the Sioux, but, as a rule, wear no scalp-lock, though some have adopted the custom,— particularly is this the case with the White River Utes.

By dressing the hair is meant the parting, braiding, and wrapping the braids with strips of otter-skin, wearing feathers, etc. The women wear the hair loose, usually cropping the ends at the neck and parting it in the middle. Both sexes make a lavish use of paint. The men are fond of pipe-clay and shell ornaments, and decorate their leggings and moccasins with a long fringe and with beads. The leggings, both for men and women, are still generally made of buckskin, and the women usually have their leggings sewed to the moccasin when the two are not cut from the same piece. The combined garment is drawn on like a stocking, and as the material is inelastic, they have to be made so large that when on they present an untidy appearance.

The Utes possess large numbers of Navajo blankets, trading directly for them or securing them from their traders. The lodges are now usually made of canvas, are small, have only a few poles, and do not compare favorably with the lodges of the Prairie Indians. I saw many made of old flour-sacks sewed together. They frequently paint the lower portion of the lodge with ochre, thinking it may shield them from bad luck. Many of them have herds of cattle, ponies, sheep, and goats; and this, as well as the possession of blankets and wicker-work vessels, shows the influence of their intercourse with the Navajos. The women wear their dresses quite short, reaching to just below the knees. The moccasins for the men are made, as a rule, with the soles separate from the uppers. Many of the men wear beards and moustaches.

Dr. A. J. McDonald, who has had quite an extensive experience with this tribe, kindly secured for me the following :

" None of the Indians present knew the meaning of the word designating the tribe. They said they had always been called Utes, and supposed that Shinnob so named them at the time of their creation."

The subjoined is a list of the several bands using the Ute language, showing the present location of each :

Tabequache, at Ouray Agency, Utah. Population, as per report of the Indian Commissioners for 1881 . . .	1500
Muache, Capota, Weeminnache, at Southern Ute Agency. Population, as per report of the Commissioners for 1881 .	1100
Yampa, Grand River, Uintah, at Uintah Valley Agency, Utah. Population of the White Rivers, as per report of the Indian Commissioners for 1879	900
Population of Uintahs as per report of 1881 . . .	474
Total	3974

The above is extracted from the Annual Report of the late Honorable Commissioner of Indian Affairs.

The following story of the origin of the Ute Indians was related by Tabby.   It is very quaint and amusing :

"Shinnob (*i.e.*, God) having a deep-rooted antipathy to white people went to war against them.   After a long and fierce fight Shinnob was killed.

" But his enemies had not got rid of him, for not long afterwards he came to life again.   Immediately after his resurrection from the dead, he determined to revenge himself by creating races of men who would be inimical to the white people, and who would, in the course of a brief period of time, sweep them from the face of the earth.   Shinnob commenced operations by procuring several large bags (probably made of buckskin, the Indian said), and filling them with loose earth, sticks, small pebbles, sand, etc., and having tied up the mouths of the bags very securely, he left them under a large tree, intending to return in proper time to open them, when each sack would have contained several Indians perfect in form and understanding.   But, unfortunately, the devil (Shinnob's brother) happened to visit the spot where the sacks were.   His curiosity was excited to a high degree, and he longed ardently to find out what his brother had been doing, but he feared Shinnob too much to dare to touch the bags.   At length the temptation became too strong for resistance, and one night, when there was no moon, he carried off the bags, one by one, and deposited them in a place where Shinnob could not possibly discover them.   Having secured all the sacks, he loosened the strings.   Out of one rushed forth Utes, from another Navajos, from another Sioux, and so on, and from these created Indians sprung all the several tribes that now inhabit the earth. Had the devil not interfered with the work of Shinnob, the Indians in the bags would have been in all respects perfect ; but as it was, they were thrust out into the world prematurely (before they were thoroughly hatched), and consequently Indians are subject to death, disease, and the other numerous ills of life."

In the above narrative, I have, as far as practicable, used the very words of the interpreter.

The Utes with whom I conversed could give no information as to how the several bands became separated, nor could they say what caused the reduction in the number of the people ; in fact, they did not seem to know that the number had at any time been reduced. According to Tabby's account the Utes believe that the earth always has been as it now is ; that Shinnob, ages ago, for some good reason of his own, created great numbers of people, animals, fishes, insects, etc.   He said that all the Indians believe that houses, stables, agricultural implements, machinery, and, in short, all things, were first planned by Shinnob.   Tabby, to illustrate his meaning, said that Shinnob, after making the first plough, left the implement where it would surely be found by white men, who would be able to imitate it.   The Utes have no Sun-Dance.   Their annual dance, which is a religious ceremony, generally takes place some time during the month of February or March. With willow-boughs a large circular enclosure is formed, and the ground within is stamped smooth and hard. Places are set apart for fires, so that the " dance-hall" may be properly illuminated. At one end is the orchestra. I will endeavor to give a brief description of the musical instrument used. A hole is dug in the ground, and into it is fitted snugly a large tin bucket, bottom upwards. Each musician takes a stick, about eighteen inches long, notched from one end to the other. One extremity of this stick is held in the left hand, and placed in contact with the edge of the tin bucket. In the right hand the performer holds a small piece of wood, square or rectangular in shape, and from three to four inches in thickness, and scraping this upwards and downwards on the notched stick, he produces the ravishing music which so delights the dusky dancers. The men and the squaws arrange themselves into two lines, so that the sexes stand opposite and facing each other. When the music commences two squaws clasp hands, advance to the male line, and choose their partners ; then two more in the same manner make their selection, and so on until all are supplied. Now the males and the females from their respective lines advance towards each other with a trot and a swaying motion of their bodies, until the couples are almost face to face, and then with similar backward movements return to the places from which they started. This alternate advance and retreat is all there is to the dance, but the participants apparently enjoy the exercise immensely, and often continue the dance until they are completely exhausted. What are termed " Bear-Dances" are frequently indulged in merely for sport, they have no religious significance.

The marriage customs are very simple and unceremonious. At night the would-be husband consults the parents of the girl he wishes to marry. If the paternal and maternal consent is obtained to the nuptials a bed is at once made, the happy couple "turn in," and are thenceforth man and wife. It is usual for the husband to offer some present to his bride, but this is not compulsory.

If a man be detected in the crime of adultery with another's wife, the wronged husband satisfies himself by killing a horse belonging to the offender, or by taking from him some blankets or other valuable property. The offending wife is perhaps chastised by her husband, but is not divorced or separated from him.

Names are given to Indian children, both male and female, by the father. If the child bears any resemblance, or fancied resemblance, to any person or thing, the name of that person or thing is given to the child. It often, perhaps generally, happens that in after-life the name is changed. It has been frequently noticed by many persons that the Utes object to give their own names when asked, requesting some other Indian to answer for them. On making inquiries respecting this matter, they one and all declared that no objection existed among them. Nevertheless, it is evident to any one acquainted with these Indians that many of them are extremely unwilling to themselves mention their own names. There is a superstitious belief held by some few that the act of signing papers, either by writing the name or by making a mark, is apt to result in the death of the party concerned. Nowadays chiefs are elected by consent of the majority. No special ceremony attends the election. A number of Utes may desire to make a certain member of the tribe a chief; they talk about it for a while, and spread the information throughout the whole band, and, if it is found that the greater number are willing that the promotion should be made, the lucky man from that time becomes a chief. But formerly the choice of chiefs was conducted differently. The frequently-recurring wars that then took place between the Utes and other tribes of Indians brought to light the fighting qualities of the warriors, and the bravest men were made chiefs.

Within the memory and knowledge of the oldest Ute living, so says Tabby, there never have been any "soldier bands,"—every able-bodied male is a soldier. So far as I could ascertain, they recognize no form of oath; but they believe that one who falsifies will be subjected to very severe punishment after death.

Tabby and the other Indians present denied that any superstition existed against killing any animal, bird, fish, or insect. On my mentioning that some persons claimed that a Ute was averse to taking the life of the coyote and of the crow, he ridiculed the very idea.

I questioned them as to "names of moons in a year," and also as to whether they had named any of the stars. The "moons" are designated by names, as are also many of the planets, and I at the time made a note of said names, but having mislaid my memoranda, I am not able to reproduce them here. The "Milky-Way" (Nah-rah-wa-aek) they suppose divides the heavens into two equal parts. I next talked with them concerning comets and eclipses, and was much astonished to find them quite well informed on such topics. They entertain no superstitious ideas whatever in connection with any of the heavenly bodies. Tabby said he supposed Shinnob had made stars, comets, etc., for some wise reason of his own, and that he (Shinnob) probably intended that man should know very little of such matters.

Tabby, who is now, I should judge, about seventy years of age, first saw a "Spaniard with horses" when a very young child. He thinks he must have been about ten years old when he first saw an "American," but it was so long ago that he does not now remember many of the circumstances attending the meeting.

The Utes all firmly believe in the immortality of the soul. The story of the future as told to me was as follows: After death all Indians go straight to heaven; on their arrival there they are required to appear before Shinnob for trial. If the Indian while on earth led a good life according to the judgment of Shinnob, he is permitted to remain in heaven; but if, on the other hand, he meets with the disapproval of the Almighty Judge, he is sent off somewhere or another, nobody knows where.

They claim that in ages past Shinnob taught Indians how to construct arrows, pipes, etc., and commanded that the children should be instructed in the art from generation to generation.

The Utes keep no account of individual age. The custom of wrapping the hair with strips of otter-skin has no significance beyond mere ornamentation, and this is true also respecting their use of paint.

I could not discover that any superstition existed against suicide. Tabby seemed to think it a very foolish practice, but in his opinion, if a person desired to destroy his own life he had a perfect right to please himself.

It seems that in this tribe there are no peculiarities in the treatment of "mothers-in-law." In the treatment of sickness "sweat-houses" are occasionally constructed and used. They are made by digging a hole in the ground and covering the opening with willow-branches and blankets. Very hot stones are placed in the hole and water poured thereon.

A custom is prevalent of requiring women during the menstrual period to lodge by themselves. A small tent is usually erected for this purpose within a few feet of the family lodge. During childbirth the woman is assisted by old and experienced squaws; but in cases of difficult labor, the native medicine-men are called in, and, recently, some such cases have been turned over to the care of white physicians. The sitting posture is, I am told, the most common, but sometimes the recumbent and other positions are assumed. In the former it is customary for the assistants, as soon as the pains set in, to frequently lift the patient up by the arms. After parturition the woman is required to remain in a special lodge set apart for her use for the period of one "moon." She is forbidden to eat meat, her principal diet being bread and large draughts of warm water.

The Utes do not make a practice of eating dog-meat, but do so in times of famine or great scarcity of other more palatable provisions.

In October, 1881, I was travelling over the Uintah range of mountains, and during a snow-storm at night came on a Ute camp, consisting mostly of Uintahs, but some few White Rivers were with them. After some little persuasion they took me into one of the tepees, and, by the flickering light of the lodge fire, while the squaw was preparing my supper, I obtained from the chief and headmen, by means of gestures and their poorly-spoken English, a brief history of their tribe as they understood it. They claimed that for many generations they had been divided into bands, which occupied different parts of the country, extending from Great Salt Lake to the head-waters of the Cimarron River. These bands were known by some familiar custom which they practised, or from some physical feature of the particular part of the country they occupied. To oppose the invasion of the Sioux, Cheyennes, Arapahoes, Comanches, Kiowas, and other tribes, these bands were at times united, and lived and fought together, quickly separating and going to what might be called their respective homes after the necessity for the concentration had passed away. The present Uintahs and some other bands were called Pah-go-wee Nutzes, or Big Water Utes; the White Rivers, Yam-pah-recks, or Root-Eaters. The Uncompahgres, Monatz, or Cedar-Tree Utes, and several bands are consolidated with what are known as the Southern Utes, viz., Travois band, Willow band, Skin and Painted Lodge band, etc.

The White Rivers are more conversant with the sign language than the other bands, their geographical position having thrown them into more constant and intimate relations with the Plains tribes, particularly of late years with the Arapahoes.

V.

Vaccinate. Make signs for WHITES, MEDICINE, MAN, and then thrust the extended right index, other fingers and thumb closed, at left arm, tip striking it midway between elbow and shoulder.

Deaf-mutes thrust index at left arm.

Many of the Indians at the different agencies are now regularly vaccinated, and the older men are extremely anxious to have the operation performed. They rightly have an unqualified horror of smallpox, knowing their powerlessness to cope with it.

Vigilant. Make signs for LOOK in different directions, moving the hand quickly, for MUCH, for SLEEP, and NO.

Deaf-mutes fix the hands as in GUARDING, and then move them into different positions.

Village. Make sign for TEPEE and for CAMP.

Deaf-mutes make their sign for HOUSE in different directions, and SMALL. (A small collection of houses.)

Vine. For a vine on the ground, make a serpentine motion of the right hand, index finger alone extended.

For on a pole or tree : The left arm or hand represents the object to which the vine clings and winds about, and the right index traces the course about it.

Deaf-mutes use the same gesture.

Vine. (Poisonous.) Make sign for VINE (above), for BAD, and then indicate that the vine kills the part of body it touches.

Virgin. Make sign for FEMALE, for MARRY, or SLEEP WITH, and for NO.

Volley. See HEAVY FIRING.

Vomit. Hold compressed right hand, back to right, fingers pointing upwards, in front of and close to neck ; move the hand slightly upwards, then turn, and, by wrist action, move it outwards and downwards on curve, repeating motion.

Deaf-mutes use both hands, and imitate motion of a person vomiting.

W.

Wagon. Conception : Wheels. Hold hands, backs down, in front of body, equally advanced, same height and a few inches apart, edges pointing to front, index fingers well curved, others and thumbs closed ; move the hands so that index fingers will describe a small vertical circle. Sometimes the hands are held backs up.

Deaf-mutes hold the hands, backs out, index fingers extended, others and thumbs closed, right index pointing to left, left index to right ; then, mostly by wrist action, move the hands so that tips of index fingers describe vertical circles.

Wagon-Road. Make sign for ROAD and WAGON.

Deaf-mutes use the same gesture.

Wait. Make sign for SIT or HALT, repeating same ; making gesture more gently and not stopping hand so abruptly as in HALT.

Deaf-mutes make their sign for STOP.

Walk. Conception : Motion of feet. For a person : hold hands, backs up, in front of body, equally advanced, same height and a few inches apart, fingers pointing to front ; move the right to front, upwards and downwards to same height as when starting ; move left to front similarly ; and as left is brought down, draw right hand to rear and repeat first motion ; same with left, repeating motions.

For an animal : close the hand and execute similar movements.

Deaf-mutes use same as the first-described gesture.

Want. Conception : Give me. Hold right hand, back to right, in front of and close to chin, and form an incomplete circle with curved thumb and index, back of index about height of mouth, space of about half an inch between tips of index and thumb, other fingers closed, plane of circle vertical ; move the hand on a small curve downwards, outwards, and then upwards, the upward movement being mostly made by turning hand by wrist action, so as to bring little finger nearly as high as index.

This sign is not very much used by some tribes, and by a few not known, even with those who use gesture speech to a great extent. An Indian, instead of saying, "I want you to do so and so," would say, "I think it good for you to do it."

The sign is so much like WATER or DRINK that, unless the connection is clear, it is liable to be misunderstood.

Deaf-mutes make signs for WITH and NEED ; for the former they hold hands, backs down, equidistant from body, at same height and several inches apart, edges pointing to front, fingers curved and separated ; the hands are drawn in a few inches, and the motion repeated two or three times. For NEED, they hold the right hand, back up, in front of body about height of shoulder, index finger curved, others and thumb closed ; mostly by wrist action, make a downward motion with right hand few inches, repeating motion several times.

War. Make sign for FIGHT. It has been often asserted, and quite generally believed, that Indian warfare is but simple assassination and murder. Viewed from our stand-point, it does partake strongly of the characteristics that we associate with these crimes, and certainly success with Indians is due mainly to the constant practice of stealth and crafty vigilance. Regarding it, however, from the stand-point of the savage or barbarian, which is that the object to be attained in war is to inflict the greatest possible amount of damage upon the enemy with the least possible risk to themselves; and considering, also, the necessities which crowd upon them to pursue such a course, though we cannot justify their wanton atrocities, yet we find our opinions modified somewhat in regard to them.

The original conquest of their tribal domain, and the maintenance of their prestige and position as tribes, depended entirely on their prowess; and where existence depended upon the possession of warlike qualities, it is no wonder that they were fostered; that war was the burden of all oratory and song, and that the highest ambition of an Indian should be to gain distinction as a warrior, especially as this ambition was stimulated by the knowledge that success in war would be rewarded by the highest honors and greatest powers in peace. Nearly every tradition of the tribe was richly colored with deeds of valor and daring; and the murder of a helpless woman and the stealing of a few ponies took rank not from the act, but from the *blow* inflicted on the enemy. Not only was the hope of reward held out to those who survived the dangers of the "warpath," but those killed in battle were (according to their belief) received with great demonstrations of joy, and made chiefs in the life beyond death. Indians possess as much courage as any people, and when young, sometimes not only scorn the fear of, but really court death. Age brings wisdom and recognition of the fact that more is accomplished by craft and cunning than by reckless daring. The cheap bravado which has led so many to imagine them cowardly wretches was the result of their training to constantly remember their maxim of war,—"Greatest amount of damage to the enemy with the least amount to one's self."

Again, people in the hunter state have no pension lists, and the death of the head of the family left that family to the mercy and charity of their people; and in savagery as in civilization, mercy and charity are at times both blind and deaf to the sufferings of humanity. This, taken in connection with the fact that their wars were, as a rule, waged for glory and spoils alone, bred in them a courage capable of great things for a sudden dash, but left them without the fibre of true bravery in tenacity of purpose and capacity for prolonged endurance under a severe strain.

Their war tactics are the stealthy approach and sudden onslaught, when, if the surprise and numbers sweep everything before them, an heroic display of courage is sometimes made ; but a determined or unexpected resistance, and they scatter and retire.

The practice of the custom of trusting everything to a single effort undoubtedly has had its effect in their not harassing an enemy after their effort was made ; but at any rate, it is a fact that they are wofully lacking in enterprise in this way. It is a common custom among all the Northern tribes for war-parties to start out and go hundreds of miles through an enemy's country on foot,—these are usually horse-stealing expeditions. Their equipment consists of the ordinary dress of an Indian,—a lariat wound diagonally over the right shoulder and around the breast, a waist-belt full of cartridges and a breech-loading rifle of modern pattern, and an extra pair of moccasins at the waist-belt. These small parties on foot leave no trail, are less liable to detection through being seen, can cross any kind of country, have no care of animals at night, and for many other reasons find it to their advantage to go in this way.

"The return of a successful war-party was an occasion of most extravagant demonstration. Men, women, and children united in welcoming the victorious braves. The following night a Scalp-Dance was celebrated, in which each one had opportunity to magnify his exploits. Prisoners, unless women and children, were rarely taken, and hence scenes of fiendish delight in inflicting exquisite torture were unusual. If, on the contrary, the party had been unfortunate and suffered loss, its return was quiet, and gave rise to dejection and unrestrained lamentation on the part of the friends of the lost.

" Many of the most daring adventures were made by braves who, unaccompanied, penetrated the enemy's country and watched opportunity to inflict some signal stroke of surprise. This was a favorite mode of warfare, and sometimes stoical scalps were brought back as the trophies of one such exploit, and secured for the adventurers a life-long notoriety. Trips of this character might be extended hundreds of miles and require weeks of absence in their accomplishment." (*J. B. Dunbar.*)

In all of our Indian wars it has *seemed* necessary to use Indian allies, and these have usually been permitted to perpetrate all kinds of savage atrocities, mutilating the dead in the most horrible manner, so that we have not taught the Indians by example any more civilized warfare. I do not here refer to the excesses of savage fury which have from time to time broken out, as in the Minnesota massacre in 1862. These isolated cases, filled with more horrors than pen can picture, are to Indian warfare generally what the savage actions of an infuriated mob are to civilized war.

The Apaches in the Southwest at present and the Eastern Indians of the past seem to have far exceeded all others in fertility of resources, so far as fiendish cruelty and excruciating torture inflicted on prisoners are concerned ; still, all Indians make war as horrible as possible so as to strike terror to the hearts of their enemies.

I was once in command of some Indian scouts where an engagement was anticipated in a day or two, and I was having a smoke and council with them. The chief in the most friendly and pleasant way explained to me that they "killed the women and children, for that made them (the enemy) afraid." He spoke of the killing just as he would have spoken of the destruction of any other property of the enemy; he looked at it merely in the light of a blow to be inflicted.

War, To Go To. (Go on the war-path.) Hold right hand, back nearly to front, in front of and close to right breast, index and thumb spread, index finger pointing to left, thumb upwards, other fingers closed; move hand well out to front and slightly upwards, or to right or left. This sign is also used for horse-stealing expeditions; following the general rule to indicate, if possible, the direction to be taken or that which was taken; this being one of the legitimate and proper acts of war.

For other people to go to war against one or one's people, hold the hand as above well out in front; turn the wrist as much as possible, so as to make a movement similar to the above, towards the body.

Deaf-mutes make their sign for FIGHT.

War-Bonnet. Carry the extended hands from front to rear, parallel and close to sides of head, fingers pointing upwards, tips little higher than top of head, palms of hands towards head; then sweep the right hand from the crown of the head well down to rear of body. Sometimes the sign for the tail-feather of the golden eagle is added.

The tail-feathers of the golden eagle are used for making these gorgeous head-dresses. There are twelve feathers in the tail, and as many as sixty or seventy are used in making the bonnet. The feathers for the cap proper are fastened to cloth or skin made to fit the head in the shape of a brimless and crownless hat (old hats are now frequently used). The feathers are placed side by side, touching, and when the bonnet is put on the head assume a nearly vertical position, the whole forming a cylinder-shaped head-gear. Fastened to the head-piece behind is a long strip of skin or cloth (red cloth is now generally used), which, when the person is standing, reaches to, and sometimes trails on, the ground. The feathers are fastened on one side of this cloth in the same way as on the cap. The latter is also frequently decorated with real or imitation buffalo-horns; and some tribes have, besides, masses of ermine-skin fastened on near the base of the feathers. Some bird, or the special medicine which belongs to the owner of the bonnet, is also fastened on, usually in front. At the tips of the feathers a few horse-hairs are fastened with glue, and ribbons are also sometimes fastened to the tail-piece. Many Indians place the most implicit confidence in the medicine, which may be only a dirty little bag given them by their magician or medicine-man, and are firm in the belief that it turns aside all the missiles of their enemies.

"Whirlwind," the once famous chief of the Southern Cheyennes, when I asked him to tell me of the hardest fight he had ever been in, said, "It was with the Sacs and Foxes, who were behind cover, dismounted ; I charged them, and was met with such a perfect storm of bullets that *every feather in my bonnet was cut away.*" I asked how it was that he was not hit, and he replied, "My medicine was on my head," and seemed to express from his manner that this was a full, complete, and perfect explanation. The lodge was full of his people, many of whom had seen him in this fight, and they corroborated his story.

Where eagles are plentiful, war rare, and provisions scarce, the bonnets are comparatively cheap ; but with many tribes they readily bring in barter a good pony, and some Indians will not for any price part with them, feeling that their good luck would desert them. I have had many Indians tell me about bullets which were coming straight for the centre of their breasts, but which the power of their medicine on the head drew up and made them pass harmlessly by. The Crow Indians are, by some tribes, given the credit of inventing this head-dress. One of this tribe claimed to have had a dream or vision in which he was told to make and wear a head-gear of eagle-feathers, and then his enemies could not kill him. He did this, and his "medicine" was so strong that the others adopted the same, and other tribes learned it from them. The Crow became so rash and confident—felt so strong and secure in his medicine—that he allowed a Mexican to shoot at him at short range,—only a few feet distant,—and the Mexican killed him.

The usual explanation for its use is that it makes a man as brave as the bird from which the feathers are taken, carries fear to the hearts of the enemy, and is handsome. (See EAGLE.)

War-Club. Indicate size of war-club stone ; clasp left index with right hand, to denote the raw-hide covering to handle, and then strike forward and downwards with right hand. Some make sign like AXE, only closing hand.

There are several varieties of war-clubs, but an excellent one, much in use by the Northern Indians, is made of a small quartz or other hard rock, about three inches in diameter and five inches in length, elliptical in form but rather pointed at the ends. The rock is carefully dressed into shape by means of much pounding with other stones; around the centre a slight depression is made, and a strip of green raw-hide is put on, which on drying shrinks firmly into position. This strip is sufficiently long and wide enough to wrap around the handle, which is of wood, three-quarters of an inch in diameter, and about four feet long. At the end of the handle a scalp is frequently fastened, and near the stone some horse-hair wrapped with porcupine-quills. Sometimes the handle is ornamented with a piece of a buffalo's tail, eagle's feather, etc.

Frequently the club is simply a piece of hard wood, with three or four butcher-knife blades carefully fastened at the large end. In fact, both material and shape vary according to the fancy of the individual. As will be seen from the gesture, the Indians do not call these weapons war-clubs, but simply something to strike a blow with.

War-Dance. Usually the sign for WAR, TO GO TO, is made, and then the sign for DANCE.

I have seen the following, but do not think it common : Hold left hand, nearly closed, well out and to left of body ; strike at it with partially-closed right hand, and then make sign for DANCE. This may come from the custom which, it is claimed, was formerly practised by some of the tribes, of "striking the post," which was an announcement that the man had joined the war-party.

War-Pony. Make signs for PONY and for FAST.

Indians do not, so far as I have observed, call their ponies *war-ponies ;* but any pony which is fast they sometimes say is a good pony to go to war with.

Warrior. Make signs for MAN and for WAR, TO GO TO.

Sometimes the signs for MAN and FIGHT are made.

The warriors of a tribe are all the men, old and young, who are physically competent to use a weapon. Any young man or boy who has been to war is called a warrior.

Wash. Make sign for WATER, and imitate motions made in washing.

Deaf-mutes use the same sign.

Watch. Form a horizontal circle with thumb and index of left hand, other fingers closed ; hold extended right index over and close to it, other fingers and thumb of right hand closed ; move the right index round over the horizontal circle. Make sign for LOOK, holding fingers so as to point at the circle formed by left thumb and index. Make sign for KNOW, for SUN, holding right hand in different position. These gestures indicate the size of the watch ; the right index, motion of hands ; *look* at these and one *knows* where the *sun* is ; *i.e.,* what time it is.

Deaf-mutes make motion of drawing watch from vest-pocket and holding same to right ear.

Water. Conception : Drinking out of palm of hand. Hold partially-compressed right hand, back down, in front of, close to, and little above mouth, fingers pointing to left and upwards ; move the hand downwards, turning palm towards mouth.

Deaf-mutes make their sign for the letter W, holding tip of index against lips, and moving hand out two or three inches, repeating motion.

Weak. Make signs for STRONG and NO, or touch arms and thighs and make sign for TIRED.

Deaf-mutes hold extended left hand, back down, in front of body, fingers pointing to front ; place tips of vertical and separated first and second fingers on left palm, back of these fingers outwards, others and thumb closed ; move the hand slightly and bend the second joint of fingers a little, indicating weak knees.

Wearing Apparel. With exception of breech-clout or cloth, blankets, and other articles previously enumerated, wearing apparel is usually represented by passing spread thumb and index close to and about parallel to surface of body covered by the articles.

Deaf-mutes pass extended hands instead of spread thumb and index.

When. Make sign for INTERROGATE, for HOW MANY, and then specify time by proper gesture for NIGHTS, MOONS, or WINTERS. In such sentences as "When will you return to-day?" make sign for INTERROGATE, and indicate two or three positions of the sun, point to person, and make sign for ARRIVE HERE. At night, one can say middle of night, a little after sunset, or a little before sunrise.

Some tribes know about the times when certain stars rise or set, and note the time at night by these means; but such attainment is by no means common.

Deaf-mutes hold left index extended and vertical, others and thumb closed; make a circle round left with tip of extended right index, others and thumb closed, and when the index reaches the starting-point, stop it and point it at tip of left index,—intended to represent an interrogation-mark.

Where. Conception: What point? Point with extended index of right hand, back up, in different directions, in front of and to right and left of body, other fingers and thumb closed, holding hand higher than shoulders, and moving it outwards and downwards, index finger pointing upwards and outwards, and when lowered to last position being horizontal, stopping hand in downward movement when little lower than shoulders.

Deaf-mutes use the same gestures.

Whetstone. Make sign for HARD or ROCK; then hold, extended and touching, first and second fingers of left hand in front of body, pointing to front, other fingers closed; with extended and touching index and second finger of right hand, others and thumb closed, placed on side of left index at right angles; move the hands outwards and inwards, as though sharpening a knife. It must be remembered that Indians sharpen a knife only on one side. Sometimes the sign for KNIFE is first made.

Deaf-mutes use the same gestures, only turn fingers as though sharpening knife on both sides.

Whip. Strike with closed right hand from front to right and rear of body, as though astride of a riding animal, and whipping him on the flank.

Deaf-mutes indicate the striking, but usually as though animal were in front.

Mr. Belden describes the Indian whip so well that I quote the following:

"Riding-whips are made in great numbers by the Indians. They are of various kinds and curious patterns. Some are twisted out of horse-hair and wrapped with fine sinew, to make them stiff and elastic, others are woven of buffalo-fur, and others of grass or bark. The regular Indian riding-whip is made of leather, fastened to a wooden handle. A bone, or piece of round, hard wood, about six inches in length, is taken, and through each end a small hole is bored across the grain. Another longer hole is then bored in the end of the stick along the grain, until it intersects the first hole. The lash, with a loop on its end, is next inserted in the end of the whip, and a peg driven through the small hole and loop, to keep it from coming out. A loop or wrist-strap is then put in the other end of the handle, and the whip is ready for use. The lashes of these whips are two or three feet long and very heavy, being made generally of buckskin, elk, or buffalo hide. They are frequently not plaited, but knotted every five or six inches. These knots are called bellies, and are intended to make the punishment more severe than it would otherwise be. The elk-horn whip is very pretty, being usually beautifully carved and painted many colors. Sometimes the long prong of a black-tail deer is used, studded with brass tacks or pieces of silver. Frequently the handles are covered with fur or buckskin, which is ornamented with bead-work.''

Whip (To). The same gestures are used as in WHIP (above).

Whirlwind. Hold right hand, back up and to front, hand held loosely at wrist, so as to drop with its own weight, forearm nearly horizontal, in front of right breast and about height of waist, the fingers separated and slightly curved, fingers pointing about downwards; raise the hand, at same time, by wrist action, give a swinging motion to hand; *i.e.*, so that tips of fingers describe a spiral curve.

Deaf-mutes make their sign for WIND, and then about the same as above.

Whiskey. The most usual signs for this among the Plains Indians are for DRINK or WATER and MEDICINE.

Whiskey has been and is called "black-water," "white-man's-water," "crazy-water," "fire-water," the latter by the Sacs and Foxes, Shawnees, Nez Perces, Shoshones, and the Eastern tribes generally. Of course the sign, as a rule, follows the name.

Deaf-mutes make signs same as TEA, DRINK, and then imitate motion of a drunken person.

Indians seem to have a natural fondness for whiskey, and the Hudson's Bay and American Fur Companies traded it to them in former years in unlimited quantities, working incalculable damage to the different tribes. To those Indians who have come in close contact with civilization it has been a greater curse than either war or disease, and perhaps one might say both. They never mix water with it,—the stronger it is the better; and they drink it as though it were some pure and mild cordial, softened by care and age. I have known some who had perfect control of their appetites, but the vast majority have not; and many wars, much unnecessary bloodshed, and great wretchedness to them have grown out of their fondness for liquor, and the cupidity and rascality of white traders in selling the article to them, never thinking, or at least not caring for the consequences. We have certainly in some cases made them savages, and then cursed and killed them for being such.

Scattered all along the frontier the same sad spectacle is presented. First robes, skins, and bead-work are sold, then the ponies; then the women are debauched and diseased, and thefts and murders are committed, either to secure whiskey, or as the result of drinking it. None of the Northern tribes have ever manufactured anything at all like it, but they claim that the gall of the buffalo produces intoxication.

Indians drink as they smoke,—seated in a circle on the ground ; the bottle or vessel is passed round and round until empty.

The name "fire-water" was probably given from some action similar to that described by Professor J. D. Butler, who says,—

"In 1683, Perrot having built a fort near the outlet of Lake Pepin, paid a visit to the Sioux up the great river. He was placed by them on their car of state, which was a buffalo-robe. He was thus lifted on high by a score of warriors, not like Sancho Panza tossed in a blanket, but borne as reverentially as the Pope on his *sedia gesta-toria*, or portable throne, into the house of council. There, holding a bowl of brandy, which the Indians thought to be water, he set it on fire. He thus made them believe that he could at will burn up their lakes and rivers. A score of years before—certainly as early as 1665—he had become a potentate among Pottawattomies near Green Bay. Perrot was worshipped with clouds of incense from a hundred calumets, because he brought iron,—especially in the shape of guns and tomahawks. The farther west he went the more unheard of his iron and powder, and the more they proved him a God."

Whistle. Hold right hand, back to right, in front of mouth, index finger extended and pointing upwards and to front, other fingers closed ; move the hand briskly a few inches in the direction of index several times.

Indians make whistles out of the wing-bones of eagles, hawks, geese, and some other birds, the eagle's wing being the most highly prized. These large bones from the wings are cut off at the end, and a small orifice made near the end like a boy's whistle, producing, when skilfully played upon, a sound exactly like that made by the bird itself; usually, as in the case of the turkey, like the plaintive note of the turkey.

They wear them, attached to a string, around the neck, and use them for various purposes. In dances, in courting a girl,—*i.e.*, making a signal for a meeting,—in battle, particularly in making a charge ; and when small parties are scouting, to give the alarm whether their game be of the human family or the brute creation ; but whenever used these sounds convey a meaning, easily and quickly understood, from a love-note to the shrill cry of war. With small scouting-parties they are particularly useful in giving a warning.

Deaf-mutes imitate the motion with the lips.

Whites. Conception : Hat or cap. Hold right hand, back up and to right, in front of, close to, and a little to left of face, index finger extended pointing to left, others and thumb closed ; draw the hand to right, index finger passing horizontally in front, close to, and opposite eyes.

Some tribes nearly close the hand in drawing it from left to right ; and I have also seen the hat represented with spread thumbs and index fingers of both hands. Some Indians call the whites "knife

men," and make signs accordingly; some call the Americans, in con-
tradistinction to the British, "Long Knives." The Sioux call the
whites vocally by a name which they claim meant God before the
missionaries came among them.

The general sign means "the people with hats or caps," and
includes all those who are not indigenous to the soil; and pictographically this was the manner of distinguishing them from the
natives.

Deaf-mutes make the sign for WHITE PEOPLE, usually distinguishing the nationality, as Spaniard or Mexican, English, etc.

White Man. Make sign for WHITES and MAN.

Why. Make the sign for INTERROGATE, but turn the hand more
slowly.

Deaf-mutes hold right hand, back out, in front of face; move the
hand downwards and outwards, and assume an inquiring expression
of countenance.

Wichita (Indian). Conception: Tattooed rings. Hold right hand,
back outwards and to left, in front and to right of lower part of face,
index finger extended and pointing towards face, other fingers and
thumb closed; by wrist action swing hand so that tip of index will
describe a curve, the diameter of which shall be about six inches.
The hand is held loosely at wrist.

After a careful study of the subject Mr. Dunbar classes this tribe
as a member of the Pawnee family, but admits that others differ with
him in this opinion, saying that "Catlin, who visited them in 1833,
is very emphatic in denying any relationship between them and the
Pawnees, claiming that in stock, language, and customs they are
altogether different. Gallatin mentions them as presumed, from
similarity of name (Pawnee Picts), to be related to the Pawnees.
Their first settlement was near the eastern extremity of the Wichita
Mountains, longitude 99° 20′, latitude 34° 50′. Before 1805 they
had for some reason moved southeast to the Red River. In 1850
they were upon the head-waters of Rush Creek, a tributary of the
False Wichita."

Mr. Dunbar also includes in this family the Caddos, Wacos, Kee-
chers, and Ta-wa-conies. (See CADDO and PAWNEE.)

The Wichita women formerly, in summer, usually wore only a
short bark skirt about the loins, no waist. They painted or tattooed
the face and rings around the breasts, and from this custom sprang
the tribal sign. There is no evidence that the men tattooed any part
or portion of their face or body.

Their permanent village lodge was made in a conical shape similar
to the skin tepee, but larger, and thatched with willows and grass.
On this account some tribes called them "the people of the dark
lodge." In the fall, after they had harvested their corn, etc., they
abandoned their thatched lodges and went out for their annual hunt
after buffalo, and did not return until mid-winter. Their corn,
beans, dried pumpkins, and personal effects were "cached" in huge
cistern-like holes, and so much care was exercised in concealing the

locations of these "caches" that no one ever thought of looking for them.

It has only been five years (1877) since quite a successful buffalo-hunt was made by these Indians from the vicinity of their present agency on the Wichita River, Indian Territory.

At present many of them wear citizen's dress, crop the hair squarely off round the neck, and have no scalp-lock. They possess quite a number of wagons, and have partially adopted the forms of worship of the Christian religion. They gather together at their little church on Saturday evening, bringing food and tentage, and many remain until Monday morning, though the less enthusiastic leave on Sunday afternoon. With their singing, preaching, and praying they mix a great deal of feasting. About Christmas-time they have a sort of "camp-meeting" service, which lasts about a week. In personal appearance they are rather inferior, dark complexion, stout, and short in stature. They are conversant with the sign language.

The agent, in his report for 1880, gives the population of the Wichitas as one hundred and ninety-eight.

Wickey-Up. Hold the hands several inches apart in front of body, index finger extended, others and thumb closed; raise the hands on curve, bringing them sufficiently near to lap the index fingers, inner surface of left to second joint placed on back of right, backs of index fingers up; then from this position change the hands, back up, edges pointing about to front, fingers partially separated and slightly curved, index fingers near each other; move the right hand to right and downwards on curve.

I suppose the word came from the wicker-work-like appearance of the willow or brush frame-work over which Indians throw pieces of canvas or cloth when out on the war-path and camp for the night, or for a short time only. Willows are cut and trimmed; the larger ends are sharpened and stuck in the ground, and then bent down into the shape desired, and the smaller ends fastened together. The manner of making and the shape may disclose the tribe. The Cheyennes, Sioux, and some others first put in two rows three or four feet apart, the length of the rows being determined by the number who are to occupy the little house, the space between the willows being about three feet. The tops of the willows are bent over and twisted together, making an oval-shaped roof, at the highest point about three feet from the ground; then canvas or cloth of some kind is fastened over the top and brought down to the ground at the ends and on one side, the other side being left open. The Crow Indians make their war-houses, as they are sometimes called, nearly circular in shape, and sometimes large enough to have a fire in the centre if necessary, and they all sleep with their feet towards the fire. These Indians also used very frequently (as they all do more or less) quite large logs to make these war-houses, for protection in case their camp should be fired into at night. Of course the little wicker-work house is not proof that the Indians are on the war-path; it shows only that a camp was made by moving Indians.

Indians take every precaution against a surprise *except keeping awake*. Their arms are placed within reach, usually near the head of the bed, and everything is as carefully arranged as though they fully expected to be (as the frontier word has it) "jumped" before daylight; but they do not keep sentries posted to give warning of the approach of an enemy. (See CAMP.)

Wife. Make sign for FEMALE and MARRY.

The Blackfeet, Flatheads, and some other tribes make sign for SIT by the right side, bringing right hand down from near shoulder, instead of UNITE or MARRY. (The wife is the woman who sits by the right side.)

Deaf-mutes make sign for WOMAN and MARRY.

The conception of the Blackfoot sign indicates a higher order or better tone than the other; but unfortunately, they do not hold their wives as sacredly even as some of the other tribes. The Jesuits have nearly eradicated polygamy from the Flatheads, Pend d'Oreilles, Koutenays, and many other tribes west of the Rocky Mountain range, but the Plains Indians and others still practise it. I once said to an Indian, in reply to his question why I was not married, "I have no wife, and therefore am at liberty to travel about, go to war, etc., at my pleasure, and, as a consequence, can, as a chief, rise more easily,"—illustrating this by the index finger of my right hand, raising it slowly and showing that nothing pulled it down. He cleverly said that this was wrong, a mistake. He had two wives, and they formed a support on each side of the index and helped to raise it.

I think there are more female children born to Indians than males, and when the number of young warriors killed in their tribal wars is considered, it will readily be seen that the number of females must be greatly in excess of the males; and polygamy, therefore, is a necessity with barbarism.

Wild. Make sign for BY ITSELF, and then bring the slightly-compressed right hand well in front of body, about height of shoulders, back of hand nearly outwards, forearm about horizontal, hand bent at wrist and knuckles, so that fingers point downwards. This is the sign frequently made to denote a group or "bunch" of animals, and these gestures would seem to indicate a group of animals unfettered by any surrounding influences; entirely by themselves. I have also seen the sign for LOOK made to the rear of body, and then the sign for GO made sharply. (A look and they run away.)

Deaf-mutes raise the hands with a wavy motion in front of and higher than shoulder, fingers extended, separated, and pointing upwards, and assume an astonished, wild expression of countenance.

Win. Make sign for KILL; usually represent in what way. A person wins twenty dollars from another,—the person "kills" the other for that amount.

Deaf-mutes sometimes make their signs for MONEY, LAID DOWN, and GET VICTORY, or sign for OVERCOME. For VICTORY, the right is raised in front of body with a wavy circular motion. For OVERCOME, the hands are brought in front of body, back of right to right, left to left, hands closed, with exception of thumbs, which are extended and pointing upwards, the right hand is a few inches in rear of left and a little higher (perhaps an inch); by wrist action turn the hands simultaneously, so that thumbs point to front, moving right hand a trifle to front as though it had forced the left over.

This metaphoric idiom is much used, as Indians are constantly gambling; and the same expression is also used in regard to winning a girl's affection. (See PHRASES.)

Winchester Rifle. Conception: Putting cartridge in chamber of piece. Make sign for GUN; then hold extended left hand, back to left, in front of left breast, fingers pointing to front, back of thumb height of side of index, and side of thumb pressed against side of index. Make thrusting motion with extended index of right hand, other fingers and thumb closed, from rear to front alongside of palmar surface of thumb, as though putting cartridge in chamber of gun.

Wind. Hold hands, backs up, near body about height of shoulders, hands same height and nearly in the same horizontal plane, fingers extended, slightly separated, and pointing in the direction the hands are moved (which is the direction the wind is supposed to blow), hands few inches apart; move the hands outwards with a wavy, tremulous motion. For wind blowing towards one, execute a similar movement towards body; the movement is sometimes accompanied with a blowing of the breath.

Deaf-mutes make a waving motion of hands in front of body.

Some tribes believe that wind is caused by the movement of the immense ears of a huge animal in the mountains, called at times a black-tailed deer.

The Bannacks and Snakes say their God, "the Wolf," causes it; the Cheyennes claim that the old woman in the cave who gave them the seeds, tobacco, etc., makes it. A Mandan chief said to me, "Long ago a war-party of Mandans started out after their enemies, two of them got separated from the rest, and came across a monster on the prairie. It looked something like a huge turtle, but contracted and enlarged like a pair of monster bellows. One of them said they ought not to touch it, that it would bring them bad luck; that disaster would overtake them if they molested it; but the other said he did not care, he was going to shoot an arrow into it any way; he did not care what the consequences might be; and, suiting the action to the word, he fired. The arrow half buried itself, and they both went to pull it out, when a great gust of wind, like an explosion, blew them high in the air and far out to sea. They landed on an island, and, when nearly starving, the huge animal, which so much resembled a turtle, appeared, told them to get on its back and he would take them to the shore. This animal causes, since the arrow was fired into it, the hurricane and strong winds. Before this time there were only mild and gentle breezes."

Wing. Hold the left forearm in front of left breast, pointing to front and right ; pass the extended right hand from shoulder down, over and little to left of arm, wrist passing over arm and close to it, back of hand up, fingers pointing to left.

Deaf-mutes imitate motion of wings, then place right hand near and to left of left shoulder.

Winter. Hold closed hands in front of body, forearms about vertical, hands several inches apart ; give a shivering, tremulous motion to hands. Sometimes, and particularly with Northern Indians, the sign for SNOW is also made.

Years, as I have remarked, are called winters by the Indians.

Deaf-mutes make sign for COLD and denote three months.

Wiped Out. See EXTERMINATE.

Wise. Make sign for HEART ; touch forehead, and make sign for GOOD. (Heart and head both good.)

Deaf-mutes place the back of curved index against centre of forehead, other fingers and thumb closed ; move the index up and down few times.

With. Hold extended left hand, back to left, in front of body, fingers pointing to front ; bring side of extended right index horizontally against centre of left palm, other fingers and thumb closed, index pointing to front. Frequently the thumb is not closed.

Deaf-mutes bring the closed hands together in front of body, balls of thumbs resting on second joints of index fingers, and sides of thumbs touching, hands touching at exposed palmar surface and backs of fingers between first and second joints.

Wolf. Hold the right hand, palm out, near right shoulder, first and second fingers extended, separated, and pointing upwards, others and thumb closed ; move the hand several inches to front and slightly upwards, turning hand a little, so that extended fingers point to front and upwards. Sometimes both hands are used, left being similarly fixed to right and held opposite left shoulder.

Some tribes not thoroughly conversant with the gesture language make signs for GRAY, size of animal, large tail, and long, sharp nose.

Woman. Make sign for FEMALE and indicate height. I have also seen among the Chippewas the hands swept about the body near the ankles to denote skirts of the dress.

Deaf-mutes use the same signs.

Even among tribes that are thoroughly conversant with gesture speech the women, as a rule, only possess a limited knowledge of it ; the exceptions being with such as the Arapahoes and Cheyennes, where for years intimate relations and daily intercourse between the tribes have been kept up, both languages being difficult to acquire and each tribe preserving its own. In savagery and barbarism women are merely beasts of burden, prized and valued for their skill in fancy or capacity for heavy work, rather than for any beauty of face or figure. The men are fond of and will fight for them, but their affection is something of the character of the love which a wild beast has for its young. A life of filth, drudgery, and exposure, sustained by the coarsest of food, is not conducive to female perfection of form and feature. The beautiful Indian maiden is so rare that one might be justified in calling her a myth, but the hideously repulsive old hags of an Indian village are sad and wretched realities, and yet, judging from appearances, their lives are not unhappy ones. They expect and anticipate the burdens of life, are bred and reared to them, and no vain and hopeless longings and yearnings poison and embitter the hard duties of their daily life. Though not, as a rule, permitted to be present at the councils, and not allowed to join the men in the more important feasts, they exercise a great influence over the warriors. Their shrill, metallic-voiced songs of encouragement urge on the de-parting war-party to greater exertions, to braver deeds, and the same shrill voices give them praise and welcome on their return, and should any have fallen, for days their weird wild chanting fills the air of the camp with the great deeds of those who have been slain, and this honor is dearly prized by the savage heart. In this and many other ways they shape and control the public feeling and opinion of the camp, and this is the greatest force which controls the destiny of all Indian tribes. (See FEMALE.)

Wonderful. Make sign for MEDICINE.

Deaf-mutes make a sign like that they make for NEW.

Woodpecker. Make sign for BIRD ; then hold left forearm about vertical, in front of left shoulder, left hand extended, back to left ; bring partially-compressed right hand, and place palm against left forearm on right side near elbow, fingers pointing upwards (direction of forearm) ; move the hand with a jerk or jump to left side of fore-arm, and little higher up, then again to right side, imitating the pe-culiar manner of hopping on the surface of a tree of this bird ; then lower the left hand, and tap the palm several times with the tip of curved index of right hand, others and thumb closed.

The first time I saw this sign made was in a conversation with an Indian who claimed to be a medicine-man of high degree, and he informed me he had learned a wonderful remedy for a special disease from the whisperings of this bird at night. His gestures were graceful, and the peculiar habit of the bird so clearly imitated that I recognized and understood the sign instantly.

Deaf-mutes indicate in the same manner.

Work. Bring extended hands in front of body, fingers pointing to front, back of right hand to right, left to left, hands few inches apart, right hand a little higher and slightly in rear of left, so that tips of right fingers are about opposite left wrist ; lower hands by wrist action, so that fingers point downwards and to front ; raise them in same way, carrying right hand a trifle to front, then as hands are raised carry them a little to right, reversing position of hands ; *i.e.,* right in front ; lower and raise as before, and carry to first posi-tion, repeating motion.

This sign is used very often in the sense of *make* and *work,* and frequently in such sentences as "I will try and fix it for you," "We are farming," "Will go to my people and work hard for them,"

"With them," "For peace." (Rather more in the sense of *work* than *make*.)

I saw a Piegan Indian simply push his hands downwards, closing and opening them as though clutching at something; and I have also seen others give a more tremulous motion to hands. These gestures are not common.

A Sioux who was not very proficient in sign language said, when I asked him the gesture for *work*, that he would make signs for " coming to agency; white man talks to me; tells me to chop wood; move about," etc.

Deaf-mutes make motion with hands to right and left as though rapidly bringing the keys for business. They close the hands and cross the wrists, backs of hands up; striking back of left with right hand two or three times.

Wound. Hold right hand well out in front of body, index finger extended and pointing towards body, other fingers and thumb closed, back of hand to left and front; move the hand briskly towards body, turning index finger to left or right, so that its tip just grazes surface of body, and moving well to right or left, as though glancing as finger passes by body.

Deaf-mutes use about the same gesture.

Wrap. Bring the slightly-compressed hands, backs about outwards, in front of body, backs of fingers of right hand resting against inner surface of left, index fingers about horizontal; move the hands around each other in rotary motion.

Deaf-mutes use the same gesture.

Wrinkle. Wrinkle the skin of forehead and clasp same with tip of fingers and thumb.

Deaf-mutes make same sign, and also draw lines on the face with tip of right index.

Write. Hold extended left hand, back to front and downwards, in front of body, fingers pointing nearly to right, then, as though holding pencil between thumb and index of right hand, make motion of writing on left palm.

Deaf-mutes use the same sign.

Y.

Yankton, Yanktonais (Sioux Indian).   Make sign for SIOUX, then for PIERCED NOSE, as in NEZ PERCE.

The above is the gesture made by the Teton Sioux for the Eastern bands, including the above.   Mr. Mark Wells, the Sioux interpreter at Crow Creek Agency, informed me that the word Yankton, or more correctly, I-hanke-ya-ton-won-wa, meant "Farthest Village." Yanktonais, or more correctly, I-hanke-ya-ton-won-ya, or smallest of farthest village, or smallest band of Yanktons.

I am not entirely satisfied with this, as the root seems to me similar to that of Uncapapa, and though not positive, yet I think I once saw the sign made for this band similar to that for UNCAPAPA. (See SIOUX.)

Year.   Make sign for WINTER.   For *this* year, add sign for Now. Many Indians use the expression as we do, but it is better to denote the time by the *season* of the year.

Deaf-mutes hold extended left hand, back down, in front of left breast, fingers pointing to front; hold the closed right hand two or three inches over left palm, back of hand about to right; move the right hand on a small horizontal circle, and then rest same on left palm.

Yes.   Conception : Bowing the head and body.   Hold right hand, back to right, in front of right breast, height of shoulder, index finger extended and pointing upwards, other fingers nearly closed, thumb resting on side of second finger ; move the hand slightly to left and a little downwards, at same time closing index over thumb.

The index finger represents a person standing, and the bending of the body and head in assent.   (See How.)

Deaf-mutes incline the head to the front.

Yesterday.   Make sign for NIGHT, then, still holding left hand in position, sweep the right upwards and to right on curve, bringing it down to same height as left hand, during movement turning back of hand down.

There are two conceptions for the sign, viz., the *night laid aside*, and *beyond the night*, the latter probably being the best.

Deaf-mutes make sign for DAY and AGO ; latter by throwing right hand over right shoulder.

Younger.   Make signs for PARTURITION and AFTER.

APPENDIX.

SIGNALS.

THE signs or signals made by the Indians to communicate information over great distances with Pony, Blanket, Mirror, Smoke, Fire, Arrows, Flint, Steel, etc., although showing a crafty shrewdness and quick perception, yet fall far short of the supernatural powers of communication which some people accredit them with.

With a Pony. Considered separately, we have first the pony; used to attract attention, denote danger, indicate presence of enemy, game, etc. ; and yet there is but one general well-defined signal, which is by riding in a small circle, or backwards and forwards. With some, the size of the circle or the distance ridden, up and down behind the crest of a hill, determine the size of the party or the quantity of game seen. This attracts attention, gives warning, and is intended to concentrate or scatter the party. If a hunting-party is out and one of the number discovers game, this signal is used ; or if one of a scouting-party discovers the enemy. Indians can usually tell whether it is intended to give information and warning of their foes or of game by the care taken by the rider to conceal the movements of his pony and himself, as well as the circumstances of the particular case. If nothing is discovered, the Indian in advance rides up on the crest of the eminence, and usually dismounts, but the riding on top in full view is sufficient. *The rapidity of riding backwards and forwards, or in a circle,* determines the importance and necessity for immediate concentration. Very fast would call for desperate exertions and violent efforts to reach the rider as soon as possible. Should the Indian in advance, after riding rapidly in the circle, suddenly secrete himself, those with whom he is communicating will do the same. The enemy is close at hand and too numerous for them to attack.

Indians notice every moving object. Ages of transmitted power have given them a wonderful keenness of vision. I have seen large numbers of Indians scattered out over the country, only one now and then being visible as he rode on some eminence, when suddenly this signal would be made, and they would come pouring in from every direction, as much commotion among them as in a disturbed ant-hill, and the cause of alarm communicated, apparently, as mysteriously as these little creatures give the alarm to their fellows, and call for help when molested. Before the Indians had ponies, corresponding movements were made by the men on foot,—*i.e.*, running in circle, appearing on the crest of bluffs, running in zigzag way down side of same, if they discovered an enemy; in short, attracting attention and giving information in about the same way. The return of a successful war-party is announced by some one of the party riding on in advance, and riding furiously up and down the crest of some bluff near camp.

With a Blanket. To attract attention, question, interrogate, to ask the reason for anything, etc.

Grasp the corners of the blanket with right and left hands, so as to spread blanket to full size; extend and spread arms, held nearly vertical, to full length. This might be called the first motion. Swing the arms two or three times to left and right, keeping blanket in same vertical plane, hands describing a vertical curve. The full surface of the blanket is thus presented, and can be seen a long distance. The blanket is of course held in front of body. In swinging blanket to left, the left hand goes nearly to the ground, and then, as it is swung back, the right goes nearly down, and so on.

If either before, during, or after a battle, engagement, or skirmish, etc., it is desired to call for a cessation of hostilities for any purpose whatever, make sign for question, etc., described above (first position), then bending forwards, bring the blanket near the ground, repeat this, and second time lay the blanket on the ground by opening the hands as they come near it. This leaves the blanket about spread out on the ground, and expresses the idea of a weaker party, having had enough, and for any party of laying down hostilities; calls, in fact, for an armistice.

To request all of a party to come in or to approach. Make sign for QUESTION; then, by bending body forwards, bring blanket near ground; repeat this; then lower extended arms till horizontal from shoulders, and bring the hands together in front of body, keeping arms about horizontal; then hold one corner of blanket with right hand, arm extended, and pointing to front and horizontal from shoulder; sweep the right arm to left and in towards body. This latter means come or approach.

To request only one of a number to approach. Make sign for QUESTION, and, by bending forward, bring blanket near ground; repeat this; then hold blanket by one corner with right hand, held high in front of body; compress blanket with left hand as it rests in this vertical position by grasping it near centre, then make sign for COME or APPROACH as described above.

Discovery of a party. Grasp one corner of blanket with right hand, arm extended pointing to front and horizontal from shoulder; hold the other corner with left hand at right shoulder; move the right arm horizontally to right and left. The Comanches formerly swung a shield, instead of a blanket, if they discovered an enemy instead of game.

A great many. Hold blanket as in QUESTION, and then sweeping hands downwards, then slightly upwards, and bringing them together in front of body.

To indicate a herd of buffalo. Spread the blanket on the ground, bringing it down so that the action can be seen at a distance, then with hands or feet raise a dust near the robe or blanket.

To ask how many have been killed. Make sign for QUESTION; then grasp blanket with right hand, arm extended to full length, held in front of and nearly vertical from shoulder; then bend the body forward and swing blanket to front on the ground. In reply the number killed would be expressed by the number of times the blanket was swung forward on to the ground.

A person in front of a party; to direct them to secrete themselves, or to retreat, would be expressed by grasping the blanket with right hand at corner, arm extended pointing to front and horizontal from shoulder; by holding the other corner with left hand at right shoulder, and then swinging the blanket to right and downwards, well down to the ground, and repeating motion.

To say, *Do not approach,* or to express any negative. Grasp one corner of blanket with right hand, other with left; carry left hand to right shoulder, and right hand to left of left shoulder; swing the right arm nearly horizontally to front and right, terminating movement when right hand is little to right of body; repeat motion; being careful by dropping right hand in bringing blanket to first position, as if brought directly back; it might be mistaken for approach.

Information is frequently conveyed by means of preconcerted signals, as, suppose an Indian in advance of two parties on an elevation, where he can be seen by both, to be watching the approach of an enemy; one of his parties circles to right, the other to left, both keeping concealed. At a favorable moment the blanket is raised, and both parties charge in on the enemy from opposite sides. Topography favoring manœuvres of this kind might be rare. So are any orders given by one Indian to others in battle.

One in advance, desiring to have those in rear come forward, would turn towards the party, grasp blanket with right hand at one corner, arm horizontal from shoulder; hold the other corner with left hand to right shoulder; sweep right arm to left and in towards body quickly and repeat motion.

In all of these motions, if blanket is too large to be held, or managed readily, fold it to suitable size.

There are some other signals with a blanket, such as denoting whether the enemy is afoot or mounted; but as they are not generally understood, I have not described them.

Little Bull, chief of the Turtle Mountain or Pembina band of Chippewas, told me that by swinging a blanket towards the setting sun from the east the tribes generally knew that this represented "Chippewas." I could not confirm this, however.

I was told by an Uncapapa Sioux that they used the blanket more in communicating information in regard to game (buffalo) than anything about their enemies. For an enemy discovered, the Indian who made the discovery would fall back behind the crest and bow nearly to the ground, first in one direction, then in another. Indians of other bands of Sioux did not confirm this.

Should a person not have a blanket, motions of the arms are made as though holding a blanket. This is not very clear except to tell a party to approach or go away. For the former, sweep the right arm, hand back out, from well out in front and to right of body in towards body. For the latter, the hand is held palm out, and swept out to front and right of body.

With a Mirror. There is not a very extensive code with a mirror. Its principal use is to attract attention, give warning, etc., and the number of flashes are often determined on, just prior to its use, by special decision of the participants. Its particular value is the power to communicate intelligence over great distances in an instant of time, provided always that the sun shines.

Though there is no special code, yet the mirror is used to impart information in regard to the pursuits of life which are nearest and dearest to an Indian heart, namely, love, war, feasting, and hunting.

A young man, armed with a looking-glass, will seat himself on some little eminence near the camp, where he can see the tepee of his sweetheart; she appears at the door of the lodge, the flash of light from the mirror falls upon her, and then moves to the right or left. Even if this arrangement has not been preconcerted she divines the meaning, and is suddenly seized with a desire to go after wood or water in the direction which the flash indicated, and a meeting is the result.

To call people to a feast some previous arrangement has to be made. Sometimes it is understood that the invitation will be issued in this way, and of course the flashes are looked for, and they are not particular as to the number. An old Indian illustrated its use by saying, "Suppose eight or ten of us were seated here smoking and became hungry. Knowing some one in camp who had plenty to eat, one of our number would go to the man's lodge and hint that something be cooked. His suggestion meeting with success, he would excuse himself for a moment, step outside the tepee, and signal us to come; and on the strength of this information we would, one after another, happen around to the lodge, and of course be invited to eat when everything was ready."

In hunting, suppose the scout sent on in advance discovered four bands or herds of buffalo, and then many scattered over the country, four distinct flashes would be made, and then a fluttering motion given to the mirror.

Information in regard to any other game would be communicated in a similar manner, and its location to right or left of the advance scout be made known by turning the flash to the right or left. By preconcerted arrangement the kind of game would be determined by the number of flashes.

For war purposes. Suppose the scouts sent on ahead discover a large number of the enemy close at hand, a continuous, quick, vibratory, tremulous motion is given the mirror; no distinct flashes. The party in rear scatter and secrete themselves. Should there be distinct flashes, the party in rear hurry forward, moving to right or left as the flashes may indicate.

The system to be used is talked over, thoroughly understood, and agreed upon by the party before the scout or scouts are sent on in advance.

With Smoke. The remarks in regard to mirror apply with equal force to *smoke.* It attracts attention, gives warning, and by previous special arrangement, or the peculiar circumstances of the occasion, may communicate many phases of information; may request a concentration or direct a scattering out; may announce a victory or disclose a defeat.

This method of communication is especially valuable in a mountainous country or one covered with forests. As it is sure to attract attention, it might be well to remember that it has in many instances discovered small and helpless parties of white people to hostile Indians.

Quite a common way of announcing the success of a war-party is to build two fires a short distance from each other, sending up two parallel columns of smoke (two columns signify good luck). If the war-party has not been successful they return very quietly, probably going into the village at night.

Signal smokes are made peculiar in some way, as by suddenly appearing and as quickly disappearing,—this being a sure way of attracting attention. A small fire is sometimes built of perfectly dry wood without the bark, making but little smoke; then some brush, grass, or evergreens are thrown on, and a blanket is held over the fire and removed at intervals; this sends up great puffs of smoke.

The Plains Indians use signal smokes in a very limited manner.

Fire-Arrows. These are rarely used at present, and the stories in regard to them have, I think, been exaggerated.

Any highly inflammable material is fastened to an arrow lighted and discharged into the air. The chief of the Santee Sioux said to me that they used them mostly to burn bears, raccoons, etc., out of hollow trees.

Flint and Steel. Small parties creeping up on a camp at night receive information from the scout in advance by means of a flint and steel. The Indian faces his own party, draws his blanket over his head and arms, and only leaving a small open space, by means of the sparks struck from the flint gives information as to the number of lodges, distance, etc., of the enemy.

Figures or Pictures are made on the ground, on the bark of trees, on pieces of skin, and these sketches give information as to where a party has gone, what it has accomplished, as well as its friendly or warlike desires.

For peace a pipe is usually drawn, and people shaking hands represented ; *war*, a tomahawk and a broken pipe.

The marks made by the enemy determine whether peace or war is wished for.

PHRASES.

The following phrases show something of the construction of the language, and present some of the metaphoric idioms by means of which Indian gesture speech is so enriched as to be able to convey the expression of difficult ideas. Many of them are noted in the description of the gestures under the words ; but it seemed best to group them together here even at the risk of repetition.

I have deemed it necessary to note the deaf-mute manner of arriving at the expression in but a few instances.

Do as you please, it makes no difference to me. Make sign for TRAIL, and indicate, by holding up fingers, that there are two or more ; then hold the left hand, back up, in front of body with as many fingers extended and separated as there have been trails indicated ; point to person and make sign for LOOK, the fingers of the right hand pointing at those of the left, representing the trails ; point to person, then with index and thumb of right hand make motion of picking up one or more of the fingers ; point to person ; make signs for THINK and GOOD ; sign for SAME or EVEN, and for I. Literally translated, this would then be, Trails two or more ; you look at them ; take or pick up the one you think good or best ; same or even to me. The trails are here used in the sense of plans or courses of action.

Deaf-mutes say, Please yourself ; I do not care. For *yourself* they push the closed right hand towards person, thumb extended, ball resting on side of index, back of hand to right. For *do not care* they touch the forehead with palmar surface of extended and touching fingers of right hand, and then wave the hand to right and downwards, turning palm up.

I am free from crime. Raise the extended hands to full length of arms at each side of head, palms up ; make sign for GOD, for LOOK, holding right hand high above and little in front of head, left little lower than the position first described, first and second fingers of right hand pointing downwards towards left palm. (Sometimes the sign for LOOK is also made with left hand, fingers pointing at right palm.) Make sign for BLOOD, and touch left palm with tips of right fingers, right palm with tips of left ; then make sign for No. "God looks at the palms of the hands and sees no blood on them." This is used mostly in the sense of murder.

Deaf-mutes make their signs for LAW, BREAK, and NOT.

To become old. Make signs for OLD and for ARRIVE THERE.
Deaf-mutes make signs for OLD and TO BECOME. For the latter, the left hand is held, back down, in front of left breast, at height of waist, fingers pointing to front; right hand is held, back up, in front of right breast, fingers pointing to front; move the left hand to right and right to left and downwards.

For murder; free-gift (to perform any act gratuitously, without hoping for or anticipating a reward or payment); **faint; accident,** the sign for BY ITSELF is used, with the descriptive gesture. In the first case some one is killed, and the addition seems to convey the idea that nothing is in view but the killing; everything else is cut away; there is no cause, provocation, or justification. In the second, nothing is in sight but the gift; there is no anticipation of or looking for any return gift, as is the usual custom among them. In the third, the condition of the person is plainly that of death, though he returns to life. In the fourth, it happened *by itself;* there was no cause or reason for it.

To win in gambling; to win a woman's affection, the sign for KILL is used. The person is killed to the extent of the amount won from him; and to win a girl's affection is also to kill her; *i.e.,* meaning, I suppose, that all opposition is destroyed.

To keep a camp together; allow no one to go beyond certain limits, is to hold or *soldier* it, and the men appointed for this purpose exercise their authority, even to the killing of those who resist, if necessary. First dogs will be shot, then ponies, then the men whipped, and shot if they resist. Tepees are cut up, property destroyed, to enforce the law or punish a violation of same. The sign for HOLD is made.

Wounded, but not fatally. The sign for WOUND is made, and the sign for RECOVER.

To expend, trade, or **lose a portion** and **have a remainder left,** the sign for LIVE or RECOVER is used; to denote the amount that remains, amount that lives, recovers or survives the action.

My people. Make sign for MY; then the signs for MEN, WOMEN, and CHILDREN; or hold the right index at different heights in front and to right of body.

To travel through an unknown country is expressed usually by making signs for STREAMS, BLUFFS, etc., and KNOW, NO. Indicate the moving; make sign for NIGHT and SAME. To travel through an unknown country is the same as travelling at *night* or in the *dark.*

I am glad to see you. This is variously expressed. The most common way perhaps is to make signs for I, look at person, HEART, and GOOD. Frequently part of the sign for DAY is used after making sign for HEART; and I have also seen in addition to this, for emphasis, sign made for CLOUD, and then the hands raised or pushed up. "The clouds rise and disappear when one meets a friend." After HEART the sign for LIGHT is sometimes made.

I am sad or disappointed. Make sign for I, for HEART, and then from this position of the right hand, carry it outwards and downwards as though laying it on the ground. The weight of care or sorrow presses it down ; the burden is too great to be carried, and the heart is laid on the ground.

Is such a person dead or alive? Make sign for INTERROGATE, point to person, make sign for KNOW. Make sign for the individual about whom the inquiries are being made ; for DIE and ALIVE.

What is your name? Make sign for INTERROGATE, point to person. Make sign for CALL and for POSSESSION.

To be raised into prominence on another person's merits. Give the description by proper gestures, then the act of being raised into view ; brought into notice. Hold the right hand in front of body, height of breast, back to right, index finger extended and pointed upwards, other fingers and thumb closed. (This represents the person of merit, through whose power the other is to be elevated to renown.) Place the centre of palmar surface of extended left index on tip of right, left index pointing to right and upwards, other fingers and thumb of left hand closed. (This index represents the person brought into prominence.) Raise the hands. The left index reclines on the right, and is pushed up.

They paid no attention to your advice and orders ; now they obey you. This is frequently expressed by saying, they had no ears, or their ears were small ; now their ears are open. They listen.

To listen is used in the sense of obeying. Aggressive and violent measures to force persons to obey are frequently called "opening their ears, making them large, so that they can listen."

I live here. Make sign for I, for LIVE, and for SIT. The latter is frequently used in the sense of *this place.*

I will remain here three years, in signs, would be, I, SIT, WINTER, and then indicate THREE by holding up fingers.

To pay no attention to a person; to ignore, suppress, and in a certain sense **depose,** is expressed by saying that a blanket has been thrown over the person.

I am old; my teeth are worn, are bad, and loose, and I suffer from indigestion on account of these afflictions. Make signs for I, for OLD ; place the palmar surface of fingers of right hand near ends on front teeth, and move the hand to right and left. Make sign for BAD ; then take hold of the front teeth with thumb and index of right hand and shake them ; then hold right hand, back out, near the teeth, fingers pointing up, extended and separated, and give a tremulous motion to the hand. Make sign for EAT, for GOOD, and No, and SICK, opposite stomach.

Literally translated, "I—old—teeth worn—bad—teeth loose— eat—good no—sick." This phrase illustrates the fact that frequently gestures convey many ideas other than those sketched by the signs. The air-picture is the skeleton merely, but suggests the rounded lines and rich coloring.

An old Indian usually has his teeth worn. They do not decay, but wear off, and become loose, and this condition is suggested by speaking of old age. The condition of the teeth again suggests imperfect mastication, and this indigestion and consequent discomfort and sickness.

I was made a scout. To be made a scout is to be made a wolf, and to be sent on in advance to spy out all that keen-eyed and crafty cunning may learn. The usual way of expressing this is to say that the chiefs met in council and made me a wolf; giving, as a rule, any special instructions. (See Scout.)

You are nothing; you are a low fellow; a dog. I scorn, detest, defy, dare you to do your worst against me, is expressed by pushing the right hand towards the person vituperated, thumb between index and second finger.

I knocked him over with a single shot. In this sense it is usual to use one clap of the hands, as in Volley or Heavy Firing, to denote the discharge of a gun, and the right hand is swept outwards to right and downwards from its position, after clapping the hands sharply together once. These gestures are also used to express the idea of shooting and hitting the object fired at in a vital part.

Such expressions as **Very poor; hard up; extremely destitute; intense physical suffering,** are usually expressed by adding the sign for Brave to the descriptive gestures.

To obey orders; accept and follow advice given, is frequently expressed by saying that the road or trail made for them was picked up and held on to; using here for *hold on to* the second described sign for Remember.

To express the idea of **riding rapidly and continuously a long distance.** Make the sign for Gallop, but move the hands slowly to front, and at same time give them a tremulous motion similar to that in Wind; sometimes adding Sleep and No. This corresponds to our metaphor of "Riding on the wings of the wind."

To induce a girl to elope is to steal her; and to picture the preliminaries necessary to effect this, after making sign for the Girl or Female, hold the left hand, back to left, in front of body, index finger extended and pointing upwards (to represent the girl); then make sign for Little Talk, holding right hand near left, and snapping the thumb and index at tip of left index. Make sign for By and By, and again holding left index as at first, make sign for Kill towards it; then make sign for Night and Steal. This represents the girl or female as standing; hence she has stopped to listen. After a time the words spoken to her take effect; in fact, *kill* her mentally and physically; all opposition dies. The maiden perishes, the woman appears. In defiance of custom, public opinion, and scorning fear of punishment, she, when, as they say, "darkness like two huge blankets spreads over the earth," goes with her lover; and, as he has made no presents for the valuable animal he has secured, he is said to have stolen her.

To be near death and recover. Make first part of sign for Die; but just as right index or hand is about to pass under left stop it; draw it back a little, and from its then position make sign for Recover.

To ride against anything and be thrown off. Indicate riding on horseback, and make sign for gait at which riding; then hold left hand, back out, well in front of body, fingers touching and pointing to right; carry right hand briskly outwards, and strike left palm sharply with backs of fingers of right hand; then sweep the right hand outwards, upwards, and slightly to right and downwards, turning palm up, terminating movement when right hand is a little lower than left.

He reached here yesterday, came into my lodge, sat down, and I told him to tell me the truth. Make signs for or point to person, for ARRIVE HERE, for YESTERDAY, for MY, TEPEE, SIT, for I, TALK, —making this gesture towards the person or where he has been represented as seated,—TALK to me, and TRUE.

Living in a certain part of the country. To illustrate: To indicate the Indians living in the Indian Territory, make sign for RIVER (Arkansas), CALL, FLINT, for on other side or BEYOND; then hold the partially-compressed right hand, fingers separated slightly and pointing about upwards, well out in front of body (or in the direction of the country described) and little higher than shoulders; by wrist action turn the hand slowly two or three times from left to right or the reverse. The Northern tribes call the Indian Territory the country beyond Flint River.

To learn to read and write. Make sign for WRITE, for LOOK (fingers pointing towards left palm), sign for BY AND BY, then for KNOW or UNDERSTAND, sometimes repeating the sign for LOOK. Some tribes simply express KNOW and COUNT, as in HOW MANY.

The beautiful and sublime, the grand and gloomy, the destructive and revivifying forces of nature, are in constant use by the Indians to express their emotions and thoughts.

A large village is a forest of tepee-poles.

A multitude, the people are compared to the blades of grass on the prairie.

A charge is like the rush of a tornado, or the fierce onslaught of a mighty flood sweeping all before it.

A braggart talks fire; his mouth is brave, his heart a coward.

Men are frequently compared to animals. The scout is a wolf, skulking through ravines, seeing without being seen.

Some years ago Red Cloud called some of the employés about the agency "long-tailed rats," who got away with the Indian provisions at night, carrying off the stores to their own nests.

Many of the same metaphors are used by all the tribes I have come in contact with, though life at an agency, or being thrown in contact with the white race, seems to quench the eloquence as well as many other of the best qualities of the Indians.

The two following phrases are very similarly expressed in gestures, and I have at times had difficulty in securing an instantaneous recognition of the difference when used by themselves. In any conversation which naturally led up to the question, of course there would be no trouble.

Where were you born? Make sign for INTERROGATE, point to person, make sign for PARTURITION and for WHERE. The latter gesture should be made distinctly, and the index finger brought deliberately down at several different points in front of body.

Where are your children? Make sign for INTERROGATE, point to person, sometimes sign for POSSESSION (see MY or MINE), for PARTURITION (sometimes repeating this gesture), and for WHERE. I have sometimes seen after gesture for WHERE sign for SIT, at others for LIVE.

To freeze any part of the body. Make sign for COLD and for KILL; the latter gesture made towards the afflicted member or part of body; the cold kills the part.

PROPER NAMES.

The following proper names are some of them interesting on account of their peculiar formation, some are difficult to express in gestures, and others give a correct interpretation to the Indian word, something that has not been done in the vocal and written translations.

Where the tribe is not well known, or where it is desirable to particularize, the tribal sign is first made, then the sign for CALL, and then the gesture or gestures for the name. Should the man be a chief, that follows immediately after the tribal sign. To illustrate, take the following: I, to-day, shook hands with Black Eagle, chief of the Pawnees; in gestures: I, NOW, SHAKE HANDS, PAWNEE CHIEF, CALL, EAGLE, BLACK.

I give the names as they are usually interpreted, some as I remember them, some that I have copied from a printed list of the names of the Indians at one of our agencies, and others from some old muster-rolls of enlisted scouts. Some of the tribes seem to revel in smutty personal names, and particularly is this the case with the Shoshones, though at every agency, I think, there are many names which civilized taste will not permit to be used in printed or vocal form. Some of the names in my list I found could not be expressed in accordance with the translation. I made some little investigation, and, as far as I went, found that it was equally impossible to express them in the vocal language of the Indians. In ordinary conversation the personal names are usually very much abbreviated, only enough given to clearly mark or distinguish the person.

American Horse. Make sign for HORSE and sign for WHITES. I have also seen the signs for a big pony or horse made to denote this name; a big pony being an American horse.

Whistling Elk. Make sign for ELK, and then sign for WHISTLE, or a snorting, whistling sound.

End-of-the-Woods. Make sign for TREE, separating hands well, to denote the trees or forest or woods, then make sign for FINISHED.

Running Horse. Make sign for HORSE and for FAST, or for RACE, repeating this to show that the horse has been run, though this would more properly be translated Race-horse.

I have also seen for this the sign for GALLOP, moving the hand sharply and quickly.

Spotted Weasel. Make gestures to denote a small white animal with black tip to tail, and then make sign for SPOTTED.

Bad-Wild-Horse. Make signs for HORSE, for BAD, and for BY ITSELF.

Count-Coup-One-by-One. Make signs for COUNT-COUP, for AFTER, then COUNT-COUP again, repeating this once or twice.

Dog-Walks-on-the-Ground. Make signs for DOG, for WALK, and point to ground. If not in the open air, some dirt or dust would be picked up, or the sign made for DIRT or DUST.

Spotted Tail. Make signs for TAIL and SPOTTED.

Crazy Horse. Make signs for POSSESSION, for HORSE, and for CRAZY. This gives a correct interpretation as I understand the vocal word in the Sioux language. It should not be *Crazy Horse*, but *His-Horse-is-Crazy*.

Man-Afraid-of-his-Horses. Make signs for POSSESSION, for HORSE, and AFRAID.

The remarks made about Crazy Horse apply with equal force here. The man is not afraid, but his horses are afraid of him.

The fertile brain of some interpreter has also given us "Young-Man-Afraid-of-his-Horses." The old man was at one time chief of the Ogalalla Sioux, I think, just before Red Cloud became their famous chief, and he gave his own name to his son, it being simply, "His-Horses-are-Afraid," or "His-Horse-is-Afraid."

Little Warrior. Make signs for WAR, To Go To, for MAN, and then for LITTLE. Either one of three, according to the idea desired to be represented; *i.e.*, SHORT, LITTLE, or SMALL.

No Neck. Touch neck and then make sign for No or WIPED OUT.

I have seen both used, one about as much as the other.

Thundering Eagle. Make signs for EAGLE and THUNDER. I know of no way to represent thundering.

The-Horse-comes-Last. Make sign for HORSE; then bring right hand from well out in front towards body, fingers extended, separated, and pointing towards body and upward. This represents animal coming; then make sign for BEHIND.

Waiting. Usually sign for SIT; but sometimes for WAIT or HOLD ON are made.

Touch-the-Cloud. Make sign for CLOUD, and then, holding extended left hand, back up, in front of and higher than head, place the tip of extended right index against palm. As the tip of index strikes left palm the right hand rather pushes up left, and this idea is in the vocal word more of a push than touch the cloud.

Swift Bear. Make signs for BEAR and for FAST. There is no difference in either the vocal language or gesture speech of Indians, so far as I know, between the words SWIFT and FAST.

Pretty Lance. Make signs for LANCE and for GOOD. The lance might be painted or decorated, and these attributes could be described, but the sign for PRETTY, HANDSOME, etc., seems to refer especially to people.

Sitting Bull. Sometimes the general sign for BUFFALO is made, and then sign for SIT. As often, however, and more properly, the sign for BUFFALO BULL is made, and then sign for SIT.

INDIAN NAMES OF STREAMS AND MOUNTAINS WHICH HAVE NOT BEEN PRESERVED ON MAPS, ETC.

Many of the Indian names for streams, mountains, and prominent bluffs have not been preserved on our maps, and this sometimes leads to serious confusion.

During the Sioux and Cheyenne war of 1876–77 friendly Indian scouts were sent out to locate the hostiles and bring the information to a large military command located near the Black Hills, Dakota.

The hostiles had only a short time before been south of the Yellowstone River. The scouts returned and reported that the hostiles had gone north; had, in fact, crossed the Missouri River. Subsequent events proved that the hostiles had *not* crossed the Missouri, but had crossed to the north of the Yellowstone, and these hitherto reliable scouts were credited with lying and mischievously bringing in a false report with the deliberate intention of deceiving. As a matter of fact the scouts were honest and had faithfully performed their work, and the mistake grew out of the ignorance of the interpreters.

The Indians call the Yellowstone Elk River, but the majority only so name it as far from its source as the mouth of Powder River, and some only as far as the mouth of the Rosebud. From these points to its confluence with the Missouri it is called by the same name as that by which they designate the latter stream, viz., Muddy, or Big Muddy. The junction of the Yellowstone and Missouri they call the Forks of the Big Muddy. The scouts said the hostiles had crossed the Big Muddy going north; and the interpreter, not knowing the distinction made by the Indians, naturally supposed they had gone north of the Missouri River.

I only give a few of the more prominent names which have come under my personal observation.

NAMES ON MAP.	INDIAN NAMES.
Missouri River.	Big River, but more properly Big Muddy River. I once heard it called Medium River.
Milk River.	Little River.
Yellowstone River.	Elk River, as explained above.
Clarke's Fork (of Yellowstone).	Rotten Buffalo Tongue.
Prior's Fork (of Yellowstone).	Arrow River.
Clear Fork (of Powder).	Lodge Pole.

NAMES ON MAP.	INDIAN NAMES.
Little Missouri River.	Thick Timber by Sioux, and Antelope by Cheyennes.
Grand River.	Ree, or Corn River.
Cheyenne River.	Good River.
White River.	Smoking Earth River.
North Platte River.	Shell River, sometimes Shell on Neck River.
South Platte River.	Greasy, or Fat River. I have also heard this called Goose River.
Republican River.	Shield River.
Arkansas River.	Flint River. The Indian Territory is called by the Northern Indians the country beyond Flint River.
Cimarron River.	Buffalo Bull River.
Canadian River.	Red River.
Washita River.	Lodge-Pole River.
Mississippi River.	I have only heard the Mississippi called Big River.

MOUNTAINS.

The Rocky Mountain Range.	The Backbone of the World.
Big Horn Mountains.	White Mountains.

It may be said that not more than one-third of the bluffs and buttes, which are the landmarks of the great plains, have retained their Indian names. Different tribes have, of course, in many instances different names for them, but it is a remarkable fact that they are in most cases, where known at all, known by the same name.

INDEX,

WITH SYNONYMES.

APPENDIX.

SIGNALS.

PHRASES.

THE END.